Security Yearbook 2024

Fifth Edition

Security Yearbook 2024

A History and Directory of the IT Security Industry

Fifth Edition

RICHARD STIENNON

WILEY

Published by John Wiley & Sons, Inc., Hoboken, New Jersey.
Published simultaneously in Canada and the United Kingdom.

ISBN: 9781394220809

Library of Congress Control Number: 2024906902

Cover image: © JuSun/Getty Images
Cover design: Wiley

SKY10075520_052024

Contents at a Glance

Contents

Acknowledgments

Creating the directory in *Security Yearbook 2024* was made possible through the dedicated efforts of several individuals. Sambath Ramesh and his team in India played a pivotal role in collecting the foundational data. They meticulously reviewed and updated vendor records each month throughout much of 2023, feeding this crucial information into the Analyst Dashboard. While automation has begun to simplify this process, the contributions of Sambath and his team remain invaluable.

Maximillian Schweizer was instrumental in shaping this data for publication. His expertise in no-code development, spanning multiple database platforms like Xano, front-end technologies like Bubble, and a variety of APIs, was crucial. His integration with OpenAI's large language models and the creation of APIs for real-time data access are critical to our success. Erika Jones also deserves special recognition for her diligent input of more than 1,000 new entries into our database, a testament to her commitment and precision.

I extend my gratitude to Salaar Aamir Jan for his exceptional work in identifying new vendors through global conference listings and adding this information to the Analyst Dashboard, providing our subscribers with valuable insights into industry events.

A special thanks goes to Louis Bedigian for his outstanding contribution to authoring Chapter 14 and compiling both the open-source solutions and a comprehensive list of significant cyber incidents.

Lastly, I am profoundly grateful to the community of security industry leaders and pioneers. Their unwavering support for the concept of this historical compendium and their generous allocation of time and expertise have been a cornerstone of this project.

CHAPTER 1

2023 in Review

Security Yearbook 2024 is the fifth edition of the annual Security Yearbook series, a desktop reference for the entire cybersecurity industry. In this edition, there are completely updated sections on funding rounds, mergers and acquisitions, and cyberattacks. There is a chapter dedicated to the industry pioneers who left us. In addition, the book's directory contains 3,240 vendors arranged alphabetically, by country/state, and by category. Each entry gives the headquarters location, number of employees at the end of the year, and percent change in head count for 2023.

The world has come to live with the constant threat of surges in new strains of SARS-CoV-2. Though many companies are pushing back on remote work and mandating a return to office, the lasting impact of COVID has seen an increase in remote connectivity security and the rapid adoption of secure access service edge (SASE) solutions for extending headquarter protections to everyone regardless of where they are located.

This chapter sums up 2023.

The AI Tsunami

ChatGPT was launched in November 2022. The year 2023 was one of rapid adaptation to what is possibly the biggest technology evolution to occur since the introduction of the Internet. Existing security solutions quickly harnessed large language models to interpret data and provide analysis. Microsoft announced Security Copilot, using its ownership/partnership with OpenAI to "summarize vast data signals into key insights to cut through the noise, detect cyberthreats before they cause harm, and reinforce your security posture."

Dozens of vendors that already had threat-hunting and data-intensive threat detection solutions added a layer of natural language communication by incorporating API access to GPT-3.5 and GPT-4.

In the meantime, startups introduced protections for AI models as well as solutions that could protect an organization from data leaks as employees uploaded confidential information for analysis by LLMs.

The year 2024 will see many more companies come out of stealth that have been working on leveraging LLMs to improve threat hunting, defense, and automated response. It will also see attackers leveraging AI to automate their campaigns.

Silicon Valley Bank Failure

The failure of the biggest bank serving the startup world had a devastating impact in March 2023. Silicon Valley Bank had to recognize a loss on the long-term bonds it held and seek additional capital even though it was technically solvent. Regulators shut it down on Friday, March 10. Luckily, the doors opened on Monday, and depositors had full access to their funds. The experience spooked many investors and slowed their activity for the rest of 2023. Vendors were also frightened and have sought protections against such an event recurring, opening accounts at multiple banks. There were more than 500 cybersecurity companies that banked with Silicon Valley Bank.

2023 Funding

There were 315 companies (6% of total) that had funding rounds in 2023. The total invested came to $10.05 billion, matching the amount in 2020 ($10.7 billion) but well below the $17 billion in 2022 and the record $26 billion in 2021. Last year, there were 452 vendors to receive funding, so 2023 saw a 30% drop in number of investments.

There were 22 investment rounds that exceeded $100 million, down from 36 last year. There were 23 that raised between $50 and $100 million.

The biggest investment of 2023 was $500 million put into Google spin-out SandboxAQ for post-quantum readiness. Wiz took in an additional $300 million valuing it at $10 billion, the largest valuation for a private cybersecurity vendor on record.

Mergers and Acquisitions in 2023

There were 250 acquisitions of cybersecurity vendors in 2023, according to data provided by investment bank AGC Partners. That is 6% of the entire vendor number. That compares to 332 in 2022, a drop of 25%. If valuations were dropping because of the much talked about economic headwinds, you would think that there would be more acquisitions at bargain prices. But the economic uncertainty also led to a smaller appetite for acquiring companies. As certainty returns to the market, look for an increase in acquisitions in 2024, as acquirers gain confidence ahead of investors.

The biggest deal of 2022, Broadcom acquiring VMware, finally closed in 2023. This was a $68 billion deal if you include the acquired debt.

By far the biggest deal of 2023, and the biggest in cybersecurity industry history, was the announcement that Cisco was acquiring publicly traded Splunk for $28 billion in cash. In some ways, these two companies are similar. They deal in machine-generated data (packets for Cisco, logs for Splunk), with primarily command-line interfaces.

There were a total of six take-private deals as the number of public companies diminished.

Public Cybersecurity Companies

January 6, 2023, was the bottom of the market for the major cybersecurity companies tracked by IT-Harvest. Most of them, including CrowdStrike, Palo Alto Networks, Zscaler, and Fortinet, had fallen 50–60% from their all-time highs in November 2021. All of these companies were up significantly in 2023, with CrowdStrike up 200%. At the time of writing, Palo Alto Networks is up 147% and became the first cybersecurity pure play to surpass a $100 billion market cap. Zscaler is up 117% but still well below its all-time high. Even stock market laggards Check Point Software and Trend Micro are up 25% for the year.

The New Guy

The story of Guy Guzner has been added to the growing list of pioneers in *Security Yearbook 2024*. He founded Fireglass and sold it to Symantec, and he is currently the founder and CEO of Savvy, which uses identity to secure SaaS applications. Guy is the youngest founder to add his story.

Updates to the Directory

In this fifth edition of *Security Yearbook*, we return to listing all of the vendors in the directory by country and category as well as alphabetically. The data is extracted from the IT-Harvest Analyst Dashboard, the only platform that collects and curates data on all the vendors in cybersecurity. Vendors are put in one of the primary categories and further cataloged by subcategory and tags. Head count changes are recorded every month. Data from multiple sources are used to enhance each vendor's page. As we go to print, we are ingesting product data for every cybersecurity product in the market.

There are several use cases for a data-driven approach to the cybersecurity industry.

Vendor/Product Selection

Many chief information security officers (CISOs) already refer to *Security Yearbook* when they are searching for a replacement vendor or interested in adding to their security stack. With the IT-Harvest Analyst Dashboard, they will be able to generate short lists by filtering by category, size, funding, and location. They will be able to evaluate vendor health based on head count growth and investment. Assisted by OpenAI, we have ingested thousands of product names and features from the dashboard. Instead of relying on analyst reports that just include the top 10 or 12 vendors in a category, CISOs and their teams will be able to review the entire list of available products to find the right fit.

Investment Thesis Validation

Investors looking for acquisitions or equity opportunities will be able to take advantage of the extensive directory of vendors in their target segment. They can quickly sort by size, growth, location, and category and download the data to their own tools.

Industry Analysis

The dashboard was created to assist IT-Harvest in its research. Information about which industry segments are growing the fastest and which are shrinking, as well as the leaders in each space, from quarter to quarter, is invaluable. Creating market reports on a segment is easy when all the vendors are already being tracked. All cybersecurity industry analysts can benefit from having access to the same data.

Strategic Evaluation

Corporate development teams can quickly find and evaluate targets for acquisition or partnership.

Marketing

Event organizers, public relations/analyst relations teams, and companies that sell their own technology to cybersecurity vendors can find partners and customers quickly and easily.

OEM Relationship Development

Many cybersecurity vendors sell their enhanced data to other vendors. The dashboard has become a critical tool to such vendors to estimate total addressable market size as well as pursuing opportunities to partner.

Ever since the first appearance of *Security Yearbook 2020* at the RSA Conference just before COVID hit, the most frequent request has been for an e-book version. Because e-books are pirated as soon as they are published, it has not been possible to publish the directory electronically. The dashboard finally makes all the data available in a searchable database. Just as *Security Yearbook 2024* is meant to be an indispensable guide to the cybersecurity industry, the dashboard will contain the data of record on the entire industry updated continuously.

CHAPTER 2

Introduction

This book presents the history of the IT security industry. Like many good histories, it must begin with an apology. Winston Churchill, in writing the preface to his *History of the Second World War*, took credit for being in a position of one who "bore the chief responsibility for the war and policy of the British Commonwealth and Empire." Yet, he declined to call his Nobel Prize–winning work a history so much as a "contribution to history." For example, John Lewis Gaddis, in the original preface to *The United States and the Origins of the Cold War*, claimed it is impractical to attempt a "definitive study of the origins of the Cold War," in light of the fact that the inner workings of the Kremlin were unavailable to him at the time. The self-effacing Gandhi wrote this in the preface to his autobiography: "I hope and pray that no one will regard the advice interspersed in the following chapters as authoritative." Machiavelli practically groveled before his benefactor in the opening words of his *Discourses on the First Ten Books of Livy* by saying, "You may well complain of the poverty of my endeavor since these narrations of mine are poor, and of the fallacy of (my) judgment when I deceive myself in many parts of my discussion." So, I must be doubly apologetic, first for this attempt at conveying the breadth and depth of the lives and experiences of so many founders, inventors, and builders of IT security, and second for even mentioning the monumental works of these historians.

With that said, this book is meant to redress something that is missing from our world: a concise recounting of what has gone before in an entire industry that has arisen alongside the information age. When an industry has surpassed 30 years of existence and experienced tremendous growth in size and relevance, there may be participants who are oblivious to its past. Founders, marketers, salespeople, researchers, admins, policy makers, and students just beginning their journeys, who stumble into security through various paths, have a view of the industry that is just a snapshot in time. Only through understanding the continuum of what has come before and has led to the present can they begin to understand what the future holds.

Thirty years is a very short time span from the perspective of the 800-year history of the Roman Empire or even the 248-year history of the United States, and it may be considered too soon to write a history of the IT security industry. By all measures, the industry continues to grow each year. In addition to the spending on IT security, this means that every year, there are more people who make their living practicing security. They are threat hunters, researchers, reverse engineers, developers, system administrators, network architects, data privacy professionals, cryptographers, managers, and executives. In addition, there are the marketing, sales, legal, product managers, and finance people who build products, take them to market, and grow the companies that provide the technology to counter the looming threat of bad actors.

The participants in this industry are on a mission. Yes, they are building careers, striving to get ahead, and showing up to work, just as anyone does. But they are also fighting a battle. They are the good guys fighting the bad guys. They are driving toward a better world, one where data, privacy, and the future are sacrosanct. This is their story.

Students of history have learned to question the perspective of the historian. Are they from the school of liberalism? Or are they neoliberals? Are they realists? Constructivists? Which events do they choose to highlight? And from what perspective? This history of the IT security industry is from the perspective of an industry analyst.

What is an industry analyst? It's someone whose job is to make sense of industry trends. They are tasked with predicting the technology future accurately and providing guidance that buyers of technology can use to make their purchasing decisions. An analyst has biases and their own experiences that color their perspective. One who comes from the financial world may focus on the numbers. A geek at heart is going to focus on the technology. A practitioner may even have an animosity toward vendors. But every analyst in every industry acquires a broad perspective, and like them, a security industry analyst must have a very wide purview. There are more than 3,700 vendors of IT security products in more than 200 separate categories. Grasping the entirety of that industry is a challenge *Security Yearbook 2024* hopes to achieve.

This analyst is a technologist at heart. An aerospace engineer by training and a structural engineer by experience, I jumped into the world of security in 1995. It was the advent of the Internet that led me to networking as I launched an Internet service provider for the automotive industry, appropriately named Rustnet, and then to security as I joined Netrex, the managed security service provider (MSSP) acquired by ISS that is now part of IBM's managed security service.

My experience of stumbling into security is not uncommon. In the early days, people did not study security in school. There were no cybersecurity programs. They came from all walks of life. Some may have had computer science backgrounds, but many were just caught up in the excitement of countering hackers, or perhaps they were hackers themselves. The founders whose stories appear in this book illustrate the diversity of their backgrounds and the paths they took. Like all entrepreneurs, they recognized a problem, thought of a solution, and attempted to build it.

Gil Shwed, Shlomo Kramer, and Marius Nacht, the founders of Check Point Software, saw the problem with network access and invented the stateful firewall. John McAfee, Dr. Solomon, Eugene Kaspersky, Eva Chen, and Kailash Katkar tackled the problem of viruses spread though shared floppy disks. As the industry grew to incorporate more and more defensive components, there were inventors and pioneers of each new category.

I played some small part in this industry. While at Netrex, I introduced Shlomo Kramer to Robert Moskowitz, who convinced Check Point to pivot from SWAN to IPSec as the basis for what became VPN-1. I attended the first IPSec bake-offs in Andover, Massachusetts, and Plano, Texas. I went on to PricewaterhouseCoopers, where I conducted risk assessments and penetration tests of large technology, transportation, and financial services companies. I was drafted into Gartner as its second analyst covering security. I served stints at Webroot Software, Fortinet, and Blancco Technology Group. Some of my writing and research have influenced the direction of some of the largest players.

There are thousands of books on security, and they are predominantly how-to guides. There are also hundreds of books that could be considered histories, but they are histories of cyber incidents. I have written two such books, one on the history of state-sponsored attacks (*Surviving Cyberwar*, 2010) and one on network warfare (*There*

Will be Cyberwar, 2015). But there is no history of the people and companies that comprise the IT security industry. *Security Yearbook 2024* is an attempt at compiling that history. This is the fifth time the history and the directory of vendors have been published. It is also the first edition published by Wiley. The directory includes all the vendors of cybersecurity products with more than 10 employees. There are three sections: an alphabetical listing, by country, and by category. The list and head count growth numbers are exported from the IT-Harvest Analyst Dashboard, the only platform for tracking and researching the entire cybersecurity industry.

CHAPTER 3

Getting to Know the IT Security Industry

Today, the IT security industry comprises more than 3,700 vendors and more than two million employees. Of course, there are many more people who work in IT security from level-one analysts in a security operations center (SOC) to systems administrators who ensure that the servers under their purview are configured as optimally as possible to the directors, vice presidents, and chief information security officers (CISOs) who lead the way in the meticulous effort of maintaining a defensible posture and warding off an ever-growing number of threat actors.

The architecture of security lends itself to a simple way to approach the industry. A layered defense at the network, endpoint, identity, and data security levels provide an appropriate way to think about the industry as a whole. While large, mature vendors of security products may seek to encompass all of the sectors, it is rare for them to dominate a market in more than one major category. There is a reason for that, which derives from the way IT security staff are specialized in these categories. Network security professionals have obtained their expertise studying network protocols, routing, Domain Name System (DNS), and, at least in the early days, the intricacies of telecom architectures.

In the meantime, those in endpoint security have grown into their professions either from a system-centric focus on operating systems and applications or from fighting the daily battle to ensure that virus signatures are up-to-date and systems are properly patched. Data security practitioners are familiar with encryption, data governance, key management, and privacy concerns, while those who manage identities are expert in directory services and myriad means of authentication.

In the modern enterprise with large security teams, this specialization has evolved over 20 years, and purchasing decisions are made independently, with each team responsible for choosing the best solution for their areas of expertise.

It's no wonder then that a firewall vendor that grew to success through a relentless pursuit of enterprise customers—enhancing their product to stay competitive and seeking always to claim the fastest throughput, the largest number of connections per second, the lowest latency, and the best management—would be well-versed in competing for the attention of network security teams but completely lacking in the connections, messaging, or evolved products needed to sell an endpoint security solution to completely different teams. Cisco has tried and failed to get on the endpoint, even though the company has had moments when it dominated in both networking and firewalls. Fortinet, a company that relentlessly introduces products of its own making into every hot segment of security, has never succeeded at gaining success on the endpoint. Only the still unproven strategy of attempting to be the single source of security products for large customers justifies a network security company like Fortinet investing in the research and development of its Forticlient software.

The endpoint security vendors have even more trouble trying to cross boundaries into network security. They have teams of hundreds if not thousands of developers who are expert in reverse engineering, malware capture and analysis, and deployment to endpoints. Because they have to continuously enhance their endpoint protections, their client software tends to get bloated and consumes more and more of a desktop's resources. Most end users of traditional endpoint security products have no great love for the products themselves. Frequent antivirus (AV) updates slow systems down, and AV products are prone to false positives and generate continuous alerts. The AV admins have no great loyalty to the products they use and are always ready to listen to a vendor that promises a smaller footprint, fewer false positives, and better catch rates.

If a vendor like Symantec, at one time the largest AV company with a market cap hovering around $14 billion on August 1, 2019 (with a jump to $16 billion after the announcement that Chinese chip maker Broadcom planned to acquire it), were to introduce a gateway security product, it would be met with derision by the network security teams within the enterprise. Network people are interested in avoiding slowdowns and false positives, and AV products are things that slow down performance. Symantec is a good example because it has tried many times to enter the network security space. The 2016 merger with Blue Coat was only the latest, and last, such attempt.

Network Associates is another example. The company was formed as a roll-up of a swath of security products and desktop management tools. One of those products, the Gauntlet Firewall acquired from Trusted Information Systems, was eventually at end-of-life. It had only managed to penetrate the market to the tune of 3,000 customers by 2003 when Network Associates stopped support and turned those customers over to Secure Computing.

Identity and access management (IAM) is a separate major category that resists the efforts of vendors to include other products in their portfolios. This space had the additional burden of Microsoft entering the directory services market with Active Directory, a move that pretty much ended the opportunity for IAM vendors until recently, when a new crop of cloud services came about.

Finally, there is data security. From the vibrant days of competition between RSA, SafeNet, Entrust, Gemalto, and hundreds of others, the space has consolidated somewhat, and the products have been commoditized. Yet, there are still 523 vendors in this major category, and each addresses the need to protect data and make encryption ubiquitous.

Main Categories

It is this striation of security vendors into categories that follows the overall IT security defense posture of layered defense and will help you in understanding this space. In fact, most vendors fall into one of 17 major categories.

Figure 3.1 shows the six main categories, covered next, and then we'll talk about the other categories.

Network Security

Network security vendors make up 11.2% of the total industry. Companies include Cisco, Palo Alto Networks, Check Point Software, Fortinet, SonicWall, and WatchGuard in the firewall space. Numerous vendors provide *Intrusion prevention system* (IPS), virtual private networking (VPN),

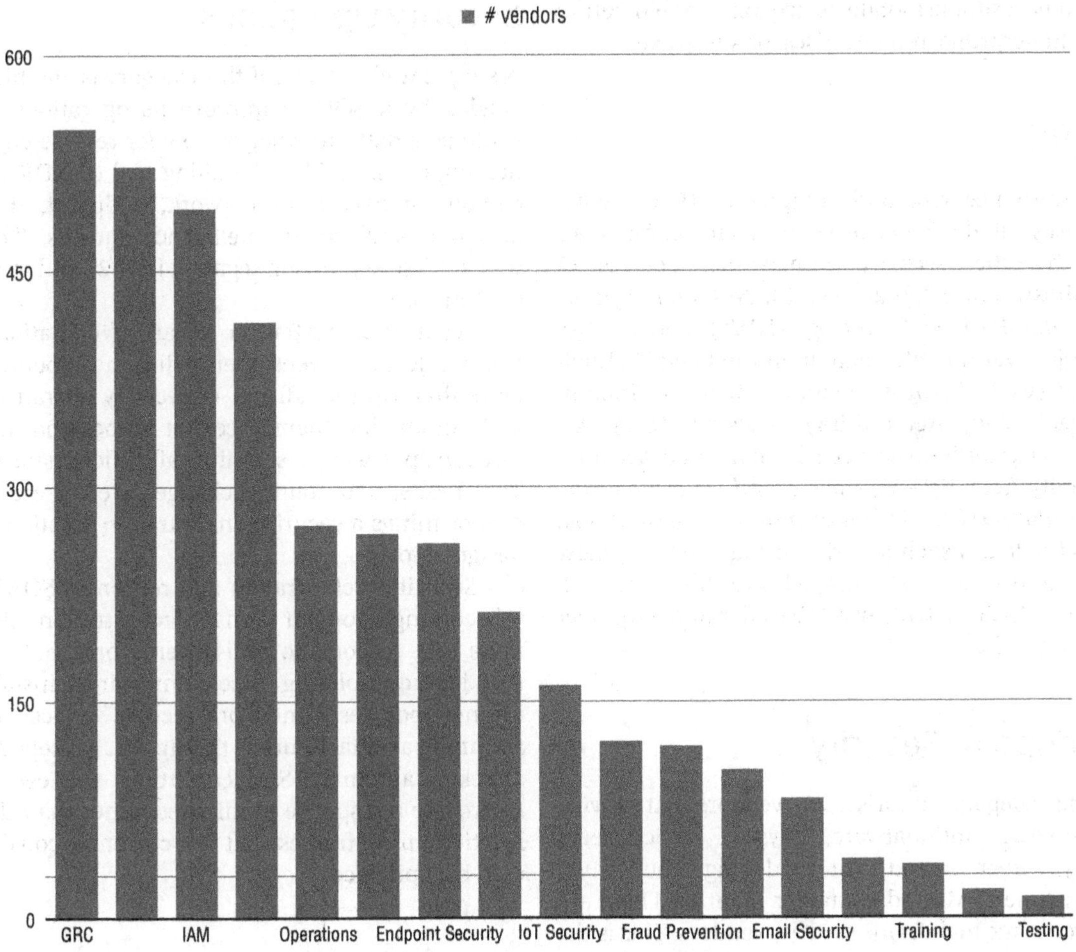

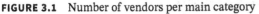

FIGURE 3.1 Number of vendors per main category

and network scanning solutions. This category also includes all the web-filtering vendors and net flow recording and analysis.

Data Security

This category is large because it includes all of the data encryption vendors and the technologies needed for encryption, such as certificate creation, key management, and the SSL certificate authorities (CAs). It also includes information rights management (IRM).

Identity and Access Management

IAM is such a big category—493 companies—because in addition to directory services such as Microsoft Azure, Okta, and Ping Identity, it includes all the password managers and a multitude of solutions for strong authentication. These can be a simple mobile device token or biometrics of fingerprints, retinas, irises, or keystrokes.

GRC

Governance risk and compliance (GRC) comprises all the tools used to ensure compliance with either security frameworks such as IT Infrastructure Library (ITIL), *National Institute of Standards & Technology* (NIST), and Control Objectives for Information and Related Technology (COBIT), or regulations such as Gramm-Leach-Bliley Act (GLBA), *Sarbanes–Oxley* Act (SOX), Health Insurance Portability and Accountability Act (HIPAA), and *General Data Protection Regulation* (GDPR). For the purposes of this book, technologies such as risk scoring, posture analysis, and logging are lumped into this major category. In 2023, GRC was the leader in the number of vendors, 547.

Endpoint Security

This category comprises 261 vendors that provide antivirus, anti-malware, physical device security, server or endpoint hardening, and virtual machine (VM) and container security. There are even some mainframe security vendors. This is the first category to experience consolidation as Norton Lifelock has acquired Avast, AVG, and others and changed its name to Gen Digital in 2022.

Other Categories

In addition to these categories, there are several technologies that deserve their own classification because they are still new and their buying centers (the team within the enterprises that makes the purchasing decision) and their usage prevent them from fitting into one of the other categories. The following six sections cover these.

Security Operations

A simple way to think of this category is anything needed by a SOC to improve its operations. It could be a malware analysis tool for reverse engineering or an incident handling tool or XDR for combining data from network, endpoint, user behavior, and threat intelligence sources. This was the fastest growing segment in 2021 and grew 9.6% in 2023.

Security orchestration is part of operations. It's simple in concept: identifying the repetitive tasks that sap the efficacy of security operations and automating them. Account suspension and recovery, password resets, firewall policy changes, TCP resets, and routing changes are all examples of things a security orchestration solution is designed to do.

Security orchestration and response (SOAR) is becoming a popular term for orchestration solutions that respond to a discovered breach. This may include isolating infected machines, installing new policies in network security devices, or shunning an attack source through TCP resets. As attackers automate, SOAR solutions will evolve to provide a response in minutes rather than the multiday time frames that are currently considered best practice.

IoT Security

The Internet of Things (IoT) is a broad category of products that have been found lacking in security controls. Closed-circuit TV cameras (like those used at traffic intersections), baby monitors, thermostats, mobile devices like bar code scanners, and industrial control systems (ICSs) all fall into this category. Add in the sensors and controls for ships, trains, bridges, and medical devices, all built and deployed with little thought of the way hackers would attack them, and you have a recipe for future disasters. Thus, a new category of vendors has cropped up just in the past seven years to address the problem with IoT security. Because of the special requirements for different segments, these vendors tend to focus on specific categories: consumer IoT, medical devices, automobiles, maritime, and ICS.

Managed Security Service Providers

Most organizations are not prepared to invest in all the product categories listed here, and even if they did, they would not have the resources to manage them. Managed security service providers (MSSPs) offer a broad range of products that they will deploy and remotely manage for their customers. The 266 listed in the directory are primarily MSSPs. There are thousands more that may be consulting firms that offer managed services as a sideline or may be resellers that manage the products they sell. MSSPs invest in monitoring automation, analyzing security, and finding and retaining staff who thrive in the stressful environment of dealing with continuous attacks against all of their customers.

Managed services are evolving into a category called *managed detection and response*. Companies like eSentire deploy network monitoring sensors on a customer's network and endpoint detection and response (EDR) such as Carbon Black, SentinelOne, or CrowdStrike on desktops and servers. If an attack is detected, they use network defenses to shut it down or quarantine the misbehaving endpoint for remediation.

Application Security

Application security encompasses code scanning, containerization, application hardening, and mobile app analysis and protection. In academic circles and the US military, this is often called *software assurance*, but the category has become very broad with 213 solution providers.

API Security

API security is a subset of application security, but we are breaking it into its own category to make it easier to track this important subcategory. There are 41 vendors including the well-funded Noname Security and Salt Security. Application programming interfaces (APIs) are rapidly becoming the dominant way for applications to communicate with one another. A simple handshake relying on poorly controlled credentials has given rise to a ripe environment for attackers. Recognizing this, entrepreneurs and investors have rushed to solve this looming security problem.

Security Analytics

One dramatic change in the makeup of the IT security industry over the last five years is the rise of security analytics. Most security information and event management (SIEM) solutions have morphed from aggregators of security alerts with a few algorithms meant to highlight the important events to full-fledged threat hunting and breach detection platforms. In 2019, Microsoft, Google, and AT&T made major announcements in this space. Microsoft and Google hoped that their ability to monitor and collect information from vast swaths of the Internet would power something new. Google's Chronicle, announced with great fanfare and high expectations, stumbled out of the gate and has been reabsorbed into Google. AT&T acquired cloud SIEM vendor AlienVault and appointed its CEO, Barmak Meftah, as CEO of its newly formed AT&T Cybersecurity, which includes AT&T's managed services along with AlienVault's SIEM solution. Meftah left in 2021 to found Ballistic Ventures, and in 2023, AT&T sought to spin out the division as a separate entity. After OpenAI's GPT-4 engine hit the market in November 2022, Microsoft announced an integration that would allow customers to have conversations with their Sentinel data. Many other vendors rushed to announce integrations with GPT-4 to enhance usability.

Security analytics is an answer to the flood of alerts from a plethora of detection solutions, which by their nature are usually tuned to fire off an alert with the least provocation. Detection has an interesting history. Clifford Stoll in *The Cuckoo's Egg* describes his archaic technique of hooking up a thermal printer to his network at Berkeley Labs and poring over the printouts to see connection attempts that eventually led him to attackers in Eastern Europe. In the late '90s, products from ISS and the open-source Snort were deployed on network taps to log network events triggered by rules meant to detect hacking attempts through regular expression or signature matches. The problem with intrusion detection systems (IDSs) is that they generated far too many alerts to be dealt with. This question was raised: if you could truly detect an attack, why would you generate an alert if you could block the attack before it did anything bad?

One response was the creation of intrusion prevention system (IPS), which eventually became a feature in firewalls. A limited number of things such as worms, direct attacks over vulnerable protocols like Telnet, and other attacks against known vulnerabilities were simply blocked at the gateway.

Managing alerts from firewall logs, system logs, and IDS systems gave rise to two separate industry segments. One was SIEM solutions like QRadar (now owned by IBM) and ArcSight (now part of Micro Focus, which was acquired in 2022 by Open Text). The other was MSSPs. Because most organizations could not staff a 24/7/365 operation to monitor thousands of alerts a day, outsourcing to an MSSP became the preferred solution. MSSPs would also offer to manage the firewall and IDS devices to maintain their configurations and tune them.

But as major breaches at Target and SONY Entertainment made clear, simply logging and monitoring such events was not effective. In retrospect, it was found that Target's deployment of FireEye products had seen the original attacks against their point-of-sale systems, yet the alert got lost in the noise.

So, the latest trend in cyber defense is extended detection and response (XDR). The idea is that network and endpoint agents are deployed that capture suspicious behavior either from network traffic or from endpoint activity. Vendors like Cybereason, Ensilo (acquired by Fortinet in 2019), and Stellar Cyber attempt to turn all of that data into strong indicators that an attack is underway. The goal is early detection and fast response. It is the automation of what is called *threat hunting*, usually a manual process of digging through all the data by an expert analyst assisted by tools such as Sqrrl (now part of AWS) and Arbor Networks for network data. It is expected that AI applied to alert data will be the next evolution of security analytics.

Fraud Prevention

Fraud prevention solutions have a lot of overlap with identity and access management, but instead of focusing on an organization's employees, they address the wider world of customers. Banks and online retailers are the usual buyers of fraud prevention products. These products may verify or assign risk scores to customers during the onboarding process, or they may monitor for unusual behavior. There are products to detect account takeover attempts and products that will check against a database of breached accounts to alert a user to change their password. Fraud prevention and deception are the only categories that usually shrink year over year, although in 2023, fraud prevention saw a small increase.

Threat Intelligence

Countering targeted attacks has become the most pressing requirement for cyber defense. Long the domain of firewalls, antivirus, and access controls, the cybersecurity industry began a reinvention that dates to the 2013 release of the now-famous APT1 report by Mandiant, which was primarily a breach response forensics company. (Mandiant spun off the FireEye products to private equity in 2021 and changed its ticker symbol to MNDT shortly before being acquired by Google in 2022.) As always, the industry is driven by threat actors: hackers, cyber criminals, hacktivists, and now nation-states. However, for years the industry's driving philosophy was to ignore the threat actors and focus on the actual attacks. Firewalls were deployed to limit access to corporate networks, and IPSs were deployed to block known worms and network exploits. Frequently updated antivirus on the endpoint helped control the spread of malicious software such as Trojans, spyware, and worms. Defenders did not worry about who was attacking them, only the signature of the attack.

The rise of targeted attacks, specifically from nation-state actors, can be traced to the 2003–2004 Titan Rain incidents, when a lone analyst at Sandia Labs, Shawn Carpenter, discovered widespread infiltration of many government research labs and military bases. While well-known inside the defense industrial base (DIB), it was not until Mandiant published its APT1 report that the industry started to respond to the devastating impact of targeted attacks with new tools and services. That report, published the week before the RSA Conference in San Francisco, caused an entire industry to pivot. One vendor, Cyphort, scrapped its product and re-tooled to become a breach detection vendor in the weeks following. Breach detection, sandbox analysis of target-specific malware, network monitoring, packet capture, and threat intelligence services became the fastest growing sectors in the IT security industry.

Types of Threat Intelligence Vendors

The threat intelligence category can be broken into several subcategories: reputation services, malware analysis, threat actor research, and Dark Web research. The vendors provide feeds and reports that, once consumed by their customers, can identify ongoing attacks, infections, and exfiltration activity. Reputation services have long been a differentiator for IPS vendors. Identifying and blocking attack traffic at the gateway based on signatures is compute-intensive because it requires full packet analysis. It is much easier to block all connection attempts from a particular IP address or Internet domain. Thus, Cisco, TippingPoint (Tried Micro), Corero, McAfee, and small vendors like Sentinel IPS (renamed Comic Networks in 2023), have incorporated IP reputation into their products.

In the meantime, stand-alone IP reputation services have sprung up to offer raw feeds of IP addresses scored on a risk scale. These services can scan IP addresses and websites looking for the presence of malware or can lay traps that identify attacks from particular IP addresses. The now essentially defunct Norse Corporation had more than 35 such honeynets deployed around the world to attract attack traffic. It claimed to have records of more than five million IP addresses (out of four billion) that it considered malicious. Of course, IP reputation is a fluid quality. An IP address of a server associated with a particular denial-of-service (DoS) attack could become completely benign if the administrator cleans the machine. So, IP reputation services have to be updated continuously, creating the business model for a subscription service.

MSSPs such as SecureWorks, Symantec, NTT, AT&T, and TrustWave collect security event information from all their customers. They are able to correlate and scrub that data and often provide those feeds to customers.

Threat feeds based on malware analysis mirror the types of infrastructure that every AV firm has built to inform their own signature update ability. Providers like ThreatGRID (acquired by Cisco) and LastLine (acquired by VMware) spin up thousands of virtual machines (sandboxes) and instrument them to extract indicators of compromise (IoC), which can include source IP addresses, command-and-control (C&C) IP addresses, MD5 hashes of the payload and its constituent parts, and other data. Team Cyrmu is perhaps the firm with the longest history, founded in 1998.

Threat actor research firms such as Intel 471 and iSIGHT Partners (sold to FireEye) have processes that require much greater human resources to provide. In addition to automated systems, these vendors rely on analysts to track particular cyber criminals, hacktivist groups, or teams associated with nation-state cyber espionage. Their products are primarily in the form of research reports that contain detailed descriptions of the threat actors, including their tactics, techniques, and procedures (TTP). This type of report does not lend itself to a feed, but most vendors are building APIs so that their data can be queried. Intel 471 has based its offering on a dashboard and feed of the activities of more than nine million separate threat actor identifiers.

Another category of threat research service is that provided for the purposes of brand protection or early alerting. Vendors such as GroupSense, Flashpoint Security, BrandProtect, Digital Shadows, and Recorded Future (the largest all-source threat intelligence vendor) attempt to identify when a customer is being targeted or even the early planning stages of an attack. They use open-source intelligence (OSINT) and tools for mining pastebins, chat channels, and anonymous sites hidden within the Tor network to gather their intelligence—the so-called Deep Web.

Deep and Dark Web Defined

While the Deep Web is the vast portion of the Internet that is not indexed by search engines, estimated at more than 90% of the entire web, the Dark Web is accessed by Tor (the Onion Router) or I2P (the Invisible Internet Project). In this way, the anonymity of participants is protected. Researchers at many vendors and law enforcement agencies infiltrate these deep and dark corners of the Internet to collect intelligence on threat actor intentions, tools, capabilities, and methods.

Most organizations track mentions of their key executives, products, and company via Google News alerts and frequent searches of social media and various paste and data dump sites where cybercriminals often share known exploits or pilfered material. But by the time this material is publicly available, it has already been discussed, shared, and exploited by the communities active in the Deep and Dark Webs. Monitoring public paste sites is not sufficient for effective research, and the data that shows up there is often out-of-date.

Though extremely valuable to both cyber and physical security teams, gathering data and gleaning intelligence from the Deep and Dark Webs is extraordinarily difficult. Thus, subscribing to a service that provides that monitoring is necessary.

Email Security

Email security comes in many flavors. Because email-born malware does not detonate until it lands on the desktop, it could be considered a form of endpoint security, but because most protections are deployed somewhere in the network, it could as easily fall into the network security bucket. It is easier to give email security its own category. When email was primarily managed on-prem, typically on a Microsoft Exchange server, solutions like Brightmail, Trend Micro, and IronPort were delivered as an appliance. As email moved to the cloud, primarily Office 365, email security has followed. There are 83 vendors of email security products. Because most breaches are credited to some sort of email delivery of a malicious payload or URL, these solutions attempt to identify and block these attacks before a user can open an attachment or click a link.

Training

Not to be confused with security awareness training, which is part of GRC, training encompasses technology that helps IT security teams and students learn how to deploy and operate security tools effectively. This is usually accomplished within a cyber range: virtual environments where defenders can square off against attackers.

Deception

Deception as a means of defense is as old as physical conflict. Massive engineering works were deployed in World War II to trick bomber squadrons into targeting decoys built from timber and tarps to look like factories. In IT security, the first commercial concept of deception was separate servers that were instrumented to detect changes to files, login attempts, and exfiltration of data. These were often deployed in the Internet-facing demilitarized zone (DMZ) with the hope that attackers would waste time poking around in this honeypot and also identify themselves and the techniques and tools they had at their disposal. These early commercial products did not fare well because targeted attacks were not very sophisticated and the primary defenses of firewalls, IPS, and privileged user management could address most of the attack methodologies. But today, attackers have gained that sophistication, and discovering them on the corporate network has become a critical component of breach discovery and response.

A modern deception solution has these four components:

- **Honeypots:** Many honeypots are distributed throughout the network as tempting VMs. A solution from the likes of Attivo (acquired by SentinelOne in March 2022), Illusive Networks (acquired by Proofpoint in December 2022), or TrapX (acquired by Commvault in February 2022) will manage the deployment of such virtual honeypots and monitor them continuously. An alert that an attack is underway is usually a good indicator that some security control has failed or a sophisticated attack is actually occurring.
- **Honeynets:** A complete network of endpoint honeypots is configured to look like a real network. In this way, attackers can be monitored as they encroach on one server, escalate privileges, and traverse toward a goal.
- **Tainted data:** Files with tempting data in them are spread through the network, even the production network. They are configured with technology that will phone home if they are opened, thus giving the organization a heads-up that a breach has occurred and possibly identifying where the attacker is.
- **Credential deception:** This is rare, but the idea is to seed social networks, especially LinkedIn, with fake identities of employees. If a security team sees attempted logins using variants of these fake identities, it would be an early warning that reconnaissance was occurring. This, and early warning from mining the Dark Web, are two of the few ways that recon can be detected.

The deception space has failed to take off. Most organizations are not yet mature enough to manage deception solutions or the high-value alerts they provide.

Security Testing

With such a complex collection of security technology deployed, it is becoming necessary to test frequently. One method is automated attack and penetration testing. These tools attempt to mimic the capabilities of a red team. In addition to vulnerability scanning, the tools will attempt exploits. This can be a scary prospect for a CISO. A safer approach is security instrumentation.

The overall philosophy of layered defense, in addition to providing a framework for breaking out the history of each layer, also leads to a complicated range of solutions deployed in most organizations. Breach detection and response in particular crosses over several boundaries as network, endpoint, and identity systems are mined for indications of an attack underway. Just as in other complex systems, it is becoming necessary to test and optimize the entire system of security controls that are in place. Infrastructures are complex, and simple misconfigurations can dramatically undercut efforts to secure them, as we are learning from recent cloud breaches. Security instrumentation addresses the blind spots that will inevitably develop in multilayer defenses. Vendors such as Verodin (now part of Google), Spirent, and AttackIQ are leading in this space.

The concept of security instrumentation is straightforward. Deploy sensors, generally as virtual machines in a cloud or on small, dedicated hardware devices across your network zones such as partner, desktop, and server networks; DMZs; and Internet. These sensors, which live in your production environment, measure the efficacy of your security tools across networks, endpoints, email, and the cloud.

The sensors run a large and growing library of test behaviors against other sensors, thus operating safely and ensuring that your assets aren't targeted while validating whether the security tools you purchased to protect those assets are working.

Security instrumentation also requires integration with security management solutions such as firewall managers, endpoint security managers, log managers, SIEMs, and other devices. These control points are instrumented to measure the response to the attacks generated by all the sensors.

For example, it could be that a test attack is not blocked, and perhaps it was not even detected. Or a test was detected on a firewall manager but the events never made it to the SIEM. All too often, events that do make it to the SIEM don't result in a notable or correlated event because of faulty configurations as well as problems around alerting, parsing, time stamping, routing, etc., meaning the likelihood of a human seeing and responding to the event is very low.

Security instrumentation automatically identifies these issues and provides actionable, prescriptive information on how to mitigate them. Best of all, once you apply a fix such as a signature, firewall rule change, endpoint security adjustment, or SIEM correlation rule, you can revalidate to ensure the changes work and then continuously validate to ensure there isn't drift from a known good state. This automated, continuous validation results in end-to-end security measurement and improvement across your entire security stack.

Summary

Think of the overall IT security industry in terms of the layers of defense. Thus, network, endpoint, data, identity, and GRC are the major buckets, with several new categories included at the higher level: threat intelligence, testing, deception, breach detection and response, and IoT.

The task for a CISO is to choose the products that, when combined, provide the most effective defense. The best product for any one organization depends on many factors. While cost is usually the top concern, that has to be weighed against efficacy, ease of management, available support, and even skill sets of existing personnel. There are also regional considerations. In what appears to be a trend toward digital mercantilism, many countries are encouraging the purchase of home-grown solutions. If this trend continues, it will only serve to increase the number of vendors in the space. If corporate ownership becomes a deciding factor in whether a security product can be trusted, then each country will need at least one vendor in each of these categories, or even in each of 660 subcategories!

It is often claimed that there are too many vendors and the IT security industry is ripe for consolidation. Yet, each of the vendors listed in this book has demonstrated viability and growth, indicating that customers have decided that they need their products. Despite the temptation to call it *consolidation* when a big vendor acquires a smaller vendor, it is not consolidation. It is the market process at work. A large vendor such as Cisco, Palo Alto Networks, or CrowdStrike cannot rely on its teams to invent the next product that will develop into significant revenue for them.

These companies look out into the market and choose the startups that are experiencing rapid growth and acquire them to add their people and products to their portfolios. In this way, they stay relevant and often take future competitors off the table. That said, 2021–2022 marked the first signs of consolidation in the traditional AV industry. NortonLifeLock, the consumer side of the old Symantec, acquired Avast for $8 billion. There are two drivers for consolidation in the AV space. First, is Microsoft's Windows Defender product, which is free and "good enough." Consumers do not need to invest in AV software. The other is the rise of EDR products like CrowdStrike and SentinelOne, which do a better job of endpoint protection for the enterprise.

Startups get funded thanks in large part to the lucrative exits of these large acquirers. There are spectacular stories of such success. Aorata, an Israeli startup, developed technology to detect attacks that took advantage of weaknesses in Microsoft Active Directory. The company had barely gotten off the ground before Microsoft snapped it up for a rumored $200 million. Another startup, Demisto, which developed orchestration capabilities, was acquired by Palo Alto Networks in early 2019 for $560 million after only four years.

One way for an established vendor to adjust to major market changes is to acquire. Gateway hardware security vendors are facing such a challenge from cloud security solutions. As computer workloads move to the cloud and employees become increasingly mobile, there is less need for stacks of appliances to protect the data center. How is a Cisco, Palo Alto Networks, or Fortinet going to protect its market share? Look to each of these to continue to acquire cloud security vendors to fill out the gaps in their offerings and provide a path to transition away from hardware.

CHAPTER 4

A Brief History of the IT Security Industry

The IT security industry is different from all technology sectors in a fundamental way—there is an outside driver.

If one were to write the history of data storage from the early days of magnetic grids, acoustic coils, and huge platter arrays the size of washing machines all the way up to the present day of solid-state drives (SSDs), you would have a history of how vendors strove to create denser storage capability at ever-higher reliability and lower cost. The only driver for that industry segment was the competitive market.

The outside driver for the IT security industry is threat actors. Early viruses and worms were created with no more nefarious purpose than to demonstrate vulnerabilities. Over time, as the Internet became ubiquitous, criminal threat actors evolved to steal account credentials for banking, steal clicks for affiliate networks, or deface websites to promulgate some hacktivist's agenda. Although nation-state threat actors were busy behind the scenes from the very beginning, it was not until 2003 and Titan Rain that we learned just how mature cyber espionage was. The APT1 report of 2013 began the shift in the industry to countering targeted attacks. Destructive nation-state attacks, such as Stuxnet and the 2015 attacks on Ukraine's power grid, demonstrated the need for defenses for industrial control systems.

The dual revelations from Edward Snowden and a still-unknown leaker to *Der Spiegel* of the TAO ANT catalog identified the intelligence community as a category of threat actor that is better funded, better organized, and more targeted than any before. For vendors, the intelligence community is a worrisome threat because they often target the products of firewall, network, and endpoint security vendors. Take, for example, the FLAME virus, identified by Kaspersky Labs, which used a tool that spoofed Microsoft's update service to gain a foothold in the target.

While the history of threat actors and their attacks is a fascinating study, tracking the history of the industry itself has value as well. That history is the story of the people, products, and companies that counter this outside driver. Within each company, there were the usual drivers to create products that were faster, easier to manage, and profitable, but each vendor is also under the constant threat of becoming obsolete as a better solution arrives to counter the latest threat.

A new vendor can start with a new technology to address the latest attack methodology and then expand its capability to encompass the features offered by legacy vendors.

Missed Opportunity

A great example of a missed opportunity was the nascent market for anti-spyware solutions. In the early 2000s, there were thousands of spyware products that fit into a confusing spectrum of maliciousness. A free tool like WeatherBug could be downloaded to a PC to give real-time updates on the weather. It would then generate pop-up ads or jigger search results to provide revenue for the creator and the thousands of affiliates it worked with. Because these tools were installed with the user's permission, the antivirus vendors of the day decided that they would not include them in their anti-malware solutions. They called them potentially unwanted programs (PUPs). This opened the door for specialist anti-spyware products like SpySweeper from Webroot Software in Boulder, Colorado.

Webroot, which in 2004 had 10 different products from MacCleaner to SpySweeper, took in $108 million from Technology Crossover Ventures and doubled down on its anti-spyware business. Within three months of launching an enterprise solution, it was selling $1 million each month in business anti-spyware and began the move to incorporate antivirus features, too. It had a very short window to gain market share based on its new feature. But by 2005, all the major AV vendors, led by McAfee, simply added anti-spyware features to their AV products. It was a rare instance of established vendors recognizing a market trend and responding effectively. It would be 15 years before Webroot could pivot into a different space and ultimately be sold to Carbonite for $615 million in 2019. Carbonite, in turn, was acquired by OpenText in November 2019 for $1.42 billion.

The lesson learned from Webroot's experience is the danger of an entrenched vendor recognizing a competitive threat early enough to fend it off by developing its own product.

An arena that experienced better results was that of email security gateways. The driving feature for Brightmail, IronPort, and CipherTrust was anti-spam. Symantec acquired Brightmail for $370 million in 2004. Cisco acquired IronPort for $830 million, and CipherTrust was acquired by Secure Computing for $274 million in 2006.

The history of network security has seen successful entrants leveraging a defining feature to become major players. Fortinet built a platform to deliver an inline antivirus solution, while Palo Alto went to market with an "application-aware" feature. Both quickly evolved into full-function firewalls to compete successfully with Check Point Software, Cisco, and Juniper in the enterprise.

Acquisition Replaces R&D in the Security Space

Market success in the security industry has two paths. Both require fast growth. One path leads to an acquisition, and the other to independence and usually an IPO.

The dynamic for the industry was, for much of the 2000s, a feeder system of venture-backed startups being acquired by the big vendors Symantec, Network Associates (McAfee), Cisco, and even CA. Each acquisition, at attractive multiples of 10 times the revenue and more, encouraged more investment on the part of venture capital and would launch a new batch of wealthy founders back into the ecosystem to try their hand at serial entrepreneurship.

This ecosystem made sense for large companies in a fast-paced industry. Innovation, engineering, and going to market require a combination of luck, ingenuity, and, most importantly, timing. Having the latest product to counter the latest threat is one thing. Having it ready for market when the threat arises is another.

The idea that a Network Associates or Symantec could lead such innovation from the top down and continue to succeed is unlikely compared to the ability to recognize when a particular product is doing well and fills a gap in their product portfolio. Thus, since its inception, Symantec has acquired more than 80 companies. McAfee itself started during the frenzied '90s as a roll-up of several disparate businesses.

While this churn of startups feeding the big players is still part of the IT security industry dynamic, something happened in the late 2000s to disrupt the success of the big players. Instead of being happy with steady growth in an industry that apparently books higher revenue each year, the large vendors often get spooked by big moves by their competition.

In September 2006, EMC, the storage giant, made a move into the security space when it acquired RSA Security, which included the SecurID product line. RSA Security was formed when publicly traded Security Dynamics acquired RSA, the encryption company in 1996. EMC may have been reacting to Symantec's oversized investment in Veritas, an EMC competitor, in 2004. Symantec paid $13.5 billion for Veritas, effectively turning it into a holding company with two major business units. This move began the slow decline of Symantec as a driving force in security. Spinning Veritas back out in 2015 after 11 years of a failed effort left Symantec thrashing around to regain its position of leadership. A desultory merger with Blue Coat in 2016 did not re-inject growth, and ultimately, Symantec was put on the block for sale. Chinese chip maker Broadcom, on its own path to enter the security industry, had already acquired CA for $18.9 billion in 2018 and paid $10.7 billion for Symantec's enterprise business in a deal announced in August 2019.

Meanwhile, Network Associates had its own issues. Like all tech companies in the early 2000s, it was reeling from the drop-off in sales and valuations after the dot-com bust. Network Associates had several leadership changes and decided to remake itself by first divesting most of its product line, including the Gauntlet Firewall. It then went on a buying binge, quickly acquiring Foundstone, a vulnerability management company; Intruvert, an early IPS vendor; and Entercept, an endpoint intrusion prevention company. It then made the ill-fated decision to rebrand itself as McAfee, after its flagship product. This rebranding proved to be ill-advised because John McAfee, the highly erratic figure who had originally combined his AV company with Network General to form Network Associates rose seemingly from the dead to leverage the name recognition for his own purposes, including making a bid as a candidate for President of the United States. (John McAfee died in June 2021 at the age of 75.)

In 2010, McAfee's new CEO, Dave DeWalt, negotiated an astounding deal. Intel, a chip manufacturer, bought into the idea that an AV company would be synergistic with a silicon company. McAfee was sold to Intel for $7.68 billion. Intel attempted to repair the brand by renaming the company Intel Security. It would be five years of stagnation and new management at Intel before Intel Security was spun off again and re-rebranded as McAfee.

McAfee's story continued in 2021. In April, private equity firm Symphony Technology Group (STG) acquired the enterprise business from publicly traded McAfee, which kept the consumer business. This was similar to the split of Symantec when it sold its enterprise business to Broadcom leaving NortonLifeLock behind as the public company. The announcement claimed revenue for the enterprise business part of McAfee of $1.3 billion.

In October 2021, STG announced it had also acquired a big chunk of FireEye's enterprise products, paying $1.2 billion. While FireEye went on to rebrand as Mandiant, the combined McAfee+FireEye are being branded as Trellix, an XDR platform. STG launched the McAfee Enterprise Secure Service Edge (SSE) portfolio as a separate business in March 2022. The new business is branded Skyhigh Security and is led by former

Cisco Executive Gee Rittenhouse. At the end of 2023, Skyhigh had 620 people.

In November 2022, what was left of the publicly traded McAfee was acquired by a group of large investors, including Advent International Corporation, Permira Advisers LLC, Crosspoint Capital Partners, Canada Pension Plan Investment Board, GIC Private Limited, and a wholly-owned subsidiary of the Abu Dhabi Investment Authority for $14 billion. At the end of 2023, McAfee had 5,641 employees, down 6% for the year.

There are other games played at the top of the security industry food chain. As the center of focus shifted to defense against nation-state adversaries and as the Pentagon stood up US Cyber Command on May 21, 2010, it seemed to make sense that defense contractors would start to make acquisitions. In fact, Raytheon entered the market with its acquisition of a majority stake in Websense in 2015. It combined its other cyber products in the newly branded Forcepoint in 2016. Lockheed Martin acquired Industrial Defender, one of the first industrial control systems security plays, in 2014. (Industrial Defender was spun out to Capgemini in 2018 as Leidos Cyber. In January 2020, Capgemini sold Industrial Defender to Teleo Capital Management. As a newly independent company, Industrial Defender had 49 employees, down to 43 at the end of 2023.)

But no defense contractor made a strategic decision to lead in cyber security, leaving Symantec, McAfee, and Cisco to continue to play their own part in the industry. The Defense Industrial Base is primarily a customer, not a vendor, of security products.

That all leads to today. There are at least 3,700 vendors of IT security products. This number includes the managed security service providers and the new realm of cloud-delivered services. As we go to press, IT-Harvest has ingested data on 6,800 products from these vendors. We estimate there are 18,000 products.

Of 3,700 vendors, 1,947 are based in the United States, with Israel second (307) and the UK third (267). Within the United States, the center of the industry is based in California, with 566 in the Bay Area alone. The second major concentration is around Washington, DC. These proportions have not changed very much over the last decade. The only force at work appears to be a form of digital mercantilism that is driving each country to favor home-grown vendors over foreign.

Digital Mercantilism

Digital mercantilism began after Edward Snowden revealed the deep relationship between the National Security Agency (NSA) and US technology vendors. European countries were the loudest protestors, and the EU has taken measures to protect the privacy of its member states' data with the General Data Protection Regulation enacted in 2018 to impose fines on companies that did not take extraordinary measures to protect the data entrusted to them. To date, there have been more that 1,956 enforcement actions, with the largest targeting Facebook.

Ironically, the United States is fueling digital mercantilism by singling out Huawei, a Chinese network gear manufacturer. The intelligence community has been waging a campaign to keep Huawei out of the United States. Former US Secretary of State Mike Pompeo made strong demands on US trading partners to do the same. One view was that blocking Chinese manufacturers from competing with US network gear companies would be "protective," but in actuality, accusing a vendor of having insecure products is a tactic that could easily backfire. If every vulnerability is deemed a backdoor, then US vendors could be tarred with the same brush. Digital mercantilism could spread, and each country could push a buy-local message, leading to more security vendors, or at least the continued success of the existing local vendor: Panda Security in Spain (sold in 2020 to WatchGuard), AVG in Germany, Kaspersky in

Eastern Europe, and AhnLab in South Korea. Look for each category of vendor, from threat intelligence to deception to security analytics, to have its own participant in each country.

The IT security industry ecosystem has been decapitated by the wayward path of Symantec and McAfee. Luckily, Cisco, Palo Alto Networks, and even Microsoft are filling the gap. Meanwhile, private equity firms have become the primary acquirers of cybersecurity vendors.

CHAPTER 5

The History of Network Security

Among the many threads that weave together to form the history of the IT security industry, one stands out in sharp contrast: the addition of Check Point's Firewall-1 to Sun Microsystem's catalog of software products. The origin story of Check Point always points to this seminal event in its early history. Founded by Gil Shwed, Shlomo Kramer, and Marius Nacht in 1993, Check Point not only gave rise to the network security industry, it was the spark that fueled what is today a booming startup ecosystem in Israel. Shwed holds the patent for the stateful inspection firewall, a critical innovation that simplified and dramatically improved the performance of gateway firewalls. He, like so many cybersecurity startup founders coming out of Israel, spent four years within the Israeli Defense Force. Shwed joined at age 18 in 1986. He and his co-founders launched Check Point Software Technologies Ltd. in 1993.

Firewall-1 was the first stateful inspection firewall. It was all software and could run on most flavors of Unix, eventually including IRIX from Silicon Graphics, HPUX from HP, AIX from IBM, and, most importantly, Solaris from Sun Microsystems. The mid-'90s, before Microsoft introduced Windows NT to disrupt the market, were notable for the battles between microcomputer vendors to win the enterprise market. They each encouraged software developers to port their products to their platforms and, like Sun, published an ever-expanding catalog of available software solutions. Much like a listing in the AWS Marketplace today will generate a flow of new revenue, being in Sun's catalog meant low-friction sales for a software company.

Soon after launching, Firewall-1 was listed in Sun's catalog, immediately turning on the spigot of sales driven by Sun's large professional sales organization and its myriad resellers. Check Point was selling products in the United States before it had hired its first US salesperson. The timing was perfect. The Internet was booming, Sun was the leader in Internet-facing servers, and it quickly became apparent that to connect an organization to the Internet, you needed a firewall.

Check Point turned in phenomenal growth numbers in those early years at tremendous gross margins, as to be expected from a software-only company. Its revenue was $9.5 million in 1995, followed by $31.9 million in 1996.

Check Point orchestrated a masterful IPO on Nasdaq. It opened an office for its US headquarters in Redwood City, California; recruited Deb Triant away from Adobe to be its US CEO; and went to market with the story that operations would be led from the United States while R&D would reside in Israel.

By 2001, CHKP clocked $528 million in revenue (on track to do $2.4 billion in 2023). It had the largest share of the firewall market but was starting to see weakness in its software-only strategy. It has never been explained why Check Point did not try to enforce its patent for stateful inspection, a technology incorporated in all of its successful competitors, most notably the Cisco PIX line of firewalls.

Cisco had acquired the PIX technology from a team of developers at Network Translation, Inc., in November 1995. The software was incorporated in a series of appliances dramatically improving the form factor and purchasing ease for a standalone gateway firewall. Check Point still required a customer to purchase and configure a server from Sun, HP, or Microsoft and then install the software separately. Much of that configuration and integration was carried out by the reseller channel eventually dominated by Nokia, which developed a set of purpose-built appliances to primarily run Firewall-1. Check Point leadership was probably influenced by the previous decade's war between the two go-to-market models: that of Apple Computer, which controlled all of its own software running on its own hardware platform, and the much more successful model of Microsoft, which stuck to software that would run on any PC hardware. But endpoint models rarely translate to networking models where throughput, low latency, and reliability are paramount.

Check Point eventually addressed the appliance model by acquiring Nokia's hardware business. But by that time, it had given up market share to Cisco, which far outsold Check Point with its multipurpose ASA appliance that incorporated networking, a PIX firewall, and VPN capability.

Check Point was also late in recognizing that firewalls were evolving rapidly.

The Rise of Intrusion Prevention

Nir Zuk was a Check Point engineer who moved to the United States in 1997, where he created a WAN optimization product for Check Point that he claims was never rolled out because of jealousy from the Israeli development team. He left Check Point in 1999 and soon after started OneSecure with the initial goal of creating a managed VPN service, but he quickly pivoted to one of the first intrusion prevention solutions (IPSs). IPS must have been an idea whose time had come because there were actually four other vendors that all introduced IPS products in the same timeframe of 2002–2003: IntruVert, TippingPoint, ISS, and Sourcefire.

IntruVert Networks was founded in San Jose California, in the fall of 2000 by Parveen Jain. IntruVert used the term *intrusion prevention* in its original marketing, although in a press release in which it announced $15 million in Series B funding in 2002, it referred to itself as "IntruVert Networks, a developer of next generation intrusion detection systems (IDS)." IntruVert was acquired by Network Associates in April 2003 for a reported $100 million. It gave NAI (soon to be rebranded to match its flagship product, McAfee) a network security component that fared much better than the Gauntlet Firewall, which reached end-of-life that year, and its customers were turned over to Secure Computing for support.

Another of these vendors was TippingPoint, which began life as a network appliance vendor in January 1999 called Shbang! It experienced a rocky few years, which included an IPO as Netpliance in 2000, in which it raised $144 million. In 2002, it discontinued the appliance operations and restarted as a network security vendor selling an intrusion prevention appliance. Under CEO John McHale it raised additional funds through a private investment in a public entity (PIPE). It was then acquired by networking company 3Com in late 2004 for an announced $430 million. At the time, quarterly revenue was $9.7 million.

By April 2010, 3Com itself was acquired by HP for $2.7 billion. Finally, the TippingPoint division was spun off to Trend Micro in 2015 for $300 million.

Internet Security Systems

Internet Security Systems (ISS) also pivoted into the IPS space. It was founded in 1993 by Chris Klaus, who had developed the first version of its flagship vulnerability scanner while working as an intern for the Department of Energy. While he was enrolled at Georgia Institute of Technology, he released the first version of Internet Security Scanner as freeware. While Klaus served as CTO, he brought in Tom Noonan to be CEO in 1995. Venture backing was provided by Greylock Ventures and Sigma Partners, with further rounds coming from Ted Schlein at Kleiner Perkins, as well as AT&T Ventures. They continued to roll out additional assessment tools, including System Scanner for servers. In 1998, ISS formed X-Force, a professional service arm, as well as one of the first research teams that led the way for future research arms at major security vendors. ISS went public on Nasdaq on March 23, 1998.

In 1999, ISS acquired Netrex Security Solutions, a Michigan-based MSSP that had been one of the first resellers of Check Point Software. Netrex had developed the backend systems to allow a Security Operations Center to manage the firewalls and security for many of its customers, becoming one of the first to introduce what became known as *managed security services*.

In 2001, ISS acquired BlackICE, an endpoint protection platform created by Rob Graham, and in 2002, it launched its own managed security service. In 2003, ISS introduced Proventia, a line of gateway security appliances that, with the addition of German web filtering company Cobion, became one of the first UTM solutions.

In 2004, Klaus stepped down as CTO to be replaced by Chris Rouland (later founder of Endgame Systems, Bastille Networks, and Phosphorus, an IoT security startup that extended its A round with an additional $27 million in December 2023.)

In 2006, ISS was acquired by IBM for $1.93 billion. IBM X-Force and managed services are still major components of ISS in use today. Many of the alumni of what was a tight-knit community can be found at an annual get-together at the RSA Conference in San Francisco.

Sourcefire

Sourcefire was founded by Martin (Marty) Roesch in 2001. In his own words, he is "a computer-building, Neuromancer-reading, software-writing, hardware-hacking, hopelessly passionate geek." Roesch was the developer of Snort, an open-source IDS. He believed firmly in a business model, much like Red Hat's for Linux, of supporting an open-source product to generate a community of users and then creating a for-profit venture to support those users who needed enterprise-class features and capabilities. As he wrote in his popular blog, "The value of an open-source technology to the company that develops and supports it is the community that grows around it." Roesch, a technologist at heart, recruited Wayne Jackson as CEO to run Sourcefire. Jackson took the company public in 2007 and stepped down in 2008 to be replaced by John Burris, who passed away in 2012. Roesch was acting CEO until John Becker was brought in to lead the company to its eventual sale to Cisco in July 2013. Roesch stayed on until 2019 to guide Cisco's security strategy.

The idea behind IPS was to look deeper into every session and look for signature matches with known attacks. It was primarily a defense against network-born worms, but there were hundreds of attacks over various protocols that could be identified and blocked. Unlike IDS, an IPS device would be inline and able to do that blocking.

In 2003, Gartner made the unusual move of removing all firewall vendors from the Leaders Quadrant of the Magic Quadrant for enterprise firewalls, with the challenge put forth that a vendor would not be put back into the Leaders Quadrant until IPS functionality was incorporated into its firewall product.*

Netscreen Technology was one of the fastest growing hardware appliance firewall vendors in 2003. It was started by Ken Xie, Yun Ke, and Feng Deng. Its form factor and throughput were competitive with the Cisco PIX products at a lower total cost of ownership than a Nokia/Check Point firewall. When Netscreen acquired Zuk's OneSecure in 2002, it quickly incorporated IPS into its appliances and became the only firewall in the Leaders Quadrant. Soon after, Juniper Networks acquired Netscreen for $4.5 billion.

Multifunction to UTM to Next-Gen Firewall

A pattern was beginning to emerge following the dictate articulated by Gartner analyst John Pescatore: what can be done in the network should be done in the network. Entrepreneurs began to bundle multiple security functions into one appliance. Fortinet was one of those.

Ken Xie, one of the founders of Netscreen, left in 2000 to form Fortinet. The initial idea behind Fortinet was to perform antivirus filtering with a network appliance. This was particularly challenging because a virus signature could be a snippet of code embedded anywhere in a relatively large package, not just in the headers where firewalls looked or the early packets of an attack where IPS looked. It required massive amounts of memory and specialized chipsets to do AV inline. Thus, Fortinet spent years and millions of dollars creating application-specific integrated circuits (ASICs) to handle the inspection and memory requirements.

As it turned out, doing AV inline was not the killer feature of this next generation of firewalls. The killer feature, arguably still driving firewall innovation today, was not initially even considered to be a security function. It was content URL filtering.

Content URL filtering, or web filtering, addressed a completely different requirement than security. As enterprises became more and more dependent on the Internet for productivity, they began to recognize that their employees were either wasting time or exposing other employees to what was termed a hostile work environment by their browsing behavior. In the first instance, it was watching movies or browsing sports sites. In the second, it was viewing pornography or other objectionable material from their work computers. Companies like Websense and Blue Coat saw this and introduced products that sat behind the firewall and proxied all web traffic. They scrambled to classify all the websites and content on the Internet and provide a policy engine that would allow administrators to decide what kind of content was appropriate for the work environment. It was only much later that websites began to deliver malware and pose a security threat. Eventually, the web filter evolved into the Secure Web Gateway. But in the meantime, Blue Coat and Websense sold their products to most large enterprises at costs that were often as high or higher than the primary firewall: $50,000 or more.

So Fortinet simply took advantage of all of its processing power in its appliances to add URL content filtering as a feature. This paved the way for what became known as *unified threat management* (UTM), the concept of incorporating many security functions in a single appliance. A Fortinet salesperson could now target companies that were simultaneously looking to refresh their firewalls and were approaching contract renewal time for its web filtering solution.

Meanwhile, Zuk left Juniper to found Palo Alto Networks. The PAN firewalls were also appliance-based but used off-the-shelf network processing silicon instead of developing ASICs. Palo Alto Networks quickly rose to the Leaders Quadrant in

*The author of the MQ was Richard Stiennon

the Gartner Magic Quadrant and went public July 20, 2012, to great fanfare. Palo Alto wisely came up with a new term for its multifunction security gateway, calling it a next-gen firewall. It was truly Zuk's next generation of security appliance after Netscreen. Gartner had discounted the term UTM, which was coined by Charles Kolodgy at IDC, and in a rare move adopted Palo Alto Networks' term.

Local Internet Breakouts

Another aspect of the industry that has driven the success of multifunction firewalls is a long-term trend away from corporate networks to local Internet breakouts. This is simply an architecture that uses the Internet as a means of transporting corporate traffic instead of a traditional hub-and-spoke MPLS network. This trend is accelerating dramatically thanks to cloud transformation.

Organizations with many locations, such as retail stores and chain restaurants, may have hundreds if not thousands of locations. Their architecture choice is to backhaul all traffic to the corporate data center over expensive leased lines and apply firewall, IPS, anti-malware, sandboxing, and content URL filtering there, or deploy lower-cost UTM devices to each location and purchase broadband access from a local provider. There is no way they can deploy the expensive stack of equipment for all these functions that they have in their data center, so they are driven to lower-cost stand-alone appliances that provide all these protections. This is an efficient use of bandwidth because traffic destined for the Internet goes directly to the desired websites and traffic for the corporate data center can be connected via an authenticated VPN.

But note that the primary feature that drove the transition to UTM was content URL filtering.

Over time there are innovations in network security that could give rise to new products. Startups with such new ideas should be aware of just how quickly a UTM vendor can add their features to their existing products, usually with a software update. One such feature was bot detection, basically monitoring outbound traffic for signs of infected hosts. That feature is already incorporated in most UTM products today.

The idea of combining multiple security functions in a single appliance is so common that it is surprising that some analysts give credit to a particular vendor for inventing it. All firewall vendors eventually migrate to this multifunction model. WatchGuard, SonicWall, Untangle, Clavister, and the startup Red Piranha in Perth, Australia, are just a few of the gateway security appliances that combine functionality. They each target different market segments or bring a different twist to their approach. WatchGuard, SonicWall, and even Fortinet do well in the distributed enterprise companies that have hundreds or thousands of locations. Think restaurant and retail chains.

If any company deserves credit for approaching network security with a revolutionary innovation, it is iPolicy. Founded in 1997, it billed itself as the first intrusion prevention firewall. Its technology was based on the concept of single-pass inspection of all packets. Then policies would be applied based on traditional factors such as source, destination, and protocol, but also on the content of the packets. But iPolicy was early with this concept and eventually ran out of funds and was sold to Tech Mahindra in 2007.

Palo Alto Networks

Palo Alto Networks is the largest firewall vendor, based on a market cap of $89 billion at the end of 2023 (and surging over $100 billion at publication). Compare that to Check Point's $17.7 billion and Fortinet's $44.8 billion.

Zuk is a driven entrepreneur and is well-known for his outspoken criticism of Check Point, where he was an early employee. He joined in 1994, only a year after it was founded, and moved to the United States in 1997, the year Check Point went public.

When asked in an interview what he found difficult about working at Check Point, he said,

> *"We started a small engineering group here in the United States and we built a product called Floodgate, a quality-of-service product Check Point started serving, and then in 1998 we had a complete implementation of a bandwidth optimization product. The product was ready to be released, and then Check Point decided not to release it. The reason given to me for not releasing it was that the engineers in Israel were really angry that someone in the US was having fun building new products. I'm not kidding you, that was the reason! Then I said, okay, this is an organization that I don't want to work for, and I left that day."*

With initial funding of $9.4 million and 25 engineers from Netscreen/Juniper, he was able to quickly create a viable product. Launched in 2005, PAN introduced its first product in 2007. The go-to-market message for PAN was that traditional firewalls could not distinguish between applications delivered over ports 80 and 443 and, therefore, could not apply firewall policies based on application. In this case, an "application" would be software as a service such as Salesforce or NetSuite. It could also be an application within an application, such as a game within Facebook.

One of the strategic successes of PAN was to raid the vaunted Check Point reseller network. Check Point is famous for protecting its channel jealously, although also famous for reducing the points (percentage of a sale) it shares with its channel over time. A newcomer wanting to sell through those channel partners would offer much higher margins, but would also have to disguise the fact that they were selling a firewall or Check Point could cut the reseller off from a lucrative renewal business. PAN went to market as a device that could sit behind a Check Point or Cisco firewall and merely provide visibility into what applications were in use. Once in place, it was just a matter of time before they could demonstrate there was no need for the legacy firewall since it was redundant.

By the time PAN went public in 2012, it reported having 6,500 customers compared to the 125,000 enterprise customers claimed by Fortinet. Check Point probably had twice as many. But PAN had won the hearts and minds of its customers, and the authors of the Gartner Magic Quadrant granted it Leader status in the 2011 Magic Quadrant for enterprise firewalls, a fact made clear in PAN's S-1 filing.

The Other UTM Vendors

There are many other UTM vendors around the world. Like the endpoint security space, there are often local vendors that established a market foothold in their own country or region with products that fit the local demand, like AhnLab in South Korea or Astaro in Germany and Cyberoam in India, both acquired by Sophos.

SonicWall was founded in 1991 by two brothers, Sreekanth and Sudhakar Ravi, to build Ethernet cards for Apple products. In the late '90s, they pivoted to hardware firewalls and VPN appliances. They addressed the small-to-medium business market segment but eventually built larger appliances that at times were challengers for the fastest feeds and speeds in the firewall segment measured in connections per second and throughput. They also built a graphical management interface that was competitive with Firewall-1. SonicWall continued to add features to become a full-fledged UTM and even predated Fortinet with many features. Remote offices and retail outlets had special demands for the appliances they wanted, including Wi-Fi access points, multiple ports for network segmentation, and eventually slots for cellular access cards that would allow a store to have a backup wireless connection in case its broadband connection failed.

SonicWall went public in 1999 with only 54 employees and a run rate of $10 million in annual revenue. By the time SonicWall was acquired by Dell in March 2012, it had 950 employees. Valuation was estimated between $1 billion and $1.5 billion.

Dell spun SonicWall out to Francisco Partners, a private equity firm that also owns WatchGuard, and Elliot Management. Bill Conner was appointed as CEO. Conner was the previous CEO of encryption company Entrust, which he joined in 2001. He continued to lead Entrust after it was taken private by Thoma Bravo, another private equity firm, until it was sold to what became Entrust Datacard and has now been rebranded back to Entrust.

WatchGuard is a UTM vendor based in Seattle, Washington. It was founded as Seattle Software Labs in 1996, but changed its name to WatchGuard Technology a year later and went public on Nasdaq in July 1999, when it reported having 134 employees. It was then taken private by Francisco Partners and Vulcan Capital in a deal announced in July 2006 for $151 million. WatchGuard's CEO, Prakash Panjwani, is an experienced IT security executive who led SafeNet to a successful sale to Gemalto in January 2015. WatchGuard grew 9% in employment in 2023 to 1,023 employees. It also acquired Spanish AV vendor Panda in 2022.

Sophos, primarily an antivirus vendor, has made two acquisitions in the UTM space. The first was Germany's Astaro, acquired in 2011. At the time of the announcement, Astaro was doing $56 million in revenue for its small appliances and had 200 employees around the world. It had recently introduced a unique product, Astaro RED, which was a simple little box that acted as an Ethernet bridge back to the home office. Even after the Sophos acquisition, this was a volume leader in shipments for the company. Astaro also sold a "virtual UTM," a set of security capabilities that could be installed in a VM on the customer's premises, much like Untangle, which was acquired by Arista Networks in 2022.

Sophos then acquired Cyberoam, a UTM vendor based in India, in February 2014. Cyberoam sold mid-range UTM devices throughout India, the Middle East, and Africa and was beginning to move into the United States, where its CEO, Hemal Patel, resided half of the time. When acquired, it had 550 employees. Cyberoam's unique approach was to focus firewall policy enforcement on user identities instead of network and protocol designators. This was a harbinger of the modern identity-defined perimeter.

Sophos has rebranded the Astaro UTM products as Sophos SG and maintains a separate brand for Cyberoam. It was a public company traded on the London Exchange, and its market cap was $2.6 billion as of mid-2019. Thoma Bravo announced an acquisition of Sophos in October 2019 for $3.9 billion.

AhnLab was created by Ahn Cheol-soo in 1995 as an antivirus vendor. It has since added UTM products under the product name TrusGuard. It went public on the KOSDAQ exchange in 2001. It was valued at $450 million at the end of 2023.

From Hardware Sales to Subscription Model

Tom Noonan, CEO of ISS, which he took public and then sold to IBM, once related a conversation he had with John Thomson, CEO of Symantec: "Tom, I have booked 85% of my quarterly revenue on the first day of the quarter." He was referring to the subscription model used for virus signature updates. This subscription model is very enticing, especially to the CEO of a publicly traded firm. Wall Street watches quarter-over-quarter growth and will punish any company that misses on expectations. A company that starts each quarter with zero revenue and has to meet or beat its previous quarter is under constant pressure, and the CEO faces diminished bonuses or even termination if they miss. So, John Thomson at Symantec was in the enviable position of having most of his revenue already committed and often already collected thanks to the subscription model prevalent in the AV world, something Tom Noonan was very cognizant of as ISS pivoted into subscription services for its Preventia line of security appliances.

The introduction of IPS and later content URL filtering and anti-malware functions into UTM devices opened the door to subscription models for hardware and software vendors. In the past, the model was an up-front fee for the hardware and software and several tiers of annual support fees, from 10–25% of the license cost. But with these new features that needed constant updates, they were able to charge for subscriptions. Those updates were pre-sold for one to three years. The vendor would collect the subscriptions up front (billings) but not recognize the revenue on their bottom line until the time had passed (revenue recognition).

Mobile Devices Side-Step Firewall Controls

The UTM vendors took advantage of the need for smaller all-in-one security appliances at remote offices to displace the large pieces of equipment that resided in the data center. But how are controls to be applied to the browsing activity of employees on their mobile devices? Most productivity tools have mobile apps and every web page is available from a mobile device. Or an employee could simply tether their mobile device to their laptop and bypass all the security on the office network.

The solution is to redirect all web and app connections from mobile devices to the cloud, where filters and controls can be applied. Blue Coat attempted to leapfrog the competition it faced from UTM vendors with just such a solution, but as is so often the case, it is hard for an entrenched vendor to introduce a product that will compete with its core offering. On top of that, an effective cloud-delivered service requires specialized architectures and faces technological challenges that are hard to overcome.

The Zscaler Story

In 2008, Jay Chaudhry was looking for his next venture. Chaudhry is arguably one of the most successful company founders in the security space. His first security company, SecureIT, in Atlanta, Georgia, provided professional services and integration for security solutions. He sold it to Verisign in 1998 for $69 million in Verisign stock, which was trading at $43 at the time. Chaudhry went on to found several other companies, which resided in the same office building in Atlanta and shared a cafeteria. Air2Web was a wireless application company, and AirDefense was a wireless security solution sold eventually to Motorola. His next venture was extremely well-timed.

CipherTrust was one of the first secure email gateway solutions. It went to market with the concept that any two CipherTrust email appliances would use SSL to talk to each other, guaranteeing that all email between two servers would be encrypted all the time. But that feature was a non-starter. Typically, people just don't care about data security. What's the point of encrypting email in transit when an attacker can just retrieve it from the victim's inbox? The feature that led to CipherTrust becoming a runaway success was anti-spam. At the time, Chaudhry described customers who would not relinquish proof-of-concept devices that CipherTrust would loan them because they reported immediate 85% reductions in email volumes thanks to the spam filtering.

Chaudhry accepted outside investment from Greylock Ventures and Asheem Chandna (another Check Point alumnus). CipherTrust eventually sold to Secure Computing in 2006 for $185 million. But that valuation was far below the $370 million that Symantec paid for competitor Brightmail or the $830 million that Cisco paid for IronPort, both email gateway devices that caught spam.

After a stint at Secure Computing, Chaudhry left to work on his next venture. He wanted to address two mega-trends that were becoming apparent in 2008. He saw the combination of mobility, where devices were no longer under corporate control, and cloud computing, where apps were moving out of the data center, as two trends that would challenge the security status quo.

He envisioned a born-in-the-cloud security solution that would replace all of the functionality of the security stack in a traditional data center: firewall, IPS, anti-malware, and, yes, content URL filtering. He recruited a team of developers with security, OS, and network expertise, and they built out a series of their own data centers around the world to essentially create a reverse content delivery network (CDN). Zscaler looks like an Akamai that has edge servers to push cached copies of content to users with as few hops as possible between them and the YouTube videos they want to watch. But in Zscaler's case, the distributed edge network provides network access. Any user on any device can connect to any cloud app through these edge nodes.

The Zscaler cloud runs on specialized hardware that is built for multi-tenancy. There is a policy control plane that sits on top of the whole infrastructure, which allows a customer company to define granular policies for every user and every app they want to use. There is an enforcement engine that applies filters to decrypted traffic to prevent malware and attacks from spreading. Unknown executables can be sequestered while they are detonated in a sandbox and observed to determine if they pose a threat. Finally, there is a logging component that either stores all the logs per customer or directs them to a destination of the customer's choice. The network infrastructure requires peering relationships with the major cloud and app providers that gets a user's traffic to its destination as efficiently as possible. The move to Office365 by most large enterprises has driven many customers to either sign up for Microsoft's ExpressRoute service or take advantage of Zscaler's established routes to Microsoft's data centers.

One final aspect that Zscaler has brought to market is an implementation of Zero Trust networking. Zscaler Private Access (ZPA) is a separate product designed to allow corporate users to gain access to internal applications whether they reside in the cloud or the corporate data center. It uses much of the same infrastructure for access to the Zscaler edge but does not require the security filters because authorized users accessing corporate apps are not exposed to the threats of the untrustworthy Internet. ZPA acts as a broker for access to corporate apps. No IP address is needed for the app, as only Zscaler needs to know where the app resides. A user authenticates to the corporate directory service, be it Active Directory, AzureAD, Okta, or Ping Identity, and Zscaler makes the connection to the app. This zero trust networking connects users to apps. The apps are not visible at all to the Internet as a whole; thus, they are "stealthed" from attackers.

Zscaler went public on Nasdaq at $26 in March 2018. As of the end of December 2023, it was trading at $217 and had 7,050 employees.

You can see that Zscaler completes the story of network security evolution that started as standalone software running on generic servers, grew to specialized hardware appliances, and now has migrated to the cloud. All of the traditional vendors have also recognized the importance of cloud architectures and are scrambling to evolve. Most simply virtualize their software and ask customers to run their software in the cloud in front of their apps. Palo Alto has acquired cloud capabilities by acquiring Evident.io for cloud configuration monitoring, Twistlock for container security, PureSec for serverless security, and RedLock for cloud compliance. Meanwhile, Check Point has acquired Dome9, a cloud firewall.

As is so often the case, and as Chris Blask points out, technology finds solutions when they are needed. The flurry of network security startups in the 1993–1995 time frame is just one example, as are the simultaneous invention of IPS, the rapid move to all-in-one appliances in the mid-2000s, and now the rush to cloud offerings.

In 2003, Gartner made the unusual move of removing all firewall vendors from the Leaders Quadrant of the Magic Quadrant for enterprise firewalls, with the challenge put forth that a vendor would not be put back into the Leaders Quadrant until IPS functionality was incorporated into its firewall product.* The author of that Gartner MQ is the author of *Security Yearbook* 2023.

Story: Chris Blask

Chris Blask contributed to the invention of the gateway firewall and network address translation (NAT) while he was at BorderWare. He is the VP of strategy at Cybeats. He is also chair of the industrial control system ISAC.

A lot of folks take an odd path to a security career. I was just another odd-pather. I didn't finish high school; I was running a baling room, making huge bales out of strips of paper and dust, into my early 20s. After getting married, I took some classes and got a computer job, and one thing led to another.

My first job was a little company called Enterprise Computer Systems, which was a Data General VAR building systems for lumberyards. Soon after I joined, my bosses left. I was left holding the technical bag and spent a year or two doing that.

When I left that job, I was teaching landscaping, Unix, and C at Greenville Tech. I ended up being a "Kelly girl" at General Electric, a full-time contract role. My job was to take care of the networks for these plants, making 150-ton turbines for power generation in a building one-quarter of a mile long. Sixty percent of the computer terminals were down when I got there. So, I took a clipboard and a pencil and I walked all of the cables to map out the network and take inventory.

I did that for a few weeks until they were all working. About that time, they were installing a video conference center. I wanted to have mobile videoconferencing, so I got some catalogs and ordered RF modulators and things. I connected the industrial control network, the plant floor network with the machine tools and terminals, and data to the Internet via the IT network. I stacked up various pieces of equipment and ran cables between them so that I could have a rolling box of video gear and I could plug in to the network anywhere and be part of a global GE videoconferencing network.

This is ironic in that, of course, I worry about OT security now, and in 1990, I was the guy who connected IT to OT for what seemed like a really good purpose. And it was effective. We had a German-made machine go down, so we got the supplier's engineers to a GE videoconference location, and I crawled around underneath the machine holding a camera to troubleshoot it. I was wearing a headset and would point the camera where the engineer said to resolve the problem. The economic and functional reasons for doing it were perfect, but, of course, I hadn't thought of security.

After GE, I moved to Toronto and got a job with a little company called C Change. The two founders were former NCR guys that had figured out how to basically hack the drivers on NCR disk drives. I needed the job, so I came on as a sales guy.

We were selling Internet connections and the gear for connecting. As one of the first ISPs in Canada, we were housing Livingston Portmasters in a closet at 1 Young Street in Toronto. Each Portmaster had 32 ports for dial-up modems. We also became a reseller for Livingston.

We also sold Rockwell NetHoppers. These neat little boxes had Ethernet on one side and a phone port on the other side with a modem and a little router in it. They were selling like hotcakes, which is fantastic, but every time we sold a Rockwell NetHopper, the customer would call us back and say it didn't work.

We were having problems associated with people using the same IP addresses on both ends. I remember sitting in a Chinese restaurant in Mississauga, Ontario, near the Meadowview GO station with the other sales guys, Clyde Stephens and Paul Hunt, and going over and over and over this. I had a Mac, and I drew a little cloud: That's C-NET and the line down here is our customer's network. We're selling this little box in the middle. What we need to do is build a box that will solve their problems.

The web wasn't popular at that time. We had DNS and mail and FTP and Gopher. I stared at the picture and thought we have to do security because the one thing between our customers and the Internet is this little box. So, we'll sell that too. Now everyone just calls that box the firewall. So, the BorderWare firewall server was invented. This put me in a weird situation when I first met Marcus Ranum and the other people who had been writing the history before me, because at that point, you did not put servers by definition on a firewall. You stripped code out, you did less, you examined it, and you had the best people in the world read the code.

I went to one of the first security conferences. Dennis Richie was up on stage with Marcus Ranum of firewall toolkit fame. I stood up and asked whether it was possible to have a firewall without reading all the code yourself. Marcus being Marcus said, "No. There's no way I would trust anything," and everybody agreed. I said, "You have it all wrong. My mom needs a firewall, and she's not reading the code." And a big debate began about how then we can't have security. Maybe, but my mom still needs a firewall.

And tens and tens of thousands and millions and millions of companies need firewalls. So, everything we've done to this point is fine, but it doesn't address this next issue. I found myself coming back to that over and over again. The war story is that me and the two guys stayed up for three days; I bought the Mountain Dew, and we just got it done in time.

As we went down this path of creating the BorderWare firewall, I had a conversation with an older guy from a big tech company who told me my sales plan for selling millions of firewalls was all wrong. I could sell only to the Fortune 1000, and then I would be done. The reason he gave? There were not enough IP addresses!

I freaked out. I got off the phone, and I ran into my boss John Alsop's office. I told him, "Look, there are not enough IP addresses. The world is going to end. The whole thing's a bad idea." And he didn't even blink an eye. He just sat there with his hands folded and said, "Look, I realize when there is enough demand for something technical solutions are a challenge, so don't worry about it; it will work out." And over the next 15 minutes in a little conference room with our one whiteboard; Omaya Algundi, who was our technical lead engineer; and Andrew Flint, who was the first hired engineer building BorderWare. We stood at the whiteboard and drew a little box in the center and a line on each side and then a little Gopher server.

I put 10 dots on the left side and said, "We're building a physical box with two-way network interfaces. We have to have a real IP address on the outside, even if it's only one or two. And on the inside is our class C that says that 10 dots can't be used anywhere else, so all of our customers can have 15 million addresses on the inside. If we can figure out some way to just build a table or something. . . ." And we invented network address translation right there. But that's not the point. The point is that John Mayes also invented NAT at the same time, as did others. To John Alsop's point: it had to be done.

And it was, and now not only does my mom have a firewall in several of her rooms, but they all do NAT. And we're not out of IP addresses even though we're out of IP addresses. And IPv6 isn't taking over the world because we continue to hack our way through things well enough.

Later, I ran into John Mayes at one of the early Internet World conferences. We had chili dogs. We weren't competing because PIX wasn't a firewall; yes, it sort of did NAT, but it did other things, too.

As far as I can tell, he went home and added security to PIX.

In fact, Check Point launched with Sun at Interop in Atlanta, and I relaunched BorderWare at the same place, right across the hall. I had a 10 by 10-foot booth with nobody but me, and I was up till 4 a.m. at Kinko's getting documentation, while Check Point had banners all up and down the escalators. BorderWare was number two in the early days before it got bought by Secure Computing.

When BorderWare was sold, I joined TIS for a year or so before they got pulled into McAfee, and then in June of '98, I joined Cisco to take over the Century firewall product line, which was put into end-of-life in the first month. I was also given the PIX, which was end-of-life in the next month as well. PIX was supposed to die in late '98.

To my point, everybody on the earth needs firewalls. At a certain point in the market, somebody like Cisco needs to come along and sell billions of dollars' worth of individual units. So I took over project management for the PIX team just as Cisco had determined to announce the end-of-life of the product.

We got really black ops about it. Intel stopped making parts for the PIX 510, so we now had only the 520, and we engineered the 515 sort of in secret. We announced it late '98 or '99 and then the gold series that lived there for 515, 525, 535.

The takeaway is that at that point, the security market thought it was really grown up. That was 1998, and look at the industry today!

Story: Gil Shwed

Gil Shwed is the cofounder and CEO of Check Point Software Technology in Israel.

I founded Check Point with my good friends Marius Nacht and Shlomo Kramer. I met Shlomo during my military service in Israel. We served in the same unit, and we always knew that we wanted to develop a product, to be entrepreneurs. I don't think we used the term *entrepreneurs*, but we wanted to develop our own product and do something, and throughout our army service we shared many ideas and many thoughts about what we could do together and what products we could develop.

I left the army at the age of 22, in 1991, after four years of service. Then I started consulting for several companies, and my main job quickly became one in which I worked for Marius Nacht, in a company called, back then, Optrotech, which became Orbotech. (Orbotech Ltd. is an Israeli technology company used in the manufacturing of consumer and industrial products throughout the electronics and adjacent industries.) We also thought about entrepreneurship and technologies and things we could develop together. That was 1987–1989 with Shlomo and 1991 with Marius. And around the end of '92 or the beginning of '93, I realized that it was time to start what became Check Point.

The idea for Check Point was actually based on an idea that I'd had since about 1990: technology for securing networks for screening traffic that runs on the network. The challenge was to connect two classified networks and make sure that only the things that should pass between these two networks actually passed. I looked at commercial solutions but didn't find anything adequate. I came up with the simple idea of defining a language that allowed you to describe the characteristics of the communication protocol.

Based on that language, I created a virtual machine code, and then I had a virtual machine that scanned every IP packet to determine whether it should pass. But I did some market research, and my conclusion was that it wasn't the right time for that idea. Most of the market was not ready for the concept that their networks needed to be compartmentalized and that they needed to separate between different departments. It was doable, but just not very exciting. It was a niche market that would require us to do a lot of work, and we weren't sure there would be an adequate return. It was too early.

At the end of '92, the United States changed its regulations regarding the Internet, and suddenly the Internet became, instead of a purely academic network, a network that could be open to everyone. Dozens of companies started to connect. In 1993, I suddenly saw that the Internet was going to have a big impact. And the first question for everyone was, "We connect to the Internet, but how do we keep our network separate from the 15,000 universities and students that are out there?" Two things came to me. First, the technology that I had in mind was the right technology to solve this problem, and second, the Internet is going to be something very, very exciting and important because it can really open the world, especially for me sitting in Israel. I actually worked with companies in the United States, and the fact that I could instantly send my code or an email looked like a revolution that would change the world.

That was actually a year before the web was invented, so it wasn't even about surfing or things like that. Just the fact that we could communicate in real time with low cost with everyone around the world looked to me revolutionary. That's when I went to Marius and Shlomo and asked them if they remembered the idea that I had discussed with them a few years before. I said it's time to take that idea and try to bring it to market and develop a product.

We then asked ourselves how we go to the customers. The first channel that we thought would take us to market were the ISPs, because they were pretty much the only people who saw the potential of the Internet. The IT community didn't really see the potential. So, the first people we tried to convince to become our partners were the ISPs.

We debated the right approach to developing this idea. Should we work at night, wait until we had a product, and then start to sell it? We were thinking about going to some big organizations in Israel and maybe offer them our idea and develop the first few versions for them. We considered many different alternatives. In the end, our analysis and our brainstorming suggested that if the market was moving really, really fast we couldn't do it as a side job or at night; we needed to dedicate all our time to the new idea. Today, this sounds obvious. But then it wasn't obvious, because up to that point I was doing three or four things in parallel at any given time.

We began to look for investors. Back then there wasn't a big venture capital industry in Israel. There were a few, but we didn't approach them. We didn't think they would even listen to us. Instead, we took a systematic approach. We looked at some people with financial backgrounds, and we contacted some software companies that we knew in Israel and a few organizations. We presented the idea to all of them, based on a basic plan that said that we needed around $100,000 to bootstrap our company, to buy computers, for travel expenses to the United States, and so on.

Finally, we had two competing companies that wanted to invest with us. One of them was BRM, which was a small antivirus software company from Jerusalem. They actually OEMed their product to a company called Fifth Generation Systems that was acquired around then by Symantec. So, they had a great OEM contract to develop a new backup system for Symantec. The other was Aladdin Knowledge Systems. To us they both looked like giant software companies. But I think BRM had 30 employees. Aladdin had a few more. We ended up choosing BRM as an investor, and actually they gave us $250,000.

From that point, we worked night and day to develop a product and to find a go-to-market strategy. That all happened between February and June 1993.

In February'93, the first Internet security conference was held in San Diego. I spent most of my savings buying an airline ticket, and Marius and I flew to San Diego to figure out what was going on in the industry and whether other people had the same idea.

At first, BRM gave us a lot of support and pushed us in many good directions. We also had some disagreements because, for example, they didn't always believe that we could make it, and they also weren't a huge believer in the Internet. They believed in networks and security, but they weren't sure whether the Internet was going to be the right thing. For example, they were developing a network product for a Novell environment, and they really wanted us to develop a Novell version of our software, which we felt was not the right direction.

Around a year and a half later, in early or mid-1995, BRM felt that it wanted to sell some of its shares and maybe even raise more money for Check Point. We didn't really want to raise money because we didn't need to. It was a year and a half since we'd started working with them, and we were already profitable and didn't need any money. But BRM hired a small boutique investment firm called Broadview, an M&A high-tech company based in New Jersey.

That led to a parade of venture capitalists to come see us, which was a very strange experience, because usually entrepreneurs run after investors and convince them to invest. In our case, we didn't want any money, and we looked at the process as a nuisance. I mean, we were ready to help and assist BRM, but conversations with investors took time from our running the business—and we simply didn't need the money.

When BRM started the process, it felt Check Point would be valued at around $12 million.

A few months later, after speaking to almost every possible VC, BRM sold its shares at $50 million. It tried to convince Marius, Shlomo, and me to sell some shares too, but we didn't want to, because we didn't feel it was the right time. Only six months later, Check Point went public at a valuation of $500 million, and after the first day on the market, it rose to $800 million. So obviously, BRM didn't have the right timing. But it was a very valuable experience. I spoke to almost every major VC firm in Silicon Valley, and the winners ended up being Venrock and US Venture Partners.

We went from nearly zero sales in '93 to a little bit less than $1 million in '94—that was the first year we started selling—to almost $10 million in '95. And $32 million in 1996. So we moved from 1 to 10 to $32 million in three years. And the next year, 1997, revenue was $80 million.

We developed our go-to-market strategy along the way. In the spring of 1994, we understood that we were three guys sitting in Tel Aviv. If we wanted to be successful, we needed to do it in the United States, because technology products that are successful in the United States can succeed all over the world. It doesn't work the other way around. If you're successful in any other country, it doesn't translate to worldwide success or to success in the United States.

We defined the United States as our primary market, and the marketing strategy was to find partners: resellers, distributors, ISPs, OEMs, and so on. OEMing to a big company was one of them. Even though that wasn't the only thing we tried—quite the contrary—we looked at five companies in the market that could be a major OEM for us. Sun Microsystems was number one on our list. But we said we couldn't build the business plan based on the fact that one out of five would decide to work with us. So we actually started by recruiting resellers, like ISPs and other software resellers. Since at the time there weren't really software resellers that specialized in Internet products, we looked at different people who sold, for example, Unix software and were resellers of Sun Microsystems, people who were selling networking equipment, and a few others.

Early on, I had a good relationship with Sun in Israel. Actually, I worked for the Sun

Microsystems distributor in Tel Aviv as a consultant for many years, so every time someone came to visit Tel Aviv from Sun, they helped me get a meeting. One of these people was in the CIO organization of Sun. When he came to Tel Aviv in early '94, I showed him our product. I explained to him why I thought it was interesting, and he said, "You know what? I think we can use something like that at Sun because we are connected to the Internet, and we have a lot of networks. I want to evaluate the product. And if we become a user, maybe I can also recommend to our business development people that they meet with you and consider distributing the software."

At that point, we had about 20 beta sites of the product around the world, and we were getting good feedback on the product. Nineteen out of those 20 beta sites told us they would like to buy the product, but we didn't have any distribution. We hadn't found anyone that would sell the software and support it. In April '94, Marius and Shlomo sent me to the United States, telling me, "Gil, you need to go there. Your task is very simple. Don't come back home without a million-dollar check."

The guy from the CIO's office at Sun had arranged a meeting with Sunsoft, the software arm of Sun, which was looking at ways to distribute their software to the Internet. When I went to the United States, one of my first meetings was in Silicon Valley with the business development people at Sun.

But we didn't rely just on Sun. The major effort was signing small resellers in different states in the United States to become our initial resellers. These things worked in parallel really fast. By June '94, I had become a very good friend of the Sun people. I spent almost every weekend with them. But in April, my first meeting was actually with a company called JVNC Network, which was the spinoff ISP from Princeton University. They were in charge of the network in the states of New York and New Jersey. They told me, "Gil, there's a big trade show next week in Las Vegas, Interop. Why don't you come and show your product in the trade show?"

That was a very important moment for us. But it was probably the longest night for me. I came to the United States in the morning, had a bunch of meetings with JVNC in New Jersey, and then I went almost all the way to DC to meet with TIS, Trusted Information Systems. It was offering a proxy server as a free toolkit. I wanted to see if we could get some sort of cooperation agreement with them. I finished the day again in Princeton. I spent the whole night talking to Marius and Shlomo on the phone and convincing them that we could put up part of the Interop booth of JVNC Network within 10 days. And we ended up doing that.

We won the best of show award as a new network product. Plus, at Interop we found some business development guys at the Digital booth and the Cisco booth, and we invited them to our booth around the same time as the Sun team was coming by. So when the Sun people came to see our product, they saw the buzz we were building.

That was the beginning of May '94. By June, the people from Sun told us, "We've got all the opinions. We want to do business with you." We were still clueless about what the business terms would be. They said, "Let's meet and start discussing business. We can even fly to Tel Aviv and see your business and meet there."

We consulted our lawyer, a very good friend of mine and a very smart person. He said, "No way. Don't make them come to Tel Aviv. If they come to Tel Aviv and see that you are sitting in the rooming house and that you are three people, even though they know all of that, they will know that you are a small company. If they see that, you won't get a good deal. Also, don't go to Mountain View and sit with them at their office, because there they don't have any motivation to close the deal. They can put you off. They'll say, 'Whatever we disagree on, let's continue tomorrow,' and weeks and months can pass like that."

So we ended up meeting in New York, in the offices of a big law firm. Sun sent three people to the meeting: a product marketing person, the business development person, and a lawyer.

From Check Point we brought 10 people to the meeting. Yes, we were only three employees at the company, so we got two lawyers from Israel, a lawyer from the United States, a business consultant from the United States, and two of our board members. So when the Sun people came into the room, they felt that they were meeting with a big company. They came with jeans and T-shirts; we came with suits and ties. By the end of the week we had agreed on the business terms. We still had nothing written, but over the weekend, I sat in the hotel room with the business development person from Sun, and we documented what we agreed on. And a few weeks later, we had that letter of intent signed, and I was able to go back home with a million-dollar deal—actually more than that. Over the next three years, the deal was for $3 to $5 million.

From there, we had to do two things. First, we needed to build the company, because to scale up and work with Sun we needed to recruit people. Second, we needed to find more distribution channels, not to compete with Sun but to augment that. We had to develop our own independent channel in parallel to Sun. Our strategy was to look at people who were not in the Sun reseller network.

By the way, one of the things that helped us in negotiations was that many Sun resellers were already interested, so we showed that interest to Sun, and it told them there was potential. They understood that their resellers wanted it, and if they didn't sign the deal with us, we'd work directly with the resellers. Basically, that started Check Point as a company. What we understood very quickly was that the number-one priority was a sales and marketing organization to support all the resellers, to grow the business, and to support Sun. So, Marius, Shlomo, and I knew that we would have to become a virtual sales and marketing organization. We had to recruit people and resellers.

Marius spent almost all his time with his suitcase in the United States, traveling from one city to another every day. He didn't have a house; he didn't have an office. He literally had a carry-on bag and a beeper. There were no cell phones back then. He would collect messages every few hours and, based on the messages, decide which city to go to the next day. He became our sales, marketing, and support organization. Shlomo took responsibility for Europe. He had a family, so he said, "I'll be in charge of development and Europe so I can leave early in the morning and be back late at night. My wife won't even pay attention that I traveled." That was his theory, at least.

My first tasks were to recruit a head of Check Point sales and marketing in the United States and to start an R&D organization in Israel. So the first few recruitments that we did in Israel were R&D people, the first three, four, and five developers who would keep developing the Firewall-1 product. The product itself was pretty good in the first version, but you can't be in technology without devoting most of your resources to improving the technology. So that's what we did.

About six or seven months later, we recruited our head of sales and marketing, Deb Triant. She had been the VP of marketing for Adobe in Silicon Valley. And that was the first major sales and marketing person we had. I worked with her very closely to build a sales team and recruit more resellers to support Sun and really build the company around that idea. When we were three people, we were spending, I don't know, $10,000 to $20,000 a month. Now we had a million-dollar contract from Sun Microsystems, which allowed us to do everything we needed. It gave us a secure future for the next few years, which we used smartly to develop a business. We could have just sat back in Israel and developed the software and enjoyed the benefit of that business, and that would have been a pretty good business for the three of us. But we really insisted on building an entire company, with sales and marketing and so on, so we could be independent and not 100% reliant on Sun.

One of the first people who showed interest in Check Point was a salesperson at BBN, a research firm that was a big government contractor, in Boston. BBN was running the network for all the

Boston educational institutions: Harvard, MIT, Boston University, and probably 50 others. He took us to many big Boston-area accounts like Digital, Gillette, and State Street Bank. They all showed interest in the product. I remember going to Gillette, a very conservative company. They wanted to connect to the Internet, and because they saw our product, they switched from Digital to Sun because they were excited about that potential.

That sales guy demonstrated the potential. He tried to convince the bosses at BBN to become a Check Point reseller, but they didn't want to. Our experience with ISPs at that point was that most of them had plenty of business selling connectivity. The ones that came from academia didn't have much interest in doing more business. They liked the product, but they didn't want to become a reseller. And so this guy decided that he would quit his job and become the first Check Point reseller. And that's what he did. The name of that business was Internet Security Corporation. They even owned the domain Security.com, by the way.

Here's one example of how we started the channel for network security products: BRM tried to convince me to go public in the summer of '95, when we were forecasted to have sales of around $10 million that year. I remember that vividly because Deb reminded me over the years about it. She came to Tel Aviv. The investors called us in to a big meeting with all our accountants and lawyers and shareholders and told me, "Gil, we see you have a nice business—$10 million." Back then $10 million was actually enough to go public. And they said, "You should go public now."

I was the youngest person in the room, maybe 27 years old. All the other people were grayer and older than me, and very authoritative, all of them running big businesses. And I told them, "No way, guys. We are building a business here. We are not here to sell it; we are not here to be involved in financing. That will distract us from the main goal, which is to develop the best security and the best business around it." Deb was shocked at how I could sit there as the kid in the room and tell them, "No way." I think maybe that's what also triggered them to sell part of their share to our VCs later in '95.

At that point, I didn't want to go public. But at the beginning of '96, around February or March, I pretty much had no choice because we already had a subsidiary in the United States with sales and marketing, we had already built a development organization, and we already had several offices around the world. The investors came to me again and said, "Gil, it's time to go public." By then the US investors had also joined us. Just to be clear, they closed the share purchase from BRM around November '95, and by February, they were already convincing me to go public. We went public at the end of June 1996 on Nasdaq. So less than three years after we started, we had an IPO. For me it was too early; for the investors it was too late.

Doing an IPO is like doing basic training in the Army. It's a difficult process that tests your abilities. It took two or three months to get all the documents done and to select the bankers. And then we did a three-week road show around the world. We started in Switzerland, on my 28th birthday, and moved to London, and then to the United States. We visited 35 cities in three weeks, and it was completely crazy. It's one of the most intense experiences that I have had.

We were in New York for the opening of trading. Both the New York Stock Exchange and Nasdaq were customers by then. I remember the morning of the IPO because I met with Deb and with our head of sales in the United States, who had been with us only three or six months. They were both excited by our stock's performance. We priced the IPO at $14 a share. The trading opened at $24 a share, so everybody was very happy. But I gave them a very hard time. I told them, "You see, it's now June 29 or June 30. We're lucky because we are public and the quarter is going to be great. But you didn't make your numbers. The quarter is great from all the previous business that you had. Your goal was to bring new resellers and new customers, but sales are coming from the old channels, not from you."

I think they were completely shocked that I was obsessed with the challenges that we had in the quarter. The next quarter was much better for them, and for the whole company.

I think it's amazing to see where the industry has gone, because for most high-tech industries after 10, or definitely 20, years, you see that demand stabilizes. We had a period like that, between the years of 2002 to 2007 or 2008. The industry flattened out. But still, if you look at our industry for the last 26 years, it's amazing to see how much the market has grown well beyond our expectations. In the early days, I said the Internet was going to be big, and it's going to change the world, but I couldn't imagine how big it would become. I couldn't imagine how big of an impact it would have on our lives.

I think we see the same thing in terms of the security and the cyber requirements. In the early days of cyber, a firewall was a simple thing to protect your network from students and universities. Today your overall cyber strategy is critical for running your business. It's critical for infrastructure. It's an important element in the relationships between countries and particularly for modern militaries. Even more important, every small business and every large business needs to protect themselves from the same powers that superpowers need to deal with. Our industry has evolved, both in terms of size and also in terms of the complexities. If in the early days you needed to have a firewall and antivirus software, you were pretty secure. Today there's probably 18 major categories of technologies. Out of these 18 categories, there's probably three or four subcategories in each one. That's why today there are close to 3,000 cyber companies around the world.

It creates a huge challenge for everyone, because whether you're a small company or a big company, if you are coming up with a new idea, you need to fight for mindshare with 2,000 other companies, not to mention the 1,000 or so that are still in stealth mode. We need to have products that actually work together. So if I recognize an attack with a malicious file, I can block that file on the network, and I can block that file on the cloud, as well as on the mobile device. If I recognize a new malicious website, I need to be able to block its access in all the posts and all the vectors. There can be at least 16 different attack vectors, and we now have several dozen technologies to combat them.

The main focus for Check Point today is on what we call threat cloud. It's a unified cloud that connects all the security elements and makes sure that every threat is recognized by all elements in real time.

Story: Guy Guzner

Guy Guzner is the cofounder and CEO of Savvy Security.

My cybersecurity story begins in my early years, the '80s, where my passion for technology and hacking first took root (or "got root?" as the case may be). I got my first computer, a Commodore 64, when I was just six years old and immediately became fascinated with programming. Then as a curious teenager, I discovered online bulletin boards and the hacking community. I began making friends who shared my interests and started learning as much as I could about the craft. Later when BITNET, an early pre-cursor to the modern-day Internet, and Internet Relay Chat (IRC), came along, my fascination turned to obsession. I was hooked.

By the age of 16, I had hacked into most of the universities in Israel, my home country, along with many of the companies that were connected to them. It was the early '90s then, and there wasn't a lot of awareness of cybersecurity. It was later in the mid-'90s that news about hacking began to increase. Folks like Kevin Mitnick and others gained notoriety as pioneers in the field. Most organizations, however, still weren't aware that they needed to protect themselves. Like me, they were all quite naïve.

While my friends and I did come across sensitive data like credit card numbers, theft or malicious intent wasn't our goal at all. My hacking escapades were driven primarily by curiosity and a desire to solve puzzles, along with a healthy measure of bragging rights and thrill seeking. However, that doesn't mean that we didn't eventually get into trouble because of our actions.

While still in high school, my friend and I learned how to "blue box" the telephone system to make long-distance calls billed to others' accounts. It was great for us, because now we had a much wider range of systems that we could try to break into. As those confused and angry subscribers began to complain to the police, however, it led the police to investigate the incidents and eventually trace the activity to us. First my partner was raided by the authorities; then a couple of days later, I received the choice of getting the same treatment or I could politely turn myself in. I took the less dramatic route.

I cooperated fully with the investigation because it was clear that we were caught. We ended up being charged and prosecuted in court, but the laws around computer crimes were less clear than they are today. We ended up striking a deal to repay those affected for costs and damages, a sizeable debt for a teenager, and had to serve community service. I feel like we were lucky, in hindsight, that we didn't end up with criminal records.

That experience was a turning point for me and is what would become the catalyst for my cybersecurity career.

NetGuard: My First Cybersecurity Startup

After my encounter with the law, I served in Israel's mandatory military service from the age of 18 until I was 21. When I got out, I still had a lot of debt I had to pay off. I started working with Israel's first Internet service provider until I landed a job with a small cybersecurity startup called NetGuard. I started there with no degree or formal training, but with this incredible early experience. NetGuard was a small company, which afforded me experience in a lot of different roles, like tech support, QA, and product management. At startups, you get the opportunity to do a lot.

NetGuard was developing a revolutionary type of network firewall for the times. Until then, firewalls were sold as software, but NetGuard wanted to create a hardware-based firewall appliance. Instead of buying server hardware, installing the operating system, and installing the firewall software, you would buy it ready to use. It was one of the first to do this. Even more interesting is that the firewall was built on top of Windows, which wasn't a very popular system for appliances. We created a firewall running on an embedded version of Windows NT.

It was around 2001, and we had roughly $8 million in annual sales. We were growing the business, but we needed more funding. Then the Internet bubble burst. Funding dried up, and we ran out of money. It was a real shame because we had cool technology, but we had to close the company and go home. There were a lot of companies that met similar fates.

Life at Check Point

While pursuing an opportunity that a friend introduced me to with Check Point, I was offered a networking job outside of cybersecurity. I was looking for job security in this tough economic climate, so I reluctantly accepted. On my first day, however, I decided I wanted to stay in cybersecurity and wanted to give the Check Point opportunity more time. Check Point did eventually get back to me and offered me a job in project management and assigned me to one of their flagship Firewall-1 projects.

My Check Point experience would span 13 years. During this time, I worked my way up from project management to development. Then I was promoted to team leader and then group manager. Throughout all of this, I stayed close to the firewall business. In a strange twist, I was put on a project to deliver Check Point's first appliance-based hardware firewall. The firewall business was changing with the introduction of players like NetScreen, Juniper, and Fortinet. They were all coming together with integrated hardware solutions. Delivering the first Check Point appliance was super interesting and challenging because it required transforming a software company into a hardware company. It was a very big shift in the DNA. It required a high degree of coordination across the company. Ultimately, it turned out to be very successful for Check Point.

After that I advanced again to managing an entire area, the threat prevention business. Network security continued to evolve, and we saw intrusion detection and prevention become integrated with the firewall. I also worked on the first Check Point IPS. The competition was increasing from the up-and-coming Palo Alto Networks, but also from dedicated players like Sourcefire. The concept of deep packet inspection was introduced, along with creating signatures to detect various threats. During this time, vendors often competed on performance along with detection rate.

A little later, I also began to witness the rise of unified threat management where additional security layers, like antivirus, were integrated into a single appliance. So, I helped Check Point get into UTM as well.

I remember we did an evaluation to acquire FireEye when they had just 11 employees. Check Point was not known for being a great acquirer, however, and we ended up developing our own sandbox technology in-house.

After that, we developed a next-generation firewall to compete with Palo Alto Networks. We began to look deeper and deeper into network traffic to protect against increasingly sophisticated attacks. When you do that, you begin to realize that looking only at network traffic is not enough. You can create signatures that will catch the proof of concepts for some exploits, and I remember there was always such a rush to publish those protections when Microsoft disclosed new security vulnerabilities as part of its Patch Tuesday process.

But as the exploits got more and more sophisticated, people started exploiting browsers. For example, you create an exploit in JavaScript. You find that there are many ways to write the JavaScript code that will perform the same function but would look totally different. It was then that I realized that creating a signature to detect the code was no longer enough.

Browser Isolation and FireGlass

I started to think about what we could do next, and this is when we started to take on the concept of isolation. If you can't detect or prevent these things on the wire, the malicious payload will find its way into the endpoint eventually, because of the many types of evasion that existed. So we thought, "What if we can create a situation where the payload doesn't get into the endpoint? What if it's executed somewhere else?" That was the whole idea of isolation: to run the browser, the target, somewhere else in a controlled environment. Think of it as a type of detonation chamber. We started pioneering this with container technology. The only thing that we would send to the endpoint itself, to the user, was the visual stream of what they were doing on the web. In terms of what the user was seeing, they weren't aware that all execution wasn't happening on the endpoint. This way, if there was an exploitation, it isn't really happening on the endpoint itself. This was the idea behind FireGlass.

It didn't make sense to me to continue to fight the network security fight at Check Point. I felt like an entirely new solution was needed. I met my cofounder Dan Amiga, and we started FireGlass, working on web isolation products. We raised money and went through the whole process of building a company from scratch. It was a great experience. We started to gain momentum and customers that understood what we were doing and why it was so much better than the traditional network security stack.

We did a seed round and then a Series A. We built the sales team out, and we were growing. This got the attention of bigger players in network and web security, because we started positioning this solution as an alternative to the standard web security products, like proxies. It was less in the cloud. People bought something like a Blue Coat or a Websense. Even next-generation firewalls were starting to add web filtering, but in the end, it was all based on network analysis of the traffic.

We realized, if we're isolating the web traffic, we can also do the other things that those products are doing. You need the proxy to create some kind of acceptable usage policy, like preventing access to porn or gambling websites. We can do that as well. We can integrate with some service and block that kind of access. So we kind of started positioning ourselves as the next generation of proxy technology. We told customers, "Look, we're going to replace your existing proxies, so work with us, partner with us." Then that started to get the attention of those proxy players.

Acquisition by Symantec

In the beginning, Symantec said, "We want to buy you. We like what you're doing." We told them that we weren't interested in selling the company; we were building the business and doing well. They then said, "Why don't we partner with you? We should do an OEM." This was much more appealing to us at the time, so we started working together as partners. After some time working together, we realized that there was real potential between our technologies and companies. For us, Symantec represented an opportunity to scale what we'd been doing into something really big. We liked this vision and asked them to make us a really nice offer. Selling to Symantec was beneficial for the founding team, for the investors, for the employees, and for everyone. This was also an opportunity for Symantec because it didn't have any presence in Israel. We were their first acquisition in Israel, and Symantec believed in the vision of Israel as one of the biggest hubs in the world for cybersecurity.

I became the general manager for the Israeli site. We made three other acquisitions in Israel and had some really big plans. I was committed to stay with Symantec for two years. We grew the business from just a couple of million dollars of ARR when they acquired us to a run rate of $50 million in ARR. We worked on the integration of the isolation tech and how to transform it into the next generation of their web security.

Then Symantec kind of imploded. The company went through a crisis. The entire leadership team at Symantec left or was fired. At that point, there wasn't much innovation going on. Some activist investors began to devise ways to take the company's assets and capitalize on them. Symantec ended up selling its enterprise business to Broadcom. Symantec wasn't looking to conquer the market and do a lot of innovation. For me, that was a sign that it was time to do the next thing.

Becoming Savvy

At FireGlass, we effectively learned how to isolate people so that outside attacks didn't affect them. But that doesn't protect a person from themselves. It couldn't stop employees from making mistakes such as submitting their corporate credentials on sites where they shouldn't or sharing sensitive data to places they shouldn't. We realized that technology could take us to a point, but if someone opens a door and lets someone else in, this kind of behavior is difficult to isolate.

This was the problem we set out to solve at Savvy. Ultimately, there are some decisions that a human would need to make. How do you affect those decisions? You can try to educate people to improve awareness. But that approach hasn't been very effective for some time, and we see a lot of organizations doing awareness training just to meet compliance requirements. It isn't drastically moving the needle in terms of improving security posture or lowering risk.

I remember talking with security professionals, and they were all doing awareness and simulation exercises. End users kept failing them. Then one professional told me, "It's not really about awareness because when you talk with people, they are aware of cybersecurity." The insight is that even if you're aware of security risk, you may not take the right action when deciding in real time. Our premise became, "How do we support people making those decisions? In real time?" Let's forget about training or education and understand that that isn't the problem. The problem is with decision-making. It's more about behavior.

Given our own limited experience in cognitive science, we set off to study human psychology to better understand decision-making and the biases that affect all decisions we make. We studied how people make decisions using heuristics that are subject to biases and then asked how we could encourage more objective conclusions. Thus, the name was chosen to reflect this mission.

We also understood that we needed to have something that was able to engage people in real time. That is, we needed to help them make those decisions while seamlessly integrating into their work environment. Nobody will leave their current work context to go and look for security answers someplace else. Nobody will stop in the middle of their work and then say, "What's the security policy here? What should I do?"

All of this thinking went into the approach that we use today. We introduced an interactive assistant that gets your attention and breaks you out of your way of thinking and encourages a slower and more complex mode of decision making. It provides education and context and helps to prevent intentional or accidental actions that lead you to a security incident or data breach. We want to provide you with just enough guidance at just the right time to let you do your work, be productive, and drive innovation forward.

Another trend that we factored into our approach is around the rapid rate of SaaS adoption. Already SaaS applications are estimated to be 70% of all business software use, and some experts predict SaaS will make up 85% of software use by 2025. A particular focus on SaaS and building a solution for the future was top of mind. To that end, we understood that to get ourselves in front of users in real time, we needed to be able to layer ourselves on top of applications. We looked at possible ways to do this and ultimately decided to build a browser extension and integrations for email and instant messaging. This allowed us to integrate seamlessly into the work environment and meet the user where they are working.

Our solution introduces nudges or guardrails directly into the workflow of the user. We do it in a way that is supportive to the user accomplishing their objective. That is, we provide guidance and context to make smarter security decisions. Nobody likes to be blocked from doing something when it's key to their productivity or efficiency in the workplace. That's what we've been doing for many years in the cybersecurity industry. For example, with firewalls it comes down to a binary decision to either allow or block. That doesn't really work well when you start blocking too many things, because then users get frustrated and find even less secure workarounds to get their job done.

Our philosophy is that organizations are looking to empower users to help them be more productive. Security has been associated with friction for far too long. Shadow IT is becoming business-led or business-managed IT. We want to help provide security teams with visibility into what's happening without getting in the way of the end user. We want people to have a positive association with the security team. Rather than "controlling" a user, we want them to feel like the security team is looking out for them and protecting them.

Conclusion

Throughout all of this, I've gained experience from every angle. I've been on the hacker side, and I've been on the defender side. I've done software development, and I've provided support and testing for software. It's all relevant for roles where you're building, managing, and marketing products. It hasn't been the most straightforward path—I didn't go to college or earn a computer science degree—but I think all the perspectives I've gained have given me many advantages.

Ultimately, I believe my journey emphasizes the importance of resilience, adaptability, and innovation in navigating the dynamic cybersecurity landscape. Together, we must embrace a proactive and human-centric approach to security, constantly seeking new ways to empower one another to make smarter security decisions.

Story: Martin Roesch

Martin Roesch is the creator of Snort and founder of Sourcefire, which sold to Cisco for $2.7 billion in 2013, and where he went on to serve as chief architect for the Security Business Group. Today he is the CEO of Netography, Inc.

I graduated from college in the early '90s with a computer engineering degree from Clarkson University. There were no formal degrees in information security at the time, so we had to teach ourselves the security discipline. I got into security originally working as a government contractor and found that one of the most effective ways to teach myself the discipline was by building tools that performed security functions, such as port scanners and vulnerability scanners, sniffers, firewalls, and honeypots. Ultimately, I got to the point where I thought it would be interesting to keep tabs on what was going on in my home network while I was at work during the day. So, I started writing a little program that I called Snort. I laid down the first lines of code for Snort in 1998 to perform basic network sniffing and packet logging. Even with that basic set of features, it was enough for me to see who was knocking on the door on my home network.

After working on Snort for about a month, I decided to release it as an open-source project to see if people would use it and to get some experience in the open-source development community. I thought that if things went well, Snort would be an interesting project for evenings, rainy days, and weekends. With all of that in mind, I sent the first release of Snort to the maintainer of one of the main security tool sites of the day, PacketStorm Security, and asked if he'd post it. He posted the package on the site near the end of December 1998, and I got a few emails at first. I then did another release and got more emails, and things started to snowball.

Snort Catches Fire

By the spring of 1999, I began sharing Snort on a few more sites and receiving a slowly increasing number of emails with the bi-weekly release cadence that the project had in the early days. I'd work on it during the evenings after my day job, downloading exploits from tool websites to run network-based attacks on my home network and figuring out how to detect them with Snort.

I would steadily add features, and when I got to what felt like a good stopping point, I would put together a release, test it, and write the documentation. I usually did releases around 2 a.m. or 3 a.m. and got emails and feedback from individual users while I slept.

In the late summer of 1999, I didn't do a very good job of QA'ing a release before pushing it out, and it ended up being particularly buggy. When I checked my email the next morning, I had dozens of emails from people I had never heard of before sending me bug reports and asking for help. This was a bit of a shock, and the volume of emails got so heavy that I started a Snort-users mailing list to coordinate bug reporting and resolution while quickly developing patches for the burgeoning user community. List membership grew rapidly until thousands of users signed up for it a few months later, and it became the hub of the Snort community.

Originally, I viewed Snort as an interim career step to demonstrate that I had security skills, not the trigger in my journey to do something interesting and relevant in security. But it turned out to be that trigger in three ways. First, because of the popularity of Snort and the subsequent notoriety it brought to me personally, I was recruited to go build an intrusion detection engine for a new security company. I found the fast pace of the company intoxicating after having spent years working within a government environment, and that was when I knew startup life was for me. But that company turned out to have substantial challenges that I wasn't going to be able to change, and I left in late 2000.

I started thinking about what I wanted to do next. I sent out an email to the Snort mailing list to let them know I was back to being a free agent, and I quickly received multiple job offers. This response was the second trigger, validating that I had a broad set of career options. However, my startup experience taught me that if I wanted to have a real impact on the industry, it probably wasn't going to happen if I worked for somebody else.

As I was mulling this over, Stephen Northcutt, one of my mentors and the founding president of SANS, shared with me some SANS survey results from the fall of 2000 that showed Snort had been massively adopted. In a survey they sent to SANS students, respondents were asked to check all the intrusion detection systems they used, both commercial and open source. Snort was checked 92% of the time. In less than two years, Snort had become the most popular IDS on the planet. That was the third trigger that convinced me to go for it and figure out a path forward with Snort as the core and a model for building an enterprise security product company around it as a disruptive idea.

Hacking a Business Model

In January 2001, Sourcefire was incorporated, and I worked out of my house with a tiny team of people who were excited to build something truly new. I had insights from user feedback about Snort's ability to scale and turned that into the business model to build a value-added platform around the open-source core, an idea known today as the Open Core model. Enterprises wanted the Snort functionality, but it also had to be manageable, scalable, performant, and automated and have a support organization around it.

Our initial funding to build the company from the ground up came from Stephen Northcutt and personal credit cards. Working out of my house, we would do product builds in the kitchen, shipping and receiving happened in the front hallway, customer calls took place from the quiet of the back deck, and marketing consisted of the mailing list. We operated like this for 10 months, and it proved to be an effective launching pad. We closed four six-figure deals in a row with customers that all came out of the Snort community: PricewaterhouseCoopers, Intel, SAIC, and International Paper.

The gorillas in the market at the time were companies like Cisco and Internet Security

Systems, along with a few others. It became obvious to me that if we didn't have money to compete with them, we'd get bulldozed, so we needed to start looking for additional funding. The dot-com crash was in progress when the company started, and it was hard to attract the attention of venture capitalists with a crazy idea about getting people to pay for something free. But once we started closing these significant deals, we attracted the attention of venture capitalists who saw we could, in fact, sell stuff that was free. In April 2002, we secured $7.65 million in our Series A round of funding.

Sourcefire Heats Up

With this first round raised, we moved into an office and started hiring. The flip side of the dot-com crash was that a lot of great talent became available, and Sourcefire was able to benefit. Part of my journey and upside in building a company is turning into a more capable person. I had an engineering degree and had read a book on managing software development, but I realized there are a few things I'm great at, several things I'm good at, and lots of things I'm not very good at because I'd never done them before. I made a very conscious decision to bring in the right people to fill the experience gaps. My approach was to bring them up to speed on what we were doing at Sourcefire, let them do their thing, and watch and learn.

Sourcefire CEO Wayne Jackson came on board as I completed raising our Series A round, and very quickly, COO Tom McDonough and CFO Todd Headley joined the team. I learned from each of them, our SVPs, and many of the great individual contributors who all had something to bring to the table. Over the next several years, I paid close attention to how they spoke with investors, discussed financial models, and interacted with customers, partners, and potential acquirers. All the way up to our multibillion-dollar acquisition, I was surrounded by great people who did their jobs incredibly well.

Once investment and a strong management team were onboard, we began to land more customers, and we were turning into a "real" company, but there were some tumultuous moments that tested us over the years. One of the first was in 2003 and the IDS to IPS market transition. Two startups launched IPSs, and simultaneously, Gartner defined the IPS category, saying it was the future of network attack detection and prevention and that "IDS is dead." We rapidly started to encounter pushback in the market when engaging with customers as a result, and we needed to address this market evolution.

Fortuitously, the Snort community—even before Sourcefire—had been a test bed for trying out some of the ideas around IPS, and we understood the changes that would need to be made in our product to bring a competitive offering to market. Simultaneously, we worked on another technology that I had been considering from the very first days of Sourcefire, real-time network awareness (RNA), to passively map networks and use that information to drive context into Snort for more accurate and relevant detection and prevention. We eventually became the leader in the IPS market, leveraging the powerful capabilities that we brought forth with the combination of RNA and Snort and the differentiation that it delivered over the early entrants to the market.

We soon faced another inflection point when in the fall of 2005, Check Point Software offered to acquire Sourcefire for $225 million in cash. The Sourcefire board decided to accept the offer, but the deal was subject to US government review by the Council on Foreign Investment in the US (CFIUS) because Check Point was a foreign-owned company. As Snort was used extensively by the US government and military, there were concerns about a change of ownership to a foreign-held company. After months of delays, Check Point shut down the deal in March 2006.

At that point in the company's history, we had raised $36 million in venture capital and weren't looking to raise additional funding at that time. But, because of the canceled acquisition, our competitors started to whisper to customers and prospects, casting doubts about our long-term prospects to stay in business. Our response was to immediately raise another round of funding. We closed a $20 million Series D round in April 2006, and announced our intentions to go public in a year. Sourcefire was a very cash-efficient business and never touched that last $20 million; we went public and became profitable without having to ever dip into those funds. One of the key questions over the years that we built Sourcefire was, what kind of eventual "exit" did we anticipate for the company—would we IPO and go public, or would we be acquired? My answer to that question was always to build the best company we possibly could, and good things would happen. Those good things—the opportunity to innovate, stay competitive, and increase value—propelled us to our IPO in 2007.

We had a bumpy start in the public markets as the financial crisis hit in 2008, but we kept moving forward. John Burris joined as CEO in July 2008 as we entered a new phase, and Sourcefire continued to grow. John was another great mentor and example to me on how to be an effective manager and leader. He recognized the talent that we had in the company and focused on what was really important—continuing the mission to build a great company.

A case in point, Sourcefire's next major milestone came in 2010 with our acquisition of Immunet. Developments in hackers' techniques and tactics had shifted where attacks were detected and combatted to the endpoints themselves, and, in those days, Sourcefire didn't have a lot of capability to combat advanced persistent threats from landing attacks and seizing control of networks, outside the purview of our IPS technology.

I had known the Immunet founders, Oliver Friedrichs and Al Huger, for many years and was intrigued when they started talking about cloud-based malware detection in 2008. Sourcefire had always focused on network-based threat detection, but customers were also looking for help dealing with client-side attacks primarily delivered via malware. I asked Matt Watchinski, head of the Sourcefire Vulnerability Research Team (VRT), our threat research group, to keep tabs on them as they developed their new cloud-based anti-malware technology platform, which was a radical departure from the industry standard methods of dealing with malware.

As they developed their offering, it became apparent that Immunet's metadata-driven cloud detection architecture was extremely powerful because of its write once and detect everywhere model. Since all detection on their platform happened in the cloud instead of on the devices themselves, users could define a detection one time in the cloud back end, and it would be applied instantly across the entire, globally deployed footprint. One of the things I'm good at is seeing technology not just for what it is but for what it could be. One of the things I saw was that, because of how it was designed, I knew we would be able to do a lot with their approach, including moving that anti-malware capability to the network as well. I talked to the executive team and board about how it would expand our offerings and make us a multi-product company, which aligned with our overall goal to be a strategic security provider for dealing with threats. We acquired the company during the last week of 2010 for $21 million, and the technology became the foundation for Sourcefire Advanced Malware Protection (AMP), our endpoint detection and response (EDR) solution.

Capping the Sourcefire Journey

By 2013, Sourcefire was delivering a multiproduct threat management platform for both the network and endpoint, and we had evolved our network product offering to deliver a next-generation firewall (NGFW). Our 12-month trailing revenue was approaching $250 million with an annual growth rate of 40%, and Cisco approached us with an offer to acquire the company for $2.7 billion. Given the synergies the two companies had and all that we had accomplished over the preceding 12 years, we felt the price tag was justified. Over that time, we had gone from offering a single model of IDS appliance to being a real security powerhouse with the consistently top-ranked IPS engine in the industry, our NGFW technology, and our cutting-edge EDR technology that was just emerging.

We also felt that Cisco was a good home for our people, our customers, and our technology. Cisco broadened our market access and the scale at which we could deliver new features and functionality to the market and was also a great place to work. A testament to that was many of us stayed with Cisco for years, and many former Sourcefire folks are still there. I stayed on as the chief architect of the Security Business Group, a role I was well-suited for—shaping technology strategy and influencing the design of the security portfolio and overseeing threat research. But I'm an engineer who likes to make stuff happen, and it's hard to make a giant ship move fast. Plus, I'd been working for 35 years, since my first job as a farmhand when I was a teenager, and I was ready for a break. So roughly five and a half years later, I quite literally sailed off into the sunset in February 2019 and resigned to go spend some time recharging on the ocean.

Back to Startup Life

In 2021, I got back in the saddle and joined a startup called Netography as its CEO. I've returned to startup life because the world has changed dramatically since I founded Sourcefire. And while Snort has remained relevant as a core technology of Cisco's network security offerings, there's a need to evolve the way security is done. Netography is solidly targeted at driving that evolution.

Since the pandemic hit, networks have rapidly transformed into composites of multicloud, hybrid-cloud, and on-prem infrastructure with mobile and remote workforces. I coined a term to describe this transformation, the *atomized network*. But it's important to recognize that the implications for network security in this new world are massive. The atomized network is distributed, ephemeral, encrypted, and diverse, and most organizations are blind to the composition of their networks and the activities of devices, which leaves them poorly defended for entire categories of attack. The limitations of the classic architectures still being used to defend most enterprises today are introducing major gaps in coverage and capability that attackers are taking advantage of every day. As I like to say, attackers live in the gaps.

The need for real-time network security has not gone away; detecting and responding to threats as they emerge is essential. Today, that requires an architecture that reconstitutes capabilities disrupted and displaced by atomization. At Netography, we recognize the world for what it has become, we understand what will remain relevant, and we're applying new thinking and passion for technology to build for that world—which is what drove me in the first place.

CHAPTER 6

DDoS Defense

One of the clearest segmentations of the IT security industry is that of distributed denial-of-service (DDoS) defense. Traditional network security is concerned with blocking attacks meant to breach a network, whereas DDoS is an attempt by attackers to disable a network-attached service. In its most direct form, attackers merely overwhelm a server by initiating more requests than it can handle, causing it to crash, reboot, or simply be too busy to respond to legitimate requests. Or, even more difficult to counter, the network pipes connecting to the service can be flooded with traffic as simple as a UDP ping request.

Place a firewall or other network defense in front of a server, and it bears the brunt of the DDoS attack. However, the firewall often fails, which accomplishes the attacker's aim. Thus, specialized equipment evolved to handle those attacks.

One of the first and more elegant denial-of-service attacks took advantage of a weakness in TCP/IP. A SYN flood is a stream of connection requests to establish a TCP connection. The TCP socket on a server becomes overwhelmed because the short SYN requests, often from spoofed sources, are never acknowledged, leaving all available sockets open waiting for a response. Check Point Software quickly added SYN flood defense to Firewall-1. Later, as more DDoS methodologies were devised by attackers, specialized equipment was developed. Hardware appliances from Top Layer (rebranded Corero), Arbor Networks, and Radware would be deployed in front of the rest of the security stack. Often, multiple DDoS defense devices with load balancers to multiply their power were required to squelch the flood of requests targeting the servers behind them.

But an appliance cannot stop an attack that fills the pipes in front of it. For that, you need to build something special, something that Barrett Lyon was one of the first to create.

Cloud Proxies

Lyon was working at an IT consulting firm when one of its clients, Don Best Sports, came under fire from DDoS extortionists in Eastern Europe. Don Best provided a sports data service to Las Vegas casinos. Lyon deployed a sufficient number of proxies in a data center and contracted with carriers to have large enough available bandwidth to counter the impending attacks and successfully warded them off.

Another type of attack, the GET flood, mimics thousands of web browsers requesting pages. This type of attack makes the web server work at maximum capacity, serving up its pages and effectively preventing legitimate traffic from getting through.

Flood attacks using SYN and GET can be blocked if the source is known. Just block all traffic from a specific IP address.

It did not take long for hackers to develop techniques for distributing their attacks among hundreds, thousands, and potentially millions of attacking hosts. One of the largest, the Mirai botnet, was made up of 100,000 compromised IoT devices. Another, attributed to North Korea, was a botnet recruited from compromised PCs by a worm. It was used to attack dozens of websites associated with the United States and South Korea, including Whitehouse.gov, CIA.gov, and Korean banks. Recruiting hundreds of thousands of devices makes the task of identifying and blocking the sources almost impossible. These are the most effective attack techniques known and can be very expensive to counter. The winner is usually the one with the most available bandwidth.

Lyon, after demonstrating that there are effective countermeasures to DDoS, began to get requests from a very specific niche industry: online gaming sites. In 2003, millions of US citizens participated in poker, slot machines, craps, and sports betting online. There were dozens of companies providing such services, most of them hosted offshore in the Caribbean, Costa Rica, or Gibraltar. These were very lucrative businesses. One small operation consisting of teleoperators and a closet of servers in an office in Costa Rica claimed to do $2 billion in annual revenue. At that level of turnover, it is easy to understand why they were prime targets for extortion threats that targeted their online presence. Being down for even a day meant millions in lost gaming revenue.

Prolexic

Super Bowl Sunday is the biggest day of the year for sports betting sites serving the United States. Leading up to Super Bowl XXXVIII in 2004, the gaming sites began to receive extortion emails from Eastern Europe. The letters said, in effect, pay us $30,000 via Western Union by a set date, or we will take you offline. The owners of the gaming sites began to call on Lyon to replicate the defenses he had created for Don Best Sports.

It was then that Lyon invented DDoS defense as a service. He took funding from one of the Costa Rican gambling operations. The new company was named Prolexic Technologies. Within a year, Prolexic hosted 80% of the online gaming websites in the world and succeeded in putting a stop to the nascent extortion racket emanating from Eastern Europe.

The architecture designed by Lyon and his team of network security engineers used three primary elements to defend against DDoS, elements that are worth studying.

First, Prolexic would proxy a customer's web servers in its own data centers placed strategically around the world. A proxy is just a server that mimics the original site. A request for a web page would go to the Prolexic server, which would, in turn, retrieve the relevant web page from the original server in Costa Rica and serve it back to the requestor. By positioning a proxy server in between all transactions, Prolexic could apply various defenses. These included hardened operating systems that would not be vulnerable to common exploits found in off-the-shelf operating systems. Lyon called on the expertise of one of the world's top BSD developers based in Hawaii.

BSD is an open-source version of Unix. The community of BSD developers has focused on creating as secure an operating system as possible. Prolexic customized BSD by removing all the components not needed by a web server. Then it enhanced its ability to thwart the type of resource restrictions (memory, open ports, etc.) that usually caused servers to fail when they received too many connections. They also developed load balancing technology so that an attack of millions of requests could be served across multiple servers.

The next investment Prolexic made was in off-the-shelf network gear from the likes of Arbor Networks and Top Layer. These devices could detect attacks, send alerts, and throttle attack packets. The cost for such devices can exceed $100,000, and the special security knowledge to run them is not readily available to a typical organization. Prolexic could make that investment because it was protecting multiple paying clients.

The final component of Prolexic's defense was bandwidth. The typical heavily trafficked website of the day used 10–20 MB per second of bandwidth. Through its relationships with major backbone Internet providers, Prolexic could use up to 18 GB per second of bandwidth, an unprecedented amount. Most Internet services see the largest amount of bandwidth for outward bound traffic. YouTube, Google's video hosting service, has to supply terabits of data to its consumers of streaming video. So, negotiating contracts with carriers for large amounts of incoming traffic is relatively easy and inexpensive. The largest attack Prolexic experienced was 11 GB of traffic. These measures are the core of DDoS defense: hardened, load-balanced servers, defensive devices, and massive amounts of available bandwidth.

Lyon, the technical founder, lost control of Prolexic, which was eventually sold to an operation in the Philippines and then acquired by the large content delivery network (CDN) company Akamai; it is still the core of Akamai's security offering. Lyon has since founded several network delivery companies.

He worked with David Cowan at Bessemer to launch Defense.net, which was acquired by F5 in 2014. He went on to found Netography and to bring on Marty Roesch as CEO. Meanwhile, CDNs like Cloudflare provide DDoS defense for the masses just by dispersing websites to its edge. An attack from Eastern Europe would hit Cloudflare's European data center. Visitors to the attacked website would just experience a slowdown as their requests are served from another data center.

As web hosting in general moves to cloud services like Google Cloud Platform, Amazon Web Services, or Microsoft Azure, customers get automatic DDoS defense because these providers have massive bandwidth available to them. Elasticity, the concept of spinning up servers in response to demand, also serves as a DDoS defense. Cowan believes the opportunity for new DDoS defense vendors is limited.

CHAPTER 7

Endpoint Protection from AV to EDR

Antivirus (AV) products predated the Internet. The 1980s were a time when viruses were transferred from machine to machine via floppy disks. The original antivirus vendors grew from companies that provided a variety of utilities for the nascent PC industry. File storage, system optimization, disk cleaning, data erasure, backup and recovery, and antivirus made up bundles sold by software companies that primarily addressed the consumer market. As PCs invaded the workplace, so did viruses, and as networks became predominant in the '90s, viruses began to spread over the wire instead of through dirty diskettes. As viruses became more and more virulent, the importance of AV grew, as did the AV market.

Symantec

Symantec has always been a company in search of an identity. The year 2019 marked, if not the demise of Symantec, perhaps the end of Symantec's market relevance. It's worth reviewing the twisted path it took over 25 years.

The Symantec name came from a small software company founded in 1982 by Stanford grads to create a database program for the new IBM PC. It was acquired by a smaller competitor, C&E Software, in 1984. The combined company retained the Symantec name and shipped its first major product called Q&A in 1985. Sales that year were $1.4 million.

Under its CEO at the time, Gordon Eubanks, Symantec embarked on a strategy of acquiring niche products and taking them to market. In 1987 Symantec acquired tools for project management (TimeLine), presentations (ThinkTank) and compilers for the Macintosh (THINK C and THINK Pascal), and an email system called InBox.

Symantec went public in 1989, and its stock took off, giving it the currency to continue to acquire companies including Peter Norton's PC software company, Norton Utilities, for $60 million in stock. Symantec also acquired a C++ compiler and pcAnywhere for remote desktop management. By 1993, Symantec even got into the contact management business when it acquired the makers of Act! from Contact Software International.

In October 1993, Symantec finally entered the AV market when it acquired Cleveland-based Certus International Corp. Five years later, it acquired the AV products of both Intel and IBM. Symantec also acquired Fifth Generation Systems, which had a contract with a small company in Jerusalem called BRM for antivirus software. That acquisition gave BRM the capital to invest in Check Point Software.

Eubanks stepped down from Symantec in 1999 to be replaced by John W. Thompson, an executive from IBM. Thompson had a 28-year career at IBM, rising to the role of general manager of the Americas. He had little experience with security products but was tasked with growing the enterprise security business. He embarked on divesting the company of nonsecurity products like the Internet Tools division and the Visual Café product line, as well as Act! He then started acquiring security companies such as firewall vendor Axent Technologies, L-3 Network Security for vulnerability management, and Seagate's Network Storage Management Group. He also looked briefly at Finjan Software. He passed on that investment but was so impressed with Finjan's CTO, Ron Moritz, that he later hired him as Symantec's CTO. Moritz defined Symantec's acquisition strategy, which he termed the NSSSM strategy: networks, systems, storage, and security management.

Very early in his tenure, Thompson relates, Symantec suffered a breach on a Friday. He asked, "Who's our CISO?" They did not have one. By the following Monday morning, Symantec had appointed its first CISO.

Under pressure to keep Symantec's stock price up, Thompson continued an aggressive acquisition strategy, culminating in 2004 with the largest acquisition in the software industry for the time: the $13.5 billion purchase of Veritas, a data center software and storage company. The best evidence that this was a major blunder for Symantec is the valuation for the Veritas division when it was spun out to investors led by the Carlyle Group in 2015, for only $8 billion.

Under John Thompson, Symantec continued to grow through acquisitions. It played an important role in the overall industry, offering an alternative to an IPO to many high-flying startups with good technology. The big paydays for investors and founders fueled more startups and more investments.

Sygate, acquired on August 16, 2005, had a series of desktop tools including a popular PC firewall that Symantec discontinued after the acquisition. It also gave Symantec a network access control (NAC) product.

Altiris was acquired on April 6, 2007, for $830 million. It produced system and asset management software. At the time Thompson told analysts, "Added to our portfolio, (Altiris) makes us infinitely more competitive with the likes of a Microsoft."

Vontu, a data loss prevention (DLP) company, was acquired November 5, 2007, for $350 million.

PC Tools, another PC utility company focused on security, was acquired August 18, 2008. PC Tools was run as a separate company until Symantec killed it in May 2013.

AppStream, a provider of application virtualization software, was acquired on April 18, 2008.

MessageLabs was one of Symantec's larger acquisitions. It paid $695 million in November 2008 for the online messaging and web filtering company.

PGP was acquired June 4, 2010, for $300 million. The Pretty Good Privacy software was originally a free encryption solution that mirrored RSA's encryption algorithms. It was created by Phil Zimmermann. The technology was acquired by Network Associates and then spun out to PGP Corporation, formed by Phil Dunkelberger and Jon Callas. The acquisition, along with Guardian Edge that was announced at the same time (for an additional $70 million), gave Symantec an endpoint encryption solution.

The Verisign certificate business was acquired August 9, 2010, for $1.28 billion. It was the end of an era for the first certificate authority to sell SSL certs recognized by the major browsers. Verisign, which eventually got out of the security business, had decided to focus on its remarkable cash cow of maintaining the top-level domain servers and collecting a fee for every `.com`, `.net`, and `.name` domain. Symantec later spun this business off to DigiCert in November 2017, for $1 billion.

RuleSpace, acquired in January 2010, provided content URL filtering services for many ISPs.

Clearwell Systems was acquired May 19, 2011, for $390 million. It provided e-discovery solutions for legal firms.

LiveOffice, a cloud email and messaging archiving company, was acquired on January 17, 2012, for $115 million. The products were already integrated with Clearwell's discovery solutions.

Odyssey Software for device management including mobile devices was acquired March 2, 2012. It was followed by Nukona, acquired April 2, 2012, which was a mobile application management solution.

NitroDesk, a nine-person shop with application container technology for Android devices, was acquired May 2014.

Then came the divestiture of Veritas. Splitting off Veritas in 2015 was the first acknowledgement that Symantec was suffering and was in need of restructuring. The following year, Symantec acquired Blue Coat, the manufacturer of secure web gateway appliances, for $4.65 billion. It was almost a reverse merger as the CEO of Blue Coat, Greg Clark, became the CEO of the merged companies.

Blue Coat had its own troubles over the years. It was initially launched as CacheFlow in 1996. In early 2002, CacheFlow's CEO, Brian NeSmith, took the company public. Its stock jumped almost fivefold on opening day. NeSmith then pivoted the company into secure gateway appliances and renamed it Blue Coat.

Blue Coat quickly became the largest vendor of content URL filtering appliances. Every large organization needed a way to block employee access to inappropriate or time-wasting websites. Adding a category for malicious websites made these devices security products and gave rise to the category of secure web gateways. Blue Coat had a problem, though. A gateway appliance that sits in the data center is very expensive. It has to handle tens of thousands of simultaneous sessions.

In the early 2000s, large distributed enterprises such as retail stores, distribution centers, car dealerships, and restaurants were moving to local Internet breakouts. Instead of back-hauling all the traffic from the remote location to HQ over very expensive MPLS circuits, each location would go directly to the Internet over low-cost broadband. To provide security, they needed to replicate the stack of security gear found at HQ, but without the million-dollar price tag associated with data center–grade equipment.

This gave rise to the inexpensive, all-in-one security appliance industry led by WatchGuard, SonicWall, and Fortinet. They each added content URL filtering as a subscription service to these devices. At price points of $1,000 or less, Blue Coat could not compete.

Blue Coat stopped growing and in February 2012, was taken private by Thoma Bravo for $1.3 billion. Considering the $4.65 billion Symantec paid for Blue Coat, this was a good outcome for Thoma Bravo. But it was not so good for Symantec.

Shortly after Greg Clark took the reins in November 2016, Symantec acquired consumer credit protection company LifeLock for $2.3 billion. Combined with the Norton consumer AV business, this represented $2.2 billion in annual revenue for the consumer division.

But growth was lackluster under Clark, and he stepped down in May 2019. The announcement caused a 15% tumble in Symantec's stock price.

The newly appointed interim CEO, Richard Hill, soon announced a sale of the company to Broadcom, but it fell apart in July. It was later restructured, and on November 5, 2019, Symantec's enterprise security business was acquired by Broadcom, while its consumer business remained a public company called NortonLifeLock. This spelled the end of Symantec as a security behemoth. It is likely that it will not play the same role in the industry as it has in the past.

Meanwhile, NortonLifeLock remained a publicly traded company and began to finally consolidate the AV industry by acquiring Avira, Avast, and

AVG. The combined companies were rebranded as Gen Digital in 2022. Revenue was $3.3 billion in 2023, up $500 million for the year.

Network Associates

Network Associates was formed from the combination of McAfee Associates with Network General and its Sniffer product. This was one of the early attempts to create a security company that would cover both endpoint and network security, a combination that continues to fail as a strategy. Back then, the goal was to dominate the enterprise software space. Security had not become a big enough sector to inspire pure-play roll-ups. That would change.

Aryeh Goretsky, now a distinguished researcher at ESET, was the first employee of John McAfee. He conducted a reddit AMA (Ask Me Anything) in 2019. During the AMA he also provided this short summary of his experience in the AV industry:

> *Heady days, indeed. When I entered the field in 1989, the number of computer viruses was in the tens, with slightly more of them targeted at the Classic Mac OS than for DOS. That flipped in a year or so to DOS, and hasn't changed back since.*
>
> *We used to advise customers to update their software once a quarter, and monthly for high-risk computers like those belonging to secretaries and technicians who might be accessing floppy diskettes from untrusted sources. That recommendation changed to two months and then a single month as the number of new viruses being seen increased. When I left McAfee in 1995, there was already work underway to automate the download of updates by dialing into a dedicated BBS system. These days, anti- malware programs update themselves hourly with continuous checking between that for additional types of telemetry, which might mean a threat was detected.*
>
> *At the beginning, we might have received 2-3 floppy diskettes a month with new viruses on them. That increased to weekly, and uploads of suspect files were occurring multiple times a day to our BBS.*
>
> *Computer viruses were initially spread mostly through floppy diskettes at the speed at which they could be couriered around the globe, and sometimes through BBS (intentionally or otherwise). Worms like the Morris Worm were not really thought about in the same way as computer viruses, and would not be for years until internet access started to become ubiquitous, and consumer desktop operating systems started to come with TCP/IP stacks, and dial-up networking began to replace BBS.*
>
> *Dozens became hundreds and hundreds became a couple of thousand by the time I left McAfee Associates in 1995. That was a steep hockey curve back then, but a blip by today's standards, where you might see 250,000-300,000 malware samples arrive on a daily basis.*

In his AMA, Goretsky credits John McAfee with the successful growth of one of the first AV vendors, going from one employee to an IPO in three years. McAfee formed McAfee Associates in 1989, and raised $42 million in its IPO in 1992. McAfee's AV software was one of the first to be distributed over a network rather than shrink-wrapped boxes of instruction manuals and floppy disks (later CDs).

In 1993, John McAfee suffered a mild heart attack and turned the reins of McAfee Associates over to Bill Larson, who became CEO. Larson had been VP of sales and marketing for Sun Microsystems. He proceeded on an acquisition binge. He acquired Brightwork Development in 1994 and Saber Software in 1995, both LAN management companies. In 1997, he acquired Jade KK, a Japanese AV company for $21 million. Finally, he merged the company with Network General later that year. The company was renamed Network Associates.

Network Associates continued to operate as a collection of endpoint and network solutions until 2003, when the newly appointed president, Gene Hodges, embarked on a major restructuring. The plan was to double down on security and divest the desktop management, LAN management, and other tools. The Gauntlet Firewall product line was handed over to Secure Computing, and the other divisions were spun out. Left with only the AV product, the company was rebranded as simply McAfee, which seemed like a logical move until John McAfee reemerged from Belize and came into the spotlight.

McAfee, the company, focused on security. It acquired Foundstone, the vulnerability scanning software company along with its founders, Kevin Mandia, Stuart McClure, and George Kurz. Mandia left to create Mandiant, which was acquired by FireEye. He rebranded the public company to Mandiant and it was acquired by Google in 2022. McClure left McAfee to found Cylance, which sold to BlackBerry in late 2018, for $1.4 billion. McClure agreed to become CEO of ShiftLeft in 2022 and quickly rebranded it to Qwiet.

Kurtz left to found CrowdStrike. After an IPO in 2019, CrowdStrike's market cap hit $21.7 billion. CrowdStrike found itself caught up in the news in 2019 as the US President and Republican leadership promulgated a Russian disinformation narrative that somehow CrowdStrike was a Ukrainian company, and it had transferred a server containing hacked Democratic National Committee emails to Ukraine. CrowdStrike has become the largest endpoint protection vendor (after Microsoft) and had a $59 billion market cap at press time.

Hodges also acquired an endpoint intrusion prevention company, Entercept, and a network intrusion prevention company, IntruVert, in 2003, led by Parveen Jain.

In 2007, Dave DeWalt took over at McAfee. Gene Hodges moved on from McAfee to become CEO of Websense, a content URL filtering company, where he acquired PortAuthority, one of the leading data leak prevention companies. Hodges retired in 2013, and passed away in 2018 at the age of 67.

Dave DeWalt had been president of Documentum before joining McAfee, where he acquired Secure Computing, bringing the Gauntlet Firewall back into the fold in addition to multiple other firewall brands that Secure Computing had consolidated. He then went on to sell McAfee to Intel for $7.68 billion, where for a short time it was branded Intel Security.

The Intel acquisition made no sense at all, although all of the executives involved spun a story of how Intel would somehow embed security into its chips. The last year before the acquisition, McAfee reported just over $2 billion in revenue. Even four years later, the Intel Software and Services Group was reporting $2.216 billion in revenue. McAfee sales completely stalled out while it was part of Intel.

In 2016, Intel spun out McAfee to TPG, a private equity firm, at a valuation of $4.2 billion, a $3.48 billion dollar loss from when it acquired McAfee in 2011. Intel maintained a 49% ownership and continued to finance $2 billion in debt from the acquisition.

McAfee, led by Peter Leav, former CEO of BMC and Polycom, went public again in October 2020. It had 8,965 employees, down slightly in 2020, and claimed 97 million corporate endpoints and 522 million consumer endpoints protected by its software.

McAfee's story continued in 2021. In April, Symphony Technology Group (STG) completed acquisition of the enterprise business from publicly traded McAfee, which kept the consumer business. This was similar to the split of Symantec when it sold its enterprise business to Broadcom, leaving behind NortonLifeLock as the public company. The announcement claimed revenue for the enterprise business part of McAfee of $1.3 billion.

In October 2021, STG announced it had also acquired a big chunk of FireEye's enterprise products, paying $1.2 billion. While FireEye went on to rebrand as Mandiant, the combined McAfee+FireEye are being branded as Trellix, an XDR platform. STG launched the McAfee Enterprise Secure Service Edge (SSE) portfolio as a separate business, Skyhigh Security, in March 2022.

In November 2021, what was left of McAfee was acquired by a group of large investors including Advent International Corporation, Permira Advisers LLC, Crosspoint Capital Partners, Canada Pension Plan Investment Board, GIC Private Limited, and a wholly owned subsidiary of the Abu Dhabi Investment Authority for $14 billion. This remaining McAfee brand sells consumer endpoint protection.

Trend Micro

Founder-led companies like Trend Micro tend to have less complicated histories than those that pass through the hands of multiple CEOs and investors. Trend Micro never succumbed to the temptation to develop or acquire a firewall vendor. It stuck to its mission of countering malware. Thus, endpoint protection, email protection, and server protection have been Trend's focus from its founding, with recent incursions into cloud security.

Trend was founded in 1988 by successful entrepreneur Steve Chang; his wife, Jenny Chang; and his wife's sister Eva Chen. The company soon moved its headquarters to Taipei from Los Angeles. In 1992, Trend developed an OEM agreement with Intel, whereby Intel sold a LAN AV product produced by Trend. In 1998, it went public on the Tokyo stock exchange, where it is still listed. Eva served as Trend's CTO until taking over from Steve as CEO in January 2005.

Although focused, Trend has made several strategic acquisitions over the years. InterMute anti-spyware was acquired May 2005, for $15 million, and incorporated into Trend's AV products by the end of the year. Incidentally, this was the same time frame in which McAfee decided to write spyware signatures for its products. These moves put an end to Webroot Software's grand plans for its Spy Sweeper product line. Until that point, all the antivirus vendors treated spyware as applications that the end user wanted to install and, therefore, as "potentially unwanted," not as malware.

Kelkea, acquired in June 2005, was an anti-spam vendor with 20 employees. Major ISPs such as AOL used their IP blacklists. Provilla was a data leak prevention company that employed 22 people. It was acquired in October 2007. Identum, an identity-based encryption company, was acquired in February 2008. Third Brigade, a Canadian endpoint intrusion prevention solution, was a transformative acquisition for Trend in April 2009. Many of the Third Brigade executives joined Trend in senior roles. The product formed the basis of Trend's cloud workload protection suite.

TippingPoint, the intrusion prevention pioneer that had been acquired by HP, was acquired by Trend in October 2015, for $300 million. IPS from TippingPoint is still supported by Trend. Immunio, a container and application scanning tool, was acquired in November 2017. Trend's latest acquisition, in February 2023, was Analyz, a maker of SOC software solutions.

Part of the reason Trend Micro has been able to resist nonstrategic acquisitions is the more sober environment of the Japanese stock market. It is not subject to the same pressures that a Nasdaq-listed company is under to increase revenue each quarter at the risk of increasing costs and confusing the customer base. Trend dominates the market for AV in Japan and continues to evolve as computing infrastructure moves to the cloud.

Kaspersky Lab

Kaspersky Lab is the AV company founded in 1997 by husband and wife Eugene and Natalya Kaspersky, and Alexey De-Monderik, who now serves as an advisor. Eugene and Natalya divorced in 2007, and by 2011, Natalya was bought out by

Eugene. Kaspersky Lab, still private, reports that its revenue has exceeded $1 billion annually. Its research team is well regarded and responsible for uncovering many samples of nation-state malware, including Stuxnet and Flame (attributed to the Equation Group, which is thought to be part of the NSA's Tailored Access Operation).

Endpoint Detection and Response

Antivirus solutions are the best depiction of the arms race that occurs between threat actors and defenders. From the early days of a handful of new viruses every month to today, when AV companies have to analyze more than half a million variants a day, there has been a steady increase in threats targeting endpoints. This has led to new approaches that leverage machine learning, such as that employed by Cylance to memory inspection, alerting, and blocking such as that of CrowdStrike and others. These new solutions are termed *endpoint detection and response* (EDR). The response part means isolating an infected machine and cleaning it before an attack can spread to do damage.

There are 261 endpoint security vendors tracked in the IT-Harvest Analyst Dashboard. They run the gamut from antivirus to container security to the control of physical devices and their ports. These histories of the major endpoint product vendors are just a small part of many transactions, investments, and startups that have occurred, with many more to come.

Story: Eva Chen and Trend Micro

It takes more than market-leading technology to remain at the apex of the cybersecurity industry for more than 30 years. To do that, companies need inspirational leaders who forge authentic, people-first corporate culture with a coherent long-term vision for continuous innovation. Eva Chen is the CEO and cofounder of Trend Micro.

The Early Years

The early stages of my life weren't what most people would expect for someone who has spent decades in the tech industry. Growing up with parents who were passionate about liberal arts, I didn't think about a career in STEM. I liked playing GO and chess, and I wanted to someday build a career in literature. My first degree, from Taipei's National Chengchi University, was in philosophy, and it wasn't until graduate school that I realized I had a knack for technology. I moved to the United States in the early 1980s and earned a dual master's degree in information management and international management from the University of Texas. After a brief stint working as a technical writer for Acer back in Taiwan, I actually considered switching careers and becoming a sports reporter. But in 1988, my brother-in-law Steve Chang and sister Jenny asked me to open an office in Taiwan and become cofounder of a business they were starting in Los Angeles: Trend Micro.

We soon moved the company to Taipei before establishing a permanent headquarters in Tokyo (today, the firm has joint head offices in the Japanese capital and in Irving, Texas). I served as executive vice president until 1996, when I became CTO. I spent almost a decade in that position, and during that time, we developed a number of services that propelled the company to the top of the industry, including InterScan VirusWall for

Internet gateway protection, ScanMail for email security, and the InterScan Web Manager for web filtering.

The early years weren't easy. It was a very different business landscape back then—which is a polite way of saying that opportunities for women in technology were few and far between. I often dealt with men who didn't know how to work with a woman, but I didn't care. We often hear about the gender pay gap, but just as telling is the "self-promotion" gap that often exists between men and women in the workplace. Being confident in my own abilities and leadership was critical to moving myself—and the company—forward.

Never Stop Innovating

In 2005, I assumed the role of CEO at Trend. Around that time, I also learned to overcome my phobia of butterflies that I'd had since childhood. It sounds like a bad joke, but this irrational fear used to significantly impact my daily life. So I decided to frame and hang images of butterflies all over the house, forcing me to confront my fears. I bought butterfly-themed stationery and even visited Singapore's Butterfly Garden. Fears big and small can hold female entrepreneurs back from becoming the best versions of themselves, and I didn't want to be held back anymore.

Research has shown that when women join the C-suite, companies become more open to embracing transformation and reducing risks. Women don't just present new ideas to the executive team; their presence makes the team more open to change. In a similar way, firms that add female executives find themselves shifting from an M&A-centric strategy of "knowledge buying" to one of R&D or "knowledge building." The latter is the philosophy that has driven our innovations over three decades.

One of my first jobs as CEO was to re-organize the business from a product to a customer-focused organization and to recategorize those customers according to size and sector. We embraced agile management across the organization, from product development to operations, and I introduced a concentric management model designed to break down departmental barriers and siloed KPIs, fostering more balanced and nonhierarchical decision-making.

That change in structure is part of the reason that an organization of 7,000+ employees can remain so nimble today—a critical success factor for any security vendor facing constantly evolving cyberthreats. Another crucial ingredient comes from a formula that has served us well over the years. It's all about monitoring infrastructure technology shifts and changes in user behavior and then predicting how threat actors may seek to exploit both to their advantage.

This formula helped us anticipate the global need for cloud computing security back in the mid-2000s, becoming one of the very first organizations to begin preparing for it. We began using cloud internally in 2008 to power the Smart Protection Network threat intelligence platform. In 2010, we started producing security optimized for VMware as the first wave of virtualization took off. Three years later, it did the same for AWS workloads.

Today, Trend is one of AWS's oldest and closest partners and delivers tight integration with all the main cloud platforms. But the security landscape is also shifting again. Accelerated digital transformation during the pandemic has driven an explosion in cloud infrastructure and applications, home working endpoints, and connected technologies. Together, they threaten to send the size of the typical corporate attack surface spiraling out of control as industry skills shortages and tool bloat restrict in-house teams.

This sea of changes has seen another evolution in Trend's offerings to customers with a new focus on platform-based security. Trend Micro One is a unified platform that we introduced in 2022, enabling customers to discover their entire attack surface and then assess and mitigate risk across it. It's about delivering visibility and then using that intelligence to power wide-ranging prevention, detection, and response capabilities with a high degree of automation to enhance security and compliance. And as IoT devices continue to proliferate in number and complexity, including through connected cars, I have seen great value in launching R&D programs and new business units through Trend to face the challenges to come.

Some of the most critical decision points in my time at Trend have been in mergers and acquisitions. Among these were the 2009 acquisition of Canadian startup Third Brigade, which gave us a crucial leg up in the cloud security space, and the $300 million purchase of TippingPoint from HP in 2015. The latter not only brought more network security expertise and capabilities in-house but also the Zero Day Initiative (ZDI), the world's largest vendor-agnostic bug bounty program. The ZDI was responsible for nearly two-thirds (64%) of all CVEs published in 2021 and today ensures that Trend customers are protected even before vendor patches are released.

Culture Is Everything

If leadership sits at the heart of Trend, culture is its pulse. This begins and ends with people. To be a "Trender" means caring about the world and having the passion to make it a safer and better place. We hire people who will continue to ensure that this attitude permeates the company from the top down. It is a family of thousands of passionate security advocates all pulling in the same direction. There's no room for ego here, and our culture empowers and encourages those closer to the action to take more decision-making responsibility. This was especially important during the pandemic when, for example, colleagues in California opted to allow local government officials to download Trend products for free to protect their home offices.

I aim to foster this culture throughout our leadership through an empathetic and consultative management style that brings out the best in people. I learned this when I was CTO and led all the engineers. Often technical leaders insist on always doing things their way and end up competing with the engineers, but I always try to understand their position and figure out how to make both of us happy. Male leaders can often be more competitive and think that for them to win the other person has to lose. But understanding what the other side wants to do and getting it to work in a way that everybody wins is how we've developed some of our best innovations.

Above and Beyond

The Trend corporate culture is not just focused on securing customer environments, as important as that is. It goes much further than that, driven by our philanthropy and passionate advocacy for diversity. That's why you'll find a growing list of global citizenship programs at Trend, of which the long-running Internet Safety for Kids & Families is perhaps the best known. It's also why we've helped to launch initiatives like Close the Gap, designed to provide more opportunities for women in the tech industry.

Partnering with the nonprofit Girls in Tech, Trend has also helped to develop a Cybersecurity Fundamentals course for its members. And we're leading by example to enhance diversity by accepting job candidates from a range of backgrounds, even outside of tech. One of our top sales staff members, for example, used to be a barista.

This perspective comes from my belief that instead of just focusing on programming and learning how to code, we should focus on how technology is applied. This also creates more room for women in areas such as management, marketing, public relations, and other communication and interaction areas. Women in leadership often bring different perspectives to the table.

My philosophies on leadership and creating a thriving culture have defined my career thus far, and I hope will continue to do so long into the future. If there's one thing I know after more than three decades, it's that the journey in cybersecurity is never over.

Story: Kailash Katkar: Quick Heal: Building a Successful Global Cybersecurity Company Out of India

Kailash Katkar is founder and chairman of Quick Heal Technologies. The company was founded 30 years ago as Cat Computer Services, a computer and peripherals repair and maintenance business. The company was renamed Quick Heal Technologies Limited in 2007, roughly one year before becoming the largest-selling cybersecurity brand in India. Kailash was named an Amazing Entrepreneur at the 2014 EY World Entrepreneur of the Year Event.

The Genesis

I founded Quick Heal Technologies with my younger brother, Sanjay Katkar, in 1995. Back then, I did not have any knowledge of the cybersecurity market, nor did I have any plans of making it big. It all started with a resolve to address the computer virus–related challenges that users were facing. We focused on the issue at hand. We went step-by-step, creating a solution to each of the challenges we encountered—and Quick Heal was born.

I come from a lower middle-class family from the city of Pune, Maharashtra. During my schooling, I realized how my father struggled to make ends meet. My father was then employed with Philips India, and in his spare time he undertook repairing radio and electronic items and even screen-printing logos on the company uniforms. The extra income from these jobs helped him to afford good English medium schooling for us.

Based on his experience, he was of an opinion that having a good formal education would brighten our career prospects. Personally speaking, English medium schooling was difficult, as it was neither my native language nor did anyone at home know English.

With a keen desire to help my father financially, I chose to drop out of school. I started to help him in his side jobs of screen printing, and, from there, my entrepreneurial journey began. I kept on doing these small jobs, which seemed so big for me and brought me tremendous satisfaction because I was able to earn and help my family. I have two younger siblings, a brother and a sister, who were still in school. I made sure they focused on their studies and completed their schooling.

During my early years, I learned to repair home appliances and electrical items just by observing my father. I later did some professional courses in radio and television repair and took exams for the 10th standard. This is how I completed my formal education until "matric."

After the professional courses, I was proficient in radio and TV repair and started earning more money. Eventually, I stopped the screen-printing work and focused on electronic repairing only. During the same period, I came across a job advertisement seeking an electronic engineer for calculator repair support by a local firm, Data Star Electronics, in Pune. Even though I didn't have any formal engineering education, I decided to apply and take a chance. To my surprise, I was selected out of more than 25 candidates who had formal education.

My practical knowledge and experience in radio and TV repair helped me to crack this interview. I was selected for a two-month training course on calculator repair. I was earning much more with electronics repairs. Still, I went ahead and chose a comparatively less-paying job of calculator repair just because it was about learning something new and advanced.

I was sent to Mumbai for training (Bombay at that time), and after two months I was back in Pune, handling a calculator repair job. During those days, most of the calculators were used in banks, and they were our major customers. This was the late '80s; we can call that time the "pre-computer era."

During my time at Data Star Electronics, I observed that banks were using German-made semi-automatic ledger posting machines for maintaining the ledgers for their customers. They were a combination of electronic and mechanical, which used to have the functionality of a calculator, as well as printing and storing smaller records while being used for keeping the print copies of these ledgers. I learned how to repair it just by observing the engineers who were sent for these repairs.

One day, when I visited one of the banks to make a repair, I realized the employees were protesting against new machines the bank planned to install. They wanted to replace all of the old ledger posting machines and calculators. These new machines were called "computers." Somehow, I knew that soon the old machines would be out and computers would be the future. Thus, I started to learn more about computers by reading whatever information was available in the form of books.

Incidentally, while I was learning about computers, my younger brother, Sanjay, was about to finish 12th grade and was keen to pursue electronics engineering. I suggested he studied computer science instead. He took a formal admission in bachelor's in computer science, which was new and relatively far less understood back then.

As I furthered my learning in computer repair and maintenance, in less than a year I was competent in repairing computers. This included the most difficult components, such as floppy drives as well as printers, because of my expertise and past experience in mechanical repairs. This really helped me to create a niche for myself.

Soon I discovered that very few could do the task of printer, printer head, monitor, and floppy drive repairs. I decided to quit my calculator repair job and embarked on the next phase of my entrepreneurial journey. I started with a small workshop, offering computer and peripherals repair and maintenance by the name of Cat Computer Services.

The business of repairing computers picked up, and I started getting good annual maintenance contracts from small organizations. This was in the early '90s, and my brother, since he was pursuing his degree in computer science, visited my workshop for his submissions and to further practice programming. At that time, a lot of my customers were facing virus problems. Being an expert in the hardware repair domain, a software-based challenge was something new for me. With the MS-DOS operating system back then, I knew very little about the software and the operating system. A few computers at my workshop were getting infected by these viruses as well because of the floppies that I was using on different customer PCs and at my office. Viruses spread through floppies in those days, as there was no Internet connectivity and email was not common.

Many times these viruses would create hardware issues to grab attention. My retainer clients used to expect us to even solve these virus-related issues. Those were the early days of viruses, and they were not cyberthreats as such. During the MS-DOS era, most of the viruses were developed by smart computer hackers and engineers who simply wanted to show off their skills. They used to have visible payloads with an intent to frighten or disturb the computer user. You could say the virus writers were happy to show that they had control over other people's computers.

Some of the prominent viruses at that time were C-Brain, Jerusalem, Cascade, and Michelangelo. Viruses like Cascade used to drop typed letters at the bottom of the screen as a payload, whereas some variants of Jerusalem disturbed the printer spool. Some variants of C-Brain created too many floppy disk operations, which made too much noise.

When I discussed these things with my younger brother, who often visited my workshop, he told me that these problems are caused by computer viruses. It wasn't a hardware malfunction; it was a virus causing these hardware-related issues.

I also observed that Sanjay had developed some tools that he used to execute on computers when he visited my workshop. Those tools helped him use the virus-infected computer smoothly. As soon as he would leave (and if I restarted the computer), the virus-related problem would emerge yet again. Later, he gave me tools to remove the virus infection from the computer memory and from the disks. It was a command-line tool for the virus Michelangelo.

This gave me an idea, and I started using the same tool to clean the computers of my existing clients. As new viruses started to appear, I would ask Sanjay to develop an update for the tool to combat new threats. During those days, new viruses appeared once every two weeks—or sometimes just once a month. Since computers were not connected to the Internet or had email functionality, viruses spread much more slowly. Physical movement of disks (from one office to another) was the primary way that viruses spread.

After some time, the frequency of new viruses increased to one emerging almost every week. Sometimes multiple new viruses would appear in a single week! The trouble caused by these viruses was increasing and becoming a bigger challenge for the user. The market started to see an influx of antivirus software, such as McAfee, Dr. Solomon, CPAV, and so on. The price of these solutions was high. Since I used the tools developed by Sanjay to combat the viruses, our customers started to demand an updated version of our tool. I also realized that Sanjay's tools were being used by many IT service providers to solve their customers' virus problems.

Quick Heal Was Born

In the meantime, Sanjay finished his degree and was now pursuing a master's in computer science. During that time he was offered placement in some IT software services company. He discussed that opportunity with me, and I said, "Why don't you join me?" He could develop antivirus software (a solution), and I could sell it to my customers. Without thinking much, Sanjay said yes. He liked the idea of working on antivirus software to combat viruses, and this indeed became his passion.

In 1993–94, the last year of his master's program, he developed an antivirus solution. It took him almost 12–15 months to finish work on the MVP version of the product, and the first Quick Heal antivirus was born. This is how, in 1995, we went from a command-line tool to a full-fledged UI-based MS-DOS antivirus solution.

At that time, the company name was still Cat Computer Services. Computer maintenance and hardware repair were its core business. Sanjay finished his master's and joined me full-time to work on developing further updates to Quick Heal Antivirus. Driven by his passion to develop an antivirus product on par with international solutions that were available in the market when he joined, he was our first and only software developer.

With the first version of Quick Heal ready and introduced to the market, the real challenges began. Sanjay and I were technical people with no experience in marketing and sales. This was the period just before the Internet and email had been introduced in the market. At that time, having a personal computer was considered a luxury, but software piracy was rampant. Everything from the DOS operating system to solutions like antivirus, WordStar, Lotus 1-2-3, and games was easily available on floppies. People already found owning a computer an expensive affair, and now factoring in software solutions became a difficult proposition. Antivirus solutions were not budgeted for at all. In this situation, selling antivirus to consumers in India was an uphill task.

Even though we had released Quick Heal's first version, it was basically distributed for free so that I could keep my annual computer maintenance customers satisfied. It also served as a key differentiator in the computer maintenance space.

I kept the hardware repair and maintenance business running to generate revenue and to fund development of Quick Heal's next version.

We tried to appoint national distributors by approaching the big ones. All our efforts were unsuccessful, as most of the big national distributors were only interested in selling MNC-branded solutions, as they did not believe that a regional company could compete with the big players.

We tried appointing small-city distributors, but they too failed to deliver positive results. With little success (and hardly any revenue coming from the antivirus offering), we lost a couple of years after the release of the first version. On the other hand, my computer maintenance business was doing well, so I could invest more money in developing an advanced version of Quick Heal.

Sanjay now could hire a couple of developers, as he wanted to work on the Windows version of Quick Heal for Windows 95, which was becoming popular. However, more complex and sophisticated viruses were beginning to appear. At Quick Heal, we were focusing on developing not only detection and protection from the virus, but we were rather competent at cleaning the virus-infected computers, restoring the infected files, and rectifying any other changes done by the malware. This was a unique differentiator in the market.

Viruses like OneHalf and Dir-II caused havoc, as removing these viruses used to make the computers stop functioning due to the encryption done by the virus or due to changes made to the directory structure. In such situations, Quick Heal's cleaning capabilities really made a big difference in the market, and it started gaining popularity among all the computer repair vendors.

Quick Heal, the Most Popular Antivirus in Pune, India

By 1998, we tried a different approach to sell our antivirus solutions. Because of my experience, I knew all the computer repair and maintenance vendors along with the computer accessories sales network across Pune. I discovered that many of these were already using free or pirated versions of Quick Heal antivirus to solve their customers' virus problems. Thus, I started approaching these vendors and convinced them to start selling our antivirus solutions along with their services.

These vendors had never sold software before; for them it was new. I motivated them to earn extra by selling antivirus to their customers. All they had to do was sell; I assured them that we would handle and provide the technical support-related requirements and issue resolutions. A few vendors in Pune started to show interest and pushed sales . . . and it worked! They were able to convince customers to go for a paid version of antivirus for better service and support. They started generating additional revenue as a result.

Gradually, in three to four quarters, most of the popular computer vendors and repair workshops were selling Quick Heal. In a year's time, Quick Heal became popular in Pune as the best antivirus that could not only protect computers from viruses but also clean the badly infected systems.

Revenue started to flow in, and to our surprise, we now had more revenue from Quick Heal sales than the hardware repair business. I then decided to shut down our computer repair and services division and focus on selling Quick Heal.

With our sole business focused on Quick Heal, we were soon the largest-selling antivirus in Pune. We stacked up well against a lot of international solutions available in the market, and even some regional solutions. Since our approach in Pune worked, I now wanted to replicate similar efforts in other cities in India.

Becoming the Largest-Selling Cybersecurity Brand in India

Around 2001–2002, I opened another branch office in Nashik, which is not as big as Pune. No other international company wanted to focus on selling their solutions in smaller towns. We replicated a similar approach by reaching out to small computer repair and sales shops, training them to sell Quick Heal's antivirus solutions, and assured them we'd provide the best support service possible, as we now had a branch office in Nashik. This worked, and we were able to break even on our operations in Nashik in less than three months. In a few more months, we were the largest-selling antivirus in that city.

Looking at the success in Nashik, I decided to follow a similar strategy for other cities across India. We started with smaller cities and later approached bigger cities. I opened a new branch office every four to five months by building a team that reached out to all the computer vendors in that city and nearby smaller towns as well. On one hand, we were increasing our presence across different cities, and on the other, Sanjay was developing newer versions with much better features and releasing them much more frequently. In those 8 to 10 years, our revenue grew by 100% year on year, and we became the largest-selling antivirus brand across India. We were able to achieve the market share of more than 30% of the country's consumer antivirus market. We now had more than 25 branch offices and a network of more than 25,000 resellers across different cities in India.

Repairing Computers to Securing Computers: Cat Computer Services to Quick Heal Technologies

Around 2007, given our impressive footprint and continued growth, we renamed our company from Cat Computer Services to Quick Heal Technologies. By 2008–2009, Quick Heal was the market leader in the consumer antivirus market of India. We were a profitable, cash-rich company with no debt.

In the year 2009–2010, some venture capital funds started to approach us about an investment. Since we already had enough cash to invest in our research and development (as I said, our revenues were growing year on year), I never thought about raising money. We kept on saying "no" to the private equity funds that approached us.

In 2010, someone from Sequoia Capital India had approached us; they were really chasing us to think about our decision and consider raising some money. They insisted that additional capital would help the company in many ways and allow us to go global. They also insisted that there would be competition from big-time MNC players in India, requiring us to invest heavily in R&D, sales, and marketing. But we were still skeptical about bringing investors into the company.

Months passed before Vipul Shah and Mehul Savla, from RippleWave, approached us to assist us with financial planning and convinced us to go for private equity (PE) funds to raise money. Sanjay and I were now convinced, so we decided to pitch to multiple private equity funds, including Sequoia Capital. After evaluating the pros and cons of the different investors, we finally selected Sequoia Capital and brought them onboard as a PE investor by diluting a 10% stake.

We further invested the funds into developing solutions for enterprises, starting with micro and small businesses. We released solutions like Endpoint Security and UTM. By 2014, we were able to generate around 10% of our revenue from the sale of enterprise security solutions alone.

From the Leading Consumer Cybersecurity Brand to Full-Scale Enterprise Security Solutions Provider

Since Quick Heal was a very strong consumer Internet security brand, it was a little difficult to convince or even communicate that we had enterprise security solutions as well. This prompted us to create a new brand, SEQRITE, which housed all our enterprise solutions under the SEQRITE brand. This helped us to keep the consumer and enterprise businesses separate.

We built a separate enterprise sales team and support team under the SEQRITE brand. This worked, and we were able to see acceptance of our enterprise solutions in small and medium-size businesses. Our revenue share from enterprise sales grew year on year. By 2015, around 15% of our revenue came from the enterprise segment. At the same time, we realized we had much bigger competition from existing international market players in this segment. As we started to further proliferate our solutions portfolio across India, we saw a huge opportunity in the micro and small organizations market.

I believe at this stage there was great potential for us in the enterprise market as our strengths were to serve small and medium businesses, catering to their cybersecurity needs. These segments are the fastest-growing segments in most developing economies. In markets like India, the Internet penetration is still growing. There will be great opportunities for consumer security solutions, as well as anti-malware and privacy protection solutions.

Because the country was rapidly adopting mobile services, we focused on developing specific solutions. We then launched Quick Heal Gadget Securance for mobile security and insurance, a solution that secured customers on their mobile phones.

Going Public

The year 2016 was a marquee year for us. This is the year when Quick Heal became a publicly listed firm. We completed our IPO, and Quick Heal was listed on both NSE and BSE stock exchanges. We were now in the public eye—every solution, each new expansion, and the expenditures were now in the public domain.

The year 2017 was a year of recognitions both for me personally and for Quick Heal. One of our solutions, Quick Heal Total Security, received the Top Product rating from AV-TEST and received the BEST+++ certification from AVLab.

I was awarded a doctor of literature degree by Chitkara University, and the following year, Sanjay Katkar was awarded an honorary doctorate by MIT–ADT University, Pune. And with this, Quick Heal reached its 25-year milestone.

Thereafter, our market share continued to grow in both the consumer and enterprise segments. Our solutions were scoring high on customer satisfaction and were getting acclaim by technology platforms and media houses.

SEQRITE, our enterprise brand, received the Best Enterprise IT Security Brand award at the 11th NCN Innovative Product Awards. The flagship solution from the SEQRITE suite, Endpoint Security, was certified as "Approved Corporate Endpoint Protection" for Windows by AV-Test. Quick Heal Total Security (Windows) achieved one of the best protection ratings in an AV-Comparatives test.

The following year was no different; our solutions were being appreciated by key platforms in the ICT space, and we gained some key patents as well. Quick Heal Technologies was recognized by NASSCOM's DSCI as Cybersecurity Product Pioneer in India. We were granted US patents for anti-ransomware technology and for signatureless behavior-based detection technology. With all of this, I was now working with top government agencies and corporations across industries and sectors. Business was thriving more than ever before; I was now the founder and managing director of a globally acclaimed business and India's number-one cybersecurity solutions provider.

Coronavirus Pandemic: The World Quarantines Itself

While I was focused on our determined growth trajectory and our goals, humanity was hit hard by the COVID-19 virus in 2020. People, business, and our healthcare infrastructure were not prepared to address the stress COVID-19 brought upon us. By the time economies understood the severity of the disease, it was too late. Businesses were badly hit across the world. Some totally shut down. Some were forced to evolve. With this, people started working from home and staying at home. And it brought us another set of critical challenges.

I saw these challenges as opportunities in the realm of cybersecurity. I now, with my team, have much greater responsibility to secure data beyond the periphery of office premises. Our world has become more digitally available than ever before. Our solutions were the answer to keeping them secure online, anywhere, anytime.

Gearing Up for the Future

While it took a couple of years for things to regain momentum, I have been witnessing a massive increase in the number of cybercrimes and their level of sophistication. Cybercriminals are more active than ever. Therefore, I, along with Sanjay, am far more focused on investing heavily in R&D to develop solutions that are built on the most advanced tech stack and are future-ready. Sanjay is rolling out technologies that are intuitive and much more comprehensive to assure the security of data and IT assets of our customers.

These technologies are being built using artificial intelligence and are self-aware and block threats in real time. Sanjay has worked on bringing a portfolio of solutions based on Zero Trust fundamentals for SEQRITE and GoDeep, as well as AI for Quick Heal (among many other solutions). His passion to address newer challenges and anticipate them well in advance is working to our advantage. We continued to expand our market share in the enterprise segment over the past few years and became number one in the micro-SMB segment.

Quick Heal's international presence is rapidly growing; I have the right partnerships and a very strong footprint across the country. With business on the right path, the industry's best talent, and Sanjay's next generation suite of solutions, I am convinced that Quick Heal can triple its revenue in the next three years.

I have observed that one major hurdle in securing people against cybercrimes is the lack of awareness of cybersecurity and how to stay safe online. In last 27 years, I have worked hard to create an ESG-centric organization with United Nations Goals embedded into our ways of working. Quick Foundation, our CSR initiative, is more active than ever before in touching millions of lives possible through our cyber-awareness programs and various community-centric interventions. We have collaborated with local administrations, industry bodies, and police across many states in India to help spread cybersecurity awareness. Quick Heal's academy has also joined forces to bridge the skills gap in India's cybersecurity industry.

As a leader in the cybersecurity domain, I feel accountable to secure people and businesses in the cyberworld. Hence, we at Quick Heal are directing all our energy toward ensuring that our efforts contribute toward a larger goal of making "cyber safety a fundamental right for all."

CHAPTER 8

Identity and Access Management

Identity and access management (IAM) is the sector devoted to onboarding users, assigning unique credentials, defining and enforcing what systems, networks, and applications they are authorized to use, and revoking that access when users depart as employees or customers. There are 494 vendors that fit in this classification, primarily because there are so many ways to authenticate users, from one-time password (OTP) tokens to grids displayed on the screen (a user remembers the coordinates, and in response to a challenge, fills in the corresponding numbers and letters they see in the grid) to biometrics and location.

Strong authentication relies on requiring at least two of these three things:

- Something you know, such as your username/password.
- Something you have, such as a one-time password generator or a digital certificate.
- Something you are, such as your face, fingerprint, voice, gait, or even the way you type.

1. This is often called *two-factor* or *multifactor* authentication.

The largest vendors of IAM products provide directory services, a specialized database usually based on the Lightweight Directory Access Protocol.

LDAP was first created in 1993. In the late 1990s and early 2000s, there was significant competition between Computer Associates, IBM, Oracle, and Novell for directory services. But then Microsoft entered the market with Active Directory, which effectively dominated the industry, and Microsoft won the enterprise.

It All Began with RACF

Barry Schrager describes in the next story how he developed the idea of applying controls to every file and service on mainframe computers. He was working within a university IT department and attending the SHARE user group meetings for mainframe computers. He put together a presentation of his ideas meant to address a looming problem of students and staff messing with each other's files. Shortly after, IBM introduced Resource Access Control Facility (RACF) for its systems. But Schrager felt RACF did not even come close to implementing the controls he envisioned, so he commercialized his ideas with Access Control Facility 2 (ACF2). He saw rapid adoption by the US government, starting with the CIA and then General Motors. But Computer Associates began giving away its competing product, Top Secret, bundled with its other software. While ACF2 and later versions of RACF were resource-centric (based on who can access each file or service), Top Secret was user-centric (based on what resources a user can access). Schrager describes it as two approaches with the same result. He eventually sold ACF2 to a small company that was immediately snapped up by CA.

With the rise of the web came a handful of startups to address the need for what was called *web access management*, a type of single sign-on. Vendors included Netegrity with its SiteMinder product, Oblix COREid, and Novell iChain. CA acquired Netegrity in 2004 for $430 million. Oracle acquired Oblix in 2005. Novell, in the meantime, was eventually acquired by the Attachmate Group in 2011, which in turn was acquired by Micro Focus in 2014, which was in turn acquired by Canadian Open Text in January 2023.

While Microsoft established a near monopoly in IAM through Active Directory, a new generation of IAM vendors arose to address a new opportunity: the cloud.

Okta was founded in 2009 by two former Salesforce executives. They saw that granular access controls for software-as-a-service and cloud resources would become needed. Most IAM solutions were hosted on legacy systems in the data center. If cloud services were taking off, there would be a need for a cloud-native IAM solution. The market proved them right. Okta raised $225 million in venture backing before going public in 2017. It had a market cap of $15 billion in November 2019, before dropping to $13 billion at the end of 2023.

ForgeRock was created in 2010 to fork and commercialize Sun Microsystem's identity platform after Oracle acquired what remained of the once high-flying computer company. Founded by ex-Sun employees in Norway, ForgeRock is now headquartered in San Francisco. In October 2022, Thoma Bravo announced it was acquiring ForgeRock.

Ping Identity was founded in 2002 by Andre Durand and Bryan Field-Elliot and is often used for cloud identity services. It was acquired by Vista Equity Partners in 2016 and went public in 2019. With close to 1,000 employees and a market cap of $1.8 billion, it is growing quickly. Thoma Bravo also took Ping private in 2022.

OneLogin was founded in 2009. It is one-fourth the size of Ping Identity. Although it grew rapidly over the years 2017 and 2018, the last six months of 2019 saw growth flatten out, and it was acquired by One Identity, part of Quest Software in 2021.

The identity space is still growing with 494 solution providers.

As Microsoft reacted to the cloud era and built its Azure cloud, it did not miss that along with moving Exchange servers from customer premises, it would need to provide a cloud version of Active Directory. It announced Azure Active Directory for its developer community on July 12, 2012. Azure AD is going to be the one to beat for all cloud IAM solutions. But differentiating on multicloud environments and messaging against vendor lock-in will give the Oktas and Pings a chance to succeed against Microsoft's messaging.

Story: Barry Schrager

Barry Schrager is responsible for the work that led to the creation of RACF at IBM and ACF2 as a commercial product for mainframe access control. He was the assistant director of the University of Illinois–Chicago Circle Computer Center from 1968 to 1978.

I first started going to SHARE, the first enterprise IT user group, in 1969. It was my first travel experience, and SHARE was a great organization. We now look at social media to exchange ideas, thoughts, plans, and assistance with research. That usage didn't exist at the time. SHARE was a vehicle for this because you got mainframe people together in a room. Out of 600 to 800 people, you found a bunch who shared your interest in certain issues. You were able to sit down with them and compare notes and come up with potential solutions. We eventually got to the point of trading code that we had written.

One of the issues that came up was that we were getting dinged on security by our organizations. I was working for the University of Illinois in Chicago, and we had students who were deleting other kids' data, deleting graduate students' material, and deleting the professors' sample data that the students were going to write programs against. Some other people were having similar issues where stuff would accidentally be deleted or, God forbid, somebody would do it on purpose. That started the whole issue of data security. Then in 1972, I met Eldon Worley, who also had ideas about data security.

He and I and a guy from Boeing got together. I gave a SHARE presentation on our thoughts for data security and how we thought the IBM community should go with it. Not much happened with it, but at that time I also formed the SHARE security and compliance project, and we came up with a series of requirements. I wrote a paper in 1974 and gave a presentation about what was needed, and one of the main issues was system integrity. We still see that in the mini and desktop computers of today. We determined that nobody should be able to modify the operating system or bypass the standard interfaces. The operating system was a requirement because we felt that in a multiuser system, like OS/360, if you gave people the capability of bypassing the standard interfaces, they could do anything they wanted.

That was the system integrity part. And then we came up with a series of requirements for future security. Fast-forward two years. IBM announced RACF as a resource access control facility, but it didn't meet the crucial requirements we had described. It did not provide protection by default, which meant that everything was protected unless you gave permission.

For example, in '78, the audit team at General Motors was complaining to me that they had a Delco division and a GM research group. Each had RACF installed for two years. One had 3% of their data protected, and the other had 5% of their data protected. One of the auditors said, "We don't really know what percentage of that data has to be protected, but we know 3% ain't it."

I sat down with a co-worker. We'd developed a prototype for ACF2, which we decided to develop into a commercial product. We attempted to get the University of Illinois to back the project, but it declined. But then Rod Murray from London Life Insurance asked us to develop a commercial version of ACF.

We created a working version of ACF2 running at London Life. Then Jerry Lyons from Pontiac Motor Division came to look at it. London Life was raving about it. General Motors decided they were going to have Pontiac install it on a trial basis and see what happened. We went to Pontiac, Michigan, and installed it and got it up in production. Three months later Pontiac Motors was at 100% data protection. So here you have General Motors Research and Delco at 5% data protection—and Pontiac at 100%. They asked us to go to Chevrolet. They were up and running and 100% protected in two months. After that ACF2 took off.

Through SHARE I became friendly with Barry Lewis from the Central Intelligence Agency. We set up a trial at the CIA, and a month later he called me and said, "Barry, got some good news and some bad news." I said, "OK, give me the bad news." He said, "We found a way to bypass your products, the system integrity requirement." And I said, "OK, Barry, tell me how you did it, and I'll fix it." He said, "Nah, it wasn't your fault. It was IBM's fault, but you could have blocked it." I said, "OK, tell me how we block it." He said, "Nah, we may have to use it." In 1978, the CIA was already looking at hacking into computers.

What was the good news? He said, "We're going to buy it. We're going to recommend it to a hundred of our collaborators and subcontractors."

I said, "Great, give me their names and I'll call them." He said, "I can't give you the names; you'll just get calls." So out of that we got the NSA and MI-6 and the entire Australian government. But the nice thing was Lewis was really supportive of us. Linda Vetter from General Motors was another big supporter. They both came to SHARE to present on their use of ACF2.

From then on our salespeople could go to a prospect who objected to buying from an itty-bitty company instead of IBM and say, "First of all, our product is better. Second, it's being used by the CIA and General Motors."

When we started, a perpetual license was $27,000 for the first CPU and $18,000 for subsequent CPUs. Maintenance was some percentage of that. General Motors negotiated a license of $18,000 plus maintenance. GM eventually had more than 100 systems.

We were doing about $17–$18 million a year, but more than $12 million was going out the door in expenses. Around '84, another company developed a product called Top Secret. It took a different approach, almost the opposite of that used by RACF and ACF2. Instead of assigning permissions based on a resource like ACF2 does, Top Secret assigned permissions to users.

If you think about it, it's a matrix. In one way, you're looking at it from the bottom. In the other, you're looking at it from the side, but the answer is in the middle, and they're both perfectly OK.

Top Secret never gained any traction against ACF2. In the meantime, IBM rewrote RACF in the early '80s to be what you see in use today. Then the company that developed Top Secret sold it to CA, and CA started giving it away with its other software. We could not compete with free, so we sold ours to University Computing in 1986. Little did we know, about eight or nine months later, University Computing was acquired by CA. So that's how ACF2 ended up at CA.

Story: Venkat Raghavan

Venkat Raghavan's career began at DASCOM and includes more than 15 years with IBM, where he served as VP of the AI Thomas J Watson Research Center and VP of IBM Research Strategic Business Development. He is the founder and CEO of Stack Identity and the operating partner of Benhamou Global Ventures.

My career started when I came to the United States to get my master's. I had a bachelor's in electrical engineering from PSG College of Technology in Tamil Nadu, India, and then I earned a master's in computer science from Clemson University in South Carolina.

I entered the software engineering space as a developer shortly thereafter. That was always my lens for cybersecurity; I was very enamored with computer science and software development, building early-generation applications. We built a lot of the early-generation distributor systems.

My first job was at Harris Corporation in Melbourne, Florida. This was the nondefense part of Harris; it built large-scale distributed systems for power maintenance and things like that. I got the chance to build a lot of the early technologies there, such as many of the remote procedure call (RPC) technologies back in the day. Then I really got my teeth into the distributed systems architecture of the product itself.

We came across a technology called distributed computing environment (DCE), which was the first RPC-based technology that allowed you to build distributed applications. As DCE technology evolved, I became more interested in it, and for the first time, we had directory services. We had layers of abstraction to build software applications. Our large teams could build on the same interface and plug in their modules.

Today we take these sorts of architectures for granted, but then it was a very advanced innovation. Those technologies started to include a lot of cybersecurity aspects. But there were questions: How do we discover our services? How do we secure them? I also remember how Kerberos was the de facto distributor, the public security system from MIT, and I was very interested in it.

I think this was really the progenitor for today's open-source movement. Kerberos and Athena was such a groundbreaking technology. In fact, DCE derived a lot of the concepts from Kerberos. My interest in these technologies really paved the way for my entry into cybersecurity. It was not even called *cybersecurity*. It was just called *distributed computing*, and security was the foundation of that.

Then I started to look at securing RPCs. BSAFE from RSA was another technology, along with encryption and understanding all these ciphers. I had a strong interest in the convergence of applications and securing applications using crypto technologies. That led to discussing how we can apply these technologies in real enterprise environments.

I also worked with Bell Atlantic as well as Freddie Mac. I then joined DASCOM, the first startup pioneer that built on the distributed framework (like DCE technologies) to build and solve problems around web access control, web single sign-on, and network-based access control. We built our first generation of technologies, which lined up with the big burst of Java and web technologies that drove this first generation of Internet 1.0. Then we got acquired by IBM on January 1, 2000. Within IBM, I started to round up some of the product lines it was using: provisioning, access management, and privileged access management.

The identity management (IM) suite was filled out, and then I had the chance to acquire some companies at IBM within AppSec, data security, IDS, IPS, SIEM—all these things that were actually on-premises technologies but had great businesses. The process built up the new case of what is today the IBM security business, which is a fantastic business, but a lot of the time, it's just pulling all these pieces together.

In the course of doing this, I enjoyed different roles but mostly did product management, then strategy and brand engineering, followed by general management of business areas and things like that. I was still an IM guy primarily. Identity and access are still the foundation of any security market, so I built that.

After many years with IBM, I left to join Blue Coat Systems in 2013. Blue Coat was another pioneer in building gateways for proxy technologies. We used the company's technology to build up and accelerate an advanced threat management program and rounded out the portfolio.

I took a hiatus from cybersecurity following Blue Coat's exit to Symantec, working in AI research, which is obviously a very different space. I came back to cybersecurity because of two broad trends: Kubernetes, which was completely earth-shattering. And with everything becoming cloud native, we had to rebuild all the foundations that we had built over the last 20 years, this time on a new foundation of cloud-native and Kubernetes space architectures. That's why I got interested and started to look at how I could invest in the space and ultimately decided to do my own startup, Stack Identity.

The inspiration for Stack Identity, which protects cloud data by prioritizing identity and access vulnerabilities via a live data attack map, came after I witnessed the fallout of the Capital One breach. With approximately 100 million Americans and 6 million Canadians affected by the incident (including 140,000 Social Security numbers and 80,000 linked bank account numbers),[1] this incident was quite significant. But when this happened in 2019, Capital One was (and still is) the leader in cloud-native transformation. The company had moved its data centers to Kubernetes and had every product imaginable—cloud

[1] "Information on the Capital One cyber incident," Capital One, www.capitalone.com/digital/facts2019

infrastructure products, CSPM, etc.—and yet they got breached.

I dug into this a bit more to see what the heck had happened. I was enamored with a lot of the things that I'd built, like metadata services, assumed role functions, and all those things now built within AWS, but they're all in silos. AWS gives you all the foundational tools, but you've got to put it together to create a layer of operational security, which is missing. Capital One had point tools, but it couldn't figure out if there were any risks in the environment. Capital One didn't know if someone could grab and export a credential and walk across the pathway to obtain someone's data and then exploit a lot of customer data from S3 buckets.

This sends a powerful, if not harrowing, message: if a company as advanced as Capital One can have all of these problems, there is a big market opportunity for any business that can help. And then when I saw the growth of Snowflake as a data cloud, I felt that really the lens of security is going to be focused on identity and data. Those were the planes that we were talking about at the time. If you fast-forward three years to now, you see a lot of technology tools, like Wiz, Orca, and Palo Alto that are very much focused on infrastructure as the perimeter.

As I said, I felt that at the end it was all going to be about identity and data and that applications were going to be the driver of modern security. I saw an opportunity for me to build something in a new layer, a new foundation that was cloud native and cloud data native. I couldn't pass up the opportunity to create something out of this and work my way through this problem, and that's how I got enthusiastic about going back and doing a startup of my own.

As far as my transition to becoming an investor, I should say that I have always felt that I am fundamentally an operator. I like to build things; I'm a builder at heart. To me, as part of IBM, we were dealing with lots of portfolio management questions, which are really more investor kinds of questions. What do we do? Where do we invest? Do we build or buy? These were problems that I had to encounter on a daily basis. Now in the VC world, it's all about shifting it left, because we're talking about not established businesses like IBM, but really early-stage, newly invented, fresh opportunities. And that requires a very sharp focus on looking at the market but also looking at technologies at a deeper sense. To be frank, I wasn't trying to be a VC; it just happened. I was fortunate in knowing great general partners who guided me along. But I felt that my deeper knowledge of technologies, both security and application technologies, and, of course, AI, helped me understand and have a clarity around where this is going in the next 10 years.

Being an operator, I felt I was able to get closer to the technology and that I'm better able to have a genuine discussion with the founders of these startups, and I really enjoyed working with them. They have an idea, and I enjoy being able to help them figure out what to do with it and how to execute. More than becoming a VC, it was mostly an opportunity for me to bring in secular experience. I've driven the larger companies, but I also understand the technology fabric.

I think the third thing is, when you talk to startups day in and day out, your knowledge improves dramatically, like 100x. It inspires you to push yourself to keep up with the new talent coming in who look at things quite differently. So for me personally, it was a much easier transition. But I've seen other cases where it's rough to break into this VC side. If you're a deep operator, you can get in if you have the passion and enthusiasm. But if you're just doing operational work and not building something, it's going to be much more difficult. I've seen a lot of my colleagues also try to break into the VC world and doing corporate development work, but those things don't translate well to an early-stage VC type of role.

If there were any advice I'd like to share, it would be the same I've followed for the last 25 years: keep on learning. When I became enamored with Kubernetes, I spent a ton of time learning that because I didn't have that opportunity previously because of my bigger role at IBM, and I had lost track of the deeper technology. You just have to keep on pounding at this; I don't think there is any other way around it. If you're a curious learner, it's not difficult!

CHAPTER 9

Data Security

Data security, among all the aspects of IT security, has the distinction of having a history that is thousands of years old. Hiding the true meaning of written messages predates all information technology. But, as an industry, encryption is much younger. Before the Internet, encryption devices were the realm of defense and intelligence agencies. The commercial industry came about after Whitfield Diffie invented nonsymmetric key exchange, paving the way for the first vendor of modern encryption tools, RSA.

Data security, as an industry, has a different set of drivers. Data security is foundational to all security. In a layered model, it is the last, best defense against an attack. But data security is based on math, and the attacks are against the algorithms and the way they are implemented. At any point in time the underlying cryptography is bulletproof, but all it takes is for a single demonstration of an attack methodology to render all the defenses ineffective and set off a rush of innovation to improve the algorithms and replace them wherever they are used. Attackers include the intelligence agencies that have waged a continuous battle to be able to decrypt captured data and communications of their adversaries. Another major class of attackers is cryptanalysts, researchers who have an academic interest in finding ways to break the latest cryptography. Their frequent publication of these techniques drives the industry as a whole to constantly improve.

So to understand the history of data security, some understanding of the history of cryptography is required. Just as Check Point Software ushered in the era of commercial network security, RSA and Verisign were the pioneers of commercial data security.

When Whitfield Diffie had his eureka moment that led to the invention of asymmetric key exchange, there were already many encryption algorithms, including DES, RC1, 2, 3, 4, etc. These were block cyphers that performed various operations on a block of clear text to create cypher text based on the input of a secret key. To simplify the concept to its basic functionality, imagine a string of 1s and 0s that represent the clear text of a message. Take a secret key, another string of 1s and 0s, and munge it with the clear text in such a way that you can reverse the process (decrypt) only if you know the secret key. That is the basic concept of symmetric key encryption.

But how, over the Internet, do you let someone know what the secret key is without exposing it to attackers? During World War II, secret key distribution required an out-of-band communications method. It could be embedded in the typewriter-like devices used on German U-boats. Or a spy behind enemy lines would have a code book they carried on their missions. On the Internet, how do you let the recipient of an encrypted email or document know what the secret key is?

Ralph Merkle first proposed a key transmission for the intended recipient to solve but extremely difficult for an eavesdropper to solve. It was Whitfield Diffie who struck upon the idea of using a property of exponential math, the discrete algorithm problem, to devise the first public key encryption scheme. A recipient could publish a key that anyone could use to encrypt a message, while only the recipient had the key to decrypt the message. Public key distribution thus depends on a system that is easy to compute for the intended recipient but enormously difficult for an eavesdropper.

Ron Rivest, Adi Shamir, and Leonard Adleman, three computer scientists working at MIT in 1977, built on the Diffie-Hellman concept. It's reported that after a late-night celebration of Passover at the house of an MIT student, Rivest came up with a one-way function that would serve as the basis of most modern public key cryptographic systems. A one-way function is meant to be easy to compute in one direction and extremely difficult to compute in the other direction. Rivest's function was simply factoring the product of two large prime numbers. It is easy to multiply two large prime numbers (100+ digits long), while it is computationally close to impossible to factor that product back to its two prime numbers.

The RSA algorithm made commercial encryption possible. The three inventors went on to found RSA Data Security in 1982, and soon after Verisign, which was spun out and funded and chaired by David Cowan of Bessemer Venture Partners. Cowan is still at Bessemer today, a VC firm that manages a small portion of the Bessemer Trust was set up by Henry Phipps in 1907 to manage the investment of his wealth derived from the sale of Carnegie Steel. Cowan played a formative role in the IT security industry, first with Verisign and then with many other investments, including LifeLock (acquired by Symantec), Good Technology (acquired by BlackBerry), Endgame (acquired by Elastic in 2019), iSight Partners (acquired by FireEye), Tripwire (now part of Fortra), Auth0, Axonius, Claroty, Illusive Networks, Virtru, and **Defense.net** (one of Barrett Lyon's startups, which was another stab at DDoS defense, and that was sold to F5 in 2014).

Data security requires confidentiality, integrity, and availability (CIA). Encryption addresses the confidentiality part, but what about integrity and authenticity? This is accomplished by encapsulating the plain text in an envelope along with a hash of the original and signing the envelope with a digital signature created from the author's private key. The one-way hash proves the text was not tampered with because any attempt at changing it would result in a different hash. Only the owner of the private key could have encrypted the message, thus providing authenticity.

RSA, which sold software libraries for encryption, was acquired by Security Dynamics in 1996 for stock that was valued at $251 million shortly after the announcement. The combined companies were branded RSA Security in 1999. Security Dynamics had developed the widely used one-time password token, SecurID.

In 2006, EMC acquired RSA Security for $2.1 billion. It also acquired Network Intelligence, a network monitoring and alerting platform. The combination formed the basis of a separate division for EMC dubbed RSA, the security division of EMC. The division went on to acquire NetWitness in 2006, a packet capture and analysis vendor led by Amit Yoran, previously the founder of MSSP Riptech and currently the CEO of Tenable.

RSA continued to be an acquirer of security vendors until Dell acquired EMC for $67 billion in 2016. RSA was spun out of Dell and appears to be positioning each of the products such as Archer and Netwitness for eventual sale as stand-alone companies.

Digital Certificates

As David Cowan relates in the next story, Verisign was formed to issue SSL certificates "from the cloud." While it had a good run in the beginning, it eventually sold what was left of the digital certificate business to Symantec. In the meantime, Verisign made the surprising move of acquiring Network Solutions. Now, it oversees the operation of the biggest domain business in the world and is valued at $20 billion.

Entrust was founded as a spinoff from Nortel Networks in Ottawa, Canada, in 1994. It sold public key infrastructure (PKI) software to banks and large enterprises that needed their own certificate authority. PKI is the pyramid of trusted signers of digital certificates. At the top of the pyramid in the PKI model is a certificate authority (CA) that signs digital certificates for the next tier down. In its original design, there was supposed to be a government agency or consortium that would sign the certificates of all the other CAs. This never happened, but there was still a market for CA software. As an enterprise software play, Entrust had the exact model that Verisign was created to counter. It went public in 1998 and had a market cap of $5 billion by 2000. In 2001, after a drop in revenue, Bill Conner came on board as CEO. He had been an executive at Nortel, which still owned 25% of Entrust. Conner expanded the focus on authentication products. Entrust provided digital certificates embedded in passports and identity cards, often called *smart cards*.

In 2009, Conner oversaw the sale of Entrust to private equity firm Thoma Bravo for $125 million. He continued to lead Entrust until it was acquired in 2013 by Datacard Group, a manufacturer of machines that made credit cards and identity cards. After paying $500 million for Entrust, the companies were combined to form Entrust Datacard. The company was eventually re-branded back to just Entrust. Connor went on to lead Sonicwall for six years.

SafeNet started out as Industrial Resource Engineering in 1983. IRE went public in 1989 in the over-the-counter market. It raised $4 million. IRE produced one of the first VPN solutions that was rapidly adopted by banks, and it was resold by MCI. In the 2000s, SafeNet acquired many companies, including Cylink, Raqia Networks, SSH, and Datakey. Vector Capital took SafeNet private in 2007, paying $634 million. As a private company, it continued to make acquisitions, including Ingrian Networks in 2008, which made appliances for their concept of "network attached encryption." SafeNet was sold to Gemalto in 2014, for $890 million.

Gemalto was formed in 2006 by the merger of two smart card companies, Gemplus and Axalto. It employs close to 9,000 people. Gemalto was sold to Thales Group in 2017, for about $6 billion. To get regulatory approval for the sale, Gemalto had to spin off its hardware security module (HSM) business to Entrust.

Other Data Security Categories

There are many more products that fit into the data security category. Digital rights management (DRM) is copy protection for software and content. Information rights management (IRM) is similar but is usually deployed to control corporate documents.

There are many vendors, especially since the enactment of GDPR, that provide data discovery and tracking for personal information. Many of these are becoming DSPM, data security posture management solutions, which do discovery, identification, and remediation, primarily in the cloud.

It is surprising how many vendors provide secure file transfer services, 34 at last count. There are also secure messaging platforms from Telegram to WhatsApp to Symphony. There are also secure data rooms where boards or investors can share the files needed for board meetings or due diligence for M&A.

Secure data erasure companies like Blancco, which acquired competitor White Canyon, address the need to sanitize devices when they are sold or recycled.

As the root of security, data security will always be a major component of the overall industry. New means of communication, storage, and processing of data will lead to new products and new companies.

The fear of quantum computing disrupting the industry is already being addressed by companies with post-quantum encryption stories. SandboxAQ was spun out of Google in 2021, and then took in a $500 million investment at the beginning of 2023. It has had steady growth in employment to 219 people.

Story: David Cowan

David Cowan is a partner at Bessemer Ventures, one of the most prominent VC firms in technology and security. He founded Verisign and has made dozens of investments since.

When I was a kid, my father gave me a *Scientific American* article to read about public-key cryptography. It was the first public explanation, if you will, of the RSA invention. And I remember talking to him about the implications that it had for sharing secrets but also for authenticating messages and authenticating people and providing nonrepudiation of communications, which was all mentioned in the article.

Fifteen years later, when I joined Bessemer Venture Partners and was thinking about where I could find big opportunities to build tech companies, I thought back on that *Scientific American* article. That was because in 1992, when I joined Bessemer, one of the first companies that I looked at was PSINet. PSINet was the first—an Internet security provider in upstate New York that had spun out of the SUNY system. And I did the deal. We funded it at Bessemer. It was the first venture-funded ISP.

And with this commercial ISP, I realized that for the first time there would be companies sharing networks. Until then, there were some companies sharing the ARPANET with the government, but now it would be companies sharing networks with each other. And I realized that this was the first time this network, this ARPANET, which was now being opened up to companies, meant that parties with different interests would be sharing the same networking infrastructure. So there had to be some rules in order to allow for privacy and to prevent parties from obstructing communications among other parties and all the things that today we worry about in the cybersecurity realm.

I asked the PSI guys, particularly Marty Schoffstall, the CTO, how they planned to provide this to their clients. And he said, "That's all figured out. None of that is an issue. We put up something called a firewall, and we buy this little box from Morningstar, and it allows everyone to control exactly what traffic goes in and out of their networks."

Yes, the firewalls worked, but it seemed like there were other security issues going on. So I kept talking to some other smart people around at that time. In fact, I went on a three-month journey talking to smart people out there, like Eric Schmidt, who was at Sun at the time; Al Lill, who was a Gartner analyst; Rick Sherlund, who was a Goldman analyst; and various technologists. I went around asking them questions about where tech was going.

The only person I talked to who had any actual operational background in security was this guy who had been the CEO of Codex, which Motorola bought. Back then, being in cybersecurity meant you were building encryption/decryption boxes. This was before public-key encryption. So you put a secret key in at one end, and the same secret key had to be available at the other end so you could encrypt messages. Codex sold these boxes to the Navy and a few other government installations where they wanted to be able to send messages securely. But it was only within the military where the secret key was available on both sides.

So I went to the CEO and I said, "Now, it looks like there are going to be a lot of companies sharing this ARPANET thing, and it seems like security is now going to be a much more important issue." He literally put his arm around my shoulder and said, "Son, don't ever invest in security." That was something I remember pretty clearly. And that kind of made sense if you were looking backward at what you were able to do in security at the time.

But I thought, OK, it seems like we need to figure out how we're going to secure messages on the Internet with all these different parties where they can't share secrets. And I remembered that article that my father had given me. I looked up this RSA and asked, "Is anybody doing this?" And I found this little company in Foster City, California. It had no venture backing because no investors would give them money, let alone even meet with them, because, of course, there was no security industry at the time.

I reached out to Jim Bidzos, who was the CEO of Verisign, and asked if I could talk to him. Here I was, a brand-new associate at a venture firm without a very illustrious background or track record. But he took the meeting. At the time, they were doing two things with this RSA invention. They were selling tool kits to make it easy for developers to create symmetric keys and then use them for encryption/decryption.

They were also licensing apps on public-key cryptography to companies who wanted to embed it in their products. The big licensers of that were Lotus and IBM, which were probably the two largest customers of those patents. Novell might've been a customer, too. The company was doing a few million dollars of revenue a year between the two businesses but wasn't growing very much. I thought, This seems very important, and it seems like one day this has to be a ubiquitous technology.

Then I went back home to Boston. I used to host poker games with CEOs who would meet two or three times a year with various other CEOs and founders. For the one in Boston, I invited Ron Rivest, to whom Jim Bidzos introduced me. I started talking to Ron about what RSA was doing. He pointed out something that Jim hadn't mentioned, which was this idea of using a certificate authority to issue certificates, which we could then use to authenticate servers and enable very, very easy encryption on the Web.

A year later, when Netscape had come onto the scene, people thought nobody really trusts this, and nobody is going to want to enter their credit card information and things like that. Ron explained that you could build a certificate authority that would allow you to encrypt communications with unique keys. It was potentially a much bigger business. I thought maybe we could build a certificate authority. It would be something that would be much, much bigger than selling tool kits and licenses.

I went back to Jim and suggested Bessemer should invest, with the goal of building a certificate authority. Jim said, "I would love to build a certificate authority, but it would take a lot of money, and I don't have it. And I can't take your money because I don't control the company." At the time the company was 51% controlled by an eccentric billionaire who bought it from Rivest, Shamir, and Adleman. He told me the billionaire would need to agree to it.

I got on a plane, flew to Miami, and then drove across Florida to the Everglades to this shack with a corrugated tin roof. And in that shack in the middle of the swamp was the office of Addison Fischer. He asked, "What are you doing here?" And I said, "I'm with Bessemer Venture Partners, and I want to invest in this company you control, RSA, in California." And he said, "This is a very valuable company because we hold these key patents." And I said, "Patent licensing is not really a great business. But we could build a certificate authority, and we could do something really big."

He said, "Well, I think these patents are really valuable, and I would not be willing to let you invest at any valuation below 20 million pre." 20 million pre in 1994 would be like saying $1 billion today.

Nobody invested in private companies at 20 million pre back then, so I left. In the next month or so, I moved to California and hosted my next poker game out in Los Altos. Jim Bidzos came to that one. I told him about my trip to the Everglades and the disappointing outcome. We thought it was too bad there was no way for Bessemer to invest. But then Jim had an idea. He said, "What if we created a spinout and we fund it to do the certificate authority?"

If Bessemer funded the spinout, then Addison had no dilution in his ownership of the patents because Bessemer would have no rights to those. It sounded like a good idea.

In January 1995, I hired a lawyer from Cooley, and I had him file incorporation papers for Digital Certificates International. At the time, I was the only officer on the documents. Bessemer put whatever we had to put into the entity to make it real. Then I went to Jim and said, "Now, let's negotiate an exchange of assets from RSA to this entity for equity."

We agreed that RSA would get a third of this new entity in exchange for everything that we needed from the company in order to build a certificate authority. It wasn't clear that legally or technically we really needed anything from RSA to do this, but it was important to be working amicably with them. They might've come after us for the patents. They did have a lot of technical expertise in how to build public-key software. I was OK giving up a third of the company to make RSA our ally instead of our competitor, which in retrospect was a good decision.

As part of that deal, we also agreed that we would take strategic investment from some companies that had been working closely with RSA. I approached Visa, Mitsubishi, Intel, and some others. They all said they wanted to participate. Bessemer led a Series A round into this entity along with Visa, Mitsubishi, and Intel. The remainder—whatever wasn't held by RSA—we set aside for an option pool. It was Jim's genius that when we did the original Series A deal, we gave 1% of the company to Netscape.

We closed that deal in March 1995. Jim agreed to serve as interim CEO in addition to serving as CEO of RSA. We set up Digital Certificates International to collocate with RSA in Foster City. Jim took a bunch of people from RSA and hired them into DCI. He was running both, and I was serving at the time as chairman and CFO of DCI. He got the team to start working on the software that we needed to stand up a certificate authority.

Jim and I hired Steve Combs to recruit a CEO. Steve started bringing us candidates. The first one was Chuck Boesenberg, who was a proven CEO. I thought he was great and tried to hire him, but he would not join this little, weird thing. You have to understand that this company, DCI, wasn't a software company, and it wasn't a hardware company. At the time, those were the only two kinds of tech companies that existed. I remember trying to get the partners at Bessemer to even put in the initial money to seed this thing. It was very difficult because they kept asking me, "What does this company do?"

I told them, "We're going to sell integers, but they're really big integers." No wonder Chuck Boesenberg said no. We had a similar experience with some other potential execs. But then Steve brought us this young buck, Stratton Sclavos, who hadn't yet struck it big and had a little more appetite for risk. He seemed like a really smart, aggressive, well-regarded sales leader, who also had experience from his previous job dealing with joint ventures because he had worked in one between two big tech companies.

In June 1995, we hired Stratton as CEO. He came in and started hiring a full team. The company moved out of the RSA office to another nearby in Foster City. He hired a whole bunch of people, including Dana Evans as CFO. He looked at this whole thing we were doing, and he really simplified it to focus on the biggest opportunity and make it more understandable to the world. He came up with this idea that a digital certificate was like a driver's license for the Internet. He told the board it was about bringing trust to the Web.

It was mid-1995. Netscape was going public. Everyone was excited about this new application of the Internet. Dana said, "We're not going to do user authenticating. We're not going to do the non-repudiation. We're not going to do all these things. We can bring trust to this by issuing certificates of servers that enable communications with the server in a secure way." It's what people today are looking to blockchain to do.

Thanks to their 1% ownership, Netscape put our public key into the Netscape browser. By late 1995, we had it operational. Anyone with a Netscape browser who went to a server that had a certificate would see the little lock go on and would be able to have an encrypted session. And as soon as Microsoft saw Netscape doing that, they came to us and asked for the public key. We gave it to them, and they put it in Internet Explorer. But we didn't have to give them 1% of the company. They just did it because they needed to have parity with Netscape.

Stratton also hired a marketing firm to come up with a name. They came up with Verisign. We all agreed: great, great name. And we changed the name to Verisign a couple of months after he joined the company.

Within a year of starting the company we now had an effective monopoly on encrypted communications for the Web. Anyone who wanted to have trust with users on the Web had to come and get an SSL cert, for which we charged about $250 a year. That quickly turned into a phenomenal business. Eventually other people figured out how to set up certificate authorities, and certificates got cheaper.

This isn't really part of cybersecurity history, but the next brilliant thing that Stratton did was parlay the company's value into a much bigger success by acquiring Network Solutions, which was the SAIC spinout that manages .com, .net, and .org to this day and gets paid annual fees from every one of those domains every year for managing them, which is really the most profitable government-mandated monopoly in history.

By the time the SSL market lost most of its value, it didn't really matter because Verisign was now running an even more valuable business. Ultimately, they sold the SSL business to Symantec. So that's the history of Verisign.

Back in the early 190s, bringing trust to the Web didn't seem like the most important thing because there really was no Web. When I funded PSINet, there was no Web. It didn't exist. What companies were doing on the Internet primarily was file transfer and email.

But you could see email was the fastest-growing traffic. The question was, how are we going to provide security around email to know that they're encrypted and authenticated and all of that?

So the first security investment I made was in Worldtalk. Worldtalk built a MIME gateway for email servers to encrypt and decrypt messages using enterprise-level keys that were certified by CAs like Verisign. Obviously, they weren't relying on Verisign in 1993, when certificate authorities didn't exist. But that's ultimately what Worldtalk evolved into. It was one of the first email security companies.

Then I invested in Tumbleweed, which was another similar email security company. After Verisign, I invested in Valicert, which was Chini Krishnan's company and was the first to provide certificate revocation abilities on top of certificate authorities.

Ultimately, all three of those companies went public: Worldtalk, Tumbleweed, and Valicert. As a public company, Tumbleweed acquired the other two, and they all were acquired by Axway. The other early investment Bessemer made back then was in Altiga, which was one of the first VPN boxes. That was in 1996, I think. Cisco bought that, and it turned into the Cisco VPN product.

After I met with the PSI guys and they explained to me what a firewall was, I took a meeting from Gil Shwed, who was raising a round for his startup, Check Point. He told me that he was going to make a firewall that would compete with Morningstar. He was going to compete with them by getting distribution through partners. That sounded to me like a terrible idea. Selling something that was effectively commoditized and relying on big partners to sell it for you never really seemed to work for startups. But he did it. He cut a deal with Sun. And Sun ended up selling the heck out of those Check Point firewalls.

Gil built one of the most valuable security companies ever. I admit I missed that one. It wasn't because I didn't appreciate the importance of firewalls early on. It was because I had underestimated the ability to work with Sun as a distributor.

One other thing worth mentioning is that there was another source of certificates at the time—Entrust. Entrust was the company run by Alberto Perez, and basically was a certificate authority software that people could use to make their own certificates. Without all the nomenclature we have today about cloud computing, it just seemed pretty obvious that it was a lot better for one person to build a certificate authority and then sell the certs than to expect everyone out there who wants a cert to build their own certificate authority and then somehow get their public keys out there.

Verisign was actually in some ways the first cloud company because it took this on-premise model of Entrust and said, "We're going to do the exact same thing they're doing, but we're going to do it ourselves in this multi-tenant way and then give access to everybody." Within a year, we saw that Verisign was really taking off. At Bessemer, I started looking for other examples of that where we could take on-premise software and host and sell access to it.

Keynote was basically Mercury Interactive in the cloud. Flycast competed with the prevailing ad software company, moving that aspect to the cloud. I met with Marc Benioff in 1999, because he was moving Siebel into the cloud, but he wanted $100 million pre-money, which was in 1999 pretty much like the $20 million Addison Fischer wanted. I said, "That's crazy," which was another terrible, terrible, terrible decision.

I got off the board of Verisign in I think 2003, when my day job at Bessemer required that I free up time.

What's next? The good news for the security industry is bad news: things are getting worse, not better. There's still a lot to be fixed and all kinds of new problems cropping up. I've always felt that the cybersecurity industry is unlike other tech industries, because in those others technology matures. In microprocessors, you get an Intel. In networking, you get a Cisco. In databases, you get an Oracle. In search, you get a Google. In cybersecurity, though, there's no such thing as mature technology because you have so many people constantly working to render your technology obsolete all the time.

And there's no such thing as a mature product. The ones that become mature are soon obsolete. There's a constant need for reinvention in cyber. I don't see how it ever ends. As long as technology is dynamic and there are new ways to hack it, the cyber industry is always going to need startups, reinvention, and innovation.

I think that the major problem facing enterprises today is the historical artifact of the SIEM model, where security products throw alerts into a SIEM to be resolved by network professionals there. This was fine early on in the industry when you were truly just sending exceptions because you had some kind of perimeter defense, which was basically deterministic like a firewall. If something weird happened, you sent it off to a human being to investigate. But in today's world, where there's no perimeter, enterprise is just drowning underneath these alerts. SOC analysts are unable to deal with them to the point where most alerts don't ever get dealt with. It leads to a situation where people say, "Target knew there was an attacker in the system and didn't do anything about it." That's a very simplistic way of saying there were just too many alerts to get to.

The other issue I see, which I blame on stupid venture capitalists, is that one-third to half of the money that's been invested in cyber has been wasted because of singular mistakes. That is the idea that a bunch of extremely smart engineers—and they are all extremely smart engineers—have found a way to identify an attack in the system due to some anomaly that points to an adversarial presence in your network. The thinking is that by baselining your network and finding anomalies, we can find intruders. This has been, in my opinion, disastrous because any anomaly-based system creates false positives. If you have false positives in a product, then you cannot operationalize the product. All you can do is create an alert and just add more and more alerts onto the SIEM.

And more alerts are not what people need. You're not solving a problem by saying something suspicious is going on. Every analyst sees thousands of suspicious things every day. They don't need to be told that there are two more on the list. There's no value in that. There is a lot of value in helping enterprises somehow tame this monster. I put all of those technologies roughly into the category of orchestration—how you make a SOC effective. There are different ways of doing it. You can do it by using machine learning to reduce alerts by discounting those common to the whole Internet, like what GrayNoise does. You can do it by realizing an alert is basically the same as these 12 other alerts, so let's put them together into a single alert. You can take an alert that suggests there's an attack going on, but it is not a severe attack. Or, you can take an alert that suggests a severe attack, but it's not against a system in your company that has any crown jewels or is near any system with crown jewels. So don't worry about it, or don't worry about it as much. In other words, don't prioritize it.

That kind of alert management technology is great. Technology that focuses on the productivity of the analysts, kind of like what call center software does. Technology that automates responses to alerts, like what Phantom and Demisto do, are great. Anything that's allowing you to tame that monster I think is really solving the biggest problem that enterprises have.

There are two other technologies that I really like that qualify as new categories, which I think are under-appreciated today, but I am very confident will be important for deterministic defenses. One of them is the idea of a simulated attack. We all know that pen testing is silly. You pay somebody to get into your network. Big deal. They show you one path in. You block that path, but so what? There are like a thousand other paths. But, a simulated attack, which I think of as 24/7 pen testing, is where you do what Verodin and AttackIQ do. I think SafeBreach is really powerful, better than pen testing.

The other area that I love is deception technology. I have an investment in that space in Illusive Networks, because deception is the only way out there to deterministically catch human intruders on your network. If you're trying to track somebody who's traversing your network with an APT that's going after your crown jewels, all the anomaly-based systems are just going to throw off alerts that you have to investigate. A deception product is going to give you a 100% certain alarm that there is a human intruder. Operationally, it's much more valuable.

I know a lot of people talk about IoT as being the next big area for security. But I've never been able to get that excited about it, because it's such a broad thing that encompasses so many different kinds of devices. If you're talking about the security issues of an RFID tag-like sensor, and you're comparing that to nuclear reactor equipment in a SCADA environment, lumping them all into one word like "IoT" is just meaningless.

For example, with a baby monitor in your home the only thing you're scared of is somebody looking at videos of your home. That's it. Whereas, if you're looking at a nuclear reactor, you're mostly worried about somebody sabotaging your nuclear plant and causing a meltdown. The threats are different. The vectors are different. And the solutions are different. So IoT is just too general a term.

I invested in Claroty because I think SCADA systems represent an enormous vulnerability. But SCADA systems are SCADA systems. Calling it IoT is not very helpful.

I've spent a lot of time in the last two years studying quantum computing, so I believe I'm as up-to-date as anyone on the cyber implications of quantum computers. The panic is a little bit premature on the impact of quantum on encryption. Undoubtedly, there will come a time when quantum computers can break conventional RSA encryption. And there will be some period of time where some nation-states do but no one else has access to quantum computers with that capability.

However, there are other algorithms out there that are quantum-proof. And like Y2K, there will be a retooling of encryption using these other algorithms. There will be a period of time where people claim the sky is falling just like we did in 1999. But then the retooling will happen, and it will be over. So to me, it's a one-time thing that does not present opportunities for entrepreneurs and venture investors to build new companies.

I think DDoS is done because it's one of the many, many markets that are being steamrolled by the major cloud providers. When you put your application onto Amazon, you pretty much don't have to worry about DDoS anymore. As everything moves into the cloud, either Google or Amazon or Azure, DDoS just becomes less and less an issue.

I spend no time on blockchain. Back in the 1990s, when we started Verisign, we looked at using public key for doing nonrepudiation, and nobody wanted it. Then, Stuart Haber started a company. It was a brilliant idea. He said, "Look, we provide nonrepudiation. You give us any data. We'll hash it. We'll hash all our hashes together. And every week, we'll publish the hash within the *New York Times*. And then we can prove nonrepudiation for anybody who wants it."

It was a perfect solution, but nobody wanted it. Blockchain is basically the same concept: it's nonrepudiation using public keys, which is then married with a decentralized infrastructure. Doing those two things for Bitcoin is great. For currency that you want to be decentralized without regulation by any governments, it's perfect. But while there may be a few other things where you need decentralization, for almost every other application that anybody has ever come to me involving blockchain, I asked them, "Why do you need decentralization to do this? Why can't the organizing company behind this simply use public keys to sign data and then publish the hashes?" Nobody has ever been able to say why that's not good enough and why they have to go through this whole blockchain thing. It's kind of bizarre.

Story: Sandra Toms

Sandra Toms is head of Experience Marketing at Google. Her career at RSA spanned 20 years.

In 1991, the first year of the RSA Conference was a bunch of cryptographers talking about the science behind cryptography. It was totally different than today. There were a lot of concerns about what was happening with the key escrow debates, Skipjack algorithm, and all these things that were happening with the government, and it felt like at that time, RSA was definitely poking a stick in the eye of the NSA.

There were posters when I joined that were still up and had to do with "NSA is listening to your calls" and all that kind of stuff. Kurt Stammberger and his team had created those. But then those wars subsided a bit. It became all about controlling the export of strong encryption, which was another way the RSA Conference was able to grow and pull the industry along with it.

We were all in it together. We all wanted to ship products with strong encryption. So the thinking was, let's get together and do something about it. It was a pretty incredible way to draw competitors in, where they could lay down their arms because we all had bigger issues to tackle. It was incredible to be a part of that.

My first conference in 1998: it was cryptographers, it was standards, and it was developers. At that point, I realized that there was a bigger audience of people who were using security, the enterprise and information security professionals. So at that point in time, I took a look at the agenda. I was largely left to my own devices, so I just experimented.

At my first RSA conference I thought, This event's going to go away because we're going to solve the security issue. It's going to be easy. Little did I know what I was really getting into, as it just kept growing.

As I looked at the agenda, I realized, we don't have anything called hackers and threats. That would be an interesting talk. It would be an interesting track and could play throughout the years and add more tracks. At the first RSA Conference there were six tracks. One of them was called an RSA products track, talking about the software development kits (SDKs). It was part of security dynamics. There was a little bit about SecurID, and I realized that the only people who sat through those sessions were other RSA employees. I thought, "OK, so maybe this isn't the most useful track in the world. Let me change things up."

As information security became more commonplace among consumers, the conference grew organically, and we were always thinking, OK, what's next? What do we need to do? What are the tracks that'll be most interesting and continue to grow the event?

In 1998, we said it was 2,000 attendees, but I do believe that was a lie. It was probably that 2,000 people registered. That doesn't mean they showed up. For the latest event, RSAC 2019, we had more than 42,000 people show up. We don't get the number of registrations anymore. It's just who shows up, because that's the most telling number.

The very first RSA conferences were at the Hotel Sofitel. Then it went to the top of Knob Hill and multiple hotels there, and then it moved to San Jose. We were always trying to get space at Moscone Center in San Francisco, but we were always such a small event that they could not fit us in to the schedule.

We jumped back and forth between San Francisco and San Jose, and then eventually landed in San Francisco because we were finally big enough.

If we had 42,000 in 2019, of that about 10,000 to 12,000 were full conference attendees. That number could fluctuate based on various things. During the SARS scare, we saw our numbers go down. Definitely after 9/11, the numbers went down. No one wanted to travel. One thing that can impact it too is the hotel room prices in San Francisco. It's really hard to justify to your boss that you are staying in San Francisco, and the hotel room is going to cost $700 a night. The price of the ticket to attend a conference is dwarfed in comparison to the hotel room prices.

The RSA Conference didn't start off as an exhibition. It started off as a meeting and then started to become important to people, and they wanted to have some kind of presence there. The management was always outsourced. LKE is probably a name you have seen. They came on pretty early. One of the first people who wanted a presence there was Bruce Schneier, who was interested in getting his book, *Applied Cryptography,* out in the marketplace and thought that it was a good place to sell books.

The core team of the RSA conference when I was there was five people. They focused on content and different special programming like Innovation Sandbox and the student program and diversity programming. There were one-day events as well, such as the executive security option forum and the fraud-related meeting. We also partnered with a board of directors group to train board members.

Britta Glade is now responsible for working with a program committee of 40-plus people to select the program each year. The 40 people are volunteers, which is amazing. It shows you how much people in the industry really like the conference.

We've developed a very fair and open approach to content. If you're not selected, you can ask why. The program committee provides feedback to help you in future years to try to hit the mark with a proposal to speak.

But if people need more technical training, I would say the RSA Conference is not for them. You could instead do a SANS package, which is two days of SANS training, and then roll into the RSA Conference. I think it's best to approach the conference as a team, as an organization within information security, to figure out what you're looking to do differently over the next year and which vendors you'll need to evaluate and then visit those vendors among the 700 different booths on the show floor.

The conference content Itself is broad. It's not deep. It gives you a nice survey of what's happening in different areas, from law to hackers and threats to anything, endpoints, etc.

Story: Deborah Taylor Moore

Debbie Taylor Moore is a senior, global cybersecurity veteran at IBM. Prior to this role, she was an industry executive and independent advisor to security startups, CISOs, and investors. Her career began at Microsoft in the early 2000s. As the security industry grew, she joined one of the fastest-growing IT security consultancies, NetSec, which was acquired by MCI, which in turn was acquired by Verizon.

I began my IT career in sales in the late 1990s—working with Federal clients deploying and migrating secure messaging platforms for IBM. I was one of the most successful sellers in that line of business—at one point, I enjoyed the top spot worldwide.

I was subsequently recruited by Microsoft as a client exec to assist with cultivating a more consultative relationship with their customers. I had responsibility for increasing customer adoption of the Outlook Exchange platform, as well as the rest of the product portfolio: SharePoint, Office, BizTalk, and a variety of other solutions that were part of Microsoft's Enterprise License Agreements. I would describe Microsoft in 2002 as a very happy, marketing-centric technology firm focused on world domination.

In early 2003, we started to see customers who were getting hammered by SQL Slammer, Code Red, Nimbda—all of the worms and viruses—of the day. It was evident that Microsoft would be experiencing some turbulence and that security was going to be the next big thing. Microsoft customers were severely impacted, experiencing outages for days on end. We were pretty much caught flat-footed, and there was no real partner in our Mid-Atlantic Microsoft ecosystem that handled anything even close to IT security. It would be an understatement to say Microsoft really didn't have a remediation plan. SQL Slammer was probably the straw that broke most customers' backs. Microsoft had implemented a Trustworthy Computing initiative in the fall of 2002, but by early 2003, we were experiencing bedlam from a security standpoint. The inception of the Trustworthy Computing Initiative began as a Bill Gates memo that brought all of Microsoft's developers out of the field and into HQ to be trained on Secure Coding Best Practices.

Our Mid-Atlantic group had a plan to bring CEO Bill Gates in to calm our customers and allay their fears about Microsoft's ""Security Plan." One of my customers drove four hours to attend this meeting. The customers waited with the anticipation of breathless, admiring fans, assembled at the district office. Bill Gates arrived with an entourage and stood before the group. He took a folded sheet of paper out of his breast pocket and began to read a long statement on Trustworthy Computing. He read in a slow monotone for about 15 minutes. He read the sheet without making much eye contact with the audience. After he finished speaking, he put the paper back in his pocket and turned to leave the room, trailed by his entourage.

My customer who had experienced several days of outages, turned to me with jaw dropped, and hissed, "What the f*ck was that? That won't solve anything for us. So, he makes this decision three months ago to train developers. What does that have to do with fixing things *now*!?"

This was a common theme among customers. Pure frustration. It was rare that speaking with clients about any of the solution portfolio didn't also surface a wry joke or a combative comment about security struggles with Microsoft solutions. Microsoft was unwavering in its delivery of user-friendly, ubiquitous, and very penetrable technology—creating a new industry. Microsoft is now firmly a leader in this industry.

At this point, the security issues were becoming so pervasive that I knew there must be someone somewhere who was identifying this gap and addressing security.

I called my friend, Mike Norton of the MRC Group, and I asked him if he knew of anyone working in this field of security. He promptly introduced me to two former NSA guys who cofounded a security startup called NetSec (Network Security Technologies, Inc.). I met with the founders, Jerry Harold and Ken Ammon, and the rest is history.

NetSec could best be described as a 150-person fraternity of some of the brightest minds in security. Most everything we did was brilliant, exciting, and new, and never done before. The environment was feral, fun, and electric. Coming from a very buttoned-up corporate background, it wasn't long before I became accustomed to some of the T-shirt–wearing, whiskey flask–toting folks with their Hustler centerfold screensaver desktops. All of the laidback culture co-existed within the genius of that place. Broadly, we were an MSSP, but we also had a professional services team that funded the organization along with our investors. A critical part of our business was our work with U.S. federal intelligence agencies led by John Sleggs. His group was very close to the threat from a nation-state perspective and responsible for much of our revenue. This group also had the very first secure coding teams run by Elaine Harvey, now a principal at AWS. The combination of global, federal, and commercial client bases made NetSec the most unique professional service security organization of its time. We also had some of the most influential commercial customers in the world: clients in finance and banking, oil and gas, health, insurance, and retail.

My role was to develop the federal civilian government market. I worked with Cheryl Stockman, one of the preeminent and earliest commercial sellers I know in the security industry. I worked with federal agencies on their inaugural security programs. I wrote some of their first incident response plans, conducted certification and accreditations for agencies, and worked with the team that built a custom SOC for the DoJ and others. We had a whole division of ethical hackers led by Chris O'Ferrell that provided vulnerability assessments and were known for their storied and extreme exploits. It was not uncommon for Chris' team to hack a bank and move $10 million into a dummy personal account just to prove to them that they were vulnerable to these types of attacks. Penetrating these businesses was often the "Wild West way" in which the business was won. Back then, we would get deals through other wild practices such as war dialing and picking up conversations from mobile phones outside federal agencies. Then we would communicate what we had learned to the vulnerable customers. It's a style of selling cybersecurity that looking back was pretty gangster and eventually changed as the threat increased. Besides, you can't do that sort of thing anymore. But we had to get people's attention in the beginning.

I also believe Chris' team along with Mandiant was one of the first DFIR teams to operate. Simply called incident response teams back then, they were held on retainer by some of the world's most prominent organizations. That team rushed to the scene to help clients in the aftermath of breaches and insider threats that seem minor compared to the threat landscape of today. Chris and Ken Ammon were also the beginning of a sort of evangelist/thought leader go-to-market approach in security. They were frequently in *USA Today*, on the morning news, and talk shows, and in the press discussing this "new security threat."

The government was starting to pay attention. President George Bush put the Federal Information Security Management Act (FISMA) law into effect in 2002. FISMA was legislation that required government to implement frameworks, guidelines, and standards to protect government information and operations. The government was slow to react, putting the burden of compliance on the private sector initially. Some of them had experienced similar problems as my commercial customers at Microsoft had experienced. And they were mandated now to build their security programs to manage risk. My strategy was to leverage FISMA and NIST to move agencies into action on developing and implementing their security programs. We engaged people like Donald Upson, whose PR firm pulled together almost every CIO in the federal government for a private dinner with NetSec. This began a real period of education, growth, and influence.

So, I went to work assembling the capabilities that we'd built, and I mapped them to the requirements established by NIST and began to sell our programs and services to the federal government. We grew 14 times over in a period of 22 months.

But more importantly, there were many products that we supported, and we were also a consumer of these solutions (IDS, IPS, firewalls) on the managed services side of our business. We were frequently asked for references and data regarding the efficacy of these new security products and solutions. We also acted as a VAR to our customers. We additionally had our own in-house approach to integrating these capabilities and delivering to clients through a custom SIEM-like portal.

Government's need for its own custom solutions, similar to the private government-cloud model today, further fueled our expertise in security products and services. The government required the building of their own SOCs with redundancy independent of their physical facilities.

NetSec was only a small coterie of 150 consultants in the beginning, but it definitely included some of the brightest people that you could imagine. Our only competitors at that time were RipTech and ISS. They were in a similar business. We wielded a lot of influence in the space, and it was the beginning of major ecosystem of technology partners such as Qualys, Foundstone, Source-Fire, Check Point, etc. Those early products were the beginning of a booming industry.

We eventually sold our company to MCI/Verizon Business in 2005. Technically, we sold NetSec to MCI, which was then acquired by Verizon three months later. So actually, we all landed at Verizon Business. To celebrate, we had the greatest martini bowling party of all time. All participants had to be driven home afterward.

After that, Verizon Business relocated me and my family to Virginia to help them with a few of their acquisitions of additional cybersecurity companies. In 2006, I left and started to work full-time as a global consultant on my own.

Most of the former NetSecers scattered to new endeavors across the security industry. Many of the people from this company went on to be some of the principal creators and contributors to this vibrant industry through developing lucrative IP, becoming industry advisors and building the next generation of security startups, solutions, and platforms.

When the federal government announced its plan to spend $7.2 billion in cybersecurity, that was the tipping point, which really drove all major system integrators, entrepreneurs, and consultants into the space. Government began driving the industry as the number-one customer worldwide and encouraging the investment environment that would spawn Silicon Valley and Israel's importance in the industry we know today.

CHAPTER 10

Governance, Risk, and Compliance

Security professionals like to point out that compliance does not equal security, yet there are 548 vendors of products that fit in this category. While compliance is not security, the responsibilities of oversight by auditors and stakeholders create the need for tools to measure and report on security controls.

Governance, risk, and compliance (GRC) takes many forms. It can be the sets of policies, controls, and checks of these controls required by a particular government regulation, or it can be the set of practices meant to ensure that an organization is fulfilling its own internal mandate.

Risk management, a significant component of the GRC space, is poorly defined. An overreliance on risk management detracts from other approaches to establishing security practices. The problem with risk management is that it relies on nearly impossible methodologies, as described in the following article excerpt, originally published in *Network World* on October 15, 2012.

Risk Management

It is not an easy task, but many vendors have attempted to provide risk scores for organizations. They use a formula based on the severity of a vulnerability and some measure of an asset's criticality to make it easier to identify high-risk vulnerabilities as well as roll up an overall risk score for the organization. While metrics are useful and can drive continuous improvement, they can be misleading because they do not take into account the determination of a threat actor. A full-fledged risk management system will identify assets, rank them based on criticality, ingest vulnerability data, and track compliance with a host of security regulations and frameworks.

A new category that is seeing some traction, thanks to greater concern about supply chain risk, is vendors that provide third-party risk scores. The idea is that a large organization may want to apply pressure to its suppliers to improve their own security profile. The third-party risk scores generated by vendors such as SecurityScorecard, RiskRecon, NormShield, Black Kite, and BitSight are created by scanning from the outside. Other vendors take it much deeper by providing management tools for conducting full internal risk assessments with questionnaires and tests of security controls.

Why Risk Management Fails in IT

It is frustrating to see the amount of budget allocated to compliance when you consider that most of the money goes to documenting security controls, not improving defenses. One of the biggest reasons is that risk management, a carryover from the bigger world of business, does not work in IT security.

While few small businesses have formal risk management programs, most large businesses do. They even have risk committees that are drawn from the board of directors, often headed up by the CFO. The goal is to identify risks and either reduce their potential impact with compensating controls or purchase insurance to further reduce the business risk. For example, a large airline, thanks to its risk management program, may recognize rising fuel prices could hurt its competitiveness and decide to hedge fuel on the open market, or a car manufacturer that has gone too far down the path of Just-In-Time supply may start to warehouse critical components in case a supplier in Thailand is wiped out by a flood.

But try to translate risk management theories to IT and you run into troubles. Every risk management program starts with the dictate to identify all IT assets and weight them based on their criticality to business operations. That leads to the first big problem.

1. **It is expensive and almost impossible to identify all IT assets.**

   While at first glance identifying assets appears to be a simple problem, it is actually extremely complex; almost fractally complex. IT assets include every computer (desktop, laptop, server, print server), every application (database, email, ERP), every dataset (customer lists, earth resources data, product pricing guide), all email, all documents in all versions, all identities, and all communications.

   As companies increasingly turn to cloud computing, they need strategies to protect and recover data stored in multiple places.

   Now, add in the proliferation of devices coming in with consumerization—smartphones, iPads, even e-readers—and the data that reside on them. Then add in the dynamic nature of the cloud, where servers can be in a constant state of flux as load is elastically met with more or fewer virtual machines. Like I said, it's complicated.

   The next big problem?

2. **It is impossible to assign value to IT assets.**

   The concept behind risk management is that you assign a value to each asset. There are many algorithms for doing so. It usually involves a cross-functional team meeting and making at least high-level determinations. But it is obviously impossible to assign a dollar value to each IT asset. Is it the cost of replacing the asset? That might work for a lumberyard, but an email server might have a replacement value of $2,000 while the potential damage to a company from losing access to email for an extended period could be millions of dollars in terms of lost productivity.

   What about the value of each email? How much is one email worth? Ten cents? Zero? What about the internal email between the CFO and the CEO on the last day of the fiscal year warning that they missed their targets? Its dollar value is zero, but the risk from that email getting into the wrong hands could be the loss of billions in market capitalization.

   Most organizations give up on the dollar value asset ranking and come up with low-medium-high valuations. Try to picture a team of IT asset managers in a room and one of them agreeing that his job is to manage servers that have little or no value. If there is no value to an IT asset, it has long since been replaced or eliminated. Every IT asset is of high value. So why bother classifying them all?

3. **Risk management methods invariably fail to predict the actual disasters.**

   In the late '90s the automotive industry attempted to apply risk management techniques to product design. The method of choice was a huge spreadsheet template labeled Design Failure Mode Effects Analysis (DFMEA). The product engineers (me) would sit in a room for several days and look at every component—every fastener, every stamping, every piece of cloth in a car seat—and decide every possible way each component could fail in the federally mandated tests.

We would generate a huge list of possible failures—stripped bolt, fatigue crack, buckling, worn nap—and submit it to upper management who would never look at it. Of course, we failed to predict the failures that actually happened in production. You remember the recliner failures on the Saturn car seats?

Another example: A giant financial services data center located on the Gulf Coast of Florida used risk management techniques. Among the usual list— power failure, internet outage, fire—was a line item for a hurricane with a storm surge of greater than 20 feet (the level above sea level of the data center). Because there had not been a single such storm in 100 years this received a risk rating of 9 out of 10, with 10 being the least likely. An FDIC auditor pointed out that in that particular year there had been four such storm surges to hit the Gulf Coast. The data center risk profile had never been revisited to reflect a changing environment.

It is the changing nature of risk that is impacting risk regimes today. IT assets that were not of interest to a pimple-faced 13-year-old hacker in Canada in 1999 can be of extreme interest to a cybercriminal operation in Eastern Europe or a nation-state looking to leapfrog a Western competitor. It is impossible to know beforehand which IT assets will be of interest to an attacker.

4. Risk management devolves to "protect everything."

For risk management to work it has to be comprehensive, so comprehensive protections are deployed. Firewalls, IPS, and AV everywhere, and vulnerability management (VM) systems deployed to check the exposure of every single device on the network. Vulnerability management has to be continuous because new vulnerabilities are announced every month for just about every application, OS, and device.

A patch management system is then used to ensure that every application has the latest patch. Risk management methodologies strive for that golden state when no vulnerabilities exist anywhere. And, failing that, the desire is to minimize the total exposure time to new vulnerabilities. Organizations spend an inordinate amount of time and money on these protections. Of course, they still succumb to targeted attacks that use previously unknown vulnerabilities.

Despite these arguments there is a thriving business in vulnerability and patch management. One effective driver is that the Payment Card Industry Data Security Standard (PCI DSS) requires vulnerability scanning for every merchant that wants to accept credit cards. PCI standards carry a lot of weight because complying with them is a universal requirement and the standard has real measures that can be validated. It has given rise to offerings like those from Qualys, Trustwave, and Beyond Security (part of Fortra) for automated monitoring and reporting of vulnerabilities. The Payment Card Industry certifies 78 approved scanning services.

For internal operations, vulnerability management solutions can take two forms. One is to use that list of assets and the version numbers of the OS and all of the applications. Compare that list to known vulnerabilities and you can know which systems need to be patched or otherwise protected. An example of systems that cannot be patched regularly are high-end medical equipment. Because regulations may require re-certifying a piece of equipment when the software is changed, most medical equipment is not patched in a timely manner. Of course patching is disruptive to any production system that has to be scheduled for downtime and then tested before going back into production. So one way to avoid the risk of an unpatched system is to ensure it is not connected to a hostile network, like the internet. Unfortunately many organizations, especially hospitals, are not aware of all their network connections.

Internal scanning of IT assets for vulnerabilities is accomplished with tools that are deployed on the inside. These may be from Qualys, Tenable (which supports the open source Nessus scanner), or Rapid7, or any of the other 22 vendors in the space.

Frameworks

While PCI DSS is a proscriptive industry requirement, there are frameworks that provide the basis of many GRC programs. The ISO 27001 series specifies the documentation of a complete information security management system (ISMS). Within the ISO standards are requirements for establishing an ISMS, identifying roles, and documenting processes for incident response and reporting.

COBIT was created by ISACA, the Information Systems Audit and Control Association, in 1996. The name derived from "Control Objectives for IT." Many organizations that use COBIT require their security programs to fit within this general-purpose framework.

ITIL is a large collection of IT management guidance produced by the UK government. Its name came from Information Technology Infrastructure Library.

The U.S. National Institute for Standards and Testing (NIST) has produced a modern Cybersecurity Framework. While not mandated, it is gaining traction in the U.S. government and those that sell to government agencies.

Other GRC Solutions

Because there are so many different frameworks and regulations that call for cybersecurity controls, several vendors create tools that map the controls so a customer can generate reports for audits from multiple parties.

Logging and log management are a requirement of information management systems so tools that capture and store logs and make them easily readable are a subcategory of GRC.

The vendors of data leak prevention (DLP) may not agree that they reside in the GRC category, but their products are often deployed to comply with requirements to protect personally identifiable information). While the vision for DLP is to prevent corporate intellectual property from being exfiltrated, most solutions are tuned to alert when credit card numbers, Social Security numbers, and other PII leak.

Another requirement of many GRC programs is regular security awareness training. Thus, vendors like KnowBe4, PhishX, and Cofense create and deliver tools to not only train employees but track the effectiveness of that training.

As more countries implement data privacy regulations, the EU's GDPR being the most impactful today, there will be more investment in GRC solutions to meet new requirements for tracking and reporting. Expect the number of vendors in this space to increase dramatically beyond the 548 in the directory.

Story: Renaud Deraison

Renaud Deraison created the Nessus vulnerability scanner as an open-source project in 1998. He eventually commercialized it and co-founded Tenable, which is now publicly traded. He recently retired from his role as the company's chief technology officer.

I got into security by accident. I started with macOS, in the 1990s. Then, I discovered Linux. I had installed this weird version of Linux called MkLinux, which was a research project done by Apple at the time to put Linux on the Mac kernel running on a PowerPC CPU. It was very arcane. If Linux was a niche OS at the time, MkLinux was even more so, a unique set of multiuser permissions and all that. I fell in love with the idea of multiple people using the same computer. I discovered it 14 years after it existed, but better late than never.

As I started to get interested in how to configure systems securely, I actually came across SATAN, which was the original granddaddy of VA scanners. I installed it. Because I had an arcane version of Linux, it took me a long, long time to install it because SATAN used a lot of third-party binaries, which were not written for my OS. It took me a week. After a week, I was kind of disappointed with the end result. I mean, it was great for the times, but it was already outdated by 1987. It had not been well maintained.

The other thing I was really in love with was coding. I loved coding. I loved C programming. I felt that coding in C on the Unix system was meaningful because Unix was written in C. At the time, I was 17. When you're 17, and learn to code a little bit, you're looking for a project. I figured, "You know what? I'd like to write my own version of SATAN." That's how it got started.

I became very interested in the security world. I subscribed to the Bugtraq mailing list, which was the source of information, as you probably remember. That was where you would learn about new flaws and whatnot. The reason that also pushed me to get into writing Nessus was that on Bugtraq once a week, twice a week, there were these big zero days being published. I was like, "Hey, nobody can keep track of all of this. There's no central system, especially if you really think in terms of Linux and not Windows." At the time, even Microsoft didn't have their act together in terms of security. It was, "Hey, well, you can't keep track of all of it," so I'm going to do that software just like SATAN, but which will be up-to-date. I'm going to maintain it so that people don't have to pass through Bugtraq to remove from default CGI from their Apache installs and things like that. That's kind of how it got started.

It was the time of open source. Of course, I had to do it under the GPL. I announced Nessus on Bugtraq in 1998. Honestly, I remember I sent the email, and then I was going on a school trip the day after for a week. I left. Then when I came back, I had a ton of emails. I was very surprised by the reaction of the community. I felt that there was actually a need for some kind of tool like that at the time.

I looked at Ballista/Cybercop in detail. I liked two things about it. I liked the UI, which really was badass, with black and all that, and also the way they organized the attacks by family and type. That's an idea I took from them. Also, what they understood about VA, just like SATAN actually, is that it's more than just integrating patches. Ballista did a lot of configuration checks. We had an `.errors` file, which was open to the world. They actually spent more time on that than just if you have an old version of an FTP server. I found that interesting.

I came across ISS way later. Honestly, I loaded it, but I never ran it. I went through the UI, but I never had the opportunity to see how it worked. I just remember it as being slow to run. Ballista definitely was an inspiration.

I created Nessus in 1998, when I started college. Also, it's a dot-com thing. At the time, keep in mind, I was in France. I lived in Paris. Dot-com was just starting. It happened at a small scale in France, but you could tell, especially in the security industry, everything was happening in the United States. What started to happen is that in 1999 or 2000, you started to see companies reselling Nessus, like MSPs, who basically would take it and follow the GPL to the letter by not paying for it. I thought, "Hey, I think there's an opportunity for a business there."

The first thing I did was create a company in France called Nessus Consulting. At the time, the future of software was synthesis. Software had no value whatsoever. The future was just providing support. That's what I tried to do. I dropped out of college entirely, because I also was being invited to a lot of conferences. I did Black Hat and something in France. It was difficult to reconcile the two. The attraction of doing something and being part of that big movement was too thrilling.

At the time, I was sales engineering manager, CEO, and salesperson. I did all of that. Of course, it didn't scale well. The environment in France at the time made it difficult to create a company on your own. You had to raise money, and if you wanted to do something, you really had to commit. The French system forces you to commit because if you have to let go of somebody, there are a lot of things to pay and whatnot.

I was on my own. I got a couple of clients. One of them was the French equivalent to NIST. Another was one of the major French banks. I had a little bit of income, but it was not repeatable, and I didn't have a structure. I felt like it was fragile. I was looking at a way to go to the next level and find an actual business model that was not just support based.

That's when Ron Gula contacted me.

I knew of him thanks to the work he did with Dragon. I met him a couple of times at Black Hat and other conferences. At the time, he struck me as a down-to-earth kind of guy, not ego driven. He contacted me and said, "Hey, I'm looking at creating a company that would take VM to the next level." Also, at the time people would do VM for what was called the DMZ. The DMZ was a web server, SMTP 1, SMTP 2 (which was kind of the same, but not exactly the same as SMTP 1), and DNS. That was your attack surface at the time.

Ron said, "Hey, I'd like to take it to the next level and scan the inside of the network," which is exactly what I had been trying to get people to do with Nessus as well. I took a flight to DC, and a couple weeks after, I moved from Paris to Columbia, Maryland.

With Jack Huffard, our third cofounder, we created Tenable. The idea with Tenable was to initially keep Nessus free but build this management console to manage all your scanners across your environment and distribute results within different teams. We started that in 2002 when I moved to the United States.

We grew in an organic way for the longest time. The cool thing when we created Tenable was that we had Nessus. It was extremely popular at the time. I remember you would go to any conference, and a third of the presentations would mention it one way or the other—sometimes just a bullet point, but it was that kind of popularity. Nessus itself was a very well-known name, so it attracted a lot of people to us. We grew organically.

For the first few years, it was steady but slow growth. It was not one of these overnight unicorns that popped up, but that was by design. We thought we had a business model that was based on the console, and then we refined it over time. After a few years, we looked at the amount of investment we put into Nessus itself and the console itself. We thought, "Hey, there are a lot of companies out there doing the same model that we have, but they use Nessus." Half of the R&D they don't have to deal with.

I think it was 2008 when we made the controversial decision to close-source Nessus, which was really a big bet. I don't know of any company that did that successfully and survived to tell the tale.

When you look at companies like Red Hat, one thing I didn't really like with the open-source model is that ultimately you have a lot of people creating in it. Red Hat says everything is open source. OK, so can I deploy that OS on every system? Well, not really because we don't own the source code, but the way the RPMs are being set up, we have the copyright on that. I'm like, that's not a clean legal argument. They kind of play a little bit on that.

For Nessus here, we said, "Look, the model is not working for us, so we're going to close-source it." We're doing this new version of Nessus, version 3, which is closed source and actually brought a lot of benefit for end users. We provided binaries for the first time so people didn't have to compile them. That was a big win for a lot of end users. It was 100 times faster. It scaled better. It was really the foundation for the future.

The message was we're a commercial product. Overnight, we had a subscription for people to get the feed to get the updates. If you didn't pay for it, you had to wait a little bit. With that, sales went up dramatically. We nearly doubled in revenue overnight without any additional investment. That freed us to put resources into SecurityCenter and in other projects.

At the time, there were two things happening. One, people realized that there is no silver bullet to fix every problem. It was also a time that was very anti-agents because existing solutions were slowing down your computer. They realized that even your patch management solutions did not cover the whole spectrum of software. It would cover only a tiny sliver at the end, which is the core OS and a few apps. Also, you had the whole compliance regime of Sarbanes-Oxley coming up and a bunch of HIPAA requirements. At a very high level, you need to have a grasp on what your infrastructure is like.

That created a very strong tailwind for us, where suddenly you had a lot of customers realizing that yeah, they do need to have a better grasp on their infrastructure. Then a few years after, another big event happened, which was Heartbleed. The takeaway for a lot of customers with Heartbleed who realized they didn't have a full VM solution in place was, "Oh, we do need a full VM solution because you've got all these components that are all over the place, and I do need a way to scan through the network and see what my infrastructure is comprised of." That also was a very big movement.

Then the last one we've seen lately was with WannaCry, which was a light bulb moment for a lot of C-level execs in a lot of companies who always thought of their digital infrastructure as a way to optimize business. With WannaCry, what they realized is that the business was infrastructure. You can't do anything anymore if it's down. Fifteen years ago that was not the case. Fifteen years ago, you could still get by. Maybe you would be off of the Internet, and you could not do an AltaVista search, but now if the infrastructure is down, you can't do anything in most industries.

From a business point of view, I'm a big proponent of knowing your own limits. The fact is, if you look at the management team we had at Tenable, we kind of hit a glass ceiling because none of us had ever run a company that big. None of us had ever taken anything public. I mean, I'm a college dropout, so I barely know how to read and write. I wasn't a big help there. My two cofounders had no experience there either.

Also, you have a feeling where you can sense processes cracking at the seams a little bit. As part of the private equity coming in, it also was a way to get a new type of leadership in the company, and true leadership. I think if the three of us had remained fully in control of the company and we hired a CEO, it would not be a real CEO. It would be a puppet. I think by letting private equity come in and losing full control of the company, it was the best way to make sure that when this new CEO came in, he was actually CEO and not a puppet. It's a very important concept.

Again, if you look at the media, if you look at the Elon Musks and the Steve Jobs of the world, nobody does that. Nobody has basically the approach of we need to hire somebody better, but I feel it's important. I'm extremely proud of that decision because that's how we took Tenable to the next level.

First, you really become public two to three years before you actually become public. There are a lot of changes in the internal discipline of the company. I think from a financial point of view, you start to have very precise forecasts. If the sales team says they're going to do five this quarter, it has to be five. I'll give you an anecdote, from way before private equity came in and Accel was the only VC working with us. When we did our first board meeting, we actually blew past the number of the quarter. We came into the meeting and we thought, "It's going to be the easiest board meeting ever. We said we would do five, and we did eight. They're going to be happy. High five, and we'll leave."

When the Accel partner we worked with saw the numbers, he paused for a minute and said, "You know, the problem is that you can't really explain why you blew the numbers up. If you can't explain success, you won't be able to explain failure." We thought that was interesting. You want to have a forecast which is precise both on the upside and the downside because that's the whole discipline of being public. It's all about being regular, and you don't want big surprises because then it's uneven. Suddenly you have a big quarter. We started to have that on the sales side.

We multiplied the size of the sales team prior to the IPO. You start this whole big machine of enablement, making sure everybody knows what they're talking about. Make sure they properly understand the market and properly present the right value props to the customers and explain our vision, which was something that was missing. Before Amit Yoran came in, we were very technical. We would sell SecurityCenter, and we'd say, "Hey, we've got all these bells and whistles. You can do this, and you can do that," but we could not really articulate what the high-level mission was that we gave ourselves. The customer was like, "This is an interesting toy, but where are you going? Where will you be five years from now?"

We put all the discipline in place. On the product side, it was the same thing. We started working to be much more enterprise friendly. This means scale became the basis of everything. It's also the software setup. Customers can deal with a result of all sizes and continue to invest in research because we realize that customers come to us because of the quality of the audits.

I'm laser-focused at Tenable on still solving vulnerability management. I feel like we're in an interesting time. On the one hand, as I mentioned, the digital infrastructure has never been so strategic for any company. Ninety percent of all businesses are based on digital infrastructure, and while this has never been so strategic, it also has never been so chaotic, with things like IoT, cloud, and BYOD. I would argue in 1998 if you're really good with IT, you didn't need Nessus. You didn't need VM. You could get by. It would not be perfect, but you could have control enough to raise the bar, if you will, in terms of security.

Today, there is no central location to do that. The need for VM has never been so important. Now it's not so much about enumerating vulns; it's what you do with that data. How do you make sure that your SLAs are being respected? How do you manage your process rather than just CVEs, which is a symptom of a process that doesn't run well? I feel like we still have a lot to do. I'm still focused on that and making sure that we're solving our customers' problems and helping them get a good grasp of what we call the cyber exposure gap.

CHAPTER 11

Managed Security Services

The managed security service provider (MSSP) sector has grown dramatically over the years. MSSPs typically service small to medium-sized businesses that cannot keep up with the constant need for investment in people and technology to avoid costly breaches.

The early MSSPs included Netrex (now part of IBM), Riptech (sold to Symantec), Counterpane (sold to BT), and Guardant (sold to Verisign). They all provided a service based on managing security devices and collecting logs and alerts.

The next round of MSSPs included NTT, Unisys, SecureWorks, IBM, Solutionary, and AT&T Cyber. These grew rapidly and attracted the attention of private equity, which started to make large investments in companies like eSentire and Arctic Wolf.

Meanwhile, most large consulting firms added managed security services to bolster the offerings from their consultants. Accenture, PwC, EY, TCS, and Infosys all have growing businesses in the MSSP space.

MSSPs are evolving rapidly. In the past, they tended to be a repository for security alerts and logs, something that was required by auditors and compliance regimes. But, as attacks proliferated, customers began looking for more from their service providers. That led to the development of managed detection and response (MDR). This new breed is more akin to true outsourced security. The MSSP's SOC is peopled with several tiers of analysts to triage alerts and engage in incident response with their customers. They use security analytics and perform threat hunting, something most smaller businesses are not capable of doing well.

MDR providers will consume threat intelligence and compare indicators of compromise to traffic and files found on a customer's network. They will deploy modern endpoint solutions to have better visibility and provide a combined endpoint and network monitoring service.

Note that MDR vendors have to deal with their employees being poached because SOC analysts are in such high demand. Thus, MDR vendors like LMNTRIX, which claims more than 80 people, will instruct their SOC employees not to identify who they work for in their LinkedIn profiles.

IT-Harvest tracks 266 MSSPs globally. It has become difficult to sort through all the MSSPs because most resellers have added managed services to their offerings. Sometimes this is white-labeled from other providers. Several sources report counting tens of thousands of MSSPs worldwide. In general, these are hyper-local, serving only the customers in their immediate vicinity. To include them in our coverage, we look for multiple 24/7 SOCs and a wide geographic delivery capability.

Story: Amit Yoran

Amit Yoran was the founder of Riptech, one of the first managed security service providers. After a successful sale to Symantec, he joined the Department of Homeland Security. He went on to lead NetWitness, which he sold to RSA Security. He is the chairman and CEO of Tenable.

Like many kids in the early 1980s, my first computer was an Apple IIE, and I did what little boys do, which is play video games. But I quickly determined that my appetite for video game play was far greater than my parent's appetite for purchasing video games. I started copying other people's games and learning a little bit about how to pirate games and things like that. I've always been interested in the topic of computer security as it was.

In the early 1990s, I went to West Point and had a visiting professor from the National Security Agency. He taught the first information and security class at West Point. I thought security was a stimulating and awesome topic. I was really excited about it. For a term project I wrote a virus, and I needed a lot of help, so I went to him and he said, "Look, you have a knack for this sort of thing, and you really seem to enjoy it. I don't know what you're going to do in the Army, but if you want to consider a technical field right away and continue to pursue information security, consider transferring to the Air Force. They have a technical career track that allows you to do that." At the time, the Army was very much in the dark ages of computers and information security.

After graduation, I inter-service transferred to the Air Force and got a job at the Pentagon doing networking for some of the OS office of security of defense networks. I did my graduate work in computer security at Georgetown University, which was one of the few schools back then that offered an information security program. Then after a couple years in the Pentagon, I went to Assist, which was I think the automation security support information team or something like that, at the Defense Information Systems Agency (DISA). That organization, while I was there, shifted from Assist to form the DoD CERT program, the computer emergency ready response team.

The time, about mid-1996 to 1997, was a really exciting time because there were no or very few really commercial intrusion detection systems or network monitoring. So we were doing some pretty interesting things at the time, like aggregating, putting on network sniffers and looking at the headers and the metadata of the packets that were going across the network, and trying to look at log data and ingest this information. And, of course, there were no SIEM products or intrusion detection systems, or at least very few commercial ones. We were recording all these things and then writing a bunch of Perl scripts to find and track activities of compromised systems and hackers and things like that. I got involved in a couple of pretty high-profile cases and incidents in the late 1990s, where we were tracking individual hackers, but even some early state-sponsored activity.

Riptech

I did that for my five years in the military, got out in 1998 during the Internet boom, and tried taking some of those concepts we were working on at the DoD and applying them to the commercial world. So how do you help organizations monitor their networks? How do you look at attack identification and response in a more in-depth way than the commercial world was doing at the time?

The great temptation coming out of the military doing information security in 1998 was to go work for a contractor, make twice as much money as you're making as a military captain, and continue on that route.

I always have looked at the jobs that I've chosen to do and said, "OK, what's the life experience in this?" At the time it was 1998, which was like the 1849 of my generation. Do I want my grandchildren asking me, "What did you do in the Internet gold rush?" And I say, "Oh, I wanted to go become a government contractor?" It just didn't seem like the life journey that I was looking for.

I got together with a couple of guys who I had worked with in the military doing network monitoring and incident response and things like that and said, "Hey, could we build something like this for the commercial market?" So we formed a company called Riptech, which was one of the first—I don't know if we were number two or number three—but it was one of the first managed security service providers. At the time, our view of how to do it differently wasn't just "Hey, we're going to connect to your firewalls and make the rule changes that you're looking for." Instead we're going to ingest the data that your firewalls are producing, all of that log data, all the alert information from your intrusion detection systems, and put it into a structured database so we can start running queries and start analyzing things in a much more sophisticated way.

Not knowing a whole lot about business—approximating zero—I jumped into this with a couple of other folks. It was fascinating because at the time, we thought the mid-market would really embrace this; these were people who didn't have the sophisticated teams to go out and do the attack monitoring themselves. What we found was that the largest of enterprises—the more sophisticated security teams—could appreciate what we were doing and how we were doing it, so they were more comfortable engaging with us. This included companies like the online presence for Citigroup and First USA Bank and a lot of more sophisticated consumers of security technology. More mature security programs were comfortable signing up.

This was actually pretty funny because I remember very distinctly we were on the second floor of a furniture store. It was a two-story building. It literally was a place called the Furniture Store on the ground level, and we were upstairs in an office space, which is where we built our security operations center. And we had the folks from Network Solutions who were managing basically the dot-com boom at the time. We had the security team for the Citibank online presence come down to our offices in Alexandria, Virginia, and take a look at our operations. They said, "Hey, these guys are for real, and what they're doing is really interesting." Somehow, they were able to see past the facility and look at the technology and what we were actually doing and said, "We're comfortable taking a chance on these guys because what they're doing is really innovative and pushing the envelope of how to detect attacks and monitor activity."

It felt like we were pioneering. We knew that there was another company called Netrex, which had started right about the same time. They ended up getting acquired by ISS. Netrex was in Michigan, and ISS, of course, was in Atlanta.

It was never about us versus Netrex. It was more about us educating the market, because very few people even knew that these service offerings were available. And at the time, we didn't even call it a managed security service provider, because there was no such term.

The term was *application service provider* (ASP), the precursor to a SaaS platform.

SaaS hadn't been invented. But we thought if we called ourselves an ASP for security, investors would get it, and customers would get it, and it would be a little bit more intuitive. So we tried at the time calling ourselves a security ASP.

We eventually approached investors. We were very counter-cyclical. I've got impeccable inverse timing for success here. We ran the company basically profitably doing some pen testing work, with a little bit of security consulting for the first couple years, living hand to mouth while we developed the technology and stood up our operations. Then in late 2000 right when the dot-com boom had burst and was quickly deflating, we went out and raised a $20 million Series A round. And at the time, the logic was still that you had to spend money to be worth anything. It's not about running a business; it's about growing and showing the greatest market potential.

We ended up burning through a lot of money, and in late 2001, we closed a Series B round. I joke with folks that when the getting was good, we ran a tight ship and lived hand to mouth and ran a real business. When times got tough, we went out and raised a whole bunch of venture capital. We ended up raising in total more than $40 million, and it accelerated a lot of our growth. Ultimately, we were acquired by Symantec in late summer of 2002.

It was almost five years in total. I guess by some measures, it was phenomenally fast. But as you know, when you're doing a startup, you measure them in dog years. It didn't feel particularly fast at the time.

When we started in the MSP world, doing security services for operations centers, there were a handful of folks using the same model. Netrex was one of them. The other major players doing this sort of thing were the ISPs.

You had AT&T, and then UUNET, which many may not even recall, was the major backbone of the Internet at the time. UUNET had a phenomenal security practice, including some firewall management.

We looked at which major companies were doing firewall management and how we could get some share of that market. We looked at AT&T, UUNET, and some of the well-funded Internet service providers and said, "OK, these guys have built out their practices. But we can partner with every other colo, every other hosting facility, every other ISP that didn't or couldn't build out, didn't have the expertise to build out, a tier one security offering." We partnered with companies like Digex, which was a major colo and hosting facility. And we also partnered with the competitive local exchange carriers (CLECs). AT&T was broken up, so there were all these competitive local exchanges that were supposed to be stood up doing last mile and high-speed Internet services. We partnered with folks like Epic Internet and Rolero, which were funded to the tune of $500 million to $700 million, or Yipes Internet.

Our plan for them was, "Look, you guys have already spent so much capex building out your infrastructure. Without a single dollar of additional capex spend we can bring you a high-margin, value-added revenue stream for security services that can allow you to compete with the big guys. You can differentiate yourselves because you do it better and it's instant-on. You can allow a customer to be co-branded or private labeled, and all we want is access to the customer base so we can generate this great margin and revenue for you." We got a lot of momentum there. Then instantly the dot-com bust happened, and all of these companies that had received hundreds of millions of dollars of funding shriveled up and died almost overnight. We found ourselves out there saying, "Oh my god, our go-to-market strategy has been completely decimated. We need to really rethink how we're going to go about doing this."

So, we went direct after that. We said "OK, we know a couple of good sales folks. What we're going to do is we'll continue to have a partnership program, but we can't leave it in the hands of these CLECs." We started shifting pretty radically from a service provider, with a colo hosting–based channel program, to one that was much more reseller oriented. At the same time, we began to have a direct enterprise touch with our own sales reps going out and meeting with folks like Citibank and First USA and financial institutions like Capital One and GE Capital. Washington Mutual was another bank that was huge for us. They ended up getting in a tough spot with the lending and mortgage crisis several years later. We found out that more sophisticated security teams and programs were much more receptive to understanding what we were doing and how it could augment their internal security efforts.

We grew Riptech to north of $20 million of annual subscription-based revenue during that stretch. It was reasonable growth, especially in light of the sort of tough economic and macro-economic environment that we were living in the early 2000s and 2001, which were for the tech world and the dot-com, world pretty horrific.

We sold the company to Symantec for $145 million in the late summer of 2002.

Symantec

It made sense for Symantec because they had a very early stage, immature managed security service offering. We were competing with them and beating them pretty consistently. And it's one of those cases where it's a small world, it's a small industry, and you have to keep collegial with everyone because today's competitor is tomorrow's acquirer. And vice versa.

Partnerships are formed. One of those golden rules about just being a decent human being ends up being more important in small communities than otherwise. We ended up getting acquired by Symantec, even though they already had a managed service. We became the showcase of that platform and ended up assuming their existing offerings. It gave us deep pockets, a worldwide footprint, and access to a large customer base. That business has really been one of the great acquisitions for Symantec. I think it's remained a top-right Gartner Magic Quadrant Leader in the managed security services space ever since the acquisition.

There are certainly mid-market MSSP players and folks that address the mid-market needs at mid-market price points and at that level of sophistication. For business reasons, everyone will claim to be in the enterprise market segment because your investor attractiveness and your return as an operator are going to be a lot better through the enterprise market segment. Selling to the enterprise gives you a better ability to differentiate yourself, and therefore, typically greater margins, which make investors really excited.

The market has really evolved in a lot of interesting ways. As with many things in security, what the security team used to do is pushed off to operations. And back in the day, security teams were deploying firewalls and managing firewalls and intrusion detection systems, and now when you go to any large enterprise or large organization, you'll see firewalls managed by network operations. You'll even see intrusion detection systems managed by network operations. Antivirus and things like that, which used to be a security domain, end up, as they mature, working their way into more of an operations discipline than a security discipline.

You've seen that in managed services. We're not going to give it to our network operations, but our team doesn't need to do it; we'll outsource it to an MSSP. The flip side is you also see the MSSPs broadening their offerings.

When we were doing this, it was predominately network-based firewalls and network-based intrusion detection systems. We had a handful of host things and some logging infrastructure as well. Now those are all table stakes for managed security services, and there's also a managed vulnerability assessment and vulnerability management services and literally dozens of other service offerings, which you see coming out of the turnkey MSS market.

On the higher end of the market, you see a lot of managed detection response (MDR) types of services as well where they don't even offer to manage your firewalls. All they want to do is the very aggressive and sophisticated level of threat response for folks that can't attract that expertise in-house or they see value in the network effect of doing this through a provider. Of course, sometimes vendors are doing that as well. It is interesting how the managed service market has broadened in terms of the offering but also has stratified in the levels of sophistication.

Department of Homeland Security

I stayed at Symantec for exactly 364 days for contractual and other reasons. Then, I was surprisingly recruited back into government to join an administration that was trying to establish a national cyber policy and start generating security operations. I joined the Department of Homeland Security, which is where the U.S. President decided he wanted to put the national cyber efforts. They had formed a national cybersecurity division within the Department of Homeland Security and had approached me. They wanted somebody who understood the technology, the business side of cybersecurity because so much of cyber is in the private sector, and who also had some startup experience and wouldn't be afraid or intimidated by the mess that was DHS in the early days. When you have the intersection of those three sets, there are just a couple of completely loony people that they could approach.

We had a global infrastructure at Riptech, and we were monitoring thousands of corporations from all over the world and had really good insight into what was happening from an Internet security perspective. So, when a breakout would happen or an incident would happen, sometimes the White House folks would call us or even come down to our operations center in Alexandria. They'd say, "Hey, we're hearing about this. What are you guys seeing? You guys have this incredible intelligence network. Is this really a big deal? How prevalent is this?"

I met with a number of the White House folks during my years at Riptech, so they said, "How would you like to come help do this for the government at DHS?" My first response was thanks but no thanks. Then when I talked to Tom Ridge, the first secretary of Homeland Security, and started learning more about the mission, I thought this is a once-in-a-lifetime opportunity to do something impactful and help get things off on the right foot. Again, going back to my thought process about deciding what is the life experience in choosing this versus choosing that, I very quickly got my arms around this concept and was excited about the mission.

I joined DHS, and we did a number of things that were really exciting at the time. We had responsibility for the incident response work across the federal civilian infrastructure. There were no unifying systems, so the Department of the Interior might be attacked, the Department of Agriculture might be attacked, or the EPA might be attacked, and they would have no understanding that there were any unifying threats across these attacks or incidents or even that these incidents were happening.

We started some government-wide collaboration initiatives. GFIRST was the government form of incident response and security teams. A bunch of programs started voluntarily at first, like Einstein, which was the first cross-federal civilian network monitoring. Basically, we did what all good Internet people do: we stole it. We relied on the insight we had from the DoD days of a program called Centaur and said, "This is technology the government has already paid for; it's flow-based monitoring. Let's use the same sensors, the same queries, and the same types of analytics and apply it across federal civilian infrastructure."

We had a series of these initiatives, some of which took off and were great at establishing early momentum. Another was an effort to map out the federal IP space and really understand what the government space looked like. We also established a bunch of collaboration points with the private sector.

At the time, we had a mindset that there's a tremendous amount of work to do. It's easy for government to put itself in the middle of a diagram and say, "We're at the center." We recognized that we were engaging with other government agencies as the US-CERT, which was the organization we formed within DHS. Whether we're engaging with other government agencies or with our private-sector partners and peers, we want to make sure we are creating a value proposition that is of great interest to them. If they're having an incident, can we help them with the malware and analytics? Can we help them with additional triangulation of malicious IP addresses or similar incidents that we were aware of? Can we share threat intelligence? Can we do network monitoring with some network effect? That way, when we go to the private sector and ask them to engage, they'll ask what we have that might be of interest to them, and we can say, "Look, we've got some network monitoring intelligence across the largest network in the world. That could be interesting."

The thought was to be very entrepreneurial about this and come up with ways that we might create value and engage with other government agencies and our private-sector peers or foreign governments in a way that would add value. It was an interesting time.

Looking back on it, we had other initiatives, like convening an interdepartmental working group on cyber. We asked what the total authorities of the federal government were. Between the FBI, the intelligence community, the Department of Energy, the Department of Agriculture, and the Department of Treasury, what authorities exist within the federal government? What are the technical capabilities that exist and the pockets of expertise? How could we begin to form a national or at least a federal response if something is happening, like an incident of national consequence? How do we know what we can do, what we have the authority and ability to do, and what we should do or what each different agency might be doing?

If there's something that might be impacting the power grid, which was a great concern at the time, what authority does the federal government have? Can the FBI kick in the door? Can somebody at the Department of Energy push an operator aside and start putting fingers to keyboard? These are all things that had never been explored previously.

There were a lot of interesting operational things that we were trying to do and a lot of interesting policy things that just hadn't been tackled before. It was, and I think remains, a field that is very rapidly evolving, especially in the federal and public-sector side.

If you're an aspiring new cybersecurity professional, you can rest assured that there'll be lots of opportunity to dig into some meaty challenges.

There was a realization that came to me that the Department of Homeland Security, maybe at the bureaucratic levels because Tom Ridge was terrific, wasn't really taking cybersecurity with the same level of gravity that our other government agencies were. They seemed willing to let intradepartmental politics dictate how the department had been thinking about things. That bothered me. We were getting great cooperation from the FBI, CIA, NSA, DoD, state department, and others. But within the department, there was a lot of disappointing dialogue that was occurring. I concluded that there's a big world out there and a lot of exciting things happening.

While I loved the mission and the team and what we were doing, if our efforts weren't going to be positioned for success or they weren't going to be treated with the gravity they deserved, I concluded the best thing I could do was depart and let it be known how serious security was.

Looking back 15+ years, I tried to be very respectful about my opinions. I never came out and said, "This is happening or that's not happening or this person is a jerk." It was more, "It's been a year, and we've accomplished a lot. I'm glad I could help the ground level, and I'm going to go off and do other things." Maybe I even said something like, "Hey, I've had twins, and I'm going to go spend time with my family."

NetWitness

I always tell folks, especially entrepreneurs who have been successful or had some successful career moves, to take their time finding the next gig. As a VC or investor, you've got a nice, diverse portfolio of things that might succeed or fail. As an operator, you've got a risk profile of one. So choose wisely.

When I left government, it was late 2004. I was working hard, sitting on boards, investing, speaking, writing, doing whatever. But I didn't jump into any one full-time role until late 2006.

It used to drive my executive assistant crazy because I had probably formed seven or eight different shell companies. "If this heats up, we're going to go off and do that. If that heats up, we're going to. . . ." I also joined and invested in a bunch of things. She would say, "You're all over the map. It's fanatical. You need focus to succeed." I completely agree with that. Ultimately, you've got to have a lot of pokers in a lot of fires to have things light up. You look for something you feel is a compelling, differentiated technology in a super-attractive market opportunity where you can create economics that can be very exciting. But all of those things lining up is really, really difficult.

You might have a great company in a not-great market or a great market with a not-great technology. Or you might have a great market and a great technology, but the company has already pissed away $50 million in venture capital, is in debt up to its eyeballs, and the economics of it are hard to pull together.

Again, getting all these things to line up is a rare event. I came across NetWitness after my government time, but as part of an advisory activity, where it was technology that was developed in a joint CIA-NSA project. The NSA branch went off and became a product called SilentRunner, which you probably recall back in the day. The CIA branch became a product called NetWitness, which never really made its way out of government. I guess they had a couple hundred thousand dollars of commercial licenses as well.

But the concept was recording your network traffic and being able to replay it and re-create exactly what happened. I thought, "Man, as these attacks are getting more sophisticated and we're seeing a lot of brazen Chinese, Russian, and other nation-state activities, having that kind of forensic evidence and the forensic detail of what exactly occurred on a packet-by-packet basis is really exciting."

The government contractor developing the NetWitness product, ManTech, came to the realization that they were not going to be able to monetize it, so they'd rather sell it or encourage somebody else to do something with it. I got together with my old CTO from Riptech, Tim Belcher, saying, "Take a look at this. I think this is really exciting." He took a look at it, and said, "That's pretty cool. It'll never scale." And I said, "OK." After going off and looking at other things, I came back and said, "No, this is really freaking cool, Tim. Go have another look at it." He came back and said, "I agree, it's super cool, super valuable, not going to work, never going to scale. Sorry." I met with ManTech while I kept pulling the thread on some other things. Eventually I called Tim back and I said, "Tim, I'm going to do it." And he said, "OK, I'm in."

We raised about $10 or $11 million. We used a couple million dollars to buy the core technology patents and bring on some of the software developers from ManTech and founded a company around it where we could do a couple of things. One, is we wanted to move it from a Windows application to be a piece of enterprise infrastructure, so we ported it from Windows to Linux so we could have an appliance-based solution that would distribute at scale. We wanted to open up the analytic application. Instead of just an investigative tool to sift through the data, we wanted to open APIs with reporting, alerting, and the ability to query.

Our vision was to make an enterprise infrastructure product that would open up not just the investigative features but reporting, alerting, dashboarding, and integrating with other products. We thought it would take nine months to a year. It took us about 18 months. The platform was awesome, and our early adopter customers and testers were singing our praises. "Boy, this thing is amazing, but it crashes once every day. When it crashes and you're rebuilding your index, it takes about a half-day to two-thirds of a day to re-index. It's hard to have a good forensic solution when you're missing 30% of the packets and down 30% of the time. So please, I love it, but please fix your freaking product."

I would turn to the CTO and say, "Tim, you've got to fix this thing. What the hell is wrong with you?" And he said, "What do you want from me? I told you all along this would never work." The lesson there is you may have a great vision of where you want to go, but don't underestimate how long or difficult it's going to be and how much capital you may need to get there.

I frequently tell people if you're an entrepreneur, you're probably two to three times more unrealistically optimistic than the normal human mind. So if you think it'll take a year, plan on it taking two. If you think you need $5 million to get something done, I suspect it'll take you at least $10 million. You should be prepared for that.

We finally got the platform working. It took us between 18 months and 2 years, but then it was off to the races. What I love to do is get it in front of mature security professionals, people who are battle hardened, crusty, and seen every vendor pitch in the world, because this was really a new category of network forensics. I remember speaking to John Pescatore at Gartner and saying, "John, what do you think of this thing?" He said, "It's really neat. The sum total market size for that is going to be about $25 million from people who can afford it." And like I said to Tim, "No, I love this. I'm going to do it."

What we came to realize is the best way to sell this was not to go to the CSO. We met many CSOs over the years, specifically many folks who ran security operations or the VP, EVP, or whatever. Don't go to the head honcho. They're going to look at it and say it's a big expensive thing. So we told our salespeople, "If you know the CSO, ask them for an intro to the incident response person—the total propeller-head packet junkie who's chasing the things that go bump in the night. That's our buyer. Find that person."

We showed them a demo of how you could navigate through network-level data using application-layer constructs. The whole vision behind NetWitness was capturing network traffic, reassembling session or application layer protocols, and pulling out rich metadata. It's not just the IP address, port number, and timestamp. When this is reconstructed, it's email. Who's the sender, who's the recipient, what's the subject line, and what's the header information? If you're talking about a database, who's the user, what database, what table are they attaching to, what tables are they selecting, what row and what are the application layer constructs, and how is the system responding? Instead of looking at the world as a bunch of IP addresses that are increasingly useless in today's dynamic environment, suddenly it is a world with a very rich application layer. A user is a user regardless of what application they're in.

The vision was to show these security practitioners how you can see the world through different lenses, and almost inevitably, you could capture their imagination, showing them something really interesting. Then they would say, "That's really cool. I want to see my traffic through that lens." That's when you know you had them, because you sit on the network, you start reconstructing traffic, and you say, "Oh, there's encrypted traffic." And "Oh, there's a certificate; oh, it's a self- signed certificate," and, of course, all these things are metadata. And there's a place and time for self-signed SSL certificates, but it's also typically a violation of policy and something you might want to look into.

Inevitably, we could see really interesting things. All of a sudden that security practitioner would light up with, "I've got to have this." All budgets went by the wayside. That person who didn't know anything would go to the CSO and have their respect and say, "We've got to have this. This is going to change how we do business." That was the magic of capturing people's imagination with NetWitness at what I think was an exciting point in the market, when the world was starting to deal with and understand that these advanced threat actors were out there and that we had to look at things differently.

Tenable

I ended up staying more than five-and-a-half years at RSA after it acquired NetWitness. But then I went to Tenable. A lot of my friends questioned why I would join a vulnerability management company with 20-year-old technology.

It's true that vulnerability scanning has been doing the same thing the same way for 20 years.

It's a core capability, and everybody knows they need it. But the world of compute has changed. You can't just scan desktops, servers, and workstations. You need to think about cloud-based infrastructure, web applications, DevOps environments, control systems, operational technologies, and so on, because the attack surface looks different.

Also, you can't just give people a list of vulnerabilities; you have to help them prioritize: what matters, what's more exploitable, what's not exploitable, what matters more to the enterprise from a criticality perspective or less to the enterprise? Use all these factors to start approximating risk. Ultimately, the thing that I think people fail to capture or understand in security today is for the first time, it's not just the CSO and the security practitioner. For the first time, business and corporate leadership are engaged in cybersecurity questions. They see a breach on the news, and they say, "Wow, that looked painful. Are we susceptible to that? What's our level of risk? How secure are we? How at risk are we?" And I think these questions are very different than "Can I find the bad guy? Can I keep the bad guy out?" and those types of questions.

I think the opportunity for a company like Tenable to take an established market segment and refactor it to help enterprises in this new way of thinking is a great opportunity. I'm excited about that.

CHAPTER 12

Open-Source Security

The history of open-source software in cybersecurity can be traced back to the 1960s when the first widely used operating system, Unix, was released. This operating system was originally created by Ken Thompson, a researcher at Bell Labs in 1969 and was released as open-source. (Thompson is now at Google.) This meant that anyone could use, change, and redistribute the code for their own needs.

The development of open-source software in cybersecurity gained momentum during the 1980s when several projects, such as the GNU Project, were developed. These projects aimed to create a free and open-source operating system that could be used by anyone without any restrictions. These projects were successful, and over the years, many other open-source projects have been developed in the cybersecurity domain.

In the late 1990s and early 2000s, open-source tools such as Snort, Nessus, and Nmap became widely used by security professionals. These tools allowed security professionals to audit and monitor networks and detect potential threats. Today, open-source software is a vital part of the cybersecurity industry. Open-source tools are used to detect, analyze, and respond to attacks. Open-source software is also used to create secure networks and applications and to develop secure coding practices.

Open-source software has been a cornerstone of the cybersecurity industry since its inception, and it continues to be an essential part of the industry today. The open nature of the software allows security professionals to develop innovative solutions to new threats and to create secure networks and applications for users. Open-source software provides the foundation for a secure, reliable, and cost-effective cybersecurity infrastructure.

There are viable open-source solutions that compete with many commercial solutions. But, because open-source relies on the generous contribution of time from developers, the solutions do not always keep up with the demands of end users for features and bug fixes. One successful business model is for a company, often founded by the original author of the code, to offer both the free version and one supported by the company.

Snort

Snort, created by Marty Roesch, is one of the prime examples of supporting both open-source and commercial products. His company, Sourcefire, was created to commercialize and support users of the open-source Snort for network traffic inspection. Sourcefire was acquired by Cisco in 2013.

Nmap

Nmap (Network Mapper) is a free and open-source network scanning tool created by Gordon

Lyon in 1997. It was initially released as an open-source tool in 1999, and has since become one of the most popular tools for network scanning and enumeration. The tool is used to discover hosts and services on a network and to identify the operating system and type of services running on them. Nmap can be used to audit entire networks or narrow down to a single IP address, port, or service. It provides options to scan specific ports, ping hosts, and map traceroutes. Nmap has evolved over the years and now supports a range of protocols and services including TCP/IP, UDP, ICMP, and HTTP. It also offers scripting capabilities, allowing users to automate routine tasks and create custom scripts to scan for specific vulnerabilities.

Kali Linux

Kali Linux is a Linux distribution created by Offensive Security, a security firm specializing in penetration testing for use in digital forensics, offensive security, and penetration testing. It is based on Debian. Kali Linux was initially released in March 2013, but its development traces back to earlier than that. The precursor to Kali Linux, BackTrack Linux, was first released in 2006. Many security professionals get their start using Kali Linux, which includes a suite of open-source tools for pen testing.

Nessus

Nessus is a comprehensive vulnerability scanning program supported by Tenable Network Security. It was originally released in 1998, and is used to identify security vulnerabilities in computers and networks. Nessus was created by Renaud Deraison. He developed the tool as a way to assess the security of networks quickly. Many commercial software and solutions and cloud-based hosted services use Nessus as their engine for vulnerability management.

Metasploit

Metasploit was first developed in 2003 by HD Moore, a renowned security researcher and author. The project started as a portable network toolkit containing various network security tools and network testing utilities. In 2005, the project was officially released as open-source software, and the first version of the Metasploit Framework was released.

Since then, Metasploit has become one of the most popular and powerful offensive security tools used by penetration testers, security researchers, and red teams alike. It is even used by cybercriminals. With the Metasploit Framework, users can develop and execute exploit code against a targeted system. It also includes an extensive collection of payloads, enabling users to create their own custom exploits. In 2009, Metasploit was acquired by Rapid7. Under Rapid7's stewardship, the tool's capabilities have grown to include comprehensive system auditing and vulnerability assessment capabilities.

Osquery

Osquery is an open-source, cross-platform security monitoring software created by Facebook. It was released in May 2014. Osquery exposes an operating system as a high-performance relational database. This allows you to write SQL-based queries to explore operating system data. The software was developed to provide an easy way for system administrators to query and monitor data across their infrastructure, enabling them to detect intrusions, ensure compliance, and gain valuable insight about their infrastructure. It has become the core of many commercial products that use the term *agentless* to describe their ability to gather data from workloads without deploying or maintaining an agent.

eBPF

eBPF, which stands for extended Berkeley Packet Filter, is a versatile technology in the Linux kernel that allows for the safe and efficient execution of programs directly in the kernel space. It has evolved significantly from its origins, becoming a powerful tool for a wide range of system-level tasks. eBPF extended the original BPF capabilities, transforming it from a specialized packet filtering mechanism into a general-purpose execution engine within the Linux kernel. This evolution was driven by the need for more dynamic and powerful network processing capabilities in Linux, especially with the rise of software-defined networking.

eBPF has gained wide adoption in the Linux community due to its flexibility and performance. It's used in networking, security, application profiling, and system observability. Major projects like Cilium leverage eBPF for network security and performance, and cloud providers and enterprises use it for monitoring and securing their infrastructure. Spyderbat uses it to both provide causal analysis of cyber incidents and observability of Kubernetes workloads.

Ruff

Ruff is an open-source linter designed for Python, known for its exceptional speed and efficiency compared to other similar tools. Linters are tools used in programming to analyze code for potential errors and stylistic issues. They help maintain code quality and consistency, which is especially important in large projects or teams and contributes to code quality.

The Top 100 Open-Source Security Projects

In December 2022, former industry analyst now investor Chenxi Wang collaborated with Andrew Smyth of Atlantic Bridge to create the Open Source Security Index. In Chenxi's words:

> "The index lists the top 100 most popular and fastest-growing security projects on GitHub. We emphasize *fast growing* as we believe modern security operations are different from security in the past, when most deployments happened on-premises. As such, many of the fast-growing OSS projects are newer initiatives designed for modern infrastructure environments.
>
> To build this index, we used the GitHub API to pull projects based on tags and topics and manually added projects that lack labels. To constrain our scope, we limited the search to projects that are considered direct security tools.
>
> **How We Ranked the Entries**
>
> Once we had the raw list, we ranked entries based on an 'Index Score,' which is a weighted average of six metrics retrieved from GitHub. They include:
>
> - Number of stars: 30%
> - Number of contributors (excluding bots and anonymous accounts): 25%
> - Number of commits the project had in the last 12 months: 25%
> - Number of watchers: 10%
> - Change in the number of watchers over the last month: 5%
> - Number of forks: 5%
>
> Based on this scoring methodology, we list the top 100 GitHub projects on the Open Source Security Index website. The index is an evolving, live project.

Table 12.1 lists the top 100 projects. See the current rankings at **opensourcesecurityindex.io**.

TABLE 12.1 Top 100 Open-Source Security Tools

Rank	Repo	Description
1	ruff	Fast Python linter, written in Rust from Astral
2	metasploit-framework	Exploitation framework; tools for pen testing from Rapid7
3	cilium	Provides secure network connectivity between app services deployed using containers: Docker/K8s (using e-BPF–based data plane) from Isovalent
4	vault	Secrets management tool from Hashicorp
5	openssl	Toolkit and library for Transport Layer Security (TLS)/Secure Sockets Layer (SSL) protocol
6	mitmproxy	SSL/TLS-capable intercepting proxy with a console interface for HTTP/1, HTTP/2, and WebSockets
7	teleport	Identity-aware, multiprotocol access proxy; designed to manage access to infrastructure from Teleport
8	eslint	Tool for identifying and reporting on patterns found in ECMAScript/JavaScript code from OpenJS Foundation
9	cloudquery	Data integration for security—extracts, transforms, and loads configurations from cloud APIs to databases, data lakes, or streaming platforms for analysis; from CloudQuery
10	wireshark	Network traffic analyzer, for Linux, macOS, *BSD, Unix, and Windows
11	osquery	Framework for exposing operating system information as a set of SQL tables; used to query and analyze operating system data on individual endpoints (servers and laptops) from Facebook
12	oss-fuzz	Fuzz testing for uncovering programming errors from Google
13	hackingtool	Catalog hacking tools
14	trivy	Vulnerability and misconfiguration scanner for K8s, AWS, container, and VM images from Aqua Security
15	rubocop	Ruby static code analyzer and code formatter
16	sigma	Generic signature format for SIEM systems
17	checkov	SAST for infrastructure as code (Terraform, k8s, etc.) and SCA tool for OSS packages from Bridgecrew
18	opa	Policy engine that enables fine-grained access control for administrators in cloud native environments from Styra
19	atomic-red-team	Library of detection tests mapped to the MITRE ATT&CK? framework from RedCanary
20	ockam	Tool to orchestrate encryption and authentication and key and credential management and authorization policy from Ockam

Rank	Repo	Description
21	infisical	Encrypted secret manager for API keys and configs from Infiscial
22	django-DefectDojo	Tool that automates application security vulnerability management (bug tracker) from DefectDojo
23	mkcert	Tool for making locally trusted development certificates that require no configuration
24	wazuh	Endpoint security agent and management server from Wazuh
25	tailscale	VPN built on top of Wireguard from Tailscale
26	calico	Network connectivity and security policy enforcement for Kubernetes, VMs, and bare-metal workloads from Tigera
27	fleet	Telemetry platform for servers and workstations from Fleet
28	authentik	Identity provider for authentication workflows, such as single-sign on (SSO), user enrollment, and access control from authentik
29	oauth2-proxy	Reverse proxy and static file server that provides authentication using providers (Google, GitHub, and others) to validate accounts by email, domain, or group
30	infer	Static analyzer for Java, C, C++, and Objective-C from Facebook
31	pfsense	Network firewall distribution from Netgate
32	semgrep	Static code analysis from Semgrep
33	prowler	Tool to perform AWS, Azure, and GCP security best practice assessments (audits, incident response, continuous monitoring, hardening and forensics readiness) from Prowler
34	zaproxy	Web application security scanner
35	nuclei	Fast and customizable vulnerability scanner from Project Discovery
36	inspec	Testing and auditing framework for infrastructure (servers, workstations, cloud instances, and containers) from Chef Software
37	MISP	Malware information sharing platform and threat sharing
38	kratos	Headless API-based identity server; provides authentication and user management (MFA, social login, and custom identities) from Ory
39	sniffnet	Network monitoring tool written in Rust
40	fail2ban	Scans log files and bans IP addresses conducting too many failed login attempts
41	graylog2-server	Log management platform from Graylog
42	server	The APIs, database, and other core infrastructure items needed for the "back end" of the Bitwarden Password manager from Bitwarden

(continued)

TABLE 12.1 (continued)

Rank	Repo	Description
43	zeek	Framework for network traffic analysis
44	gitleaks	Secret scanner for Git repositories, files, and directories
45	suricata	Network intrusion detection tool (IDS, IPS, and NSM engine) developed by OISF
46	kubescape	Kubernetes scanner; scans for misconfigurations inside manifest files like YAML and Helm throughout the CI/CD from ARMO
47	ThreatMapper	Runtime discovery (pods, containers, applications) and scans for in-production threats and attack path enumeration from Deepfence.io
48	purple-team-attack-automation	Tool that implements MITRE ATT&CK TTPs as Metasploit Framework post gather modules from Praetorian
49	cli	Scans and monitors projects for security vulnerabilities from Snyk
50	fingerprintjs	Browser fingerprinting library from Fingerprint
51	falco	Runtime security tool to detect and alert on behavior from making Linux system calls (Kubernetes threat detection engine) from Sysdig
52	vast	Network telemetry engine for data-driven security investigations (SIEM replacement) from Tenzir
53	yara	Tool for malware researchers to identify and classify malware samples from VirusTotal (Google)
54	sops	special-purpose encryption tool for Kubernetes secrets from Mozilla
55	trufflehog	Secrets scanning engine that helps resolve exposed secrets from Truffle Security
56	mullvadvpn-app	VPN client software for the Mullvad VPN service
57	cosign	Command-line utility that can sign and verify software artifact, such as container images and blobs from Sigstore
58	libsodium	Software library for encryption, decryption, signatures, and password hashing
59	saml2aws	CLI tool that enables you to log in and retrieve AWS temporary credentials using a SAML IDP from Versent
60	mimikatz	Credential dumper for plaintext Windows account logins and passwords
61	sysdig	Forensic tool for Linux system and container exploration and troubleshooting from Sysdig
62	PEASS-ng	Privilege escalation tools for Windows and Linux/Unix and macOS
63	st2	Workflow engine for IFTTT operations in security response and remediation

Rank	Repo	Description
64	boundary	Automates a secure identity-based user access to hosts and services across environments from Hashicorp
65	snarkOS	Decentralized operating system for zero-knowledge applications from Aleo
66	docker-slim	Tool to optimize (make 30 times smaller) and secure Docker images from Slim.ai
67	Empire	Post-exploitation and adversary emulation framework (server is written in Python 3 and is modular to allow operator flexibility) from BC Security
68	sliver	Adversary emulation/red team framework from Bishop Fox
69	clair	Static analysis of vulnerabilities in application containers (currently including OCI and Docker) from Red Hat
70	dnscrypt-proxy	Flexible DNS proxy server that encrypts DNS traffic using DNSCryp
71	opencti	Visualization tool for security threat data from Filigran.io
72	kube-bench	Tool that checks whether Kubernetes is deployed securely by running the checks documented in the CIS Kubernetes Benchmark from Aqua Security
73	k8sgpt	Tool for scanning Kubernetes clusters with a set of built-in and configurable analyzers from K8sgpt.ai
74	zitadel	Open-source alternative for Auth0 from Zitadel
75	syft	CLI tool and library for generating SBOMs from container images and filesystems from Anchore
76	adversarial-robustness-toolbox	4,233
77	adversarial-robustness-toolbox	Python library for machine learning security from IBM
78	ossec-hids	Host-based intrusion detection system that performs log analysis, file integrity checking, policy monitoring, rootkit detection, and active response
79	brakeman	Static analysis security vulnerability scanner for Ruby on Rails application
80	age	Encryption tool (and Go library) with small explicit keys, no config options, and Unix-style composability
81	subfinder	Subdomain discovery tool from Project Discovery
82	arkime	Tool to store and index network traffic in standard PCAP format
83	PentestGPT	Penetration testing tool powered by ChatGPT; can solve easy to medium HackTheBox machines and other CTF challenges
84	BloodHound	Data analysis tool for managing attack paths in Active Directory environments from SpectorOps

(continued)

TABLE 12.1 (continued)

Rank	Repo	Description
85	kubeshark	Traffic viewer for Kubernetes: protocol-level visibility, capturing and monitoring payload traffic going in, out, and across containers, pods, nodes, and clusters from Kubeshark
86	sudo-rs	Memory-safe implementation of sudo and su written in Rust
87	rengine	Web application reconnaissance suite with focus on a highly configurable streamlined recon process
88	deepeval	Evaluation framework for unit testing LLM applications from Confident AI
89	httpx	Fast and multipurpose HTTP toolkit from ProjectDiscovery
90	grype	Vulnerability scanner for container images and filesystems from Anchore
91	certificates	Private certificate authority and ACME server for secure automated certificate management (so you can use TLS everywhere and SSO for SSH)
92	netbird	NetBird is an open-source VPN management platform built on top of WireGuard from Netbird.io
93	noir	Rust-based domain-specific language (DSL) for creating and verifying zero-knowledge proofs; the easiest way to write zk applications that are compatible with any proving system
94	crowdsec	Collaborative IPS to analyze visitor behavior and provide attack responses from Crowdsec
95	firezone	Self-hosted VPN server and Linux firewall from Firezone
96	iambic	Multicloud identity and access management (IAM) control plane that centralizes and simplifies cloud access and permissions from Noq Software
97	tracee	Runtime security and forensics tool for Linux-based cloud deployments (using eBPF) from Aqua Security
98	docker-bench-security	Script that checks for dozens of common best practices around deploying Docker containers from Docker
99	clamav	Antivirus engine for detecting trojans, viruses, and malware from Cisco
100	inspektor-gadget	eBPF introspection tool for Kubernetes, containers, and Linux hosts from Inspektor Gadget

CHAPTER 13

Failures

Learning from failure is one of the most valuable reasons to study history. Successes like Check Point Software in Israel lead to more investment, economic growth for a country, and innovation as the company invests in R&D. Failures tend to be forgotten by all but those who were part of the company. Attempting research into defunct companies will often turn up all the press mentions as it got several rounds of funding, won big deals, and made acquisitions, but once it begins to fail, there is no one there to write the press releases or record its demise.

Complete failures in the IT security industry are rare. Unless one has insight into the internal operations, it is often difficult to even determine if a company has failed. Was the sale of the company just an exit for the founders and investors, or was it a fire sale of intellectual property and key people? In recent history, the crash of Norse Corporation is one of the few admitted failures. Norse, based in Kansas City, Missouri, raised its first seed round in 2011. It went on to raise $33 million total. It appeared to be a vibrant company hiring and marketing at a healthy pace when Brian Krebs reported that there had been a major round of layoffs in January 2016. With that revelation, customers who were close to buying Norse's threat intelligence feeds canceled or put their orders on hold. That led to the CEO leaving, and eventually the company was disbanded.

Was Mirage Networks' sale to Trustwave a failure? Was Finjan? One measure of failure when an acquisition occurs is whether the investors turned a profit or lost the value of their investment. Bruce Schneier's Counterpane, one of the original cohorts of managed security service providers (MSSPs), had $90 million in investment when it was sold to British Telecom in 2006, for a reported $90 million. In such cases, the founders rarely walk away with anything, a measure of failure.

Another failure attributed to the dot-com boom was Vigilinx Digital Security Solutions, an attempt by investors to build a major player in the security consulting space to compete with PricewaterhouseCoopers, KPMG, Deloitte, and EY. Investors pledged $90 million to a venture of their own creation and hired Bruce Murphy from PricewaterhouseCoopers to lead it. It was only two years before it morphed into a reseller and managed security firm and was eventually sold to TruSecure for an undisclosed amount.

Many failures are brought about by investors losing interest in supporting the companies they have funded. One of the largest failures was that of Nexi, an attempt to create the god-box of networking to compete with Cisco and Juniper in the carrier space. The VC poured $100 million into the development of Nexi's first product, a datacenter solution that, in addition to being a switch, had a full-fledged firewall. A turnover in partners at the VC firm led them to pull the plug on Nexi before it had a chance to start delivering products.

Cosine Communications, founded in 1998, was the last dot-com company to go public. It too created a god-box for switching, networking, and security. It raised $230 million in its IPO in 2000, and its stock jumped 195%. It employed more than 400 people when it ran out of money and shut down in a few short years. Its portfolio of 80 patent applications and its leftover gear and few remaining customers were handed off to Fortinet at fire-sale prices.

Crossbeam Systems was another hardware venture deemed a failure. It had gone to market with what was, in retrospect, a failed strategy. Crossbeam invested $72.5 million to create and sell a multiblade security appliance. Up to 10 cards were load balanced to handle high throughput for security software products, primarily Check Point and ISS. It was eventually sold to Thoma Bravo and then sold to Blue Coat.

In 2019, ThinAir shut down. It was a startup in the data discovery space. Its agent deployed to Windows desktops allowed a customer to discover what data was on each of its endpoints, a valuable capability for compliance with data privacy regulations. In late 2018, as it was burning through its remaining funding, it attempted to sell to a competitor that pulled out at the last minute. It had to lay off its employees and shutter operations.

2020 Failures

GigaTrust, an information rights management solution based in Herndon, Virginia, shut down its website and LinkedIn profile page in 2020, although its customer ticketing system was still active. There is no explanation and no news coverage. Glassdoor reviews by employees highlight the implosion and dissatisfaction with executive leadership. GigaTrust took in a total of $46.2 million in funding, with the final infusion of $20 million provided by private equity from Balance Point Capital Partners. It had 37 employees at the beginning of 2020.

NS8 saw a meteoric rise in early 2020, growing from 80 employees at the beginning of the year to 214 by July. That growth came after a $123 million Series A round led by Lightspeed Partners valuing the fraud prevention company at $400 million. After irregularities involving the handling of corporate funds, it was reported that the SEC was investigating the firm. The CEO left abruptly, and they laid off most employees in September. The IP of NS8 was acquired by Avolin.

NSS Labs was founded in 2007, to provide testing services of security products. It developed reports on the efficacy of firewalls, malware defense, and other critical components of the security stack. At one point, the Texas-based firm had 100 employees. It had taken in $27 million in funding over the years. There has never been a proven market for product evaluation. Enterprises apparently do not see the value, preferring to use the simple model of comparing features and conducting a proof of concept (PoC) evaluation.

2021 Failures

In 2021, there were 50 companies removed from the directory. Most were small companies that never got past two or three employees. Their websites have been taken down, and the founders have moved on. Some were companies acquired the previous year and are no longer operating as stand-alone brands. There were no high-profile failures to hit the radar.

Failures in the security space are remarkably rare, considering the number of vendors. Most vendors that survive a couple of years actually provide products that customers value. The customers renew, and companies continue to make headway as they take on investment, hire marketing and sales teams, and focus on a geographic region or an industry vertical.

2022 Failures

In April 2022, most vendors slowed hiring dramatically as they began listening to the investors spooked by drastic declines in the public market. Yet 54% of all vendors grew in head count during the year. There were no remarkable failures during the year that saw other tech sectors, particularly crypto currency exchanges, suffer dramatic losses. FTX grabbed the most headlines with its complete collapse.

In August 2022, the CEO of GigaTrust, mentioned earlier, pleaded guilty to multiple counts of fraud. The 68-year-old Robert Bernardi could have been sentenced to 30 years in prison. In early January, 2023, he was sentenced to five years in prison. According to the Justice Department press release, Bernardi "was sentenced for orchestrating a scheme to defraud investors and lenders of millions of dollars through false and misleading misrepresentations, including fabricated bank statements and audit reports, and by impersonating a purported customer, auditor, and GigaTrust lawyer."

2023 Failures

The year began not with a vendor failure, but with the dramatic and near-catastrophic collapse of Silicon Valley Bank. SVB was the primary bank of the startup ecosystem even stretching to the UK, where it had a subsidiary. There were at least 500 cybersecurity companies that kept their funds in SVB. During 2021 and 2022, SVB's deposits had skyrocketed as a record number of new venture funding poured into the accounts of the startups. Like most banks, it prudently put those excess deposits into long-term bonds. But rising interest rates pushed the current value of those bonds down to the point that SVB had to sell some of them at a loss in early 2023. By March, SVB announced it had to raise money, which led to a loss of confidence among the VC community. On Friday, March 10, panicked customers attempted to withdraw $42 billion in deposits. This caused California regulators and the FDIC to shut the bank down and freeze all its accounts.

It was a harrowing weekend as startups and VCs scrambled to find funds to meet payroll. Luckily, the regulators announced the bank would open on Monday. The crisis was resolved, but the markets were spooked, and investors pulled back, leading to reduced funding, down-rounds, and some fire sales of companies that were out of runway.

Silvergate and Signature Banks also failed in March under similar circumstances.

In early December, Boston-based VC firm OpenView announced that they were shutting down their latest fund, which had just closed at $570 million. OpenView has more than $2 billion under management and has invested in at least eight cybersecurity vendors including Acronis, Axonius, and DataDog. The reason given was that two of its partners had resigned. Only $80 million of the fund has been committed. OpenView suspended new investments as they work through this crisis.

In the vendor space, 124 small vendors (fewer than two people) were removed from the IT-Harvest Dashboard. Most were acquired in previous years, and the brand has gone away.

There were also sales of larger vendors that, while not complete failures, represented significant drops in value. The Chicago-based MSSP Trustwave, which had been acquired by Singtel in 2017 for $810 million, was spun back out to a Chertoff Group entity for $205 million.

A few vendors closed their doors while the company assets and people were "rescued." For instance, Araali Networks, a provider of cloud container patch management solutions, was acquired by Qualys in September.

Qomplx, a risk analytics company in Tysons, Virginia, was reported to have failed yet still appears to be in operation employing 52 people, down from 190. In 2021, the company had announced a reverse merger with special-purpose acquisition company TailWind. As part of the deal, they were acquiring Sentar, a vendor with more than 300 people today that sells to the government. They even announced a distinguished board of directors in June 2021, including Chris Krebs. The merger deal was called off in August 2021. Two years later, the company filed a Work Adjustment and Retraining Notification with the Virginia Employment Commission, and its state of operations remains unclear. The WARN notice specified the type of reduction as a "closure," according to the *Washington Business Journal*.

Speaking of SPACs, the storied history of IronNet came to an end in 2023. IronNet was primarily a services company. It was founded by General (Ret.) Keith Alexander who had created and commanded U.S. Cyber Command. In October 2015, IronNet received $32.5 million in funding from Trident Capital Cybersecurity (now ForgePoint Capital) and Kleiner Perkins Caufield & Byers in a Series A investment. In May 2018, IronNet raised an additional $78 million in a round led by C5 Capital, alongside existing investors ForgePoint Capital and Kleiner Perkins Caufield & Byers. In August 2021, IronNet went public on the New York Stock Exchange via a SPAC merger with LGL Systems Acquisition Corp. Alexander was later replaced by Linda Zecher on July 12, 2023, as CEO of IronNet. After two years as a public company, IronNet announced it would be delisted from the NYSE in August 2023. It has since ceased operations and has filed for bankruptcy.

Despite the tumultuous year, the massive fallout from a dismal economy, decreased spending, and the risk aversion of VCs did not materialize. The year had its challenges, but the cybersecurity industry survived with perhaps a healthy retrenching.

CHAPTER 14

In Memoriam

In 2023, the industry lost several pioneers. This chapter celebrates the lives and contributions to the cybersecurity industry of these influential founders, practitioners, and thought leaders.

Zohar Zisapel

Founder, serial entrepreneur, serial investor, and cofounder of RAD Data Communications and RAD Group

Known as the "Bill Gates of Israel," Zohar Zisapel was a serial entrepreneur who founded and invested in multiple cybersecurity companies. His first business, RAD Data Communications (which he founded with his brother, Yehuda), broke new ground with a small modem that did not need a separate power source. RAD started in the back offices of Bynet, a company founded by Yehuda. This idea—of starting a new business within an existing enterprise—became the strategy that Zisapel used to transform one of his other businesses, RAD Group, into a world-renowned incubator of startups.

Through both RAD Group (a family of independent companies) and Bynet, as well as his many personal investments, Zisapel fostered the growth of more than 1,000 organizations. He invested in Wiz (a $10 billion unicorn), Talon Cyber Security (acquired by Palo Alto Networks for $630 million), Argus Cyber Security (acquired by Continental AG for $430 million), and Adallom (acquired by Microsoft for $320 million). He also served as a cofounder of Argus and as chairman of Talon.

His contributions to cybersecurity and other sectors helped many entrepreneurs prosper, creating numerous employment opportunities while making a significant impact on the Israeli economy—and the global tech world at large.

In addition to his work as an innovator, entrepreneur, and investor, Zisapel helped establish the Nanoelectronics Center at the Technion in Israel. The science and technology research university is committed to the advancement of the State of Israel and all humanity through the creation of knowledge and the development of human capital and leadership.

Kevin Mitnick

White-hat hacker, security consultant, chief hacking officer and co-owner of KnowBe4

Kevin Mitnick was a pioneer in the telephone hacking world (phreaking). At the age of 16, he broke into DEC's network and stole source code for which he was charged and convicted in 1988. After serving 12 months in prison, he was on supervised release when he hacked into Pacific Bell. A warrant was issued for his arrest, and he spent two-and-a-half years as a fugitive.

When he was finally caught and tried for multiple crimes, including wire fraud, he served five years in prison. He was released in 2000 but still barred from most access to technology.

He was a highly sought-after global public speaker and writer and established Mitnick Security Consulting to help businesses minimize their cyber threats through testing, training, and presentations. Mitnick Security Consulting became very well known for its Global Ghost Team, an elite pentesting team with members in Argentina, Spain, Germany, and Canada, among other nations. He was also the chief hacking officer and co-owner of KnowBe4, which offers Kevin Mitnick Security Awareness Training to help employees understand the mechanisms of spam, phishing, spear phishing, and more.

Mitnick was also a notable storyteller and bestselling author. His most successful book, *Ghost in the Wires: My Adventures as the World's Most Wanted Hacker* recounted the escapades that landed him in prison, including his second hack of Pacific Bell. Co-authored with William L. Simon, the book detailed his time on the FBI's Most Wanted List and became a *New York Times* bestseller. He co-authored two other books with Simon, *The Art of Deception: Controlling the Human Element of Security* and *The Art of Intrusion: The Real Stories Behind the Exploits of Hackers, Intruders, and Deceivers*. He also wrote *The Art of Invisibility: The World's Most Famous Hacker Teaches You How to Be Safe in the Age of Big Brother and Big Data* with Robert Vamosi.

Vittorio Luigi Bertocci

Principal architect at Auth0; principal program manager at Microsoft

Vittorio Luigi Bertocci's résumé—16 years as principal program manager at Microsoft and most recently serving Auth0 as principal architect—was strong enough to stand out on its own. But it was his knowledge and expertise of identity, as well as his commitment to ensuring that others understood its importance, which created Bertocci's long-lasting legacy. In a blog post, Okta (which acquired Auth0) referred to Bertocci as one of the people who created the identity industry and helped it to become more than an afterthought.

Bertocci was credited with having a major influence on Auth0 and Okta's product roadmaps and authored two IETF RFCs that led to the OAuth 2.0 protocol. At Microsoft, he helped to conceive and launch the company's claims-based platform components, including Windows Identity Foundation and ADFS, the ADAL and MSAL SDKs, and the ASP.NET middleware. He served on the board of directors of the OpenID Foundation, a nonprofit open standards body that develops identity and security specifications.

Bertocci was also a well-known advocate and educator for identity and strived to elevate the identity IQ of others. He wanted the whole world to understand why it was important. To accomplish this goal, he wrote several books and articles on the topic and produced various training videos. He also wrote blogs and traveled the globe to share his guidance and expertise at major industry events, including Identiverse and Cloud Identity Summit. Most recently, he started his own podcast, *Identity, Unlocked*, to further educate and inform others about identity.

Steve Katz

First CISO in history; CISO of Citicorp and Merrill Lynch

Steve Katz became the first CISO after becoming one of the few people who made a career in information security in the mid-1990s. His initial titles varied between data security officer and information security officer, but his mission was always the same: to make sure that businesses were prepared for future cyber threats.

When rumors spread that Citicorp had been hacked, the company took a proactive approach to combating malicious threat actors. Instead of merely upgrading their security and following the status quo, Citicorp searched for new talent to fill a newly created role: chief information security officer. Citicorp's search concluded with Katz, who had previously led information security at J.P. Morgan. As CISO, Katz advanced Citicorp's cybersecurity efforts for six years before taking on the role of CISO at Merrill Lynch, where he established a privacy and security program for the entire company.

Katz started his own business, Security Risk Solutions, while working for Merrill Lynch and went on to serve in advisory roles for Kaiser Permanente, Deloitte, and other organizations. A lifelong learner, Katz was a strong advocate for information sharing and analysis centers (ISACs) and served on many of them, including the Financial Services-ISAC and Health-ISAC. He was also known for providing his guidance and mentorship to others in the industry, as well as those who aspired to build a career in information security.

French Caldwell

Gartner fellow; founder and chief research officer of FCInsights

French Caldwell had a lot of proud moments throughout his career, starting with his decision to join the U.S. Naval Academy in 1977. He worked his way up to submarine commander before retiring in 1994. His professional career began thereafter, starting as a diplomatic liaison for the Commission on Roles and Missions of the Armed Forces.

Often known simply as "French," Caldwell served as a director for Richard S. Carson and Associates and as a senior manager at Arthur Andersen. He joined Gartner as a vice president and fellow in 1999, a position that allowed him to inform Congress and the military about the risks of a significant cyberattack. He was concerned that a powerful attack could create a crisis of confidence that would ultimately alter the balance of power—a digital Pearl Harbor. If he did not coin the term *digital Pearl Harbor*, he elevated awareness of the threat.

Caldwell used his time at Gartner to become an expert on governance, risk, and compliance and a pillar in the GRC community. He established and led research and advisory programs on governance, risk management, compliance, knowledge management, digital society, public policy, cybersecurity, legal information technology, and disruptive trends and technologies.

Caldwell also served as chief marketing officer for MetricStream, chief financial officer for The Analyst Syndicate, and chief research officer of FCInsight, which he also founded.

CHAPTER 15

2023 Mergers and Acquisitions

According to Table 15.1 provided by AGC Partners, there were 250 acquisitions of cybersecurity vendors in 2023. That compares to 332 in 2022, a 25% drop. If valuations were dropping due to the much-talked-about economic headwinds, you would think that there would be more acquisitions at bargain prices. However, economic uncertainty also led to less appetite for acquiring companies.

The giant deal of 2022 finally closed as Broadcom overcame regulatory hurdles put up by the UK and China for its acquisition of VMware. The $68 billion deal, completed in November, included the cybersecurity division that had been put together with multiple acquisitions, including Carbon Black, Lastline, E8 Security, and Bracket Computing. After the deal closed, Broadcom laid off 2,800 people and put the security offerings into one of four new divisions called Application Networking and Security. If Broadcom follows the playbook it used when it acquired Symantec, it will focus on the top 2,000 VMware customers.

By far, the biggest deal of the year and the biggest in cybersecurity industry history was the announcement that Cisco was acquiring publicly traded Splunk for $28 billion in cash. Splunk had come to dominate the SIEM industry. It employed 8,893 people at the end of 2023. Cisco also had a busy year acquiring Valtix, Lightspin Technologies, Armorblox, Oort, and Isovalent.

In addition to Splunk, there were five other take-private acquisitions in 2023. These were Sumo Logic, acquired by Francisco Partners; Absolute Software, acquired by Crosspoint Capital Partners; Tesserent, acquired by Thales; Blancco Technology Group, acquired by Francisco Partners; and Osmium Technologies, acquired by Sailpoint Technologies.

There was also one company acquired by a special-purpose acquisition corporation (SPAC). Yubico went public on the Swedish exchange via merging with a SPAC called ACQ Bure. Yubico's market cap was $1.1 billion in early January 2024.

First Quarter M&A

In the first quarter of 2023, there were 34 acquisitions. These included Valtix by Cisco, Axis Security by Hewlett Packard Enterprise, and Baffin Bay Networks by Mastercard.

Second Quarter M&A

The period of April through June saw 39 acquisitions beginning with Ericom being acquired by a division of Ericsson. Archer, the GRC pioneer, was spun out from the remains of RSA Security to private equity firm Cinven.

Threat intelligence vendor Lookingglass was acquired by rapidly growing ZeroFox, also a threat intelligence company.

Armour, founded in 2011, was acquired by Night Dragon Management, a private equity company run by Dave DeWalt.

Maltego, the open-source tool for mapping linkages used by threat hunters and researchers, was acquired by Charles Bank, a private equity firm.

Cyren, the source for URL classification used by most gateway security vendors, went out of business and was acquired by publicly traded Data443 Risk Mitigation. Data443 has a market cap just under $2 million at the time of writing.

Third Quarter M&A

The third quarter of 2023 saw 45 transactions. In July, SCADAfence was acquired by Honeywell and RiskLens by Safe Security.

Boulder-based Resurface Labs, an API security vendor, was acquired by Houston-based GrayLog.

Thales continued to grow in cybersecurity by acquiring Imperva, one of the first web application firewall vendors, for $3.6 billion. Imperva, originally founded and taken public by Shlomo Kramer, was taken private by Thoma Bravo in 2018 for $2.1 billion.

The assets of 22-year-old Fidelis Cybersecurity were acquired by Private equity firm Partner One Capital. It was sold by Skyview Capital, which had acquired Fidelis in 2020.

Perimeter81, a direct competitor to Zscaler in the SASE space, was acquired by Check Point Software.

Fourth Quarter M&A

There were only 21 acquisitions in the last three months of 2023. Of course, the biggest acquisition ever of Splunk by Cisco made the fourth quarter the biggest by value.

Trustwave, part of Singtel, was spun out to a division of the Chertoff Group.

Atmosec was acquired by Check Point. Revelstoke was bought by Arctic Wolf. Adding to the large dollar volume of deals in the fourth quarter were two acquisitions by Palo Alto Networks: Dig Security and Talon Cyber.

Year Summary

Table 15.1 is the complete list of 2023 transactions, provided by investment bank AGC Partners.

TABLE 15.1 ACG Partners 2023 Security M&A Dataset

Date Announced	Target Name	Acquirer Name	Acquirer Type	Value (in Millions of Dollars)
12/24/23	Atom Security	Mend.io (formerly known as White Source)	Strategic	
12/21/23	Isovalent	Cisco Systems	Strategic	
12/19/23	Spera Cybersecurity	Okta	Strategic	

Date Announced	Target Name	Acquirer Name	Acquirer Type	Value (in Millions of Dollars)
12/18/23	Consigas	Exclusive Networks SA (Permira Holdings)	Private equity	
12/14/23	Grabowsky	Xalient Holdings (formerly known as Xalient)	Strategic	
12/6/23	GreyCastle Security	DeepSeas	Strategic	
12/6/23	Semnet	GSTechnologies	Strategic	$3
12/5/23	WireWheel	Osano	Strategic	
11/29/23	Conquest Cyber	BlueVoyant (formerly known as BlueteamGlobal)	Strategic	
11/28/23	Keep Secure	Jot Digital	Strategic	
11/21/23	Tenax Solutions	IP Pathways	Strategic	
11/16/23	ReachOut Technology	Yuenglings Ice Cream Corporation	Strategic	
11/16/23	WaveDancer	Firefly Neuroscience	Strategic	
11/16/23	Solutions Granted	SonicWall	Strategic	
11/15/23	Increase Your Skills	Metacompliance	Strategic	
11/15/23	SixGen	Washington Harbour Partners LP	Private equity	
11/14/23	Rush Tech Holdings	Rightworks (BV Investment Partners LP)	Private equity	
11/9/23	Decisive Group	Calian Group	Strategic	
11/9/23	Nets A/S (eID business)	IN Groupe	Strategic	
11/8/23	Krebs Stamos Group	SentinelOne	Strategic	
11/7/23	Trustmatic	Certn Holdings	Strategic	
11/6/23	Talon Cyber Security	Palo Alto Networks	Strategic	
11/6/23	Pangiam Intermediate Holdings	BigBear.ai Holdings	Strategic	$70
11/3/23	Corvus Insurance Holdings	The Travelers Companies	Strategic	$435
11/2/23	Innotec System	Accenture plc	Strategic	
10/31/23	Dig Security Solutions	Palo Alto Networks	Strategic	

(continued)

TABLE 15.1 (continued)

Date Announced	Target Name	Acquirer Name	Acquirer Type	Value (in Millions of Dollars)
10/30/23	Tessian	Proofpoint (Thoma Bravo LP)	Private equity	$300
10/26/23	Seekintoo	Cycura Data Protection	Strategic	
10/24/23	nextAuth	Belgian Mobile ID SA (doing business as itsme)	Strategic	
10/23/23	Verve Industrial Protection	Rockwell Automation	Strategic	$185
10/23/23	Mnemo Evolution & Integration Services	Accenture plc (formerly known as Accenture)	Strategic	
10/10/23	Revelstoke Security	Arctic Wolf Networks	Strategic	
10/6/23	Unoideo Technology	Truecaller AB (OMX:TRUE B)	Strategic	
10/5/23	Blue Lava	Zyston	Strategic	
10/4/23	Advanced Network Systems	Magna5 International (NewSpring Holdings)	Private equity	
10/4/23	WithUno	Okta (NASDAQ: OKTA)	Strategic	
10/4/23	Castra Managed Services	Lumifi Cyber	Strategic	
10/3/23	IMagosoft Identity Management Solutions	KPMG LLP Canada (KPMG International Coop)	Strategic	
10/2/23	Avirtek	LOCH Technologies	Strategic	
10/2/23	Trustwave Holdings	MC2 Titanium (The Chertoff Group)	Private equity	$205
10/2/23	Scientific Software & Systems	Acheron Capital	Private equity	
9/29/23	Beyond Binary	Tesserent	Strategic	$4
9/27/23	Awen Collective	Sapphire Technologies	Strategic	
9/26/23	Dark Beam	APrivate equityX Analytix (KKR & Co.)	Private equity	
9/25/23	Vector0	StrataScale (SHI International)	Strategic	
9/21/23	Splunk	Cisco Systems	Strategic	$29,006
9/21/23	SecureMix	Domotz,	Strategic	
9/20/23	CyGlass	WatchGuard Technologies (Vector Capital)	Private equity	

Date Announced	Target Name	Acquirer Name	Acquirer Type	Value (in Millions of Dollars)
9/19/23	Bionic	CrowdStrike Holdings (NASDAQ:CRWD)	Strategic	
9/18/23	Saisei Networks	FirstWave Cloud Technology	Strategic	$1
9/12/23	ERP Security	SecurityBridge	Strategic	
9/12/23	Informtica y Comunicaciones	Exclusive Networks SA (ENXTPA:EXN)	Private equity	$0
9/12/23	FraudWatch International	Netcraft (Spectrum Equity Management LP)	Private equity	$0
9/8/23	AnyTech365	Zalatoris Acquisitions	SPAC	$200
9/7/23	Ermetic	Tenable Holdings	Strategic	$265
9/6/23	Kadiska SAS	Netskope	Strategic	
9/6/23	Atmosec	Check Point Software Technologies	Strategic	
9/6/23	Advanced Network Products	Coretelligent (Norwest Equity Partners)	Private equity	$0
9/5/23	Cohere Cyber Secure (MSP business)	Dataprise (Trinity Hunt Partners, L.P.)	Private equity	
9/5/23	Stacksi	SafeBase	Strategic	
9/5/23	Infinite ID	First Advantage Corporation (Silver Lake)	Private equity	$41
9/4/23	The DataFlow Group	Arcapita Group Holdings	Private equity	
8/31/23	Ports Group AB	Bridgepoint Advisers (Bridgepoint Group plc)	Private equity	
8/30/23	Osirium Technologies	SailPoint Technologies UK	Strategic	$6
8/29/23	Cyberillium Security (Baseline)	Cyesec (CYE)	Strategic	
8/24/23	ES2 Pty	1Step Communications	Strategic	
8/24/23	StackPath	Akamai Technologies	Strategic	
8/24/23	Cyrus Labs	Malwarebytes	Strategic	$0
8/23/23	Force Security Solutions	Konica Minolta Business Solutions, U.S.A.	Strategic	
8/23/23	Sealing Technologies	Parsons Corporation (NYSE: PSN)	Strategic	$175

(continued)

TABLE 15.1 (continued)

Date Announced	Target Name	Acquirer Name	Acquirer Type	Value (in Millions of Dollars)
8/22/23	Big Bad Wolf Security	Owl Cyber Defense Solutions	Private equity	
8/22/23	Integral Partners	Xalient Holdings	Strategic	$0
8/22/23	Wellteck IT	VC3	Strategic	$0
8/21/23	Griffeye Technologies	Magnet Forensics (Thoma Bravo LP)	Private equity	$0
8/17/23	Satisnet	Gamma Communications Plc	Strategic	
8/16/23	Solutions By Design II	Evolver (Hillcrest Holdings)	Private equity	
8/14/23	SpearTip	Zurich Holding Company of America	Strategic	
8/10/23	Perimeter 81	Check Point Software Technologies	Strategic	$490
8/10/23	Complyify	Zyston	Strategic	$0
8/8/23	418SEC	Protect AI	Strategic	
8/8/23	Triaxiom Security	Strata Information Group (Fort Point Capital)	Private equity	
8/8/23	Laminar Technologies	Rubrik	Strategic	$225
8/8/23	Cybersmart	Theta Systems	Strategic	$0
8/8/23	Helixera	Seceon	Strategic	$0
8/7/23	Sastema	Bechtle AG	Strategic	$0
8/7/23	Probax	Think On	Strategic	$0
8/4/23	gridscale	OVH Groupe	Strategic	
8/3/23	Armor Defense Asia	Armor Defense (Telecom Brokerage)	Strategic	
8/3/23	Rfi Electronics	Pavion (Wind Point Partners LP)	Private equity	
8/3/23	Fidelis Cybersecurity	Partner One Capital	Private equity	$25
8/2/23	The Mako Group	Centric Consulting	Strategic	
8/2/23	Blancco Technology Group	Francisco Partners Management LP	Private equity	$207
8/2/23	Strata Consulting	BueAlly Technology Solutions (Source Capital)	Private equity	$0

Date Announced	Target Name	Acquirer Name	Acquirer Type	Value (in Millions of Dollars)
8/1/23	Code BGP	Cisco Systems	Strategic	
8/1/23	Cyber Cloud Technologies	T-Rex Solutions	Strategic	$0
8/1/23	Healthcare Technology Advisors	THE 20 MSP Group	Strategic	$0
7/27/23	Advantio	Integrity Communications (August Equity LLP)	Private equity	
7/26/23	Privatise	Coro Cyber Security	Strategic	
7/25/23	Imperva	Thales	Strategic	$3,600
7/19/23	SB Cyber Technologies	CISO Global (Jemmett Enterprises)	Strategic	
7/19/23	Resurface Labs	GrayLog	Strategic	
7/19/23	Inedge Pvt	Bureau	Strategic	
7/17/23	Phronesis Technologies	TMT Analysis	Strategic	
7/13/23	Oort, Inc	Cisco Systems	Strategic	
7/13/23	eb-Qual	Swiss Expert Group SA	Strategic	
7/12/23	RiskLens	Safe Securities	Strategic	
7/12/23	Red Team Collaborative	DeepSeas	Strategic	
7/12/23	CyberGRX	ProcessUnity (Marlin Equity Partners)	Private equity	
7/11/23	Cobwebs Technologies	Spire Capital Partners	Private equity	
7/10/23	Forcepoint (Global Governments business)	TPG Capital LP	Private equity	
7/10/23	CyVig	Global Market Innovators	Strategic	
7/10/23	Shimazaki Management Group	DC Two	Strategic	
7/10/23	SCADAfence	Honeywell International	Strategic	
7/6/23	OryxLabs Technologies	EDGE Group PJSC	Strategic	
7/6/23	Midwest Computech	Heartland Business Systems	Strategic	$0
7/5/23	Automation & Control Concepts	GrayMatter	Strategic	
7/4/23	terreActive	Die Schweizerische Post AG	Strategic	

(continued)

TABLE 15.1 (continued)

Date Announced	Target Name	Acquirer Name	Acquirer Type	Value (in Millions of Dollars)
7/4/23	The 324 Consultancy	Node4 (Providence Equity Partners)	Private equity	
7/4/23	INCIDE Digital Data	Computest Security BV	Strategic	
7/3/23	Silicom	The Carlyle Group	Private equity	
7/3/23	Wise Security Global	Var Group SpA (Sesa SpA)	Strategic	
6/28/23	Horangi	Bitdefender S.R.L.	Strategic	
6/27/23	BluBracket	HashiCorp	Strategic	
6/27/23	Epiphany Systems	Reveald	Strategic	
6/27/23	Berbix	Socure	Strategic	$70
6/23/23	Eministration	General Informatics	Strategic	
6/21/23	Revel Solutions	Dataprise (Trinity Hunt Partners, L.P.)	Private equity	
6/21/23	Happy Gears	Airgap Networks	Strategic	
6/18/23	SecuLore Solutions	Exacom	Strategic	
6/16/23	Kovert AS	ECIT AS	Strategic	
6/15/23	Telia Finland Oyj	Intragen (FPE Capital LLP)	Private equity	
6/14/23	Privitar	Informatica	Strategic	
6/13/23	IT Systems and Solution	Lyvia Group AB	Strategic	
6/13/23	HighIOT	ODI (doing business as odix)	Strategic	
6/12/23	Tesserent	Thales SA	Strategic	$149
6/7/23	Sweepatic	Outpost24 AB (Vitruvian Partners LLP)	Private equity	
6/7/23	Enso Security	Snyk	Strategic	
6/5/23	Pivot Point Security	CBIZ	Strategic	
6/1/23	Secure Innovations	iNovex Information Systems	Strategic	
6/1/23	Venzo Cyber Security	Truesec Group AB (IK Partners)	Private equity	
5/31/23	Armorblox	Cisco Systems	Strategic	
5/25/23	Systems Solution	Meriplex Communications (Vitruvian Partners)	Private equity	

Date Announced	Target Name	Acquirer Name	Acquirer Type	Value (in Millions of Dollars)
5/24/23	XOR Security	Agile Defense (Enlightenment Capital)	Strategic	
5/22/23	Airside Mobile	Onfidol	Strategic	
5/16/23	ICCS & Co.	NexusTek (ABRY Partners)	Private equity	
5/16/23	Polar Security	International Business Machines Corporation	Strategic	
5/16/23	EclecticIQ (agent software assets)	ReliaQuest	Strategic	
5/16/23	Kleverware	WALLIX Group SA	Strategic	$0
5/15/23	SITIC	Trustonic (EMK Capital LLP)	Private equity	
5/15/23	Cyren	Data443 Risk Mitigation	Strategic	
5/11/23	Plisec	Verified Global AB	Strategic	
5/11/23	Absolute Software Corporation	Crosspoint Capital Partners LP	Private equity	$826
5/10/23	Cyberlab Consulting	Chess ICT	Strategic	
5/10/23	Netsecure Sweden	Integrity Communications (August Equity LLP)	Private equity	
5/10/23	EBS	**Alarm.com** Holdings	Strategic	$10
5/8/23	OneComply	GeoComply Solutions	Strategic	
5/1/23	MAXISIQ	Millennium Corporation	Strategic	
4/26/23	Legion Star	MajorKey Technologies (The Acacia Group)	Private equity	
4/26/23	Inclusive Innovations	Smile Identity	Strategic	
4/26/23	Phalanx Security Solutions	Unified Solutions	Strategic	
4/26/23	Lookout (mobile consumer security business)	F-Secure Oyj	Strategic	$223
4/25/23	Vonahi	Kaseya (Insight Venture Management)	Private equity	
4/25/23	xdr.global	Ascenda	Strategic	
4/25/23	Vintra	**Alarm.com** Holdings	Strategic	

(continued)

TABLE 15.1 (continued)

Date Announced	Target Name	Acquirer Name	Acquirer Type	Value (in Millions of Dollars)
4/21/23	Fusion Security	Scarlet Security & Risk Group (Trilogy Capital Group)	Private equity	
4/21/23	TS-WAY	Telsy SpA (TIM SpA)	Strategic	
4/19/23	Neosec	Akamai Technologies	Strategic	
4/19/23	Yubico	ACQ Bure	SPAC	$796
4/18/23	vArmour	NightDragon Management Company	Private equity	
4/18/23	CloudComputing	Allurity AB (Trill Impact AB)	Strategic	
4/18/23	Maltego Technologies	Charlesbank Capital Partners	Private equity	$100
4/17/23	Nowcomm	4net Technologies (Palatine Private Equity)	Private equity	
4/17/23	LookingGlass Cyber Solutions	ZeroFox Holdings (NYSE:ZFOX)	Strategic	$23
4/13/23	Archer Technologies	Cinven	Private equity	
4/11/23	TrustCloud	Branddocs	Strategic	
4/11/23	ICY Security	Columbus A/S	Strategic	$6
4/5/23	FRAFOS	Frequentis AG	Strategic	
4/4/23	Set Solutions	Trace3 (American Securities)	Private equity	
4/4/23	LP Network	Pavion (Wind Point Partners)	Private equity	
4/4/23	Ericom Software	Cradlepoint (Ericsson)	Strategic	
4/4/23	ITrust	Iliad SA	Strategic	
4/4/23	Zacco	OpSec Security (OpSec Security Group plc)	Strategic	
4/4/23	conpal	Utimaco (SGT Capital)	Private equity	
4/4/23	Assently	Verified Global AB	Strategic	
4/4/23	PatchAdvisor	Core4ce	Strategic	
3/30/23	Talus Solutions	Fulcrum Technology Solutions	Strategic	
3/29/23	Lightspin Technologies	Cisco Systems	Strategic	
3/28/23	Onward Security Corporation	DEKRA SE	Strategic	

Date Announced	Target Name	Acquirer Name	Acquirer Type	Value (in Millions of Dollars)
3/28/23	Passbase	Parallel Markets	Strategic	
3/28/23	OOO "Fuzzy Logic Labs"	Public Joint Stock Company Rostelecom	Strategic	
3/27/23	Volar Security	Unified Solutions	Strategic	
3/26/23	Open Storage Solutions	Tsunati	Strategic	
3/23/23	Foxpass	Splashtop (formerly known as DeviceVM)	Strategic	
3/23/23	Volta Wireless	4 Freedom Mobile	Strategic	
3/22/23	Confluera	XM Cyber (Schwarz Group)	Strategic	
3/21/23	QuadIQ	Interactive (formerly known as Casward)	Strategic	
3/21/23	Cysiv MEA	Liquid Intelligent Technologies (Econet Wireless International)	Strategic	
3/20/23	Baffin Bay Networks	Mastercard International Incorporated	Strategic	
3/20/23	Lidera Network	V-Valley Advanced Solutions Espaa SL (Esprinet S.p.A.)	Strategic	$6
3/15/23	Minerva Labs	Rapid7 (NASDAQ: RPD)	Strategic	$38
3/14/23	IPKeys Power Partners	Parsons Corporation (NYSE: PSN)	Strategic	$43
3/10/23	Safeway Consultoria Empresarial	Stefanini Consultoria e Assessoria em Informatica SA (dba Stefanini Group)	Strategic	
3/8/23	Rewire Online	ActiveFence	Strategic	
3/8/23	Tutus Data	C-Resiliens AB (Formica Capital AB)	Private equity	
3/7/23	Nokia Oyj (DDI business unit)	Cygna Labs	Strategic	
3/7/23	Netronix Integration	Pavion (Wind Point Partners LP)	Private equity	
3/6/23	ControlMap	ScalePad Software	Strategic	
3/3/23	Identum	Visma AS (HgCapital LLP)	Strategic	
3/2/23	Trust Codes	VerifyMe	Strategic	

(continued)

TABLE 15.1 (continued)

Date Announced	Target Name	Acquirer Name	Acquirer Type	Value (in Millions of Dollars)
3/2/23	Axis Security	Hewlett Packard Enterprise Co. (aka HPrivate equity)	Strategic	$500
3/2/23	LogPoint	Summa Equity AB	Private equity	$150
3/1/23	Criterion Systems	Cherokee Federal (Cherokee Nation Businesses)	Strategic	
3/1/23	AccountChek	Informative Research (Stewart Information Services Corporation)	Strategic	
3/1/23	Key Resources	Rocket Software (Bain Capital LP)	Private equity	
2/28/23	Certwell	Oribi Software BV (Main Capital Partners BV)	Private equity	
2/24/23	Valtix	Cisco Systems	Strategic	
2/24/23	Aditinet Consulting	Nomios Group (IK Investment Partners)	Private equity	
2/23/23	Aspl Info Services Private	iValue InfoSolutions India Pvt.	Strategic	
2/22/23	fielddrive	Hubilo Technologies	Strategic	
2/22/23	Anlyz	Trend Micro Incorporated	Strategic	
2/14/23	LEET Security	Uptime Institute (Dominus Capital LP)	Private equity	
2/14/23	Canonic Security Technologies	Zscaler	Strategic	
2/13/23	Morphus Tecnologia e Seguranca da Informacao	Accenture plc	Strategic	
2/13/23	Vigilnet America	Monroe Street Partners	Private equity	
2/9/23	Arturai Italia	BV Tech S.p.A.	Strategic	
2/9/23	Sumo Logic	Francisco Partners Management, L.P.	Private equity	$1,381
2/7/23	Atlas	Archer Technologies (RSA Security)	Strategic	
2/3/23	Arcas Risk Management	GreenPages (ABRY Partners)	Private equity	
2/3/23	Complytron	SEON	Strategic	

Date Announced	Target Name	Acquirer Name	Acquirer Type	Value (in Millions of Dollars)
2/2/23	Fidus Information Security	Wavenet	Strategic	
2/1/23	Brainwave GRC	Radiant Logic (TA Associates Management LP)	Private equity	
1/26/23	Southbank Software	OpenSpan	Strategic	
1/26/23	NXTsoft	Cash Flow Management	Strategic	
1/26/23	REDLattice	AE Industrial Partners, LP	Private equity	
1/26/23	GuardSight	Iron Bow Technologies (H.I.G. Capital)	Private equity	
1/26/23	SUPrivate equityRAntiSpyware	RealDefense	Strategic	
1/19/23	NCC Group Plc (DDI business)	Cygna Labs	Strategic	
1/19/23	Spectrotel	Grain Management	Private equity	
1/19/23	TwoWay Security	Vanta	Strategic	
1/18/23	GoVanguard	Abacus Group	Strategic	
1/18/23	Passwordless.dev	Bitwarden	Strategic	
1/18/23	Immue Cyber Technologies	Forter	Strategic	
1/17/23	Trum & Associates	ProArch Technologies	Strategic	
1/15/23	DTS Solution	Beyon Cyber W.L.L. (Bahrain Telecommunications)	Strategic	
1/12/23	SecZetta	SailPoint Technologies (Thoma Bravo LP)	Private equity	
1/10/23	Ran Ingenieria De Sistemas	Cerberus Cyber Sentinel Corporation	Strategic	
1/10/23	nVisium	NetSPI (Sunstone Partners Management)	Private equity	
1/10/23	PathMaker Group	Simeio Solutions (ZelnickMedia Corporation)	Private equity	
1/5/23	Amyx	Tetra Tech	Strategic	

CHAPTER 16

2023 Funding

Despite the fears caused by the failure of Silicon Vally Bank in March, 2023 saw a healthy $10.05 billion in investments across 315 vendors. The breakdown by category put GRC at the top once again for total number of investments. Those 59 investments totaled $2.216 billion. See Table 16.1.

TABLE 16.1 2023 Investment Rounds

Category	Number	Total (in Millions of Dollars)
GRC	59	2,216
IAM	44	1,748
Data Security	38	1,159
Operations	33	688
Application Security	27	937
Network Security	21	836
Fraud Prevention	18	437
Threat Intelligence	13	234
Endpoint Security	12	321
MSSP	12	693
IoT Security	11	223
Security Analytics	11	383
API Security	6	24
Email Security	4	25
Training	3	125
TOTAL		10,050

The $10 billion matches the levels of investment recorded for 2020 in *Security Year Book 2021*. That was followed by $26 billion in 2021, and a drop to $17 billion in 2022.

The number of companies to receive new funding dropped from 451 the previous year and 474 in the record year of 2021.

There were 22 investment rounds that exceeded $100 million, down from 36 last year. There were 23 that raised between $50 and $100 million.

These were some notable investments:

- **Sandbox AQ**, a spin-out from Google, took in $500 million. In addition to a post-quantum discovery capability for finding areas where enterprises can beef up their cryptographic processes, SandboxAQ has a business selling simulation software to accelerate the development of drugs and materials. Former Google chief executive Eric Schmidt is the startup's chairman as well as investor. Other investors include Breyer Capital, T. Rowe Price funds, and SFDC founder Marc Benioff's TIME Ventures.
- **Wiz** took in an additional $300 million at an astounding $10 billion valuation. No cybersecurity vendor has ever gone public at anything near that valuation. Wiz could seek to break the record for cyber IPOs or get acquired.
- **Cato Networks** ($238 million) and **Netskope** ($401 million) took in large rounds as they both prepared for IPOs. They will do battle with Zscaler, public since 2018 and with a market cap of $34 billion.
- **Yubico** went public on the Swedish stock exchange, raising $210 million. An amazing accomplishment after a 16-year journey promoting its OTP-generating hardware tokens.
- Threat intelligence vendor **SpyCloud** took in $110 million in growth capital. The Austin-based startup uses breach data to strengthen enterprise security postures.
- **Island** took in $100 million in a frothy year for browser security vendors. Island provides a secure enterprise browser.
- **Coro** took in $75 million to help grow its SMB protection solution, an all-in-one "click here to begin" managed security service.

Note that API security is still active and possibly poised to take off when the threats become more onerous. Yet, investment is way down to only $24 million put into six players. See Table 16.2.

TABLE 16.2 New Funding in 2023

Name	Amount Invested (in Millions of Dollars)
SandboxAQ	500
NetSkope	401
Archer	365
Axiom	350
Wiz	300
KnowBe4	300
Rapid7	261.5
Cyxtera Technologies	250

Name	Amount Invested (in Millions of Dollars)
Cato Networks	238
Saviynt	205
Yubico	204.32
OneTrust	200
Blackpoint	190
deepwatch	180
Blackberry	150
BlueVoyant	140
ID.me	132
Ledger	111.73
SpyCloud	110
BioCatch	110
Avepoint	110
HiddenLayer	101.25
Netcraft	100
Maltego Technologies	100
Island	100
Cyera	100
Cybereason	100
Socure	95
Brivo	92.5
Adlumin	81
SecureW2	80
Coro	75.13
Censys	75
Dragos	74
Endor Labs	70
FusionAuth	65
Chainguard	61
Xage Security	60.15

(continued)

TABLE 16.2 (continued)

Name	Amount Invested (in Millions of Dollars)
Huntress Labs	60
ThetaRay	57
Hack the Box	55
CYGNVS	55
Semgrep	53
Descope	53
Gutsy	51
Upwind	50
Skybox Security	50
SecureCode Warrior	50
Safe Security	50
Halcyon	50
Forward Networks	50
MicroStrategy	46.6
BAE Systems	45.93
Unit21	45
DataDome	42
Grip Security	41
Prove	40
Legit Security	40
Hyperproof	40
Horizon3.ai	40
ArmorCode	40
SEKOIA.IO	39.11
Opal Dev	39
Graylog	39
Cranium	36.65
Lumu Technologies	36
HUB Security	36

Name	Amount Invested (in Millions of Dollars)
Protect AI	35
Vulcan Cyber	34
Gem	34
Dream Security	33.6
EGERIE	33.52
SpecterOps	33.5
Shift5	33
FingerprintJS	33
Fingerprint	33
Blockaid	33
DuploCloud Inc.	32
Cyble	30.2
Token	30
Sentra	30
Mine	30
Cyware	30
HarfangLab	27.93
Axuall	27
Strata Identity	26
Snyk	25
Osano	25
Avalor	25
Astrix Security	25
Altr	25
Hypori	23
Calypso AI	23
Field Effect Software	22.65
Savvy	22
Britive	20.5
Stellar Cyber	20.49

(continued)

TABLE 16.2 (continued)

Name	Amount Invested (in Millions of Dollars)
SpecTrust	20.41
Zluri	20
Zero Networks	20
Strivacity	20
Revelstoke	20
RangeForce	20
Oligo Security	20
Cado Security	20
Lynx Tech	19.68
Binalyze	19
Metomic	18.92
Kodem	18
Darwinium	18
Symmetry Systems.	17.7
AuthID	17.6
IronNet Cybersecurity	17.08
nsKnox	17
Cerby	17
Veridas	16.76
Cybersmart	16.73
Zenity	16.5
Spideroak	16.4
ArQit	16.2
dope.security	16
ScadaFence	16
Veza Technologies	15
Vali Cyber	15
Sevco Security	15
Radiant Security	15

Name	Amount Invested (in Millions of Dollars)
Push Security	15
Moderne	15
Entitle	15
DNSFilter	15
Cypago	15
Blumira	15
BlastRadius	15
Build38	14.52
1touch.io	14
Aembit	13.9
Siren	13.41
Yoti	13.12
Refine Intelligence	13
Mitiga	13
ThreatFabric	12.85
Silk Security	12.5
Conveyor	12.5
Cybeats	12.25
Wizdome	12
Sweet Security	12
Rootly	12
Riot	12
Dasera	12
CyberQP	12
ConductorOne	12
SixMap	11.76
Votiro	11.5
Recorded Future	11.33
Quside	11.17
Cleafy	11.17

(continued)

TABLE 16.2 (continued)

Name	Amount Invested (in Millions of Dollars)
NexusFlow AI	10.6
Palantir Technologies	10.08
Spera Security	10
Silent Push	10
Lakera	10
Adaptive Shield	10
Vendict	9.5
Senser	9.5
Opscura	9.4
Nu Quantum	9.19
CultureAI	9.19
SpiderSilk	9
RADICL Defense	9
InfiniDome	9
Deduce	9
Censinet	9
AuthMind	8.5
Salvador Technologies	8.2
Risk Ledger	8.2
Upfort	8
Tromzo	8
Sequretek	8
Paladin Cyber	8
Nokod Security	8
NetRise	8
Cydome	8
Cerbos	7.87
CyberVadis	7.82
Aikido	7.82

Name	Amount Invested (in Millions of Dollars)
Scrut Automation	7.5
CyberconIQ	7.02
Strike Graph	7
Sendmarc	7
Riscosity	7
Lineaje	7
Ironblocks	7
FireCompass	7
Cyemptive Technologies Inc.	6.71
Glasswall Solutions	6.56
Procyon	6.5
Monarx	6.1
Trustle	6
Tausight	6
Stamus Networks	6
SquareX	6
Sonet.io	6
Pynt	6
Myrror Security	6
Manifest	6
Lasso Security	6
Keyless	6
Exium	6
Entro Security	6
CYFIRMA	6
Accuknox	6
Oblivious	5.98
QuoIntelligence	5.59
Filigran	5.59
DriveLock	5.5

(continued)

TABLE 16.2 (continued)

Name	Amount Invested (in Millions of Dollars)
Mobb	5.4
Gomboc	5.3
Hushmesh	5.2
Tamnoon	5.1
accSenSe	5
Tidal Cyber	5
SOCRadar	5
Right-Hand Security	5
RevBits	5
Rampart Communications	5
P0 Security	5
Ostrich	5
Astran	5
AaDya Security	5
Nano Corp.	4.69
Authlete	4.55
Escape	4.52
Inigo	4.5
Fossa	4.5
Bureau	4.5
Xygeni	4.47
OverSOC	4.25
VU Security	4.2
ThreatKey	4
Stack Identity	4
Protecto	4
Hive Pro	4
Fiverity	4
Cyviation	4

Name	Amount Invested (in Millions of Dollars)
443ID	4
Secfix	3.8
Cavelo Inc	3.78
BIO-key	3.75
Cyberwrite	3.7
Tune Insight	3.69
0pass	3.65
Soveren	3.6
ComplianceRisk	3.5
BrandShield	3.38
trackd	3.35
ERMES Cyber Security	3.35
Pingsafe	3.3
Goldilock	3.24
Xeol	3.2
VulnCheck	3.2
Tauruseer	3
Soos	3
Operant AI	3
METABASE Q	3
CommandK.Dev	3
CipherStash	3
Anonybit	3
Infisical	2.93
Elba	2.79
i2Chain	2.41
Keep Aware	2.4
Intrusion Inc.	2.4
Hook Security	2.3
DryRun Security	2.3

(continued)

TABLE 16.2 (continued)

Name	Amount Invested (in Millions of Dollars)
Decentriq	2.13
1Fort	2.06
VigilantOps	2
Keyp	2
enclaive	1.84
Data443 Risk Mitigation	1.8
Corsha	1.8
Datamasque	1.79
Mesh	1.73
Polymer	1.69
Qontrol	1.68
Zymbit	1.6
Cyturus Technologies	1.5
Trickest	1.4
ThreatMate	1.4
Mithril Security	1.34
Sitehop	1.31
Hackmetrix	1.3
Slauth.io	1.2
Cybermaniacs	1.2
Evo Security	1
Threatrix	0.8
Tehama	0.76
SecureSky	0.75
Inspeere	0.67
Tenzir	0.56
3rdRisk	0.56
Vaero	0.5
Safeguard Privacy	0.5

Name	Amount Invested (in Millions of Dollars)
Quantum Resistant Cryptography	0.5
Matano	0.5
Foretrace	0.5
EdgeBit	0.5
Dapple	0.5
Blyss	0.5
OneWave	0.45
Cytix	0.43
Fingerprint Cards AB	0.35
heylogin	0.34
Hopr	0.3
GroupSense	0.23
Kriptos	0.15

CHAPTER 17

Significant Cyber Incidents in 2023

While there are many books written on hacking, espionage, and attacks, *Security Yearbook* is meant to be a history of the cybersecurity industry—the people and the companies that contribute to the response to cyberattacks. That history is closely coupled with cyberattacks, its primary driver. Solutions are rarely offered that do not counter some sort of clear and present threat. Antivirus companies like Network Associates and QuickHeal launched in response to the spread of computer viruses by the medium of the time, floppy diskettes, and later over the Internet. For a short time, a new class of malware—spyware and adware—gave rise to companies like Webroot Software (now part of OpenText). Network attacks against vulnerable systems created the market for intrusion prevention systems (IPSs). Today, companies are dealing with a continuous onslaught of ransomware attacks.

Supply chain attacks are the latest problem. In 2021, the Sunburst campaign delivered software updates that contained backdoors to 18,000 SolarWinds customs. So far, no solution has been offered that can protect a customer from malicious updates like Sunburst or Notpetya. That would require a tool to somehow inspect an update package for potentially harmful components. To date, the vendors that are profiting from the rise of supply chain attacks are those that primarily offer solutions to improve the software development lifecycle (SDLC). These are great tools for software vendors to deploy, but not something an enterprise can deploy to protect themselves from the next Sunburst or Flame.

The other cybersecurity vendors that are seeing increased traction are those that monitor third parties for best practices. They usually scan suppliers for vulnerabilities and facilitate documentation of security policies and practices.

Threats come in two flavors: random and targeted. Random attacks are those that find victims no matter who they are. Certainly, viruses, spam, and even phishing fall into this category. Ransomware started as a random attack with the cybercriminals going after anyone who was foolish enough to click a link or install their packages. But ransomware evolved quickly into targeted attacks. The cybercriminals realized they could demand much higher ransoms from organizations. They could invest in the infrastructure to support negotiations, transfer cryptocurrency, and return/recover the stolen data. In increasing severity and roughly chronologically, targeted attacks include the following:

Exploratory hacking: Imagine you have an internal open file share labeled "HR" and a spreadsheet labeled "salaries." How long before employees would access it? People can't resist poking around. Another exploratory attack may be if you exposed a customer's ID in a URL. A hacker can simply craft a URL with a different ID and potentially gain access.

Hacktivism: Hackers who are motivated by an ideology will engage in malicious behavior to promote their cause. This could be an environmental hacktivist or political hacktivist.

Web defacement: Closely associated with hacktivism is web defacement. Any vulnerability in the way a website is configured could be exploited to redirect the website or install drive-by malware for any visitor to be infected—often called a *watering hole attack*—or replace the landing page. This last technique was widely used in the 2007 attacks against Estonia and the 2008 attacks against Georgia and once again in early January 2022 against Ukraine.

DDoS: See Chapter 6 for more about distributed denial-of-service attacks.

Credential theft: Attackers seek out credentials for websites, especially online banking. They either leak them or put them up for sale on the Dark Web. Or, they systematically go through them to pilfer funds from the bank. Once leaked, other hackers use these vast troves of credentials to attempt to log in to other services. Stolen credentials from Forbes or LinkedIn could be used to attempt logins to major banks. These attacks are called *credential stuffing*.

Cyber espionage: While commercial entities can engage in competitive espionage, this is most often associated with the activities of intelligence agencies. China was the first to engage openly in such activity during the Titan Rain series of attacks in the early 2000s.

Cyber warfare: Simply, cyber warfare includes attacks carried out by a country in support of military operations. This type of attack can target communications, power, pipelines, water supplies, and logistics.

Surveillance state: Snowden revealed in 2013 that countries, the United States in particular, engage in massive efforts to collect data on everybody. The concept is that they can quickly search that data to derive intelligence on anyone.

As attack methodologies gain in sophistication and the motivations for attacks increase, there will be a continual rise in demand for cybersecurity products. The following list of 115 incidents through November 2023 is reprinted with permission from the Center for Strategic and International Studies (CSIS), a nonprofit policy think tank. They update it throughout the year at **www.csis.org/programs/strategic-technologies-program/significant-cyber-incidents** as incidents occur, with this explanation: "Significance is in the eye of the beholder, but we focus on cyberattacks on government agencies, defense, and high tech companies, or economic crimes with losses of more than a million dollars."

We have arranged the incidents by month in 2023. There is a lot to learn from reviewing the breadth of attacks that occur each year. This is why the cybersecurity industry continues to grow, takes in billions of dollars in investments each year, and experiences so much M&A activity.

January 2023

The following attacks took place in January 2023:

- Hackers sent more than 1,000 emails containing malicious links to Moldovan government accounts.
- Hackers targeted government, military, and civilian networks across the Asia Pacific, leveraging malware to obtain confidential information. The malware targeted both the data on victim machines and the audio captured by infected machines' microphones.

- Hackers launched a series of cyberattacks against Malaysian national defense networks. Malaysian officials stated that the hacking activities were detected early enough to prevent any network compromise.
- Albanian officials reported that its government servers were still near-daily targets of cyberattacks following a major attack by Iran-linked hackers in 2022.
- Hackers used ransomware to encrypt 12 servers at Costa Rica's Ministry of Public Works, knocking all its servers offline.
- Iran-linked hackers executed ransomware attacks and exfiltrated data from U.S. public infrastructure and private Australian organizations. Australian authorities claim that the data exfiltrated was for use in extortion campaigns.
- Russia-linked hackers deployed a ransomware attack against the UK postal service, the Royal Mail. The attack disrupted the systems used to track international mail.
- CISA, the NSA, and the Multi-State Information Sharing and Analysis Center released a joint advisory warning of an increase in hacks on the federal civilian executive branch utilizing remote access software. This followed an October 2022 report on a financially motivated phishing campaign against multiple U.S. federal civilian executive branch agencies.

February 2023

The following attacks took place in February 2023:

- Chinese cyber espionage hackers performed a spear-phishing campaign against government and public-sector organizations in Asia and Europe. The emails used a draft EU Commission letter as its initial attack vector. These campaigns have occurred since at least 2019.
- Hackers disabled Italy's Revenue Agency (Agenzia delle Entrate) website. While the website was disabled, users received phishing emails directing them to a false login page that mirrored the official agency site.
- Hackers launched a ransomware attack against Technion University, Israel's top technology education program. Hackers demanded 80 bitcoin ($1.7 million USD) to decrypt the university's files. Israeli cybersecurity officials blamed Iranian state-sponsored hackers for the attack.
- Iranian hacktivists claimed responsibility for taking down websites for the Bahrain international airport and state news agency.
- An Iranian hacking group launched an espionage campaign against organizations in the Middle East. Hackers used a backdoor malware to compromise target email accounts. Researchers claim the hacking group is linked to Iranian intelligence services.
- Iranian hacktivists disrupted the state-run television broadcast of a speech by Iranian president Ebrahim Raisi during Revolution Day ceremonies. Hackers aired the slogan "Death to Khamenei" and encouraged citizens to join antigovernment protests.
- Latvian officials claimed that Russian hackers launched a phishing campaign against its Ministry of Defense. The Latvian Ministry of Defense stated this operation was unsuccessful.
- A North Korean hacking group conducted an espionage campaign between August and November 2022. Hackers targeted medical research, healthcare, defense, energy, chemical engineering, and a research university, exfiltrating more than 100 MB of data from each victim while remaining undetected. The group is linked to the North Korean government.
- Polish officials reported a disinformation campaign targeting the Polish public. Targets received anti-Ukrainian refugee disinformation

via email. Officials claimed these activities may be related to Russia-linked hackers.

- A pro-Russian hacking group claimed responsibility for DDoS attacks against NATO networks used to transmit sensitive data. The attack disrupted communications between NATO and airplanes providing earthquake aid to a Turkish airbase. The attack also took NATO's sites offline temporarily.
- Russian hackers deployed malware to steal information from Ukrainian organizations in a phishing campaign. The malware is capable of extracting account information and files, as well as taking screenshots. Researchers believe the group is a key player in Russia's cyber campaigns against Ukraine.

March 2023

The following attacks took place in March 2023:

- Poland blamed Russian hackers for a DDoS attack on its official tax service website. Hackers blocked users' access to the site for approximately an hour, but no data was leaked in the attack. A pro-Russian hacking group had earlier published a statement on Telegram about its intention to attack the Polish tax service.
- Slovakian cybersecurity researchers discovered a new exploit from a Chinese espionage group targeting political organizations in Taiwan and Ukraine.
- Russian hackers launched social engineering campaigns targeting U.S. and European politicians, businesspeople, and celebrities who had publicly denounced Vladimir Putin's invasion of Ukraine. Hackers persuaded victims to participate in phone or video calls, giving misleading prompts to obtain pro-Putin or pro-Russian sound bites. They published these to discredit victims' previous anti-Putin statements.
- A Chinese cyber espionage group targeted government entities in Vietnam, Thailand, and Indonesia, using newly developed malware optimized to evade detection.
- North Korean hackers targeted U.S.-based cybersecurity research firms in a phishing campaign. The campaign was meant to deliver malware for cyber espionage.
- Estonian officials claim that hackers unsuccessfully targeted the country's Internet voting system during its recent parliamentary elections. Officials did not release details about the attacks or provide attribution.
- A South Asian hacking group targeted firms in China's nuclear energy industry in an espionage campaign. Researchers believe the group commonly targets the energy and government sectors of Pakistan, China, Bangladesh, and Saudi Arabia.
- A Chinese cyber espionage group targeted an East Asian data protection company that serves military and government entities in a campaign that lasted approximately a year.
- CISA and FBI reported that a U.S. federal agency was targeted by multiple attackers, including a Vietnamese espionage group, in a cyber espionage campaign between November 2022 and January 2023. Hackers used a vulnerability in the agency's Microsoft Internet Information Services (IIS) server to install malware.
- Russian hackers brought down the French National Assembly's website for several hours using a DDoS attack. In a Telegram post, hackers cited the French government's support for Ukraine as the reason for the attack.

April 2023

- The following attacks took place in April 2023:North Korean-linked hackers targeted people with expertise in North Korean policy issues in a phishing campaign. Hackers posed as journalists requesting interviews from targets, inviting them to use embedded links for scheduling and stealing their login credentials. The amount of information stolen and number of targets are unclear.

- Ukraine-linked hacktivists targeted the email of Russian GRU Unit 26165's leader, Lieutenant Colonel Sergey Alexandrovich, leaking his correspondence to a volunteer intelligence analysis group. The exfiltrated data contained Alexandrovich's personal information, unit personnel files, and information on Russian cyberattack tools.
- Researchers discovered Israeli spyware on the iPhones of more than five journalists, political opposition figures, and an NGO worker. Hackers initially compromised targets using malicious calendar invitations. The hackers' origin and motivations are unclear.
- North Korea–linked hackers are operating an ongoing espionage campaign targeting defense industry firms in Eastern Europe and Africa. Researchers at Kaspersky believe the hacking group shifted its focus in 2020 from financially motivated coin-mining attacks to espionage.
- A Russia-linked threat group launched a DDoS attack against Canadian prime Minister Justin Trudeau, blocking access to his website for several hours. The operation's timing coincided with the Canadian government's meeting with Ukrainian Prime Minister Denys Shmyhal, suggesting that the operation was retaliation.
- Chinese hackers targeted telecommunication services providers in Africa in an espionage campaign since at least November 2022. Researchers believe the group has targeted pro-domestic human rights and pro-democracy advocates, including nation-states, since at least 2014. Using the access from the telecom providers, the group gathers information including keystrokes and browser data, records audio, and captures data from individual targets on the network.
- Researchers at Mandiant attributed a software supply chain attack on 3CX Desktop App software to North Korea–linked hackers. During its investigation, Mandiant found that this attack used a vulnerability previously injected into 3CX software. This is Mandiant's first discovery of a software supply chain attack leveraging vulnerabilities from a previous software supply chain attack.
- Recorded Future released a report revealing data exfiltration attacks against South Korean research and academic institutions in January 2023. The report identified Chinese-language hackers. Researchers believe that this is a hacktivist group motivated by patriotism for China.
- Iranian state-linked hackers targeted critical infrastructure in the United States and other countries in a series of attacks using a previously unseen customized dropper malware. The hacking group has been active since at least 2014, conducting social engineering and espionage operations that support the Iranian government's interests.
- NSA cyber authorities reported evidence of Russian ransomware and supply chain attacks against Ukraine and other European countries that have provided Ukraine with humanitarian aid during the war in Ukraine. There were no indications of these attacks against U.S. networks.
- Sudan-linked hackers conducted a DDoS attack on Israel's Independence Day, taking the Israeli Supreme Court's website offline for several hours. Israeli cyber authorities reported no lasting damage to network infrastructure. Hackers claimed to have also attacked several other Israeli government

and media sites, but those attacks could not be confirmed. The group has been active since at least January 2023, attacking critical infrastructure in Northern Europe, and is considered religiously motivated.

May 2023

The following attacks took place in May 2023:

- Russia-linked hacktivists conducted an unsuccessful cyberattack against Ukraine's system for managing border crossings by commercial trucks through a phishing campaign.
- An unidentified group hacked targets in both Russia and Ukraine. The motive for the attacks was surveillance and data gathering.
- India's Insurance Information Bureau fell victim to a ransomware attack. Hackers encrypted nearly 30 server systems and demanded $250,000 in bitcoin. The bureau relied on its data backup system to maintain operations and did not pay the ransom.
- A likely Russian state group has targeted government organizations in Central Asia. The group is using previously unknown malware, and the attacks focused on document exfiltration.
- Chinese hackers targeted Kenyan government ministries and state institutions, including the presidential office. The hacks appeared to be aimed at gaining information on debt owed to Beijing.
- Chinese hackers breached communications networks at a U.S. outpost in Guam. The hackers used legitimate credentials, making it harder to detect them.
- Belgium's cybersecurity agency has linked China-sponsored hackers to a spearfishing attack on a prominent politician. The attack comes as European governments are increasingly willing to challenge China over cyber offenses.

June 2023

The following attacks took place in June 2023:

- Russia's Federal Security Services (FSB) alleged that Apple worked closely with U.S. intelligence agencies to hack thousands of iPhones belonging to Russian users and foreign diplomats. Apple denied the claims, and the NSA declined to comment.
- Ukrainian hackers claimed responsibility for an attack on a Russian telecom firm that provides critical infrastructure to the Russian banking system. The attack occurred in conjunction with Ukraine's counteroffensive.
- According to new reporting, North Korean hackers have been impersonating tech workers or employers to steal more than $3 billion since 2018. The money has reportedly been used to fund the country's ballistic missiles program, according to U.S. officials.
- Pro-Russian hackers targeted several Swiss government websites, including those for Parliament, the federal administration, and the Geneva airport. The DDoS attacks coincided with preparations for Ukrainian President Volodymyr Zelensky's virtual address before the Swiss parliament.
- An Illinois hospital became the first healthcare facility to publicly list a ransomware attack as a primary reason for closing. The attack, which occurred in 2021, permanently crippled the facility's finances.
- Several U.S. federal government agencies, including Department of Energy entities and the U.S. Office of Personnel Management,

were breached in a global cyberattack by Russian-linked hackers. Cybercriminals targeted a vulnerability in software that is widely used by the agencies, according to a U.S. cybersecurity agent.

- Pro-Russian hacktivists used a DDoS attack to target several Ukrainian and Italian banking institutions, including the European Investment Bank.
- A Pakistani-based hacker group infiltrated the Indian army and education sector in the group's latest wave of attacks against Indian government institutions. The hack is the latest in a series of targeted attacks from this group that have intensified over the past year.
- A group allegedly tied to the private military corporation Wagner hacked a Russian satellite telecommunications provider that services the Federal Security Service (FSB) and Russian military units. The attack comes after Wagner's attempted rebellion against President Vladimir Putin over the war in Ukraine.

July 2023

The following attacks took place in July 2023:

- A Polish diplomat's advertisement to purchase a used BMW was corrupted by Russian hackers and used to target Ukrainian diplomats. The hackers copied the flyer, embedded it with malicious software, and distributed it to foreign diplomats in Kyiv.
- Russian hackers targeted numerous attendees of the latest NATO Summit in Vilnius. The assailants used a malicious replica of the Ukraine World Congress website to target attendees.
- Chinese hackers breached the emails of several prominent U.S. government employees in the State Department and Department of Commerce through a vulnerability in Microsoft's email systems.
- Chinese-linked hackers infected a Pakistani government app with malware. A state bank and telecoms provider were also targeted in the attack.
- A South Korean government-affiliated institution fell victim to a phishing scandal that resulted in a loss of 175 million won, reportedly the first phishing incident against a South Korean government public organization.
- Russian hackers targeted 12 government ministries in Norway to gain access to sensitive information. The hackers exploited a vulnerability in a software platform used by the ministries.
- New Zealand's parliament was hit by a cyberattack from a Russian hacking group. The group said their attack was retaliation against New Zealand's support for Ukraine, such as its assistance with training Ukrainian troops and sanctions against Russia. Hackers temporarily shut down the New Zealand Parliament, Parliamentary Counsel Office (PCO), and Legislation websites in a DDoS attack.
- The Ministry of Justice in Trinidad and Tobago was hit with a DDoS attack that disrupted court operations across the country. The ministry reported outages beginning in late June, which are believed to be linked to this same attack.
- Russian-linked cyber hackers have targeted Ukrainian state services, such as the app Diia, using malware and phishing attacks. The primary targets are Ukrainian defense and security services.
- Kenya's eCitizen service was disrupted by pro-Russian cybercriminals for several days. Kenya's Ministry of Information, Communications, and the Digital Economy claimed that no data was accessed or lost.

- China claims that an earthquake monitoring system in Wuhan was hacked by "U.S. cybercriminals." Chinese state media asserts that a backdoor program with the capacity to steal seismic data was inserted into the program.

August 2023

The following attacks took place in August 2023:

- According to a new report, North Korean hackers breached computer systems at a Russian missile developer for five months in 2022. Analysts could not determine what information may have been taken or viewed.
- The United Kingdom's Electoral Commission revealed that Russian hackers breached the commission's network beginning in August 2021. They obtained information on tens of thousands of British citizens by accessing the commission's email and file-sharing system.
- Russia's military intelligence service attempted to hack Ukrainian Armed Forces' combat information systems. Hackers targeted Android tablets that Ukrainian forces use for planning and orchestrating combat missions.
- The Canadian government accused a "highly sophisticated Chinese state-sponsored actor" of hacking a prominent Canadian federal scientific research agency.
- A Canadian politician was targeted by a Chinese disinformation campaign on WeChat. The attack included false accusations about the politician's race and political views. The Canadian government believes the attacks are retaliation against the politician's criticism of China's human rights policies.
- Russian hackers launched a ransomware attack against a Canadian government service provider, compromising the data of 1.4 million people in Alberta. The organization paid the ransom and claimed that very little data was lost.
- Ukraine's State Security Service (SBU) claims that Russia's GRU is attempting to deploy custom malware against Starlink satellites to collect data on Ukrainian troop movements. SBU members discovered malware on Ukrainian tablets that were captured by the Russians before being recovered by Ukrainian forces.
- Iranian cyber spies are targeting dissidents in Germany, according to Germany's domestic intelligence unit. The spies are using false digital personas tailored to victims to build a rapport with their targets before sending a malicious link to a credential harvesting page.
- Chinese hackers obtained personal and political emails of a U.S. Congressman from Nebraska. The hackers exploited the same Microsoft vulnerability that gave them access to emails from the State Department and Department of Commerce.
- Belarusian hackers targeted foreign embassies in the country for nearly a decade, according to new reporting. Hackers disguised malware as Windows updates to get diplomats to download it onto their devices.
- Bangladesh shut down access to their central bank and election commission websites amid warnings of a planned cyberattack by an Indian hacking group. The shutdown was intended to prevent a cyberattack similar to a 2016 incident in Bangladesh where hackers stole nearly $1 billion, according to the central bank's statement.
- Suspected North Korean hackers attempted to compromise a joint U.S.-South Korean military exercise on countering nuclear threats from North Korea. Hackers launched several spear phishing email attacks at the exercise's war simulation center.

- Ecuador's national election agency claimed that cyberattacks from India, Bangladesh, Pakistan, Russia, Ukraine, Indonesia, and China caused difficulties for absentee voters attempting to vote online in the latest election. The agency didn't elaborate on the nature of the attacks.
- Ukrainian hackers claim to have broken into the email of a senior Russian politician and leaked medical and financial documents, as well as messages that allegedly connect him to money laundering and sanctions evasion plots.
- Chinese hackers targeted a U.S. military procurement system for reconnaissance, along with several Taiwan-based organizations. Attackers targeted high-bandwidth routers to exfiltrate data and establish covert proxy networks within target systems.
- Russian hacktivists disabled Poland's rail system by gaining access to the system's railway frequencies and transmitted a malicious signal that halted train operations. Attackers blasted Russia's national anthem and a speech from Putin on Russia's military operation in Ukraine during the attack.
- Russian hacktivists launched several DDoS attacks that knocked the Polish government's website offline, as well as the Warsaw Stock exchange and several Polish national banks.
- Cybercriminals are allegedly selling a stolen dataset from China's Ministry of State Security. The full data set purportedly includes personal identification information for roughly half a billion Chinese citizens and "classified document[s]," according to the criminals' post about the sale.
- Unnamed hackers took X, formerly known as Twitter, offline in several countries and demanded that owner Elon Musk open Starlink in Sudan. Attackers flooded the server with traffic to disable access for more than 20,000 individuals in the United States, UK, and other countries.
- Russian hacktivists launched DDoS attacks against Czech banks and the Czech stock exchange. The hackers cut online banking access to the banks' clients and demanded that the institutions stop supporting Ukraine. Bank representatives claim the hacks did not threaten their clients' finances.

September 2023

The following attacks took place in September 2023:

- Russian cyber criminals accessed sensitive information from South Africa's Department of Defense, including military contracts and personnel information. The department reversed its previous statement denying the data leak.
- Russian hackers stole thousands of documents from the British Ministry of Defense and uploaded them to the Dark Web. The documents contained accessibility details for a nuclear base in Scotland, high-security prisons, and other national security details. Hackers acquired the documents by breaking into a British fencing developer and gaining backdoor access to Ministry files.
- An Indian cybersecurity firm uncovered plans from Pakistani and Indonesian hacking groups to disrupt the G20 summit in India. The hacktivists are expected to use DDoS attacks and mass defacement in their attacks, which are presumed to be the latest development in the hacktivist battle between these nations according to the firm's research.
- A ransomware attack wiped four months of Sri Lankan government data. The country's

cloud services system didn't have backup services available for the data from May 17 to August 26, according to reporting. Malicious actors targeted Sri Lanka's government cloud system starting in August 2023 by sending infected links to government workers.

- Suspected Chinese hackers attacked the national power grid of an unspecified Asian country earlier this year using Chinese malware. The group corrupted a Windows application that allowed them to move laterally within their target's systems.
- The iPhone of a Russian journalist for the independent newspaper Meduza was infected with Pegasus spyware in Germany this year. The incident is the first known instance of the spyware being used against a prominent Russian target. The country behind the spyware placement is unknown, but Latvia, Estonia, Azerbaijan, Kazakhstan, and Uzbekistan are all suspects given past use of Pegasus spyware or their allegiance to Russia.
- A Russian ransomware group leaked Australian federal police officers' details on the Dark Web. The leak is the latest phase of a Russian attack, which started in April 2023 against an Australian law firm that services several Australian government agencies.
- A new Microsoft report indicates an increase of Chinese cyber operations in the South China Sea, as well as increased attacks against the U.S. defense industrial base and U.S. critical infrastructure. The increase comes amid rising tensions between China and the United States.
- Russian cybercriminals breached the International Criminal Court's IT systems amid an ongoing probe into Russian war crimes committed in Ukraine.
- Russian forces in occupied Crimea reported a cyberattack on Crimean Internet providers. The attack happened around the same time that a Ukrainian missile strike aimed at Russian naval headquarters in the area. Ukrainian officials have yet to comment.
- Russia is stepping up cyberattacks against Ukrainian law enforcement agencies, specifically units collecting and analyzing evidence of Russian war crimes, according to Ukrainian officials. Russian cyberattacks have primarily targeted Ukrainian infrastructure for most of the war.
- Cybercriminals targeted Kuwait's Ministry of Finance with a phishing ransomware attack. Kuwait isolated the Ministry and other government systems to protect them from potential further attacks.
- A massive cyberattack hit Bermuda's Department of Planning and other government services. The country's hospitals, transportation, and education centers remained functional, but other services were down for several weeks. Bermuda announced that it is investigating the attack and declined to state if any sensitive data was compromised.
- U.S. and Japanese officials warn that Chinese state-sponsored hackers placed modifying software inside routers to target government industries and companies located in both countries. The hackers use firmware implants to stay hidden and move around in their target's networks. China has denied the allegations.
- Iranian hackers launched a cyberattack against Israel's railroad network. The hackers used a phishing campaign to target the network's electrical infrastructure. Brazilian and UAE companies were also reportedly targeted in the same attack.
- Indian hacktivists targeted Canada's military and Parliament websites with DDoS attacks that slowed system operations for several hours. Hacktivists referenced Canadian Prime Minister Justin Trudeau's public accusation against India of killing Sikh independence activist Hardeep Singh Nijjar as motivation for the hack.

October 2023

The following attacks took place in October 2023:

- North Korean hackers sent malware phishing emails to employees of South Korea's shipbuilding sector. South Korea's National Intelligence Service suggested that the attacks were intended to gather key naval intelligence that could help North Korea build larger ships.
- New reporting reveals Chinese hackers have been targeting Guyana government agencies with phishing emails to exfiltrate sensitive information since February 2023.
- Vietnamese hackers attempted to install spyware on the phones of journalists, United Nations officials, and the chairs of the House Foreign Affairs Committee and Senate Homeland Security and Governmental Affairs. The spyware was designed to siphon calls and texts from infected phones, and the unsuccessful deployment comes while Vietnamese and American diplomats were negotiating an agreement to counter China's growing influence in the region.
- Hacktivists stole 3,000 documents from NATO, the second time in three months that hacktivists have breached NATO's cybersecurity defenses. Hackers described themselves as "gay furry hackers" and announced their attack was retaliation against NATO countries' human rights abuses. NATO alleges the attack did not impact NATO missions, operations, or military deployments.
- Pro-Hamas and pro-Israeli hacktivists have launched multiple cyberattacks against Israeli government sites and Hamas web pages in the aftermath of Hamas' attacks on Israel on October 7. Russian and Iranian hacktivists also targeted Israeli government sites, and Indian hacktivists have attacked Hamas websites in support of Israel.
- Researchers discovered what appears to be a state-sponsored software tool designed for espionage purposes and used against ASEAN governments and organizations.

November 2023

The following attacks took place in November 2023:

- Chinese cybercriminals targeted at least 24 Cambodian government networks, including the national defense, election oversight, human rights, national treasury, finance, commerce, politics, natural resources and telecommunications agencies. Hackers disguised themselves as cloud storage services to mask their data exfiltration. Initial research indicates the attack is part of a broader Chinese espionage campaign.
- Denmark suffered its largest cyberattack on record when Russian hackers hit 22 Danish power companies. The attack began in May 2023 and appeared to be aimed at gaining comprehensive access to Denmark's decentralized power grid. Hackers exploited a critical command injection flaw and continued to exploit unpatched systems to maintain access.
- Trinidad and Tobago's Prime Minister Dr. Keith Rowley declared the latest ransomware attack against the country's telecommunications service to be a "national security threat." Hackers stole an estimated 6 GB of data, including email addresses, national ID numbers, and phone numbers.
- Chinese hackers compromised Philippine government networks. Beginning in August 2023, hackers used phishing emails to embed malicious code into their target's systems to establish command and control and spy on their target's activities.
- Chinese-linked hackers attacked Japan's space agency during summer 2023 and compromised the organization's directory. The agency shut down parts of its network to

investigate the breach's scope but claims it did not compromise critical rocket and satellite operations information.

- Suspected Chinese hackers launched an espionage campaign against Uzbekistan and the Republic of Korea. Hackers used phishing campaigns to gain access to their target's systems and decrypt their information.

December 2023

Israeli-linked hackers disrupted approximately 70% of gas stations in Iran. Hackers claimed the attack was in retaliation for aggressive actions by Iran and its proxies in the region. Pumps restored operation the next day, but payment issues continued for several days.

Ukrainian state hackers crippled Russia's largest water utility plant by encrypting over 6,000 computers and deleting over 50 TB of data. Hackers claimed their attack was in retaliation for the Russian Kyivstar cyberattack.

Russian hackers hit Ukraine's largest mobile phone provider, Kyivstar, disabling access to its 24 million customers in Ukraine. Hackers claim to have destroyed more than 10,000 computers and 4,000 servers, including cloud storage and backup systems. The attack began hours before President Zelenskyy met with President Biden in Washington D.C.

Ukraine's military intelligence service (the GRU) claims to have disabled Russia's tax service in a cyberattack. According to the GRU, the attack destroyed the system's configuration files, databases, and their backups, paralyzing Russia's tax service.

CHAPTER 18

Research Methodology

IT-Harvest is a data-driven analyst firm. It couples advisory services with access to the only directory for researching the entire cybersecurity industry, available at **https://dashboard.it-harvest.com**. The genesis of the platform in this edition was the directory contained in *Security Yearbook 2022*. The directory is a snapshot in time of the state of the industry at the end of 2023.

Most tech industry analysts take a top-down approach. They follow what the big players are doing and keep an eye on the up-and-comers. They track the revenue of the big players and make some assumption about their market share to derive an overall number. The IT-Harvest directory is an attempt at bottom-up analysis by discovering and tracking every vendor.

What Is a Security Vendor?

To be included in this directory, a vendor must produce and sell its own IT security product. This is a simple determination for a firewall or endpoint security vendor, but what about service providers? Managed security service providers (MSSPs) are included because they are an important part of the industry. They have to develop their own tools to collect, manage, and analyze security event data.

There are several thousand consulting firms around the world that provide pentesting, audit, staff augmentation, and breach investigation services. While many of them eventually develop their own products and become vendors, as long as they are purely consulting providers, they are not included in the directory.

Systems integrators (SIs) and value-added resellers (VARs) are also not included unless they have their own products. Thus, Optiv, the biggest reseller of security products in the United States, is listed as an MSSP because it also offers managed services.

There are more than 200 cyber insurance companies. This is a category outside the scope of the directory.

A distinction is made between a "security product" and a "secure product." A vendor of any product may claim it is "secure." But, to be included in IT-Harvest's coverage, the vendor must contribute to the overall security of its customers.

How to Find Vendors?

It is surprisingly difficult to discover all of the vendors in a particular category. Many start-ups steadfastly resist any effort to be pigeonholed into a particular category. They would rather be the only vendor in a category of their own definition than a minor vendor in an existing category. Meanwhile, the large analyst firms, such as Gartner, IDC, and Forrester, rush to label new categories as they evolve, creating confusion. Thus, we have two categories for multifunction gateway appliances: UTM and Next-Gen Firewall. We also have the new category of IRM from Gartner, which they decided stands for "integrated risk management, even though that three-letter acronym was already in use for information rights management. Recently, Gartner changed the category of threat intelligence to digital risk protection. Most of the 123 threat intelligence vendors have changed their branding to DRP, making it difficult to determine what they actually do. They certainly do not *protect* digital risks.

It may not be possible to find every single vendor, especially those that have not built English-language websites, but as a vendor grows, it becomes visible by the following means:

Funding announcements: Using a comprehensive news feed from Feedly, we track all funding announcements. This identifies new companies as they come out of stealth.

Conference appearances: By the time a vendor has acquired customers and hired a marketing team, it will begin to show up in the listing of vendors exhibiting at conferences such as InfoSec Europe and RSA Conferences in San Francisco and Asia. We track 26 conferences around the world and are expanding that scope.

Social media: The first steps for any start-up today is to get a Twitter handle and create a LinkedIn page, both valuable tools for discovering new and small vendors.

Vendor briefings: As a vendor matures, it starts to reach out to the analyst community in an effort to be noticed. While the Gartner Magic Quadrant tracks the largest vendors in a space, there is always the hope of being named a Cool Vendor, a designation reserved for new vendors with technology that catches the eye of a Gartner analyst. Forrester Wave reports are another source of vendor information, and smaller independent analyst firms may cover emerging vendor spaces.

Press coverage: A mention in an article at Dark Reading, **CIO.com**, or mainstream media helps a vendor get on the radar.

Search engines: At one time, there was an argument made that industry analysis was no longer needed thanks to Google search. But search has become less and less effective for enumerating a space. Each vendor strives to be on the first page of results for its space in the hope that customers will find them. Every category soon develops a number of "top 10" sites that list the top 10 vendors, but inclusion in the top 10 is a pay-to-play game, so it is unreliable.

Artificial intelligence: Large language models (LLMs) have been trained on most of human knowledge. The expectation is that someday you will be able to ask an AI tool to list all the vendors in a particular category. IT-Harvest is at the forefront of this effort.

Once a vendor is identified, it is tracked as it grows, is acquired, becomes an acquirer, or, in a very few cases, fails and goes out of business. The *Security Yearbook* book is published each year with important updates covering the new vendors and those that have been acquired.

One difficult question is when a vendor should be removed from the directory. A small vendor like Aorato, acquired by Microsoft in 2014 for its ability to defend Active Directory, will be included in the year it was acquired but removed the following year because the acquisition was a pure technology play. The product and its brand are absorbed into the mothership. Similar acquisitions may be to acquire the team but the products are discontinued quickly. A company like SafeNet, acquired by Gemalto, which in turn was acquired by Thales, was listed in the first edition of the directory but was removed in 2021. Gemalto, too, has been removed as its website was taken down in April 2020 and now points to Thales' site.

The key factor for keeping a vendor in the directory is the brand. Thus, Lancope, Viptela, and OpenDNS are not in the directory, although the products continue to be supported. Arbor Networks has been removed from the directory because the website redirects to a product page at Netscout. We include Mandiant in the directory, although it was acquired by Google in 2022. After the Google acquisition, the head count at Mandiant dropped by 1,000. It is steady at about 1,400 today. If the Mandiant brand and website stay active, we will continue to track it.

Once a vendor is identified, its headquarters address, URL, and LinkedIn profile are recorded in the database. The LinkedIn profile will report the number of people who self-identify as an employee of the company. This number is usually accurate for companies that are growing. Generally, as people are let go from a company, they do not update their employment status until they land a new role, so the fact that a company is shrinking may not be picked up immediately. Spot testing the LinkedIn data against data provided by vendors indicates that the LinkedIn number is surprisingly accurate. The exceptions are vendors in China and Russia whose employees are less likely to have LinkedIn profiles.

Vendor briefings are required to understand a space. These hour-long sessions with industry analysts reveal the company strategy and aspirations as well as the underlying technology and how they differentiate themselves from their competitors. It is up to the analyst to determine the validity of their claims for the number of customers, growth, etc. Anecdotal evidence from end users and reference customers provides valuable confirmation. Magic Quadrants from Gartner, Forrester Wave Reports, and the vendor's own published research all help make vendors stand out.

Each edition of *Security Yearbook* is completed in February to make it into print by June, so changes to the directory are frozen at that time. Updates to the data are made available throughout the year at **https://dashboard.it-harvest.com**.

CHAPTER 19

Directory A–Z

0pass (7, 133.3%)
IAM / Authentication
Los Angeles, CA, US
0pass.com

11:11 Systems (794, 40.5%)
MSSP / MDR
Fairfield, NJ, US
1111systems.com

1E (513, 8.2%)
Endpoint Security / Patch Management
London, United Kingdom
1e.com

1Fort (7, 0.0%)
GRC / Cyber Insurance
New York, NY, US
1fort.com

1Kosmos (92, 15.0%)
IAM / Authentication
Somerset, NJ, US
1kosmos.com

1LINK (3, -40.0%)
GRC / Vulnerabilities
Ha Noi, Ba Dinh, Vietnam
1link.vn

1Password (1707, 89.0%)
IAM / Credential Security
Toronto, ON, Canada
1password.com

1touch.io (78, 39.3%)
GRC / Data Discovery
Stamford, CT, US
1touch.io

2T Security (16, 33.3%)
MSSP / Monitoring
Victoria, United Kingdom
2t-security.com

360 Security (23, 35.3%)
MSSP / Managed Security Services
Bogota, Colombia
360sec.com

3Frames Software labs (50, 19.1%)
Endpoint Security / Mobile Device Security
Bangalore, India
3frameslab.com

3rdRisk (11, 57.1%)
GRC / Risk Management
Amsterdam, Netherlands
3rdrisk.com

3wSecurity (4, -20.0%)
GRC / Penetration Testing
Tampa, FL, US
3wsecurity.com

418 Intelligence (11, 37.5%)
Threat Intelligence / Threat Intelligence Gamification
Reston, VA, US
418intelligence.com

42Crunch (44, -13.7%)
API Security
Irvine, CA, US
42crunch.com

42Gears (437, 12.1%)
Endpoint Security / Mobile Device Security
Bangalore, India
42gears.com

443ID (22, -8.3%)
IAM / Identity Verification
Austin, TX, US
443id.com

4CRisk (29, -6.5%)
GRC / Compliance Management
San Francisco, CA, US
4crisk.ai

4Secure (17, 41.7%)
Network Security / Firewalls
Northampton, Northamptonshire, United Kingdom
4-secure.com

6clicks (61, 24.5%)
GRC / Compliance Management
Melbourne, Australia
6clicks.io

6cure (16, 23.1%)
Network Security / DDoS Defense
Herouville-Saint-Clair, France
6cure.com

6WIND (112, 17.9%)
Network Security / VPN/Proxy
Montigny-le-Bretonneux, France
6wind.com

9Star (31, 40.9%)
IAM / Managed Security Services
Austin, TX, US
9starinc.com

A&O IT Group (266, 3.5%)
MSSP / MDR
Bracknell, Berkshire, United Kingdom
aoitgroup.com

A-Lign (644, -0.5%)
GRC / Compliance Management
Tampa, FL, US
a-lign.com

A10 Networks (721, -1.1%)
Network Security / DDoS Defense
San Jose, CA, US
a10networks.com

A3BC (11, -35.3%)
IAM / Authentication
Rennes, France
a3bc.io

A3Sec Grupo (119, 29.4%)
MSSP
Madrid, Spain
a3sec.com

**Numbers in parentheses indicate headcount and % change in 2023.*

AaDya Security (31, 6.9%)
MSSP / SMB Security
Plymouth, MI, US
aadyasecurity.com

Abacode (70, 18.6%)
MSSP / MDR
Tampa, FL, US
abacode.com

Abnormal Security (584, 2.8%)
Email Security / Defense Against Phishing
San Francisco, CA, US
abnormalsecurity.com

Absio (5, 0.0%)
Data Security / SDKC
Denver, CO, US
absio.com

Absolute Software (981, 14.6%)
Endpoint Security / Mobile Device Security
Vancouver, BC, Canada
absolute.com

Abusix (35, -5.4%)
Threat Intelligence
San Jose, CA, US
abusix.com

Acalvio Technologies (75, 2.7%)
Deception
Santa Clara, CA, US
acalvio.com

Accedian (336, -11.3%)
Network Security / Monitoring
Montreal, QU, Canada
accedian.com

Accenture (548423, 1.2%)
MSSP / MDR
Dublin, Ireland
accenture.com

Acceptto (9, -43.8%)
Fraud Prevention / Identity Verification
Portland, OR, US
acceptto.com

Accertify (330, 9.6%)
Fraud Prevention
Itasca, IL, US
accertify.com

Accolade Technology (8, 14.3%)
Network Security / Network Appliance Security
Franklin, MA, US
accoladetechnology.com

Accops Systems (243, 25.9%)
IAM / Access Security
Pune, India
accops.com

Accountable (6, -25.0%)
GRC / Compliance Management
Fort Worth, TX, US
accountablehq.com

accSenSe (18, 0.0%)
IAM / Secure Backup/Recovery
Ra'anana, Israel
accsense.io

Accudata Systems (98, -14.0%)
Operations / Security Management
Houston, TX, US
accudatasystems.com

Accuknox (146, 49.0%)
Endpoint Security
Cupertino, CA, US
accuknox.com

Accurics (10, -16.7%)
GRC / Policy Management
Pleasanton, CA, US
accurics.com

Aceiss (10, 25.0%)
IAM / Access Security
New Canaan, CT, US
aceiss.com

achelos GmbH (57, 21.3%)
Testing / TLS Testing
Paderborn, Germany
achelos.de

Achilleas (13, 333.3%)
MSSP / MDR
Brazil
achilleas.com.br

AckTao (5, 0.0%)
GRC / Security Awareness Training
Vaud, Switzerland
acktao.com

Acreto Cloud (20, 25.0%)
IoT Security / Segmentation
Jersey City, NJ, US
acreto.io

Acronis (2123, -3.1%)
Data Security / Secure Backup / Recovery
Schaffhausen, Switzerland
acronis.com

Acsense (19, 0.0%)
IAM
Tel Aviv, Israel
acsense.com

Actifile (22, 4.8%)
GRC / DLP
Herzliya, Israel
actifile.com

Active Countermeasures (10, 25.0%)
Security Analytics / Threat Hunting
Spearfish, SD, US
activecountermeasures.com

Active Cypher (15, 7.1%)
Network Security / DLP
Newport Beach, CA, US
activecypher.com

ActiveFence (293, -6.1%)
GRC / Monitoring
Tel Aviv, Israel
activefence.com

Actus Mobile Solutions (4, -20.0%)
Fraud Prevention
Bray, Ireland
actusmobile.com

ActZero (65, -30.1%)
MSSP / MDR
Menlo Park, CA, US
actzero.ai

Acuity Risk Management (16, 14.3%)
GRC / Risk Management
London, United Kingdom
acuityrm.com

Acumera (201, 21.1%)
MSSP / Firewalls
Austin, TX, US
acumera.net

Acunetix (Invicti) (38, -28.3%)
GRC / Vulnerabilities
Mriehel, Malta
acunetix.com

ADAMnetworks (5, 25.0%)
Network Security / Access Security
London, Canada
adamnet.works

Adaptiva (90, -10.9%)
Endpoint Security / Configuration Management
Kirkland, WA, US
adaptiva.com

Adaptive Mobile (91, -33.1%)
Endpoint Security / Mobile Device Security
Dublin, Ireland
adaptivemobile.com

Adaptive Shield (79, 19.7%)
Operations / Posture Management
Tel Aviv, Israel
adaptive-shield.com

Adaptus (11, 37.5%)
Operations
Austin, TX, US
adaptus.com

Adarma (301, -5.3%)
MSSP / MDR
Edinburgh, United Kingdom
adarma.com

**Numbers in parentheses indicate headcount and % change in 2023.*

Adaware (13, 0.0%)
Endpoint Security / Anti-virus
Montreal, QC, Canada
adaware.com

Adcy.io (5, -16.7%)
MSSP / Managed Security Services
Trivandrum, Kerala, India
adcy.io

ADF Solutions (25, 19.1%)
GRC / Forensics
Bethesda, MD, US
adfsolutions.com

ADINES MAROC (8, 0.0%)
MSSP / SOC
Casablanca, Morocco
adines.ma

Adjust (646, -5.0%)
Fraud Prevention / Bot Security
Berlin, Germany
adjust.com

Adlumin (119, 35.2%)
Security Analytics / SIEM
Washington, DC, US
adlumin.com

AdNovum (638, 7.8%)
IAM / CIAM
Zurich, Switzerland
adnovum.ch

aDolas (30, 15.4%)
IoT Security / Assurance
Victoria, BC, Canada
adolus.com

Adsero Security (3, 0.0%)
MSSP / Managed Security Services
Tampa, FL, US
adserosecurity.com

Adtran Inc. (2052, 26.0%)
Network Security / Firewalls
Huntsville, AL, US
adtran.com

ADVA Optical Networking (2011, -10.7%)
Network Security / Secure Switching
Munich, Germany
advaoptical.com

Advanced Network Systems (22, -38.9%)
MSSP / MDR
Charlottesville, VA, US
getadvanced.net

Advanced Systems International (3, -25.0%)
Endpoint Security
Lima, Peru
usb-lock-rp.com

Advenica (87, 22.5%)
Network Security / Air Gap
Sweden
advenica.com

Advens (477, 32.5%)
MSSP / SOC
Paris, France
advens.fr

Adversa (3, -25.0%)
Application Security
Tel Aviv, Israel
adversa.ai

Aegify (12, -7.7%)
GRC / Risk Management
San Jose, CA, US
aegify.com

Aegis IT Solutions (7, 16.7%)
MSSP / Managed Security Services
Boca Raton, FL, US
aegisitsolutions.net

Aembit (21, 162.5%)
IAM / Identity Management
Silver Spring, MD, US
aembit.io

Aerobyte (11, 0.0%)
Network Security / Zero Trust Networking
Boca Raton, FL, US
aerobyte.com

AerPass (6, -33.3%)
IAM / Authentication
Boulder, CO, US
aerpass.com

AET Europe (58, 18.4%)
IAM / Identity Management
Arnhem, Gelderland, Netherlands
aeteurope.com

Afero (47, -2.1%)
IoT Security / Hardware
Los Altos, CA, US
afero.io

Agari (65, 41.3%)
Email Security
Foster City, CA, US
agari.com

Agat Software (32, 14.3%)
Network Security / Security For Unified Comms
Jerusalem, Israel
agatsoftware.com

Agency (11, 37.5%)
MSSP
New York, NY, US
getagency.com

AgileBlue (36, 2.9%)
MSSP / Managed Security Services
Cleveland, OH, US
agileblue.com

Agilicus (13, -13.3%)
IoT Security / Access Security
Kitchener, Canada
agilicus.com

Agora SecureWare (7, 16.7%)
Data Security / Secure Collaboration
Bioggio, Switzerland
agora-secureware.com

Ahnlab (563, 7.8%)
Endpoint Security / Anti-virus
Gyeonggi-do, South Korea
ahnlab.com

Ahope (16, 6.7%)
Application Security / Mobile Device Security
Seoul, South Korea
ahope.net

AI Spera (23, 15.0%)
Threat Intelligence / OSINT
Seoul, South Korea
criminalip.io

Aiculus (8, 14.3%)
API Security
Melbourne, Australia
aiculus.co

Aikido (20, 11.1%)
Application Security / Vulnerabilities
Ghent, Belgium
aikido.dev

Aiprise (10, 400.0%)
Fraud Prevention / Identity Verification
Santa Clara, CA, US
aiprise.com

Airbus Cybersecurity (293, 1.4%)
Training / Cyber Range
Alancourt, France
airbus-cyber-security.com

Aircloak (5, -28.6%)
Data Security / Data Masking
Berlin, Germany
aircloak.com

Aireye (27, -27.0%)
Network Security / Wireless Security
Tel Aviv, Israel
AirEye.tech

Airgap Networks (45, 25.0%)
Network Security / Segmentation
Santa Clara, CA, US
airgap.io

Airiam (62, -17.3%)
MSSP / MDR
Miami Beach, FL, US
airiam.com

**Numbers in parentheses indicate headcount and % change in 2023.*

Airlock (12, -14.3%)
IAM / Access Security
Zurich, Switzerland
airlock.com

Airlock Digital (37, 42.3%)
Endpoint Security / Application Whitelisting
Unley, Australia
airlockdigital.com

Airside (17, -39.3%)
IAM / Mobile Identity
Herndon, VA, US
airsidemobile.com

Airtrack (3, -72.7%)
Security Analytics / Configuration Management
Melbourne, Victoria, Australia
airtrack.io

AIS (16, 33.3%)
Operations / Attack Surface Management
Saarland, Germany
ais-security.de

AIUKEN CYBERSECURITY (85, 14.9%)
MSSP / Managed Security Services
Madrid, Spain
aiuken.com

Akamai Technologies (9270, 5.7%)
Network Security / DDoS Defense
Cambridge, MA, US
akamai.com

Akana By Perforce (51, -1.9%)
API Security / API Management
Minneapolis, MN, US
akana.com

Akarion (15, 7.1%)
GRC / Compliance Management
Munich, Germany
akarion.com

Akeero (5, -44.4%)
Application Security / Software Development Security
County Cork, Ireland
akeero.com

Akeyless (95, 11.8%)
Data Security / Key Management
Tel Aviv, Israel
akeyless.io

AKITRA (42, 50.0%)
GRC / Compliance Management
Sunnyvale, CA, US
akitra.com

Akku (19, 1800.0%)
IAM / Identity Platform
Rock Hill, SC, US
akku.work

Akto (15, 114.3%)
Application Security / Visibility
Palo Alto, CA, US
www.akto.io

Aladdin-RD (43, 4.9%)
IAM / Authentication
Moscow, Russia
aladdin-rd.ru

Alcatraz.ai (97, 14.1%)
IAM / Authentication
Cupertino, CA, US
alcatraz.ai

Alert Logic (319, -30.4%)
Security Analytics / Logs
Houston, TX, US
alertlogic.com

AlertEnterprise (268, 20.7%)
IAM / Physical IAM
Fremont, CA, US
alertenterprise.com

alertsec (6, 20.0%)
GRC / Monitoring
Palo Alto, CA, US
alertsec.com

Alfahive (30, -16.7%)
GRC / Posture Management
Mississauga, ON, Canada
alfahive.com

Algosec (504, 4.6%)
Operations / Policy Management
Petah Tikva, Israel
algosec.com

Alias Robotics (14, 27.3%)
IoT Security / Anti-malware
Vitoria, Basque Country, Spain
aliasrobotics.com

ALL4TEC (26, -3.7%)
GRC / Risk Management
Massy, France
all4tec.com

AllClear ID (55, 1.9%)
Fraud Prevention / Identity Protection Service
Austin, TX, US
allclearid.com

Allegro Software (6, -25.0%)
IoT Security / Security For Embedded Systems
Boxborough, MA, US
allegrosoft.com

Allgeier IT (82, -6.8%)
MSSP / Managed Security Services
Bremen, Germany
allgeier-it.de

Allgress (23, -8.0%)
GRC / Compliance Management
Livermore, CA, US
allgress.com

Allied Telesis (926, 5.3%)
Network Security / Firewalls
San Jose, CA, US
alliedtelesis.com

Allot (955, -4.3%)
Network Security / Filtering
Hod HaSharon, Israel
allot.com

AllowMe (65, 22.6%)
IAM / Identity Management
Sao Paulo, Brazil
allowme.cloud

Allthenticate (12, 0.0%)
IAM / Authentication
Goleta, CA, US
allthenticate.net

Allure Security (36, -12.2%)
Deception / Document Security
New York, NY, US
alluresecurity.com

Allurity (13, 44.4%)
MSSP / SOC
Stockholm, Stockholms Lan, Sweden
allurity.com

Alpha Recon (22, 0.0%)
Threat Intelligence / Threat Intelligence Platform
Colorado Springs, CO, US
alpharecon.com

AlphaGuardian Networks (5, -16.7%)
IoT Security / OT Security
San Ramon, CA, US
alphaguardian.net

alphaMountain.ai (9, 28.6%)
Threat Intelligence / DNS Security
Salt Lake City, UT, US
alphamountain.ai

AlphaSOC (18, 80.0%)
Operations / Security Analytics
San Francisco, CA, US
alphasoc.com

Alsid (14, -30.0%)
Network Security / Active Directory
Paris, France
alsid.com

**Numbers in parentheses indicate headcount and % change in 2023.*

Altitude Networks (3, -50.0%)
Data Security / Monitoring
San Francisco, CA, US
altitudenetworks.com

Altr (72, 18.0%)
Data Security / Data Discovery
Austin, TX, US
altr.com

Altrnativ (19, 11.8%)
Threat Intelligence / Consumer CTI
Nice, France
altrnativ.com

Alyne (22, -24.1%)
GRC / Risk Management
Munich, Germany
alyne.com

AMI (1980, 44.6%)
Endpoint Security / Firmware
Duluth, GA, US
ami.com

AMOSSYS (66, 8.2%)
Operations / Breach And Attack Simulation
Rennes, Bretagne, France
amossys.fr

Amplify Intelligence (3, 0.0%)
GRC / Vulnerabilities
Melbourne, Victoria, Australia
amplifyintelligence.com

Amtel (78, 6.8%)
Endpoint Security / Mobile Device Security
Rockville, MD, US
amtelnet.com

AmynaSec Labs (12, -7.7%)
IoT Security / Vulnerabilities
Pune, Maharashtra, India
amynasec.io

Analyst1 (35, 59.1%)
Threat Intelligence / Threat Intelligence Platform
Reston, VA, US
analyst1.com

Ananda Networks (4, 0.0%)
Network Security / Segmentation
San Francisco, CA, US
ananda.net

AnChain.ai (36, -5.3%)
Security Analytics / Forensics
San Jose, CA, US
anchain.ai

Anchor Technologies (16, -11.1%)
GRC / Risk Management
Columbia, MD, US
anchortechnologies.com

Anchorage (336, -11.3%)
Data Security / Secure Storage
San Francisco, CA, US
anchorage.com

Anchore (82, 28.1%)
Endpoint Security / Container Security
Montecito, CA, US
anchore.com

anecdotes (109, 31.3%)
GRC / Compliance Management
Palo Alto, CA, US
anecdotes.ai

Anetac (16, 0.0%)
Stealth
Los Altos, CA, US
anetac.com

AnexGATE (25, 25.0%)
Network Security / UTM
Bangalore, India
anexgate.com/

Angoka (34, 21.4%)
IoT Security / Automotive
Belfast, United Kingdom
angoka.io

Anitian (66, -17.5%)
GRC / Compliance Management
Portland, OR, US
anitian.com

Anjuna (50, -29.6%)
Data Security / Runtime Security
Palo Alto, CA, US
anjuna.io

Anlyz (9, -66.7%)
Operations / SIEM
Lewes, DE, US
anlyz.co

Anomali (286, -1.0%)
Threat Intelligence / Threat Intelligence Platform
Redwood City, CA, US
anomali.com

Anomalix (6, 0.0%)
IAM / Identity Analysis
Las Vegas, NV, US
anomalix.com

Anonos (69, 81.6%)
Data Security / Secure Data Sharing
Boulder, CO, US
anonos.com

Anonybit (22, 15.8%)
IAM / Shards
New York, NY, US
anonybit.io

Anonyome Labs (128, 18.5%)
Data Security / Secure Communications
Salt Lake City, UT, US
anonyome.com

AnubisNetworks (BitSight) (29, 3.6%)
Email Security
Lisbon, Portugal
anubisnetworks.com

Anvilogic (81, 15.7%)
Operations / SOC
Palo Alto, CA, US
anvilogic.com

Anxinsec (34, 100.0%)
Application Security / Runtime Security
Beijing, China
anxinsec.com

ANY.RUN (89, 161.8%)
Endpoint Security / Malware Analysis
Dubai, United Arab Emirates
any.run

Apcon (231, 5.0%)
Network Security / Traffic Analysis
Wilsonville, OR, US
apcon.com

APERIO Systems (35, 25.0%)
IoT Security / OT Security
Haifa, Israel
aperio-systems.com

aPersona (3, -25.0%)
IAM / Authentication
Raleigh, NC, US
apersona.com

Apiiro (126, 22.3%)
API Security / Software Development Security
Tel Aviv, Israel
apiiro.com

APIsec.ai (53, 1.9%)
API Security
San Francisco, CA, US
apisec.ai

Apollo Information Systems (63, 65.8%)
MSSP / Managed Security Services
Los Gatos, CA, US
apollo-is.com

**Numbers in parentheses indicate headcount and % change in 2023.*

Apolloshield (5, 0.0%)
IoT Security / Drones
Palo Alto, CA, US
apolloshield.com

Apona (12, 50.0%)
Application Security / SAST
Roseville, CA, US
apona.ai

Apono (28, 27.3%)
IAM / Rights Management
Tel Aviv, Israel
apono.io

Apozy (17, -41.4%)
Endpoint Security / Filtering
San Francisco, CA, US
apozy.com

Appaegis (31, 24.0%)
IAM / Access Security
Palo Alto, CA, US
appaegis.com

Appalachia Technologies (49, 0.0%)
MSSP / Managed Security Services
Mechanicsburg, PA, US
appalachiatech.com

AppCheck (83, 0.0%)
GRC / Vulnerabilities
Leeds, United Kingdom
appcheck-ng.com

AppDetex (218, 7.4%)
Threat Intelligence / Brand
Boise, ID, US
appdetex.com

AppDome (154, 28.3%)
Application Security
Tel Aviv, Israel
appdome.com

Appgate (372, -11.2%)
IAM / Access Security
Coral Gables, FL, US
appgate.com

AppGuard (22, -15.4%)
Endpoint Security / Application Containment
Chantilly, VA, US
appguard.us

Apphaz Security Solutions (5, -16.7%)
GRC / Penetration Testing
Bear, DE, US
apphaz.com

AppKnox (73, 19.7%)
Application Security / Mobile Device Security
Singapore
appknox.com

Applied Technology Group (6, 0.0%)
MSSP / Managed Security Services
Brandon, MS, US
atgconsults.com

AppMobi (14, 0.0%)
Endpoint Security / Mobile Device Security
Poughkeepsie, NY, US
appmobi.com

appNovi (8, 60.0%)
Application Security
Durham, NC, US
appnovi.com

AppOmni (208, 48.6%)
Operations / Configuration Management
San Francisco, CA, US
appomni.com

Apporetum (4, 0.0%)
IAM
Canberra, Australia
apporetum.com.au

AppRiver (149, -20.7%)
Email Security
Gulf Breeze, FL, US
appriver.com

Approov (16, 23.1%)
API Security
Edinburgh, United Kingdom
approov.io

AppSealing (8, 33.3%)
Application Security
Los Angeles, CA, US
appsealing.com

AppSec Labs (15, 0.0%)
Application Security / Mobile Device Security
Kfar Saba, Israel
appsec-labs.com

AppSecure Security (14, 27.3%)
Application Security / Software Testing For Security
Bangalore, Karnataka, India
appsecure.security

AppTec (20, 42.9%)
Endpoint Security / Mobile Device Security
Basel, Switzerland
apptec360.com

Apptega (54, 1.9%)
GRC / Compliance Management
Atlanta, GA, US
apptega.com

AppViewX (575, 10.8%)
Data Security / Encryption
Seattle, WA, US
appviewx.com

AppVision (5, -16.7%)
Application Security / Code Security
San Francisco, CA, US
appvision.net

Apricorn (31, 10.7%)
Data Security / Secure Storage
Poway, CA, US
apricorn.com

APT Defend (5, 400.0%)
GRC / Security Awareness Training
Warszawa, Mazowieckie, Poland
aptdefend.com

Aptible (29, 0.0%)
GRC / Compliance Management
San Francisco, CA, US
aptible.com

Apura (71, 29.1%)
Threat Intelligence / OSINT
Sao Paulo, Brazil
apura.com.br

Apvera (5, 0.0%)
GRC / Monitoring
Singapore, Singapore
apvera.com

Aqua Security (605, -4.4%)
Endpoint Security / Container Security
Ramat Gan, Israel
aquasec.com

Aquila Technology (31, 14.8%)
Email Security / Defense Against Phishing
Burlington, MA, US
aquilatc.com

Araali Networks (7, -53.3%)
Application Security / Container Security
Fremont, CA, US
araalinetworks.com

Arama Tech (6, -14.3%)
GRC / Compliance Management
Glostrop, Denmark
aramatech.com

Arbit Security (12, 20.0%)
Network Security / Data Diode
Hvidovre, Denmark
arbitcds.com

**Numbers in parentheses indicate headcount and % change in 2023.*

Arc4dia (3, -25.0%)
Security Analytics / Incident Management
Montreal, QC, Canada
arc4dia.com

Arcabit (3, 0.0%)
Endpoint Security / Anti-virus
Warsaw, Poland
arcabit.pl

Arcanna AI (24, -4.0%)
Operations / SOC
Dover, DE, US
arcanna.ai

ARCANO (4, 0.0%)
Data Security / Secure Data Sharing
Zurich, Switzerland
arcano.app

Archer (661, 36.3%)
GRC / Risk Management
Overland Park, KS, US
archerirm.com

Archon (Was Attila Security) (17, 13.3%)
IoT Security / Firewalls
Fulton, MD, US
attilasec.com

Arcon (551, 53.9%)
GRC / Rights Management
Mumbai, India
arconnet.com

Arctic Security (24, -4.0%)
Threat Intelligence
Oulu, Finland
arcticsecurity.com

Arctic Wolf Networks (2251, 8.9%)
MSSP / MDR
Eden Prarie, MN, US
arcticwolf.com

arctonyx (7, 0.0%)
Operations / Attack Surface Management
Baltimore, MD, US
arctonyx.com

Ardaco (25, -16.7%)
Data Security / Secure Communications
Bratislava, Slovakia
ardaco.com

Ardent Privacy (15, 25.0%)
GRC / Data Privacy
Catonsville, MD, US
ardentprivacy.ai

Arexdata (11, 175.0%)
Data Security / Posture Management
Madrid, Spain
arexdata.com

Argus Cyber Security (210, 11.1%)
IoT Security / Automotive
Tel Aviv, Israel
argus-sec.com

Aries Security (14, 7.7%)
Training / Cyber Range
Wilmington, DE, US
ariessecurity.com

Arista Networks (4079, 12.5%)
Network Security / NDR
Santa Clara, CA, US
arista.com

Arkose Labs (214, -11.6%)
Fraud Prevention / Bot Security
San Francisco, CA, US
arkoselabs.com

Armadillo Managed Services Limited (55, -6.8%)
MSSP / Managed Security Services
Hayes, United Kingdom
wearearmadillo.com

Armarius Software (8, 0.0%)
Data Security / DLP
Warrenville, IL, US
armariussoftware.com

Armis (764, 8.2%)
IoT Security / Asset Management
Palo Alto, CA, US
armis.com

Armo Security (59, 25.5%)
Endpoint Security / Container Security
Tel Aviv, Israel
armosec.io

Armor (151, 16.1%)
MSSP / Cloud Security
Richardson, TX, US
armor.com

Armorblox (34, -71.4%)
Email Security / Defense Against Phishing
Cupertino, CA, US
armorblox.com

ArmorCode (125, 71.2%)
Application Security / Posture Management
Palo Alto, CA, US
armorcode.com

Armortext (12, 0.0%)
Data Security / Secure Collaboration
McLean, VA, US
armortext.com

ARMS Cyber (4, 0.0%)
Endpoint Security
Nashville, TN, US
armscyber.com

arnica (25, -26.5%)
Operations / Software Development Security
Alpharetta, GA, US
arnica.io

Arpeggio Software (3, 0.0%)
Data Security / ISeries
Atlanta, GA, US
arpeggiosoftware.com

ArQit (150, -8.5%)
Network Security / Quantum
London, United Kingdom
arqit.io

Array Networks (OSS Corp.) (219, 7.3%)
Network Security / VPN/Proxy
Milpitas, CA, US
arraynetworks.com

Aruba Networks (5710, 3.7%)
Network Security / Monitoring
Santa Clara, CA, US
arubanetworks.com

Aryaka (589, 1.2%)
Network Security / SASE
San Mateo, CA, US
aryaka.com

Ascend Technologies (246, -5.0%)
MSSP / Managed Security Services
Chicago, IL, US
teamascend.com

Aserto (17, 0.0%)
IAM / Access Security
Redmond, WA, US
aserto.com

Asigra (85, 13.3%)
Data Security / Secure Backup / Recovery
Toronto, ON, Canada
asigra.com

Asimily (66, 43.5%)
IoT Security / Healthcare
Sunnyvale, CA, US
asimily.com

Asparna Ltd. (5, 0.0%)
Data Security / Encrypted File Sync And Social Conversations
Afula, Israel
asparna.com

ASPG (31, 40.9%)
Data Security / Encryption
Naples, FL, US
aspg.com

**Numbers in parentheses indicate headcount and % change in 2023.*

Aspire Technology Partners (150, 5.6%)
MSSP / Managed Security Services
Eatontown, NJ, US
aspiretransforms.com

Assac Networks (15, 25.0%)
Endpoint Security / Mobile Device Security
Ramat HaSharon, Israel
assacnetworks.com

AssetNote (11, 22.2%)
Operations / Monitoring
Brisbane, Queensland, Australia
assetnote.io

Assura (46, 12.2%)
MSSP / Managed Security Services
Richmond, VA, US
assurainc.com

Assured Enterprises Inc (10, 0.0%)
GRC / Vulnerabilities
Vienna, VA, US
assured.enterprises

Assured Information Security (186, 3.9%)
Network Security / Dual Domain Control
Rome, NY, US
ainfosec.com

Assuria (19, 0.0%)
Security Analytics / SIEM
Reading, United Kingdom
assuria.com

Astra (54, 63.6%)
Application Security / Web App Protection
New Delhi, India
getastra.com

Astran (26, 8.3%)
Data Security / Secure Storage
Paris, France
astran.io

Astrix Security (63, 90.9%)
GRC / Risk Management
Tel Aviv, Israel
astrix.security

asvin (23, 15.0%)
IoT Security / Device Management
Stuttgart, Germany
asvin.io

AT&T Cybersecurity (62, -10.1%)
Security Analytics / SIEM
San Mateo, CA, US
cybersecurity.att.com

At-Bay (325, 12.8%)
GRC / Cyber Insurance
San Francisco, CA, US
at-bay.com

Atakama (43, -4.4%)
Data Security / Encryption
New York, NY, US
atakama.com

Atmosec (17, -32.0%)
Operations / Application Security
Tel Aviv, Israel
atmosec.com

Atomicorp (11, -8.3%)
Endpoint Security / IPS
Chantilly, VA, US
atomicorp.com

Atonomi (10, 25.0%)
IoT Security / Blockchain
Seattle, WA, US
atonomi.io

Atos Group (81052, -12.7%)
IAM
Bezons, France
atos.net

Atricore (8, 14.3%)
IAM
Sausalito, CA, US
atricore.com

Attack Forge (7, 0.0%)
Operations / Penetration Testing
Melbourne, Australia
attackforge.com

AttackFlow (3, -25.0%)
Application Security / Code Security
San Francisco, CA, US
attackflow.com

AttackIQ (151, -1.9%)
Testing / Security Instrumentation
San Diego, CA, US
attackiq.com

Attify (5, 0.0%)
Application Security / Mobile Device Security
Bangalore, India
attify.com

Attivo Networks (91, -32.6%)
Deception
Fremont, CA, US
attivonetworks.com

Au10Tix (199, 1.0%)
IAM / Identity Management
Hod HaSharon, Israel
au10tix.com

Auconet (9, -25.0%)
IAM / Access Security
Berlin, Germany
auconet.com

AuditBoard (781, 20.3%)
GRC / GRC Platform
Cerritos, CA, US
auditboard.com

Aujas (897, 9.0%)
IAM / Identity Management
Jersey City, NJ, US
aujas.com

Aura (733, 13.8%)
Endpoint Security / Data Privacy
Boston, MA, US
aura.com

Auth Armor (5, -16.7%)
IAM / Authentication
Los Angeles, CA, US
autharmor.com

Auth0 (448, -17.2%)
IAM / Authentication
Bellevue, WA, US
auth0.com

AUTHADA (22, -12.0%)
Fraud Prevention / Authentication
Darmstadt, Germany
authada.de

Authenteq (5, -58.3%)
Fraud Prevention / Identity Verification
Reykjavik, Iceland
authenteq.com

Authentic8 (134, 8.9%)
Network Security / Secure Web Browsing
Redwood City, CA, US
authentic8.com

Authenticid (96, -20.7%)
Fraud Prevention / Identity Verification
Kirkland, WA, US
authenticid.co

AuthID (32, 0.0%)
IAM / Authentication
Long Beach, NY, US
authid.ai

Authlete (29, 38.1%)
IAM / Gateways
Tokyo, Japan
authlete.com

AuthLogics (6, -25.0%)
IAM / Authentication
Bracknell, United Kingdom
authlogics.com

AuthMind (31, 55.0%)
GRC / Risk Management
Bethesda, MD, US
authmind.com

**Numbers in parentheses indicate headcount and % change in 2023.*

Authomate (4, 0.0%)
IAM / Authentication
Morganville, NJ, US
authomate.com

Authomize (47, 0.0%)
IAM / Monitoring
Tel Aviv, Israel
authomize.com

Authsignal (11, 22.2%)
Fraud Prevention
Auckland, New Zealand
authsignal.com

AUTOCRYPT (162, 55.8%)
IoT Security / Automotive
Seoul, South Korea
autocrypt.io

Automox (227, -12.0%)
GRC / Patch Management
Boulder, CO, US
automox.com

Autonomic Software (9, 0.0%)
Endpoint Security / Patch Management
Danville, CA, US
autonomic-software.com

Ava Security (81, -24.3%)
Security Analytics / Monitoring
Uxbridge, United Kingdom
avasecurity.com

Avalon Cyber (425, 3.7%)
MSSP / Managed Security Services
Buffalo, NY, US
avaloncybersecurity.com

Avalor (74, 39.6%)
Operations / Data Management
Tel Aviv, Israel
avalor.io

Avanan (93, 8.1%)
Email Security / Technology Deployment Management
New York, NY, US
avanan.com

Avast Software (1057, -29.4%)
Endpoint Security / Anti-virus
Prague, Czech Republic
avast.com

Avatier (39, 11.4%)
IAM / Identity Management
Pleasanton, CA, US
avatier.com

Avaya (13587, -2.8%)
Network Security / VPN/Proxy
Santa Clara, CA, US
avaya.com

Avepoint (1466, 9.7%)
Data Security / Secure Backup/Recovery
Jersey City, NJ, US
avepoint.com

Avertium (209, -10.3%)
MSSP / Managed Security Services
Phoenix, AZ, US
avertium.com

Avertro (22, 57.1%)
GRC / Risk Management
Sydney, NSW, Australia
avertro.com

Aves Netsec (4, -20.0%)
Endpoint Security / Patch Management
London, United Kingdom
avesnetsec.com

Avi Networks (38, -29.6%)
Network Security / Firewalls
Santa Clara, CA, US
avinetworks.com

Aviatrix (390, -8.9%)
Network Security / Firewalls
Palo Alto, CA, US
aviatrix.com

Avira (202, -0.5%)
Endpoint Security / Anti-virus
Tettnang, Germany
avira.com

Avnos (3, -50.0%)
Endpoint Security / Application Whitelisting
Singapore, Singapore
avnos.io

Avocado Systems (20, -48.7%)
Application Security / App Hardening
San Jose, CA, US
avocadosys.com

Awake Security (50, -3.9%)
Network Security / Monitoring
Sunnyvale, CA, US
awakesecurity.com

Aware7 (34, 183.3%)
GRC / Security Awareness Training
Gelsenkirchen, Germany
aware7.com

AwareHQ (159, -5.9%)
Network Security / Monitoring
Columbus, OH, US
awarehq.com

Awareness Technologies (36, 5.9%)
Operations / Monitoring
Westport, CT, US
awarenesstechnologies.com

Awareways (53, -10.2%)
GRC / Security Awareness Training
Utrecht, Netherlands
awareways.com

Axcrypt (24, 14.3%)
Data Security / Encryption
Stockholm, Sweden
axcrypt.net

Axiad IDS (62, 3.3%)
IAM / Authentication
Santa Clara, CA, US
axiadids.com

Axiado (62, 19.2%)
Endpoint Security / Hardware
San Jose, CA, US
axiado.com

Axio (91, 26.4%)
GRC / Risk Management
New York, NY, US
axio.com

Axiom (22, 4.8%)
IAM / Identity Management
San Francisco, CA, US
axiom.security

Axiom Cyber Solutions (3, -25.0%)
GRC / Vulnerabilities
Las Vegas, NV, US
axiomcyber.com

Axiomatics (67, 24.1%)
IAM / Access Security
Stockholm, Sweden
axiomatics.com

Axis Security (268, 103.0%)
IAM / Access Security
San Mateo, CA, US
axissecurity.com

Axonius (600, -6.2%)
GRC / Asset Management
New York, NY, US
axonius.com

Axuall (92, 95.7%)
IAM / Identity Verification
Cleveland, OH, US
axuall.com

Axur (213, 10.9%)
Threat Intelligence / Brand
Porto Alegre, Brazil
axur.com

Axway (1729, -4.9%)
GRC / Secure Data Sharing
Phoenix, AZ, US
axway.com

**Numbers in parentheses indicate headcount and % change in 2023.*

Ayyeka (34, -5.6%)
IoT Security /
Remote Devices
Jerusalem, Israel
ayyeka.com

Azul (416, -22.5%)
Application Security /
Runtime Security
Sunnyvale, CA, US
azul.com

B-Secur (76, -2.6%)
IAM / Authentication
Belfast, United Kingdom
b-secur.com

BAAR (57, 23.9%)
IAM / Identity Management
Mississauga, Canada
baar.ai

Babel (3080, 19.0%)
MSSP / SOC
Madrid, Spain
babelgroup.com

Backbox (63, 16.7%)
Operations / Orchestration
Dallas, TX, US
backbox.com

Badrap Oy (4, -33.3%)
Operations / Security
Playbooks
Oulu, Finland
badrap.io

BAE Systems (38342, 6.4%)
MSSP / Managed
Security Services
Guildford, United Kingdom
baesystems.com

Baffin Bay Networking
(8, -50.0%)
Network Security /
Threat Detection
Stockholm, Sweden
baffinbaynetworks.com

Baffle (54, 14.9%)
Data Security /
Database Security
Santa Clara, CA, US
baffle.io

Balance Theory (16, 45.5%)
Operations / Secure
Collaboration
Columbia, MD, US
balancetheory.io

Balasys (39, -27.8%)
API Security
Budapest, Hungary
balasys.hu

Balbix (146, 29.2%)
GRC / Asset Management
San Jose, CA, US
balbix.com

BalkanID (27, 35.0%)
IAM / Auditing
Austin, TX, US
balkan.id

Bandura Cyber (30, 0.0%)
Network Security / Firewalls
Columbia, MD, US
bandurasystems.com

BankVault Cybersecurity
(14, 75.0%)
IAM / Authentication
West Perth, Australia
bankvault.com

Banyan Cloud (54, 25.6%)
Operations / Posture
Management
San Jose, CA, US
banyancloud.io

Banyan Security (64, -1.5%)
Network Security / Zero
Trust Networking
San Francisco, CA, US
banyansecurity.io

Baramundi Software
(209, 14.8%)
GRC / Endpoint
Management
Augsburg, Germany
baramundi.com

Barracuda Networks
(2146, 17.0%)
Network Security / Anti-spam
Campbell, CA, US
barracuda.com

Barricade IT Security
(3, 200.0%)
MSSP / Managed
Security Services
Islip, NY, US
barricadeitsecurity.com

Basis Technology
(75, -44.4%)
Operations / Forensics
Cambridge,
MA, US
basistech.com

Bastazo (6, 0.0%)
GRC / Vulnerabilities
Fayetteville,
AR, US
bastazo.com

Bastille (64, 39.1%)
Network Security /
Wireless Security
Atlanta, GA, US
bastille.net

BastionZero (14, -26.3%)
IAM / Gateways
Boston, MA, US
bastionzero.com

BAYOOSOFT (22, 29.4%)
IAM
Darmstadt,
Germany
bayoosoft.com

Bayshore Networks
(14, 0.0%)
IoT Security / OT Security
Durham, NC, US
bayshorenetworks.com

BDO Cyber Security
(46, 27.8%)
MSSP / SIEM
Hamburg,
Germany
bdosecurity.de

Beachhead Solutions
(14, 0.0%)
Endpoint Security / Device
Management
San Jose, CA, US
beachheadsolutions.com

Beagle Security (35, 16.7%)
Application Security /
Penetration Testing
Thiruvananthapuram,
India
beaglesecurity.com

Bearer (29, 20.8%)
Application Security
San Francisco, CA, US
bearer.com

Beauceron (44, -22.8%)
GRC / Defense
Against Phishing
Fredericton, NB, Canada
beauceronsecurity.com

Becrypt (57, 23.9%)
Data Security / Encryption
London, United Kingdom
becrypt.com

Bedrock (21, 40.0%)
Data Security / Posture
Management
San Francisco, CA, US
bedrock.security

Behaviosec (24, -36.8%)
Fraud Prevention /
Monitoring
San Francisco, CA, US
behaviosec.com

Belarc Inc. (14, -12.5%)
GRC / Asset Management
Maynard, MA, US
belarc.com

Belkasoft (21, -8.7%)
Operations / Forensics
Palo Alto, CA, US
belkasoft.com

Besedo (370, 9.8%)
Fraud Prevention /
Scanning
Stockholm, Sweden
besedo.com

Beta Systems Software AG
(327, 14.3%)
IAM
Berlin, Germany
betasystems.com

**Numbers in parentheses indicate headcount and % change in 2023.*

Bettercloud (267, -22.8%)
Network Security / Monitoring
New York, NY, US
bettercloud.com

Beyond Identity (146, -18.0%)
IAM / Authentication
New York, NY, US
beyondidentity.com

Beyond Security (33, -10.8%)
GRC / Vulnerabilities
San Jose, CA, US
beyondsecurity.com

BeyondID (191, 0.5%)
MSSP / Managed Security Services
San Francisco, CA, US
beyondid.com

BeyondTrust (1452, 4.5%)
IAM / Access Security
Johns Creek, GA, US
beyondtrust.com

Bfore.ai (40, 29.0%)
Threat Intelligence / Domain Prediction
Montpellier, France
bfore.ai

BI.ZONE (257, 12.7%)
Threat Intelligence / Threat Intel Aggregator
Moscow, Russia
bi.zone

BicDroid (7, 0.0%)
Data Security / Encryption
Waterloo, ON, Canada
bicdroid.com

BigID (543, 0.2%)
GRC / Data Discovery
Tel Aviv, Israel
bigid.com

Binalyze (83, -4.6%)
Operations / Forensics
Tallinn, Harjumaa, Estonia
binalyze.com

Binare.io (8, 14.3%)
IoT Security / Firmware
Finland
binare.io

Binarly (26, 30.0%)
Endpoint Security / Firmware
Pasadena, CA, US
binarly.io

Binary Defense (178, 26.2%)
MSSP / SOC
Stow, OH, US
binarydefense.com

BinaryEdge (6, 0.0%)
Operations / Scanning
Zurich, Switzerland
binaryedge.io

Bindle Systems (17, -19.1%)
IAM / Identity Management
Ardsley, NY, US
bindlesystems.com

BIO-key (72, -13.2%)
IAM / Authentication
Wall, NJ, US
bio-key.com

BioCatch (297, 20.7%)
Fraud Prevention / Authentication
Tel Aviv, Israel
biocatch.com

BioConnect (50, 21.9%)
IAM / Authentication
Toronto, ON, Canada
bioconnect.com

BioEnable (76, 0.0%)
IAM / Access Security
Pune, India
bioenabletech.com

BioID (14, 7.7%)
IAM / Authentication
Sachseln, Switzerland
bioid.com

Biometric Signature-Id (15, 7.1%)
IAM / Authentication
Lewisville, TX, US
biosig-id.com

Biomio (4, -20.0%)
IAM / Authentication
Portland, OR, US
biom.io

Bionic (103, -8.8%)
API Security / Posture Management
Palo Alto, CA, US
bionic.ai

Biscom (202, 9.2%)
Data Security / Secure Data Sharing
Chelmsford, MA, US
biscom.com

Bishop Fox (389, -8.2%)
Operations / Breach And Attack Simulation
Tempe, AZ, US
bishopfox.com

Bitahoy (5, -37.5%)
Operations
Saarland, Germany
bitahoy.com

BitDefender (2110, 4.0%)
Endpoint Security / Anti-virus
Bucharest, Romania
bitdefender.com

Bitdiscovery (3, 0.0%)
GRC / Asset Management
Santa Clara, CA, US
bitdiscovery.com

BitGlass (36, -36.8%)
Security Analytics / Incident Management
Campbell, CA, US
bitglass.com

BitLyft (20, 17.6%)
MSSP / SIEM
Lansing, MI, US
bitlyft.com

BitNinja (30, -14.3%)
Endpoint Security / Servers
London, United Kingdom
bitninja.io

BitSight (805, 0.6%)
GRC / Security Ratings
Boston, MA, US
bitsight.com

Bittium (1526, -4.4%)
Data Security / Secure Communications
Oulu, Finland
bittium.com

Bitwarden (162, 46.0%)
IAM / Credential Security
Santa Barbara, CA, US
bitwarden.com

Bizzy Labs (8, -11.1%)
IoT Security / Vulnerabilities
Irving, TX, US
bizzylabs.tech

Black Kite (115, -2.5%)
GRC / Security Scores
Vienna, VA, US
normshield.com

Blackbelt Smartphone Defence Ltd (33, 57.1%)
Data Security / Data Erasure And Destruction
Kendal, United Kingdom
blackbeltdefence.com

Blackberry (3314, -7.4%)
Endpoint Security / Mobile Device Security
Waterloo, ON, Canada
BlackBerry.com

BlackCloak (50, 56.2%)
Threat Intelligence / Protection For Executives And Celebrities
Orlando, FL, US
blackcloak.io

BlackDice Cyber (14, 366.7%)
Network Security / Security For Gateways
Leeds, Horsforth, United Kingdom
blackdice.io

**Numbers in parentheses indicate headcount and % change in 2023.*

BlackFog (21, 23.5%)
Endpoint Security / EDR
Cheyenne, WY, US
blackfog.com

Blacklight by Owlgaze (11, -50.0%)
Operations / Threat Hunting
London, United Kingdom
blacklight.owlgaze.com

Blacklock Security (4, -20.0%)
GRC / Penetration Testing
Thorndon, Wellington Region, New Zealand
blacklock.io

Blackpoint (169, 83.7%)
MSSP / MDR
Ellicott City, MD, US
blackpointcyber.com

Blacksands (8, -11.1%)
Network Security / Software Defined Perimeter
Ann Arbor, MI, US
blacksandsinc.com

Blancco (352, 3.8%)
Data Security / Data Erasure And Destruction
Bishops Stortford, United Kingdom
blancco.com

BlastWave (19, 11.8%)
Network Security / Segmentation
Mountain View, CA, US
blastwaveinc.com

Blind Hash (3, 0.0%)
IAM / Credential Security
Boston, MA, US
blindhash.com

Blink Ops (55, 17.0%)
Operations / Automation
Tel Aviv, Israel
blinkops.com

Block Armour (36, 24.1%)
Network Security / Zero Trust Networking
Mumbai, India
blockarmour.com

BlockChain Security (20, 66.7%)
Data Security / Blockchain
Taipei, Taiwan
chainsecurity.asia

Blockdos (4, 0.0%)
Network Security / DDoS Defense
Mississauga, ON, Canada
blockdos.net

Blocmount (3, 50.0%)
IoT Security / OT Security
San Antonio, TX, US
blocmount.com

Bloombase (18, -28.0%)
Data Security / Encryption
Redwood City, CA, US
bloombase.com

Blowfish (18, 260.0%)
Data Security / Wallets
Switzerland
blowfish.xyz

Blu Sapphire (85, 97.7%)
MSSP / Threat Hunting
Madhapur, India
blusapphire.com

BluBracket (6, -60.0%)
Application Security / Software Development Security
Palo Alto, CA, US
blubracket.com

Blue Lance Inc. (11, -21.4%)
GRC / Asset Management
Houston, TX, US
bluelance.com

Blue Lava (12, -76.5%)
GRC / Security Program Management
Menlo Park, CA, US
blue-lava.net

Blue Planet-works (14, -22.2%)
Application Security / Isolation
Tokyo, Japan
blueplanet-works.com

Blue Ridge Networks (36, 2.9%)
Network Security / Segmentation
Chantilly, VA, US
blueridgenetworks.com

Blue Team Labs (193, 127.1%)
Training / Cyber Range
London, United Kingdom
blueteamlabs.online

Bluecat Networks (687, 55.1%)
Network Security / DNS Security
Bracknell, United Kingdom
bluecatnetworks.com

BlueCedar (44, 41.9%)
Endpoint Security / Mobile Device Security
San Francisco, CA, US
bluecedar.com

BlueRisc (10, -16.7%)
Application Security / Code Security
Amherst, MA, US
bluerisc.com

BlueShift Cybersecurity (12, -7.7%)
MSSP / MDR
Fort Myers, FL, US
blueshiftcyber.com

BlueVoyant (604, 2.5%)
MSSP / MDR
New York, NY, US
bluevoyant.com

Bluink (24, 9.1%)
IAM / Authentication
Ottawa, ON, Canada
bluink.ca

Blumira (63, 21.1%)
Security Analytics / SIEM
Ann Arbor, MI, US
blumira.com

BluVector (13, 0.0%)
Network Security / IDS
Arlington, VA, US
bluvector.io

BMC Software (9786, 1.8%)
Security Analytics / SIEM
Houston, TX, US
bmc.com

Bob's Business (29, 0.0%)
GRC / Security Awareness Training
Barnsley, United Kingdom
bobsbusiness.co.uk

BOLDEND (17, 13.3%)
Stealth
San Diego, CA, US
boldend.com

Boldon James (31, -8.8%)
GRC / DLP
Farnborough, United Kingdom
boldonjames.com

Bolster (75, 27.1%)
Email Security / Defense Against Phishing
Los Altos, CA, US
bolster.ai

Boolebox (13, -18.8%)
Data Security / IRM
Milan, Italy
boolebox.com

Boost Security (27, 28.6%)
Application Security / Software Development Security
Montreal, QU, Canada
boostsecurity.io

Borneo (142, 144.8%)
GRC / Compliance Management
San Francisco, CA, US
borneo.io

Bornio (12, 0.0%)
Data Security / Data Flows
Menlo Park, CA, US
bornio.com

Bosch AIShield (13, 30.0%)
Application Security
Koramangala, Bengaluru, India
boschaishield.com

**Numbers in parentheses indicate headcount and % change in 2023.*

Botdoc (13, 8.3%)
Data Security / Secure Data Sharing
Monument, CO, US
botdoc.io

BotGuard (31, 0.0%)
Fraud Prevention / Bot Security
Tallinn, Estonia
botguard.net/en/home

Bottomline (2461, 6.0%)
Data Security
Portsmouth, NH, US
bottomline.com

Bowline Security (11, 10.0%)
MSSP / SOC
Durban, KZN, South Africa
bowlinesecurity.co.za

Boxcryptor (10, -44.4%)
Data Security / Encryption
Augsburg, Germany
boxcryptor.com

Boxphish (25, 19.1%)
GRC / Security Awareness Training
London, United Kingdom
boxphish.com

Brainloop (67, 3.1%)
Data Security / Secure Collaboration
Munich, Germany
brainloop.com

Brainwave Grc (32, -37.2%)
GRC / Identity Analytics
Asnieres-sur-Seine, France
brainwaveGRC.com

Brama Systems (6, 0.0%)
Network Security / Access Security
Utrecht, Netherlands
bramasystems.com

BRANDEFENSE (64, 42.2%)
Threat Intelligence / Managed Security Services
Ankura, Turkey
brandefense.io

BrandShield (82, 9.3%)
Fraud Prevention / Brand
Ramat HaSharon, Israel
brandshield.com

Breachlock (90, 1.1%)
GRC / Penetration Testing
New York, NY, US
breachlock.com

BreachQuest (9, -35.7%)
Security Analytics / Incident Management
Dallas, TX, US
breachquest.com

BreachRx (17, 21.4%)
GRC / Incident Management
San Francisco, CA, US
breachrx.com

Bricata (10, -23.1%)
Network Security / IPS
Columbia, MD, US
bricata.com

Bridewell (230, -0.9%)
MSSP / SOC
Reading, United Kingdom
bridewell.com

Bridgecrew (10, -56.5%)
Application Security / Configuration Management
San Francisco, CA, US
bridgecrew.io

Bright Security (162, 65.3%)
Application Security / Code Security
Tel Aviv, Israel
brightsec.com

brighter AI (44, -4.3%)
Data Security / Video / Image Anonymization
Berlin, Germany
brighter.ai

Brinqa (98, -10.1%)
GRC / Risk Management
Austin, TX, US
brinqa.com

British Telecom (78799, 7.3%)
MSSP / Managed Security Services
London, United Kingdom
bt.com

Britive (58, -12.1%)
IAM / Access Security
Glendale, CA, US
britive.com

Brivo (405, 38.7%)
IAM / Identity Management
Bethesda, MD, US
brivo.com

Broadcom (24651, 1.8%)
Network Security / Hardware
San Jose, CA, US
broadcom.com

BroadForward (26, 0.0%)
Network Security / Firewalls
Amersfoort, Netherlands
broadforward.com

BSI Group (8263, 8.3%)
Training / Standards Certification
London, United Kingdom
bsigroup.com

Btech - IT Security for Credit Unions (9, 0.0%)
MSSP / Managed Security Services
Pasadena, CA, US
btechonline.com

Buckler (8, 0.0%)
GRC / Compliance Management
Columbus, OH, US
buckler.app

Bufferzone (19, 11.8%)
Endpoint Security / Sandbox
Giv'atayim, Israel
bufferzonesecurity.com

Bugcrowd (2461, 18.7%)
Operations / Bugs
San Francisco, CA, US
bugcrowd.com

BugProve (12, 9.1%)
IoT Security / Vulnerabilities
Budapest, Hungary
bugprove.com

Bugsec Group (77, -6.1%)
MSSP / Managed Security Services
Rishon LeZion, Israel
bugsec.com

Build38 (67, 52.3%)
Application Security / Mobile Device Security
Munich, Germany
build38.com

Bulletproof (101, 13.5%)
MSSP / SIEM
Stevenage, United Kingdom
bulletproof.co.uk

BullGuard Ltd. (31, -24.4%)
Endpoint Security / Anti-virus
London, United Kingdom
bullguard.com

Bundesdruckerei (1373, 30.0%)
IAM / Public Key Infrastructure
Berlin, Germany
bundesdruckerei.de

Buoyant (25, 4.2%)
Network Security / Segmentation
San Francisco, CA, US
buoyant.io

Bureau (115, 3.6%)
Fraud Prevention / Identity Verification
San Francisco, CA, US
bureau.id

Buypass As (85, 10.4%)
IAM / Public Key Infrastructure
OSLO, Norway
buypass.no

Byos (29, -6.5%)
Network Security / Segmentation
Halifax, Canada
byos.io

**Numbers in parentheses indicate headcount and % change in 2023.*

BYSTAMP (19, 0.0%)
Data Security
Paris, France
bystamp.com

C1Risk (7, 0.0%)
GRC / Policy Management
San Francisco, CA, US
c1risk.com

C1Secure (19, -20.8%)
GRC / Compliance Management
Atlanta, GA, US
c1secure.com

C2 Cyber (22, 4.8%)
GRC / Risk Management
London, United Kingdom
c2cyber.com

C2A Security (39, 18.2%)
IoT Security / Automotive
Jerusalem, Israel
c2a-sec.com

C2SEC (6, 0.0%)
GRC / Risk Management
Redmond, WA, US
c2sec.com

CACI International Inc. (19442, 7.4%)
MSSP / Managed Security Services
Arlington, VA, US
caci.com

Cado Security (53, 39.5%)
Operations / Incident Management
London, United Kingdom
cadosecurity.com

Calamu (27, -12.9%)
Data Security / Shards
Clinton, NJ, US
calamu.com

CalCom (52, 20.9%)
Endpoint Security / Servers
Lod, Israel
calcomsoftware.com

Callsign (233, -19.7%)
IAM / Authentication
London, United Kingdom
callsign.com

Calvin Risk (17, 13.3%)
Application Security / AI Model Security
Zurich, Switzerland
calvin-risk.com

Calypso AI (51, 13.3%)
Data Security / Safe AI/ML Data
San Francisco, CA, US
calypsoai.com

Calyptix Security Corporation (11, 10.0%)
Network Security / UTM
Charlotte, NC, US
calyptix.com

Cambridge Intelligence (72, -1.4%)
Security Analytics / Data Visualization
Cambridge, United Kingdom
cambridge-intelligence.com

Camel Secure (8, -27.3%)
GRC
Santiago, Chile
camelsecure.com

Canonic (14, -50.0%)
Application Security
Tel Aviv, Israel
canonic.security

Capgemini (290105, 2.4%)
MSSP / Managed Security Services
Paris, France
capgemini.com

Caplinked (14, -12.5%)
Data Security / Secure Data Sharing
Manhattan Beach, CA, US
caplinked.com

Capsule8 (4, -55.6%)
Endpoint Security / Linux Security
New York, NY, US
capsule8.com

Capture The Bug (12, 200.0%)
Application Security / Bugs
Waikato, New Zealand
capturethebug.xyz

Capzul (3, 0.0%)
Application Security
Toronto, ON, Canada
capzul.net

CardinalOps (50, 0.0%)
Operations / Automated Control Checks
Tel Aviv, Israel
cardinalops.com

Carson & Saint (Was Saint Corporation) (25, 8.7%)
GRC / Vulnerabilities
Bethesda, MD, US
carson-saint.com

Carve Systems (16, -30.4%)
GRC / Risk Management
New York, NY, US
carvesystems.com

Casa (68, 6.2%)
Data Security
Denver, CO, US
keys.casa

Castle (27, 22.7%)
Fraud Prevention / Access Security
San Francisco, CA, US
castle.io

Cato Networks (813, 22.4%)
Network Security / Cloud Security
Tel Aviv, Israel
catonetworks.com

Cavelo Inc (20, 25.0%)
GRC / Data Discovery
Kitchener, ON, Canada
cavelo.com

Caveonix (33, 43.5%)
GRC / Risk Management
Falls Church, VA, US
caveonix.com

Cavirin Systems (16, -15.8%)
GRC / Compliance Management
Santa Clara, CA, US
cavirin.com

CBL Data Recovery Technologies Inc. (39, 11.4%)
Data Security / Data Recovery
Markham, ON, Canada
cbldata.com

CDeX (27, 0.0%)
Training / Cyber Range
Poznan, Poland
cdex.cloud

Ceedo (34, -2.9%)
Endpoint Security / Secured Devices
Herzliya, Israel
ceedo.com

Ceeyu (10, -16.7%)
Operations / Attack Surface Management
Belgium
ceeyu.io

Celestix (23, 15.0%)
IAM
Fremont, CA, US
celestix.com

Cellcrypt (5, 400.0%)
Data Security / Secure Communications
London, United Kingdom
cellcrypt.com

Cellebrite (1081, 5.5%)
Endpoint Security / Forensics
Petah Tikva, Israel
cellebrite.com

Cellopoint International Corporation (31, -6.1%)
Email Security / Gateways
New Taipei City, Taiwan
cellopoint.com

**Numbers in parentheses indicate headcount and % change in 2023.*

Cellrox (14, -30.0%)
Endpoint Security / Virtualization
Tel Aviv, Israel
cellrox.com

Celltrust Corporation (20, 11.1%)
Data Security / Secure Communications
Scottsdale, AZ, US
celltrust.com

Cenobe (12, 0.0%)
Operations / Penetration Testing
Athens, Greece
cenobe.com

Censinet (39, 34.5%)
GRC
Boston, MA, US
censinet.com

CensorNet (59, -27.2%)
Network Security / Filtering
Basingstoke, United Kingdom
censornet.com

Censys (129, 14.2%)
GRC / Asset Management
Ann Arbor, MI, US
censys.io

Centraleyes (20, -13.0%)
GRC / Risk Management
New York, NY, US
centraleyes.com

Centripetal (91, 30.0%)
Network Security / Firewalls
Herndon, VA, US
centripetalnetworks.com

CenturyLink (25991, -5.1%)
MSSP / Monitoring
Monroe, LA, US
centurylink.com

Cequence Security (167, 4.4%)
API Security
Sunnyvale, CA, US
cequence.ai

Cerbos (20, 66.7%)
IAM / Authorization
London, United Kingdom
cerbos.dev

Cerby (93, 55.0%)
IAM / Credential Security
Alameda, CA, US
cerby.com

Cerdant (26, -25.7%)
MSSP / Managed Security Services
Dublin, OH, US
cerdant.com

Cereus (4, 33.3%)
GRC / Compliance Management
Eau Claire, WI, US
cereus.io

Ceritas (8, 0.0%)
IoT Security / Vulnerabilities
Cambridge, MA, US
ceritas.ai

Certes Networks (46, 4.5%)
Network Security / VPN/Proxy
Pittsburgh, PA, US
certesnetworks.com

certgate (11, -8.3%)
Endpoint Security / Mobile Device Security
Germany
airid.com

Certicom (123, -2.4%)
Data Security / Encryption
Mississauga, ON, Canada
certicom.com

CertiK (206, -14.9%)
Data Security / Blockchain
New York, NY, US
certik.com

CertiPath (43, 10.3%)
Data Security / Public Key Infrastructure
Reston, VA, US
certipath.com

Certora (74, 8.8%)
Data Security / Blockchain
Tel Aviv, Israel
certora.com

Cervello (36, 28.6%)
IoT Security / Railway
Tel Aviv, Israel
cervellosec.com

CGS Tower Networks (15, 7.1%)
Network Security / Network Taps
Rosh HaAyin, Israel
cgstowernetworks.com

Chainalysis (842, -7.3%)
Fraud Prevention / Crypto Investigations
New York, NY, US
chainalysis.com

Chainguard (97, 67.2%)
Application Security / Code Security
Kirkland, WA, US
chainguard.dev

Check Point Software (7468, 9.2%)
Network Security / UTM
Tel Aviv, Israel
checkpoint.com

Checkmarx (919, -1.8%)
Application Security / Software Development Security
Ramat Gan, Israel
checkmarx.com

CheckRed (48, 60.0%)
Operations / Posture Management
Frisco, TX, US
checkred.com

Cheq (263, 2.7%)
Fraud Prevention / Advertising-related
Tel Aviv, Israel
cheq.ai

CHEQUER (12, -40.0%)
IAM / Access Security
Seoul, South Korea
querypie.com

Chili Security (32, 0.0%)
Endpoint Security / Anti-virus
Odense, Denmark
chilisecurity.dk

Chorus Intel (38, -13.6%)
Operations / Link Analysis
Woodbridge, United Kingdom
chorusintel.com

Chronicle (part of Google) (45, 80.0%)
Security Analytics / SIEM
Mountain View, CA, US
chronicle.security

CI Security (90, 8.4%)
MSSP / MDR
Seattle, WA, US
ci.security

Cider Security (30, -64.3%)
Application Security / Software Development Security
Tel Aviv, Israel
cidersecurity.io

Cienaga Systems (5, 25.0%)
Security Analytics / Cyber Threat Management
Lakewood Ranch, FL, US
cienagasystems.net

Cigent (20, -9.1%)
Network Security / Monitoring
Fort Myers, FL, US
cigent.com

Cimcor (22, 0.0%)
GRC
Merrillville, IN, US
cimcor.com

Cinder (27, 107.7%)
GRC / Insider Abuse Management
New York, NY, US
cinder.co

**Numbers in parentheses indicate headcount and % change in 2023.*

CIPHER Security (341, 27.7%)
MSSP / Managed Security Services
Miami, FL, US
cipher.com

CipherStash (19, 18.8%)
Data Security / Encryption
Sydney, Australia
cipherstash.com

CipherTechs (58, -33.3%)
MSSP / Managed Security Services
New York, NY, US
ciphertechs.com

Ciphertex (8, 33.3%)
Data Security / Secure Storage
San Fernando, CA, US
ciphertex.com

ciphertrace (110, 17.0%)
Fraud Prevention / Anti-money Laudering
Menlo Park, CA, US
ciphertrace.com

Circadence (76, -20.0%)
Training / Cyber Range
Boulder, CO, US
circadence.com

Cisco (99793, 2.6%)
Network Security / Firewalls
San Jose, CA, US
cisco.com

CISOteria (7, 0.0%)
GRC / Risk Management
Ra'ananna, Israel
cisoteria.com

Citalid (43, 87.0%)
GRC
Versailles, France
citalid.com

Citicus (3, -25.0%)
GRC
London, United Kingdom
citicus.com

Citrix Systems (6105, -27.2%)
Network Security / Access Security
Fort Lauderdale, FL, US
citrix.com

Civic Technologies (33, -8.3%)
Data Security / Wallets
San Francisco, CA, US
civic.com

Claranet Cyber Security (81, -22.1%)
MSSP
London, United Kingdom
claranetcybersecurity.com

Clare Computing Solutions (51, 6.2%)
MSSP / Managed Security Services
San Ramon, CA, US
clarecomputer.com

Claroty (484, 16.6%)
IoT Security / OT Security
New York, NY, US
claroty.com

Clavister (120, -13.7%)
Network Security / UTM
Ornskoldsvik, Sweden
clavister.com

Cleafy (54, -6.9%)
Fraud Prevention / Anti-fraud
Milan, Italy
cleafy.com

ClearDATA (186, -3.1%)
MSSP / HIPAA Cloud Hosting
Austin, TX, US
cleardata.com

Clearnetwork (10, 11.1%)
MSSP / SOC
Hazlet, NJ, US
clearnetwork.com

ClearSky Cyber (10, 11.1%)
Threat Intelligence / Threat Analysis
Cambridge, United Kingdom
clearskysec.com

ClearSkye (38, -17.4%)
IAM / Governance
Emeryville, CA, US
clearskye.com

Clearswift (95, -15.9%)
Email Security
Theale, United Kingdom
clearswift.com

Clearwater (250, 110.1%)
GRC / Compliance Management
Nashville, TN, US
clearwatercompliance.com

Cloaked (50, 16.3%)
Data Security
Lowell, MA, US
cloaked.app

Clone Systems (16, -11.1%)
MSSP / Monitoring
Philadelphia, PA, US
clone-systems.com

Cloud Range (22, 0.0%)
Training / Cyber Range
Nashville, TN, US
cloudrangecyber.com

Cloud Raxak (7, 0.0%)
GRC / Compliance Management
Los Gatos, CA, US
cloudraxak.com

Cloud Storage Security (17, 70.0%)
Operations / Anti-virus
Rochester, NY, US
cloudstoragesec.com

Cloud24X7 (25, 8.7%)
MSSP / MSSP Enablement
Fort Lauderdale, FL, US
cloud24x7.us

Cloudanix (10, 0.0%)
Operations / Posture Management
Pune, India
cloudanix.com

Cloudbric Corporation (17, -32.0%)
MSSP / Website Security
Seoul, South Korea
cloudbric.com

Cloudcheckr (61, -51.2%)
GRC / Configuration Management
Rochester, NY, US
cloudcheckr.com

Cloudcodes Software (21, -12.5%)
IAM
Pune, India
cloudcodes.com

Cloudcoffer (4, -20.0%)
Network Security / UTM
Taipei, China
cloudcoffer.com

CloudCover (19, 26.7%)
GRC / Compliance Management
Saint Paul, MN, US
cloudcover.net

Clouddefense.ai (36, 28.6%)
Application Security / Code Security
Palo Alto, CA, US
clouddefense.ai

Cloudentity (45, -35.7%)
IAM / Identity Management
Seattle, WA, US
cloudentity.com

Cloudera (2987, -9.7%)
Operations / Cloud Security
Palo Alto, CA, US
cloudera.com

Cloudflare (4009, 18.1%)
Network Security / DDoS Defense
San Francisco, CA, US
cloudflare.com

**Numbers in parentheses indicate headcount and % change in 2023.*

Cloudmark Inc. (68, 0.0%)
Network Security /
DNS Security
San Francisco, CA, US
cloudmark.com

Cloudmask (4, 0.0%)
Email Security
Ottawa, ON, Canada
cloudmask.com

Cloudmatos (12, -29.4%)
GRC / Compliance
Management
Livermore, CA, US
cloudmatos.com

Cloudnosys (13, 0.0%)
Operations / Posture
Management
Roswell, GA, US
cloudnosys.com

Cloudrise (56, 3.7%)
MSSP / Security Platform
Management
Grand Junction,
CO, US
cloudrise.com

CloudSEK (166, 4.4%)
Threat Intelligence / Risk
Management
Bangalore, India
cloudsek.com

CloudTruth (15, 25.0%)
Application Security /
Configuration Management
Boston, MA, US
cloudtruth.com

CloudWize (9, 28.6%)
Operations / Cloud Security
Netanya, Israel
cloudwize.io

Coalfire (984, -8.2%)
GRC / Vulnerabilities
Westminster, CO, US
coalfire.com

Coalition (638, 11.0%)
GRC / Cyber Insurance
San Francisco, CA, US
coalitioninc.com

Cobalt (444, -3.3%)
Application Security /
Software Testing For
Security
San Francisco,
CA, US
cobalt.io

Cobwebs (164, 16.3%)
Threat Intelligence /
All Source
New York, NY, US
cobwebs.com

Cocoon Data (23, -17.9%)
Data Security / Secure
Data Sharing
Arlington, VA, US
cocoondata.com

CODA Intelligence
(11, 22.2%)
GRC / Vulnerabilities
Boston, MA, US
codaintelligence.com

Code 42 Software
(294, -32.4%)
Operations / Secure
Backup/Recovery
Minneapolis,
MN, US
code42.com

Code Intelligence
(62, -3.1%)
Application Security
Bonn, Germany
code-intelligence.com

Code-X (16, -5.9%)
Data Security / Shards
Tampa, FL, US
teamcode-x.com

Codean (7, 0.0%)
Application Security /
Code Security
Utrecht, Netherlands
codean.io

Codenotary (17, -26.1%)
Application Security /
SBOM
Bellaire, TX, US
codenotary.com

CodeProof (18, 20.0%)
Application Security /
Mobile Device Security
Bellevue, WA, US
codeproof.com

CodeThreat (8, 33.3%)
Application Security /
SAST
Istanbul, Turkey
codethreat.com

Codified Security
(4, 33.3%)
Application Security / Code
Security
London, United Kingdom
codifiedsecurity.com

Cofense (was Phishme)
(312, -26.4%)
GRC / Defense
Against Phishing
Leesburg, VA, US
cofense.com

Cog (19, 5.6%)
IoT Security / Virtualization
Sydney, Australia
cog.systems

Cognito (12, 20.0%)
Fraud Prevention /
Authentication
Palo Alto, CA, US
cognitohq.com

Cognitum-Software
(11, 0.0%)
IAM
Lower Saxony,
Germany
cognitum-software.com

Cognni (28, 0.0%)
Data Security /
Data Discovery
Tel Aviv, Israel
cognni.ai

CoGuard (5, 25.0%)
GRC / Configuration
Management
Waterloo, ON, Canada
coguard.io

Cohesity (2221, -3.1%)
Data Security
San Jose, CA, US
cohesity.com

Cohesive Networks
(18, 0.0%)
Network Security / Cloud
Tunnels Over IPSec
Chicago, IL, US
cohesive.net

Collax Inc. (6, 20.0%)
Network Security / UTM
Ismaning, Germany
collax.com

ColorTokens (270, -13.5%)
Network Security / Zero
Trust Networking
Santa Clara, CA, US
colortokens.com

Comae Technologies
(5, -16.7%)
Endpoint Security
/ Forensics
San Francisco, CA, US
comae.com

Comcrypto (13, 8.3%)
Email Security /
Secure Email
Chemnitz,
Sachsen, Germany
comcrypto.de

Command Zero (28, 27.3%)
Stealth
Austin, TX, US
cmdzero.io

CommandK.Dev
(13, 85.7%)
Data Security / Secrets
Management
San Francisco, CA, US
commandk.dev

Commfides Norge As
(15, -11.8%)
IAM / Public Key
Infrastructure
Lysaker, Norway
commfides.com

**Numbers in parentheses indicate headcount and % change in 2023.*

Commsec (22, -4.3%)
MSSP / Managed Security Services
Dublin, Ireland
commsec.ie

Commugen (25, 8.7%)
GRC / Risk Management
Tel Aviv, Israel
commugen.com

Communication Devices Inc (10, 25.0%)
Operations / Remote Devices
Boonton, NJ, US
commdevices.com

Communication Security Group (16, -23.8%)
Data Security / Secure Communications
London, United Kingdom
csghq.com

CommuniTake Technologies (17, -10.5%)
Endpoint Security / Mobile Device Security
Yokneam, Israel
communitake.com

CommVault (3022, 3.9%)
Operations / Secure Backup / Recovery
Tinton Falls, NJ, US
commvault.com

Comodo (663, -2.8%)
Data Security / Public Key Infrastructure
Clifton, NJ, US
comodo.com

Compass Security AG (60, -16.7%)
Data Security / Secure Data Sharing
Rapperswil-Jona, Switzerland
compass-security.com

ComplianceCow (20, 53.9%)
GRC
Fremont, CA, US
compliancecow.com

ComplianceRisk (5, 0.0%)
GRC
Dover, NH, US
compliancerisk.io

ComplyCloud (91, 7.1%)
GRC / GDPR
Copenhagen, Denmark
complycloud.com

ComplyUp (4, 0.0%)
GRC / Compliance Management
Tampa, FL, US
complyup.com

Compumatica (19, 0.0%)
Data Security / Secure Remote Access
Uden, Netherlands
compumatica.com

Compuquip (59, 0.0%)
MSSP / SOC
Miami, FL, US
compuquip.com

Comtech (94, 32.4%)
GRC / Credential Security
Reston, VA, US
comtechllc.com

Concentric AI (59, 37.2%)
Data Security / Data Classification
San Jose, CA, US
concentric.ai

ConductorOne (57, 72.7%)
GRC
Portland, OR, US
conductorone.com

Confiant Inc (46, -11.5%)
Endpoint Security / Advertising-related
New York, NY, US
confiant.com

Confidently (28, 211.1%)
GRC / Employee Protection
San Francisco, CA, US
confidently.com

Confluera (7, -46.1%)
Security Analytics / Incident Management
Palo Alto, CA, US
confluera.com

Consistec (31, 14.8%)
Fraud Prevention
Saarland, Germany
consistec.de

Constella Intelligence (143, -16.4%)
Threat Intelligence / Stolen Identities
Los Altos, CA, US
constellaintelligence.com

Containn (4, 0.0%)
Application Security / Container Security
Bay Area, CA, US
containn.com

ContentKeeper (34, -20.9%)
Network Security / Filtering
Braddon, Australia
contentkeeper.com

Continuity (63, 0.0%)
Data Security / Hygiene For Storage
New York, NY, US
continuitysoftware.com

ContraForce (21, 0.0%)
Security Analytics / XDR
Dallas, TX, US
contraforce.com

Contrast Security (304, -22.4%)
Application Security / Software Testing For Security
Los Altos, CA, US
contrastsecurity.com

ControlMap (10, -33.3%)
GRC / Compliance Management
Bellevue, WA, US
controlmap.io

ControlScan (35, -14.6%)
MSSP / Managed Security Services
Alpharetta, GA, US
controlscan.com

Contxt (17, 0.0%)
API Security
London, United Kingdom
bycontxt.com

Convergent Information Security Solutions (7, 16.7%)
MSSP / Managed Security Services
Columbia, SC, US
convergesecurity.com

Conveyor (24, 14.3%)
GRC
San Francisco, CA, US
conveyor.com

Coralogix (295, 30.5%)
Operations / OP - Configuration Management
San Francisco, CA, US
coralogix.com

Cord3 Innovation Inc. (9, 0.0%)
Data Security / Encryption
Ottawa, ON, Canada
cord3inc.com

Core Business Solutions (66, 0.0%)
GRC / CMCC Tools
Lewisburg, PA, US
thecoresolution.com

Core Security (112, 3.7%)
GRC / Vulnerabilities
Roswell, GA, US
coresecurity.com

Corelight (273, -1.8%)
Network Security / Traffic Analysis
San Francisco, CA, US
corelight.com

**Numbers in parentheses indicate headcount and % change in 2023.*

Corellium (53, 23.3%)
Application Security / Virtualization
Boynton Beach, FL, US
corellium.com

Corero Network Security (117, 13.6%)
Network Security / DDoS Defense
Marlborough, MA, US
corero.com

Corgea (4, 0.0%)
Application Security
San Francisco, CA, US
corgea.com

CORL Technologies (81, -22.9%)
GRC
Atlanta, GA, US
corltech.com

Coro (330, 24.5%)
MSSP / SMB Security
New York, NY, US
coro.net

Corrata (8, -20.0%)
Endpoint Security / Mobile Device Security
Blackrock, Ireland
corrata.com

Corsa (27, 8.0%)
Network Security / Zero Trust Networking
Ottawa, ON, Canada
corsa.com

Corsha (34, 54.5%)
API Security
Vienna, VA, US
corsha.com

Corsica Technologies (138, 9.5%)
MSSP / Managed Security Services
Centreville, MD, US
corsicatech.com

Corvid Cyberdefense (24, 20.0%)
MSSP / MDR
Mooresville, NC, US
corvidcyberdefense.com

Cosmian (20, 25.0%)
Data Security
Paris, France
cosmian.com

CoSoSys (156, 0.0%)
Network Security / DLP
Raleigh, NC, US
endpointprotector.com

CounterCraft (48, -21.3%)
Deception
Donostia-San Sebastian, Spain
countercraft.eu

Covered Security (3, -25.0%)
GRC / Security Awareness Training
Boston, MA, US
coveredsecurity.com

CovertSwarm (32, 88.2%)
Operations / Breach And Attack Simulation
London, United Kingdom
covertswarm.com

Covr Security (21, 16.7%)
IAM / Authentication
Sweden
covrsecurity.com

cPacket (119, -4.8%)
Network Security / Traffic Analysis
San Jose, CA, US
cpacket.com

Cranium (32, 166.7%)
GRC / AI Discovery
Short Hills, NJ, US
cranium.ai

Cribl (671, 37.8%)
Operations / Data Process Flow
San Francisco, CA, US
cribl.io

Criptext (8, 0.0%)
Email Security / Secure Email
New York, NY, US
criptext.com

Critical Start (281, 2.9%)
MSSP / MDR
Plano, TX, US
criticalstart.com

Critifence (4, 100.0%)
IoT Security / OT Security
Herzliya, Israel
critifence.com

Crosswire (15, -16.7%)
IAM / Access Security
New York, NY, US
crosswire.io

Crossword Cybersecurity (71, -12.3%)
GRC / Risk Management
London, United Kingdom
crosswordcybersecurity.com

CrowdSec (40, 42.9%)
Network Security / IPS
Paris, France
crowdsec.net

CrowdStrike (7569, 11.8%)
Endpoint Security / EDR
Sunnyvale, CA, US
crowdstrike.com

Crown Sterling (29, 26.1%)
Data Security / Encryption
Newport Beach, CA, US
crownsterling.io

Crypta Labs (13, -7.1%)
Data Security / Encryption
London, United Kingdom
cryptalabs.com

Cryptium (3, 50.0%)
IAM / Authentication
Portland, OR, US
cryptium.com

Crypto International AG (43, 43.3%)
Data Security / Hardware
Steinhausen, Switzerland
crypto.ch

Crypto Quantique (49, 16.7%)
IoT Security / Security For Embedded Systems
Egham, United Kingdom
cryptoquantique.com

Crypto4A Inc. (25, 8.7%)
Data Security / Entropy As A Service
Ottawa, ON, Canada
crypto4a.com

Cryptomathic (102, -1.9%)
Data Security / Key Management
Aarhus, Denmark
cryptomathic.com

Cryptomill Cybersecurity Solutions (21, -22.2%)
Data Security
Toronto, ON, Canada
cryptomill.com

CryptoPhoto (4, 0.0%)
IAM / Authentication
Australia
cryptophoto.com

cryptovision (59, 40.5%)
Data Security / Public Key Infrastructure
Gelsenkirchen, Germany
cryptovision.com

Cryptr (9, -10.0%)
IAM / Authentication
Lille, France
cryptr.co

Cryptshare (57, -1.7%)
Data Security / Secure Data
Freiburg, Germany
cryptshare.com

**Numbers in parentheses indicate headcount and % change in 2023.*

Cryptsoft Pty Ltd. (15, 0.0%)
Data Security / Public Key Infrastructure
Greenslopes, Australia
cryptsoft.com

Cryptyk (10, -9.1%)
Data Security / Secure Storage
Las Vegas, NV, US
cryptyk.io

Crysp (3, 200.0%)
IAM / Authentication
San Francisco, CA, US
crysp.com

Crytica Security (29, 3.6%)
Endpoint Security / Anti-malware
Reno, NV, US
cryticasecurity.com

Csi Tools (7, -36.4%)
IAM / SAP
Herent, Belgium
csi-tools.com

CSIS Security Group (117, 11.4%)
MSSP / MDR
Denmark
csisgroup.com

CSIT Finland Oy (13, 85.7%)
IAM
Helsinki, Finland
csit.fi

CSPi (125, 10.6%)
Network Security / Traffic Analysis
Lowell, MA, US
cspi.com

CTCI (4, 0.0%)
Threat Intelligence / OSINT
Beaverton, OR, US
ctci.ai

CTM360 (92, 55.9%)
Threat Intelligence / Dark Web
Seef, Bahrain
ctm360.com

Cubed Mobile (5, -16.7%)
Endpoint Security / Mobile Device Security
Kibbutz Einat, Drom HaSharon Regional Council, Israel
cubedmobile.com

Cubro (32, -3.0%)
Network Security / Traffic Analysis
Vienna, Austria
cubro.com

Cujo AI (171, 6.9%)
Network Security / Home Security
El Segundo, CA, US
getcujo.com

Culinda (26, 13.0%)
IoT Security / Healthcare
Irvine, CA, US
culinda.io

CultureAI (39, 44.4%)
GRC / Security Awareness Training
Manchester, United Kingdom
culture.ai

Cupp Computing (5, 0.0%)
Endpoint Security
Palo Alto, CA, US
cuppcomputing.com

Cura Software Solutions (85, 9.0%)
GRC / Risk Management
Singapore, Singapore
curasoftware.com

CuriX AG (16, 45.5%)
Operations / Monitoring
Baar, Switzerland
curix.ai

Currentware Inc. (24, 4.3%)
Endpoint Security / Monitoring
Toronto, ON, Canada
currentware.com

Curricula (12, 0.0%)
GRC / Security Awareness Training
Atlanta, GA, US
curricula.com

Curtail (4, -20.0%)
Application Security / Software Development Security
Anaheim, CA, US
curtail.com

Customerxps (236, 5.8%)
Fraud Prevention
Bangalore, India
clari5.com

CY4GATE (132, 5.6%)
Security Analytics / SIEM
Rome, Italy
cy4gate.com

Cyabra (53, 6.0%)
Threat Intelligence / Fake News Defense
Tel Aviv, Israel
cyabra.com

CYAN Network Security (4, 33.3%)
Network Security / Gateways
Vienna, Austria
cyannetworks.com

Cybeats (41, 28.1%)
Application Security / SBOM
Aurora, ON, Canada
cybeats.com

CybelAngel (156, -17.9%)
Operations / Attack Surface Management
Paris, France
cybelangel.com

Cybellum (95, 33.8%)
Endpoint Security / In-Memory Prevention
Tel Aviv, Israel
cybellum.com

Cyber adAPT (23, 0.0%)
Security Analytics / Monitoring
Dallas, TX, US
cyberadapt.com

Cyber Crucible (12, -20.0%)
Security Analytics / Incident Management
Severna Park, MD, US
cybercrucible.com

Cyber Defense Labs (36, -40.0%)
MSSP / Managed Security Services
Dallas, TX, US
cyberdefenselabs.com

Cyber Guru (80, 33.3%)
GRC / Security Awareness Training
Rome, Italy
cyberguru.it

Cyber Observer Ltd. (6, -60.0%)
GRC / Security Management
Caesarea, Israel
cyber-observer.com

Cyber Operations LLC (5, -28.6%)
Operations / Access Security
Pelham, AL, US
cyberoperations.com

CYBER RANGES (54, 35.0%)
Training / Cyber Range
Stafford, VA, US
cyberranges.com

Cyber Reliant (6, 0.0%)
Data Security / Encryption
Annapolis, MD, US
cyberreliant.com

Cyber Risk Aware (6, -14.3%)
GRC / Security Awareness Training
Dublin, Ireland
cyberriskaware.com

Cyber Risk International (3, -40.0%)
GRC / Risk Management
Kinsealy, Ireland
cyberriskinternational.com

**Numbers in parentheses indicate headcount and % change in 2023.*

Cyber Skyline (16, 77.8%)
Training /
Continuous Training
College Park, MD, US
cyberskyline.com

Cybera (20, -25.9%)
Fraud Prevention / Financial Crime
New York, NY, US
cybera.io

CyberArk Software (3188, 15.2%)
IAM / Access Security
Petah Tikva, Israel
cyberark.com

Cyberaware (3, -25.0%)
GRC / Security Awareness Training
Melbourne, Australia
cyberaware.com

Cyberbit (202, -1.5%)
Training / Cyber Range
Ra'anana, Israel
cyberbit.com

CyberCNS (7, -22.2%)
GRC / Vulnerabilities
Surrey, BC, Canada
cybercns.com

CyberconIQ (31, 63.2%)
GRC / Security Awareness Training
York, PA, US
cyberconiq.com

CyberConvoy (18, 0.0%)
MSSP / MDR
New York, NY, US
cyberconvoy.com

CyberCube (117, 11.4%)
GRC / Risk Management
San Francisco, CA, US
cybcube.com

CyberCX (1263, 14.4%)
MSSP / Managed Security Services
Melbourne, Australia
cybercx.com.au

Cybeready (36, 5.9%)
GRC / Defense Against Phishing
Tel Aviv, Israel
cybeready.com

Cybereason (814, -17.4%)
Security Analytics / Incident Management
Boston, MA, US
cybereason.com

CyberEye Research Labs & Security Solutions (15, 0.0%)
GRC / Security Awareness Training
Hyderabad, India
cybereye.io

CyberForza (10, -16.7%)
Endpoint Security / Endpoint Protection
Santa Clara, CA, US
cyberforza.com

CyberFOX (64, 8.5%)
IAM / Access Security
Tampa, FL, US
cyberfox.com

CyberGhost (47, -16.1%)
Network Security / VPN/Proxy
Bucharest, Romania
cyberghostvpn.com

CyberGRX (107, -44.0%)
GRC / Risk Management
Denver, CO, US
cybergrx.com

Cybergym (55, 0.0%)
Training / Cyber Range
Hadera, Israel
cybergym.com

Cyberhaven (116, 22.1%)
Network Security / Monitoring
Boston, MA, US
cyberhaven.io

CyberHive (32, 3.2%)
Network Security / Quantum
Newbury, United Kingdom
cyberhive.com

CyberHoot (5, 0.0%)
GRC / Security Awareness Training
Hampton, NH, US
cyberhoot.com

Cyberint (144, 10.8%)
Threat Intelligence
Petah Tikva, Israel
cyberint.com

Cyberkov (4, 0.0%)
GRC / Risk Management
Kuwait City, Kuwait
cyberkov.com

Cyberlitica (8, -33.3%)
Threat Intelligence / Dark Web
New York, NY, US
cyberlitica.com

Cybermaniacs (18, 20.0%)
GRC / Security Awareness Training
London, United Kingdom
thecybermaniacs.com

CyberMaxx (117, 244.1%)
MSSP / Managed Security Services
Nashville, TN, US
cybermaxx.com

CyberMDX (18, -64.7%)
IoT Security / Healthcare
New York, NY, US
cybermdx.com

Cybernance (4, 0.0%)
GRC / Risk Management
Austin, TX, US
cybernance.com

Cybernet (32, -8.6%)
GRC / Security Manager
Ann Arbor, MI, US
cybernet.com

Cybernite (10, -28.6%)
Email Security / Defense Against Phishing
Tel Aviv, Israel
cybernite.com

CyberOwl (51, 18.6%)
GRC / Risk Management
Birmingham, United Kingdom
cyberowl.io

Cyberpoint (64, 60.0%)
MSSP / SOC
Baku, Azerbaijan
cyberpoint.az

CyberPoint International (3, 0.0%)
Endpoint Security / File Artifact Detection (mostly PS)
Baltimore, MD, US
cyberpointllc.com

CyberProof (377, 20.1%)
MSSP / Managed Security Services
Aliso Viejo, CA, US
cyberproof.com

CyberQP (68, 54.5%)
IAM / Access Security
North Vancouver, Canada
cyberqp.com

CyberReef Solutions (21, -30.0%)
IoT Security / OT Security
Shreveport, LA, US
cyberreef.com

CyberSafe Ltd. (10, 66.7%)
IAM / Access Security
Longford, United Kingdom
cybersafe.com

CyberSafe Software (3, 0.0%)
Data Security / Encryption
Krasnodar, Russia
cybersafesoft.com

Cybersafe Solutions (56, 1.8%)
MSSP / MDR
Jericho, NY, US
cybersafesolutions.com

CyberSaint (43, -20.4%)
GRC / Risk Management
Boston, MA, US
cybersaint.io

**Numbers in parentheses indicate headcount and % change in 2023.*

CyberSecure IPS (10, 25.0%)
Network Security / IPS
Upper Marlboro, MD, US
cybersecureips.com

Cyberseer (10, 11.1%)
MSSP / Threat Intelligence
London, United Kingdom
cyberseer.net

Cybersense (10, 25.0%)
Data Security / Deception
North Rhine-Westphalia, Germany
cybersense.ai

CyberShark (Was Black Stratus) (26, -7.1%)
MSSP / SOC
Piscataway, NJ, US
cybersharkinc.com

CyberSixgill (112, -16.4%)
Threat Intelligence / Dark Web
Netanya, Israel
cybersixgill.com

Cybersmart (69, 13.1%)
GRC / Compliance Management
London, United Kingdom
cybersmart.co.uk

Cyberstanc (9, -35.7%)
Operations
Delaware, OH, US
cyberstanc.com

CYBERTRAP (14, -6.7%)
Deception
Wiener Neustadt, Austria
cybertrap.com

Cyberus Labs (7, 0.0%)
IAM / Authentication
Krakow, Poland
cyberuslabs.com

CyberVadis (89, 7.2%)
GRC / Risk Management
Paris, France
cybervadis.com

Cyberwatch (27, -3.6%)
GRC
Paris, France
cyberwatch.fr

Cyberwrite (14, 0.0%)
GRC / Risk Management
Manhattan, NY, US
cyberwrite.com

Cybexer (40, -14.9%)
Training / Cyber Range
Tallinn, Estonia
cybexer.com

Cyble (185, 58.1%)
Threat Intelligence / Dark Web
Alpharetta, GA, US
cyble.io

Cybonet (27, -12.9%)
Email Security / Sandbox
Matam, Israel
cybonet.com

Cyborg Security (32, 23.1%)
Threat Intelligence / TIP
Orlando, FL, US
cyborgsecurity.com

Cybraics (11, -50.0%)
Security Analytics
Atlanta, GA, US
cybraics.com

Cybral (24, 33.3%)
Operations / Breach And Attack Simulation
Miami, FL, US
cybral.com

Cybrary (213, -13.1%)
GRC / Training
College Park, MD, US
cybrary.it

CybrHawk (11, -8.3%)
Operations / Data Management
Fort Lauderdale, FL, US
cybrhawk.com

Cybriant (24, 0.0%)
MSSP / MDR
Alpharetta, GA, US
cybriant.com

CybSafe (105, -5.4%)
GRC / Security Awareness Training
London, United Kingdom
cybsafe.com

Cyclops (25, 38.9%)
Operations / Data Management
Tel Aviv, Israel
cyclops.security

Cycode (122, 15.1%)
Application Security / Code Security
Tel Aviv, Israel
cycode.com

Cycognito (162, -15.6%)
GRC / Vulnerabilities
Palo Alto, CA, US
cycognito.com

Cycraft (81, 44.6%)
Operations / Incident Management
Taipei City, Banqiao District, Taiwan
cycraft.com

Cycuity (38, 2.7%)
Endpoint Security
San Diego, CA, US
cycuity.com

Cycurity (8, -33.3%)
Security Analytics
Tel Aviv, Israel
cycurity.com

Cydarm (18, -21.7%)
Operations / Incident Management
Docklands, Australia
cydarm.com

Cyder (6, 50.0%)
Data Security / Data Privacy
San Francisco, CA, US
getcyder.com

Cyderes (715, -1.8%)
MSSP / Managed Security Services
Kansas City, MO, US
cyderes.com

Cydome (25, 66.7%)
IoT Security / Maritime Security
Tel Aviv, Israel
cydome.io

CYE (185, 2.2%)
Operations / Breach And Attack Simulation
Herzliya, Israel
cyesec.com

Cyemptive Technologies Inc. (83, 36.1%)
MSSP / Managed Security Services
Snohomish, WA, US
cyemptive.com

Cyera (180, 164.7%)
Data Security / Data Management
Tel Aviv, Israel
cyera.io

CYFIRMA (98, 27.3%)
Threat Intelligence
Oak Park, IL, US
cyfirma.com

CyFlare (42, 61.5%)
MSSP / Managed Security Services
Victor, NY, US
cyflare.com

CYFOX (31, 0.0%)
Security Analytics / XDR
Tel Aviv, Israel
cyfox.com

CyGlass (12, -47.8%)
Security Analytics
Littleton, MA, US
cyglass.com

**Numbers in parentheses indicate headcount and % change in 2023.*

Cygna Labs Corp (80, 56.9%)
GRC / Auditing
Miami Beach, FL, US
cygnalabs.com

CYGNVS (103, 56.1%)
Operations / Crisis Response Platform
Los Altos, CA, US
cygnvs.com

Cyjax (33, 6.5%)
Threat Intelligence
London, United Kingdom
cyjax.com

Cylera (44, 22.2%)
IoT Security / Healthcare
New York, NY, US
cylera.com

CyLock (11, 10.0%)
GRC / Penetration Testing
Roma, Italy
cylock.tech/en/home-en

Cylus (67, -11.8%)
IoT Security / Railway
Tel Aviv, Israel
cylus.com

Cymatic (5, -37.5%)
Security Analytics / Monitoring
Raleigh, NC, US
cymatic.io

Cymotive (197, 0.0%)
IoT Security / Automotive
Tel Aviv, Israel
cymotive.com

Cympire (17, -5.6%)
Training / Cyber Range
Tel Aviv, Israel
cympire.com

Cymulate (237, 2.2%)
Operations / Breach And Attack Simulation
Holon, Israel
cymulate.com

Cynalytica (6, 0.0%)
IoT Security / OT Security
Belfast, United Kingdom
cynalytica.com

Cynamics (31, 6.9%)
Network Security / Traffic Analysis
Peachtree Corners, GA, US
cynamics.ai

CyNation (4, 0.0%)
GRC / Risk Management
London, United Kingdom
cynation.com

CYNC (14, 0.0%)
Operations / Vulnerabilities
Tel Aviv, Israel
cyncsecure.com

Cynergy (11, 10.0%)
Operations / Monitoring
Tel Aviv, Israel
cynergy.app

Cynerio (66, 1.5%)
IoT Security / Healthcare
Ramat Gan, Israel
cynerio.co

Cynet (257, -8.2%)
Operations / APT Discovery
Rishon LeZion, Israel
cynet.com

Cyolo (93, 0.0%)
IAM / Access Security
Tel Aviv, Israel
cyolo.io

Cypago (35, 34.6%)
GRC / Compliance Management
Tel Aviv, Israel
cypago.com

Cyph (3, 0.0%)
Data Security / Secure Collaboration
McLean, VA, US
cyph.com

Cypher.Dog (13, -23.5%)
Data Security / Secure Data Sharing
Wroclaw, Poland
cypher.dog

Cyphere (3, 50.0%)
MSSP / Vulnerabilities
Greater Manchester, GB, United Kingdom
thecyphere.com

Cyral (47, -24.2%)
Data Security / Access Security
Redwood City, CA, US
cyral.com

Cyrebro (150, -5.1%)
MSSP / SOC
Tel Aviv, Israel
cyberhat.com

Cyren (67, -69.0%)
Threat Intelligence / Reputation
McLean, VA, US
cyren.com

Cyrus (28, -45.1%)
Data Security / Personal Cybersecurity
San Francisco, CA, US
cyrus.app

Cyscale (16, -20.0%)
Operations / Posture Management
London, United Kingdom
cyscale.com

CYSEC (50, 13.6%)
Endpoint Security
Lausanne, Vaud, Switzerland
cysec.com

CySight (5, 25.0%)
Network Security / Monitoring
Sydney, Australia
netflowauditor.com

Cysiv (27, -63.5%)
MSSP / SOC
Irving, TX, US
cysiv.com

Cysmo (3, 50.0%)
GRC / Risk Management
Hamburg, Germany
cysmo.de

Cytellix (22, 22.2%)
GRC / MDR
Aliso Viejo, CA, US
cytellix.com

Cytix (8, 166.7%)
Operations / Penetration Testing
Manchester, United Kingdom
cytix.io

CYTRIO (17, -15.0%)
GRC / Rights Management
Boston, MA, US
cytrio.com

Cyturus Technologies (12, 20.0%)
GRC / Risk Management
Addison, TX, US
cyturus.com

CyTwist (19, 35.7%)
Operations / Threat Hunting
Ramat Gan, Israel
cytwist.com

Cyvatar.Ai (26, 13.0%)
MSSP / Full Service
Irvine, CA, US
cyvatar.ai

Cyviation (18, 0.0%)
IoT Security / Trains, Planes, And Tanks
New York, NY, US
cyviation.aero

Cyware (248, -6.1%)
Threat Intelligence / TIP
New York, NY, US
cyware.com

**Numbers in parentheses indicate headcount and % change in 2023.*

Cyxtera Technologies (622, -9.7%)
Network Security / Zero Trust Networking
Coral Gables, FL, US
cyxtera.com

D-Fend Solutions (145, 2.1%)
IoT Security / Drones
Ra'anana, Israel
d-fendsolutions.com

D-ID (123, 95.2%)
IAM / Non-authentication Biometrics
Tel Aviv, Israel
deidentification.co

D-Link Systems (542, 9.1%)
Network Security / UTM
Taipei City, Taiwan
dlink.com

D3 Security (171, 17.9%)
Operations / Incident Management
Vancouver, BC, Canada
d3security.com

Dacoso (139, 10.3%)
MSSP / SOC
Langen, Germany
dacoso.com

Daon (271, 1.1%)
IAM / Assurance
Reston, VA, US
daon.com

Dapple (3, 0.0%)
IAM / Authentication
Centennial, CO, US
dapplesecurity.com

Dark Cubed (10, -58.3%)
Security Analytics / Monitoring
Charlottesville, VA, US
darkcubed.com

DarkBeam (7, -22.2%)
Threat Intelligence
London, United Kingdom
darkbeam.com

DarkInvader (9, 80.0%)
Threat Intelligence / Dark Web
Leeds, United Kingdom
darkinvader.io

DarkLight.ai (19, -20.8%)
Security Analytics
Bellevue, WA, US
darklight.ai

DarkOwl (26, -31.6%)
Threat Intelligence / Dark Web
Denver, CO, US
darkowl.com

DarkScope (8, 300.0%)
Threat Intelligence
Wellington, New Zealand
darkscope.com

Darktrace (2529, 6.4%)
Security Analytics / Incident Management
San Francisco, CA, US
darktrace.com

Darwinium (30, 76.5%)
Fraud Prevention / Monitoring
San Francisco, CA, US
darwinium.com

Dasera (46, 21.1%)
Data Security / Monitoring
Mountain View, CA, US
dasera.com

Dashlane (353, -13.9%)
IAM / Credential Security
New York, NY, US
dashlane.com

Data Encryption Systems (5, 25.0%)
Data Security / DRM
Taunton, United Kingdom
des.co.uk

Data Resolve Technologies (80, -2.4%)
Network Security / Monitoring
Noida, India
dataresolve.com

Data Sentinel (31, -11.4%)
GRC / Risk Management
Concord, Canada
data-sentinel.com

Data Theorem (91, 167.7%)
Application Security / Mobile Device Security
Palo Alto, CA, US
datatheorem.com

Data443 Risk Mitigation (23, 43.8%)
Data Security / Data Management
Morrisville, NC, US
data443.com

DataDog (5821, 14.1%)
Application Security / Logs
New York, NY, US
datadoghq.com

DataDome (179, 21.8%)
Fraud Prevention / Bot Security
New York, NY, US
datadome.co

DataGrail (127, 5.0%)
GRC / Data Privacy
San Francisco, CA, US
datagrail.io

Datakey (ATEK Access Technologies LLC) (11, 22.2%)
IAM / Authentication
Eden Prairie, MN, US
datakey.com

DATAKOM (16, -23.8%)
MSSP / Managed Security Services
Ismaning, Bayern, Germany
datakom.de

DataLocker (55, -3.5%)
Data Security / Secure Storage
Overland Park, KS, US
datalocker.com

Datamasque (15, 36.4%)
Data Security / Data Masking
Auckland, New Zealand
datamasque.com

DataMotion (41, -10.9%)
Email Security
Florham Park, NJ, US
datamotion.com

Datanchor (32, 18.5%)
Data Security / Document Security
Columbus, OH, US
anchormydata.com

DataPassports (9, -52.6%)
Data Security / IRM
Toronto, ON, Canada
datapassports.com

DATASHIELD (24, -17.2%)
MSSP / Managed Security Services
Salt Lake City, UT, US
datashieldprotect.com

Dataships (18, -10.0%)
GRC / Compliance Management
Dublin, Ireland
dataships.io

DataSunrise (117, 10.4%)
Data Security / Database Security
Mercer Island, WA, US
datasunrise.com

Datatron (8, -42.9%)
Operations / AI Operations
San Francisco, CA, US
datatron.com

Datavisor (129, 13.2%)
Fraud Prevention
Mountain View, CA, US
datavisor.com

Datawiza (9, -10.0%)
IAM / Access Security
Santa Clara, CA, US
datawiza.com

**Numbers in parentheses indicate headcount and % change in 2023.*

Datex Inc. (52, 20.9%)
Data Security / DLP
Mississauga, ON,
Canada
datex.ca

Dathena Science (6, -40.0%)
Data Security /
Data Discovery
Singapore, Singapore
dathena.io

Datiphy (13, 8.3%)
GRC / Monitoring
San Jose,
CA, US
datiphy.com

Datto (1193, -31.8%)
Email Security / Microsoft
Norwalk, CT, US
datto.com

Davinsi Labs (68, 21.4%)
MSSP / MDR
Antwerp, Belgium
davinsi.com

Dawizz (9, 0.0%)
Data Security / Data
Discovery
Vannes, France
dawizz.fr

Dazz (107, 40.8%)
Operations / Vulnerabilities
Palo Alto, CA, US
dazz.io

Dcoya (23, 64.3%)
GRC / Defense
Against Phishing
Tel Aviv, Israel
dcoya.com

Ddos-Guard (60, -6.2%)
Network Security /
DDoS Defense
Rostov-na-Donu, Russia
ddos-guard.net

DealRoom (27, -18.2%)
Data Security / Deal Room
Chicago, IL, US
dealroom.net

Debricked (29, -23.7%)
Application Security /
Vulnerabilities
Sweden
debricked.com

Decentriq (34, -2.9%)
Data Security / Secure
Collaboration
Zurich, Switzerland
decentriq.com

Deceptive Bytes (6, 20.0%)
Deception
Holon, Israel
deceptivebytes.com

Decision Focus (54, 46.0%)
GRC / Compliance
Management
Birkerod, Denmark
decisionfocus.com

Dedrone (137, 45.7%)
Network Security / Drones
San Francisco, CA, US
dedrone.com

Deduce (26, -25.7%)
Fraud Prevention /
ATO Defense
Philadelphia, PA, US
deduce.com

Deep Indentity Pte Ltd. (78, 2.6%)
GRC / Access Security
Singapore, Singapore
deepidentity.com

Deep Instinct (271, 0.0%)
Endpoint Security /
Endpoint Machine Learning
New York, NY, US
deepinstinct.com

Deep-Secure (23, 15.0%)
Network Security / Air Gap
Malvern, United Kingdom
deep-secure.com

Deepfactor (40, -2.4%)
Application Security /
Runtime Security
San Jose, CA, US
deepfactor.io

Deepfence (27, -3.6%)
Network Security / IPS
Milpitas, CA, US
deepfence.io

Deepinfo (24, 9.1%)
Operations / Attack Surface
Management
Istanbul, Turkey
deepinfo.com

Deepkeep (20, 66.7%)
Data Security / Safe
AI/ML Data
Tel Aviv, Israel
deepkeep.ai

Deepnet Security (24, 84.6%)
IAM / Identity Management
London, United Kingdom
deepnetsecurity.com

DeepSource (19, -57.8%)
Application Security /
Code Security
San Francisco,
CA, US
deepsource.io

DeepSurface (19, -13.6%)
GRC / Vulnerabilities
Portland, OR, US
deepsurface.com

DeepView (6, 20.0%)
Data Security / Monitoring
London, United Kingdom
deepview.com

deepwatch (395, 7.9%)
MSSP / MDR
Denver, CO, US
deepwatch.com

Defence Intelligence (20, -48.7%)
Operations / Anti-malware
Kanata, ON, Canada
defintel.com

DefendEdge (124, 12.7%)
MSSP / Managed
Security Services
Rosemont, IL, US
defendedge.com

Defendify (26, -3.7%)
GRC
Portland, ME, US
defendify.io

DefenseStorm (103, 0.0%)
GRC / Compliance
Management
Atlanta, GA, US
defensestorm.com

DefensX (21, 16.7%)
Endpoint Security
New York, NY, US
defensx.com

Defentry (17, -15.0%)
Operations / Scanning
Stockholm, Sweden
defentry.com

Defined Networking (11, 10.0%)
Network Security / Zero
Trust Networking
Santa Monica,
CA, US
defined.net

Dekart (9, 125.0%)
Data Security / Encryption
Chisinau, Republic
of Moldova
dekart.com

Dekko Secure (10, 25.0%)
Data Security / Encryption
Sydney, Australia
dekkosecure.com

DeleteMe (110, 74.6%)
Data Security /
Data Removal
Somerville, MA, US
joindeleteme.com

Delinea (956, 21.5%)
IAM / Access Security
Redwood City,
CA, US
delinea.com

Dellfer (11, -26.7%)
IoT Security / Automotive
Novato, CA, US
dellfer.com

**Numbers in parentheses indicate headcount and % change in 2023.*

Delphix (628, 0.2%)
Data Security / Data Management
Redwood City, CA, US
delphix.com

Delta Risk (22360, 2.0%)
MSSP / MDR
San Antonio, TX, US
deltarisk.com

Denexus (46, 2.2%)
GRC / Risk Management
Sausalito, CA, US
denexus.io

Descope (43, 34.4%)
IAM / Authentication
Los Altos, CA, US
descope.com

Detack (13, 0.0%)
IAM / Credential Security
Ludwigsburg, Germany
detack.de

Detectify (128, -25.6%)
Application Security / Scanning
Stockholm, Sweden
detectify.com

Detexian (11, 10.0%)
Operations / Monitoring
Docklands, Australia
detexian.com

DeUmbra (4, 0.0%)
Security Analytics / Visualization
Austin, TX, US
deumbra.com

Device Authority (32, -3.0%)
IAM / Authentication
Reading, United Kingdom
deviceauthority.com

DeviceTotal (12, -14.3%)
IoT Security / Vulnerabilities
Tel Aviv, Israel
devicetotal.com

Devicie (22, 46.7%)
Operations
Sydney, Australia
devicie.com

Devo (675, 4.7%)
Security Analytics / SIEM
Cambridge, MA, US
devo.com

DevOcean Security (22, 15.8%)
Operations
Tel Aviv, Israel
devocean.security

Devolutions (175, 34.6%)
IAM
Quebec, Canada
devolutions.net

DGC (9, -25.0%)
GRC / Vulnerabilities
Flensburg, Germany
dgc.org

DH2i (12, 20.0%)
Network Security / Zero Trust Networking
Fort Collins, CO, US
dh2i.com

Diamond Fortress Technologies (3, -25.0%)
IAM / Authentication
Birmingham, AL, US
diamondfortress.com

Difenda (77, 2.7%)
MSSP / MDR
Oakville, ON, Canada
difenda.com

Dig Security (80, 48.1%)
Data Security / Data Discovery
Tel Aviv, Israel
dig.security

DigiCert (1368, 7.3%)
Data Security / Public Key Infrastructure
Lehi, UT, US
digicert.com

Digify (45, 21.6%)
Data Security / IRM
Singapore, Singapore
digify.com

Digital Confidence Ltd. (4, 0.0%)
GRC / DLP
Tel Aviv, Israel
digitalconfidence.com

Digital Core Design (6, 0.0%)
Data Security / Encryption
Bytom, Poland
dcd.pl

Digital Defense (44, -24.1%)
GRC / Vulnerabilities
San Antonio, TX, US
digitaldefense.com

Digital Envoy (69, 7.8%)
Network Security / Reputation
Peachtree Corners, GA, US
digitalenvoy.net

Digital Guardian (204, -10.5%)
GRC / DLP
Waltham, MA, US
digitalguardian.com

Digital Hands (69, 9.5%)
MSSP / Managed Security Services
Tampa, FL, US
digitalhands.com

Digital Immunity (3, 0.0%)
Endpoint Security / System Hardening
Burlington, MA, US
digitalimmunity.com

Digital Shadows (45, -64.6%)
Threat Intelligence / Dark Web
San Francisco, CA, US
digitalshadows.com

Digital.ai (923, 13.4%)
Endpoint Security / Mobile Device Security
Plano, TX, US
digital.ai

DigitalXRAID (52, 13.0%)
MSSP / Monitoring
Doncaster, South Yorkshire, United Kingdom
digitalxraid.com

Digitronic (11, 22.2%)
Data Security / Encryption
Chemnitz, Sachsen, Germany
digitronic.net

DigitSec (9, 12.5%)
Application Security / Scanning
Seattle, WA, US
digitsec.com

DigitTrade (6, -14.3%)
Data Security
Teutschenthal, Germany
digittrade.de

Diligent (104, -30.7%)
GRC / Risk Management
Vancouver, BC, Canada
wegalvanize.com

Diligent Corporation (2240, -0.3%)
GRC / GRC Platform
New York, NY, US
diligent.com

Diligent eSecurity International (4, 33.3%)
GRC / Monitoring
Atlanta, GA, US
desintl.com

Disconnect (12, -36.8%)
Network Security / VPN / Proxy
San Francisco, CA, US
disconnect.me

Dispel (37, 5.7%)
IoT Security / Remote Devices
Austin, TX, US
dispel.io

**Numbers in parentheses indicate headcount and % change in 2023.*

Dispersive Networks (14, -30.0%)
Network Security / VPN / Proxy
Alpharetta, GA, US
dispersive.io

DisruptOps (6, -25.0%)
Operations / Cloud Security
Kansas City, MO, US
disruptops.com

Ditno (9, -25.0%)
Network Security / Firewalls
Sydney, Australia
ditno.com

Dmarcian (33, 0.0%)
Email Security / Technology Deployment Management
Brevard, NC, US
dmarcian.com

DNIF (65, -1.5%)
Operations / SIEM
Mumbai, India
dnif.it

DNSFilter (161, 30.9%)
Network Security / Filtering
Washington, DC, US
dnsfilter.com

DocAuthority (7, 0.0%)
GRC / DLP
Ra'anana, Israel
docauthority.com

Docker Scout (798, 1.8%)
Application Security / SBOM
San Francisco, CA, US
docker.com

DoControl (71, -5.3%)
Data Security / Access Security
New York, NY, US
docontrol.io

Dojah (21, 0.0%)
Fraud Prevention / Identity Verification
Lagos, Nigera
dojah.io

DomainTools (123, 5.1%)
Threat Intelligence / Threat Intelligence From DNS
Seattle, WA, US
domaintools.com

Domdog (5, 150.0%)
Endpoint Security / Secure Web Browsing
Chennai, India
domdog.io

dope.security (37, 19.4%)
Endpoint Security / Gateways
Mountain View, CA, US
dope.security

Doppler (34, 0.0%)
Data Security / Secrets Management
San Francisco, CA, US
doppler.com

DOSarrest (12, -7.7%)
Network Security / DDoS Defense
BC, Canada
dosarrest.com

Dover Microsystems (10, 11.1%)
IoT Security / Firmware
Waltham, MA, US
dovermicrosystems.com

Dr. Web (245, -8.9%)
Endpoint Security / Anti-virus
Moscow, Russia
drweb.com

DRACOON (97, 19.8%)
Data Security / Secure Data Sharing
Regensburg, Germany
dracoon.com

Dragonfly Cyber (3, 0.0%)
Data Security
San Diego, CA, US
dragonflycyber.com

DragonSoft (21, -19.2%)
Application Security / Firewalls
New Taipei City, Taiwan
dragonsoft.com.tw

Dragos (553, -4.3%)
IoT Security / OT Security
Hanover, MD, US
dragos.com

Drata (552, -10.1%)
GRC / Compliance Management
San Diego, CA, US
drata.com

Drawbridge (98, 27.3%)
GRC / GRC Platform
New York, NY, US
drawbridgeco.com

Dream Security (67, 570.0%)
Network Security
Tel Aviv, Israel
dream-security.com

Dreamlab Technologies (142, 21.4%)
Deception / Managed Security Services
San Isidro, Peru
dreamlab.net

DriveLock (58, 18.4%)
Endpoint Security / DLP
Munich, Germany
drivelock.com

DroneSec (11, -8.3%)
IoT Security / Drones
Melbourne, Victoria, Australia
dronesec.com

Drooms (174, 1.2%)
Data Security / Data Rooms
Frankfurt, Germany
drooms.com

Druva (1220, -1.3%)
Endpoint Security / Secure Secure Backup/Recovery
Sunnyvale, CA, US
druva.com

DryRun Security (6, 500.0%)
Application Security / Software Development Security
Austin, TX, US
dryrun.security

DryvIQ (44, -18.5%)
GRC / Risk Management
Ann Arbor, MI, US
dryviq.com

DTEX Systems (118, 32.6%)
GRC / Insider Threats
San Jose, CA, US
dtexsystems.com

DTonomy (8, 100.0%)
Security Analytics / AI Applied To Alerts
Cambridge, MA, US
dtonomy.com

Dull (11, 22.2%)
IoT Security / Secure Remote Access
Melbourne, Australia
dull.net

DuoKey (7, 0.0%)
Data Security / Encryption
Lausanne, Switzerland
duokey.com

DuoSecurity (now part of Cisco) (641, -11.0%)
IAM / Authentication
Ann Arbor, MI, US
duo.com

DuploCloud Inc. (72, 84.6%)
Application Security / Configuration Management
San Jose, CA, US
duplocloud.com

DuskRise (47, -33.8%)
Network Security / Segmentation
New York, NY, US
duskrise.com

**Numbers in parentheses indicate headcount and % change in 2023.*

DXC Technology (91269, 5.9%)
MSSP / Managed Security Services
Tysons, VA, US
dxc.technology

DynaRisk (19, -13.6%)
GRC / Risk Management
London, United Kingdom
dynarisk.com

Dynatrace (4639, 8.9%)
Application Security / Vulnerabilities
Waltham, MA, US
dynatrace.com

Early Warning (1308, 12.5%)
Fraud Prevention / Assurance
Scottsdale, AZ, US
earlywarning.com

east-tec (7, 16.7%)
Data Security / Data Erasure And Destruction
Oradea, Romania
east-tec.com

EasyDMARC (74, 23.3%)
Email Security / DNS Security
Middletown, DE, US
easydmarc.com

EBRAND (81, 11.0%)
Threat Intelligence / Brand
Leudelange, Luxembourg
ebrand.com

Echosec (6, -79.3%)
Threat Intelligence / Intel Gathering Tool
Victoria, BC, Canada
echosec.net

Echoworx (89, 4.7%)
Email Security / Secure Email
Toronto, ON, Canada
echoworx.com

EclecticIQ (82, -35.4%)
Threat Intelligence / Threat Intelligence Platform
Amsterdam, Netherlands
eclecticiq.com

Eclipz (18, -37.9%)
Data Security / IPSec Tools
Los Gatos, CA, US
eclipz.io

Eclypsium (100, 6.4%)
Endpoint Security / Firmware
Beaverton, OR, US
eclypsium.com

eCyLabs (8, 60.0%)
Application Security / Software Testing For Security
Coimbatore, India
ecylabs.com

EdgeBit (5, 66.7%)
Application Security / SBOM
San Mateo, CA, US
edgebit.io

edgescan (90, 11.1%)
Application Security / Vulnerabilities
Dublin, Ireland
edgescan.com

Edgile (214, -2.7%)
MSSP / Managed Security Services
Austin, TX, US
edgile.com

Edgio (1161, -9.3%)
Network Security / DDoS Defense
Scottsdale, AZ, US
edg.io

EfficientIP (231, -10.5%)
Network Security / DNS Security
West Chester, PA, US
efficientip.com

EFTsure (145, 39.4%)
Fraud Prevention / EFT Protection
North Sydney, Australia
home.eftsure.com.au

EGERIE (144, 63.6%)
GRC / Risk Management
Toulon, France
egerie.eu

Egis Technology (147, -2.6%)
IAM / Authentication
Taipei, Taiwan
egistec.com

Egnyte (1065, 31.3%)
Data Security / Secure Data Sharing
Mountain View, CA, US
egnyte.com

Egress (307, 4.1%)
Email Security
London, United Kingdom
egress.com

Ekco (311, 9.1%)
MSSP / MDR
Dublin, Ireland
ek.co

Ekran System (27, -6.9%)
GRC / Insider Threats
Newport Beach, CA, US
ekransystem.com

Elastic (3751, 8.4%)
Security Analytics / SIEM
Amsterdam, Netherlands
elastic.co

Elba (32, 113.3%)
GRC / Security Awareness Training
Paris, France
elba.security

Elcomsoft (15, 0.0%)
Operations / Forensics
Moscow, Russia
elcomsoft.com

Elemendar (20, 11.1%)
Threat Intelligence / Threat Intelligence Analysis
Stourbridge, NC, United Kingdom
elemendar.com

Elemental Cyber Security (5, 0.0%)
GRC / Vulnerabilities
Dallas, TX, US
elementalsecurity.com

Elephantastic (6, 200.0%)
Security Analytics / Link Analysis
Paris, France
elephantastic.io

Elevate Security (42, -14.3%)
GRC / Security Awareness Training
Berkeley, CA, US
elevatesecurity.com

Elimity (6, 50.0%)
IAM / CIAM
Mechelen, Antwerpen, Belgium
elimity.com

Elisity (69, 27.8%)
IAM / Access Security
Milpitas, CA, US
elisity.com

ELK Analytics (18, 20.0%)
MSSP / Managed Security Services
Naples, FL, US
elkanalytics.com

Elliptic (168, -17.6%)
GRC
London, United Kingdom
elliptic.co

Elysium Analytics (27, 12.5%)
Operations / Security Analytics
Santa Clara, CA, US
elysiumanalytics.ai

***Numbers in parentheses indicate headcount and % change in 2023.**

emproof (13, 18.2%)
IoT Security / Security For Embedded Systems
Eindhoven, Netherlands
emproof.com

Emsisoft (28, 7.7%)
Endpoint Security / Anti-virus
Chicago, IL, US
emsisoft.com

enclaive (9, 50.0%)
Data Security / Confidential Computing
Berlin, Germany
enclaive.io

Enclave Networks (9, -10.0%)
Network Security / Zero Trust Networking
London, United Kingdom
enclave.io

Encode (61, -24.7%)
Security Analytics
London, United Kingdom
encodegroup.com

Encore (10, 0.0%)
Operations / Attack Surface Management
Maidenhead, United Kingdom
encore.io

Endace (89, 7.2%)
Network Security / IDS
Ellerslie, New Zealand
endace.com

Endian (28, 0.0%)
Network Security / UTM
Bolzano, Italy
endian.com

Endor Labs (74, 85.0%)
Application Security / Dependency Management
Palo Alto, CA, US
endorlabs.com

Eneo Tecnologia (9, 50.0%)
Network Security / IPS
Mairena del Aljerafe, Spain
redborder.com

Engage Black (4, -20.0%)
Data Security / Code Security
Aptos, CA, US
engageblack.com

Enginsight (28, 3.7%)
GRC / Vulnerabilities
Jena, Germany
enginsight.com

Enigmatos (11, -8.3%)
IoT Security / Automotive
Yavne, Israel
enigmatos.com

Enigmedia (8, -66.7%)
Data Security / Secure Communications
San Sebastian, Spain
enigmedia.es

Enov8 (29, 7.4%)
Data Security / Data Masking
New South Wales, Australia
enov8.com

Ensighten (28, -17.6%)
Fraud Prevention / Bot Security
Menlo Park, CA, US
ensighten.com

Ensign Infosecurity (722, 20.9%)
MSSP / Managed Security Services
Kuala Lumpur, Malaysia
ensigninfosecurity.com

Enso Security (21, -40.0%)
Application Security / Code Security
Mill Valley, CA, US
enso.security

Ensure Technologies (21, 0.0%)
IAM
Ypsilanti, MI, US
ensuretech.com

Ensurity (28, -6.7%)
IAM / Authentication
Hyderabad, India
ensurity.com

Entersekt (211, 3.4%)
IAM / Authentication
Stellenbosch, South Africa
entersekt.com

Entitle (34, 9.7%)
IAM
New York, NY, US
entitle.io

Entreda (9, -10.0%)
Endpoint Security / Monitoring
Santa Clara, CA, US
entreda.com

Entro Security (24, 71.4%)
Data Security / Secrets Management
Tel Aviv, Israel
entro.security

Enveil (67, -10.7%)
Data Security / Encryption
Washington, DC, US
enveil.com

Envieta (18, -5.3%)
Data Security / Hardware
Columbia, MD, US
envieta.com

Enzoic (19, 0.0%)
Fraud Prevention / Credential Security
Boulder, CO, US
enzoic.com

eperi (26, 8.3%)
Data Security / Encryption
Pfungstadt, Germany
eperi.de

Equiinet (11, 10.0%)
Network Security / UTM
Las Vegas, NV, US
equiinet.com

erika (7, 40.0%)
Email Security / Anti-scam
London, United Kingdom
erika.app

ERMES Cyber Security (48, 23.1%)
Data Security / DLP
Turin, Italy
ermessecurity.com

Ermetic (106, -45.1%)
IAM / Access Security
Tel Aviv, Israel
ermetic.com

ERMProtect (14, -22.2%)
GRC / Security Awareness Training
Coral Gables, FL, US
ermprotect.com

esatus (40, 8.1%)
IAM
Langen, Hessen, Germany
esatus.com

EScan (204, 33.3%)
Endpoint Security / Anti-virus
Mumbai, India
escanav.com

Escape (18, 5.9%)
API Security / API Discovery
Paris, France
escape.tech

eSentire (577, -5.1%)
MSSP / MDR
Cambridge, ON, Canada
esentire.com

ESET (1719, 5.6%)
Endpoint Security / Anti-virus
Bratislava, Slovakia
eset.com

eShard (38, -11.6%)
Testing
Aquitaine, France
eshard.com

**Numbers in parentheses indicate headcount and % change in 2023.*

ESNC (4, 0.0%)
GRC / SAP
Berlin, Germany
esnc.de

ESProfiler (7, 133.3%)
Operations / Security Tool Effectiveness
Manchester, United Kingdom
esprofiler.com

essentry (16, 77.8%)
IAM
Eschborn, Hessen, Germany
essentry.com

ESTsoft (314, 3.3%)
Endpoint Security / Anti-virus
Seoul, South Korea
estsoft.ai

ETHIACK (13, 160.0%)
Application Security / Penetration Testing
Coimbra, Portugal
ethiack.com

Ethoca (171, 4.3%)
Fraud Prevention / Transaction Security
Toronto, ON, Canada
ethoca.com

Ethyca (29, -14.7%)
GRC / Privacy Tools
New York, NY, US
ethyca.com

eureka (38, 11.8%)
Data Security / Data Discovery
Tel Aviv, Israel
eureka.security

EventSentry (4, 0.0%)
Security Analytics / SIEM
Chicago, IL, US
eventsentry.com

EverCompliant (153, -13.6%)
Fraud Prevention / Banking Security
Tel Aviv, Israel
everc.com

Evernym (6, -40.0%)
IAM / Identity Attestation
Herriman, UT, US
evernym.com

Everspin (19, 26.7%)
Endpoint Security / Dynamic Image Replacement
Seoul, South Korea
everspin.global

Everykey (19, 11.8%)
IAM / Authentication
Cleveland, OH, US
everykey.com

Evident ID (69, -19.8%)
IAM / Identity Verification
Atlanta, GA, US
evidentid.com

Evo Security (28, 27.3%)
IAM / Identity Management
Austin, TX, US
evosecurity.com

evolutionQ (32, 45.5%)
Network Security / Quantum
Ontario, Canada
evolutionq.com

Exabeam (760, 5.0%)
Security Analytics / Monitoring
San Mateo, CA, US
exabeam.com

Exacttrak Ltd (8, -11.1%)
Data Security / Managed Devices To Protect Laptop Data
Banbury, United Kingdom
exacttrak.com

eXate (30, -6.2%)
API Security / Monitoring
West End, United Kingdom
exate.com

ExcelSecu (51, -17.7%)
Data Security / Public Key Infrastructure
Shenzhen, China
excelsecu.com

Exein (26, 18.2%)
IoT Security
Rome, Italy
exein.io

Exeon Analytics (37, 42.3%)
Security Analytics / Monitoring
Zurich, Switzerland
exeon.ch

Exium (37, 15.6%)
Network Security / SASE
Palo Alto, CA, US
exium.net

Exodus Intelligence (45, 36.4%)
Application Security / Research
Austin, TX, US
exodusintel.com

Exonar (5, -54.5%)
GRC / Data Discovery
Newbury, United Kingdom
exonar.com

Expanse (33, -8.3%)
GRC / Vulnerabilities
San Francisco, CA, US
expanse.co

Expel (516, 1.0%)
MSSP / SOC
Herndon, VA, US
expel.io

ExpressVPN (266, -7.3%)
Network Security / VPN / Proxy
Tortola, British Virgin Islands
expressvpn.com

ExtraHop Networks (671, 0.6%)
Security Analytics / Incident Management
Seattle, WA, US
extrahop.com

Extreme Networks (3881, 7.8%)
IAM / Access Security
San Jose, CA, US
extremenetworks.com

EY (345449, -1.6%)
MSSP / Managed Security Services
London, United Kingdom
ey.com

Eye Security (99, 32.0%)
MSSP / MDR
Zuid-Holland, Netherlands
eye.security

Eyeonid Group Ab (11, 83.3%)
IAM / Theft
Stockholm, Sweden
eyeonid.com

EYL (4, -81.0%)
Data Security / Quantum
Seoul, South Korea
eylpartners.com

F5 Networks (6174, -3.0%)
Network Security / Firewalls
Seattle, WA, US
f5.com

FaceFirst (65, 109.7%)
Fraud Prevention / Non-authentication Biometrics
Austin, TX, US
FaceFirst.com

FACEKI (15, 0.0%)
IAM
Manama, Al Manamah, Bahrain
faceki.com

Facephi Biometra (261, 17.6%)
IAM / Authentication
Alicante, Spain
facephi.com

FACT360 (12, 9.1%)
Network Security / Monitoring
Waterlooville, United Kingdom
fact360.co

Faddom (37, -22.9%)
Operations / Segmentation
Ramat Gan, Israel
faddom.com

**Numbers in parentheses indicate headcount and % change in 2023.*

Falanx Cyber (48, -2.0%)
MSSP / MDR
Reading, Berkshire, United Kingdom
falanxcyber.com

Faraday (47, 14.6%)
Operations / Manager Of Managers
Miami, FL, US
faradaysec.com

Faronics Technologies Inc. (116, 2.6%)
Endpoint Security
Vancouver, BC, Canada
faronics.com

Farsight Security (17, -15.0%)
Threat Intelligence / Threat Intelligence From DNS
San Mateo, CA, US
farsightsecurity.com

FASOO (105, -3.7%)
GRC / Digital Rights Management
Seoul, South Korea
fasoo.com

Fastly (1279, 12.3%)
Network Security / DDoS Defense
San Francisco, CA, US
fastly.com

FastpassCorp (69, -2.8%)
IAM / Credential Security
Kongens Lyngby, Denmark
fastpasscorp.com

FastPath (109, 13.5%)
GRC / Authorization
Des Moines, IA, US
gofastpath.com

FCI Cyber (128, -22.4%)
MSSP / Device Management
Bloomfield, NJ, US
fcicyber.com

Featurespace (393, -1.3%)
Fraud Prevention
Cambridge, United Kingdom
featurespace.com

Feedly (56, 0.0%)
Threat Intelligence / Feeds
Redwood City, CA, US
feedly.com

Feedzai (582, -20.1%)
Fraud Prevention / Anti-fraud
San Mateo, CA, US
feedzai.com

Feitian Technologies (101, 6.3%)
IAM
Beijing, China
ftsafe.com

Fend Incorporated (9, -10.0%)
IoT Security / Firewalls
Arlington, VA, US
fend.tech

Feroot Security (22, 0.0%)
Application Security / Scanning
Toronto, ON, Canada
feroot.com

Fidelis Cybersecurity (Skyview) (150, -23.9%)
Security Analytics
Bethesda, MD, US
fidelissecurity.com

fidentity (10, 25.0%)
IAM / Identity Verification
Basel, Switzerland
fidentity.ch

Field Effect Software (161, 9.5%)
MSSP / MDR
Ottawa, ON, Canada
fieldeffect.com

FifthDomain (16, -30.4%)
Training / Cyber Range
Canberra, Australia
fifthdomain.com.au

Fijowave (8, -11.1%)
IoT Security / Remote Devices
Dublin, Ireland
fijowave.com

FileCloud (117, 7.3%)
Data Security / IRM
Austin, TX, US
filecloud.com

Fileflex (19, -17.4%)
IAM / Access Security
Toronto, ON, Canada
fileflex.com

FileOpen Systems (7, -36.4%)
Data Security / DRM
Santa Cruz, CA, US
fileopen.com

Filestring (55, 7.8%)
Data Security / IRM
Santa Cruz, CA, US
filestring.com

Filigran (35, 250.0%)
Threat Intelligence
Paris, France
filigran.io

Findings (34, 9.7%)
GRC / Risk Management
New York, NY, US
findings.co

Fingerprint (115, 2.7%)
Fraud Prevention / Device Identification
Chicago, IL, US
fingerprint.com

Fingerprint Cards AB (185, -12.3%)
IAM / Authentication
Gothenburg, Sweden
fingerprints.com

FingerprintJS (115, -21.2%)
Fraud Prevention / Device Characteristics
Chicago, IL, US
fingerprintjs.com

Finite State (58, -10.8%)
IoT Security / Firmware
Columbus, OH, US
finitestate.io

FinLock Technologies (3, -62.5%)
Fraud Prevention / Personal Protection
South Delhi, New Delhi, India
finlock.in

FIRCY (3, 0.0%)
Threat Intelligence / Cloud Security
Adelaide, Australia
fircy.co

Fireblocks (649, 25.5%)
Data Security / Blockchain
New York, NY, US
fireblocks.com

FireCompass (81, 8.0%)
Operations / Attack Surface Management
Boston, MA, US
firecompass.com

FireDome (27, -47.1%)
IoT Security / IoT Security For Device Manufacturers
Tel Aviv, Israel
firedome.io

Firefly (46, 43.8%)
Operations / Asset Management
Tel Aviv, Israel
gofirefly.io

FireMon (235, -8.2%)
Operations / Policy Management
Overland Park, KS, US
firemon.com

FireTail (20, 100.0%)
API Security / Authentication
McLean, VA, US
firetail.io

Firetrust (3, -57.1%)
Email Security / Anti-spam
Christchurch, New Zealand
firetrust.com

**Numbers in parentheses indicate headcount and % change in 2023.*

Firewalla (18, 12.5%)
Network Security / Firewalls
San Jose, CA, US
firewalla.com

Firezone (7, 40.0%)
Network Security / VPN / Proxy
Mountain View, CA, US
firezone.dev

First Watch (18, -5.3%)
IoT Security / OT Security
Hamilton, New Zealand
firstwatchprotect.com

FirstPoint Mobile Guard (17, -34.6%)
Endpoint Security / Mobile Device Security
Netanya, Israel
firstpoint-mg.com

FirstWave (55, 5.8%)
Operations / SOC
North Sydney, New South Wales, Australia
firstwave.com

Fischer International Identity (69, -6.8%)
IAM
Naples, FL, US
fischeridentity.com

Fiverity (21, 10.5%)
Fraud Prevention / Fraud Detection
Boston, MA, US
fiverity.com

FixMeStick (12, -7.7%)
Endpoint Security / Anti-virus
Montreal, QC, Canada
fixmestick.com

Fixnix (39, -9.3%)
GRC / SMB Security
Ashok Nagar, India
fixnix.co

Flare (59, 3.5%)
Operations / Attack Surface Management
Montreal, QU, Canada
flare.systems

Flashpoint (398, 0.0%)
Threat Intelligence / Dark Web
New York, NY, US
flashpoint-intel.com

Fleet (55, 37.5%)
Endpoint Security / Asset Management
San Francisco, CA, US
fleetdm.com

Fletch.AI (69, 187.5%)
Operations / SOC
San Francisco, CA, US
fletch.ai

Flexible IR (6, 0.0%)
Operations / Incident Management
Singapore, Singapore
flexibleir.com

Flow Security (33, 32.0%)
Data Security / Data Flows
Tel Aviv, Israel
flowsecurity.com

Flowmon Networks (65, -5.8%)
Network Security / Monitoring
San Diego, CA, US
flowmon.com

Fluency Security (7, 0.0%)
Security Analytics / SIEM
College Park, MD, US
fluencysecurity.com

Fluid Attacks (156, 34.5%)
Application Security / Scanning
San Francisco, CA, US
fluidattacks.com

Flying Cloud Technology (15, 0.0%)
Data Security / Data Flows
Santa Cruz, CA, US
flyingcloudtech.com

ForAllSecure (42, -22.2%)
Application Security / Software Testing For Security
Pittsburgh, PA, US
forallsecure.com

ForcePoint (2199, -0.1%)
GRC / DLP
Austin, TX, US
forcepoint.com

Foregenix (91, 1.1%)
GRC / Vulnerabilities
Boston, MA, US
foregenix.com

ForeScout Technologies (1048, 3.2%)
Network Security / Access Security
San Jose, CA, US
forescout.com

Foresiet (10, 25.0%)
Threat Intelligence / OSINT
Bangalore, India
foresiet.com

Foresite MSP (63, -14.9%)
MSSP / Managed Security Services
Overland Park, KS, US
foresite.com

ForgeRock (896, -6.1%)
IAM
San Francisco, CA, US
forgerock.com

forghetti (3, 0.0%)
IAM / Credential Security
Winchester, United Kingdom
forghetti.com

Fornetix (49, 8.9%)
Data Security / Key Management
Frederick, MD, US
fornetix.com

Fortanix (273, 28.8%)
Data Security / Confidential Computing
Mountain View, CA, US
fortanix.com

Forter (611, -1.3%)
Fraud Prevention
Tel Aviv, Israel
forter.com

Fortify 24x7 (5, -16.7%)
MSSP / Managed Security Services
Los Angeles, CA, US
fortify24x7.com

FortifyData (19, -36.7%)
GRC / Risk Management
Kennesaw, GA, US
fortifydata.com

Fortifyedge (5, -16.7%)
IAM
Tasmania, Australia
fortifyedge.com

Fortinet (13793, 11.5%)
Network Security / UTM
Sunnyvale, CA, US
fortinet.com

Fortiphyd Logic (6, 0.0%)
IoT Security / OT Security
Norcross, GA, US
fortiphyd.com

FortKnoxster (4, -33.3%)
Data Security / Encryption
Gibraltar, United Kingdom
fortknoxster.com

FortMesa (10, 42.9%)
GRC / Risk Management
Austerlitz, NY, US
fortmesa.com

Fortra (313, -26.7%)
Endpoint Security / ISeries
Eden Prairie, MN, US
fortra.com

Fortress Information Security (248, 6.0%)
GRC / Risk Management
Oralndo, FL, US
fortressinfosec.com

Fortress SRM (53, 1.9%)
MSSP / Managed Security Services
Cleveland, OH, US
fortresssrm.com

ForumSystems (35, 12.9%)
Network Security / Firewalls
Needham, MA, US
forumsys.com

**Numbers in parentheses indicate headcount and % change in 2023.*

Forward Networks (150, 74.4%)
Network Security / Attack Surface Management
Santa Clara, CA, US
forwardnetworks.com

Fossa (72, -19.1%)
Application Security / Vulnerabilities
San Francisco, CA, US
fossa.com

FourCore (9, 28.6%)
Operations / Breach And Attack Simulation
New Delhi, Delhi, India
fourcore.io

Fox IT (424, 11.6%)
MSSP / MDR
Delft, Netherlands
fox-it.com

Foxpass (6, -45.5%)
IAM / Authentication
San Francisco, CA, US
foxpass.com

Fraud.com (28, 7.7%)
Fraud Prevention / Identity Verification
London, United Kingdom
fraud.com

Fraud.net (45, 12.5%)
Fraud Prevention / Fraud Management
New York, NY, US
fraud.net

Fraudlogix (17, -5.6%)
Fraud Prevention
Hallandale Beach, FL, US
fraudlogix.com

Fraudmarc (5, 25.0%)
Fraud Prevention / Email Fraud Prevention
Atlanta, GA, US
fraudmarc.com

Fraugster (9, -87.5%)
Fraud Prevention / Transaction Security
Berlin, Germany
fraugster.com

Freja eID Group AB (Was Verisec) (45, -13.5%)
IAM / Mobile Identity
Stockholm, Sweden
verisec.com

Friendly Captcha (15, 150.0%)
Fraud Prevention / Bot Security
Munich, Germany
friendlycaptcha.com

FRS Labs (23, 9.5%)
Fraud Prevention / Fraud Detection
Bangalore, India
frslabs.com

Fudo Security (56, 12.0%)
IAM / Access Security
Newark, CA, US
fudosecurity.com

Fujitsu (66402, 15.8%)
MSSP / Managed Security Services
Kawasaki-Shi, Japan
fujitsu.com

FullArmor (24, 0.0%)
Network Security / Policy Management
Boston, MA, US
fullarmor.com

FusionAuth (30, 20.0%)
IAM / CIAM
Broomfield, CO, US
fusionauth.io

Futurae (45, -2.2%)
IAM / Authentication
Zurich, Switzerland
futurae.com

FutureX (134, 36.7%)
Data Security / Hardware
Bulverde, TX, US
futurex.com

FYEO (10, -56.5%)
Threat Intelligence / Threat Intelligence From DNS
Denver, CO, US
gofyeo.com

G Data Software (116, -10.8%)
Endpoint Security / Anti-virus
Bochum, Germany
gdata.de

GajShield (72, -4.0%)
Network Security / Firewalls
Mumbai, India
gajshield.com

Galaxkey (33, -5.7%)
Data Security / Secure Data Sharing
London, United Kingdom
galaxkey.com

Garland Technology (49, 16.7%)
IoT Security / Network Taps
Buffalo, NY, US
garlandtechnology.com

Garner Products (22, -18.5%)
Data Security / Data Erasure And Destruction
Roseville, CA, US
garnerproducts.com

Garrison (189, 32.2%)
Network Security / Secure Web Browsing
London, United Kingdom
garrison.com

Gat Labs (17, 0.0%)
GRC / Monitoring
Dublin, Ireland
gatlabs.com

Gatefy (6, -14.3%)
Email Security
Miami, FL, US
gatefy.com

GateKeeper Access (19, 5.6%)
IAM / Authentication
College Park, MD, US
gkaccess.com

GateWatcher (118, 34.1%)
Network Security / Threat Detection
Paris, France
gatewatcher.com

GBMS Tech (16, 0.0%)
Endpoint Security / Monitoring
London, United Kingdom
gbmstech.com

GBS (37, -15.9%)
Data Security
Karlsruhe, Germany
gbs.com

Geetest (64, -8.6%)
IAM / Captchas
Wuhan, China
geetest.com

Gem (65, 225.0%)
Operations / Incident Management
New York, NY, US
gem.security

Gen Digital (2011, 44.0%)
Endpoint Security / Anti-virus
Tempe, AZ, US
gendigital.com

General Dynamics IT (24128, 6.3%)
MSSP / Managed Security Services
Drive Falls Church, VA, US
gdit.com

Genians (7, 0.0%)
IoT Security / Device Fingerprinting
Anyang-si, South Korea
genians.com

genua (226, 14.7%)
Network Security / IoT Security
Kirchheim, Germany
genua.de

GeoEdge (69, -2.8%)
Application Security / Advertising-related
New York, NY, US
geoedge.com

GeoTrust Inc. (31, -16.2%)
Data Security / Encryption
Mountain View, CA, US
geotrust.com

**Numbers in parentheses indicate headcount and % change in 2023.*

GetData Forensics (12, 0.0%)
GRC / Forensics
Kogarah, Australia
forensicexplorer.com

getidee (17, 0.0%)
IAM / Authentication
München, Germany
getidee.com

Getvisibility (51, 34.2%)
Data Security / Data Discovery
Cambridge, MA, US
getvisibility.com

GFI Software (220, -0.9%)
Email Security / Anti-spam
Austin, TX, US
gfi.com

GhangorCloud (20, 53.9%)
GRC / DLP
San Jose, CA, US
ghangorcloud.com

Ghost Security (28, 27.3%)
Application Security / Asset Management
TX, US
ghost.security

Gigamon (1175, 2.7%)
Network Security / Span Port Mirroring
Santa Clara, CA, US
gigamon.com

GigaNetworks (13, 8.3%)
MSSP / Managed Security Services
Miami, FL, US
giganetworks.com

Gita Technologies (41, 5.1%)
Network Security / SIGINT Offensive
Tel Aviv, Israel
gitatechnologies.com

GitGuardian (162, 50.0%)
IAM / Monitoring
Paris, France
gitguardian.com

Github (5327, -0.1%)
Application Security / Vulnerabilities
San Francisco, CA, US
github.com

GitLab (2351, 1.9%)
Application Security / Code Security
San Francisco, CA, US
about.gitlab.com

GK8 (48, 23.1%)
Data Security / Wallets
Tel Aviv, Israel
gk8.io

Glasswall Solutions (129, 30.3%)
Operations / Document Security
West End, United Kingdom
glasswallsolutions.com

GlassWire (3, -40.0%)
Endpoint Security / Firewalls
Austin, TX, US
glasswire.com

GLIMPSE (50, 47.1%)
Operations / Malware Analysis
Cesson-Sevigne, France
glimps.fr

Globalscape (59, -6.3%)
Network Security / Secure Data Sharing
San Antonio, TX, US
globalscape.com

GlobalSign (475, 3.5%)
IAM / Authentication
Portsmouth, NH, US
globalsign.com

Gluu (22, -18.5%)
IAM / Access Security
Austin, TX, US
gluu.org

GM Sectec (166, 32.8%)
MSSP / Managed Security Services
San Juan, Puerto Rico
gmsectec.com

GObugfree AG (20, 0.0%)
Application Security / Hackers For Hire
Zurich, Switzerland
gobugfree.com

Gold Comet (7, 75.0%)
Email Security / Secure Email
Alexandria, VA, US
goldcomet.com

Gold Lock (6, 0.0%)
Data Security / Mobile Device Security
Ramat Gan, Israel
goldlock.com.br

Goldilock (30, 25.0%)
Network Security / Air Gap
London, United Kingdom
goldilock.com

Goldkey (19, -52.5%)
Data Security / Secure Storage
Kansas City, MO, US
goldkey.com

Gomboc (12, 50.0%)
Operations / Configuration Management
New York, NY, US
gomboc.ai

GORISCON (5, 25.0%)
GRC / Compliance Management
Rosenheim, Bayern, Germany
goriscon.de

GoSecure (177, -6.3%)
MSSP / Managed Security Services
Montreal, QC, Canada
gosecure.net

GoTrustID Inc. (16, -15.8%)
IAM / Authentication
Taichung City, Taiwan
gotrustid.com

Gradiant Cyber (46, 15.0%)
GRC / Risk Management
Dallas, TX, US
gradientcyber.com

GrammaTech (65, -52.2%)
Application Security / Code Security
Ithaca, NY, US
grammatech.com

Granite (26, 8.3%)
GRC / Risk Management
Tampere, Finland
granitegrc.com

Graphite Software (3, 0.0%)
Endpoint Security / Container Security
Ottawa, ON, Canada
graphitesoftware.com

Gravitee.io (110, 1.9%)
API Security / Access Security
France
gravitee.io

Gravwell (16, 14.3%)
Security Analytics / Data Analysis
Coeur dAlene, ID, US
gravwell.io

Graylog (108, -4.4%)
Operations / Logs
Houston, TX, US
graylog.org

Great Bay Software (3, 0.0%)
IAM / Access Security
Bloomington, MN, US
greatbaysoftware.com

GreatHorn (23, -41.0%)
Email Security / Defense Against Phishing
Waltham, MA, US
greathorn.com

Green Hills Software (258, 0.4%)
Endpoint Security / Operating System Security
Santa Barbara, CA, US
ghs.com

**Numbers in parentheses indicate headcount and % change in 2023.*

Green Rocket Security Inc. (5, 400.0%)
IAM / Authentication
San Jose, CA, US
greenrocketsecurity.com

Greenview Data (7, 0.0%)
MSSP / Managed Security Services
Ann Arbor, MI, US
greenviewdata.com

Gretel.ai (72, 35.9%)
Data Security / Data Masking
San Diego, CA, US
gretel.ai

GreyCortex (33, 22.2%)
Network Security / Traffic Analysis
Brno, Czech Republic
greycortex.com

Greymatter (37, -26.0%)
API Security
Arlington, VA, US
greymatter.io

GreyNoise (62, 5.1%)
Threat Intelligence / Dark Web
Washington, DC, US
greynoise.io

Grip Security (100, 37.0%)
IAM / Access Security
Tel Aviv, Israel
grip.security

Ground Labs (44, -6.4%)
GRC / Data Discovery
Singapore, Singapore
groundlabs.com

Group-IB (103, -72.9%)
Threat Intelligence / Dark Web
Central Region, Singapore, Singapore
group-ib.com

GroupSense (38, -11.6%)
Threat Intelligence / Dark Web
Arlington, VA, US
groupsense.io

Gsmk Cryptophone (12, -14.3%)
Data Security / Secure Communications
Berlin, Germany
cryptophone.de

GTB Technologies (60, -1.6%)
GRC / Leaked Data
Newport Beach, CA, US
gttb.com

Guardian (10, 100.0%)
Endpoint Security / Firewalls
San Francisco, CA, US
guardianapp.com

Guardian 360 (13, 30.0%)
GRC / Vulnerabilities
Utrecht, Netherlands
guardian360.nl

Guardian Digital Inc. (5, -28.6%)
Endpoint Security / Secure Linux
Midland Park, NJ, US
guardiandigital.com

Guardio (85, 21.4%)
Application Security / Scanning
Tel Aviv, Israel
guard.io

GuardKnox (74, -1.3%)
IoT Security / Automotive
Tel Aviv, Israel
guardknox.com

Guardsquare (149, 16.4%)
Application Security / Mobile Device Security
Leuven, Belgium
guardsquare.com

Guardtime (106, 3.9%)
GRC / Assurance
Tallinn, Estonia
guardtime.com

GuardYoo (6, 0.0%)
GRC / Compromise Assessment
Cork, Ireland
guardyoo.com

Guidepoint Security (869, 25.4%)
MSSP / Managed Security Services
Herndon, VA, US
guidepointsecurity.com

Guidewire (3358, 2.8%)
GRC / Security Ratings
Foster City, CA, US
guidewire.com

GuruCul (200, 25.0%)
Security Analytics
El Segundo, CA, US
gurucul.com

Gutsy (35, 29.6%)
Operations
Tel Aviv, Israel
gutsy.com

Gytpol (33, 57.1%)
GRC / Configuration Management
Tel Aviv, Israel
gytpol.com

H3C (4064, -0.9%)
Network Security / Gateways
Beijing, China
h3c.com

Hack the Box (1620, 36.4%)
Training / Cyber Range
Kent, United Kingdom
hackthebox.eu

HackerOne (4418, 21.4%)
Operations / Research
San Francisco, CA, US
hackerone.com

HackersEye (7, 40.0%)
Training / Cyber Range
Ramat Gan, Israel
hackerseye.net

Hacking Lab (9, 50.0%)
Training / Cyber Range
Rapperswil-Jona, Switzerland
shop.hacking-lab.com

Hackmetrix (58, 11.5%)
GRC / Compliance Management
Santiago, Chile
hackmetrix.com

HackNotice (26, -40.9%)
GRC / Security Awareness Training
Austin, TX, US
hacknotice.com

Hackuity (51, 24.4%)
GRC / Vulnerabilities
Lyon, France
hackuity.io

HacWare (8, -27.3%)
GRC / Security Awareness Training
Brooklyn, NY, US
hacware.com

Hadrian (79, 31.7%)
Operations / Attack Surface Management
Noord-Holland, Netherlands
hadrian.io

Halcyon (105, 72.1%)
Endpoint Security / Ransomware Security
Austin, TX, US
halcyon.ai

HALOCK Security Labs (33, 10.0%)
Operations / Incident Management
Schaumburg, IL, US
halock.com

Halon (32, 23.1%)
Email Security / Anti-spam
Gothenburg, Sweden
halon.io

Haltdos (26, 8.3%)
Network Security / DDoS Defense
Noida, India
haltdos.com

**Numbers in parentheses indicate headcount and % change in 2023.*

HAProxy Technologies (100, 5.3%)
Network Security / Firewalls
Waltham, MA, US
haproxy.com

HarfangLab (85, 49.1%)
Endpoint Security / EDR
Paris, France
harfanglab.io

HashiCorp (2339, -5.4%)
Data Security / Secrets Management
San Francisco, CA, US
hashicorp.com

Havoc Shield (13, 18.2%)
GRC / SMB Security
Chicago, IL, US
havocshield.com

Hawk Network Defense (3, -25.0%)
Security Analytics
Dallas, TX, US
hawkdefense.com

Haystax (42, 27.3%)
Security Analytics / Threat Analysis
McLean, VA, US
haystax.com

HCL Technologies (254393, 15.3%)
MSSP / Managed Security Services
Noida, India
hcltech.com

HDN (16, 0.0%)
Network Security / Security Switches
Guro-gu, South Korea
handream.net

Heimdal Security (281, 48.7%)
Network Security / IPS
Copenhagen, Denmark
heimdalsecurity.com

HENSOLDT Cyber (15, -40.0%)
IoT Security
Taufkirchen, Germany
hensoldt-cyber.com

HEROIC Cybersecurity (25, 19.1%)
Threat Intelligence / Monitoring
Provo, UT, US
heroic.com

Heureka Software (5, -37.5%)
GRC / Data Discovery
Cleveland, OH, US
heurekasoftware.com

Hexagate (12, 500.0%)
IAM / Access Security
Israel
hexagate.com

Hexnode (112, 6.7%)
Endpoint Security / Device Management
San Francisco, CA, US
hexnode.com

heylogin (12, 20.0%)
IAM
Braunschweig, Germany
heylogin.com

HIAsecure (5, 0.0%)
IAM / Authentication
Courbevoie, France
hiasecure.com

Hicomply (16, -20.0%)
GRC / Compliance Management
Durham, United Kingdom
hicomply.com

HID Global (3416, 9.6%)
IAM / Authentication
Austin, TX, US
hidglobal.com

HiddenLayer (78, 271.4%)
Application Security / ML Security
Austin, TX, US
hiddenlayer.com

Hideez (12, 0.0%)
IAM / Hardware
Redwood City, CA, US
hideez.com

HighGround.io (6, 0.0%)
GRC / Compliance Management
Perth, United Kingdom
highground.io

Hillstone Networks (388, 11.2%)
Network Security / Firewalls
Santa Clara, CA, US
hillstonenet.com

Hitachi ID Systems (80, -18.4%)
IAM
Calgary, AB, Canada
hitachi-id.com

Hive Pro (68, 36.0%)
GRC / Vulnerabilities
Milpitas, CA, US
hivepro.com

HOB Networking (40, 17.6%)
Network Security / VPN/Proxy
Cadolzburg, Germany
hob.de

Holm Security (62, -19.5%)
Network Security / Vulnerabilities
Stockholm, Sweden
holmsecurity.com

Hook Security (26, 52.9%)
GRC / Security Awareness Training
Greenville, SC, US
hooksecurity.co

Hoplite Industries (15, 7.1%)
Operations / Security Alerts
Bozeman, MT, US
hopliteindustries.com

Hopr (8, 0.0%)
Operations / Key Rotation
Columbia, MD, US
hopr.co

Hopzero (9, 0.0%)
Network Security / Hop Minimization
Austin, TX, US
hopzero.com

Horangi (115, -14.8%)
Network Security / Vulnerabilities
Singapore, Singapore
horangi.com

Horizon3.ai (111, 3.7%)
Network Security / Penetration Testing
San Francisco, CA, US
horizon3.ai

Hornetsecurity (346, 11.6%)
Email Security / Managed Security Services
Hannover, Germany
hornetsecurity.com

Hoxhunt (142, -7.8%)
GRC / Security Awareness Training
Helsinki, Finland
hoxhunt.com

Huawei (174232, 0.5%)
Network Security / Firewalls
Shenzhen, China
huawei.com

HUB Security (141, -11.3%)
Data Security / Encryption
Tel Aviv, Israel
hubsecurity.com

Hubble Technology (19, 5.6%)
Operations / Asset Management
Reston, VA, US
hubble.net

Hudson Rock (5, 0.0%)
Threat Intelligence / Leaked Data
Tel Aviv, Israel
hudsonrock.com/

**Numbers in parentheses indicate headcount and % change in 2023.*

Human (481, 17.3%)
Fraud Prevention /
Bot Security
New York, NY, US
humansecurity.com

Human Presence (8, -33.3%)
Network Security /
Bot Security
Greenville, SC, US
humanpresence.io

Humio (40, -37.5%)
Security Analytics / Logs
London, United Kingdom
humio.com

Humming Heads (9, 125.0%)
Endpoint Security /
Application Whitelisting
Tokyo, Japan
hummingheads.co.jp

Hunters (216, 42.1%)
Security Analytics / Incident
Management
Tel Aviv, Israel
hunters.ai

Huntress Labs (335, 19.6%)
Operations / Anti-malware
Baltimore, MD, US
huntresslabs.com

Huntsman (22, 10.0%)
Security Analytics / SIEM
Chatswood, Australia
huntsmansecurity.com

Hushmail (256, 0.4%)
Data Security / Secure
Communications
Vancouver, BC, Canada
hushmail.com

Hushmesh (9, 50.0%)
Data Security / Key
Management
Falls Church, VA, US
hushmesh.com

Hyas (43, -23.2%)
Threat Intelligence /
Attribution Intelligence
Victoria, BC, Canada
hyas.com

Hyperproof (150, 48.5%)
GRC / Compliance
Management
Bellevue, WA, US
hyperproof.io

Hypersecu Information Systems (7, 0.0%)
IAM / OTP
BC, Canada
hypersecu.com

Hypori (114, 2.7%)
Endpoint Security / Device
Management
Austin, TX, US
hypori.com

HYPR (132, -7.7%)
IAM / Authentication
New York, NY, US
hypr.com

Hysolate (7, -22.2%)
Endpoint Security /
Secure Workspace
Tel Aviv, Israel
hysolate.com

I Am I (4, 33.3%)
IAM / Authentication
Markham, Canada
useiami.com

I-Sprint Innovations (104, -0.9%)
IAM
Singapore, Singapore
i-sprint.com

I-Tracing (443, 51.2%)
MSSP / Managed
Security Services
Puteaux, France
i-tracing.com

i2Chain (8, -20.0%)
Data Security
San Francisco, CA, US
i2chain.com

IBM (307605, 1.0%)
MSSP / Managed
Security Services
Armonk, NY, US
ibm.com

iboss (307, 1.3%)
Network Security /
Gateways
Boston, MA, US
iboss.com

Iceberg Cyber (5, 25.0%)
MSSP / Personal Protection
Toronto, ON, Canada
icebergcyber.com

Iconix (23, 4.5%)
Email Security / Sender
Verification
San Jose, CA, US
iconix.com

ICsec (29, 0.0%)
IoT Security / OT Security
Poznan, Poland
icsec.pl/en/

ID Agent (20, 5.3%)
Threat Intelligence / Dark
Web
Miami, FL, US
idagent.com

Id Insight (19, 26.7%)
Fraud Prevention / Identity
Verification
Minneapolis,
MN, US
idinsight.com

Id Quantique (110, 5.8%)
Data Security / Quantum
Carouge, Switzerland
idquantique.com

ID R&D Inc. (56, 30.2%)
IAM / Authentication
New York, NY, US
idrnd.net

ID.me (875, -2.7%)
IAM / Credential Security
McLean, VA, US
id.me

idappcom (6, 0.0%)
Network Security / Traffic
Analysis
Ludlow,
United Kingdom
idappcom.com

Idax Software (5, 25.0%)
IAM
Petersfield, United Kingdom
idaxsoftware.com

ideaBOX (4, 0.0%)
MSSP
New Rochelle, NY, US
ideabox.com

IDECSI (31, 14.8%)
Email Security / Auditing
Paris, France
idecsi.com

IDEE (17, 0.0%)
IAM / Identity Platform
Munich, Germany
getidee.com

Idemeum (10, 11.1%)
IAM / Access Security
Palo Alto, CA, US
idemeum.com

IDEMIA (12850, 10.6%)
IAM / Identity Augmentation
Reston, VA, US
idemia.com

IDENprotect (18, 63.6%)
IAM / Authentication
London, United Kingdom
idenprotect.com

Identiq (59, -7.8%)
IAM / Identity Validation
Tel Aviv, Israel
identiq.com

Identite (43, -21.8%)
IAM / Authentication
Clearwater, FL, US
identite.us

Identity Automation (83, -17.0%)
IAM / Identity Management
Houston, TX, US
identityautomation.com

Identity Science (8, 60.0%)
Application Security /
Software Development
Security
Sunnyvale, CA, US
identityscience.ai

**Numbers in parentheses indicate headcount and % change in 2023.*

IdentityLogix (3, 0.0%)
IAM / Access Security
Crown Point, IN, US
identitylogix.com

Identitypass (20, -16.7%)
IAM / Identity Verification
Lagos, Nigera
myidentitypass.com

Identiv (277, 9.5%)
IAM / Credential Security
Fremont, CA, US
identiv.com

Identos Inc. (60, 9.1%)
IAM / Mobile Identity
Toronto, ON, Canada
identos.com

IdenTrust (part of HID Global) (66, -1.5%)
Data Security / Public Key Infrastructure
Fremont, CA, US
identrust.com

IDENTT (38, 0.0%)
IAM
Wroclaw, Poland
identt.pl

Idera (270, 1.5%)
GRC / Compliance Management
Houston, TX, US
idera.com

IDmelon Technologies Inc. (12, 71.4%)
IAM
Vancouver, BC, Canada
idmelon.com

IDnow (321, 6.6%)
Fraud Prevention / Identity Verification
Munich, Bayern, Germany
idnow.io

IDology (184, 85.9%)
IAM / Authentication
Atlanta, GA, US
idology.com

IdRamp (4, 0.0%)
IAM / Authentication
Indianola, IA, US
idramp.com

idwall (361, -10.2%)
Fraud Prevention / Fraud Detection
Sao Paulo, Brazil
idwall.co

IDX (71, -27.6%)
GRC / Data Privacy
Portland, OR, US
idx.us

IGLOO Software (125, -9.4%)
GRC / Security Management
Kitchener, ON, Canada
igloosoftware.com

Ikarus Security Software GmbH (45, 21.6%)
Endpoint Security / Anti-virus
Vienna, Austria
ikarussecurity.com

Ilantus (175, -8.4%)
IAM / Identity Management
Schaumburg, IL, US
ilantus.com

Illumio (591, 2.2%)
Endpoint Security / Monitoring
Sunnyvale, CA, US
illumio.com

Illuria Security (5, -16.7%)
Deception
Yerevan, Armenia
illuriasecurity.com

illusive Networks (58, -55.4%)
Deception
New York, NY, US
illusivenetworks.com

illustria.io (14, 27.3%)
Application Security / Code Security
Tel Aviv, Israel
illustria.io

ImageWare (47, -17.5%)
IAM / Authentication
San Diego, CA, US
iwsinc.com

Immersive Labs (329, -0.3%)
Training / Cyber Range
Bristol, United Kingdom
immersivelabs.com

Immunant (5, 25.0%)
Application Security / Code Security
Irvine, CA, US
immunant.com

Immunefi (86, 43.3%)
Application Security / Bugs
Cascais, Portugal
immunefi.com

Immunity (27, -18.2%)
GRC / Vulnerabilities
Miami, FL, US
immunityinc.com

Immuniweb (34, 3.0%)
Application Security / Scanning
Geneva, Switzerland
immuniweb.com

Immuta (265, -8.6%)
Data Security / Access Security
College Park, MD, US
immuta.com

Impart Security (16, 128.6%)
API Security
Los Angeles, CA, US
impart.security

Imperva (1751, 3.1%)
Network Security / Firewalls
Redwood Shores, CA, US
imperva.com

Imprivata (1058, 36.2%)
IAM
Lexington, MA, US
imprivata.com

InBay Technologies (8, -33.3%)
IAM / Authentication
Kanata, ON, Canada
inbaytech.com

incident.io (84, 100.0%)
Operations / Slack Automation
London, United Kingdom
incident.io

Incode (340, 17.6%)
IAM / Identity Management
San Francisco, CA, US
incode.com

Incognia (178, 23.6%)
Fraud Prevention / Authentication
Palo Alto, CA, US
incognia.com

InCyber (3, 0.0%)
Operations / Monitoring
Cherry Hill Township, DE, US
incyber1.com

Indeni (28, -22.2%)
Operations / Automation
San Francisco, CA, US
indeni.com

Indusface (155, 0.7%)
Network Security / Firewalls
Vodadora, India
indusface.com

Industrial Defender (43, -2.3%)
IoT Security
Foxborough, MA, US
industrialdefender.com

IndyKite (54, -3.6%)
IAM / Identity Management
San Francisco, CA, US
indykite.com

Infineon (37071, 17.6%)
IAM / Smart Card Solutions
Neubiberg, Germany
infineon.com

**Numbers in parentheses indicate headcount and % change in 2023.*

InfiniDome (27, 8.0%)
IoT Security / Automotive
Caesarea, Israel
infinidome.com

Infinipoint (21, -25.0%)
Endpoint Security /
Device Identity
Tel Aviv, Israel
infinipoint.io

Infinite Convergence Solutions (110, 7.8%)
Data Security / Secure
Communications
Arlington Heights,
IL, US
infinite-convergence.com

Infiot (5, -44.4%)
Network Security / Secure
Remote Access
San Jose, CA, US
infiot.com

Infisical (9, 12.5%)
Data Security / Secrets
Management
San Francisco, CA, US
infisical.com

Infobay (10, 0.0%)
Data Security / Secure
Data Sharing
Petah Tikva, Israel
infobaysec.com

Infoblox (2186, 4.7%)
Network Security /
DNS Security
Santa Clara,
CA, US
infoblox.com

Infodas (157, 11.3%)
Network Security /
Air Gap
Cologne, Germany
infodas.com

InfoExpress Inc. (30, -31.8%)
IAM / Access Security
Santa Clara,
CA, US
infoexpress.com

Infopercept (136, 46.2%)
MSSP / MDR
Ahmedabad, Gujarat, India
infopercept.com

Infor (20055, 3.7%)
GRC / Monitoring
New York, NY, US
infor.com

Informatica (5720, -4.9%)
Data Security / Data Masking
Redwood City, CA, US
informatica.com

Information Security Corporation (21, 16.7%)
Data Security / Public Key
Infrastructure
Oak Park, IL, US
infoseccorp.com

Informer (15, -11.8%)
GRC / Attack Surface
Management
London, United Kingdom
informer.io

Infosec Global (35, 2.9%)
Data Security / Public Key
Infrastructure
North York, ON, Canada
infosecglobal.com

Infosequre (12, 20.0%)
GRC / Security
Awareness Training
Hilversum, Netherlands
infosequre.com

Infosys (324937, 7.1%)
MSSP / Managed
Security Services
Bangalore, India
infosys.com

Infowatch (193, -3.0%)
GRC / DLP
Moscow, Russia
infowatch.com

InGate (19, 0.0%)
Network Security / Firewalls
Sundbyberg, Sweden
ingate.com

Inigo (12, 50.0%)
API Security /
GraphQL Security
Palo Alto, CA, US
inigo.io

Inky (48, -11.1%)
Email Security / Defense
Against Phishing
Rockville, MD, US
inky.com

Innefu Labs Pvt Ltd. (190, 31.9%)
Operations /
Security Analytics
New Delhi, India
innefu.com

Innosec (16, 33.3%)
GRC / DLP
Hod HaSharon, Israel
innosec.com

Inpher (33, 13.8%)
Data Security / Data Privacy
New York, NY, US
inpher.io

InPhySec (42, -32.3%)
MSSP / Managed
Security Services
Wellington,
New Zealand
inphysecsecurity.com

Inpixon (128, -39.9%)
Network Security / Rogue
Wifi AP Location
Palo Alto,
CA, US
inpixon.com

InQuest (30, 15.4%)
Data Security / DLP
Arlington,
VA, US
inquest.net

Inseqr (12, 0.0%)
Network Security / VPN /
Proxy
Warszawa,
Poland
inseqr.pl/en/

Inside-Out Defense (6, 0.0%)
IAM / Access Security
Palo Alto, CA, US
insideoutdefense.com

Insignary (6, -25.0%)
Application Security /
Vulnerabilities
Seoul, South Korea
insignary.com

Inspeere (8, 100.0%)
Data Security / Secure
Backup / Recovery
Poitiers, France
inspeere.com

Inspira Enterprise (1557, 8.9%)
MSSP / MDR
Mumbai, India
inspiraenterprise.com

Insside Informacion (104, 16.9%)
GRC / GRC Platform
Madrid, Spain
insside.net

Insta DefSec Oy (643, -13.0%)
Network Security / VPN /
Proxy
Tampere, Finland
insta.fi

Instasafe (81, 11.0%)
Network Security /
Gateways
Bangalore,
India
instasafe.com

Intego Inc. (56, 16.7%)
Network Security /
Firewalls
Seattle, WA, US
intego.com

Integrated Corporation (19, 171.4%)
IAM
Sheungwan, Hong Kong
integrated.com

**Numbers in parentheses indicate headcount and % change in 2023.*

Integrity360 (357, 89.9%)
MSSP / MDR
Dublin, Ireland
integrity360.com

Intel 471 (157, 6.1%)
Threat Intelligence / Threat Actor Intelligence
Amsterdam, Netherlands
intel471.com

Inteligensa (125, 9.7%)
IAM / Smart Card Solutions
Caracas, Venezuela
inteligensa.com

Intelligent Waves (206, 21.2%)
Network Security / Secure Web Browsing
Reston, VA, US
intelligentwaves.com

IntelliGRC (18, 38.5%)
GRC / GRC Platform
Fairfax, VA, US
intelligrc.com

IntelliSystems (29, 11.5%)
MSSP / Managed Security Services
Augusta, GA, US
intellisystems.com

Intensity Analytics (9, -10.0%)
IAM / Monitoring
Warrenton, VA, US
intensityanalytics.com

Interface Masters Technologies (60, -17.8%)
Network Security / IPS
San Jose, CA, US
interfacemasters.com

Interguard (6, 0.0%)
Operations / Monitoring
Westport, CT, US
interguardsoftware.com

Interlink Networks (5, 0.0%)
IAM
Ann Arbor, MI, US
interlinknetworks.com

Internet 2.0 (14, -17.6%)
Network Security / UTM
Alexandria, VA, US
internet2-0.com

Interos (229, -16.7%)
GRC / Risk Management
Arlington, VA, US
interos.ai

Interpres Security (26, 136.4%)
Operations / Attack Surface Management
Bethesda, MD, US
interpressecurity.com

Intertrust Technologies (197, 0.5%)
IoT Security / Public Key Infrastructure
Sunnyvale, CA, US
intertrust.com

Intezer (42, -6.7%)
Operations / Runtime Security
New York, NY, US
intezer.com

Intigriti (422, 11.9%)
Testing / Penetration Testing
Antwerp, Belgium
intigriti.com

Intrinsic-ID (45, 2.3%)
IAM / Authentication
Sunnyvale, CA, US
intrinsic-id.com

Intruder (70, 59.1%)
GRC / Vulnerabilities
London, United Kingdom
intruder.io

Intrusion Inc. (55, -19.1%)
Network Security / IDS
Richardson, TX, US
intrusion.com

Intsights (45, -43.0%)
Threat Intelligence / Dark Web
New York, NY, US
intsights.com

Invicti Security (318, -17.0%)
Application Security / Scanning
Austin, TX, US
invicti.com

Invisiron - Cyber Defence Fortified (8, -11.1%)
Network Security / Firewalls
Singapore, Singapore
invisiron.com

InvizBox (4, -33.3%)
Network Security / VPN / Proxy
Dublin, Ireland
invizbox.com

inWebo (5, -91.4%)
IAM / Authentication
Paris, France
inwebo.com

Ioetec (6, 0.0%)
IoT Security / Endpoint Protection
Sheffield, United Kingdom
ioetec.com

iomart (392, 9.5%)
MSSP / Managed Security Services
Glasgow, United Kingdom
iomart.com

Ion Channel (4, -69.2%)
Application Security / SBOM
Washington, DC, US
ionchannel.io

Ionburst (8, 0.0%)
Data Security
Edinburgh, Scotland
ionburst.io

IONIX (83, 38.3%)
GRC / Attack Surface Management
Kirkland, WA, US
cyberpion.com

Ionu (3, 0.0%)
Data Security / Data Management
Los Gatos, CA, US
ionu.com

IoT Secure (10, 25.0%)
IoT Security / Asset Management
Duluth, GA, US
iotsecure.io

IPification (26, -13.3%)
IAM
Hong Kong
ipification.com

IPQualityScore (33, 200.0%)
Fraud Prevention / IP Intelligence
Las Vegas, NV, US
ipqualityscore.com

IProov (201, 16.2%)
IAM / Authentication
London, United Kingdom
iproov.com

IPV Security (19, -13.6%)
MSSP / Monitoring
Ra'anana, Israel
ipvsecurity.com

IPVanish (7, -12.5%)
Network Security / VPN / Proxy
Dallas, TX, US
ipvanish.com

Iraje (61, 17.3%)
IAM / Access Security
Mumbai, India
iraje.com

Irdeto (1094, 5.8%)
IoT Security / Entertainment Systems
Hoofddorp, Netherlands
irdeto.com

Iris Analytics Gmbh (47, 34.3%)
Fraud Prevention
Urbar, Germany
iris.de

Iris Network Systems (19, 11.8%)
Network Security / Traffic Analysis
Alpharetta, GA, US
irisns.com

**Numbers in parentheses indicate headcount and % change in 2023.*

IriusRisk (167, 11.3%)
Application Security / Scanning
Cuarte, Spain
iriusrisk.com

IRM Security (46, -25.8%)
GRC / Risk Management
Cheltenham, United Kingdom
irmsecurity.com

Ironblocks (14, 40.0%)
Data Security / Blockchain
Tel Aviv, Israel
ironblocks.com

Ironchip Telco (29, 20.8%)
IAM / Identity Management
Barakaldo, Spain
ironchip.com

IronNet Cybersecurity (84, -55.8%)
Network Security / Traffic Analysis
Fulton, MD, US
ironnet.com

IronScales (138, -13.8%)
GRC / Defense Against Phishing
Tel Aviv, Israel
ironscales.com

IronVest (25, 0.0%)
IAM / Authentication
New York, NY, US
ironvest.com

Ironwifi (3, -25.0%)
IAM / Authentication
Orlando, FL, US
ironwifi.com

Ironwood Cyber (19, -13.6%)
MSSP / Scanning
Fort Worth, TX, US
ironwoodcyber.com

IS Decisions (43, 4.9%)
IAM / Access Security
Bidart, France
isdecisions.com

IS3 (opens as Stopzilla) (26, 13.0%)
Endpoint Security / Anti-virus
Dover, DE, US
stopzilla.com

ISARA (18, -47.1%)
Data Security / Encryption
Waterloo, ON, Canada
isara.com

ISARR (8, 60.0%)
GRC / Asset Management
London, United Kingdom
isarr.com

Island (413, 163.1%)
Network Security / Secure Web Browsing
Dallas, TX, US
island.io

Isovalent (157, 52.4%)
Endpoint Security / Container Security
Mountain View, CA, US
isovalent.com

IStorage (27, 0.0%)
Data Security / Hardware
Perivale, United Kingdom
istorage-uk.com

ITC Secure Networking (97, -14.9%)
MSSP / Managed Security Services
London, United Kingdom
itcsecure.com

ITConcepts (36, 0.0%)
IAM
Bonn, Germany
itconcepts.net

iTrust (83, 36.1%)
GRC / Vulnerabilities
Labege, France
itrust.fr

ITsMine (24, -4.0%)
Data Security / Secure Storage
Rishon Lezion, Israel
itsmine.io

ITUS Security echnologies (4, 0.0%)
MSSP / Managed Security Services
Letterkenny, Ireland
itus-tech.com

itWatch (17, -5.6%)
Endpoint Security / DLP
Munich, Germany
itwatch.info

Ivanti (3050, -1.3%)
Endpoint Security / Endpoint Management
South Jordan, UT, US
ivanti.com

IVPN (8, -20.0%)
Network Security / VPN / Proxy
Gibraltar, United Kingdom
ivpn.net

iWelcome (10, -23.1%)
IAM / Identity Management
Amersfoort, Netherlands
iwelcome.com

IXDen (12, -7.7%)
Data Security
Tel Aviv, Israel
ixden.com

iZOOlogic (22, 69.2%)
Threat Intelligence
London, United Kingdom
izoologic.com

Jamf (2746, 3.6%)
Endpoint Security / Device Management
Minneapolis, MN, US
jamf.com

Janusnet (9, 12.5%)
Data Security / Data Classification
Milsons Point, Australia
janusnet.com

Jemurai (8, 0.0%)
Operations / Security Program Dashboard
Chicago, IL, US
jemurai.com

Jetico Inc. Oy (14, -6.7%)
Data Security / Encryption
Espoo, Finland
jetico.com

JetPatch (14, -17.6%)
Operations / Patch Management
Boston, MA, US
jetpatch.com

Jetstack (36, -32.1%)
Operations
United Kingdom
jetstack.io

JFrog (1567, 15.1%)
Application Security / Software Development Security
Sunnyvale, CA, US
jfrog.com

Jimber (20, -16.7%)
Network Security / Secure Web Browsing
Oostkamp, Belgium
jimber.io

Jio Security (60073, -2.8%)
Endpoint Security / Anti-virus
Navi Mumbai, India
jio.com

Jiran (44, -2.2%)
GRC / DLP
Daejeon, South Korea
jiran.com

Jit.io (64, 42.2%)
Application Security / Open Source Tools
Tel Aviv, Israel
jit.io

JOESecurity (8, 14.3%)
Operations / Malware Analysis
Reinach, Switzerland
joesecurity.org

**Numbers in parentheses indicate headcount and % change in 2023.*

Jscrambler (100, 8.7%)
Application Security / Code Security
San Francisco, CA, US
jscrambler.com

Jumio (714, -22.2%)
Fraud Prevention / Identity Verification
Palo Alto, CA, US
jumio.com

Jumpcloud (697, 5.9%)
IAM / Directory Services
Louisville, CO, US
jumpcloud.com

Juniper Networks (11835, 5.1%)
Network Security / Firewalls
Sunnyvale, CA, US
juniper.net

JupiterOne (141, -25.8%)
Operations / Posture Management
Morrisville, NC, US
jupiterone.com

K2 Cyber Security (10, 0.0%)
Application Security
San Jose, CA, US
k2io.com

K7Computing (416, 5.6%)
Endpoint Security / Anti-virus
Sholinganallur, India
k7computing.com

KabaCorp (5, 400.0%)
Endpoint Security / Secure Web Browsing
Boston, MA, US
kabacorp.com

Kameleon Security (5, 0.0%)
Endpoint Security
Mountain View, CA, US
kameleonsec.com

Kandji (315, -4.3%)
Endpoint Security / Device Management
San Diego, CA, US
kandji.io

Karamba Security (44, 10.0%)
IoT Security / Automotive
Hod HaSharon, Israel
karambasecurity.com

Kasada (113, 15.3%)
Fraud Prevention / Bot Security
Sydney, Australia
kasada.io

Kaseya (4862, 95.1%)
IAM / Authentication
New York, NY, US
kaseya.com

Kaspersky (3901, 3.4%)
Endpoint Security / Anti-virus
Moscow, Russia
kaspersky.com

Kaymera (33, -17.5%)
Endpoint Security / Mobile Device Security
Herzliya, Israel
kaymera.com

Kayran (10, 11.1%)
Application Security / Penetration Testing
Nitsanei Oz, Israel
kayran.io

Kazuar Advanced Technologies Ltd (37, 0.0%)
Endpoint Security / Dual Use Laptops
Tel Aviv, Israel
kazuar-tech.com

KeeeX (9, 12.5%)
Data Security / Document Security
Marseille, France
keeex.me

Keep Aware (12, 200.0%)
Endpoint Security
Austin, TX, US
keepaware.co

Keeper Security (347, -7.2%)
IAM / Credential Security
Chicago, IL, US
keepersecurity.com

Keepnet Labs (42, 23.5%)
Email Security
London, United Kingdom
keepnetlabs.com

KeepSafe (22, 10.0%)
Data Security / Encryption
San Francisco, CA, US
getkeepsafe.com

KEEQuant (16, 45.5%)
Data Security / Quantum
Fürth, Germany
keequant.com

Kela Group (106, 12.8%)
Threat Intelligence / Dark Web
Tel Aviv, Israel
ke-la.com

Kenna Security (rebranded from Risk I/O) (46, -25.8%)
GRC / Feeds
San Francisco, CA, US
kennasecurity.com

Kernelios (68, 23.6%)
Training
Rishon LeZion, Israel
kernelios.com

Ketch (93, 20.8%)
GRC / Compliance Management
San Francisco, CA, US
ketch.com

KETS Quantum Security (29, 20.8%)
Data Security / Secure Communications
Bristol, United Kingdom
kets-quantum.com

Keyavi (41, -2.4%)
Data Security / IRM
Denver, CO, US
keyavi.com

KeyCaliber (13, -23.5%)
GRC / Asset Inventory
Washington, DC, US
keycaliber.com

Keyfactor (416, 12.4%)
Data Security / Public Key Infrastructure
Independence, OH, US
keyfactor.com

Keyless (60, -3.2%)
IAM / Authentication
London, United Kingdom
keyless.io

Keypair (10, 42.9%)
IAM / Indentities
Gangnam-gu, South Korea
keypair.co.kr

Keysight (was Ixia) (522, -6.6%)
Network Security / Visibility
Calabasas, CA, US
keysight.com

Keytalk - Pki Management Solutions (5, -16.7%)
Data Security / Public Key Infrastructure
Amersfoort, Netherlands
keytalk.com

Keytos Security (7, 16.7%)
IAM / Authentication
Boston, MA, US
keytos.io

KinectIQ (14, 27.3%)
IAM / Encryption
Woodbury, MN, US
knectiq.com

Kingston Technology (1496, 11.3%)
Data Security / Secure Storage
Fountain Valley, CA, US
kingston.com

**Numbers in parentheses indicate headcount and % change in 2023.*

Kintent (70, -6.7%)
GRC / Compliance Management
Boston, MA, US
kintent.com

Kion (80, 33.3%)
GRC / Compliance Management
Fulton, MD, US
kion.io

Kiteworks (239, 6.7%)
Data Security / IRM
Palo Alto, CA, US
kiteworks.com

Kiuwan (29, 0.0%)
Application Security / Code Security
Houston, TX, US
kiuwan.com

klearis (4, 0.0%)
Data Security / Content Disarm And Reconstruction
Ankara, Turkey
klearis.com

kloudle (11, -21.4%)
Operations / OP - Configuration Management
Wilmington, DE, US
kloudle.com

KnowBe4 (1856, 4.9%)
GRC / Security Awareness Training
Clearwater, FL, US
knowbe4.com

Kobalt (24, 60.0%)
MSSP / Managed Security Services
Vancouver, BC, Canada
kobalt.io

KOBIL Systems (179, 20.1%)
IAM / Authentication
Worms, Germany
kobil.com

Kodem (38, 81.0%)
Application Security / Runtime Security
Tel Aviv, Israel
kodemsecurity.com

Kolide (35, 25.0%)
Endpoint Security / Slack Community For Security Updates
Somerville, MA, US
kolide.com

Kondukto (23, 9.5%)
Application Security
Istanbul, Turkey
kondukto.io

Konduto (73, -17.1%)
Fraud Prevention / Fraud Detection
Sao Paulo, Brazil
konduto.com

Konika Minolta (519, 7.2%)
MSSP / Managed Security Services
Mississauga, Canada
konicaminolta.ca

KoolSpan (33, 10.0%)
Data Security / Secure Communications
Bethesda, MD, US
koolspan.com

Kount (265, 0.4%)
Fraud Prevention / Identity Verification
Boise, ID, US
kount.com

Kovrr (42, -2.3%)
GRC / Risk Management
London, United Kingdom
kovrr.com

KPMG (230145, -0.4%)
MSSP / Managed Security Services
New York, NY, US
kpmg.com

Kratikal Tech (138, 7.8%)
GRC / Risk Management
Noida, India
kratikal.com

Kriptone (4, 300.0%)
GRC / Monitoring
Navsari, India
kriptone.com

Kriptos (50, 16.3%)
Data Security / Data Classification
Sausalito, CA, US
kriptos.io

Kroll (5960, 9.9%)
MSSP / Risk Management
New York, NY, US
kroll.com

Kryptus (130, 8.3%)
Data Security / Hardware
Campinas Sao Paulo, Brazil
kryptus.com

KSOC (36, 5.9%)
Endpoint Security / Kubernetes Security
San Francisco, CA, US
ksoc.com

Kyber Security (16, -5.9%)
MSSP / Managed Security Services
Fairfield, CT, US
kybersecure.com

Kymatio (18, -14.3%)
GRC / Security Awareness Training
Madrid, Spain
kymatio.com

KYND (46, 53.3%)
GRC / Risk Management
London, United Kingdom
kynd.io

LABRADOR LABS (16, 14.3%)
Application Security / Code Security
Seoul, South Korea
labradorlabs.ai

Labris Networks (42, 75.0%)
Network Security / UTM
Ankara, Turkey
labrisnetworks.com

Labyrinth (13, 0.0%)
Deception / Decoy Hosts
Zabrze, Poland
labyrinth.tech

Lacework (823, -15.8%)
Application Security / Cloud Security
Mountain View, CA, US
lacework.com

Laika (185, -7.5%)
GRC / Compliance Management
New York, NY, US
heylaika.com

Lakera (30, 0.0%)
Data Security / AI Data Security
Zürich, Switzerland
lakera.ai

Laminar (74, -12.9%)
Data Security / Data Discovery
New York, NY, US
lmnr.io

Lansweeper (323, 19.6%)
Operations / Asset Management
Dendermonde, Belgium
lansweeper.com

Lasso Security (19, 0.0%)
Data Security
Israel
lasso.security

LastLine (VMware) (8, -27.3%)
Threat Intelligence / IoC Intelligence
Redwood City, CA, US
lastline.com

**Numbers in parentheses indicate headcount and % change in 2023.*

LastPass (704, 16.0%)
IAM / Credential Security
Fairfax, VA, US
lastpass.com

Lastwall (26, 36.8%)
IAM / Access Security
Mountain View, CA, US
lastwall.com

Lavabit (132, -1.5%)
Email Security /
Secure Email
Dallas, TX, US
lavabit.com

LayerX (28, 40.0%)
Endpoint Security / Secure
Web Browsing
Tel Aviv, Israel
layerxsecurity.com

LeakSignal (8, 33.3%)
API Security / Leaked Data
Menlo Park, CA, US
leaksignal.com

Leanear (8, 0.0%)
Data Security /
Cloud Security
Paris, France
leanear.io

LeapFILE (6, 0.0%)
Data Security / Secure
Data Sharing
Cupertino, CA, US
leapfile.com

LeapYear Technologies (5, -86.5%)
Data Security / Analyze
Private Information
Berkeley, CA, US
leapyear.ai

Ledger (732, 0.1%)
Data Security / Wallets
Paris, France
ledger.com

Legit Security (79, 12.9%)
GRC / Risk Management
Palo Alto, CA, US
legitsecurity.com

Lepide (157, -4.8%)
GRC / Data Discovery
Austin, TX, US
lepide.com

LetsDefend (52, 40.5%)
Training / Cyber Range
Sterling, VA, US
letsdefend.io

Libraesva (35, 25.0%)
Email Security
Lecco, Italy
libraesva.com

Licel (15, 25.0%)
Application Security /
Mobile Device Security
Los Angeles, CA, US
licelus.com

LifeRaft (85, 3.7%)
Threat Intelligence /
Monitoring
Halifax, NS, Canada
liferaftinc.com

Lightspin (41, -29.3%)
Application
Security / Software
Development Security
Tel Aviv, Israel
lightspin.io

LimaCharlie/Refraction Point (21, 40.0%)
Network Security / SASE
Walnut, CA, US
limacharlie.io

Link11 (59, 31.1%)
Network Security /
DDoS Defense
Frankfurt, Germany
link11.de

Liopa (13, 44.4%)
IAM / Authentication
Belfast, United Kingdom
liopa.ai

Live Action (138, -13.8%)
Network Security / NDR
Palo Alto, CA, US
liveaction.com

Liverton Security (18, 20.0%)
Email Security / Gateways
Wellington, New Zealand
livertonsecurity.com

Living Security (68, -16.1%)
GRC / Security
Awareness Training
Austin, TX, US
livingsecurity.com

LMNTRIX (47, 56.7%)
MSSP / MDR
Orange, CA, US
lmntrix.com

LocateRisk (18, 28.6%)
GRC / Risk Management
Darmstadt, Germany
locaterisk.com

Locknet Managed IT (53, 8.2%)
MSSP / Managed Security
Services
Onalaska, WI, US
locknetmanagedit.com

LogDog (8, 0.0%)
Data Security
Tel Aviv, Israel
getlogdog.com

LogicGate (271, 3.4%)
GRC
Chicago, IL, US
logicgate.com

LogicHub (17, -55.3%)
Operations / Incident
Management
Mountain View, CA, US
logichub.com

LoginID (45, -6.2%)
IAM / Authentication
San Mateo, CA, US
loginid.io

LoginRadius (154, 12.4%)
IAM / CIAM
San Francisco,
CA, US
loginradius.com

LoginTC (8, -11.1%)
IAM / Authentication
Kanata, ON, Canada
logintc.com

LogMeIn (1337, -19.8%)
IAM / Credential Security
Boston, MA, US
logmein.com

Logmeonce (8, -20.0%)
IAM / Identity Management
McLean, VA, US
LogmeOnce.com

LogPoint (290, -6.2%)
Security Analytics / SIEM
Copenhagen, Denmark
logpoint.com

LogRhythm (544, -11.4%)
Security Analytics / Logs
Boulder, CO, US
logrhythm.com

Logsign (65, -13.3%)
Security Analytics / SIEM
Istanbul, Turkey
logsign.com

Logstail (3, 0.0%)
Security Analytics / Logs
Athens, Greece
logstail.com

Logz.io (184, -17.1%)
Security Analytics / Logs
Boston, MA, US
logz.io

Longbow Security (31, 0.0%)
GRC / Vulnerabilities
Austin, TX, US
longbow.security

Lookingglass Cyber Solutions (102, -37.0%)
Threat Intelligence
Reston, VA, US
lookingglasscyber.com

Lookout (830, -9.6%)
Endpoint Security / Mobile
Device Security
San Francisco, CA, US
lookout.com

**Numbers in parentheses indicate headcount and % change in 2023.*

Loop Secure (27, -41.3%)
MSSP / Managed Security Services
Melbourne, Australia
loopsec.com.au

LSoft Technologies (7, 0.0%)
Data Security / Data Erasure And Destruction
Mississauga, ON, Canada
lsoft.net

Lucent Sky (3, 0.0%)
Application Security / Code Security
San Francisco, CA, US
lucentsky.com

Lucidum (20, 11.1%)
Operations / Asset Management
San Jose, CA, US
lucidum.io

LUCY Security (20, -25.9%)
GRC / Defense Against Phishing
Zug, Switzerland
lucysecurity.com

Lumifi Cyber (69, 35.3%)
MSSP / MDR
Scottsdale, AZ, US
lumificyber.com

Lumu Technologies (121, 12.0%)
Security Analytics / Incident Management
Doral, FL, US
lumu.io

Lunio (71, 14.5%)
Fraud Prevention / Advertising-related
Chorley, Lancashire, United Kingdom
ppcprotect.com

Lupovis (10, -16.7%)
Deception / Network Decoys
Glasgow, Scotland
lupovis.io

Lux Scientiae (43, 0.0%)
Data Security / Secure Communications
Medfield, MA, US
luxsci.com

Lynx Software Technologies (91, 3.4%)
Endpoint Security / Container Security
San Jose, CA, US
lynx.com

Lynx Tech (68, 7.9%)
Fraud Prevention / Monitoring
London, United Kingdom
lynxtech.com

M2Sys Technology (86, -8.5%)
IAM / Authentication
Atlanta, GA, US
m2sys.com

MacKeeper (80, -9.1%)
Endpoint Security / Anti-virus
London, United Kingdom
kromtech.com

Macmon (53, 8.2%)
Network Security / Access Security
Berlin, Germany
macmon.eu

Mage (Was Mentis) (91, 12.3%)
Data Security / Data Masking
New York, NY, US
magedata.ai

MagicCube (28, -22.2%)
IAM / Transaction Security
Santa Clara, CA, US
magiccube.co

Magnet Forensics (566, 23.6%)
Operations / Forensics
Waterloo, ON, Canada
magnetforensics.com

Maidsafe (19, 0.0%)
Data Security / Blockchain
Ayr, United Kingdom
maidsafe.net

Mailchannels (17, 6.2%)
Email Security / SMTP Relay
Vancouver, BC, Canada
mailchannels.com

MailCleaner (4, 0.0%)
Email Security
Saint-Sulpice, Switzerland
mailcleaner.net

Mailfence (6, 0.0%)
Email Security / Secure Email
Brussels, Belgium
mailfence.com

MailInBlack (106, 20.4%)
Email Security / Anti-spam
Marseille, France
mailinblack.com

Mailprotector (42, 5.0%)
Email Security / Managed Security Services
Greenville, SD, US
mailprotector.com

Mailshell (8, 14.3%)
Email Security / Anti-spam
San Francisco, CA, US
mailshell.com

Make IT Safe (15, -25.0%)
GRC / Auditing
Rezé, France
makeitsafe.fr

Mako Networks Ltd. (70, 9.4%)
MSSP / Managed Security Services
Elgin, IL, US
makonetworks.com

Maltego Technologies (130, 32.6%)
Operations / Maltego Enhancement
Munich, Germany
maltego.com

Maltiverse (9, 0.0%)
Threat Intelligence / IoC Intelligence
Madrid, Spain
maltiverse.com

Malware Patrol (8, 14.3%)
Threat Intelligence / Feeds
Sao Paulo, Brazil
malwarepatrol.net

Malwarebytes (768, -12.4%)
Endpoint Security / Anti-virus
Santa Clara, CA, US
malwarebytes.org

Mammoth Cyber (31, 34.8%)
Network Security / Secure Web Browsing
Palo Alto, CA, US
mammothcyber.com

Managed Methods (37, 23.3%)
GRC / Access Security
Boulder, CO, US
managedmethods.com

ManageEngine (Zoho Corp.) (300, 55.4%)
GRC / Security Management
Pleasanton, CA, US
manageengine.com

Mandiant (1394, 4.2%)
Security Analytics / XDR
Milpitas, CA, US
mandiant.com

Manifest (13, 44.4%)
Application Security / SBOM
Remote, OR, US
manifestcyber.com

Mantis Networks (6, 0.0%)
Network Security / Visibility
Reston, VA, US
mantisnet.com

Mantix4 (4, 0.0%)
Security Analytics / Threat Hunting
Englewood, CO, US
mantix4.com

**Numbers in parentheses indicate headcount and % change in 2023.*

Mantra (621, 15.9%)
IAM / Authentication
Ahmedabad, India
mantratec.com

Markany (96, 28.0%)
Data Security / DRM
Seoul, South Korea
markany.com

MarkMonitor (178, 3.5%)
Threat Intelligence / Brand
San Francisco, CA, US
markmonitor.com

Marvell (7744, -3.9%)
Data Security / Hardware
Santa Clara, CA, US
marvell.com

Masergy (684, 3.5%)
MSSP / Managed Security Services
Plano, TX, US
masergy.com

Material Security (107, 87.7%)
Email Security / ATO Prevention
Redwood City, CA, US
material.security

Materna Virtual Solution (102, 21.4%)
Data Security / Secure Communications
Munich, Germany
virtual-solution.com

MATESO (11, -63.3%)
IAM / Credential Security
Neusäß, Germany
passwordsafe.com

Matrix42 (384, 9.4%)
Endpoint Security / EDR
Paris, France
matrix42.com

Mattermost (158, -31.0%)
Operations / Incident Management
Palo Alto, CA, US
mattermost.com

Max Secure Software (75, 2.7%)
Endpoint Security / Endpoint Protection
Pune, India
maxpcsecure.com

Maxmind (80, 27.0%)
Fraud Prevention / Geolocation
Waltham, MA, US
maxmind.com

Maxxsure (32, 6.7%)
GRC / Risk Management
Richardson, TX, US
maxxsure.com

MazeBolt Technologies (35, 2.9%)
Testing / DDoS Defense
Ramat Gan, Israel
mazebolt.com

MB Connect Line (20, -20.0%)
IoT Security / Firewalls
Germany
mbconnectline.com

McAfee (5641, -6.0%)
Endpoint Security / Anti-virus
Santa Clara, CA, US
mcafee.com

MDaemon Technologies (34, -2.9%)
Network Security / Gateways
Grapevine, TX, US
altn.com

MeasuredRisk (21, -8.7%)
GRC / Risk Management
Arlington, VA, US
measuredrisk.com

Medcrypt (59, 68.6%)
IoT Security / Healthcare
Encinitas, CA, US
medcrypt.co

Media Sonar (15, -11.8%)
Threat Intelligence / TIP
London, ON, Canada
mediasonar.com

MediGate (106, -6.2%)
IoT Security / Healthcare
Tel Aviv, Israel
medigate.io

MegaplanIT (28, -3.5%)
MSSP / Managed Security Services
Scottsdale, AZ, US
megaplanit.com

Mend (293, -16.5%)
Application Security / Open Source Security And License Management
Giv'atayim, Israel
whitesourcesoftware.com

Mender (39, 69.6%)
IoT Security / Linux Devices
Palo Alto, CA, US
mender.io

Menlo Security (380, -11.8%)
Network Security / Secure Web Browsing
Palo Alto, CA, US
menlosecurity.com

Merit (258, 69.7%)
IAM
Sunnyvale, CA, US
merits.com

Merlincryption (5, 0.0%)
Data Security / Encryption
Austin, TX, US
MerlinCryption.com

Merox (7, -12.5%)
Network Security / DNS Security
Montpellier, France
merox.io

Mesh (16, 128.6%)
Email Security
Sandyford, Dublin, Ireland
meshsecurity.io

Mesh Security (15, 25.0%)
Operations / Posture Management
Tel Aviv, Israel
mesh.security

MessageSolution Inc. (17, -10.5%)
GRC / Email Archiving
Milpitas, CA, US
messagesolution.com

Messageware (11, 0.0%)
Email Security / OWA Security
Mississauga, ON, Canada
messageware.com

METABASE Q (94, 27.0%)
GRC / Compliance Management
San Francisco, CA, US
metabaseq.com

MetaCompliance (197, 13.9%)
GRC / Compliance Management
London, United Kingdom
metacompliance.com

Metascan (6, 0.0%)
GRC / Scanning
Moscow, Russia
metascan.ru

Meterian (12, 33.3%)
Application Security / Open Source Management
North Kensington, United Kingdom
meterian.io

Metmox (106, -22.6%)
MSSP / SOC
Schaumburg, IL, US
metmox.com

Metomic (52, 73.3%)
Data Security / Data Discovery
Liverpool, United Kingdom
metomic.io

MetricStream (1385, -5.3%)
GRC
Palo Alto, CA, US
metricstream.com

**Numbers in parentheses indicate headcount and % change in 2023.*

Mezmo (115, -25.8%)
Security Analytics / Logs
Mountain View, CA, US
mezmo.com

Mi-Token (63, 0.0%)
IAM / Authentication
Austin, TX, US
mi-token.com

Micro Focus (5742, -40.3%)
Security Analytics / SIEM
Newbury,
United Kingdom
microfocus.com

MicroSec (35, -16.7%)
IoT Security / OT Security
Central Region, Singapore,
Singapore
usec.io

Microsec.AI (35, -18.6%)
Operations / Posture
Management
Santa Clara, CA, US
microsec.ai

Microsoft (224857, -1.4%)
IAM
Redmond, WA, US
microsoft.com

MicroStrategy (3405, -2.0%)
IAM / Mobile Identity
Tysons Corner,
VA, US
microstrategy.com

Mideye (6, 200.0%)
IAM / Authentication
Espoo, Finland
mideye.com

Mimecast (2355, 7.7%)
Email Security / Microsoft
London, United Kingdom
mimecast.com

Minded Security UK Limited (32, 14.3%)
Endpoint Security /
Anti-malware
Rome, Italy
mindedsecurity.com

Mindflow (33, 83.3%)
Operations / SOAR
Paris, France
mindflow.io

MindoLife (8, -11.1%)
Network Security / IDS
Haifa, Israel
mindolife.com

Mindshift (9, 50.0%)
GRC / Security Awareness
Training
Aotearoa, New Zealand
mindshift.kiwi

Mine (58, 70.6%)
GRC / Compliance
Management
Tel Aviv, Israel
saymine.com

Minerva Labs (10, -66.7%)
Endpoint Security /
Ransomware Security
Petah Tikva, Israel
minerva-labs.com

miniOrange (293, 148.3%)
IAM / Authentication
Pune, India
miniorange.com

Mira Security (19, -5.0%)
Network Security / Traffic
Analysis
Cranberry Township,
PA, US
mirasecurity.com

MIRACL (20, -13.0%)
IAM / Authentication
London, United Kingdom
miracl.com

Miradore (60, -18.9%)
Endpoint Security / Device
Management
Vantaa, Finland
miradore.com

Mirato (27, 8.0%)
GRC / Risk Management
Tel Aviv, Israel
mirato.com

Mission Secure (30, -23.1%)
IoT Security / OT Security
Charlottesville, VA, US
missionsecure.com

Mission: Cybersecurity (7, 0.0%)
Training / Security
Awareness Training
Ruda Slaska, Poland
misjacyber.pl/en/

Mithril Security (17, -15.0%)
Data Security / AI
Training Security
Paris, France
mithrilsecurity.io

Mitiga (84, 1.2%)
MSSP / Incident Management
Tel Aviv, Israel
mitiga.io

Mitigant (14, 55.6%)
Operations / Posture
Management
Potsdam, Brandenburg,
Germany
mitigant.io

MixMode (81, 47.3%)
Operations / Forensics
San Diego, CA, US
mixmode.ai

MMOX (6, 0.0%)
MSSP / SMB Security
The Hague, Netherlands
mmox.co

Mnemonic (383, 17.1%)
MSSP / MDR
Oslo, Norway
mnemonic.no

Mobb (25, 38.9%)
Application Security /
Vulnerabilities
Acton, MA, US
mobb.ai

Mobbeel (22, 22.2%)
IAM / Authentication
Caceres, Spain
mobbeel.com

Mobile Helix (3, 0.0%)
Data Security / Encryption
Mountain View, CA, US
mobilehelix.com

Mobiledit (Was Compelson Labs) (24, 33.3%)
GRC / Forensics
Prague, Czech Republic
mobiledit.com

MobileHop (8, 33.3%)
Network Security / VPN /
Proxy
Los Angeles, CA, US
mobilehop.com

Mobolize (13, -13.3%)
Network Security / Mobile
Wireless Protection
Santa Monica, CA, US
mobolize.com

Mocana Corporation (29, 7.4%)
Application Security /
Mobile Device Security
Sunnyvale, CA, US
mocana.com

Mode (21, 250.0%)
Data Security / Quantum
Calgary, Canada
mode.io

Moderne (33, 37.5%)
Application Security
Miami, FL, US
moderne.io

Modulo (182, 9.0%)
GRC
Rio de Janeiro, Brazil
modulo.com

Monad (36, 50.0%)
GRC / Vulnerabilities
San Francisco, CA, US
monad.security

Monarx (18, 5.9%)
Network Security / Webshell
Detection And Blocking
Cottonwood Heights, UT, US
monarx.com

**Numbers in parentheses indicate headcount and % change in 2023.*

Mondoo (40, 25.0%)
GRC / Risk Management
San Francisco, CA, US
mondoo.io

Moresec (49, 0.0%)
Application Security / Scanning
Hangzhou, China
moresec.cn

Morphisec (126, -17.6%)
Endpoint Security / Obfuscation
Be'er Sheva, Israel
morphisec.com

Mosaic451 (25, -58.3%)
MSSP / SOC
Phoenix, AZ, US
mosaic451.com

Mostly.AI (61, 3.4%)
Data Security / Data Masking
Vienna, Wien, Austria
mostly.ai

Msab (279, 10.7%)
Endpoint Security / Forensics
Stockholm, Sweden
msab.com

Msecure Data Labs (13, -7.1%)
Endpoint Security / Anti-virus
Walnut, CA, US
msecuredatalabs.com

Msignia (14, 7.7%)
Data Security / Public Key Infrastructure
Franklin, TN, US
mSIGNIA.com

MTG AG (28, 27.3%)
IoT Security / OT Security
Darmstadt, Germany
mtg.de

Multicert (83, 10.7%)
Data Security / Public Key Infrastructure
Porto Salvo, Portugal
multicert.com

Muninn (39, 56.0%)
Operations / Monitoring
Kongens Lyngby, Denmark
muninn.ai

Mutare (40, -18.4%)
Data Security / Secure Communications
Rolling Meadows, IL, US
mutare.com

My1login (15, 7.1%)
IAM / Identity Management
London, United Kingdom
my1login.com

MyCena (14, 0.0%)
IAM / Credential Security
London, United Kingdom
mycena.co

Mymobilesecurity (4, -20.0%)
Endpoint Security / Mobile Device Security
London, United Kingdom
mymobilesecurity.com

Myntex (9, 0.0%)
Data Security / Secure Communications
Calgary, AL, Canada
myntex.com

Myota (19, 58.3%)
Data Security / IRM
Blue Bell, PA, US
myota.io

MyPermissions (6, -14.3%)
Endpoint Security / Data Privacy
Ramat Gan, Israel
mypermissions.com

Myra Security (60, 5.3%)
Network Security / Web Security
Munich, Germany
myracloud.com

Myrror Security (17, 30.8%)
Application Security / Code Security
Tel Aviv, Israel
myrror.security

MyWorkDrive (10, 0.0%)
Data Security / Secure Storage
San Francisco, CA, US
myworkdrive.com

N-Able (1644, 23.6%)
Endpoint Security
Morrisville, NC, US
n-able.com

Nametag (19, 11.8%)
IAM / Authentication
Seattle, WA, US
getnametag.com

Nanitor (20, 17.6%)
GRC
Iceland
nanitor.com

Nano Corp. (20, 5.3%)
Network Security / Traffic Analysis
Paris, France
nanocorp.fr

Nano Security (3, -25.0%)
Endpoint Security / Anti-virus
Moscow, Russia
nanoav.pro

Nanolock (43, 7.5%)
IoT Security / Automotive
Nitsanei Oz, Israel
nanolocksecurity.com

NanoVMs (8, -27.3%)
Endpoint Security / Container Security
San Francisco, CA, US
nanovms.com

Napatech (94, -3.1%)
Operations / Network Acceleration Cards
Soeborg, Denmark
napatech.com

Navaho Technologies (10, 25.0%)
Endpoint Security / Secure Linux
Brockenhurst, United Kingdom
navaho.co.uk

Naval Dome (8, -27.3%)
IoT Security / Security For Ships
Ra'anana, Israel
navaldome.com

NAVEX (1340, 2.6%)
GRC / GRC Platform
Lake Oswego, OR, US
navex.com

NCP Engineering (18, -5.3%)
Network Security / VPN / Proxy
Mountain View, CA, US
ncp-e.com

Nelysis (11, 37.5%)
IoT Security / Monitoring
Wilmington, DE, US
nelysis.com

Nemassis (Was MicroWorld) (13, 116.7%)
GRC / Vulnerabilities
Novi, MI, US
nemasisva.com

NeoCertified (8, 0.0%)
Email Security / Secure Email
Centennial, CO, US
neocertified.com

neoEYED (3, -57.1%)
IAM / Authentication
Bangalore, India
neoeyed.com

**Numbers in parentheses indicate headcount and % change in 2023.*

Net Protector Antivirus (121, 18.6%)
Endpoint Security / Anti-virus
Karvenagar, India
npav.net

Netacea (72, -28.7%)
Fraud Prevention / Bot Security
Manchester, United Kingdom
netacea.com

Netcraft (167, 29.5%)
GRC / Compliance Management
Bath, United Kingdom
netcraft.com

Netdeep (6, 20.0%)
Network Security / Firewalls
Brazil
netdeep.com.br

Netenrich (885, 3.1%)
Operations / Logs
San Jose, CA, US
netenrich.com

NetFlow Logic (5, -16.7%)
Network Security / Traffic Analysis
Atherton, CA, US
netflowlogic.com

Netfoundry (78, 8.3%)
Network Security / Zero Trust Networking
Charlotte, NC, US
NetFoundry.io

Netgate (126, 37.0%)
Network Security
Austin, TX, US
netgate.com

Nethone (106, 2.9%)
Fraud Prevention / Anti-fraud
Warsaw, Poland
nethone.com

Netlib (4, 0.0%)
Data Security
Stamford, CT, US
netlibsecurity.com

NetLinkz (24, 100.0%)
Network Security / Zero Trust Networking
Sydney, Australia
netlinkz.com

NetMotion (134, 4.7%)
Network Security / SASE
Seattle, WA, US
netmotionwireless.com

Netography (47, 6.8%)
Network Security / DDoS Defense
San Francisco, CA, US
netography.com

NetRise (36, 33.3%)
Application Security / Firmware
Austin, TX, US
netrise.io

NetScout (2816, 1.9%)
Network Security / Incident Management
Westford, MA, US
netscout.com

NetSecurity (82, 12.3%)
MSSP / Managed Security Services
Sao Paulo, Brazil
netsecurity.com.br

Netsense Gmbh (3, -25.0%)
GRC / Vulnerabilities
Zurich, Switzerland
netsense.ch

NetSkope (2439, 13.7%)
Application Security
Santa Clara, CA, US
netskope.com

Netspark Ltd (77, 28.3%)
Network Security / Filtering
New York, NY, US
netspark.com

NetSPI (537, 33.2%)
GRC / Vulnerabilities
Minneapolis, MN, US
netspi.com

NetSTAR (11, 10.0%)
Network Security / Gateways
San Mateo, CA, US
netstar-inc.com

Netsurion (263, -9.3%)
MSSP / Managed Security Services
Houston, TX, US
netsurion.com

Netsweeper (70, 0.0%)
Network Security / Filtering
Waterloo, ON, Canada
netsweeper.com

Netswitch Technology Management (16, 6.7%)
MSSP / MDR
San Francisco, CA, US
netswitch.net

Nettoken (5, 25.0%)
GRC / Credential Security
London, United Kingdom
nettoken.io

NetWitness (196, 56.8%)
Operations / XDR
Bedford, MA, US
netwitness.com

Network Box Deutschland (13, 8.3%)
Network Security / UTM
Nordrhein-Westfalen, Germany
network-box.eu

Network Box USA (9, -10.0%)
MSSP / Managed Security Services
Houston, TX, US
networkboxusa.com

Network Critical (28, 27.3%)
Network Security / IPS
Caversham, United Kingdom
networkcritical.com

Network Intelligence (668, 12.3%)
Operations / Policy Management
Mumbai, India
niiconsulting.com

Network Perception (47, -21.7%)
GRC / Configuration Management
Chicago, IL, US
network-perception.com

Networking4All (35, 2.9%)
MSSP / Managed Security Services
de Meern, Utrecht, Netherlands
networking4all.com

NetWrix Corporation (751, 18.8%)
GRC / Auditing
Irvine, CA, US
netwrix.com

Neupart (21, 50.0%)
GRC / Secure ISMS
Soborg, Denmark
neupart.com

Neuro-ID (74, -11.9%)
Fraud Prevention / Monitoring
Whitefish, MT, US
neuro-id.com

Neurocat (36, 2.9%)
Data Security / Safe AI/ML Data
Berlin, Germany
neurocat.ai

NeuShield (10, 42.9%)
Data Security / Ransomware Security
Fremont, CA, US
neushield.com

Neustar (1449, -29.2%)
Network Security / DDoS Defense
Sterling, VA, US
home.neustar

**Numbers in parentheses indicate headcount and % change in 2023.*

NeuVector (17, -5.6%)
Endpoint Security / Container Security
San Jose, CA, US
neuvector.com

Nevatech (4, -33.3%)
API Security
Atlanta, GA, US
nevatech.com

New Net Technologies (28, 21.7%)
Operations / Workflow Automation
Naples, FL, US
newnettechnologies.com

NewBanking (17, 6.2%)
IAM
Copenhagen, Denmark
newbanking.com

Nexcom (282, 8.1%)
Network Security / Hardware
New Taipei City, Taiwan
nexcom.com

Next DLP (86, 4.9%)
GRC / Insider Threats
London, United Kingdom
qush.com

NextLabs (163, 19.0%)
Data Security / IRM
San Mateo, CA, US
nextlabs.com

Nexus Group Global (257, 19.0%)
IAM / Identity Management
Stockholm, Sweden
nexusgroup.com

Nexus Industrial Memory (6, 0.0%)
Data Security
West Sussex, United Kingdom
nexusindustrialmemory.com

NexusFlow AI (6, 50.0%)
Security Analytics / AI Security
Palo Alto, CA, US
nexusflow.ai

Nexusguard (136, -2.9%)
Network Security / DDoS Defense
Tsuen Wan, Hong Kong
nexusguard.com

ngrok (84, 0.0%)
IAM / Access Security
San Francisco, CA, US
ngrok.com

Niagra Networks (64, -8.6%)
Network Security / Monitoring
San Jose, CA, US
niagaranetworks.com

NICE Actimize (1357, 6.8%)
Fraud Prevention / Fraud Detection
Hoboken, NJ, US
niceactimize.com

Nightfall AI (114, 11.8%)
Data Security / Data Discovery
San Francisco, CA, US
nightfall.ai

NightVision (25, 47.1%)
API Security / Vulnerabilities
Los Angeles, CA, US
nightvision.net

NIKSUN (334, 30.5%)
Network Security / NBAD
Princeton, NJ, US
niksun.com

Nimbusddos (4, 0.0%)
Testing / DDoS Defense
Newton, MA, US
nimbusddos.com

Nimbusec (14, 16.7%)
GRC / Scanning
Linz, Austria
nimbusec.com

NinjaOne (908, 47.2%)
Endpoint Security / Endpoint Management
Austin, TX, US
ninjaone.com

NINJIO (60, -6.2%)
GRC / Security Awareness Training
Westlake Village, CA, US
ninjio.com

Nira (33, 10.0%)
Data Security
Redwood City, CA, US
nira.com

Nirmata (73, 4.3%)
GRC / Kubernetes Security
San Jose, CA, US
nirmata.com

Nisos (115, 18.6%)
Threat Intelligence / Managed Security Services
Alexandria, VA, US
nisos.com

NitroKey (6, 50.0%)
Data Security / Encryption
Berlin, Germany
nitrokey.com

Nixu Corporation (414, 5.3%)
MSSP / Managed Security Services
Espoo, Finland
nixu.com

NodeSource (18, 5.9%)
Application Security / Serverless
San Francisco, CA, US
nodesource.com

Noetic (52, 4.0%)
GRC / Asset Management
Waltham, MA, US
noeticcyber.com

NoID (12, 33.3%)
Data Security / Secure Communications
St Julians, Malta
noid.ltd

Nok Nok Labs (36, -16.3%)
IAM / Authentication
San Jose, CA, US
noknok.com

Nokia (82184, 4.5%)
Endpoint Security / Mobile Device Security
Espoo, Finland
networks.nokia.com

Nokod Security (15, 1400.0%)
Application Security / Security For No-code Applications
Tel Aviv, Israel
nokodsecurity.com

Nominet (323, 7.7%)
Network Security / Threat Detection
Oxford, United Kingdom
nominet.com

noname security (499, 41.4%)
API Security
Palo Alto, CA, US
nonamesecurity.com

Nopsec (53, 12.8%)
GRC / Vulnerabilities
Brooklyn, NY, US
nopsec.com

Noq (4, 0.0%)
IAM / Identity As Code
Irvine, CA, US
noq.dev

NordVPN (75, 29.3%)
Network Security / VPN / Proxy
Panama City, Panama
nordvpn.com

Norma (9, 80.0%)
IoT Security
Seoul, South Korea
norma.co.kr

Normalyze (66, 112.9%)
Data Security / Data Discovery
Los Altos, CA, US
normalyze.ai

**Numbers in parentheses indicate headcount and % change in 2023.*

NorthStar.io (16, -5.9%)
GRC / Vulnerabilities
Chicago, IL, US
northstar.io

nostra (229, 36.3%)
MSSP / Managed Security Services
Dublin, Ireland
nostra.ie

Notakey (3, -25.0%)
IAM / Access Security
Riga, Latvia
notakey.com

Notebook Labs (5, 0.0%)
IAM / Identity Management
Stanford, CA, US
notebooklabs.xyz

Nova Leah (21, 0.0%)
IoT Security / Healthcare
Dundalk, Ireland
novaleah.com

Novetta (411, -23.0%)
Network Security / Monitoring
McLean, VA, US
novetta.com

NoviFlow (50, -3.9%)
Network Security / SDN
Montreal, QC, Canada
noviflow.com

NowSecure (137, -16.5%)
Endpoint Security / Mobile Device Security
Chicago, IL, US
nowsecure.com

Nozomi Networks (268, -30.2%)
IoT Security / OT Security
San Francisco, CA, US
nozominetworks.com

NPcore (18, 5.9%)
Endpoint Security / EDR
Seoul, South Korea
npcore.com

NS1 (126, -25.9%)
Network Security / DNS Security
New York, NY, US
ns1.com

NSFocus (369, -47.5%)
Network Security / DDoS Defense
Santa Clara, CA, US
nsfocus.com

nsKnox (46, -4.2%)
Fraud Prevention / Payment Verification
Tel Aviv, Israel
nsknox.net

nSure.ai (49, 13.9%)
Fraud Prevention / Chargeback Prevention
Tel Aviv, Israel
nsureai.com

NTrepid (179, -6.3%)
Operations / Forensics
Herndon, VA, US
ntrepidcorp.com

NTT Ltd. (18412, -8.1%)
MSSP / Managed Security Services
London, United Kingdom
hello.global.ntt

Nu Quantum (39, 69.6%)
Data Security / Quantum
London, United Kingdom
nu-quantum.com

Nubo Software (8, 0.0%)
Endpoint Security / Virtualization
New York, NY, US
nubosoftware.com

Nucleon Cyber (6, -33.3%)
Threat Intelligence / Aggregation
Tampa, FL, US
nucleon.sh

Nucleus Security (73, 1.4%)
GRC / Vulnerabilities
Sarasota, FL, US
nucleussec.com

NuData Security (52, -42.9%)
Fraud Prevention / Fraud Detection
Vancouver, BC, Canada
nudatasecurity.com

Nudge Security (19, 26.7%)
GRC
Austin, TX, US
nudgesecurity.com

Nuix (436, 1.4%)
Security Analytics / Investigation
Sydney, Australia
nuix.com

Nullafi (15, 0.0%)
Data Security / Secure Storage
Chicago, IL, US
nullafi.com

Nuspire (183, -9.0%)
MSSP / Managed Security Services
Commerce, MI, US
nuspire.com

Nuts Technologies Inc. (6, 0.0%)
Data Security / Encryption
Chicago Area, IL, US
nutstechnologies.com

NXM Labs (17, 13.3%)
IoT Security / Endpoint Protection
San Francisco, CA, US
nxmlabs.com

Nym (55, 22.2%)
Data Security / Encryption
Neuchatel, China
nymtech.net

Oasis Labs (32, -25.6%)
Data Security / Governance
San Francisco, CA, US
oasislabs.com

Oblivious (32, 88.2%)
Data Security / Secure Data Sharing
Dublin, Ireland
oblivious.ai

ObserveID (10, 42.9%)
IAM / Monitoring
Los Angeles, CA, US
observeid.com

Obsidian Security (144, 22.0%)
Network Security / Cloud Security
Newport Beach, CA, US
obsidiansecurity.com

Occamsec (37, -2.6%)
GRC / Penetration Testing
New York, NY, US
occamsec.com

Ockam (24, 26.3%)
Data Security / Orchestration
San Francisco, CA, US
ockam.io

Octatco (6, 20.0%)
IAM / Authentication
Seongnam, South Korea
octatco.com

Octiga (5, 0.0%)
MSSP / Managed Security Services
Galway, Ireland
octiga.io

OctoXlabs (10, 66.7%)
GRC / Attack Surface Management
Istanbul, Turkey
octoxlabs.com

odix (26, -7.1%)
Data Security / Document Security
Rosh HaAyin, Israel
odi-x.com

Odyssey Technologies (155, 14.8%)
IAM / Public Key Infrastructure
Chennai, India
odysseytec.com

**Numbers in parentheses indicate headcount and % change in 2023.*

Offensive Security (964, 11.1%)
Training / Cyber Range
New York, NY, US
offensive-security.com

Okera (24, -72.4%)
Data Security / Governance
San Francisco, CA, US
okera.com

Okta (7108, -12.4%)
IAM
San Francisco, CA, US
okta.com

Olfeo (55, 12.2%)
Network Security / Gateways
Paris, France
olfeo.com

Oligo Security (58, 65.7%)
Application Security
Tel Aviv, Israel
oligo.security

Oloid (46, 9.5%)
IAM / Identity Management
Sunnyvale, CA, US
oloid.ai

Omada (322, 20.1%)
IAM
Copenhagen, Denmark
omada.net

Omega Systems (173, 0.0%)
MSSP / SIEM
Reading, PA, US
omegasystemscorp.com

Omniquad Ltd. (23, -11.5%)
Endpoint Security / Anti-spyware
London, United Kingdom
omniquad.com

Omny (32, 77.8%)
GRC / Risk Management
Oslo, Norway
omnysecurity.com

On Security (3, 50.0%)
MSSP / SOC
Sao Paulo, Brazil
on-security.com

ON2IT Cybersecurity (85, 4.9%)
MSSP / Managed Security Services
Zaltbommel, Netherlands
on2it.net

Onapsis Inc. (345, -5.0%)
Data Security / SAP
Boston, MA, US
onapsis.com

Onclave Networks (19, -32.1%)
IoT Security / OT Security
North Mclean, VA, US
onclave.net

Onda (39, 457.1%)
GRC / Risk Management
Minneapolis, MN, US
onda.ai

Ondeso - Industrial It Made In Germany (22, -15.4%)
IoT Security / OT Security
Regensburg, Germany
ondeso.com

One Identity (596, 1.5%)
IAM / Identity Management
Aliso Viejo, CA, US
oneidentity.com

OneKey (12, 500.0%)
Data Security / Wallets
Hong Kong Island, Hong Kong
onekey.so

OneLayer (30, 0.0%)
Network Security / Cellular Network Security
Galicia, Spain
one-layer.com

OneLeet (15, 7.1%)
GRC / Penetration Testing
Amsterdam, Netherlands
oneleet.com

OneLogin (100, -17.4%)
IAM / Identity Management
San Francisco, CA, US
onelogin.com

OnePath (356, -5.3%)
MSSP / Managed Security Services
Kennesaw, GA, US
1path.com

OneSpan (741, -1.5%)
IAM
Chicago, IL, US
onespan.com

OneTrust (2500, -5.2%)
GRC / Risk Management
Atlanta, GA, US
onetrust.com

OneVisage (7, -12.5%)
IAM / Authentication
Lausanne, Switzerland
onevisage.com

OneWave (29, -9.4%)
IAM / Authentication
Rennes, France
onewave.io

OneWelcome (Was Onegini) (4, -50.0%)
IAM / CIAM
Woerden, Netherlands
onegini.com

Onfido (588, -17.3%)
Fraud Prevention / Identity Verification
London, United Kingdom
onfido.com

Onpage (31, 0.0%)
Operations / Security Alerts
Waltham, MA, US
OnPage.com

onShore Security (41, -2.4%)
MSSP / Managed Security Services
Chicago, IL, US
onShore.com

Onspring (85, 6.2%)
GRC / Auditing
Overland Park, KS, US
onspring.com

OnSystem Logic (6, 0.0%)
Endpoint Security / Application Hardening
Catonsville, MD, US
onsystemlogic.com/

Ontic (188, 12.6%)
Threat Intelligence / Personal Protection Platform
Austin, TX, US
ontic.co

Ontinue (197, 99.0%)
MSSP / MDR
Redwood City, CA, US
ontinue.com

Onwardly (8, 14.3%)
GRC / Policy Management
Aukland, New Zealand
onwardly.io

Onyxia Cyber (21, 40.0%)
Operations
New York, NY, US
onyxia.io

Oodrive (415, -1.9%)
Data Security / Secure Backup/Recovery
Paris, France
oodrive.com

Oort (29, -37.0%)
IAM / Incident Management
Boston, MA, US
www.oort.io

Opal Dev (50, 51.5%)
IAM / Identity Management
San Francisco, CA, US
opal.dev

Open Raven (38, -19.1%)
Data Security / Data Discovery
Olympia, WA, US
openraven.com

Open Systems (426, -17.6%)
MSSP / Managed Security Services
Zurich, Switzerland
open-systems.com

**Numbers in parentheses indicate headcount and % change in 2023.*

Open Zeppelin (92, 10.8%)
Application Security / Blockchain
San Francisco, CA, US
openzeppelin.com

OpenIAM (11, 37.5%)
IAM / Identity Management
Cortlandt Manor, NY, US
openiam.com

OpenText (21752, 45.1%)
IAM / Federated Identity
Waterloo, ON, Canada
opentext.com

OpenVPN (164, 9.3%)
Network Security / VPN/Proxy
Pleasanton, CA, US
openvpn.net

OpenVRM (6, 0.0%)
GRC / Risk Management
Columbus, OH, US
openvrm.com

Operant AI (23, 21.1%)
Application Security / Runtime Security
San Francisco, CA, US
operant.ai

Opora (14, -54.8%)
Threat Intelligence / Adversary Tracking
San Francisco, CA, US
opora.io

OpsCompass (24, 14.3%)
Operations / Posture Management
Omaha, NE, US
opscompass.com

Opscura (28, 12.0%)
IoT Security
CA, US
opscura.io

OpsHelm (12, 50.0%)
Operations / Configuration Management
Seattle, WA, US
opshelm.com

OPSWAT (732, 11.4%)
Endpoint Security / SDKs
San Francisco, CA, US
opswat.com

Optimal IdM (11, 0.0%)
IAM / Authentication
Lutz, FL, US
optimalidm.com

Optimeyes (65, 62.5%)
GRC / Risk Management
San Diego, CA, US
optimeyes.ai

Optiv (2381, -2.6%)
MSSP / Managed Security Services
Denver, CO, US
optiv.com

Opus Security (31, 24.0%)
Operations / Cloud Security
Tel Aviv, Israel
opus.security

Oracle (201930, -1.7%)
IAM
Redwood Shores, CA, US
oracle.com

Orange Cyberdefense (3449, 14.4%)
MSSP / Managed Security Services
Nanterre, France
orangecyberdefense.com

Orca Security (506, 14.7%)
Operations / Vulnerabilities
Tel Aviv, Israel
orca.security

Orchestra Group (45, -16.7%)
IoT Security / Monitoring
Tel Aviv, Israel
orchestragroup.com

Ordr (121, 21.0%)
IoT Security / Device Management
Santa Clara, CA, US
ordr.net

Orpheus Cyber (32, 0.0%)
Threat Intelligence / OSINT
London, United Kingdom
orpheus-cyber.com

Ory (25, -34.2%)
IAM
Munich, Germany
ory.sh

Osano (107, 78.3%)
Data Security / Compliance Management
Austin, TX, US
osano.com

Osirium (40, -14.9%)
IAM / Access Security
Theale, United Kingdom
osirium.com

Ostendio (37, -21.3%)
GRC / Compliance Management
Arlington, VA, US
ostendio.com

Ostrich (21, 61.5%)
GRC / Risk Management
Cottonwood Heights, UT, US
ostrichcyber-risk.com

OTORIO (94, -2.1%)
IoT Security / OT Security
Tel Aviv, Israel
otorio.com

Outpost24 (228, 38.2%)
GRC / Vulnerabilities
Karlskrona, Sweden
outpost24.com

Outseer (216, -3.1%)
Fraud Prevention / Authentication
Palo Alto, CA, US
outseer.com

OutThink (43, 34.4%)
GRC / Monitoring
London, United Kingdom
outthink.io

Ovalsec (10, -9.1%)
Operations / Attack Surface Management
Tel Aviv, Israel
ovalsec.com

Overe.io (4, 0.0%)
Application Security / SaaS Security
London, United Kingdom
overe.io

OverSOC (26, 44.4%)
Operations / Attack Surface Management
Lille, France
oversoc.com

Owl Cyber Defense (163, -11.9%)
Network Security / Air Gap
Danbury, CT, US
owlcyberdefense.com

OwnData (1264, -10.8%)
Data Security
Englewood Cliffs, NJ, US
owndata.com

OwnID (16, -5.9%)
IAM / Authentication
Tel Aviv, Israel
ownid.com

OX Security (85, 107.3%)
Application Security / Software Development Security
Tel Aviv, Israel
ox.security

oxeye (30, -9.1%)
Application Security / Software Testing For Security
Tel Aviv, Israel
oxeye.io

Oxford Biochronometrics (8, -11.1%)
Fraud Prevention / Click Fraud Prevention
London, United Kingdom
oxford-biochron.com

**Numbers in parentheses indicate headcount and % change in 2023.*

P0 Security (11, 22.2%)
IAM / Access Security
San Francisco,
CA, US
p0.dev

P3 Audit (5, 0.0%)
GRC / Compliance
Management
Covent Garden,
United Kingdom
p3audit.com

P3KI (6, -25.0%)
IAM / Access Security
Berlin, Germany
p3ki.com

PacketViper (16, 0.0%)
Deception
Pittsburgh, PA, US
packetviper.com

Paladin Cyber (36, 89.5%)
Email Security / Defense
Against Phishing
San Francisco,
CA, US
meetpaladin.com

Palantir Technologies (4031, 0.1%)
Security Analytics / Link
Analysis
Palo Alto,
CA, US
palantir.com

Palitronica (16, -11.1%)
Network Security / IDS
Ontario, Canada
palitronica.com

Palo Alto Networks (14805, 5.8%)
Network Security / UTM
Santa Clara,
CA, US
paloaltonetworks.com

Palqee (11, -26.7%)
GRC / Compliance
Management
London, United Kingdom
palqee.com

Panaseer (135, -2.9%)
Operations / Security
Management
London, United Kingdom
panaseer.com

Panda Security (402, 0.8%)
Endpoint Security /
Anti-virus
Bilbao, Spain
pandasecurity.com

Pangea (56, 80.7%)
Operations / Security APIs
Palo Alto, CA, US
pangea.cloud

Pango (91, 26.4%)
IAM / VPN/Proxy
Redwood City, CA, US
pango.co

Panorays (147, -2.0%)
GRC / Vulnerabilities
New York, NY, US
panorays.com

Panther (245, 17.2%)
Security Analytics / SIEM
San Francisco, CA, US
runpanther.io

Paperclip (26, -3.7%)
Data Security /
Document Security
Hackensack, NJ, US
paperclip.com

Paraben Corporation (17, -10.5%)
GRC / Forensics
Aldie, VA, US
paraben.com

Parablu (44, 29.4%)
Data Security / Secure
Backup/Recovery
Santa Clara, CA, US
parablu.com

Parasoft (271, 0.0%)
Application Security /
Software Testing For Security
Monrovia, CA, US
parasoft.com

Pareto Cyber (12, -20.0%)
GRC / Risk Management
St. Louis, MO, US
paretosecurity.com

Passage (4, -66.7%)
IAM / Authentication
Austin, TX, US
passage.id

Passbase (5, -83.9%)
IAM / User Verification
Berlin, Germany
passbase.com

Passbolt (28, -15.2%)
IAM / Credential Security
Esch-sur-alzette,
Luxembourg
passbolt.com

PassMark Software Pvt Ltd. (8, 0.0%)
IAM
Surry Hills, Australia
passmark.com

Passware (25, 8.7%)
Operations / Red Team
Tools
Mountain View,
CA, US
passware.com

Password Depot (13, 8.3%)
IAM / Credential Security
Darmstadt, Germany
password-depot.de

Patch My PC (86, 8.9%)
GRC / Patch Management
Castle Rock, CO, US
patchmypc.com

Patronus.io (3, 0.0%)
Application Security
/ Scanning
Berlin, Germany
patronus.io

Patrowl (20, 11.1%)
Operations / Attack Surface
Management
Paris, France
patrowl.io

Paubox (51, -16.4%)
Email Security /
Secure Email
San Francisco, CA, US
paubox.com

Paygilant (14, -6.7%)
Fraud Prevention /
Transaction
Security
Ramat Gan, Israel
paygilant.com

PC Matic (63, 8.6%)
Endpoint Security /
Application Whitelisting
Sioux City, IA, US
pcmatic.com

Peloton Cyber Security (16, -20.0%)
MSSP / SOC
Brunswick, Australia
pelotoncyber.com.au

Penfield.ai (7, -22.2%)
Security Analytics / Threat
Analysis
Toronto, ON,
Canada
penfield.ai

Penta Security (81, 0.0%)
Network Security / Firewalls
Seoul, South Korea
pentasecurity.com

Penten (110, 5.8%)
Data Security / Encryption
Braddon, Australia
penten.com

Pentera (was Pcysys) (374, 25.5%)
Operations / Penetration
Testing
Petah Tikva, Israel
pcysys.com

Perception Point (126, 1.6%)
Email Security / Defense
Against Phishing
Tel Aviv, Israel
perception-point.io

**Numbers in parentheses indicate headcount and % change in 2023.*

Perch (9, -30.8%)
MSSP / SOC
Tampa, FL, US
perchsecurity.com

Perimeter 81 (206, -14.5%)
Network Security / Gateways
Tel Aviv, Israel
perimeter81.com

PerimeterX (66, -37.1%)
Network Security / Website Security
Tel Aviv, Israel
perimeterx.com

Permiso Security (33, 17.9%)
Operations / Vulnerabilities
Palo Alto, CA, US
permiso.io

Perseus. (41, -21.1%)
Email Security / Defense Against Phishing
Berlin, Germany
perseus.de

Persona (280, 27.3%)
IAM / Identity Verification
San Francisco, CA, US
withpersona.com

Personam (3, 200.0%)
Network Security / Insider Threats
McLean, VA, US
PersonamInc.com

Pervade Software (10, 0.0%)
GRC
Cardiff, United Kingdom
pervade-software.com

Perygee (9, 28.6%)
IoT Security / OT Security
Boston, MA, US
perygee.com

PFP Cybersecurity (25, -3.9%)
Endpoint Security / Endpoint Protection
Vienna, VA, US
pfpcyber.com

Phantom (127, 89.5%)
Data Security / Wallets
San Francisco, CA, US
phantom.app

Phin Security (32, 146.2%)
GRC / Security Awareness Training
Newark, DE, US
phinsec.io

PhishCloud (9, 12.5%)
Email Security / Defense Against Phishing
Renton, WA, US
phishcloud.com

PhishFirewall (11, -15.4%)
GRC / Security Awareness Training
Huntsville, AL, US
phishfirewall.com

PhishLabs (109, -18.7%)
GRC / Defense Against Phishing
Charleston, SC, US
phishlabs.com

PhishX (20, 5.3%)
GRC / Security Awareness Training
Cotia, Brazil
phishx.io

Phoenix Security (6, 20.0%)
Endpoint Security
Los Altos, CA, US
r6security.com

Phoenix Technologies (726, 31.8%)
Endpoint Security / Secured Devices
Campbell, CA, US
phoenix.com

Phosphorus (62, 10.7%)
IoT Security / Patch Management
Nashville, TN, US
phosphorus.io

Phylum (22, -33.3%)
Application Security / Code Security
Evergreen, CO, US
phylum.io

PHYSEC (40, -13.0%)
IoT Security / OT Security
Bochum, Nordrhein-Westfalen, Germany
physec.de

Picnic (38, -17.4%)
Data Security / Employee Protection
Washington, DC, US
getpicnic.com

Picus Security (234, 8.3%)
Operations / Breach And Attack Simulation
Ankara, Turkey
picussecurity.com

Piiano (27, -6.9%)
GRC / Data Privacy
Tel Aviv, Israel
piiano.com

PiiqMedia (5, -16.7%)
GRC / Security Awareness Training
Cambridge, MA, US
piiqmedia.com

Pikered (6, 0.0%)
Operations / Breach And Attack Simulation
Milan, Italy
pikered.com

Ping Identity Corporation (1387, -0.2%)
IAM
Denver, CO, US
pingidentity.com

Pingsafe (69, 109.1%)
Network Security / Posture Management
Bengaluru, India
pingsafe.com

Pinochle.AI (15, -40.0%)
Operations / XDR
Vernon Hills, IL, US
pinochle.ai

Pipeline Security (26, -10.3%)
MSSP
Chuo-ku, Tokyo, Japan
ppln.co

Pirean (Echostar) (30, -9.1%)
IAM / Identity Management
London, United Kingdom
pirean.com

PivotPoint Security (31, -20.5%)
GRC / Risk Management
Hamilton, NJ, US
pivotpointsecurity.com

PixAlert (10, 0.0%)
GRC / Data Discovery
Dublin, Ireland
pixalert.com

PIXM (11, -8.3%)
Email Security / Defense Against Phishing
Brooklyn, NY, US
pixm.net

PKWARE (149, 4.2%)
Data Security / Data Privacy
Milwaukee, WI, US
pkware.com

PlainID (91, -12.5%)
IAM / Authorization
Tel Aviv, Israel
plainid.com

Plextrac (95, -15.9%)
GRC / Security Report Management Platform
Boise, ID, US
plextrac.com

Plixer (96, -6.8%)
Network Security / Traffic Analysis
Kennebunk, ME, US
plixer.com

**Numbers in parentheses indicate headcount and % change in 2023.*

Plurilock (45, -8.2%)
IAM / Authentication
Victoria, BC, Canada
plurilock.com

PNF Software (3, 0.0%)
Application Security / Reverse Engineering
Redwood City, CA, US
pnfsoftware.com

PointSharp AB (58, 13.7%)
Endpoint Security / Mobile Device Security
Stockholm, Sweden
pointsharp.com

Polar Security (29, -9.4%)
Data Security / Data Management
Tel Aviv, Israel
polar.security

Polarity (34, -15.0%)
Operations / Onscreen Data Augmentation
Farmington, CT, US
polarity.io

PolicyCo (8, -46.7%)
GRC / Policy Management
Nashville, TN, US
policyco.io

Polymer (24, 9.1%)
GRC / DLP
New York, NY, US
polymerhq.io

PolySwarm (24, -11.1%)
Endpoint Security / Anti-malware
San Diego, CA, US
polyswarm.io

Polyverse (6, 0.0%)
Endpoint Security / Operating System Security
Bellevue, WA, US
polyverse.io

Portnox (66, 0.0%)
Endpoint Security / Device Management
Israel
portnox.com

Portshift (12, 33.3%)
Application Security / Identity-Based Workload Protection
Tel Aviv, Israel
portshift.io

PortSwigger (196, 40.0%)
GRC / Vulnerabilities
Knutsford, United Kingdom
portswigger.net

PortSys (6, -25.0%)
IAM / Access Security
Marlborough, MA, US
portsys.com

Post-Quantum (9, -25.0%)
IAM / Authentication
London, United Kingdom
post-quantum.com

PQShield Ltd (62, 34.8%)
Data Security / Quantum
Oxford, United Kingdom
pqshield.com

Praetorian (141, 6.0%)
Operations / Secure Remote Access
Austin, TX, US
praetorian.com

Prancer (27, 50.0%)
Operations / Vulnerabilities
San Diego, CA, US
prancer.io

PreEmptive Solutions (44, 76.0%)
Application Security / App Hardening
Mayfield Village, OH, US
preemptive.com

Prelude (31, 3.3%)
Testing / Breach And Attack Simulation
New York, NY, US
prelude.org

Presidio (3799, 3.8%)
MSSP / Managed Security Services
New York, NY, US
presidio.com

Prevalent AI (136, 6.2%)
GRC / Risk Management
London, United Kingdom
prevalent.ai

Prevalent Networks (152, 23.6%)
GRC / Risk Management
Warren, NJ, US
prevalent.net

Prevasio (5, 0.0%)
Operations / Container Security
Sydney, Australia
prevasio.com

PreVeil (61, 17.3%)
Data Security / Encryption
Boston, MA, US
preveil.com

Preventon (3, 0.0%)
Endpoint Security / Anti-virus
Mayfair, United Kingdom
preventon.com

PrimeKey Solutions (36, -28.0%)
Data Security / Public Key Infrastructure
Solna, Sweden
primekey.com

Primx (48, -2.0%)
Data Security / Encryption
Lyon, France
primx.eu/en

Prismo Systems (5, -72.2%)
Network Security / Zero Trust Networking
San Francisco, CA, US
prismosystems.com

Privacera (140, -1.4%)
Data Security / Governance
Fremont, CA, US
privacera.com

Privacy Analytics (98, -4.8%)
Data Security / Healthcare
Ottawa, ON, Canada
privacy-analytics.com

Privacy Engine (34, 6.2%)
GRC / Data Privacy
Blackrock, Ireland
privacyengine.io

Privacy4Cars (32, 33.3%)
Data Security / Automotive
Kennesaw, GA, US
privacy4cars.com

Privado (173, 130.7%)
Application Security / Code Security
San Francisco, CA, US
privado.ai

Privafy (83, -3.5%)
IAM / Access Security
Burlington, MA, US
privafy.com

Privakey (7, 75.0%)
Fraud Prevention / Transaction Security
Philadelphia, PA, US
privakey.com

Private AI (81, 113.2%)
GRC / Data Discovery
Toronto, ON, Canada
private-ai.com

Privitar (67, -54.7%)
Data Security / Data Masking
London, United Kingdom
privitar.com

Privo (39, 8.3%)
GRC / Data Privacy
Dumfries, VA, US
privo.com

Privoro (55, 0.0%)
Endpoint Security / Hardened Cases For Mobile Phones
Chandler, AZ, US
privoro.com

Privus (7, -22.2%)
Data Security / Secure Communications
Zug, Switzerland
privus.global

**Numbers in parentheses indicate headcount and % change in 2023.*

Privva (8, -20.0%)
GRC / Risk Management
Arlington, VA, US
privva.com

Privy (721, 8.6%)
Data Security
Jakarta Selatan, DKI
Jakarta, Indonesia
privy.id

Privya.AI (23, -11.5%)
GRC / Compliance
Management
Tel Aviv, Israel
privya.ai

Probely (33, 43.5%)
Application Security
/ Scanning
Lisbon, Portugal
probely.com

Process Software (15, 7.1%)
Email Security
Framingham, MA, US
process.com

ProcessUnity (174, 28.9%)
GRC / Risk Management
Concord, MA, US
processunity.com

Procivis AG (29, 11.5%)
IAM / Credential Security
Zurich, Switzerland
procivis.ch

Procyon (17, 325.0%)
IAM / Access Security
Santa Clara, CA, US
procyon.ai

Prodaft (52, 15.6%)
Threat Intelligence / OSINT
Yverdon-les-Bains,
Switzerland
prodaft.com

ProDevice (5, 0.0%)
Data Security / Data Erasure
And Destruction
Wieliczka, Poland
pro-device.com/en/pro-device.com/en/

Profian (9, -40.0%)
Data Security / Hardware
Raleigh, NC, US
profian.com

Proficio (242, 22.2%)
MSSP / MDR
Carlsbad, CA, US
proficio.com

Profitap (35, 16.7%)
Network Security /
Traffic Analysis
Eindhoven, Netherlands
profitap.com

Progress (3516, 6.3%)
Network Security / Secure
Data Sharing
Bedford, MA, US
progress.com

Prohacktive.Io (9, -30.8%)
GRC / Vulnerabilities
Gap, France
prohacktive.io

Promisec (31, 0.0%)
Endpoint Security /
Endpoint Security
Intelligence
Holon, Israel
promisec.com

Promon (109, 7.9%)
Application Security /
Mobile Device Security
Oslo, Norway
promon.co

Proof Authentication (12, 50.0%)
IAM / Application
Authenticity
Boston, MA, US
proofauthentication.com

Proofpoint (4508, 4.3%)
Email Security / Defense
Against Phishing
Sunnyvale, CA, US
proofpoint.com

PropelAuth (6, -14.3%)
IAM / Authentication
Redwood City, CA, US
propelauth.com

Prophecy International (78, 14.7%)
Operations / Logs
Adelaide, Australia
prophecyinternational.com

Protect AI (38, 153.3%)
Data Security
Seattle, WA, US
protectai.com

Protected Media (18, 100.0%)
Network Security /
Advertising-related
Petah Tikva, Israel
protected.media

Protectimus Ltd (49, 13.9%)
IAM / Authentication
Dublin, Ireland
protectimus.com

Protecto (26, 0.0%)
Data Security / Posture
Management
Cupertino, CA, US
protecto.ai

ProtectStar (3, 50.0%)
Data Security / Data Erasure
And Destruction
Miami, FL, US
protectstar.com

Protectt.ai (54, 35.0%)
Endpoint Security / Mobile
Device Security
Gurgaon, Haryana, India
protectt.ai

Protegrity (369, -1.6%)
Application Security
Stamford, CT, US
protegrity.com

Protenus (101, -11.4%)
GRC / Healthcare
Baltimore, MD, US
protenus.com

Proteus Cyber (5, 0.0%)
GRC
London, United Kingdom
proteuscyber.com

Protexxa (70, 2233.3%)
GRC / Security Awareness
Training
Toronto, ON, Canada
protexxa.com

Prove (414, 35.3%)
Fraud Prevention / Anti-fraud
New York, NY, US
payfone.com

Proxim (130, -4.4%)
Network Security / Wireless
Security
San Jose, CA, US
proxim.com

Pryvate Now (46, 12.2%)
Data Security / Secure
Communications
Jersey, United Kingdom
pryvatenow.com

Psafe Technology (3, -80.0%)
Endpoint Security / Anti-virus
San Francisco, CA, US
psafe.com

Pulse Secure (151, -18.4%)
IAM / Authentication
San Jose, CA, US
pulsesecure.net

PureID (12, -7.7%)
IAM / Authentication
Heydon, Royston,
United Kingdom
pureid.io

Purevpn (205, 75.2%)
Network Security / VPN /
Proxy
Hong Kong, Hong Kong
purevpn.com

Purplemet (4, 0.0%)
Application Security /
Scanning
Paris, France
purplemet.com

Push Security (26, 52.9%)
Operations / Application
Security
London, United Kingdom
pushsecurity.com

**Numbers in parentheses indicate headcount and % change in 2023.*

PwC (277228, 6.5%)
MSSP / Managed Security Services
Mclean, VA, US
pwc.com

PXL Vision (34, -2.9%)
IAM / Identity Verification
Zurich, Switzerland
pxl-vision.com

Pynt (17, 13.3%)
API Security / API Testing
Tel Aviv, Israel
pynt.io

Pyramid Computer GmbH (72, 2.9%)
Network Security / Firewalls
Freiburg, Germany
pyramid-computer.com

Q-Net Security (16, 0.0%)
Network Security / Segmentation
St. Louis, MO, US
qnetsecurity.com

Q6 Cyber (51, 4.1%)
Threat Intelligence / Dark Web
Miami, FL, US
q6cyber.com

QEDit (14, 16.7%)
Data Security / Data Privacy
Tel Aviv, Israel
qed-it.com

QEYnet (11, 22.2%)
Data Security
Vaughan, ON, Canada
qeynet.com

Qgroup (21, 10.5%)
Network Security / Firewalls
Frankfurt am Main, Germany
qgroup.de

QI-ANXIN (87, 13.0%)
Endpoint Security / Anti-virus
Beijing, China
qianxin.com

Qihoo 360 Total Security (3044, 18.7%)
Endpoint Security / Anti-virus
Beijing, China
360.cn

qikfox (35, 94.4%)
Fraud Prevention / Secure Web Browsing
San Mateo, CA, US
qikfox.com

Qingteng (101, -1.9%)
Operations / Asset Management
Beijing, China
qingteng.cn

Qmulos (87, 11.5%)
GRC
Arlington, VA, US
qmulos.com

Qohash (43, -21.8%)
GRC / Data Discovery
Quebec, Canada
qohash.com

Qomplx (92, 31.4%)
Security Analytics / Incident Management
Reston, VA, US
qomplx.com

Qontrol (12, 71.4%)
GRC / Compliance Management
Paris, France
qontrol.io

Qrator Labs (34, 0.0%)
Network Security / DDoS Defense
Prague, Czech Republic
qrator.net

Qredo (124, -24.9%)
Data Security / Encryption
London, United Kingdom
qredo.com

Qrypt (52, 6.1%)
Data Security / Quantum
New York, NY, US
qrypt.com

Quad Miners (25, 13.6%)
Network Security / Monitoring
Seoul, South Korea
quadminers.com

Quadrant Information Security (41, 17.1%)
MSSP / SIEM
Jacksonville, FL, US
quadrantsec.com

Qualys (2528, 11.6%)
GRC / Vulnerabilities
Foster City, CA, US
qualys.com

Quantinuum (397, 13.4%)
Data Security / Quantum
Charlotte, NC, US
quantinuum.com

QuantLR (10, 25.0%)
Data Security / Quantum
Jerusalem, Israel
quantlr.com

Quantropi (31, 0.0%)
Data Security / Quantum
Ontario, Canada
quantropi.com

Quantum (11, -47.6%)
MSSP / MDR
Singapore, Singapore
quantum.security

Quantum Dice (23, 76.9%)
Data Security / Quantum
Oxford, United Kingdom
quantum-dice.com

Quantum Integrity (4, -20.0%)
IAM / Identity Verification
Lausanne, Switzerland
q-integrity.com

Quantum Knight (10, 400.0%)
Data Security / Quantum
Palo Alto, CA, US
quantumknight.io

Quantum Resistant Cryptography (5, 0.0%)
Data Security / Encryption
Lausanne, Switzerland
qrcrypto.ch

Quantum Xchange (17, 13.3%)
Data Security / Quantum
Newton, MA, US
quantumxc.com

Quarkslab (93, 0.0%)
Application Security / Code Security
Paris, France
quarkslab.com

Quasar Scan (4, 0.0%)
Data Security / Data Discovery
Wellington Region, New Zealand
quasarscan.com

Query.Ai (42, 2.4%)
Operations / Search
Brookings, SD, US
query.ai

Quest Software (3736, -4.1%)
IAM / Access Security
Aliso Viejo, CA, US
quest.com

Quick Heal (1513, 5.1%)
Endpoint Security / UTM
Pune, India
quickheal.com

Quicklaunch (41, 13.9%)
IAM / Identity Management
Miami, FL, US
quicklaunch.io

Quickpass (67, 67.5%)
IAM / Access Security
North Vancouver, Canada
getquickpass.com

QuintessenceLabs (48, -7.7%)
Data Security / Quantum
Deakin, Australia
quintessencelabs.com

**Numbers in parentheses indicate headcount and % change in 2023.*

Quiver (3, -40.0%)
Data Security / Secure Data Sharing
Amsterdam, Netherlands
quivercloud.com

QuoIntelligence (45, 15.4%)
Threat Intelligence / Managed Security Services
Frankfurt am Main, Hesse, Germany
quointelligence.eu

Quorum Cyber (223, 11.5%)
MSSP / MDR
Edinburgh, United Kingdom
quorumcyber.com

Quotium (12, -20.0%)
GRC / Monitoring
Paris, France
quotium.com

Qusecurity (76, 7.0%)
Data Security
San Mateo, CA, US
qusecure.com

Quside (47, 34.3%)
Data Security / Quantum
Barcelona, Spain
quside.com

Qustodio (89, 1.1%)
Endpoint Security / Mobile Parental Controls
Redondo Beach, CA, US
qustodio.com

Quttera (5, 0.0%)
Network Security / Website Security
Herzliya Pituach, Israel
quttera.com

Qwiet AI (42, -22.2%)
Application Security / Code Security
Santa Clara, CA, US
shiftleft.io

R&K Cyber Solutions (6, 0.0%)
MSSP / Managed Security Services
Manassas, VA, US
rkcybersolutions.com

R-Vision (114, 2.7%)
Operations / Incident Management
Moscow, Russia
rvision.pro

Racktop Systems (59, 1.7%)
Data Security / Secure Storage
Fulton, MD, US
racktopsystems.com

Radarfirst (63, -14.9%)
Operations / Incident Management
Portland, OR, US
radarfirst.com

Radiant Logic (166, 23.9%)
IAM / Authentication
Novato, CA, US
radiantlogic.com

Radiant Security (41, 78.3%)
Operations / SOC
San Francisco, CA, US
radiantsecurity.ai

RadiFlow (69, 40.8%)
IoT Security / OT Security
Tel Aviv, Israel
radiflow.com

Radware (1472, -1.0%)
Network Security / IPS
Tel Aviv, Israel
radware.com

Raito (15, -6.2%)
Data Security / Access Security
Brussels, Belgium
raito.io

Rambus (973, -6.8%)
Data Security / Semiconductor Security R&D
Sunnyvale, CA, US
rambus.com

Rampart Communications (55, 66.7%)
Network Security / Wireless Security
Hanover, MD, US
rampartcommunications.com

Randori (90, -6.2%)
GRC / Attack Surface Management
Waltham, MA, US
randori.com

RangeForce (80, -8.1%)
Training / Cyber Range
White Plains, NY, US
rangeforce.com

Raonsecure (78, 36.8%)
IAM / Authentication
Santa Clara, CA, US
raonsecure.com

Rapid7 (2825, -0.2%)
GRC / Vulnerabilities
Boston, MA, US
rapid7.com

RapidFort Inc. (33, 32.0%)
Application Security / Attack Surface Management
Sunnyvale, CA, US
rapidfort.com

Ravel Technologies (10, -16.7%)
Data Security / Encryption
Paris, France
raveltech.io

RavenWhite Security (3, 0.0%)
IAM / Cookies
Menlo Park, CA, US
ravenwhite.com

RAWCyber (3, 0.0%)
Endpoint Security / Mobile Device Security
Warszawa, Poland
rawcyber.pl

Rawstream (3, 0.0%)
Network Security / DNS Security
London, United Kingdom
rawstream.com

Raz-Lee Security (22, -8.3%)
Endpoint Security / ISeries
Herzliya, Israel
razlee.com

RazorSecure (46, 9.5%)
IoT Security / Automotive
Basingstoke, United Kingdom
razorsecure.com

RCDevs (19, 5.6%)
IAM
Belvaux, Luxembourg
rcdevs.com

Reach Security (11, 0.0%)
Operations
San Francisco, CA, US
reach.security

RealCISO (6, -25.0%)
GRC
Boston, MA, US
realciso.io

RealDefense (40, 37.9%)
Endpoint Security / Microsoft
Pasadena, CA, US
realdefen.se

Realsec (23, 0.0%)
Data Security / Hardware
Madrid, Spain
realsec.com

RealTheory (7, -12.5%)
Endpoint Security / Container Security
Atlanta, GA, US
realtheory.io

**Numbers in parentheses indicate headcount and % change in 2023.*

RealVNC (108, 12.5%)
Network Security / Access Security
Cambridge, United Kingdom
realvnc.com

ReaQta (14, -48.1%)
Endpoint Security / EDR
Amsterdam, Netherlands
reaqta.com

Reblaze (45, -30.8%)
Application Security / Web App Protection
Tel Aviv, Israel
reblaze.com

Reciprocity (90, -46.4%)
GRC / Risk Management
San Francisco, CA, US
reciprocity.com

Reco Labs (62, 29.2%)
Data Security / Secure Collaboration
New York, NY, US
recolabs.ai

Recorded Future (1104, 9.5%)
Threat Intelligence
Somerville, MA, US
recordedfuture.com

Red Access (26, 62.5%)
Network Security / Secure Web Browsing
Tel Aviv, Israel
redaccess.io

Red Balloon Security (25, 0.0%)
Endpoint Security / Security For Embedded Systems
New York, NY, US
redballoonsecurity.com

Red Button (10, 25.0%)
Network Security / DDoS Defense
Tel Aviv, Israel
red-button.net

Red Canary (418, -5.6%)
MSSP / MDR
Denver, CO, US
redcanary.com

Red Piranha (59, 3.5%)
Network Security / UTM
Melbourne, Australia
redpiranha.net

Red Sift (111, 3.7%)
Endpoint Security / Open Platform
London, United Kingdom
redsift.com

Redborder (10, 11.1%)
Network Security / IDS
Sevilla, Spain
redborder.com

RedJack (36, 33.3%)
Network Security / Monitoring
Silver Spring, MD, US
redjack.com

RedLegg (58, 18.4%)
MSSP / Managed Security Services
Geneva, IL, US
redlegg.com

RedScan (87, -23.0%)
MSSP / MDR
London, United Kingdom
redscan.com

RedSeal (178, 7.2%)
GRC / Posture Management
San Jose, CA, US
redseal.net

RedShield Security (37, -7.5%)
MSSP / Managed Security Services
Wellington, New Zealand
redshield.co

RedShift Networks (35, -10.3%)
Network Security / VoIP Security
San Ramon, CA, US
redshiftnetworks.com

Redstout (3, -50.0%)
Network Security / UTM
Lisbon, Portugal
redstout.com

Redwall Technologies (5, 0.0%)
Endpoint Security / Mobile Device Security
Beavercreek, OH, US
redwall.us

Refine Intelligence (20, 0.0%)
Fraud Prevention / Monitoring
Tel Aviv, Israel
refineintelligence.com

Reflectiz (38, 11.8%)
Application Security / Website Security
Ramat Gan, Israel
reflectiz.com

Regdata (16, 23.1%)
Data Security / Compliance Management
Geneva, Switzerland
regdata.ch/en/

RegScale (55, 96.4%)
GRC / Compliance Management
Tysons, VA, US
regscale.com

Regulativ.ai (7, 16.7%)
GRC / Compliance Management
London, United Kingdom
regulativ.ai

Regulus (15, 25.0%)
IoT Security / Automotive
Haifa, Israel
regulus.com

Reliaquest (1002, 5.1%)
Operations / Threat Hunting
Tampa, FL, US
reliaquest.com

Relyance AI (70, 0.0%)
GRC / Compliance Management
Mountain View, CA, US
relyance.ai

Remediant (9, -66.7%)
IAM / Access Security
San Francisco, CA, US
remediant.com

remote.it (16, -23.8%)
Network Security / Zero Trust Networking
Palo Alto, CA, US
remote.it

Remy Security (4, -33.3%)
Operations
San Francisco, CA, US
remysec.com

Report-Uri (3, -25.0%)
Network Security / Website Security
Clitheroe, United Kingdom
report-uri.com

Reposify (13, -23.5%)
Operations / Asset Management
Bnei Brak, Israel
reposify.com

Rescana (17, 54.5%)
GRC
Tel Aviv, Israel
rescana.com

ReSec Technologies (20, -16.7%)
Data Security / Document Security
Caesarea, Israel
resec.co

Resecurity (85, 57.4%)
Endpoint Security / EDR
Los ANgelas, CA, US
resecurity.com

Resilient Network Systems (3, 0.0%)
IAM / Access Security
San Francisco, CA, US
resilient-networks.com

Resmo (17, 6.2%)
Operations
Wilmington, DE, US
resmo.com

Resolve (127, -19.6%)
Operations / Orchestration
Campbell, CA, US
resolve.io

**Numbers in parentheses indicate headcount and % change in 2023.*

Resolver (363, 13.4%)
GRC / Risk Management
Toronto, ON,
Canada
resolver.com

Resourcely (28, 12.0%)
Operations / Technology
Deployment Management
San Francisco, CA, US
resourcely.io

Responsible Cyber (14, -6.7%)
GRC / Risk Management
Central Business District,
Singapore
responsible-cyber.com

RevBits (13, 0.0%)
Endpoint Security
Mineola, NY, US
revbits.com

RevealSecurity (47, 4.4%)
Application Security /
Monitoring
Tel Aviv, Israel
trackerdetect.com

Revelstoke (9, -82.7%)
Operations / Orchestration
San Jose, CA, US
revelstoke.io

Reversing Labs (298, 13.3%)
Operations / Malware
Analysis
Cambridge,
MA, US
reversinglabs.com

revyz (11, 83.3%)
Data Security
Fremont, CA, US
revyz.io

Rezilion (42, -32.3%)
Endpoint Security
Be'er Sheva, Israel
rezilion.co

Rezonate (27, 50.0%)
IAM / Identity Management
Boston, MA, US
rezonate.io

Rhea Group (675, 13.4%)
Training / Cyber Range
Wavre, Belgium
rheagroup.com

Rhebo (36, 0.0%)
IoT Security / OT Security
Leipzig, Germany
rhebo.com

Ricoh USA (18703, -1.1%)
IAM / Authentication
Exton, PA, US
ricoh-usa.com

Ridge Security (33, 50.0%)
GRC / Penetration Testing
Santa Clara,
CA, US
ridgesecurity.ai

Ridgeback Network Defense (9, -18.2%)
Deception
Baltimore, MD, US
ridgebacknet.com

Right-Hand Security (48, 54.8%)
GRC / Security
Awareness Training
Lewes, DE, US
right-hand.ai

RioRey (16, 0.0%)
Network Security /
DDoS Defense
Bethesda, MD, US
riorey.com

Riot (34, 54.5%)
GRC / Security
Awareness Training
San Francisco,
CA, US
tryriot.com

Rippleshot (20, -9.1%)
Fraud Prevention /
Fraud Detection
Chicago, IL, US
rippleshot.com

Riscosity (26, 52.9%)
GRC
Austin, TX, US
riscosity.com

Riscure (173, 1.8%)
Testing / Security For
Embedded Systems
Delft, Netherlands
riscure.com

Risk Based Security (4, -20.0%)
GRC / Vulnerabilities
Richmond, VA, US
riskbasedsecurity.com

Risk Ledger (33, -23.3%)
GRC / Risk Management
London, United Kingdom
riskledger.com

Risk.Ident (74, 5.7%)
Fraud Prevention /
Fraud Detection
London, United Kingdom
riskident.com

Riskified (753, -3.2%)
Fraud Prevention /
Transaction
Security
Tel Aviv, Israel
riskified.com

RiskLens (14, -79.4%)
GRC / Risk Management
Spokane, WA, US
risklens.com

RiskRecon (118, 0.8%)
GRC / Risk Management
Salt Lake City,
UT, US
riskrecon.com

RiskSense (27, -12.9%)
GRC / Vulnerabilities
Albuquerque, NM, US
risksense.com

RiskWatch International (12, -7.7%)
GRC / Risk Management
Sarasota, FL, US
riskwatch.com

River Security (26, 62.5%)
Operations / Attack Surface
Management
Oslo, Norway
riversecurity.eu

RMRF TECH (11, 22.2%)
Deception / Host
Environments
Kyiv, Ukraine
rmrf.tech

Robust Intelligence (72, 4.3%)
GRC / Governance
San Francisco, CA, US
robustintelligence.com

Rocketcyber (22, 4.8%)
Operations / SOC
Dallas, TX, US
rocketcyber.com

Romad (21, -12.5%)
Endpoint Security / Anti-virus
Kiev, Ukraine
romad.io

Room 40 Labs (27, 145.4%)
Operations
Bethesda, MD, US
room40labs.com

Rootly (35, -7.9%)
Operations / Incident
Management
San Francisco, CA, US
rootly.com

Rootshell Security (46, 12.2%)
GRC
Basingstoke, Hampshire,
United Kingdom
rootshellsecurity.net

Route 1 (43, -12.2%)
IAM
Toronto, ON, Canada
route1.com

RSA Security (Symphony Technology Group) (2826, 0.3%)
IAM / Authentication
Bedford, MA, US
rsa.com

Rthreat (23, -14.8%)
Operations / Breach And
Attack Simulation
Bellingham, WA, US
rthreat.net

**Numbers in parentheses indicate headcount and % change in 2023.*

Rublon (18, 20.0%)
IAM / Authentication
Zielona Gora, Poland
rublon.com

Rubrik (3540, 14.7%)
Data Security / Data Discovery
Palo Alto, CA, US
rubrik.com

Rudder (46, 228.6%)
Operations / Configuration Management
Paris, France
rudder.io

Rugged Tooling (8, 0.0%)
Network Security / Monitoring
Oulu, Finland
ruggedtooling.com

Runecast Solutions (68, -8.1%)
Operations / Vulnerabilities
London, United Kingdom
runecast.com

RunSafe Security (18, 5.9%)
Application Security / Application Hardening
McLean, VA, US
runsafesecurity.com

Runtime Verification (48, 17.1%)
Application Security / Code Security
Urbana, IL, US
runtimeverification.com

runZero (57, -29.6%)
Network Security / Asset Management
Austin, TX, US
runzero.com

S2 Grupo (679, 13.4%)
MSSP / SOC
Valencia, Spain
s2grupo.es

S2T (51, 21.4%)
Threat Intelligence / Dark Web
Slough, United Kingdom
s2t.ai

S2W Inc. (59, -6.3%)
Threat Intelligence / Investigation
Pangyo, South Korea
s2w.inc

SaaS Alerts (35, 20.7%)
Operations / Monitoring
Wilmington, NC, US
saasalerts.com

Saaspass (11, -8.3%)
IAM
San Francisco, CA, US
saaspass.com

Saf.ai (6, 0.0%)
Data Security / IRM
Bethesda, MD, US
saf.ai

Safe Security (301, -34.6%)
GRC / Risk Management
Palo Alto, CA, US
safe.security

Safe-T (21, 5.0%)
IAM / Access Security
Herzliya Pituach, Israel
safe-t.com

SafeBase (72, 56.5%)
GRC / Secure Storage
San Francisco, CA, US
safebase.io

SafeBreach (134, -20.2%)
Operations / Breach And Attack Simulation
Tel Aviv, Israel
safebreach.com

SafeDNS (21, 31.2%)
Network Security / DNS Security
Alexandria, VA, US
safedns.com

SafeGuard Cyber (62, -13.9%)
GRC / Employee Social Media Management
Charlottesville, VA, US
safeguardcyber.com

Safeguard Privacy (27, 42.1%)
GRC / Compliance Management
New York, NY, US
safeguardprivacy.com

SafeHats (7, 16.7%)
Application Security / Bugs
Bangalore, India
safehats.com

Safeheron (13, 0.0%)
Data Security / Encryption
Singapore City, Singapore
safeheron.com

Safehouse Technologies (66, 10.0%)
Network Security / VPN/Proxy
Tel Aviv, Israel
safehousetech.com

SafeLiShare (13, 160.0%)
Data Security
Morristown, NJ, US
safelishare.com

SafeLogic (13, 18.2%)
Data Security / Cryptographic Libraries
Palo Alto, CA, US
safelogic.com

SaferPass (16, -11.1%)
IAM / Credential Security
Bratislava, Slovakia
saferpass.net

SaferVPN (3, 0.0%)
Network Security / VPN/Proxy
New York, NY, US
safervpn.com

SafeStack (19, -24.0%)
Training / Software Development Security
Aukland, New Zealand
safestack.io

Safetica (94, -8.7%)
Data Security / DLP
Brno, Czechia
safetica.com

SafeUM (3, 50.0%)
Data Security / Secure Communications
Iceland
safeum.com

SailPoint (2464, 9.2%)
IAM / Governance
Austin, TX, US
sailpoint.com

Salem Security (8, 0.0%)
Operations
Winston-Salem, NC, US
salemcyber.com

Salt Security (202, -1.0%)
API Security
Palo Alto, CA, US
salt.security

SaltDNA (16, -20.0%)
Data Security / Secure Communications
Belfast, United Kingdom
saltdna.com

SaltyCloud (10, -9.1%)
Operations / Workflow Automation
Austin, TX, US
saltycloud.com

Salvador Technologies (26, 36.8%)
IoT Security
Rehovot, Israel
salvador-tech.com

**Numbers in parentheses indicate headcount and % change in 2023.*

Salviol Global Analytics (22, 15.8%)
Fraud Prevention / Fraud Detection
Reading, United Kingdom
salviol.com

SAM for Compliance (3, 0.0%)
GRC / Compliance Management
Hastings, New Zealand
samcompliance.co

SAM Seamless Network (74, -7.5%)
Network Security / Gateways
Tel Aviv, Israel
securingsam.com

SandboxAQ (219, 71.1%)
Data Security / Quantum
New York, NY, US
sandboxaq.com

Sandfly Security (10, 11.1%)
Endpoint Security / EDR
Christchurch, New Zealand
sandflysecurity.com

Sangfor (2101, -0.5%)
Network Security / UTM
Shenzhen, China
sangfor.com

Sapien Cyber (10, -56.5%)
Security Analytics / Incident Management
Joondalup, Australia
sapiencyber.com.au

Saporo (30, 7.1%)
IAM / Identity Management
Lausanne, Vaud, Switzerland
saporo.io

SAS Institute (16426, 2.9%)
Fraud Prevention / Anti-fraud
Cary, NC, US
sas.com

Sasa Software (32, -5.9%)
Data Security / File Scrubbing
Sasa, Israel
sasa-software.com

Satori Cyber (136, 58.1%)
Data Security / Data Flows
Tel Aviv, Israel
satoricyber.com

Saviynt (845, -5.0%)
IAM / Governance
El Segundo, CA, US
saviynt.com

Savvy (50, -2.0%)
Operations / SaaS Security
Tel Aviv District, Israel
savvy.security

Sayata Labs (73, 7.3%)
GRC / Risk Management
Tel Aviv, Israel
sayatalabs.com

ScadaFence (56, -15.2%)
IoT Security / OT Security
Tel Aviv, Israel
scadafence.com

Scalarr (21, -27.6%)
Fraud Prevention / Advertising-related
Wilmington, DE, US
scalarr.io

scanmeter (7, 75.0%)
Application Security / Penetration Testing
Zurich, Switzerland
scanmeter.io

Scantist (26, -16.1%)
GRC / Vulnerabilities
Singapore, Singapore
scantist.com

SCIS Security (62, -1.6%)
MSSP / MDR
Houston, TX, US
scissecurity.com

SCIT Labs (8, -11.1%)
Endpoint Security / Servers
Clifton, VA, US
scitlabs.com

ScoutDNS (3, 0.0%)
Network Security / DNS Security
Grand Prairie, TX, US
scoutdns.com

Scram Software (3, -25.0%)
Data Security / Encryption
Melbourne, Australia
scramsoft.com

Scribe Security (33, 37.5%)
Application Security / SBOM
Tel Aviv, Israel
scribesecurity.com

Scrut Automation (145, 119.7%)
GRC / Compliance Management
Bangalore, Karnataka, India
scrut.io

Scybers (61, 29.8%)
MSSP / SOC
Singapore
scybers.com

Scytale (54, 25.6%)
GRC / Compliance Management
Tel Aviv, Israel
scytale.ai

SCYTHE (32, -33.3%)
Testing / Breach And Attack Simulation
Arlington, VA, US
scythe.io

SDG Corporation (577, 10.3%)
GRC
Norwalk, CT, US
sdgc.com

Seagate Technology (16127, -2.7%)
Data Security / Encryption
Cupertino, CA, US
seagate.com

Seald (10, 25.0%)
Data Security
Paris, France
seald.io

Sealit (11, -15.4%)
Data Security / Secure Communications
London, United Kingdom
sealit.id

Sealpath (26, 0.0%)
Data Security / IRM
Bilbao, Spain
sealpath.com

Searchguard (6, 50.0%)
Data Security / Security For Elasticsearch
Berlin, Germany
search-guard.com

SearchInform (110, 12.2%)
Operations / Monitoring
Moscow, Russia
searchinform.com

Searchlight Cyber (57, 26.7%)
Threat Intelligence / Dark Web
Portsmouth, United Kingdom
slcyber.io

SEC Consult (137, 0.0%)
Application Security / Code Security
Vienna, Austria
sec-consult.com

Secberus (20, -33.3%)
GRC / Compliance Management
Miami, FL, US
secberus.com

**Numbers in parentheses indicate headcount and % change in 2023.*

Seccom Global (46, -4.2%)
MSSP / Managed Security Services
Sydney, Australia
seccomglobal.com

Seceon (121, 9.0%)
Security Analytics / SIEM
Westford, MA, US
seceon.com

Secfense (16, 23.1%)
IAM / Access Security
Krakow, Poland
secfense.com

Secfix (21, 50.0%)
GRC / Compliance Management
Berlin, Germany
secfix.com

Seckiot (34, 6.2%)
IoT Security
Paris, France
seckiot.fr

Seclab (20, -13.0%)
Data Security / Secure Data Sharing
Montpellier, France
seclab-security.com

SecLogic (38, 46.1%)
GRC / Posture Management
Jacksonville, FL, US
seclogic.io

Seclore (325, 15.7%)
Data Security / IRM
Mumbai, India
seclore.com

Seclytics (15, 0.0%)
Security Analytics / Threat Intelligence
San Diego, CA, US
seclytics.com

Secnap (18, 12.5%)
MSSP / Managed Security Services
Fort Lauderdale, FL, US
secnap.com

SECNOLOGY (14, -6.7%)
Security Analytics / Big Data
El Granada, CA, US
secnology.com

Secomea A/S (101, 5.2%)
IoT Security / Remote Devices
Herlev, Denmark
secomea.com

Secon Cyber (211, 74.4%)
MSSP / MDR
Surrey, United Kingdom
seconcyber.com

Seconize (17, 6.2%)
GRC / Risk Management
Singapore, Singapore
seconize.co

SecOps Solution (10, -9.1%)
GRC / Vulnerabilities
Bengaluru, India
secopsolution.com

Secpod (112, 21.7%)
Endpoint Security / Endpoint Management
Tulsa, OK, US
secpod.com

SecPoint (15, -11.8%)
GRC / Vulnerabilities
Copenhagen, Denmark
secpoint.com

Secret Double Octopus (41, -21.1%)
IAM / Authentication
Tel Aviv, Israel
doubleoctopus.com

SecSign (4, 0.0%)
IAM / Authentication
Henderson, NV, US
secsign.com

Sectigo (410, 25.0%)
Data Security / Public Key Infrastructure
Roseland, NJ, US
sectigo.com

Sectona (56, 21.7%)
IAM / Access Security
Mumbai, Maharashtra, India
sectona.com

Sectra Communications (1363, 21.5%)
Data Security / Secure Communications
Linkoping, Sweden
sectra.com

Sectrio (39, 34.5%)
IoT Security / Segmentation
CO, US
sectrio.com

Secude (108, -25.0%)
Data Security / SAP
Luzern, Switzerland
secude.com

SecuGen (18, -14.3%)
IAM / Authentication
Santa Clara, CA, US
secugen.com

SecuLetter (16, 0.0%)
Operations / Malware Analysis
Seongnam-si, South Korea
seculetter.com

secunet (762, 47.4%)
Data Security
Germany
secunet.com

SecuPi (50, 21.9%)
Application Security / Monitoring
London, United Kingdom
secupi.com

Securco (24, 33.3%)
Data Security / Secure Communications
New York, NY, US
secureco.com

Securden (75, 31.6%)
IAM / Access Security
Newark, DE, US
securden.com

Secure Decisions (4, 0.0%)
Security Analytics / Visualization
Northport, NY, US
securedecisions.com

Secure Exchanges (10, 42.9%)
Data Security / Document Security
Canada
secure-exchanges.com

Secure-Nok (15, 15.4%)
IoT Security / OT Security
Hamar, Norway
securenok.com

Secure64 (41, 0.0%)
Network Security / DNS Security
Fort Collins, CO, US
secure64.com

SecureAge Technology (37, -9.8%)
Data Security / Encryption
West Chester, PA, US
secureage.com

Secureauth Corporation (175, -8.4%)
IAM / Access Security
Irvine, CA, US
secureauth.com

SecureCode Warrior (259, 2.0%)
Training / Software Development Security
Sydney, Australia
securecodewarrior.com

Secured Communications (12, -55.6%)
Data Security / Secure Communications
San Francisco, CA, US
securedcommunications.com

**Numbers in parentheses indicate headcount and % change in 2023.*

Secured2 (5, -16.7%)
Data Security /
Secure Storage
Minneapolis,
MN, US
secured2.com

SecureData (57, -26.0%)
Data Security / Secure
Storage
Los Angeles, CA, US
securedata.com

SecureEnvoy (3, -25.0%)
GRC / DLP
Cardiff, United Kingdom
geolang.com

SecureFlag (24, 33.3%)
Training
London, United Kingdom
secureflag.com

Secureframe (153, 5.5%)
GRC / Compliance
Management
San Francisco,
CA, US
secureframe.com

SecureIC (112, 2.8%)
IoT Security / Hardware
France
secure-ic.com

SecureLink (132, -21.0%)
IAM / Access Security
Austin, TX, US
securelink.com

SecureLogix Corporation (77, 0.0%)
Network Security /
VoIP Security
San Antonio,
TX, US
securelogix.com

SecurelyShare (24, -22.6%)
Data Security / Secure
Storage
Indira Nagar,
India
securelyshare.com

SecureMac (6, 0.0%)
Endpoint Security /
Anti-malware
Las Vegas, NV, US
securemac.com

Securemailbox (3, 0.0%)
Data Security / Secure
Communications
Stockholm, Sweden
securemailbox.com

Secureme2 (17, 54.5%)
MSSP / MDR
Rijen, Netherlands
secureme2.eu

SecurEnds (62, -26.2%)
IAM / Governance
Atlanta, GA, US
securends.com

SecurEnvoy (24, 0.0%)
IAM / Authentication
Basingstoke,
United Kingdom
securenvoy.com

SecureSky (19, 18.8%)
MSSP / MDR
Omaha, NE, US
securesky.com

SecureStack (8, 33.3%)
GRC / Configuration
Management
Docklands,
Australia
securestack.com

SecureTeam (11, -8.3%)
Data Security / DRM
Rishon LeZion, Israel
secureteam.net

SecureThings (26, 23.8%)
IoT Security / Automotive
Sunnyvale, CA, US
securethings.ai

SecureW2 (73, 0.0%)
IAM / Authentication
Seattle, WA, US
securew2.com

SecureWorks (1903, -21.8%)
MSSP / Managed
Security Services
Atlanta, GA, US
secureworks.com

Securicy (Now Carbide) (34, -27.7%)
GRC / Policy Management
Sydney, NS, Canada
securicy.com

Securithings (72, 2.9%)
IoT Security / Device
Management
Ramat Gan, Israel
securithings.com

Securiti (703, 34.4%)
Data Security /
Data Discovery
San Jose, CA, US
securiti.ai

Security Code (123, -3.9%)
Network Security / UTM
Moscow, Russia
securitycode.ru

Security Compass (259, 13.1%)
GRC / Compliance
Management
Toronto, ON, Canada
securitycompass.com

Security Innovation (225, 22.3%)
Training / Cyber Range
Wilmington, MA, US
securityinnovation.com

Security Journey (60, -3.2%)
Training / Software
Development Security
Raleigh, NC, US
securityjourney.com

Security Mentor (5, 25.0%)
GRC / Security
Awareness Training
Pacific Grove, CA, US
securitymentor.com

Security Mind (4, 0.0%)
GRC / Security Awareness
Training
Veneto, Italy
securitymind.cloud

Security Weaver (59, -21.3%)
Data Security / IRM
Lehi, UT, US
securityweaver.com

SecurityBox (4, -33.3%)
Network Security / Gateways
Hanoi, Vietnam
securitybox.vn

SecurityBridge (43, 65.4%)
Application Security / SAP
Ingolstadt, Germany
securitybridge.com

SecurityGen (35, 0.0%)
Network Security / Firewalls
Rome, Italy
secgen.com

SecurityHQ (383, 26.0%)
MSSP / MDR
London, United Kingdom
securityhq.com

SecurityMetrics (260, 0.8%)
GRC / Vulnerabilities
Orem, UT, US
securitymetrics.com

SecurityScorecard (544, -0.2%)
GRC / Risk Management
New York, NY, US
securityscorecard.com

SecurityStudio (13, -35.0%)
GRC / Risk Management
Minnetonka, MN, US
securitystudio.com

SecurityTrails (17, -39.3%)
Operations / Asset Inventory
Los Angeles, CA, US
securitytrails.com

**Numbers in parentheses indicate headcount and % change in 2023.*

SecurityZONES (5, -28.6%)
Threat Intelligence / Spamhaus
London, United Kingdom
securityzones.net

SecurLinx (9, -10.0%)
IAM / Authentication
Morgantown, WV, US
securlinx.com

Securonix (750, -20.6%)
Security Analytics / Monitoring
Addison, TX, US
securonix.com

Securosys (29, 20.8%)
Data Security / Hardware
Zurich, Switzerland
securosys.com

Secutech Solutions (8, -20.0%)
Data Security / USB Token Security
North Ryde, Australia
esecutech.com

Secuware (9, -25.0%)
Data Security / Database Security
London, United Kingdom
secuware.com

SecZetta (17, -56.4%)
IAM
Fall River, MA, US
seczetta.com

Sedicii (12, -33.3%)
IAM / Authentication
Carriganore, Ireland
sedicii.com

Seedata (5, -28.6%)
Deception / Leaked Data
London, United Kingdom
seedata.io

Seela (24, -22.6%)
Training / Interactive Courses
Boulogne Billancourt, France
seela.io

SeeMetrics (23, 21.1%)
Operations / Monitoring
Tel Aviv, Israel
seemetrics.co

Seemplicity (67, 48.9%)
Operations
Tel Aviv, Israel
seemplicity.io

SEKOIA.IO (115, 30.7%)
Security Analytics / SIEM
Paris, France
sekoia.io

Semgrep (147, 0.0%)
Application Security / Code Security
San Francisco, CA, US
semgrep.dev

Semperis (396, 14.4%)
IAM / Active Directory
New York, NY, US
semperis.com

Sendio (17, -5.6%)
Email Security / Anti-spam
Newport Beach, CA, US
sendio.com

Sendmarc (64, 68.4%)
Email Security / Defense Against Phishing
ROSEBANK, Gauteng, South Africa
sendmarc.com

SendSafely (34, 9.7%)
Data Security / Secure Data Sharing
New York, NY, US
sendsafely.com

SendThisFile (8, 60.0%)
Data Security / Secure Data Sharing
Wichita, KS, US
sendthisfile.com

Senetas Corporation Limited (41, -8.9%)
Data Security / Encryption
South Melbourne, Australia
senetas.com

Sennovate (73, -16.1%)
MSSP / Managed Security Services
San Ramon, CA, US
sennovate.com

SensCy (17, 6.2%)
GRC / Healthcare
Ann Arbor, MI, US
senscy.com

Senseon (83, -1.2%)
Security Analytics / Incident Management
London, United Kingdom
senseon.io

Senser (16, -5.9%)
Operations / Workload Security
Ramat Gan, India
senser.tech

Senserva (7, 16.7%)
GRC / Posture Management
St Paul, MN, US
senserva.com

Sensible Vision (4, -20.0%)
IAM / Authentication
Cape Coral, FL, US
sensiblevision.com

SensiPass (7, 0.0%)
IAM / Authentication
Dublin, Ireland
sensipass.com

Sensor Fleet (9, -10.0%)
Network Security / Monitoring
Oulu, Finland
sensorfleet.com

Sentar (313, 3.3%)
Application Security / Code Security
Huntsville, AL, US
sentar.com

SentiLink (101, 16.1%)
Fraud Prevention / Anti-fraud
San Francisco, CA, US
sentilink.com

Sentinel IPS (9, 0.0%)
MSSP / Firewalls
Dallas, TX, US
sentinelips.com

SentinelOne (2293, 20.7%)
Endpoint Security / Endpoint Protection
Mountain View, CA, US
sentinelone.com

Sentor (78, -6.0%)
MSSP / SIEM
Stockholm, Sweden
sentor.se

Sentra (84, 44.8%)
Data Security / Data Discovery
Tel Aviv, Israel
sentra.io

SentryBay (32, -11.1%)
Endpoint Security / Anti-malware
London, United Kingdom
sentrybay.com

Seon (254, -13.9%)
Fraud Prevention / Fraud Detection
Budapest, Hungary
seon.io

Sepio Systems (69, -15.8%)
IoT Security / Asset Management
Gaithersburg, MD, US
sepiocyber.com

Sepior (8, 33.3%)
Data Security / Encryption
Aarhus, Denmark
sepior.com

Seppmail (12, 20.0%)
Email Security / Secure Email
Neuenhof, Switzerland
seppmail.com

Septier Communication (30, 3.5%)
Network Security / SIGINT Offensive
Petah Tikva, Israel
septier.com

**Numbers in parentheses indicate headcount and % change in 2023.*

Seqrite (171, 185.0%)
Endpoint Security / Encryption
Pune, India
seqrite.com

Sequretek (353, 4.8%)
Endpoint Security / Anti-virus
Mumbai, India
sequretek.com

Sera-Brynn (13, 44.4%)
GRC / Risk Management
Suffolk, VA, US
sera-brynn.com

Seraphic Security (29, 31.8%)
Network Security / Secure Web Browsing
Wilmington, DE, US
seraphicsecurity.com

Sergeant Laboratories (15, 0.0%)
GRC / Risk Management
Onalaska, WI, US
sgtlabs.com

Sertinty (20, 0.0%)
Data Security / IRM
Nashville, TN, US
sertainty.com

ServiceNow (24941, 14.4%)
Operations / Orchestration
Santa Clara, CA, US
servicenow.com

SessionGuardian (14, 27.3%)
IAM / Identity Verification
New York, NY, US
sessionguardian.com

Set In Stone (3, 0.0%)
Data Security / IRM
Paris, France
setinstone.io

Sevco Security (63, 21.1%)
GRC / Asset Management
Austin, TX, US
sevco.io

Seworks (28, 133.3%)
Operations / Penetration Testing
San Francisco, CA, US
se.works

ShadowDragon (48, 71.4%)
Threat Intelligence / OSINT
Wilmington, DE, US
shadowdragon.io

ShardSecure (35, 29.6%)
Data Security / Shards
New York, NY, US
go.shardsecure.com

SHAREKEY (25, -3.9%)
Data Security / Encryption
Zug, Switzerland
sharekey.com

SharePass (5, 66.7%)
IAM / CIAM
Melbourne, Victoria, Australia
sharepass.com

ShareVault (38, 2.7%)
Data Security / Secure Storage
Los Gatos, CA, US
sharevault.com

Sharkgate (12, -20.0%)
Network Security / Firewalls
London, United Kingdom
sharkgate.net

Sharktech (21, 40.0%)
Network Security / DDoS Defense
Las Vegas, NV, US
sharktech.net

Shield (157, 6.8%)
Fraud Prevention / Device Fingerprinting
San Francisco, CA, US
shield.com

ShieldIOT (17, -15.0%)
IoT Security
Herzliya, Israel
shieldiot.io

Shift5 (114, 28.1%)
IoT Security / Trains, Planes, And Tanks
Arlington, VA, US
shift5.io

Shodan (12, 50.0%)
IoT Security / Attack Surface Management
Austin, TX, US
beta.shodan.io

Sicura (26, 8.3%)
GRC / Compliance Management
Baltimore, MD, US
sicura.us

SideChannel (34, 3.0%)
Network Security / Segmentation
Worcester, MA, US
sidechannel.com

SideDrawer (27, 22.7%)
Data Security / Secure Data Sharing
Toronto, Canada
sidedrawer.com

SIEMonster (14, 75.0%)
Security Analytics
New York, NY, US
siemonster.com

Sierraware (13, -13.3%)
Endpoint Security / Mobile Device Security
Sunnyvale, CA, US
sierraware.com

Sift (369, 14.9%)
Fraud Prevention / Identity Verification
San Francisco, CA, US
sift.com

Siga OT Solutions (35, 9.4%)
IoT Security / Monitoring
Wilmington, DE, US
sigasec.com

SigmaRed (16, 60.0%)
Data Security / AI Debiasing
Toronto, ON, Canada
sigmared.ai

SignaCert (6, 0.0%)
Endpoint Security / Whitelisting OEM
Austin, TX, US
signacert.com

Signal Science (24, 26.3%)
API Security / Bot Security
Culver City, CA, US
signalsciences.com

Signicat (438, -0.5%)
IAM / Identity Verification
Rotterdam, Netherlands
signicat.nl

Signifyd (555, 2.0%)
Fraud Prevention / E-Commerce Fraud Prevention
San Jose, CA, US
signifyd.com

Silence Laboratories (24, -25.0%)
IAM / Authentication
Central Region, Singapore, Singapore
silencelaboratories.com

Silent Circle (23, 0.0%)
Data Security / Secure Communications
Fairfax, VA, US
silentcircle.com

Silent Push (28, 55.6%)
Threat Intelligence / OSINT
Reston, VA, US
silentpush.com

Silicon Forensics (11, 22.2%)
Operations / Forensics
Pomona, CA, US
siliconforensics.com

Silk Security (25, 66.7%)
GRC / Risk Management
Santa Clara, CA, US
silk.security

Silobreaker (66, -1.5%)
Threat Intelligence / Threat Intelligence Management
London, United Kingdom
silobreaker.com

**Numbers in parentheses indicate headcount and % change in 2023.*

SilverLakeMasterSAM (29, -6.5%)
IAM / Access Security
Singapore, Singapore
mastersam.com

Silverskin Information Security (20, -9.1%)
GRC / Compliance Management
Helsinki, Finland
silverskin.com

SilverSky (417, 27.5%)
MSSP / Managed Security Services
Durham, NC, US
silversky.com

Simeio Solutions (719, 1.8%)
IAM
Atlanta, GA, US
simeiosolutions.com

Simplex (215, 0.9%)
Fraud Prevention / Transaction Security
Givatayim, Israel
simplex.com

SimSpace (173, -13.9%)
Training / Cyber Range
Boston, MA, US
simspace.com

Singular Security (8, 14.3%)
GRC
Tustin, CA, US
singularsecurity.com

Siren (84, 29.2%)
Security Analytics / Data Analysis
Galway, Ireland
siren.io

SIRP (21, 31.2%)
Operations
London, United Kingdom
sirp.io

SISA (638, -12.7%)
Data Security / Data Discovery
Bengaluru, India
sisainfosec.com

Sitehop (13, 85.7%)
Network Security
Sheffield, United Kingdom
sitehop.co.uk

SiteLock (98, -10.1%)
Network Security / Website Security
Scottsdale, AZ, US
sitelock.com

SixMap (26, 420.0%)
Operations / Attack Surface Management
San Francisco, CA, US
sixmap.io

Skiff (30, 30.4%)
Data Security / Secure Communications
San Francisco, CA, US
skiff.org

Skopenow (45, -6.2%)
Threat Intelligence / OSINT
New York, NY, US
skopenow.com

Skout Cybersecurity (20, -20.0%)
Security Analytics / Data Analysis
New York, NY, US
getskout.com

Skurio (33, -13.2%)
Threat Intelligence / Brand
Belfast, United Kingdom
skurio.com

Skybox Security (300, -7.4%)
Operations / Security Management
San Jose, CA, US
skyboxsecurity.com

Skyflow (132, 17.9%)
Data Security / Secure Storage
Palo Alto, CA, US
skyflow.com

Skyhawk Security (34, 25.9%)
Operations / Breach Detection
Tel Aviv, Israel
skyhawk.security

Skyhigh Security (620, -2.4%)
Network Security / Gateways
Santa Clara, CA, US
skyhighsecurity.com

Skymatic (5, 25.0%)
Data Security
Sankt Augustin, Germany
skymatic.de

SlashID (14, 0.0%)
IAM / Access Security
Chicago, IL, US
slashid.dev

SlashNext (168, 31.2%)
Email Security / Defense Against Phishing
Pleasanton, CA, US
slashnext.com

Slauth.io (4, 0.0%)
GRC / Policy Management
Tel Aviv, Israel
slauth.io

Slim.AI (38, -9.5%)
Application Security / Container Security
Acton, MA, US
slim.ai

Sling (26, -7.1%)
GRC / Risk Management
Tel Aviv, Israel
slingscore.com

Smallstep (22, -18.5%)
Data Security / Public Key Infrastructure
San Francisco, CA, US
smallstep.com

Smartfense (32, -8.6%)
GRC / Security Awareness Training
Cordoba, Argentina
smartfense.com

Smarttech247 (190, 38.7%)
MSSP / MDR
New York, NY, US
smarttech247.com

Smoothwall (151, 11.8%)
Network Security / UTM
Leeds, United Kingdom
smoothwall.com

SMX (26, 44.4%)
Email Security
Auckland, New Zealand
smxemail.com

SnapAttack (26, 0.0%)
Operations / Threat Hunting
Columbia, MD, US
snapattack.com

Snowbit (16, 23.1%)
MSSP / MDR
Tel Aviv, Israel
snowbit.io

SnowHaze (3, 0.0%)
Endpoint Security / Secure Web Browsing
Zurich, Switzerland
snowhaze.com

Snowpack (16, 45.5%)
Network Security / VPN/Proxy
Orsay, France
snowpack.eu

Snyk (1128, -11.5%)
Application Security / Vulnerabilities
London, United Kingdom
snyk.io

**Numbers in parentheses indicate headcount and % change in 2023.*

SoBug (3, 0.0%)
Application Security /
Bugs
Shenzhen, China
sobug.com

SOC Prime (99, -10.8%)
Threat Intelligence / Threat
Intelligence Platform
Kiev, Ukraine
socprime.com

SOCAutomation (6, 50.0%)
Operations / XDR
Witney, United Kingdom
socautomation.com

Social Links (96, 100.0%)
Operations / OSINT
New York, NY, US
sociallinks.io

SOCRadar (166, 19.4%)
Threat Intelligence / TIP
Middletown,
DE, US
socradar.io

SOCSoter (21, 16.7%)
MSSP / Managed
Security Services
Hagerstown, MD, US
socsoter.com

Socura (22, 15.8%)
MSSP / MDR
London, United Kingdom
socura.co.uk

Socure (440, -8.0%)
IAM / Identity Verification
New York, NY, US
socure.com

Soffid (14, 40.0%)
IAM / Authentication
Palma de Mallorca,
Spain
soffid.com

Sofistic (81, -3.6%)
MSSP
Castellon, Spain
sofistic.com

Softcamp (29, 3.6%)
Data Security
Eongnam-Si,
South Korea
softcamp.co.kr

Softex (22, 266.7%)
IAM / Authentication
Austin, TX, US
softexinc.com

Software Diversified Services (20, 17.6%)
Endpoint Security / Z / OS
Security
Minneapolis, MN, US
sdsusa.com

Software Engineering of America (85, -5.6%)
Endpoint Security / ISeries
Garden City,
NY, US
seasoft.com

SOFTwarfare (31, 63.2%)
Application Security /
Integration Security
Prairie Village,
KS, US
softwarfare.com

Softwin SRL (176, -9.7%)
Endpoint Security /
Anti-virus
Bucharest, Romania
softwin.com

Solarwinds (2540, 0.2%)
Security Analytics / SIEM
Austin, TX, US
solarwinds.com

SolCyber (34, 0.0%)
MSSP / Managed Security
Services
Dallas, TX, US
solcyber.com

SolidWall (17, 112.5%)
Application Security /
Firewalls
Moscow, Russia
solidwall.io

solo.io (229, 2.7%)
Network Security /
Segmentation
Cambridge, MA, US
solo.io

SolonTek (4, -55.6%)
GRC / Configuration
Management
Raleigh, NC, US
solontek.net

SolSoft (24, 4.3%)
Operations / Policy
Management
Bristol, United Kingdom
solsoft.co.uk

Solutions-II (85, 11.8%)
MSSP / Monitoring
Littleton, CO, US
solutions-ii.com

Solvo (30, 25.0%)
Operations / Configuration
Management
Tel Aviv, Israel
solvo.cloud

Somansa (38, -9.5%)
GRC / DLP
San Jose, CA, US
somansatech.com

Somma (8, -27.3%)
Security Analytics / XDR
Seongnam-si, South Korea
somma.kr

Sonar (527, 5.6%)
Application Security /
Code Security
Vernier, Switzerland
sonarsource.com

Sonatype (573, -10.5%)
Application Security /
Code Security
Fulton, MD, US
sonatype.com

Sonet.io (12, 33.3%)
IAM / Access Security
San Jose, CA, US
sonet.io

SonicWall (1944, 3.9%)
Network Security / UTM
Milpitas, CA, US
sonicwall.com

Sonrai Security (90, -21.1%)
IAM / Data Security
New York, NY, US
sonraisecurity.com

Soos (15, -6.2%)
Application Security / SBOM
Winooski, VT, US
soos.io

Sophos (4592, -1.3%)
Endpoint Security /
Anti-virus
Abingdon, United Kingdom
sophos.com

SoSafe (403, 12.6%)
GRC / Security Awareness
Training
Cologne, North Rhine-
Westphalia,
Germany
sosafe-awareness.com

Sotero (19, -36.7%)
Data Security / Encryption
Burlington, MA, US
soterosoft.com

Source Defense (46, -9.8%)
Network Security /
Client-Side
Protection Against Third
Party Attacks
Be'er Sheva, Israel
sourcedefense.com

South River Technologies (17, -10.5%)
Data Security / Secure
Data Sharing
Annapolis, MD, US
southrivertech.com

Soveren (28, -12.5%)
API Security / Compliance
Management
London, United Kingdom
soveren.io

**Numbers in parentheses indicate headcount and % change in 2023.*

SPAMfighter (16, -11.1%)
Endpoint Security / Anti-spam
Miami, FL, US
spamfighter.com

Spanalytics (11, -8.3%)
IoT Security / Wireless Security
Glen Allen, VA, US
spanalytics.com

SparkCognition (309, -17.8%)
Endpoint Security / Anti-virus
Austin, TX, US
sparkcognition.com

Sparrow (19, 26.7%)
Application Security / Code Security
Mapo-gu, South Korea
sparrowfasoo.com

Specfile (4, 0.0%)
Data Security / Encryption
Poznan, Poland
specfile.pl

Specialized Security Services Inc. (66, -20.5%)
MSSP / Managed Security Services
Plano, TX, US
s3security.com

Specops Software Inc. (68, -17.1%)
IAM / Credential Security
Stockholm, Sweden
specopssoft.com

SpecterOps (115, 51.3%)
IAM
Alexandria, VA, US
specterops.io

SpecTrust (81, 68.8%)
Fraud Prevention
San Jose, CA, US
spec-trust.com

SpeechPro (25, -26.5%)
IAM / Authentication
New York, NY, US
speechpro-usa.com

SpeQtral (31, 55.0%)
Data Security / Quantum
Singapore, Singapore
speqtral.space

Spera Security (34, 0.0%)
IAM / Posture Management
Tel Aviv, Israel
spera.security

SPHERE Technology Solutions (109, 34.6%)
IAM / Access Security
Hoboken, NJ, US
sphereco.com

Spherical Defence (4, 0.0%)
API Security
San Francisco, CA, US
sphericaldefence.com

SpiderAF (45, 0.0%)
Fraud Prevention / Advertising-related
Tokyo, Japan
spideraf.com

Spideroak (38, 0.0%)
Data Security
Mission, KS, US
spideroak.com

SpiderSilk (43, 2.4%)
GRC / Attack Surface Management
Dubai, United Arab Emirates
spidersilk.com

Spin Technology (76, 5.6%)
GRC / Risk Management
Palo Alto, CA, US
spin.ai

Spirent Communications (2053, -1.0%)
Testing / Security Instrumentation
Crawley, United Kingdom
spirent.com

Spirion (was Identity Finder) (81, -17.4%)
GRC / Data Discovery
St. Petersburg, FL, US
spirion.com

SplashData (10, 0.0%)
IAM / Authentication
Los Gatos, CA, US
splashdata.com

SplitByte (4, 0.0%)
Data Security / Shards
Los Gatos, CA, US
splitbyte.com

Splunk (8893, 1.9%)
Security Analytics / SIEM
San Francisco, CA, US
splunk.com

Spring Labs (68, 28.3%)
Data Security / Data Masking
Marina del Rey, CA, US
springlabs.com

Sprinto (227, 83.1%)
GRC / Compliance Management
San Francisco, CA, US
sprinto.com

Sprocket Security (18, 80.0%)
GRC / Penetration Testing
Madison, WI, US
sprocketsecurity.com

SpruceID (25, 4.2%)
IAM / Credential Security
New York, NY, US
spruceid.com

Spur (7, 0.0%)
Fraud Prevention / Reputation
Mount Dora, FL, US
spur.us

SpyCloud (213, 27.5%)
Threat Intelligence / Dark Web
Austin, TX, US
spycloud.com

Spyderbat (26, 8.3%)
Operations / Runtime Security
Austin, TX, US
spyderbat.com

Sqreen (4, -42.9%)
Application Security / Monitoring
Saint-Cloud, France
sqreen.com

Squadra Technologies (27, 3.9%)
GRC / DLP
Las Vegas, NV, US
squadratechnologies.com

SquareX (15, 1400.0%)
Network Security / Secure Web Browsing
Singapore
sqrx.com

SS8 (124, 6.9%)
Security Analytics
Milpitas, CA, US
ss8.com

SSenStone (17, 6.2%)
IAM / Authentication
Mapo-Gu, South Korea
ssenstone.com

SSH Communications Security (516, -4.3%)
Data Security / Secure Data Sharing
Helsinki, Finland
ssh.com

SSHTeam (19, 58.3%)
GRC / Penetration Testing
LogroÃƒÆ'Ã‚Â±o, La Rioja, Spain
sshteam.com

SSL.com (43, 26.5%)
Data Security / Public Key Infrastructure
Houston, TX, US
ssl.com

**Numbers in parentheses indicate headcount and % change in 2023.*

Stack Identity (33, 57.1%)
Operations / Access Security
Los Gatos, CA, US
stackidentity.com

stackArmor (49, 11.4%)
GRC / Monitoring
Tysons, VA, US
stackarmor.com

StackGuardian (21, 75.0%)
GRC / Compliance Management
Munich, Germany
beta.stackguardian.io

StackHawk (56, 3.7%)
Application Security / Vulnerabilities
Denver, CO, US
stackhawk.com

Stacklet (25, -34.2%)
GRC / Policy Management
Washington, DC, US
stacklet.io

StackPath (249, -18.4%)
Network Security / DDoS Defense
Dallas, TX, US
stackpath.com

Stairwell (65, 6.6%)
Security Analytics / Graph Search
Palo Alto, CA, US
stairwell.com

Stamus Networks (24, 20.0%)
Network Security / NDR
Indianapolis, IN, US
stamus-networks.com

Star Lab (42, -2.3%)
Application Security / Research
Washington, DC, US
starlab.io

STASH Global (4, 0.0%)
Data Security / DRM
Wilmington, DE, US
stash.global

STEALIEN (37, 8.8%)
Application Security
Seoul, South Korea
stealien.com

Stealth Software (5, 25.0%)
Data Security / Encryption
Scottsdale, AZ, US
stealth-soft.com

Stealthbits (61, -25.6%)
Security Analytics / Threat Prevention
Hawthorne, NJ, US
stealthbits.com

StealthMole (12, 20.0%)
Threat Intelligence / Dark Web
Singapore
stealthmole.com

SteelCloud (66, 3.1%)
GRC / Configuration Management
Ashburn, VA, US
steelcloud.com

Steganos (11, -8.3%)
Data Security / Encryption
Munich, Germany
steganos.com

Stellar Cyber (120, 29.0%)
Security Analytics / Threat Detection
Santa Clara, CA, US
stellarcyber.ai

Sternum (38, -13.6%)
IoT Security / Healthcare
Tel Aviv, Israel
sternumiot.com

StickyPassword (7, 0.0%)
IAM
Brno, Czech Republic
stickypassword.com

StormShield (was NetASQ/Arcoon) (384, 4.9%)
Network Security / UTM
Issy-les-Moulineaux, France
stormshield.com

StormWall (26, 8.3%)
Network Security / DDoS Defense
Bratislava, Slovakia
stormwall.network

Storro (6, 0.0%)
Data Security / Secure Storage
Hengelo, Netherlands
storro.com

Strac (6, 20.0%)
Data Security / DLP
Bellevue, WA, US
strac.io

Strata Identity (70, 6.1%)
IAM / Orchestration
Boulder, CO, US
strata.io

Strata Security Solutions (7, 16.7%)
GRC / Asset Management
Croydon, United Kingdom
stratasecurity.co.uk

Stratejm (69, 21.1%)
MSSP / SOC
Ontario, Canada
stratejm.com

StratoKey (4, 0.0%)
Data Security / Encryption
Austin, TX, US
stratokey.com

Stratus Digital Systems (3, 0.0%)
Endpoint Security / Servers
Eugene, OR, US
stratusdigitalsystems.com

Stream.Security (43, -28.3%)
GRC / Posture Management
Tel Aviv, Israel
stream.security

Strike Graph (44, -15.4%)
GRC / Compliance Management
Seattle, WA, US
strikegraph.com

Strike.sh (36, -2.7%)
GRC / Penetration Testing
London, United Kingdom
strike.sh

StrikeForce Technologies (25, 13.6%)
IAM / Authentication
Edison, NJ, US
strikeforcetech.com

StrikeReady (35, -2.8%)
Operations / SOC
Fremont, CA, US
strikeready.co

Strivacity (50, 31.6%)
IAM / Customer Registration
Herndon, VA, US
strivacity.com

Strobes (53, 15.2%)
GRC / Vulnerabilities
Frisco, TX, US
strobes.co

Strong Network (32, 3.2%)
Application Security / Workspace Security
Lausanne, Switzerland
strong.network

strongDM (108, -26.5%)
IAM / Access Security
Burlingame, CA, US
strongdm.com

StrongKey (12, 20.0%)
Data Security / Key Management
Durham, NC, US
strongkey.com

Sttarx (4, 33.3%)
Data Security / Encryption
Washington, DC, US
sttarx.com

Styra (61, -38.4%)
Endpoint Security / Access Security
Redwood City, CA, US
styra.com

**Numbers in parentheses indicate headcount and % change in 2023.*

Stytch (64, -19.0%)
IAM
San Francisco, CA, US
stytch.com

Subgraph (5, 25.0%)
Endpoint Security /
Operating System Security
Montreal, QC, Canada
subgraph.com

SubpicoCat (5, 0.0%)
Network Security / IPS
Sydney, Australia
subpicocat.com

Sucuri (51, 4.1%)
Network Security / Website
Security
Menifee, CA, US
sucuri.net

Sudoviz (8, 100.0%)
Application Security
US
sudoviz.com

Sumo Logic (914, -15.2%)
Security Analytics / SIEM
Redwood City, CA, US
sumologic.com

Sunnic (55, 77.4%)
Data Security / Encryption
Singapore
sunnic-sec.com

Sunny Valley Networks (9, -18.2%)
Network Security /
Firewalls
Cupertino, CA, US
sunnyvalley.io

Supplywisdon (115, -5.7%)
GRC
New York, NY, US
supplywisdom.com

Surance.io (10, 25.0%)
IoT Security / Home
Security
Ramat HaSharon, Israel
surance.io

SureCloud (99, -18.2%)
GRC / Cloud Security
Plano, TX, US
surecloud.com

SurePass ID (13, 8.3%)
IAM / Authentication
Winter Garden, FL, US
surepassid.com

suresecure (79, 16.2%)
MSSP / SOC
Nordrhein-Westfalen,
Germany
suresecure.de

Surety (45, 40.6%)
Data Security
Naples, FL, US
surety.com

Surevine (23, -8.0%)
Data Security / Secure
Collaboration
Guildford, United Kingdom
surevine.com

Surf Security (36, 157.1%)
Network Security / Secure
Web Browsing
London, United Kingdom
surf.security/

Suridata (38, 11.8%)
Data Security / SaaS Data
Protection
Tel Aviv, Israel
suridata.ai

Susteen (36, 12.5%)
Endpoint Security
/ Forensics
Irvine, CA, US
susteen.com

Swascan (78, 13.0%)
GRC / Scanning
Cassina de' Pecchi, Italy
swascan.com

Sweepatic (16, -15.8%)
Threat Intelligence / Brand
Leuven, Belgium
sweepatic.com

Sweet Security (20, 0.0%)
Endpoint Security /
Workload Protection
Tel Aviv, Israel
sweet.security

swIDch (9, -10.0%)
IAM
London, United Kingdom
swidch.com

Swimlane (238, 30.1%)
Operations / Incident
Management
Louisville, CO, US
swimlane.com

SwissSign Group (90, 12.5%)
Data Security / Public Key
Infrastructure
Glattbrugg, Switzerland
swisssign.com

SwivelSecure (39, -11.4%)
IAM / Authentication
Wetherby, United Kingdom
swivelsecure.com

Sword Active Risk (56, -20.0%)
GRC / Risk Management
Maidenhead,
United Kingdom
sword-activerisk.com

Syhunt (7, 40.0%)
Application Security /
Code Security
Rio de Janeiro,
Brazil
syhunt.com

SYlink (24, 4.3%)
Network Security / UTM
Clermont-Ferrand,
France
sylink.fr

Sym (36, 63.6%)
Operations / Workflow
Automation
San Francisco, CA, US
symops.com

Symantec (13600, -3.3%)
Endpoint Security /
Anti-virus
San Jose, CA, US
broadcom.com / products /
cybersecurity

Symmetrium (12, 100.0%)
Data Security /
Access Security
Tel Aviv, Israel
symmetrium.io

Symmetry Systems. (47, -6.0%)
Data Security / Monitoring
San Francisco, CA, US
symmetry-systems.com

Symphony (769, 8.3%)
Data Security / Secure
Collaboration
Palo Alto, CA, US
symphony.com

Synack (264, -22.8%)
Testing
Redwood City, CA, US
synack.com

Syncdog (12, -36.8%)
Endpoint Security / Mobile
Device Security
Reston, VA, US
syncdog.com

Syncplicity by Axway (36, 56.5%)
Data Security /
Secure Storage
Santa Clara, CA, US
syncplicity.com

SynerComm (50, 6.4%)
Network Security / Network
& Security Infrastructure
Brookdfield, WI, US
synercomm.com

Synergy Quantum (8, 33.3%)
Data Security / Encryption
Geneva, Switzerland
synergyquantum.swiss

**Numbers in parentheses indicate headcount and % change in 2023.*

Synopsys (18348, 7.5%)
Application Security / Software Testing For Security
Mountain View, CA, US
synopsys.com

Synsaber (8, -27.3%)
IoT Security / Monitoring
Chandler, AZ, US
synsaber.com

SysCloud (138, -9.2%)
Data Security / Secure Backup / Recovery
Red Bank, NJ, US
syscloud.com

Sysdig (879, 3.8%)
Endpoint Security / Kubernetes Security
Davis, CA, US
sysdig.com

Systancia (115, -3.4%)
IAM
Sausheim, France
systancia.com

Syxsense (81, 15.7%)
Operations / Vulnerabilities
Aliso Viejo, CA, US
syxsense.com

TAC Security (155, 31.4%)
GRC
San Francisco, CA, US
tacsecurity.com

Tailscale (122, 87.7%)
Network Security / Zero Trust Networking
Toronto, ON, Canada
tailscale.com

Tala Secure (6, -14.3%)
GRC / Compliance Management
Mountain View, CA, US
talasecure.com

Talon Cyber Security (147, 54.7%)
Network Security / Secure Web Browsing
New York, NY, US
talon-sec.com

Tamnoon (19, 137.5%)
MSSP / Managed Security Services
Remote, WA, US
tamnoon.io

TamosSoft (4, 0.0%)
Network Security / Monitoring
Christchurch, New Zealand
tamos.com

Tanium (1952, -4.4%)
Endpoint Security / Visibility
Emeryville, CA, US
tanium.com

Tascent (8, -61.9%)
IAM / Authentication
Los Gatos, CA, US
tascent.com

Tascet (7, 0.0%)
GRC / Risk Management
Madison, WI, US
tascet.com

Tata Communications (15430, 9.9%)
MSSP / Managed Security Services
Mumbai, India
tatacommunications.com

Tata Consultancy Services (583267, -8.1%)
MSSP / Managed Security Services
Nariman Point, India
on.tcs.com

Tauruseer (23, 155.6%)
Operations / Code Security
Jacksonville Beach, FL, US
tauruseer.com

Tausight (29, 31.8%)
GRC / Healthcare
Boston, MA, US
tausight.com

Tavve Software (21, 40.0%)
Network Security / Packet Routing
Morrisville, NC, US
tavve.com

Team Cymru (128, 1.6%)
Threat Intelligence / IoC Intelligence
Lake Mary, FL, US
team-cymru.com

TECH5 (61, 29.8%)
IAM / Identity Management
Geneva, Switzerland
tech5.ai

Technical Communications Corporation (15, -28.6%)
Data Security / Secure Communications
Concord, MA, US
tccsecure.com

TechR2 (36, 12.5%)
Data Security / Data Erasure And Destruction
Reynoldsburg, OH, US
techr2.com

TecSec (45, 80.0%)
Data Security / Key Management
McLean, VA, US
tecsec.com

TeejLab (13, 0.0%)
API Security / API Discovery
British Columbia, Canada
apidiscovery.teejlab.com

Tego Cyber (17, 70.0%)
Threat Intelligence / TIP
Las Vegas, NV, US
tegocyber.com

Tehama (29, -47.3%)
Network Security / Virtualization
Ottawa, ON, Canada
tehama.io

TEHTRIS (271, 21.0%)
Security Analytics / XDR
Paris, France
tehtris.com

TELEGRID Technologies (5, -44.4%)
Data Security / Monitoring
Florham Park, NJ, US
telegrid.com

Telemate Software (23, 15.0%)
Security Analytics / SIEM
Norcross, GA, US
telemate.net

Telemessage (113, 31.4%)
GRC / Secure Communications
Petah Tikva, Israel
telemessage.com

Teleport (153, -27.1%)
IAM / Access Security
Oakland, CA, US
goteleport.com

TeleSign Corporation (773, 9.7%)
IAM / Identity Verification
Marina del Rey, CA, US
telesign.com

Telesoft Technologies (109, 34.6%)
Network Security / Monitoring
Annapolis Junction, MD, US
telesoft-technologies.com

Telos (736, -4.5%)
GRC / Compliance Management
Ashburn, VA, US
telos.com

**Numbers in parentheses indicate headcount and % change in 2023.*

Telstra (35161, 5.5%)
MSSP / Managed Security Services
Melbourne, Australia
telstra.com

Tempest Security Intelligence (425, -7.0%)
GRC / Data Discovery
Recife, Brazil
tempest.com.br

Tenable (2219, 7.9%)
GRC / Vulnerabilities
Columbia, MD, US
tenable.com

Tenacity (7, -46.1%)
Operations / Posture Management
Ann Arbor, MI, US
tenacitycloud.com

Tencent (108056, -0.3%)
Endpoint Security / Anti-virus
Shenzhen, China
tencent.com

Tenchi Security (45, 60.7%)
GRC / Risk Management
Sao Paulo, Brazil
tenchisecurity.com

Tenzir (16, 23.1%)
Operations / Data Management
Hamburg, Germany
tenzir.com

TeraDact (9, 12.5%)
Data Security / Secure Data Sharing
Missoula, MT, US
teradact.com

Terafence (15, -11.8%)
IoT Security / Gateways
Haifa, Israel
terafence.com

Teramind (104, 50.7%)
Operations / Monitoring
Aventura, FL, US
teramind.co

Terranova Security (107, 4.9%)
Training
Laval, QC, Canada
terranovasecurity.com

TerraTrue (38, -22.4%)
GRC / Software Development Security
San Francisco, CA, US
terratrue.com

Teskalabs (18, 5.9%)
Network Security / Gateways
London, United Kingdom
teskalabs.com

Tesorion (122, 2.5%)
MSSP / Managed Security Services
Leusden, Netherlands
tesorion.nl

Tesseract (5, 25.0%)
Data Security / Encryption
Mexico City, Mexico
tesseract.mx

Tesseract Intelligence (9, -30.8%)
Threat Intelligence / Dark Web
Sofia, Bulgaria
tesseractintelligence.com

Tessian (212, -17.8%)
Email Security / Defense Against Phishing
New York, NY, US
tessian.com

Tetra Defense (46, -57.4%)
MSSP / MDR
Madison, WI, US
tetradefense.com

Tetrate (126, -2.3%)
Operations / Posture Management
Milpitas, CA, US
tetrate.io

TG Soft (10, 0.0%)
Endpoint Security / Anti-virus
Rubano, Italy
tgsoft.it

Thales (666, 12.1%)
Data Security / Authentication
Plantation, FL, US
thalesesecurity.com

thatDot (17, 21.4%)
Fraud Prevention / Fraud Analytics
Portland, OR, US
thatdot.com

The Cyberfort Group (107, 15.1%)
MSSP / SOC
Thatcham, United Kingdom
cyberfortgroup.com

The DigiTrust Group (19, -5.0%)
MSSP / Firewalls
Los Angeles, CA, US
digitrustgroup.com

The Media Trust (69, -4.2%)
Fraud Prevention / Advertising-related
McLean, VA, US
themediatrust.com

The Whisper Company (3, 0.0%)
IAM / Authentication
Austin, TX, US
thewhispercompany.com

TheGreenBow (32, 10.3%)
Network Security / VPN/Proxy
Paris, France
thegreenbow.com

Theom (25, 4.2%)
Data Security / Posture Management
San Francisco, CA, US
theom.ai

Theon (5, -68.8%)
Data Security / Quantum
Newport Beach, CA, US
theontechnology.com

Theta (282, 10.2%)
Operations / Attack Surface Management
Auckland, New Zealand
theta.co.nz

Theta Lake (92, -8.0%)
GRC / Compliance Management
Santa Barbara, CA, US
thetalake.com

ThetaRay (160, 26.0%)
Security Analytics
Hod HaSharon, Israel
thetaray.com

Think Cyber Security (14, 55.6%)
GRC / Security Awareness Training
London, United Kingdom
thinkcyber.co.uk

Thinking Objects (59, 7.3%)
MSSP / SOC
Stuttgart, Germany
to.com

Thinkst Canary (5, 150.0%)
Deception / Target Agents Deployed In Operations
Edinvale, South Africa
canary.tools

ThinScale (57, -28.8%)
Endpoint Security / Remote Desktop Agent
Dublin, Ireland
thinscale.com

ThirdPartyTrust (16, -71.4%)
GRC / Risk Management
Chicago, IL, US
thirdpartytrust.com

ThisIsMe (9, -10.0%)
IAM / Onboarding
Cape Town, South Africa
thisisme.com

**Numbers in parentheses indicate headcount and % change in 2023.*

Thistle Technologies (6, -40.0%)
IoT Security / Security For Embedded Systems
San Francisco, CA, US
thistle.tech

Thoropass (185, 0.5%)
GRC / Compliance Management
New York, NY, US
thoropass.com

Threat Intelligence (21, 0.0%)
Threat Intelligence / Leaked Data
Sydney Nsw, Australia
threatintelligence.com

Threat Mark (82, -19.6%)
Fraud Prevention / Identity Verification
Brno, Czechia
threatmark.com

Threat Stack (8, -68.0%)
Network Security / Monitoring
Boston, MA, US
threatstack.com

ThreatAware (19, 0.0%)
Operations / Asset Management
London, United Kingdom
threataware.com

ThreatBook (88, 57.1%)
Threat Intelligence / TIP
Haidian District, China
threatbook.cn

ThreatConnect (168, 5.0%)
Threat Intelligence
Arlington, VA, US
threatconnect.com

ThreatFabric (52, 67.7%)
Fraud Prevention / Bot Security
Amsterdam, Netherlands
threatfabric.com

ThreatKey (12, 20.0%)
GRC / Configuration Management
New York, NY, US
threatkey.com

ThreatLocker (314, 34.8%)
Endpoint Security / Application Whitelisting
Maitland, FL, US
threatlocker.com

ThreatMate (8, 700.0%)
Operations
Dover, DE, US
threatmate.com

ThreatModeler Software (53, 8.2%)
Application Security / Vulnerabilities
Jersey City, NJ, US
threatmodeler.com

ThreatNG (11, 120.0%)
Threat Intelligence / Dark Web
Shrewsbury, MA, US
threatngsecurity.com

ThreatOptix (12, 33.3%)
Operations / XDR
San Francisco, CA, US
threatoptix.ai

ThreatQuotient (106, -9.4%)
Threat Intelligence / Threat Intelligence Platform
Reston, VA, US
threatquotient.com

Threatray (12, 20.0%)
Threat Intelligence / IoC Intelligence
Biel/Bienne, Switzerland
threatray.com

Threatrix (14, -12.5%)
GRC / Supply Chain Security
Dallas, TX, US
threatrix.io

Threatscape (36, 28.6%)
MSSP / MDR
Dublin, Ireland
threatscape.com

Threatspan (4, -20.0%)
IoT Security / Maritime Security
Rotterdam, Netherlands
threatspan.com

ThreatSpike (20, 17.6%)
MSSP / MDR
London, United Kingdom
threatspike.com

ThreatSTOP (20, 5.3%)
Network Security / Reputation
Carlsbad, CA, US
threatstop.com

ThreatWarrior (13, -23.5%)
Network Security / Monitoring
Austin, TX, US
threatwarrior.com

ThreatX (63, -4.5%)
API Security / Firewalls
Louisville, CO, US
threatx.com

TIBCO Software Inc. (3470, -22.4%)
Data Security / Big Data
Palo Alto, CA, US
tibco.com

Tidal Cyber (25, 25.0%)
Threat Intelligence / OSINT
Washington, DC, US
tidalcyber.com

Tidelift (66, -17.5%)
Application Security / SBOM
Boston, MA, US
tidelift.com

Tiempo (31, 34.8%)
Endpoint Security / Hardware
Montbonnot-Saint-Martin, France
tiempo-secure.com

Tigera (124, -9.5%)
Endpoint Security / Kubernetes Security
San Francisco, CA, US
tigera.io

Timus Networks (66, 106.2%)
Network Security
Boston, MA, US
timusnetworks.com

Tines (249, 40.7%)
Operations / Orchestration
Dublin, Ireland
tines.com

TitanHQ (158, 9.0%)
Network Security / DNS Security
Galway, Ireland
titanhq.com

Titania Ltd. (90, 57.9%)
GRC / Configuration Management
Worcester, United Kingdom
titania.com

Titaniam (31, 0.0%)
Data Security / Encryption
San Jose, CA, US
titaniam.io

TITUS (73, -4.0%)
GRC / DLP
Ottawa, ON, Canada
titus.com

Todyl (67, 67.5%)
Network Security / Access Security
New York, NY, US
todyl.com

Token (40, 11.1%)
IAM / Authentication
Rochester, NY, US
tokenring.com

TokenEx (90, 11.1%)
Data Security / Tokenization
Edmond, OK, US
tokenex.com

**Numbers in parentheses indicate headcount and % change in 2023.*

TokenOne (3, 0.0%)
IAM
Sydney, Australia
tokenone.com

Tonic.ai (98, -6.7%)
Data Security / Data Masking
San Francisco, CA, US
tonic.ai

ToothPic (11, 10.0%)
Operations / Forensics
Turin, Italy
toothpic.eu

Tophat Security (4, 0.0%)
MSSP / SIEM
Wilmington, DE, US
tophatsecurity.com

Topia Technology (23, 9.5%)
Data Security / Encryption
Tacoma, WA, US
topiatechnology.com

Topsec Network Security (152, -0.7%)
Network Security / Firewalls
Haidian District, China
topsec.com.cn

Torq (126, 0.8%)
Operations / Automation
Portland, OR, US
torq.io

Torsion Information Security (12, -25.0%)
Data Security / Monitoring
London, United Kingdom
torsionis.com

Tosibox (77, 28.3%)
IoT Security / Remote Devices
Oulu, Finland
tosibox.com

Total Defense (27, -3.6%)
Endpoint Security / PC, Mobile & Internet Security
Hauppauge, NY, US
totaldefense.com

ToucanX (3, -25.0%)
Endpoint Security / Sandbox
Southfield, MI, US
toucanx.com

Townsend Security (13, 0.0%)
Data Security / Encryption
Olympia, WA, US
townsendsecurity.com

Tozny (19, 18.8%)
IAM / Secure Identity
Portland, OR, US
tozny.com

TR7 (25, 38.9%)
Network Security / Firewalls
Ankara, Turkey
tr7.com

Traceable (186, 24.0%)
API Security / API Security Cloud
San Francisco, CA, US
traceable.ai

TraceSecurity (108, 1.9%)
GRC
Baton Rouge, LA, US
tracesecurity.com

trackd (9, 80.0%)
GRC / Vulnerabilities
US
trackd.com

Trail of Bits (105, 4.0%)
Data Security / Vulnerabilities
New York, NY, US
trailofbits.com

Traitware (18, 5.9%)
IAM / Credential Security
Reno, NV, US
traitware.com

Transmit Security (324, -11.7%)
Fraud Prevention / Anti-fraud
Boston, MA, US
transmitsecurity.com

Trapezoid (9, -30.8%)
IoT Security / Firmware
Miami, FL, US
trapezoid.com

Trapmine (4, -77.8%)
Endpoint Security
Tallinn, Estonia
trapmine.com

Treebox Solutions (17, 21.4%)
Data Security / Secure Communications
Singapore, Singapore
treeboxsolutions.com

Trellix (3353, 8.7%)
Security Analytics / XDR
Milpitas, CA, US
trellix.com

Trend Micro (7735, 1.8%)
Endpoint Security / Anti-virus
Irving, TX, US
trendmicro.com

Tresorit (130, -1.5%)
Data Security / Secure Data Sharing
Budapest, Hungary
tresorit.com

Tresys (28, -3.5%)
Data Security / Data Erasure And Destruction
Columbia, MD, US
tresys.com

TriagingX (9, -10.0%)
Operations / Sandbox
San Jose, CA, US
triagingx.com

Tricerion (4, -20.0%)
IAM / Credential Security
Reading, United Kingdom
tricerion.com

Trickest (15, 15.4%)
Operations / Penetration Testing
Dover, DE, US
trickest.com

TripleBlind (53, -15.9%)
Data Security / Secure Data Sharing
Kansas City, MO, US
tripleblind.ai

TripleCyber (16, 14.3%)
MSSP / SOC
Tel Aviv, Israel
triplecyber.co.il

TripWire (Fortra) (202, -20.8%)
GRC / Monitoring
Portland, OR, US
tripwire.com

TrojAI (19, 5.6%)
GRC / Governance
New Brunswick, Canada
troj.ai

Tromzo (27, 80.0%)
Application Security / Software Development Security
Mountain View, CA, US
tromzo.com

Trovares (11, 57.1%)
Security Analytics / Graph Analytics
Seattle, WA, US
trovares.com

True Digital Security (10, -41.2%)
MSSP / SIEM
Tulsa, OK, US
truedigitalsecurity.com

TrueFort (89, 6.0%)
Application Security / Monitoring
Weehawken, NJ, US
truefort.com

TrueVault (16, -5.9%)
Data Security / Secure Storage
San Francisco, CA, US
truevault.com

**Numbers in parentheses indicate headcount and % change in 2023.*

Truffle Security (31, 24.0%)
Data Security / Secrets Management
San Francisco, CA, US
trufflesecurity.com

TruGrid (6, -14.3%)
IAM / Access Security
Schaumburg, IL, US
trugrid.com

TruKno (8, 0.0%)
Threat Intelligence / TIP
Denver, CO, US
trukno.com

Trulioo (398, 3.1%)
IAM / Identity Verification
Vancouver, BC, Canada
trulioo.com

Truops (19, -5.0%)
GRC / Risk Management
Norwalk, CT, US
truops.com

Trusona (37, 0.0%)
IAM / Authentication
Scottsdale, AZ, US
trusona.com

TrustArc (396, -7.9%)
GRC / Privacy Assessments
San Francisco, CA, US
trustarc.com

TrustBrands (61, -1.6%)
GRC / Scanning
Ogden, UT, US
trustbrands.com

TrustBuilder (62, 82.3%)
IAM / CIAM
Ghent, Flemish Region, Belgium
trustbuilder.com

Trusted Objects (13, 8.3%)
IoT Security
Aix-en-Provence, France
trusted-objects.com

Trustero (12, -36.8%)
GRC / Compliance Management
Palo Alto, CA, US
trustero.com

Trustifi (27, 0.0%)
Email Security / Encryption
Las Vegas, NV, US
trustifi.com

TrustLayer (45, 0.0%)
GRC / Risk Management
San Francisco, CA, US
trustlayer.io

Trustle (14, 16.7%)
IAM / Access Security
Walnut Creek, CA, US
trustle.io

Trustless.ai (3, -40.0%)
Endpoint Security / Secured Devices
Geneva, Switzerland
trustless.ai

TrustLogix (18, 38.5%)
GRC / Governance
Mountain View, CA, US
trustlogix.io

Trustlook (9, -25.0%)
Endpoint Security / Malware Analysis
San Jose, CA, US
trustlook.com

TrustMAPP (14, -6.7%)
GRC / Monitoring
Minneapolis, MN, US
trustmapp.com

Trustonic (109, 14.7%)
Endpoint Security / Mobile Device Security
Austin, TX, US
trustonic.com

Trustpage (3, -81.2%)
Data Security / Secure Storage
Detroit, MI, US
trustpage.com

TrustSpace (6, -33.3%)
GRC / Compliance Management
Berlin, Germany
trustspace.io

TrustWave (a Singtel Company) (1202, -7.4%)
MSSP / Managed Security Services
Chicago, IL, US
trustwave.com

TruU (69, 21.1%)
IAM / Authentication
Palo Alto, CA, US
truu.ai

TryHackMe (2118, 45.4%)
Training / Cyber Range
London, United Kingdom
tryhackme.com

Tu Identidad (20, 66.7%)
IAM / Authentication
Mexico City, Mexico
tuidentidad.com

Tufin (462, -12.3%)
Operations / Policy Management
Boston, MA, US
tufin.com

Tune Insight (13, 18.2%)
Data Security / Secure Collaboration
Lausanne, Switzerland
tuneinsight.com

TunnelBear (14, 7.7%)
Network Security / VPN/Proxy
Toronto, ON, Canada
tunnelbear.com

Turbot (46, 2.2%)
IAM / Encryption
New York, NY, US
turbot.com

Tutus (47, 42.4%)
Data Security / Encryption
Danderyd, Sweden
tutus.se

Twingate (78, 11.4%)
IAM / Access Security
Redwood City, CA, US
twingate.com

TwinSoft (33, 10.0%)
IAM / Authentication
Darmstadt, Hessen, Germany
twinsoft-biometrics.de

TwoSense (13, -13.3%)
IAM / Authentication
New York, NY, US
twosense.ai

Tychon (49, 36.1%)
GRC / Risk Management
Fredericksburg, VA, US
tychon.io

Tyk (156, -22.4%)
API Security / Gateways
London, United Kingdom
tyk.io

Typing DNA (144, -11.7%)
IAM / Authentication
New York, NY, US
typingdna.com

Ubble.ai (70, -26.3%)
Fraud Prevention / Identity Verification
Paris, France
ubble.ai

UBIKA (74, 32.1%)
API Security / Firewalls
Meudon, France
ubikasec.com

Ubiq Security (23, -17.9%)
Data Security / Encryption
San Diego, CA, US
ubiqsecurity.com

Ubiqu (16, 23.1%)
IAM / Public Key Infrastructure
Delft, Netherlands
ubiqu.com

**Numbers in parentheses indicate headcount and % change in 2023.*

Ubirch (28, -34.9%)
IoT Security / OT Security
Berlin, Germany
ubirch.de

Ubisecure (66, 15.8%)
IAM
Espoo, Finland
ubisecure.com

ULedger (21, 5.0%)
Data Security / Blockchain
Boise, ID, US
uledger.co

ULTRA RED (22, 0.0%)
Operations / Breach And Attack Simulation
Tel Aviv, Israel
ultrared.ai

UltraViolet Cyber (205, 15.8%)
MSSP / MDR
McLean, VA, US
uvcyber.com

UM-Labs (9, 12.5%)
Endpoint Security / Operating System Security
London, United Kingdom
um-labs.com

UncommonX (22, 0.0%)
MSSP / MDR
Chicago, IL, US
uncommonx.com

UnderDefense (104, 31.6%)
MSSP / MDR
New York, NY, US
underdefense.com

unico (1031, -3.6%)
IAM / Authentication
Sao Paulo, Brazil
unico.io

UnifyID (5, -28.6%)
IAM / Authentication
Redwood City, CA, US
unify.id

Uniken (163, 14.0%)
IAM / Authentication
Chatham Twp., NJ, US
uniken.com

Uniqkey (56, 5.7%)
IAM / Credential Security
Herlev, Hovedstaden, Denmark
uniqkey.eu

Unistal Systems (231, 2.2%)
Endpoint Security / Anti-virus
Mumbai, India
unistal.in

Unisys Stealth (24225, 4.5%)
Network Security / Cloaking
Blue Bell, PA, US
unisys.com

Unit21 (125, 0.8%)
GRC / Compliance Management
San Francisco, CA, US
unit21.ai

United Security Providers (75, -3.9%)
Network Security / Firewalls
Bern, Switzerland
united-security-providers.com

Unitrends (156, -6.6%)
Data Security / Encryption
Burlington, MA, US
unitrends.com

Universign (85, -8.6%)
IAM / Authentication
Paris, France
universign.com

Unmukti (8, -33.3%)
Network Security / Firewalls
New Delhi, India
unmukti.in

Uno (14, 16.7%)
Operations / Threat Analysis
Palo Alto, CA, US
uno.ai

Untangle (18, -18.2%)
Network Security / UTM
San Jose, CA, US
untangle.com

Unxpose (8, -20.0%)
Operations / Attack Surface Management
Sao Paulo, Brazil
unxpose.com

Upfort (36, 9.1%)
Email Security / SMB Security
San Francisco, CA, US
upfort.com

UpGuard (195, 48.9%)
GRC / Monitoring
Mountain View, CA, US
upguard.com

Uppsala Security (26, 8.3%)
Data Security / Tracking Of Crypto Currencies
Singapore, Singapore
uppsalasecurity.com

Upstream Security (128, -3.0%)
IoT Security / Automotive
Herzliya, Israel
upstream.auto

Uptycs (344, 18.6%)
Security Analytics / OSQuery
Waltham, MA, US
uptycs.com

Upwind (72, 53.2%)
Operations
CA, US
upwind.io

usecure (40, 25.0%)
GRC / Security Awareness Training
Manchester, United Kingdom
usecure.io

Usercube (17, -37.0%)
IAM
Marseille, France
usercube.com

Utimaco (510, 14.6%)
Data Security / Hardware
Aachen, Germany
utimaco.com

V-Key (122, 16.2%)
Endpoint Security / Sandbox
Ottawa, ON, Canada
v-key.com

V5 Systems (30, -21.1%)
IoT Security / OT Security
Fremont, CA, US
v5systems.us

Vade Secure (264, 16.8%)
Email Security / Defense Against Phishing
San Francisco, CA, US
vadesecure.com

Vairav Technology (94, 27.0%)
MSSP / Managed Security Services
Kathmandu, Nepal
vairav.net

Valence Security (49, 36.1%)
API Security
Tel Aviv, Israel
valencesecurity.com

ValeVPN (4, 100.0%)
Network Security / VPN/Proxy
Washington, DC, US
valevpn.com

Vali Cyber (32, 23.1%)
Endpoint Security / Linux Security
Charlottesville, VA, US
valicyber.com

**Numbers in parentheses indicate headcount and % change in 2023.*

Valid Networks (8, -38.5%)
Application Security / Blockchain
New York, NY, US
valid.network

Valimail (109, 6.9%)
Email Security / Defense Against Phishing
San Francisco, CA, US
valimail.com

Valtix (22, -42.1%)
Network Security / Zero Trust Networking
Santa Clara, CA, US
valtix.com

Vandyke Software (18, -5.3%)
Data Security / Secure Data Sharing
Albuquerque, NM, US
vandyke.com

Vanguard Integrity Professionals (91, 8.3%)
GRC / Monitoring
Las Vegas, NV, US
go2vanguard.com

Vanta (484, 33.7%)
GRC / Compliance Management
San Francisco, CA, US
vanta.com

VantagePoint (53, 1.9%)
Operations
Wesley Chapel, FL, US
thevantagepoint.com

Vario Secure Networks (12, -14.3%)
MSSP / Managed Security Services
Tokyo, Japan
variosecure.net

vArmour (91, -34.5%)
Endpoint Security / Servers
Mountain View, CA, US
varmour.com

Varonis (2207, 5.2%)
Data Security / Secure Collaboration
New York, NY, US
varonis.com

Vault Security (3, -66.7%)
IAM / Authentication
CA, US
linktr.ee/vault_security

Vault Vision (3, 0.0%)
IAM
Denver, CO, US
vaultvision.com

Vault12 (14, -6.7%)
Data Security / Wallets
Mountain View, CA, US
vault12.com

Vaultize (10, -23.1%)
Data Security / IRM
San Francisco, CA, US
vaultize.com

Vaultmatix (4, 0.0%)
Data Security / Data Rooms
London, United Kingdom
vaultmatix.com

Vaultree (64, 3.2%)
Data Security / Encryption
Cork, Ireland
vaultree.com

Vdoo (15, -37.5%)
IoT Security / Security For Embedded Systems
Tel Aviv, Israel
vdoo.com

VectorZero (22, 83.3%)
Data Security / Secure Storage
Reston, VA, US
vectorzero.ai

Vectra AI (624, 0.3%)
Security Analytics / Incident Management
San Jose, CA, US
vectra.ai

Vehere (155, 14.0%)
Network Security / NDR
San Francisco, CA, US
vehere.com

Velona Systems (5, 0.0%)
GRC / Scanning
Cork, Ireland
velonasystems.com

Velotix (39, -4.9%)
Data Security
Tel Aviv, Israel
velotix.ai

Venafi (430, -10.0%)
Data Security / Key Management
Salt Lake City, UT, US
venafi.com

Venari Security (51, -3.8%)
Network Security / Traffic Analysis
London, United Kingdom
venarisecurity.com

Vendict (36, 89.5%)
GRC / Security Questionnaire Automation
Tel Aviv, Israel
vendict.com

Venminder (236, -3.3%)
GRC / Risk Management
Elizabethtown, KY, US
venminder.com

Venustech (368, -18.0%)
Network Security / UTM
China
venustech.com.cn

Vera (19, -9.5%)
Data Security / IRM
Palo Alto, CA, US
vera.com

Veracity Industrial Networks (7, 16.7%)
IoT Security / OT Security
Aliso Viejo, CA, US
veracity.io

Veracode (692, -13.6%)
Application Security / Code Security
Burlington, MA, US
veracode.com

Verafin (802, -2.8%)
Fraud Prevention / Fraud Management
St. John's, NL, Canada
verafin.com

Vereign (17, 13.3%)
IAM
Zug, Switzerland
vereign.com

Veriato (22, -4.3%)
Operations / Monitoring
Palm Beach Gardens, FL, US
veriato.com

VeriClouds (9, -10.0%)
Fraud Prevention / Credential Security
Seattle, WA, US
vericlouds.com

Veridas (197, 50.4%)
IAM / Authentication
Pamplona, Navarra, Spain
veridas.com

Veridify Security (20, 11.1%)
IoT Security / Authentication
Shelton, CT, US
veridify.com

Veridium (42, -2.3%)
IAM / Authentication
Boston, MA, US
veridiumid.com

Verif-y (29, 7.4%)
IAM / Identity Verification
Philadelphia, PA, US
verif-y.com

Veriff (380, -24.8%)
Fraud Prevention / Identity Verification
Tallinn, Estonia
veriff.com

**Numbers in parentheses indicate headcount and % change in 2023.*

Verificient Technologies (215, -11.9%)
IAM / Identity Verification
New York, NY, US
verificient.com

Verifyoo (3, 0.0%)
IAM / Authentication
Tel Aviv, Israel
verifyoo.com

Verimatrix (280, -3.1%)
Data Security / DRM
San Diego, CA, US
verimatrix.com

Verimi (107, 0.9%)
IAM / Identity Management
Berlin, Germany
verimi.de

Veriscan Security (12, 9.1%)
GRC / Security Measurement
Karlstad, Sweden
veriscan.se

Veriti (39, 129.4%)
Operations / Posture Management
Tel Aviv, Israel
veriti.ai

Verizon Business Security Solutions (17038, -14.2%)
MSSP / Managed Security Services
Basking Ridge, NJ, US
verizon.com

Versa (662, 4.6%)
Network Security / SDN
San Jose, CA, US
versa-networks.com

Versasec (23, -11.5%)
IAM
Stockholm, Sweden
versasec.com

Verve (134, 0.8%)
IoT Security / OT Security
Chicago, IL, US
verveindustrial.com

Very Good Security (233, 34.7%)
GRC / Secure Storage
San Francisco, CA, US
verygoodsecurity.com

Veza Technologies (195, 77.3%)
IAM / Access Security
Palo Alto, CA, US
veza.com

vFeed (3, -25.0%)
GRC / Vulnerabilities
Middletown, DE, US
vfeed.io

VIA3 Corperation (4, -66.7%)
Data Security / Secure Communications
Scottsdale, AZ, US
via3.com

Viakoo (22, -4.3%)
IoT Security / Vulnerabilities
Mountain View, CA, US
viakoo.com

Viascope (7, -36.4%)
IAM / Access Security
Seoul, South Korea
viascope.com

Vicarius (58, 9.4%)
Application Security / Code Security
Jerusalem, Israel
vicarius.io

VigilantOps (3, 0.0%)
GRC / Healthcare
Pittsburgh, PA, US
vigilant-ops.com

Vigiles (4, 33.3%)
GRC / Security Awareness Training
Miami, FL, US
vigiles.cloud

VigiTrust (129, 16.2%)
GRC / Risk Management
Dublin, Ireland
vigitrust.com

Vijilan Security (52, -3.7%)
MSSP / SIEM
Ft. Lauderdale, FL, US
vijilan.com

VikingCloud (574, 9.8%)
MSSP / MDR
Chicago, IL, US
vikingcloud.com

Vinca Cyber (128, 10.3%)
MSSP
Bangalore, India
vincacyber.com

Vipre (182, 15.2%)
Endpoint Security / Anti-virus
Clearwater, FL, US
vipre.com

Vir2us (6, 0.0%)
Endpoint Security / Virtualization
Petaluma, CA, US
vir2us.com

Vircom (31, 0.0%)
Email Security / Threat Prevention
Montreal, QC, Canada
vircom.com

Virgil Security (15, -6.2%)
Data Security / Encryption
Manassas, VA, US
virgilsecurity.com

VirnetX (24, 4.3%)
Network Security / Zero Trust Networking
Zephyr Cove, NV, US
virnetx.com

Virsec Systems (150, -14.8%)
Application Security / Web App Protection
San Jose, CA, US
virsec.com

Virta Laboratories (4, 0.0%)
IoT Security / Healthcare
Seattle, WA, US
virtalabs.com

Virtru (178, -3.3%)
Data Security / Secure Communications
Washington, DC, US
virtru.com

VirtualArmour (48, 6.7%)
MSSP / Managed Security Services
Centennial, CO, US
virtualarmour.com

VirusBlokAda (15, 25.0%)
Endpoint Security / Anti-virus
Minsk, Belarus
anti-virus.by

VirusRescuers (26, -3.7%)
MSSP / MDR
Dubai, United Arab Emirates
virusrescuers.com

VisibleRisk (5, -70.6%)
GRC / Risk Management
New York, NY, US
visiblerisk.com

Viso Trust (45, 15.4%)
GRC / Risk Management
San Francisco, CA, US
visotrust.com

Visual Click Software (12, 0.0%)
GRC / Auditing
Austin, TX, US
visualclick.com

Vitrium (28, 27.3%)
Data Security / DRM
Vancouver, BC, Canada
vitrium.com

Vkansee (5, 0.0%)
IAM / Authentication
Beijing, China
vkansee.com

VMRay (118, 11.3%)
Security Analytics / Threat Analysis
Boston, MA, US
vmray.com

**Numbers in parentheses indicate headcount and % change in 2023.*

VMWare (30796, -12.7%)
Endpoint Security / EDR
Palo Alto, CA, US
vmware.com

Volexity (41, 13.9%)
Data Security / Forensics
Reston, VA, US
volexity.com

Vonahi Security (16, -11.1%)
Operations /
Penetration Testing
Atlanta, GA, US
vonahi.io

Vorpal (8, 0.0%)
IoT Security / Drones
Tel Aviv, Israel
vorpal-corp.com

Votiro (57, 23.9%)
Network Security / File
Scrubbing
Tel Aviv, Israel
votiro.com

VoxCroft (39, -9.3%)
Threat Intelligence /
OSINT
Western Cape,
South Africa
voxcroft.com

VTS (36, 227.3%)
IoT Security / IDS
Auckland, New Zealand
vts.energy

VU Security (180, -28.0%)
IAM / VPN/Proxy
Buenos Aires, Argentina
vusecurity.com

Vulcan Cyber (118, 16.8%)
GRC / Vulnerabilities
Tel Aviv, Israel
vulcan.io

Vulidity (5, 0.0%)
Threat Intelligence /
OSINT
Burghausen, Bayern,
Germany
vulidity.de

VulnCheck (13, 116.7%)
Threat Intelligence /
Vulnerabilities
Lexington, MA, US
vulncheck.com

Vulners (3, -25.0%)
Threat Intelligence /
Vulnerabilities
Wilmington, DE, US
vulners.com

VuNet Systems (195, 33.6%)
Security Analytics / Logs
Bangalore, India
vunetsystems.com

Wabbi (16, -5.9%)
Application
Security / Software
Development Security
Boston, MA, US
wabbisoft.com

Wallarm (112, 21.7%)
API Security
San Francisco, CA, US
wallarm.com

Wallix (261, 11.1%)
IAM / Access Security
Paris, France
wallix.com

Waratek (31, -20.5%)
Application Security
Dublin, Ireland
waratek.com

WaryMe (16, 6.7%)
GRC
Cesson-Sevigne,
France
waryme.com

Watchdata (204, 5.2%)
IAM / Public Key
Infrastructure
Singapore, Singapore
watchdata.com

WatchGuard (1023, 9.1%)
Network Security / UTM
Seattle, WA, US
watchguard.com

watchTowr (21, 5.0%)
Operations / Attack Surface
Management
Central Region, Singapore,
Singapore
watchtowr.com

Waterfall (124, 25.2%)
IoT Security / Firewalls
Rosh HaAyin, Israel
waterfall-security.com

Wault (9, 28.6%)
Data Security / Secure
Data Sharing
London, United Kingdom
wault.com

Wavecrest Computing (16, 14.3%)
Network Security /
Gateways
Melbourne, FL, US
wavecrest.net

Wazuh (197, 26.3%)
Operations / SOC
San Jose, CA, US
wazuh.com

WebTitan (TitanHQ) (5, -16.7%)
Network Security /
Filtering
Salthill, Ireland
webtitan.com

Wedge Networks (34, -5.6%)
Network Security
Calgary, AB, Canada
wedgenetworks.com

WetStone Technologies (14, 40.0%)
Data Security / Forensics
Cortland, NY, US
wetstonetech.com

Whistic (84, -34.9%)
Operations / Vendor
Management
Pleasant Grove,
UT, US
whistic.com

White Cloud Security (15, 0.0%)
Endpoint Security /
Application Whitelisting
Austin, TX, US
whitecloudsecurity.com

White Hawk Software (4, 0.0%)
Application Security /
Tamper Proofing
Palo Alto, CA, US
whitehawksoftware.com

Whiteswan (8, 700.0%)
IAM / Access Security
Belmont,
CA, US
whiteswansecurity.com

WhoisXML API (31, 6.9%)
Threat Intelligence /
DNS Security
Covina, CA, US
whoisxmlapi.com

WIB (70, 25.0%)
API Security
Tel Aviv, Israel
wib.com

Wickr (22, -29.0%)
Data Security / Secure
Communications
San Francisco,
CA, US
wickr.com

Widevine Technologies (6, -14.3%)
Data Security / DRM
Kirkland,
WA, US
widevine.com

WiJungle (53, 76.7%)
Network Security / UTM
Gurugram, Haryana,
India
wijungle.com

WiKID Systems (4, 0.0%)
IAM / Authentication
Atlanta, GA, US
wikidsystems.com

**Numbers in parentheses indicate headcount and % change in 2023.*

Wing Security (44, 2.3%)
Application Security / SaaS Management
Tel Aviv, Israel
wing.security

WinMagic Inc. (89, 2.3%)
Data Security / Encryption
Mississauga, ON, Canada
winmagic.com

WipeDrive (Was White Canyon Inc.) (10, -16.7%)
Data Security / Data Erasure And Destruction
American Fork, UT, US
whitecanyon.com

Wipro Limited (237905, -18.9%)
MSSP / Managed Security Services
Bangalore, India
wipro.com

Wirewheel (20, -57.5%)
Data Security / Customer Data Security
Arlington, VA, US
wirewheel.io

WireX Systems (21, 16.7%)
Operations / Forensics
Sunnyvale, CA, US
wirexsystems.com

Wisekey (104, -3.7%)
IoT Security / Hardware
Geneva, Switzerland
wisekey.com

WitFoo (11, -21.4%)
Operations / Security Operations Platform
Dunwoody, GA, US
witfoo.com

WithSecure (1671, 63.3%)
Endpoint Security / Anti-virus
Helsinki, Finland
withsecure.com

WiTopia (9, 12.5%)
Network Security / VPN / Proxy
Reston, VA, US
witopia.com

Wiz (1114, 74.3%)
GRC / Configuration Management
Tel Aviv, Israel
wiz.io

Wizdome (10, -63.0%)
Threat Intelligence / TIP
Tel Aviv, Israel
wizdome.com

Woleet (3, -62.5%)
Data Security / Blockchain
Rennes, France
woleet.io

wolfSSL (41, 5.1%)
Network Security / Open Source Internet Security
Edmonds, WA, US
wolfssl.com

Wontok (24, 4.3%)
Fraud Prevention / Anti-fraud
Pyrmont, Australia
wontok.com

WootCloud (3, -40.0%)
Endpoint Security / Endpoint Control
San Jose, CA, US
wootcloud.com

Workspot (158, -6.0%)
Operations / Secure Remote Access
Campbell, CA, US
workspot.com

WoSign (5, -44.4%)
Data Security / Public Key Infrastructure
Shenzhen, China
wosign.com

WWN Software LLC (7, -12.5%)
Data Security / Secure Data Sharing
Washington, DC, US
wwnsoftware.com

WWPass (19, 26.7%)
IAM / Authentication
Nashua, NH, US
wwpass.com

X-Ways Software (5, 66.7%)
Data Security / Forensics
Germany
x-ways.net

Xage Security (102, 54.5%)
IoT Security / OT Security
Palo Alto, CA, US
xage.com

Xahive (12, 20.0%)
Data Security / Secure Communications
Ottawa, ON, Canada
xahive.com

Xantrion (84, 5.0%)
MSSP / Managed Security Services
Oakland, CA, US
xantrion.com

Xaptum (4, -20.0%)
Network Security
Palo Alto, CA, US
xaptum.com

Xcitium (139, 6.9%)
Endpoint Security
Bloomfield, NJ, US
xcitium.com

Xello (7, 75.0%)
Deception
Moscow, Russia
xello.ru

Xeol (3, 0.0%)
API Security
New York, NY, US
xeol.io

XignSys (18, 0.0%)
IAM / Authentication
Gelsenkirchen, NRW, Germany
xignsys.com

Xiid (5, 25.0%)
IAM / Identity Management
Cupertino, CA, US
xiid.com

Xiphera (16, 14.3%)
Data Security / Encryption
Espoo, Finland
xiphera.com

XM Cyber (297, 63.2%)
Operations / Breach And Attack Simulation
Herzliya, Israel
xmcyber.com

Xorlab (28, 3.7%)
Email Security / Zero Day Defense
Zurich, Switzerland
xorlab.com

XplicitTrust (6, 0.0%)
Network Security
Karlsruhe, Germany
xplicittrust.com

XQmessage (30, -25.0%)
Data Security / IRM
Oakland, CA, US
xqmsg.co

XTN Cognitive Security (25, 0.0%)
IAM / Identity Verification
Boston, MA, US
xtn-lab.com

Xygeni (22, 120.0%)
Application Security / SBOM
Madrid, Spain
xygeni.io

YazamTech (8, 33.3%)
Data Security
Ra'anana, Israel
yazamtech.com

**Numbers in parentheses indicate headcount and % change in 2023.*

Yes Security (9, 800.0%)
Application Security
South Yorkshire,
United Kingdom
yes-security.com

YeshID (17, 54.5%)
IAM / Identity
Management
Denver, CO, US
yeshid.com

YesWeHack (237, 37.8%)
Operations / Bugs
Paris, France
yeswehack.com

Yoggie (8, 14.3%)
Network Security /
Firewalls
Beth Halevy, Israel
yoggie.com

Yogosha (189, 41.0%)
Operations / Bugs
Paris, France
yogosha.com

Yoti (390, 5.4%)
Fraud Prevention / Identity
Verification
London, United Kingdom
yoti.com

Yottaa (103, -18.2%)
Network Security / DDoS
Defense
Waltham, MA, US
yottaa.com

YouAttest (20, -9.1%)
GRC / Governance
Newport Beach,
CA, US
youattest.com

Yubico (460, 15.3%)
IAM / Authentication
Stockholm, Sweden
yubico.com

Zafehouze (5, 150.0%)
IAM
Roskilde, Denmark
zafehouze.com

Zama (92, 37.3%)
Data Security /
Encryption
Paris, France
zama.ai

Zartech (41, 20.6%)
GRC / GRC Platform
Dallas, TX, US
zartech.net/grc

ZecOps (16, -30.4%)
Operations / Automated
Defense
San Francisco,
CA, US
zecops.com

Zecurion (38, 5.6%)
Data Security /
Database Security
Moscow, Russia
zecurion.com

Zemana (11, -8.3%)
Endpoint Security /
Anti-virus
Ankara, Turkey
zemana.com

ZenGo (60, -1.6%)
Data Security / Wallets
Sarona, Israel
zengo.com

Zenity (37, 42.3%)
GRC / No-code/Low-
code Security
Tel Aviv, Israel
zenity.io

Zentera Systems (19, -24.0%)
Network Security / Zero
Trust Networking
San Jose,
CA, US
zentera.net

Zero Day Initiative (Trend Micro) (13, 30.0%)
Application Security /
Bugs
Austin, TX, US
zerodayinitiative.com

Zero Networks (54, 35.0%)
Network Security /
Segmentation
Tel Aviv, Israel
zeronetworks.com

Zerocopter (45, 2.3%)
Application Security /
Hackers For Hire
Amsterdam, Netherlands
zerocopter.com

ZERODIUM (5, 400.0%)
Application Security / Bugs
Washington, DC, US
zerodium.com

ZeroFOX (823, 30.0%)
Threat Intelligence /
Monitoring
Baltimore, MD, US
zerofox.com

Zeronorth (5, -28.6%)
GRC / Vulnerabilities
Boston, MA, US
zeronorth.io

ZeroSpam (4, -42.9%)
Email Security / Anti-spam
Montreal, QC, Canada
zerospam.ca

ZeroTier (16, 33.3%)
Network Security /
Segmentation
Irvine, CA, US
zerotier.com

Zertid (24, 71.4%)
IAM
Melbourne,
Victoria, Australia
zertid.com

Zertificon Solutions (62, -15.1%)
Email Security / Secure Email
Berlin, Germany
zertificon.com

Zettaset (16, -5.9%)
Data Security / Encryption
Mountain View, CA, US
zettaset.com

Zeva (25, -7.4%)
Data Security / Encryption
Fairfax, VA, US
zevainc.com

Zighra (11, 10.0%)
IAM / Authentication
Ottawa, ON, Canada
zighra.com

Zignsec (26, 4.0%)
IAM / Identity Verification
Solna, Sweden
zignsec.com

Zilla Security (41, 28.1%)
GRC / Compliance
Management
Boston, MA, US
zillasecurity.com

Zimperium (228, -4.2%)
Endpoint Security / Mobile
Device Security
Dallas, TX, US
zimperium.com

Ziperase (5, 0.0%)
Data Security / Data Erasure
And Destruction
Austin, TX, US
ziperase.com

Ziroh Labs (74, -6.3%)
Data Security /
Data Discovery
Bangalore, India
ziroh.com

ZITADEL (14, -17.6%)
IAM / Identity Management
St. Gallen, Schweiz,
Switzerland
zitadel.com

Zivver (136, -8.7%)
Email Security / Secure Email
Amsterdam, Netherlands
zivver.eu

Zix Corp. (275, -13.2%)
Data Security / Secure
Communications
Dallas, TX, US
zixcorp.com

**Numbers in parentheses indicate headcount and % change in 2023.*

Zluri (239, 151.6%)
Operations / Asset Management
San Francisco, CA, US
zluri.com

Zoloz (4, -55.6%)
IAM / Authentication
Haidian District, China
zoloz.com

Zorus (25, -16.7%)
Network Security / VPN / Proxy
Monroe, CT, US
zorustech.com

ZPE Systems (143, 19.2%)
Network Security / Access Security
Fremont, CA, US
zpesystems.com

Zscaler (7050, 11.3%)
Network Security / Cloud Security
San Jose, CA, US
zscaler.com

Zumigo (28, 33.3%)
IAM / Identity Verification
San Jose, CA, US
zumigo.com

Zuul (11, 0.0%)
IoT Security / OT Security
Columbia, MD, US
zuuliot.com

Zvelo (40, -4.8%)
Network Security / URL Categorization
Greenwood Village, CO, US
zvelo.com

Zwipe (39, -26.4%)
IAM / Authentication
Oslo, Norway
zwipe.com

ZyLAB (61, -18.7%)
GRC / E-discovery
Amsterdam, Netherlands
zylab.com

Zymbit (12, 71.4%)
IoT Security / Device Security Modules
Santa Barbara, CA, US
zymbit.com

Zyston (66, 20.0%)
MSSP / Managed Security Services
Dallas, TX, US
zyston.com

ZyXEL Communications Corp. (18, 5.9%)
Network Security / Firewalls
Anaheim, CA, US
zyxel.com

**Numbers in parentheses indicate headcount and % change in 2023.*

CHAPTER 20

Directory by Country

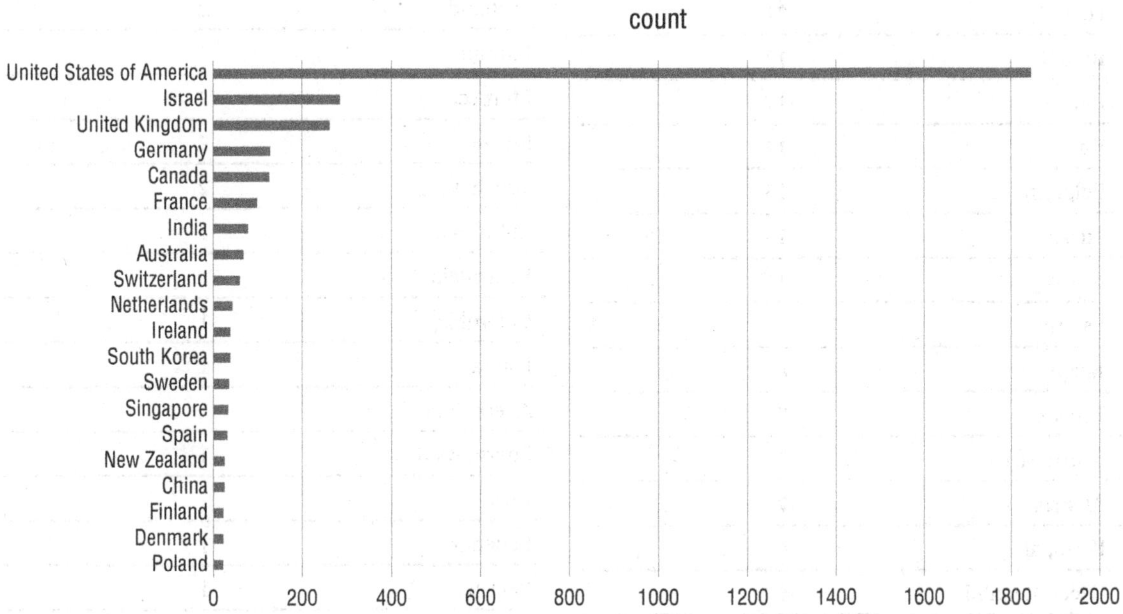

Vendors by Country

Country	Count
United States of America	1846
Israel	285
United Kingdom	262
Germany	129
Canada	126
France	99
India	79
Australia	68
Switzerland	60
Netherlands	43
Ireland	38
South Korea	38
Sweden	35

(continued)

Vendors by Country (continued)

Country	Count
Singapore	33
Spain	31
New Zealand	25
China	25
Finland	22
Denmark	22
Poland	21
Brazil	18
Italy	17
Russia	17
Belgium	15
Turkey	13
Norway	11
Estonia	8
Japan	8
Taiwan	8
South Africa	7
Austria	7
Portugal	6
Czech Republic	5
Hong Kong	5
Slovakia	4
Hungary	4
Romania	4
Luxembourg	3
Ukraine	3
Vietnam	3
Iceland	3
United Arab Emirates	3
Malta	2
Argentina	2
Nigera	2
Greece	2
Chile	2
Peru	2
Malaysia	2
Scotland	2
Bahrain	2
Morocco	2
Mexico	2
Czechia	2
Indonesia	1
Venezuela	1
Colombia	1
Latvia	1
Azerbaijan	1
Puerto Rico	1
Kuwait	1
Ecuador	1
Belarus	1
Armenia	1
Serbia	1
British Virgin Islands	1
Panama	1
Bulgaria	1
Croatia	1
Georgia	1
Nepal	1
Republic of Moldova	1

Argentina

Smartfense (32, -8.6%)
GRC / Security Awareness Training
Cordoba, Argentina
smartfense.com

VU Security (180, -28.0%)
IAM / VPN/Proxy
Buenos Aires, Argentina
vusecurity.com

Armenia

Illuria Security (5, -16.7%)
Deception
Yerevan, Armenia
illuriasecurity.com

Australia

6clicks (61, 24.5%)
GRC / Compliance Management
Melbourne, Australia
6clicks.io

Aiculus (8, 14.3%)
API Security
Melbourne, Australia
aiculus.co

Airlock Digital (37, 42.3%)
Endpoint Security / Application Whitelisting
Unley, Australia
airlockdigital.com

Airtrack (3, -72.7%)
Security Analytics / Configuration Management
Melbourne, Victoria, Australia
airtrack.io

Amplify Intelligence (3, 0.0%)
GRC / Vulnerabilities
Melbourne, Victoria, Australia
amplifyintelligence.com

Apporetum (4, 0.0%)
IAM
Canberra, Australia
apporetum.com.au

AssetNote (11, 22.2%)
Operations / Monitoring
Brisbane, Queensland, Australia
assetnote.io

Attack Forge (7, 0.0%)
Operations / Penetration Testing
Melbourne, Australia
attackforge.com

Avertro (22, 57.1%)
GRC / Risk Management
Sydney, NSW, Australia
avertro.com

BankVault Cybersecurity (14, 75.0%)
IAM / Authentication
West Perth, Australia
bankvault.com

CipherStash (19, 18.8%)
Data Security / Encryption
Sydney, Australia
cipherstash.com

Cog (19, 5.6%)
IoT Security / Virtualization
Sydney, Australia
cog.systems

ContentKeeper (34, -20.9%)
Network Security / Filtering
Braddon, Australia
contentkeeper.com

CryptoPhoto (4, 0.0%)
IAM / Authentication
Australia
cryptophoto.com

Cryptsoft Pty Ltd. (15, 0.0%)
Data Security / Public Key Infrastructure
Greenslopes, Australia
cryptsoft.com

Cyberaware (3, -25.0%)
GRC / Security Awareness Training
Melbourne, Australia
cyberaware.com

CyberCX (1263, 14.4%)
MSSP / Managed Security Services
Melbourne, Australia
cybercx.com.au

Cydarm (18, -21.7%)
Operations / Incident Management
Docklands, Australia
cydarm.com

CySight (5, 25.0%)
Network Security / Monitoring
Sydney, Australia
netflowauditor.com

Dekko Secure (10, 25.0%)
Data Security / Encryption
Sydney, Australia
dekkosecure.com

Detexian (11, 10.0%)
Operations / Monitoring
Docklands, Australia
detexian.com

Devicie (22, 46.7%)
Operations
Sydney, Australia
devicie.com

Ditno (9, -25.0%)
Network Security / Firewalls
Sydney, Australia
ditno.com

DroneSec (11, -8.3%)
IoT Security / Drones
Melbourne, Victoria, Australia
dronesec.com

Dull (11, 22.2%)
IoT Security / Secure Remote Access
Melbourne, Australia
dull.net

EFTsure (145, 39.4%)
Fraud Prevention / EFT Protection
North Sydney, Australia
home.eftsure.com.au

Enov8 (29, 7.4%)
Data Security / Data Masking
New South Wales, Australia
enov8.com

FifthDomain (16, -30.4%)
Training / Cyber Range
Canberra, Australia
fifthdomain.com.au

FIRCY (3, 0.0%)
Threat Intelligence / Cloud Security
Adelaide, Australia
fircy.co

FirstWave (55, 5.8%)
Operations / SOC
North Sydney, New South Wales, Australia
firstwave.com

Fortifyedge (5, -16.7%)
IAM
Tasmania, Australia
fortifyedge.com

GetData Forensics (12, 0.0%)
GRC / Forensics
Kogarah, Australia
forensicexplorer.com

Huntsman (22, 10.0%)
Security Analytics / SIEM
Chatswood, Australia
huntsmansecurity.com

Janusnet (9, 12.5%)
Data Security / Data Classification
Milsons Point, Australia
janusnet.com

Kasada (113, 15.3%)
Fraud Prevention / Bot Security
Sydney, Australia
kasada.io

**Numbers in parentheses indicate headcount and % change in 2023.*

Loop Secure (27, -41.3%)
MSSP / Managed Security Services
Melbourne, Australia
loopsec.com.au

NetLinkz (24, 100.0%)
Network Security / Zero Trust Networking
Sydney, Australia
netlinkz.com

Nuix (436, 1.4%)
Security Analytics / Investigation
Sydney, Australia
nuix.com

PassMark Software Pvt Ltd. (8, 0.0%)
IAM
Surry Hills, Australia
passmark.com

Peloton Cyber Security (16, -20.0%)
MSSP / SOC
Brunswick, Australia
pelotoncyber.com.au

Penten (110, 5.8%)
Data Security / Encryption
Braddon, Australia
penten.com

Prevasio (5, 0.0%)
Operations / Container Security
Sydney, Australia
prevasio.com

Prophecy International (78, 14.7%)
Operations / Logs
Adelaide, Australia
prophecyinternational.com

QuintessenceLabs (48, -7.7%)
Data Security / Quantum
Deakin, Australia
quintessencelabs.com

Red Piranha (59, 3.5%)
Network Security / UTM
Melbourne, Australia
redpiranha.net

Sapien Cyber (10, -56.5%)
Security Analytics / Incident Management
Joondalup, Australia
sapiencyber.com.au

Scram Software (3, -25.0%)
Data Security / Encryption
Melbourne, Australia
scramsoft.com

Seccom Global (46, -4.2%)
MSSP / Managed Security Services
Sydney, Australia
seccomglobal.com

SecureCode Warrior (259, 2.0%)
Training / Software Development Security
Sydney, Australia
securecodewarrior.com

SecureStack (8, 33.3%)
GRC / Configuration Management
Docklands, Australia
securestack.com

Secutech Solutions (8, -20.0%)
Data Security / USB Token Security
North Ryde, Australia
esecutech.com

Senetas Corporation Limited (41, -8.9%)
Data Security / Encryption
South Melbourne, Australia
senetas.com

SharePass (5, 66.7%)
IAM / CIAM
Melbourne, Victoria, Australia
sharepass.com

SubpicoCat (5, 0.0%)
Network Security / IPS
Sydney, Australia
subpicocat.com

Telstra (35161, 5.5%)
MSSP / Managed Security Services
Melbourne, Australia
telstra.com

Threat Intelligence (21, 0.0%)
Threat Intelligence / Leaked Data
Sydney Nsw, Australia
threatintelligence.com

TokenOne (3, 0.0%)
IAM
Sydney, Australia
tokenone.com

Wontok (24, 4.3%)
Fraud Prevention / Anti-fraud
Pyrmont, Australia
wontok.com

Zertid (24, 71.4%)
IAM
Melbourne, Victoria, Australia
zertid.com

Austria

Cubro (32, -3.0%)
Network Security / Traffic Analysis
Vienna, Austria
cubro.com

CYAN Network Security (4, 33.3%)
Network Security / Gateways
Vienna, Austria
cyannetworks.com

CYBERTRAP (14, -6.7%)
Deception
Wiener Neustadt, Austria
cybertrap.com

Ikarus Security Software GmbH (45, 21.6%)
Endpoint Security / Anti-virus
Vienna, Austria
ikarussecurity.com

Mostly.AI (61, 3.4%)
Data Security / Data Masking
Vienna, Wien, Austria
mostly.ai

Nimbusec (14, 16.7%)
GRC / Scanning
Linz, Austria
nimbusec.com

SEC Consult (137, 0.0%)
Application Security / Code Security
Vienna, Austria
sec-consult.com

Azerbaijan

Cyberpoint (64, 60.0%)
MSSP / SOC
Baku, Azerbaijan
cyberpoint.az

Bahrain

CTM360 (92, 55.9%)
Threat Intelligence / Dark Web
Seef, Bahrain
ctm360.com

FACEKI (15, 0.0%)
IAM
Manama, Al Manamah, Bahrain
faceki.com

Belarus

VirusBlokAda (15, 25.0%)
Endpoint Security / Anti-virus
Minsk, Belarus
anti-virus.by

**Numbers in parentheses indicate headcount and % change in 2023.*

Belgium

Aikido (20, 11.1%)
Application Security / Vulnerabilities
Ghent, Belgium
aikido.dev

Ceeyu (10, -16.7%)
Operations / Attack Surface Management
Belgium
ceeyu.io

Csi Tools (7, -36.4%)
IAM / SAP
Herent, Belgium
csi-tools.com

Davinsi Labs (68, 21.4%)
MSSP / MDR
Antwerp, Belgium
davinsi.com

Elimity (6, 50.0%)
IAM / CIAM
Mechelen, Antwerpen, Belgium
elimity.com

Guardsquare (149, 16.4%)
Application Security / Mobile Device Security
Leuven, Belgium
guardsquare.com

Intigriti (422, 11.9%)
Testing / Penetration Testing
Antwerp, Belgium
intigriti.com

Jimber (20, -16.7%)
Network Security / Secure Web Browsing
Oostkamp, Belgium
jimber.io

Lansweeper (323, 19.6%)
Operations / Asset Management
Dendermonde, Belgium
lansweeper.com

Mailfence (6, 0.0%)
Email Security / Secure Email
Brussels, Belgium
mailfence.com

Raito (15, -6.2%)
Data Security / Access Security
Brussels, Belgium
raito.io

Rhea Group (675, 13.4%)
Training / Cyber Range
Wavre, Belgium
rheagroup.com

Sweepatic (16, -15.8%)
Threat Intelligence / Brand
Leuven, Belgium
sweepatic.com

TrustBuilder (62, 82.3%)
IAM / CIAM
Ghent, Flemish Region, Belgium
trustbuilder.com

Brazil

Achilleas (13, 333.3%)
MSSP / MDR
Brazil
achilleas.com.br

AllowMe (65, 22.6%)
IAM / Identity Management
Sao Paulo, Brazil
allowme.cloud

Apura (71, 29.1%)
Threat Intelligence / OSINT
Sao Paulo, Brazil
apura.com.br

Axur (213, 10.9%)
Threat Intelligence / Brand
Porto Alegre, Brazil
axur.com

idwall (361, -10.2%)
Fraud Prevention / Fraud Detection
Sao Paulo, Brazil
idwall.co

Konduto (73, -17.1%)
Fraud Prevention / Fraud Detection
Sao Paulo, Brazil
konduto.com

Kryptus (130, 8.3%)
Data Security / Hardware
Campinas Sao Paulo, Brazil
kryptus.com

Malware Patrol (8, 14.3%)
Threat Intelligence / Feeds
Sao Paulo, Brazil
malwarepatrol.net

Modulo (182, 9.0%)
GRC
Rio de Janeiro, Brazil
modulo.com

Netdeep (6, 20.0%)
Network Security / Firewalls
Brazil
netdeep.com.br

NetSecurity (82, 12.3%)
MSSP / Managed Security Services
Sao Paulo, Brazil
netsecurity.com.br

On Security (3, 50.0%)
MSSP / SOC
Sao Paulo, Brazil
on-security.com

PhishX (20, 5.3%)
GRC / Security Awareness Training
Cotia, Brazil
phishx.io

Syhunt (7, 40.0%)
Application Security / Code Security
Rio de Janeiro, Brazil
syhunt.com

Tempest Security Intelligence (425, -7.0%)
GRC / Data Discovery
Recife, Brazil
tempest.com.br

Tenchi Security (45, 60.7%)
GRC / Risk Management
Sao Paulo, Brazil
tenchisecurity.com

unico (1031, -3.6%)
IAM / Authentication
Sao Paulo, Brazil
unico.io

Unxpose (8, -20.0%)
Operations / Attack Surface Management
Sao Paulo, Brazil
unxpose.com

British Virgin Islands

ExpressVPN (266, -7.3%)
Network Security / VPN/Proxy
Tortola, British Virgin Islands
expressvpn.com

Bulgaria

Tesseract Intelligence (9, -30.8%)
Threat Intelligence / Dark Web
Sofia, Bulgaria
tesseractintelligence.com

Canada

1Password (1707, 89.0%)
IAM / Credential Security
Toronto, ON, Canada
1password.com

Absolute Software (981, 14.6%)
Endpoint Security / Mobile Device Security
Vancouver, BC, Canada
absolute.com

Accedian (336, -11.3%)
Network Security / Monitoring
Montreal, Quebec, Canada
accedian.com

**Numbers in parentheses indicate headcount and % change in 2023.*

ADAMnetworks (5, 25.0%)
Network Security / Access Security
London, Canada
adamnet.works

Adaware (13, 0.0%)
Endpoint Security / Anti-virus
Montreal, QC, Canada
adaware.com

aDolas (30, 15.4%)
IoT Security / Assurance
Victoria, BC, Canada
adolus.com

Agilicus (13, -13.3%)
IoT Security / Access Security
Kitchener, Canada
agilicus.com

Alfahive (30, -16.7%)
GRC / Posture Management
Mississauga, ON, Canada
alfahive.com

Arc4dia (3, -25.0%)
Security Analytics / Incident Management
Montreal, QC, Canada
arc4dia.com

Asigra (85, 13.3%)
Data Security / Secure Backup/Recovery
Toronto, ON, Canada
asigra.com

BAAR (57, 23.9%)
IAM / Identity Management
Mississauga, Canada
baar.ai

Beauceron (44, -22.8%)
GRC / Defense Against Phishing
Fredericton, NB, Canada
beauceronsecurity.com

BicDroid (7, 0.0%)
Data Security / Encryption
Waterloo, ON, Canada
bicdroid.com

BioConnect (50, 21.9%)
IAM / Authentication
Toronto, ON, Canada
bioconnect.com

Blackberry (3314, -7.4%)
Endpoint Security / Mobile Device Security
Waterloo, ON, Canada
BlackBerry.com

Blockdos (4, 0.0%)
Network Security / DDoS Defense
Mississauga, ON, Canada
blockdos.net

Bluink (24, 9.1%)
IAM / Authentication
Ottawa, ON, Canada
bluink.ca

Boost Security (27, 28.6%)
Application Security / Software Development Security
Montreal, Quebec, Canada
boostsecurity.io

Byos (29, -6.5%)
Network Security / Segmentation
Halifax, Canada
byos.io

Capzul (3, 0.0%)
Application Security
Toronto, Canada
capzul.net

Cavelo Inc (20, 25.0%)
GRC / Data Discovery
Kitchener, ON, Canada
cavelo.com

CBL Data Recovery Technologies Inc. (39, 11.4%)
Data Security / Data Recovery
Markham, ON, Canada
cbldata.com

Certicom (123, -2.4%)
Data Security / Encryption
Mississauga, ON, Canada
certicom.com

Cloudmask (4, 0.0%)
Email Security
Ottawa, ON, Canada
cloudmask.com

CoGuard (5, 25.0%)
GRC / Configuration Management
Waterloo, ON, Canada
coguard.io

Cord3 Innovation Inc. (9, 0.0%)
Data Security / Encryption
Ottawa, ON, Canada
cord3inc.com

Corsa (27, 8.0%)
Network Security / Zero Trust Networking
Ottawa, ON, Canada
corsa.com

Crypto4A Inc. (25, 8.7%)
Data Security / Entropy As A Service
Ottawa, ON, Canada
crypto4a.com

Cryptomill Cybersecurity Solutions (21, -22.2%)
Data Security
Toronto, ON, Canada
cryptomill.com

Currentware Inc. (24, 4.3%)
Endpoint Security / Monitoring
Toronto, ON, Canada
currentware.com

Cybeats (41, 28.1%)
Application Security / SBOM
Aurora, ON, Canada
cybeats.com

CyberCNS (7, -22.2%)
GRC / Vulnerabilities
Surrey, British Columbia, Canada
cybercns.com

CyberQP (68, 54.5%)
IAM / Access Security
North Vancouver, Canada
cyberqp.com

D3 Security (171, 17.9%)
Operations / Incident Management
Vancouver, BC, Canada
d3security.com

Data Sentinel (31, -11.4%)
GRC / Risk Management
Concord, Canada
data-sentinel.com

DataPassports (9, -52.6%)
Data Security / IRM
Toronto, ON, Canada
datapassports.com

Datex Inc. (52, 20.9%)
Data Security / DLP
Mississauga, ON, Canada
datex.ca

Defence Intelligence (20, -48.7%)
Operations / Anti-malware
Kanata, ON, Canada
defintel.com

Devolutions (175, 34.6%)
IAM
Quebec, Canada
devolutions.net

Difenda (77, 2.7%)
MSSP / MDR
Oakville, ON, Canada
difenda.com

Diligent (104, -30.7%)
GRC / Risk Management
Vancouver, BC, Canada
wegalvanize.com

DOSarrest (12, -7.7%)
Network Security / DDoS Defense
BC, Canada
dosarrest.com

Echosec (6, -79.3%)
Threat Intelligence / Intel Gathering Tool
Victoria, BC, Canada
echosec.net

**Numbers in parentheses indicate headcount and % change in 2023.*

Echoworx (89, 4.7%)
Email Security / Secure Email
Toronto, ON, Canada
echoworx.com

eSentire (577, -5.1%)
MSSP / MDR
Cambridge, ON, Canada
esentire.com

Ethoca (171, 4.3%)
Fraud Prevention / Transaction Security
Toronto, ON, Canada
ethoca.com

evolutionQ (32, 45.5%)
Network Security / Quantum
Ontario, Canada
evolutionq.com

Faronics Technologies Inc. (116, 2.6%)
Endpoint Security
Vancouver, BC, Canada
faronics.com

Feroot Security (22, 0.0%)
Application Security / Scanning
Toronto, ON, Canada
feroot.com

Field Effect Software (161, 9.5%)
MSSP / MDR
Ottawa, ON, Canada
fieldeffect.com

Fileflex (19, -17.4%)
IAM / Access Security
Toronto, Canada
fileflex.com

FixMeStick (12, -7.7%)
Endpoint Security / Anti-virus
Montreal, QC, Canada
fixmestick.com

Flare (59, 3.5%)
Operations / Attack Surface Management
Montreal, Quebec, Canada
flare.systems

GoSecure (177, -6.3%)
MSSP / Managed Security Services
Montreal, QC, Canada
gosecure.net

Graphite Software (3, 0.0%)
Endpoint Security / Container Security
Ottawa, ON, Canada
graphitesoftware.com

Hitachi ID Systems (80, -18.4%)
IAM
Calgary, AB, Canada
hitachi-id.com

Hushmail (256, 0.4%)
Data Security / Secure Communications
Vancouver, BC, Canada
hushmail.com

Hyas (43, -23.2%)
Threat Intelligence / Attribution Intelligence
Victoria, BC, Canada
hyas.com

Hypersecu Information Systems (7, 0.0%)
IAM / OTP
BC, Canada
hypersecu.com

I Am I (4, 33.3%)
IAM / Authentication
Markham, Canada
useiami.com

Iceberg Cyber (5, 25.0%)
MSSP / Personal Protection
Toronto, Canada
icebergcyber.com

Identos Inc. (60, 9.1%)
IAM / Mobile Identity
Toronto, ON, Canada
identos.com

IDmelon Technologies Inc. (12, 71.4%)
IAM
Vancouver, BC, Canada
idmelon.com

IGLOO Software (125, -9.4%)
GRC / Security Management
Kitchener, ON, Canada
igloosoftware.com

InBay Technologies (8, -33.3%)
IAM / Authentication
Kanata, ON, Canada
inbaytech.com

Infosec Global (35, 2.9%)
Data Security / Public Key Infrastructure
North York, ON, Canada
infosecglobal.com

ISARA (18, -47.1%)
Data Security / Encryption
Waterloo, ON, Canada
isara.com

Kobalt (24, 60.0%)
MSSP / Managed Security Services
Vancouver, BC, Canada
kobalt.io

Konika Minolta (519, 7.2%)
MSSP / Managed Security Services
Mississauga, Canada
konicaminolta.ca

LifeRaft (85, 3.7%)
Threat Intelligence / Monitoring
Halifax, NS, Canada
liferaftinc.com

LoginTC (8, -11.1%)
IAM / Authentication
Kanata, ON, Canada
logintc.com

LSoft Technologies (7, 0.0%)
Data Security / Data Erasure And Destruction
Mississauga, ON, Canada
lsoft.net

Magnet Forensics (566, 23.6%)
Operations / Forensics
Waterloo, ON, Canada
magnetforensics.com

Mailchannels (17, 6.2%)
Email Security / SMTP Relay
Vancouver, BC, Canada
mailchannels.com

Media Sonar (15, -11.8%)
Threat Intelligence / TIP
London, ON, Canada
mediasonar.com

Messageware (11, 0.0%)
Email Security / OWA Security
Mississauga, ON, Canada
messageware.com

Mode (21, 250.0%)
Data Security / Quantum
Calgary, Canada
mode.io

Myntex (9, 0.0%)
Data Security / Secure Communications
Calgary, AL, Canada
myntex.com

Netsweeper (70, 0.0%)
Network Security / Filtering
Waterloo, ON, Canada
netsweeper.com

NoviFlow (50, -3.9%)
Network Security / SDN
Montreal, QC, Canada
noviflow.com

NuData Security (52, -42.9%)
Fraud Prevention / Fraud Detection
Vancouver, BC, Canada
nudatasecurity.com

OpenText (21752, 45.1%)
IAM / Federated Identity
Waterloo, ON, Canada
opentext.com

Palitronica (16, -11.1%)
Network Security / IDS
Ontario, Canada
palitronica.com

**Numbers in parentheses indicate headcount and % change in 2023.*

Penfield.ai (7, -22.2%)
Security Analytics / Threat Analysis
Toronto, ON, Canada
penfield.ai

Plurilock (45, -8.2%)
IAM / Authentication
Victoria, BC, Canada
plurilock.com

Privacy Analytics (98, -4.8%)
Data Security / Healthcare
Ottawa, ON, Canada
privacy-analytics.com

Private AI (81, 113.2%)
GRC / Data Discovery
Toronto, ON, Canada
private-ai.com

Protexxa (70, 2233.3%)
GRC / Security Awareness Training
Toronto, Canada
protexxa.com

QEYnet (11, 22.2%)
Data Security
Vaughan, ON, Canada
qeynet.com

Qohash (43, -21.8%)
GRC / Data Discovery
Quebec, QC, Canada
qohash.com

Quantropi (31, 0.0%)
Data Security / Quantum
Ontario, Canada
quantropi.com

Quickpass (67, 67.5%)
IAM / Access Security
North Vancouver, Canada
getquickpass.com

Resolver (363, 13.4%)
GRC / Risk Management
Toronto, ON, Canada
resolver.com

Route 1 (43, -12.2%)
IAM
Toronto, ON, Canada
route1.com

Secure Exchanges (10, 42.9%)
Data Security / Document Security
Canada
secure-exchanges.com

Securicy (Now Carbide) (34, -27.7%)
GRC / Policy Management
Sydney, NS, Canada
securicy.com

Security Compass (259, 13.1%)
GRC / Compliance Management
Toronto, ON, Canada
securitycompass.com

SideDrawer (27, 22.7%)
Data Security / Secure Data Sharing
Toronto, Canada
sidedrawer.com

SigmaRed (16, 60.0%)
Data Security / AI Debiasing
Toronto, Canada
sigmared.ai

Stratejm (69, 21.1%)
MSSP / SOC
Ontario, Canada
stratejm.com

Subgraph (5, 25.0%)
Endpoint Security / Operating System Security
Montreal, QC, Canada
subgraph.com

Tailscale (122, 87.7%)
Network Security / Zero Trust Networking
Toronto, ON, Canada
tailscale.com

TeejLab (13, 0.0%)
API Security / API Discovery
British Columbia, Canada
apidiscovery.teejlab.com

Tehama (29, -47.3%)
Network Security / Virtualization
Ottawa, ON, Canada
tehama.io

Terranova Security (107, 4.9%)
Training
Laval, QC, Canada
terranovasecurity.com

TITUS (73, -4.0%)
GRC / DLP
Ottawa, ON, Canada
titus.com

TrojAI (19, 5.6%)
GRC / Governance
New Brunswick, Canada
troj.ai

Trulioo (398, 3.1%)
IAM / Identity Verification
Vancouver, BC, Canada
trulioo.com

TunnelBear (14, 7.7%)
Network Security / VPN/Proxy
Toronto, ON, Canada
tunnelbear.com

V-Key (122, 16.2%)
Endpoint Security / Sandbox
Ottawa, ON, Canada
v-key.com

Verafin (802, -2.8%)
Fraud Prevention / Fraud Management
St. John'S, NL, Canada
verafin.com

Vircom (31, 0.0%)
Email Security / Threat Prevention
Montreal, QC, Canada
vircom.com

Vitrium (28, 27.3%)
Data Security / DRM
Vancouver, BC, Canada
vitrium.com

Wedge Networks (34, -5.6%)
Network Security
Calgary, AB, Canada
wedgenetworks.com

WinMagic Inc. (89, 2.3%)
Data Security / Encryption
Mississauga, ON, Canada
winmagic.com

Xahive (12, 20.0%)
Data Security / Secure Communications
Ottawa, ON, Canada
xahive.com

ZeroSpam (4, -42.9%)
Email Security / Anti-spam
Montreal, QC, Canada
zerospam.ca

Zighra (11, 10.0%)
IAM / Authentication
Ottawa, ON, Canada
zighra.com

Chile

Camel Secure (8, -27.3%)
GRC
Santiago, Chile
camelsecure.com

Hackmetrix (58, 11.5%)
GRC / Compliance Management
Santiago, Chile
hackmetrix.com

China

Anxinsec (34, 100.0%)
Application Security / Runtime Security
Beijing, China
anxinsec.com

Cloudcoffer (4, -20.0%)
Network Security / UTM
Taipei, China
cloudcoffer.com

**Numbers in parentheses indicate headcount and % change in 2023.*

ExcelSecu (51, -17.7%)
Data Security / Public Key Infrastructure
Shenzhen, China
excelsecu.com

Feitian Technologies (101, 6.3%)
IAM
Beijing, China
ftsafe.com

Geetest (64, -8.6%)
IAM / Captchas
Wuhan, China
geetest.com

H3C (4064, -0.9%)
Network Security / Gateways
Beijing, China
h3c.com

Huawei (174232, 0.5%)
Network Security / Firewalls
Shenzhen, China
huawei.com

Moresec (49, 0.0%)
Application Security / Scanning
Hangzhou, China
moresec.cn

Nym (55, 22.2%)
Data Security / Encryption
Neuchatel, China
nymtech.net

QI-ANXIN (87, 13.0%)
Endpoint Security / Anti-virus
Beijing, China
qianxin.com

Qihoo 360 Total Security (3044, 18.7%)
Endpoint Security / Anti-virus
Beijing, China
360.cn

Qingteng (101, -1.9%)
Operations / Asset Management
Beijing, China
qingteng.cn

Sangfor (2101, -0.5%)
Network Security / UTM
Shenzhen, China
sangfor.com

SoBug (3, 0.0%)
Application Security / Bugs
Shenzhen, China
sobug.com

Tencent (108056, -0.3%)
Endpoint Security / Anti-virus
Shenzhen, China
tencent.com

ThreatBook (88, 57.1%)
Threat Intelligence / TIP
Haidian District, China
threatbook.cn

Topsec Network Security (152, -0.7%)
Network Security / Firewalls
Haidian District, China
topsec.com.cn

Venustech (368, -18.0%)
Network Security / UTM
China
venustech.com.cn

Vkansee (5, 0.0%)
IAM / Authentication
Beijing, China
vkansee.com

WoSign (5, -44.4%)
Data Security / Public Key Infrastructure
Shenzhen, China
wosign.com

Zoloz (4, -55.6%)
IAM / Authentication
Haidian District, China
zoloz.com

Colombia

360 Security (23, 35.3%)
MSSP / Managed Security Services
Bogota, Colombia
360sec.com

Czech Republic

Avast Software (1057, -29.4%)
Endpoint Security / Anti-virus
Prague, Czech Republic
avast.com

GreyCortex (33, 22.2%)
Network Security / Traffic Analysis
Brno, Czech Republic
greycortex.com

Mobiledit (Was Compelson Labs) (24, 33.3%)
GRC / Forensics
Prague, Czech Republic
mobiledit.com

Qrator Labs (34, 0.0%)
Network Security / DDoS Defense
Prague, Czech Republic
qrator.net

StickyPassword (7, 0.0%)
IAM
Brno, Czech Republic
stickypassword.com

Czechia

Safetica (94, -8.7%)
Data Security / DLP
Brno, Czechia
safetica.com

Threat Mark (82, -19.6%)
Fraud Prevention / Identity Verification
Brno, Czechia
threatmark.com

Denmark

Arama Tech (6, -14.3%)
GRC / Compliance Management
Glostrop, Denmark
aramatech.com

Arbit Security (12, 20.0%)
Network Security / Data Diode
Hvidovre, Denmark
arbitcds.com

Chili Security (32, 0.0%)
Endpoint Security / Anti-virus
Odense, Denmark
chilisecurity.dk

ComplyCloud (91, 7.1%)
GRC / GDPR
Copenhagen, Denmark
complycloud.com

Cryptomathic (102, -1.9%)
Data Security / Key Management
Aarhus, Denmark
cryptomathic.com

CSIS Security Group (117, 11.4%)
MSSP / MDR
Denmark
csisgroup.com

Decision Focus (54, 46.0%)
GRC / Compliance Management
Birkerod, Denmark
decisionfocus.com

FastpassCorp (69, -2.8%)
IAM / Credential Security
Kongens Lyngby, Denmark
fastpasscorp.com

Heimdal Security (281, 48.7%)
Network Security / IPS
Copenhagen, Denmark
heimdalsecurity.com

LogPoint (290, -6.2%)
Security Analytics / SIEM
Copenhagen, Denmark
logpoint.com

Muninn (39, 56.0%)
Operations / Monitoring
Kongens Lyngby, Denmark
muninn.ai

**Numbers in parentheses indicate headcount and % change in 2023.*

Napatech (94, -3.1%)
Operations / Network Acceleration Cards
Soeborg, Denmark
napatech.com

Neupart (21, 50.0%)
GRC / Secure ISMS
Soborg, Denmark
neupart.com

NewBanking (17, 6.2%)
IAM
Copenhagen, Denmark
newbanking.com

Omada (322, 20.1%)
IAM
Copenhagen, Denmark
omada.net

Secomea A/S (101, 5.2%)
IoT Security / Remote Devices
Herlev, Denmark
secomea.com

SecPoint (15, -11.8%)
GRC / Vulnerabilities
Copenhagen, Denmark
secpoint.com

Sepior (8, 33.3%)
Data Security / Encryption
Aarhus, Denmark
sepior.com

Uniqkey (56, 5.7%)
IAM / Credential Security
Herlev, Hovedstaden, Denmark
uniqkey.eu

Zafehouze (5, 150.0%)
IAM
Roskilde, Denmark
zafehouze.com

Estonia

Binalyze (83, -4.6%)
Operations / Forensics
Tallinn, Harjumaa, Estonia
binalyze.com

BotGuard (31, 0.0%)
Fraud Prevention / Bot Security
Tallinn, Estonia
botguard.net/en/home

Cybexer (40, -14.9%)
Training / Cyber Range
Tallinn, Estonia
cybexer.com

Guardtime (106, 3.9%)
GRC / Assurance
Tallinn, Estonia
guardtime.com

Trapmine (4, -77.8%)
Endpoint Security
Tallinn, Estonia
trapmine.com

Veriff (380, -24.8%)
Fraud Prevention / Identity Verification
Tallinn, Estonia
veriff.com

Finland

Arctic Security (24, -4.0%)
Threat Intelligence
Oulu, Finland
arcticsecurity.com

Badrap Oy (4, -33.3%)
Operations / Security Playbooks
Oulu, Oulu, Finland
badrap.io

Binare.io (8, 14.3%)
IoT Security / Firmware
Finland
binare.io

Bittium (1526, -4.4%)
Data Security / Secure Communications
Oulu, Finland
bittium.com

CSIT Finland Oy (13, 85.7%)
IAM
Helsinki, Finland
csit.fi

Granite (26, 8.3%)
GRC / Risk Management
Tampere, Finland
granitegrc.com

Hoxhunt (142, -7.8%)
GRC / Security Awareness Training
Helsinki, Finland
hoxhunt.com

Insta DefSec Oy (643, -13.0%)
Network Security / VPN/Proxy
Tampere, Finland
insta.fi

Jetico Inc. Oy (14, -6.7%)
Data Security / Encryption
Espoo, Finland
jetico.com

Mideye (6, 200.0%)
IAM / Authentication
Espoo, Finland
mideye.com

Miradore (60, -18.9%)
Endpoint Security / Device Management
Vantaa, Finland
miradore.com

Nixu Corporation (414, 5.3%)
MSSP / Managed Security Services
Espoo, Finland
nixu.com

Nokia (82184, 4.5%)
Endpoint Security / Mobile Device Security
Espoo, Finland
networks.nokia.com

Rugged Tooling (8, 0.0%)
Network Security / Monitoring
OULU, Finland
ruggedtooling.com

Sensor Fleet (9, -10.0%)
Network Security / Monitoring
Oulu, Finland
sensorfleet.com

Silverskin Information Security (20, -9.1%)
GRC / Compliance Management
Helsinki, Finland
silverskin.com

SSH Communications Security (516, -4.3%)
Data Security / Secure Data Sharing
Helsinki, Finland
ssh.com

Tosibox (77, 28.3%)
IoT Security / Remote Devices
Oulu, Finland
tosibox.com

Ubisecure (66, 15.8%)
IAM
Espoo, Finland
ubisecure.com

WithSecure (1671, 63.3%)
Endpoint Security / Anti-virus
Helsinki, Finland
withsecure.com

Xiphera (16, 14.3%)
Data Security / Encryption
Espoo, Finland
xiphera.com

France

6cure (16, 23.1%)
Network Security / DDoS Defense
Herouville-Saint-Clair, France
6cure.com

6WIND (112, 17.9%)
Network Security / VPN/Proxy
Montigny-le-Bretonneux, France
6wind.com

**Numbers in parentheses indicate headcount and % change in 2023.*

A3BC (11, -35.3%)
IAM / Authentication
Rennes, France
a3bc.io

Advens (477, 32.5%)
MSSP / SOC
Paris, France
advens.fr

Airbus Cybersecurity (293, 1.4%)
Training / Cyber Range
Alancourt, France
airbus-cyber-security.com

ALL4TEC (26, -3.7%)
GRC / Risk Management
Massy, France
all4tec.com

Alsid (14, -30.0%)
Network Security / Active Directory
Paris, France
alsid.com

Altrnativ (19, 11.8%)
Threat Intelligence / Consumer CTI
Nice, France
altrnativ.com

AMOSSYS (66, 8.2%)
Operations / Breach And Attack Simulation
Rennes, Bretagne, France
amossys.fr

Astran (26, 8.3%)
Data Security / Secure Storage
Paris, France
astran.io

Atos Group (81052, -12.7%)
IAM
Bezons, France
atos.net

Bfore.ai (40, 29.0%)
Threat Intelligence / Domain Prediction
Montpellier, France
bfore.ai

Brainwave Grc (32, -37.2%)
GRC / Identity Analytics
Asnieres-sur-Seine, France
brainwaveGRC.com

BYSTAMP (19, 0.0%)
Data Security
Paris, France
bystamp.com

Capgemini (290105, 2.4%)
MSSP / Managed Security Services
Paris, France
capgemini.com

Citalid (43, 87.0%)
GRC
Versailles, France
citalid.com

Cosmian (20, 25.0%)
Data Security
Paris, France
cosmian.com

CrowdSec (40, 42.9%)
Network Security / IPS
Paris, France
crowdsec.net

Cryptr (9, -10.0%)
IAM / Authentication
Lille, France
cryptr.co

CybelAngel (156, -17.9%)
Operations / Attack Surface Management
Paris, France
cybelangel.com

CyberVadis (89, 7.2%)
GRC / Risk Management
Paris, France
cybervadis.com

Cyberwatch (27, -3.6%)
GRC
Paris, France
cyberwatch.fr

Dawizz (9, 0.0%)
Data Security / Data Discovery
Vannes, France
dawizz.fr

EGERIE (144, 63.6%)
GRC / Risk Management
Toulon, France
egerie.eu

Elba (32, 113.3%)
GRC / Security Awareness Training
Paris, France
elba.security

Elephantastic (6, 200.0%)
Security Analytics / Link Analysis
Paris, France
elephantastic.io

Escape (18, 5.9%)
API Security / API Discovery
Paris, France
escape.tech

eShard (38, -11.6%)
Testing
Aquitaine, France
eshard.com

Filigran (35, 250.0%)
Threat Intelligence
Paris, France
filigran.io

GateWatcher (118, 34.1%)
Network Security / Threat Detection
Paris, France
gatewatcher.com

GitGuardian (162, 50.0%)
IAM / Monitoring
Paris, France
gitguardian.com

GLIMPSE (50, 47.1%)
Operations / Malware Analysis
Cesson-Sevigne, France
glimps.fr

Gravitee.io (110, 1.9%)
API Security / Access Security
France
gravitee.io

Hackuity (51, 24.4%)
GRC / Vulnerabilities
Lyon, France
hackuity.io

HarfangLab (85, 49.1%)
Endpoint Security / EDR
Paris, France
harfanglab.io

HIAsecure (5, 0.0%)
IAM / Authentication
Courbevoie, France
hiasecure.com

I-Tracing (443, 51.2%)
MSSP / Managed Security Services
Puteaux, France
i-tracing.com

IDECSI (31, 14.8%)
Email Security / Auditing
Paris, France
idecsi.com

Inspeere (8, 100.0%)
Data Security / Secure Backup/Recovery
Poitiers, France
inspeere.com

inWebo (5, -91.4%)
IAM / Authentication
Paris, France
inwebo.com

IS Decisions (43, 4.9%)
IAM / Access Security
Bidart, France
isdecisions.com

iTrust (83, 36.1%)
GRC / Vulnerabilities
Labege, France
itrust.fr

KeeeX (9, 12.5%)
Data Security / Document Security
Marseille, France
keeex.me

**Numbers in parentheses indicate headcount and % change in 2023.*

Leanear (8, 0.0%)
Data Security /
Cloud Security
Paris, France
leanear.io

Ledger (732, 0.1%)
Data Security / Wallets
Paris, France
ledger.com

MailInBlack (106, 20.4%)
Email Security / Anti-spam
Marseille, France
mailinblack.com

Make IT Safe (15, -25.0%)
GRC / Auditing
Rezé, France
makeitsafe.fr

Matrix42 (384, 9.4%)
Endpoint Security / EDR
Paris, France
matrix42.com

Merox (7, -12.5%)
Network Security /
DNS Security
Montpellier, France
merox.io

Mindflow (33, 83.3%)
Operations / SOAR
Paris, France
mindflow.io

Mithril Security (17, -15.0%)
Data Security / AI
Training Security
Paris, France
mithrilsecurity.io

Nano Corp. (20, 5.3%)
Network Security /
Traffic Analysis
Paris, France
nanocorp.fr

Olfeo (55, 12.2%)
Network Security / Gateways
Paris, France
olfeo.com

OneWave (29, -9.4%)
IAM / Authentication
Rennes, France
onewave.io

Oodrive (415, -1.9%)
Data Security / Secure
Backup/Recovery
Paris, France
oodrive.com

Orange Cyberdefense (3449, 14.4%)
MSSP / Managed
Security Services
Nanterre, France
orangecyberdefense.com

OverSOC (26, 44.4%)
Operations / Attack Surface
Management
Lille, France
oversoc.com

Patrowl (20, 11.1%)
Operations / Attack Surface
Management
Paris, France
patrowl.io

Primx (48, -2.0%)
Data Security / Encryption
Lyon, France
primx.eu/en

Prohacktive.Io (9, -30.8%)
GRC / Vulnerabilities
Gap, France
prohacktive.io

Purplemet (4, 0.0%)
Application Security
/ Scanning
Paris, France
purplemet.com

Qontrol (12, 71.4%)
GRC / Compliance
Management
Paris, France
qontrol.io

Quarkslab (93, 0.0%)
Application Security /
Code Security
Paris, France
quarkslab.com

Quotium (12, -20.0%)
GRC / Monitoring
Paris, France
quotium.com

Ravel Technologies (10, -16.7%)
Data Security / Encryption
Paris, France
raveltech.io

Rudder (46, 228.6%)
Operations / Configuration
Management
Paris, France
rudder.io

Seald (10, 25.0%)
Data Security
Paris, France
seald.io

Seckiot (34, 6.2%)
IoT Security
Paris, France
seckiot.fr

Seclab (20, -13.0%)
Data Security / Secure
Data Sharing
Montpellier, France
seclab-security.com

SecureIC (112, 2.8%)
IoT Security / Hardware
France
secure-ic.com

Seela (24, -22.6%)
Training / Interac-
tive Courses
Boulogne Billancourt, France
seela.io

SEKOIA.IO (115, 30.7%)
Security Analytics / SIEM
Paris, France
sekoia.io

Set In Stone (3, 0.0%)
Data Security / IRM
Paris, France
setinstone.io

Snowpack (16, 45.5%)
Network Security / VPN/Proxy
Orsay, France
snowpack.eu

Sqreen (4, -42.9%)
Application Security /
Monitoring
Saint-Cloud, France
sqreen.com

StormShield (was NetASQ/ Arcoon) (384, 4.9%)
Network Security / UTM
Issy-les-Moulineaux, France
stormshield.com

SYlink (24, 4.3%)
Network Security / UTM
Clermont-Ferrand, France
sylink.fr

Systancia (115, -3.4%)
IAM
Sausheim, France
systancia.com

TEHTRIS (271, 21.0%)
Security Analytics / XDR
Paris, France
tehtris.com

TheGreenBow (32, 10.3%)
Network Security
/ VPN/Proxy
Paris, France
thegreenbow.com

Tiempo (31, 34.8%)
Endpoint Security
/ Hardware
Montbonnot-Saint-Mar-
tin, France
tiempo-secure.com

Trusted Objects (13, 8.3%)
IoT Security
Aix-en-Provence, France
trusted-objects.com

**Numbers in parentheses indicate headcount and % change in 2023.*

Ubble.ai (70, -26.3%)
Fraud Prevention / Identity Verification
Paris, France
ubble.ai

UBIKA (74, 32.1%)
API Security / Firewalls
Meudon, France
ubikasec.com

Universign (85, -8.6%)
IAM / Authentication
Paris, France
universign.com

Usercube (17, -37.0%)
IAM
Marseille, France
usercube.com

Wallix (261, 11.1%)
IAM / Access Security
Paris, France
wallix.com

WaryMe (16, 6.7%)
GRC
Cesson-Sevigne, France
waryme.com

Woleet (3, -62.5%)
Data Security / Blockchain
Rennes, France
woleet.io

YesWeHack (237, 37.8%)
Operations / Bugs
Paris, France
yeswehack.com

Yogosha (189, 41.0%)
Operations / Bugs
Paris, France
yogosha.com

Zama (92, 37.3%)
Data Security / Encryption
Paris, France
zama.ai

Germany

achelos GmbH (57, 21.3%)
Testing / TLS Testing
Paderborn, Germany
achelos.de

Adjust (646, -5.0%)
Fraud Prevention / Bot Security
Berlin, Germany
adjust.com

ADVA Optical Networking (2011, -10.7%)
Network Security / Secure Switching
Munich, Germany
advaoptical.com

Aircloak (5, -28.6%)
Data Security / Data Masking
Berlin, Germany
aircloak.com

AIS (16, 33.3%)
Operations / Attack Surface Management
Saarland, Germany
ais-security.de

Akarion (15, 7.1%)
GRC / Compliance Management
Munich, Germany
akarion.com

Allgeier IT (82, -6.8%)
MSSP / Managed Security Services
Bremen, Germany
allgeier-it.de

Alyne (22, -24.1%)
GRC / Risk Management
Munich, Germany
alyne.com

asvin (23, 15.0%)
IoT Security / Device Management
Stuttgart, Germany
asvin.io

Auconet (9, -25.0%)
IAM / Access Security
Berlin, Germany
auconet.com

AUTHADA (22, -12.0%)
Fraud Prevention / Authentication
Darmstadt, Germany
authada.de

Avira (202, -0.5%)
Endpoint Security / Anti-virus
Tettnang, Germany
avira.com

Aware7 (34, 183.3%)
GRC / Security Awareness Training
Gelsenkirchen, Nordrhein-Westfalen, Germany
aware7.com

Baramundi Software (209, 14.8%)
GRC / Endpoint Management
Augsburg, Germany
baramundi.com

BAYOOSOFT (22, 29.4%)
IAM
Darmstadt, Germany
bayoosoft.com

BDO Cyber Security (46, 27.8%)
MSSP / SIEM
Hamburg, Germany
bdosecurity.de

Beta Systems Software AG (327, 14.3%)
IAM
Berlin, Germany
betasystems.com

Bitahoy (5, -37.5%)
Operations
Saarland, Germany
bitahoy.com

Boxcryptor (10, -44.4%)
Data Security / Encryption
Augsburg, Germany
boxcryptor.com

Brainloop (67, 3.1%)
Data Security / Secure Collaboration
Munich, Germany
brainloop.com

brighter AI (44, -4.3%)
Data Security / Video/ Image Anonymization
Berlin, Germany
brighter.ai

Build38 (67, 52.3%)
Application Security / Mobile Device Security
Munich, Germany
build38.com

Bundesdruckerei (1373, 30.0%)
IAM / Public Key Infrastructure
Berlin, Germany
bundesdruckerei.de

certgate (11, -8.3%)
Endpoint Security / Mobile Device Security
Germany
airid.com

Code Intelligence (62, -3.1%)
Application Security
Bonn, Germany
code-intelligence.com

Cognitum-Software (11, 0.0%)
IAM
Lower Saxony, Germany
cognitum-software.com

Collax Inc. (6, 20.0%)
Network Security / UTM
Ismaning, Germany
collax.com

**Numbers in parentheses indicate headcount and % change in 2023.*

comcrypto (13, 8.3%)
Email Security / Secure Email
Chemnitz, Sachsen, Germany
comcrypto.de

Consistec (31, 14.8%)
Fraud Prevention
Saarland, Germany
consistec.de

cryptovision (59, 40.5%)
Data Security / Public Key Infrastructure
Gelsenkirchen, Germany
cryptovision.com

Cryptshare (57, -1.7%)
Data Security / Secure Data
Freiburg, Germany
cryptshare.com

Cybersense (10, 25.0%)
Data Security / Deception
North Rhine-Westphalia, Germany
cybersense.ai

Cysmo (3, 50.0%)
GRC / Risk Management
Germany
cysmo.de

Dacoso (139, 10.3%)
MSSP / SOC
Langen, Germany
dacoso.com

DATAKOM (16, -23.8%)
MSSP / Managed Security Services
Ismaning, Bayern, Germany
datakom.de

Detack (13, 0.0%)
IAM / Credential Security
Ludwigsburg, Germany
detack.de

DGC (9, -25.0%)
GRC / Vulnerabilities
Flensburg, Germany
dgc.org

Digitronic (11, 22.2%)
Data Security / Encryption
Chemnitz, Sachsen, Germany
digitronic.net

DigitTrade (6, -14.3%)
Data Security
Teutschenthal, Germany
digittrade.de

DRACOON (97, 19.8%)
Data Security / Secure Data Sharing
Regensburg, Germany
dracoon.com

DriveLock (58, 18.4%)
Endpoint Security / DLP
Munich, Germany
drivelock.com

Drooms (174, 1.2%)
Data Security / Data Rooms
Frankfurt, Germany
drooms.com

enclaive (9, 50.0%)
Data Security / Confidential Computing
Berlin, Germany
enclaive.io

Enginsight (28, 3.7%)
GRC / Vulnerabilities
Jena, Germany
enginsight.com

eperi (26, 8.3%)
Data Security / Encryption
Pfungstadt, Germany
eperi.de

esatus (40, 8.1%)
IAM
Langen, Hessen, Germany
esatus.com

ESNC (4, 0.0%)
GRC / SAP
Germany
esnc.de

essentry (16, 77.8%)
IAM
Eschborn, Hessen, Germany
essentry.com

Fraugster (9, -87.5%)
Fraud Prevention / Transaction Security
Berlin, Germany
fraugster.com

Friendly Captcha (15, 150.0%)
Fraud Prevention / Bot Security
Munich, Germany
friendlycaptcha.com

G Data Software (116, -10.8%)
Endpoint Security / Anti-virus
Bochum, Germany
gdata.de

GBS (37, -15.9%)
Data Security
Karlsruhe, Germany
gbs.com

genua (226, 14.7%)
Network Security / IoT Security
Kirchheim, Germany
genua.de

getidee (17, 0.0%)
IAM / Authentication
München, Germany
getidee.com

GORISCON (5, 25.0%)
GRC / Compliance Management
Rosenheim, Bayern, Germany
goriscon.de

Gsmk Cryptophone (12, -14.3%)
Data Security / Secure Communications
Berlin, Germany
cryptophone.de

HENSOLDT Cyber (15, -40.0%)
IoT Security
Taufkirchen, Germany
hensoldt-cyber.com

heylogin (12, 20.0%)
IAM
Braunschweig, Germany
heylogin.com

HOB Networking (40, 17.6%)
Network Security / VPN/Proxy
Cadolzburg, Germany
hob.de

Hornetsecurity (346, 11.6%)
Email Security / Managed Security Services
Hannover, Germany
hornetsecurity.com

IDEE (17, 0.0%)
IAM / Identity Platform
Munich, Germany
getidee.com

IDnow (321, 6.6%)
Fraud Prevention / Identity Verification
Munich, Bayern, Germany
idnow.io

Infineon (37071, 17.6%)
IAM / Smart Card Solutions
Neubiberg, Germany
infineon.com

Infodas (157, 11.3%)
Network Security / Air Gap
Cologne, Germany
infodas.com

Iris Analytics Gmbh (47, 34.3%)
Fraud Prevention
Urbar, Germany
iris.de

ITConcepts (36, 0.0%)
IAM
Bonn, Germany
itconcepts.net

**Numbers in parentheses indicate headcount and % change in 2023.*

itWatch (17, -5.6%)
Endpoint Security / DLP
Munich, Germany
itwatch.info

KEEQuant (16, 45.5%)
Data Security / Quantum
Fürth, Germany
keequant.com

KOBIL Systems (179, 20.1%)
IAM / Authentication
Worms, Germany
kobil.com

Link11 (59, 31.1%)
Network Security / DDoS Defense
Frankfurt, Germany
link11.de

LocateRisk (18, 28.6%)
GRC / Risk Management
Darmstadt, Germany
locaterisk.com

Macmon (53, 8.2%)
Network Security / Access Security
Berlin, Germany
macmon.eu

Maltego Technologies (130, 32.6%)
Operations / Maltego Enhancement
Munich, Germany
maltego.com

Materna Virtual Solution (102, 21.4%)
Data Security / Secure Communications
Munich, Germany
virtual-solution.com

MATESO (11, -63.3%)
IAM / Credential Security
Germany
passwordsafe.com

MB Connect Line (20, -20.0%)
IoT Security / Firewalls
Germany
mbconnectline.com

Mitigant (14, 55.6%)
Operations / Posture Management
Potsdam, Brandenburg, Germany
mitigant.io

MTG AG (28, 27.3%)
IoT Security / OT Security
Darmstadt, Germany
mtg.de

Myra Security (60, 5.3%)
Network Security / Web Security
Munich, Germany
myracloud.com

Network Box Deutschland (13, 8.3%)
Network Security / UTM
Nordrhein-Westfalen, Germany
network-box.eu

Neurocat (36, 2.9%)
Data Security / Safe AI/ML Data
Berlin, Germany
neurocat.ai

NitroKey (6, 50.0%)
Data Security / Encryption
Berlin, Germany
nitrokey.com

Ondeso - Industrial It Made In Germany (22, -15.4%)
IoT Security / OT Security
Regensburg, Germany
ondeso.com

Ory (25, -34.2%)
IAM
Munich, Germany
ory.sh

P3KI (6, -25.0%)
IAM / Access Security
Berlin, Germany
p3ki.com

Passbase (5, -83.9%)
IAM / User Verification
Berlin, Germany
passbase.com

Password Depot (13, 8.3%)
IAM / Credential Security
Darmstadt, Germany
password-depot.de

Patronus.io (3, 0.0%)
Application Security / Scanning
Berlin, Germany
patronus.io

Perseus. (41, -21.1%)
Email Security / Defense Against Phishing
Berlin, Germany
perseus.de

PHYSEC (40, -13.0%)
IoT Security / OT Security
Bochum, Nordrhein-Westfalen, Germany
physec.de

Pyramid Computer GmbH (72, 2.9%)
Network Security / Firewalls
Freiburg, Germany
pyramid-computer.com

Qgroup (21, 10.5%)
Network Security / Firewalls
Frankfurt am Main, Germany
qgroup.de

QuoIntelligence (45, 15.4%)
Threat Intelligence / Managed Security Services
Frankfurt am Main, Hesse, Germany
quointelligence.eu

Rhebo (36, 0.0%)
IoT Security / OT Security
Leipzig, Germany
rhebo.com

Searchguard (6, 50.0%)
Data Security / Security For Elasticsearch
Berlin, Germany
search-guard.com

Secfix (21, 50.0%)
GRC / Compliance Management
Berlin, Germany
secfix.com

secunet (762, 47.4%)
Data Security
Germany
secunet.com

SecurityBridge (43, 65.4%)
Application Security / SAP
Ingolstadt, Germany
securitybridge.com

Skymatic (5, 25.0%)
Data Security
Sankt Augustin, Germany
skymatic.de

SoSafe (403, 12.6%)
GRC / Security Awareness Training
Cologne, North Rhine-Westphalia, Germany
sosafe-awareness.com

StackGuardian (21, 75.0%)
GRC / Compliance Management
Munich, Germany
beta.stackguardian.io

Steganos (11, -8.3%)
Data Security / Encryption
Munich, Germany
steganos.com

suresecure (79, 16.2%)
MSSP / SOC
Nordrhein-Westfalen, Germany
suresecure.de

Tenzir (16, 23.1%)
Operations / Data Management
Hamburg, Germany
tenzir.com

Thinking Objects (59, 7.3%)
MSSP / SOC
Stuttgart, Germany
to.com

TrustSpace (6, -33.3%)
GRC / Compliance Management
Berlin, Germany
trustspace.io

*Numbers in parentheses indicate headcount and % change in 2023.

TwinSoft (33, 10.0%)
IAM / Authentication
Darmstadt, Hessen, Germany
twinsoft-biometrics.de

Ubirch (28, -34.9%)
IoT Security / OT Security
Berlin, Germany
ubirch.de

Utimaco (510, 14.6%)
Data Security / Hardware
Aachen, Germany
utimaco.com

Verimi (107, 0.9%)
IAM / Identity Management
Berlin, Germany
verimi.de

Vulidity (5, 0.0%)
Threat Intelligence / OSINT
Burghausen, Bayern, Germany
vulidity.de

X-Ways Software (5, 66.7%)
Data Security / Forensics
Germany
x-ways.net

XignSys (18, 0.0%)
IAM / Authentication
Gelsenkirchen, NRW, Germany
xignsys.com

XplicitTrust (6, 0.0%)
Network Security
Karlsruhe, Germany
xplicittrust.com

Zertificon Solutions (62, -15.1%)
Email Security / Secure Email
Berlin, Germany
zertificon.com

Greece

Cenobe (12, 0.0%)
Operations / Penetration Testing
Athens, Greece
cenobe.com

Logstail (3, 0.0%)
Security Analytics / Logs
Athens, Greece
logstail.com

Hong Kong

Integrated Corporation (19, 171.4%)
IAM
Sheungwan, Hong Kong
integrated.com

IPification (26, -13.3%)
IAM
Hong Kong
ipification.com

Nexusguard (136, -2.9%)
Network Security / DDoS Defense
Tsuen Wan, Hong Kong
nexusguard.com

OneKey (12, 500.0%)
Data Security / Wallets
Hong Kong
Island, Hong Kong
onekey.so

Purevpn (205, 75.2%)
Network Security / VPN/Proxy
Hong Kong, Hong Kong
purevpn.com

Hungary

Balasys (39, -27.8%)
API Security
Budapest, Hungary
balasys.hu

BugProve (12, 9.1%)
IoT Security / Vulnerabilities
Budapest, Hungary
bugprove.com

Seon (254, -13.9%)
Fraud Prevention / Fraud Detection
Budapest, Hungary
seon.io

Tresorit (130, -1.5%)
Data Security / Secure Data Sharing
Budapest, Hungary
tresorit.com

Iceland

Authenteq (5, -58.3%)
Fraud Prevention / Identity Verification
Reykjavik, Iceland
authenteq.com

Nanitor (20, 17.6%)
GRC
Iceland
nanitor.com

SafeUM (3, 50.0%)
Data Security / Secure Communications
Iceland
safeum.com

India

3Frames Software labs (50, 19.1%)
Endpoint Security / Mobile Device Security
Bangalore, India
3frameslab.com

42Gears (437, 12.1%)
Endpoint Security / Mobile Device Security
Bangalore, India
42gears.com

Accops Systems (243, 25.9%)
IAM / Access Security
Pune, Maharastra, India
accops.com

Adcy.io (5, -16.7%)
MSSP / Managed Security Services
Trivandrum, Kerala, India
adcy.io

AmynaSec Labs (12, -7.7%)
IoT Security / Vulnerabilities
Pune, Maharashtra, India
amynasec.io

AnexGATE (25, 25.0%)
Network Security / UTM
Bangalore, India
anexgate.com/

AppSecure Security (14, 27.3%)
Application Security / Software Testing For Security
Bangalore, Karnataka, India
appsecure.security

Arcon (551, 53.9%)
GRC / Rights Management
Mumbai, India
arconnet.com

Astra (54, 63.6%)
Application Security / Web App Protection
New Delhi, India
getastra.com

Attify (5, 0.0%)
Application Security / Mobile Device Security
Bangalore, India
attify.com

Beagle Security (35, 16.7%)
Application Security / Penetration Testing
Thiruvananthapuram, Kerala, India
beaglesecurity.com

BioEnable (76, 0.0%)
IAM / Access Security
Pune, India
bioenabletech.com

Block Armour (36, 24.1%)
Network Security / Zero Trust Networking
Mumbai, India
blockarmour.com

Blu Sapphire (85, 97.7%)
MSSP / Threat Hunting
Madhapur, India
blusapphire.com

**Numbers in parentheses indicate headcount and % change in 2023.*

Bosch AIShield (13, 30.0%)
Application Security
Koramangala, Bengaluru, India
boschaishield.com

Cloudanix (10, 0.0%)
Operations / Posture Management
Pune, India
cloudanix.com

Cloudcodes Software (21, -12.5%)
IAM
Pune, India
cloudcodes.com

CloudSEK (166, 4.4%)
Threat Intelligence / Risk Management
Bangalore, India
cloudsek.com

Customerxps (236, 5.8%)
Fraud Prevention
Bangalore, India
clari5.com

CyberEye Research Labs & Security Solutions (15, 0.0%)
GRC / Security Awareness Training
Hyderabad, India
cybereye.io

Data Resolve Technologies (80, -2.4%)
Network Security / Monitoring
Noida, India
dataresolve.com

DNIF (65, -1.5%)
Operations / SIEM
Mumbai, India
dnif.it

Domdog (5, 150.0%)
Endpoint Security / Secure Web Browsing
Chennai, India
domdog.io

eCyLabs (8, 60.0%)
Application Security / Software Testing For Security
Coimbatore, India
ecylabs.com

Ensurity (28, -6.7%)
IAM / Authentication
Hyderabad, India
ensurity.com

EScan (204, 33.3%)
Endpoint Security / Anti-virus
Mumbai, India
escanav.com

FinLock Technologies (3, -62.5%)
Fraud Prevention / Personal Protection
South Delhi, New Delhi, India
finlock.in

Fixnix (39, -9.3%)
GRC / SMB Security
Ashok Nagar, India
fixnix.co

Foresiet (10, 25.0%)
Threat Intelligence / OSINT
Bangalore, India
foresiet.com

FourCore (9, 28.6%)
Operations / Breach And Attack Simulation
New Delhi, Delhi, India
fourcore.io

FRS Labs (23, 9.5%)
Fraud Prevention / Fraud Detection
Bangalore, India
frslabs.com

GajShield (72, -4.0%)
Network Security / Firewalls
Mumbai, India
gajshield.com

Haltdos (26, 8.3%)
Network Security / DDoS Defense
Noida, India
haltdos.com

HCL Technologies (254393, 15.3%)
MSSP / Managed Security Services
Noida, India
hcltech.com

Indusface (155, 0.7%)
Network Security / Firewalls
Vodadora, India
indusface.com

Infopercept (136, 46.2%)
MSSP / MDR
Ahmedabad, Gujarat, India
infopercept.com

Infosys (324937, 7.1%)
MSSP / Managed Security Services
Bangalore, India
infosys.com

Innefu Labs Pvt Ltd. (190, 31.9%)
Operations / Security Analytics
New Delhi, India
innefu.com

Inspira Enterprise (1557, 8.9%)
MSSP / MDR
Mumbai, India
inspiraenterprise.com

Instasafe (81, 11.0%)
Network Security / Gateways
Bangalore, India
instasafe.com

Iraje (61, 17.3%)
IAM / Access Security
Mumbai, India
iraje.com

Jio Security (60073, -2.8%)
Endpoint Security / Anti-virus
Navi Mumbai, India
jio.com

K7Computing (416, 5.6%)
Endpoint Security / Anti-virus
Sholinganallur, India
k7computing.com

Kratikal Tech (138, 7.8%)
GRC / Risk Management
Noida, India
kratikal.com

Kriptone (4, 300.0%)
GRC / Monitoring
Navsari, India
kriptone.com

Mantra (621, 15.9%)
IAM / Authentication
Ahmedabad, India
mantratec.com

Max Secure Software (75, 2.7%)
Endpoint Security / Endpoint Protection
Pune, India
maxpcsecure.com

miniOrange (293, 148.3%)
IAM / Authentication
Pune, India
miniorange.com

neoEYED (3, -57.1%)
IAM / Authentication
Bangalore, India
neoeyed.com

Net Protector Antivirus (121, 18.6%)
Endpoint Security / Anti-virus
Karvenagar, India
npav.net

Network Intelligence (668, 12.3%)
Operations / Policy Management
Mumbai, India
niiconsulting.com

Odyssey Technologies (155, 14.8%)
IAM / Public Key Infrastructure
Chennai, India
odysseytec.com

**Numbers in parentheses indicate headcount and % change in 2023.*

Pingsafe (69, 109.1%)
Network Security / Posture Management
Bengaluru, India
pingsafe.com

Protectt.ai (54, 35.0%)
Endpoint Security / Mobile Device Security
Gurgaon, Haryana, India
protectt.ai

Quick Heal (1513, 5.1%)
Endpoint Security / UTM
Pune, India
quickheal.com

SafeHats (7, 16.7%)
Application Security / Bugs
Bangalore, India
safehats.com

Scrut Automation (145, 119.7%)
GRC / Compliance Management
Bangalore, Karnataka, India
scrut.io

Seclore (325, 15.7%)
Data Security / IRM
Mumbai, India
seclore.com

SecOps Solution (10, -9.1%)
GRC / Vulnerabilities
Bengaluru, India
secopsolution.com

Sectona (56, 21.7%)
IAM / Access Security
Mumbai, Maharashtra, India
sectona.com

SecurelyShare (24, -22.6%)
Data Security / Secure Storage
Indira Nagar, India
securelyshare.com

Senser (16, -5.9%)
Operations / Workload Security
Ramat Gan, India
senser.tech

Seqrite (171, 185.0%)
Endpoint Security / Encryption
Pune, India
seqrite.com

Sequretek (353, 4.8%)
Endpoint Security / Anti-virus
Mumbai, India
sequretek.com

SISA (638, -12.7%)
Data Security / Data Discovery
Bengaluru, India
sisainfosec.com

Tata Communications (15430, 9.9%)
MSSP / Managed Security Services
Mumbai, India
tatacommunications.com

Tata Consultancy Services (583267, -8.1%)
MSSP / Managed Security Services
Nariman Point, India
on.tcs.com

Unistal Systems (231, 2.2%)
Endpoint Security / Anti-virus
Mumbai, India
unistal.in

Unmukti (8, -33.3%)
Network Security / Firewalls
New Delhi, India
unmukti.in

Vinca Cyber (128, 10.3%)
MSSP
Bangalore, India
vincacyber.com

VuNet Systems (195, 33.6%)
Security Analytics / Logs
Bangalore, India
vunetsystems.com

WiJungle (53, 76.7%)
Network Security / UTM
Gurugram, Haryana, India
wijungle.com

Wipro Limited (237905, -18.9%)
MSSP / Managed Security Services
Bangalore, India
wipro.com

Ziroh Labs (74, -6.3%)
Data Security / Data Discovery
Bangalore, India
ziroh.com

Indonesia

Privy (721, 8.6%)
Data Security
Jakarta Selatan, DKI Jakarta, Indonesia
privy.id

Ireland

Accenture (548423, 1.2%)
MSSP / MDR
Dublin, Ireland
accenture.com

Actus Mobile Solutions (4, -20.0%)
Fraud Prevention
Bray, Ireland
actusmobile.com

Adaptive Mobile (91, -33.1%)
Endpoint Security / Mobile Device Security
Dublin, Ireland
adaptivemobile.com

Akeero (5, -44.4%)
Application Security / Software Development Security
County Cork, Ireland
akeero.com

Commsec (22, -4.3%)
MSSP / Managed Security Services
Dublin, Ireland
commsec.ie

Corrata (8, -20.0%)
Endpoint Security / Mobile Device Security
Blackrock, Ireland
corrata.com

Cyber Risk Aware (6, -14.3%)
GRC / Security Awareness Training
Dublin, Ireland
cyberriskaware.com

Cyber Risk International (3, -40.0%)
GRC / Risk Management
Kinsealy, Ireland
cyberriskinternational.com

Dataships (18, -10.0%)
GRC / Compliance Management
Dublin, Ireland
dataships.io

edgescan (90, 11.1%)
Application Security / Vulnerabilities
Dublin, Ireland
edgescan.com

Ekco (311, 9.1%)
MSSP / MDR
Dublin, Ireland
ek.co

Fijowave (8, -11.1%)
IoT Security / Remote Devices
Dublin, Ireland
fijowave.com

Gat Labs (17, 0.0%)
GRC / Monitoring
Dublin, Ireland
gatlabs.com

GuardYoo (6, 0.0%)
GRC / Compromise Assessment
Cork, Ireland
guardyoo.com

Integrity360 (357, 89.9%)
MSSP / MDR
Dublin, Ireland
integrity360.com

**Numbers in parentheses indicate headcount and % change in 2023.*

InvizBox (4, -33.3%)
Network Security / VPN/Proxy
Dublin, Ireland
invizbox.com

ITUS Security Technologies (4, 0.0%)
MSSP / Managed Security Services
Letterkenny, Ireland
itus-tech.com

Mesh (16, 128.6%)
Email Security
Sandyford, Dublin, Ireland
meshsecurity.io

nostra (229, 36.3%)
MSSP / Managed Security Services
Dublin, Ireland
nostra.ie

Nova Leah (21, 0.0%)
IoT Security / Healthcare
Dundalk, Ireland
novaleah.com

Oblivious (32, 88.2%)
Data Security / Secure Data Sharing
Dublin, Ireland
oblivious.ai

Octiga (5, 0.0%)
MSSP / Managed Security Services
Galway, Ireland
octiga.io

PixAlert (10, 0.0%)
GRC / Data Discovery
Dublin, Ireland
pixalert.com

Privacy Engine (34, 6.2%)
GRC / Data Privacy
Blackrock, Ireland
privacyengine.io

Protectimus Ltd (49, 13.9%)
IAM / Authentication
Dublin, Ireland
protectimus.com

Sedicii (12, -33.3%)
IAM / Authentication
Carriganore, Ireland
sedicii.com

SensiPass (7, 0.0%)
IAM / Authentication
Dublin, Ireland
sensipass.com

Siren (84, 29.2%)
Security Analytics / Data Analysis
Galway, Ireland
siren.io

ThinScale (57, -28.8%)
Endpoint Security / Remote Desktop Agent
Dublin, Ireland
thinscale.com

Threatscape (36, 28.6%)
MSSP / MDR
Dublin, Ireland
threatscape.com

Tines (249, 40.7%)
Operations / Orchestration
Dublin, Ireland
tines.com

TitanHQ (158, 9.0%)
Network Security / DNS Security
Galway, Ireland
titanhq.com

Vaultree (64, 3.2%)
Data Security / Encryption
Cork, Ireland
vaultree.com

Velona Systems (5, 0.0%)
GRC / Scanning
Cork, Ireland
velonasystems.com

VigiTrust (129, 16.2%)
GRC / Risk Management
Dublin, Ireland
vigitrust.com

Waratek (31, -20.5%)
Application Security
Dublin, Ireland
waratek.com

WebTitan (TitanHQ) (5, -16.7%)
Network Security / Filtering
Salthill, Ireland
webtitan.com

Israel

accSenSe (18, 0.0%)
IAM / Secure Backup/Recovery
Ra'anana, Israel
accsense.io

Acsense (19, 0.0%)
IAM
Tel Aviv, Israel
acsense.com

Actifile (22, 4.8%)
GRC / DLP
Herzliya, Israel
actifile.com

ActiveFence (293, -6.1%)
GRC / Monitoring
Tel Aviv, Israel
activefence.com

Adaptive Shield (79, 19.7%)
Operations / Posture Management
Tel Aviv, Israel
adaptive-shield.com

Adversa (3, -25.0%)
Application Security
Tel Aviv, Israel
adversa.ai

Agat Software (32, 14.3%)
Network Security / Security For Unified Comms
Jerusalem, Israel
agatsoftware.com

Aireye (27, -27.0%)
Network Security / Wireless Security
Tel Aviv, Israel
AirEye.tech

Akeyless (95, 11.8%)
Data Security / Key Management
Tel Aviv, Israel
akeyless.io

Algosec (504, 4.6%)
Operations / Policy Management
Petah Tikva, Israel
algosec.com

Allot (955, -4.3%)
Network Security / Filtering
Hod HaSharon, Israel
allot.com

APERIO Systems (35, 25.0%)
IoT Security / OT Security
Haifa, Israel
aperio-systems.com

Apiiro (126, 22.3%)
API Security / Software Development Security
Tel Aviv, Israel
apiiro.com

Apono (28, 27.3%)
IAM / Rights Management
Tel Aviv, Israel
apono.io

AppDome (154, 28.3%)
Application Security
Tel Aviv, Israel
appdome.com

AppSec Labs (15, 0.0%)
Application Security / Mobile Device Security
Kfar Saba, Israel
appsec-labs.com

Aqua Security (605, -4.4%)
Endpoint Security / Container Security
Ramat Gan, Israel
aquasec.com

Argus Cyber Security (210, 11.1%)
IoT Security / Automotive
Tel Aviv, Israel
argus-sec.com

Armo Security (59, 25.5%)
Endpoint Security / Container Security
Tel Aviv, Israel
armosec.io

**Numbers in parentheses indicate headcount and % change in 2023.*

Asparna Ltd. (5, 0.0%)
Data Security / Encrypted File Sync And Social Conversations
Afula, Israel
asparna.com

Assac Networks (15, 25.0%)
Endpoint Security / Mobile Device Security
Ramat HaSharon, Israel
assacnetworks.com

Astrix Security (63, 90.9%)
GRC / Risk Management
Tel Aviv, Israel
astrix.security

Atmosec (17, -32.0%)
Operations / Application Security
Tel Aviv, Israel
atmosec.com

Au10Tix (199, 1.0%)
IAM / Identity Management
Hod HaSharon, Israel
au10tix.com

Authomize (47, 0.0%)
IAM / Monitoring
Tel Aviv, Israel
authomize.com

Avalor (74, 39.6%)
Operations / Data Management
Tel Aviv, Israel
avalor.io

Ayyeka (34, -5.6%)
IoT Security / Remote Devices
Jerusalem, Israel
ayyeka.com

BigID (543, 0.2%)
GRC / Data Discovery
Tel Aviv, Israel
bigid.com

BioCatch (297, 20.7%)
Fraud Prevention / Authentication
Tel Aviv, Israel
biocatch.com

Blink Ops (55, 17.0%)
Operations / Automation
Tel Aviv, Israel
blinkops.com

BrandShield (82, 9.3%)
Fraud Prevention / Brand
Ramat HaSharon, Israel
brandshield.com

Bright Security (162, 65.3%)
Application Security / Code Security
Tel Aviv, Israel
brightsec.com

Bufferzone (19, 11.8%)
Endpoint Security / Sandbox
Giv'atayim, Israel
bufferzonesecurity.com

Bugsec Group (77, -6.1%)
MSSP / Managed Security Services
Rishon LeZion, Israel
bugsec.com

C2A Security (39, 18.2%)
IoT Security / Automotive
Jerusalem, Israel
c2a-sec.com

CalCom (52, 20.9%)
Endpoint Security / Servers
Lod, Israel
calcomsoftware.com

Canonic (14, -50.0%)
Application Security
Tel Aviv, Israel
canonic.security

CardinalOps (50, 0.0%)
Operations / Automated Control Checks
Tel Aviv, Israel
cardinalops.com

Cato Networks (813, 22.4%)
Network Security / Cloud Security
Tel Aviv, Israel
catonetworks.com

Ceedo (34, -2.9%)
Endpoint Security / Secured Devices
Herzliya, Israel
ceedo.com

Cellebrite (1081, 5.5%)
Endpoint Security / Forensics
Petah Tikva, Israel
cellebrite.com

Cellrox (14, -30.0%)
Endpoint Security / Virtualization
Tel Aviv, Israel
cellrox.com

Certora (74, 8.8%)
Data Security / Blockchain
Tel Aviv, Israel
certora.com

Cervello (36, 28.6%)
IoT Security / Railway
Tel Aviv, Israel
cervellosec.com

CGS Tower Networks (15, 7.1%)
Network Security / Network Taps
Rosh HaAyin, Israel
cgstowernetworks.com

Check Point Software (7468, 9.2%)
Network Security / UTM
Tel Aviv, Israel
checkpoint.com

Checkmarx (919, -1.8%)
Application Security / Software Development Security
Ramat Gan, Israel
checkmarx.com

Cheq (263, 2.7%)
Fraud Prevention / Advertising-related
Tel Aviv, Israel
cheq.ai

Cider Security (30, -64.3%)
Application Security / Software Development Security
Tel Aviv, Israel
cidersecurity.io

CISOteria (7, 0.0%)
GRC / Risk Management
Ra'ananna, Israel
cisoteria.com

CloudWize (9, 28.6%)
Operations / Cloud Security
Netanya, Israel
cloudwize.io

Cognni (28, 0.0%)
Data Security / Data Discovery
Tel Aviv, Israel
cognni.ai

Commugen (25, 8.7%)
GRC / Risk Management
Tel Aviv, Israel
commugen.com

CommuniTake Technologies (17, -10.5%)
Endpoint Security / Mobile Device Security
Yokneam, Israel
communitake.com

Critifence (4, 100.0%)
IoT Security / OT Security
Herzliya, Israel
critifence.com

Cubed Mobile (5, -16.7%)
Endpoint Security / Mobile Device Security
Kibbutz Einat, Drom HaSharon Regional Council, Israel
cubedmobile.com

Cyabra (53, 6.0%)
Threat Intelligence / Fake News Defense
Tel Aviv, Israel
cyabra.com

**Numbers in parentheses indicate headcount and % change in 2023.*

Cybellum (95, 33.8%)
Endpoint Security / In-Memory Prevention
Tel Aviv, Israel
cybellum.com

Cyber Observer Ltd. (6, -60.0%)
GRC / Security Management
Caesarea, Israel
cyber-observer.com

CyberArk Software (3188, 15.2%)
IAM / Access Security
Petah Tikva, Israel
cyberark.com

Cyberbit (202, -1.5%)
Training / Cyber Range
Ra'anana, Israel
cyberbit.com

Cybeready (36, 5.9%)
GRC / Defense Against Phishing
Tel Aviv, Israel
cybeready.com

Cybergym (55, 0.0%)
Training / Cyber Range
Hadera, Israel
cybergym.com

Cyberint (144, 10.8%)
Threat Intelligence
Petah Tikva, Israel
cyberint.com

Cybernite (10, -28.6%)
Email Security / Defense Against Phishing
Tel Aviv, Israel
cybernite.com

CyberSixgill (112, -16.4%)
Threat Intelligence / Dark Web
Netanya, Israel
cybersixgill.com

Cybonet (27, -12.9%)
Email Security / Sandbox
Matam, Israel
cybonet.com

Cyclops (25, 38.9%)
Operations / Data Management
Tel Aviv, Israel
cyclops.security

Cycode (122, 15.1%)
Application Security / Code Security
Tel Aviv, Israel
cycode.com

Cycurity (8, -33.3%)
Security Analytics
Tel Aviv, Israel
cycurity.com

Cydome (25, 66.7%)
IoT Security / Maritime Security
Tel Aviv, Israel
cydome.io

CYE (185, 2.2%)
Operations / Breach And Attack Simulation
Herzliya, Israel
cyesec.com

Cyera (180, 164.7%)
Data Security / Data Management
Tel Aviv, Israel
cyera.io

CYFOX (31, 0.0%)
Security Analytics / XDR
Tel Aviv, Israel
cyfox.com

Cylus (67, -11.8%)
IoT Security / Railway
Tel Aviv, Israel
cylus.com

Cymotive (197, 0.0%)
IoT Security / Automotive
Tel Aviv, Israel
cymotive.com

Cympire (17, -5.6%)
Training / Cyber Range
Tel Aviv, Israel
cympire.com

Cymulate (237, 2.2%)
Operations / Breach And Attack Simulation
Holon, Israel
cymulate.com

CYNC (14, 0.0%)
Operations / Vulnerabilities
Tel Aviv, Israel
cyncsecure.com

Cynergy (11, 10.0%)
Operations / Monitoring
Tel Aviv, Israel
cynergy.app

Cynerio (66, 1.5%)
IoT Security / Healthcare
Ramat Gan, Israel
cynerio.co

Cynet (257, -8.2%)
Operations / APT Discovery
Rishon LeZion, Israel
cynet.com

Cyolo (93, 0.0%)
IAM / Access Security
Tel Aviv, Israel
cyolo.io

Cypago (35, 34.6%)
GRC / Compliance Management
Tel Aviv, Israel
cypago.com

Cyrebro (150, -5.1%)
MSSP / SOC
Tel Aviv, Israel
cyberhat.com

CyTwist (19, 35.7%)
Operations / Threat Hunting
Ramat Gan, Israel
cytwist.com

D-Fend Solutions (145, 2.1%)
IoT Security / Drones
Ra'anana, Israel
d-fendsolutions.com

D-ID (123, 95.2%)
IAM / Non-authentication Biometrics
Tel Aviv, Israel
deidentification.co

Dcoya (23, 64.3%)
GRC / Defense Against Phishing
Tel Aviv, Israel
dcoya.com

Deceptive Bytes (6, 20.0%)
Deception
Holon, Israel
deceptivebytes.com

Deepkeep (20, 66.7%)
Data Security / Safe AI/ML Data
Tel Aviv, Israel
deepkeep.ai

DeviceTotal (12, -14.3%)
IoT Security / Vulnerabilities
Tel Aviv, Israel
devicetotal.com

DevOcean Security (22, 15.8%)
Operations
Tel Aviv, Israel
devocean.security

Dig Security (80, 48.1%)
Data Security / Data Discovery
Tel Aviv, Israel
dig.security

Digital Confidence Ltd. (4, 0.0%)
GRC / DLP
Tel Aviv, Israel
digitalconfidence.com

DocAuthority (7, 0.0%)
GRC / DLP
Ra'anana, Israel
docauthority.com

Dream Security (67, 570.0%)
Network Security
Tel Aviv, Israel
dream-security.com

**Numbers in parentheses indicate headcount and % change in 2023.*

Enigmatos (11, -8.3%)
IoT Security / Automotive
Yavne, Israel
enigmatos.com

Entro Security (24, 71.4%)
Data Security / Secrets Management
Tel Aviv, Israel
entro.security

Ermetic (106, -45.1%)
IAM / Access Security
Tel Aviv, Israel
ermetic.com

eureka (38, 11.8%)
Data Security / Data Discovery
Tel Aviv, Israel
eureka.security

EverCompliant (153, -13.6%)
Fraud Prevention / Banking Security
Tel Aviv, Israel
everc.com

Faddom (37, -22.9%)
Operations / Segmentation
Ramat Gan, Israel
faddom.com

FireDome (27, -47.1%)
IoT Security / IoT Security For Device Manufacturers
Tel Aviv, Israel
firedome.io

Firefly (46, 43.8%)
Operations / Asset Management
Tel Aviv, Israel
gofirefly.io

FirstPoint Mobile Guard (17, -34.6%)
Endpoint Security / Mobile Device Security
Netanya, Israel
firstpoint-mg.com

Flow Security (33, 32.0%)
Data Security / Data Flows
Tel Aviv, Israel
flowsecurity.com

Forter (611, -1.3%)
Fraud Prevention
Tel Aviv, Israel
forter.com

Gita Technologies (41, 5.1%)
Network Security / SIGINT Offensive
Tel Aviv, Israel
gitatechnologies.com

GK8 (48, 23.1%)
Data Security / Wallets
Tel Aviv, Israel
gk8.io

Gold Lock (6, 0.0%)
Data Security / Mobile Device Security
Ramat Gan, Israel
goldlock.com.br

Grip Security (100, 37.0%)
IAM / Access Security
Tel Aviv, Israel
grip.security

Guardio (85, 21.4%)
Application Security / Scanning
Tel Aviv, Israel
guard.io

GuardKnox (74, -1.3%)
IoT Security / Automotive
Tel Aviv, Israel
guardknox.com

Gutsy (35, 29.6%)
Operations
Tel Aviv, Israel
gutsy.com

Gytpol (33, 57.1%)
GRC / Configuration Management
Tel Aviv, Israel
gytpol.com

HackersEye (7, 40.0%)
Training / Cyber Range
Ramat Gan, Israel
hackerseye.net

Hexagate (12, 500.0%)
IAM / Access Security
Israel
hexagate.com

HUB Security (141, -11.3%)
Data Security / Encryption
Tel Aviv, Israel
hubsecurity.com

Hudson Rock (5, 0.0%)
Threat Intelligence / Leaked Data
Tel Aviv, Israel
hudsonrock.com/

Hunters (216, 42.1%)
Security Analytics / Incident Management
Tel Aviv, Israel
hunters.ai

Hysolate (7, -22.2%)
Endpoint Security / Secure Workspace
Tel Aviv, Israel
hysolate.com

Identiq (59, -7.8%)
IAM / Identity Validation
Tel Aviv, Tel Aviv, Israel
identiq.com

illustria.io (14, 27.3%)
Application Security / Code Security
Tel Aviv, Israel
illustria.io

InfiniDome (27, 8.0%)
IoT Security / Automotive
Caesarea, Israel
infinidome.com

Infinipoint (21, -25.0%)
Endpoint Security / Device Identity
Tel Aviv, Israel
infinipoint.io

Infobay (10, 0.0%)
Data Security / Secure Data Sharing
Petah Tikva, Israel
infobaysec.com

Innosec (16, 33.3%)
GRC / DLP
Hod HaSharon, Israel
innosec.com

IPV Security (19, -13.6%)
MSSP / Monitoring
Ra'anana, Israel
ipvsecurity.com

Ironblocks (14, 40.0%)
Data Security / Blockchain
Tel Aviv, Israel
ironblocks.com

IronScales (138, -13.8%)
GRC / Defense Against Phishing
Tel Aviv, Israel
ironscales.com

ITsMine (24, -4.0%)
Data Security / Secure Storage
Rishon Lezion, Israel
itsmine.io

IXDen (12, -7.7%)
Data Security
Tel Aviv, Israel
ixden.com

Jit.io (64, 42.2%)
Application Security / Open Source Tools
Tel Aviv, Israel
jit.io

Karamba Security (44, 10.0%)
IoT Security / Automotive
Hod HaSharon, Israel
karambasecurity.com

Kaymera (33, -17.5%)
Endpoint Security / Mobile Device Security
Herzliya, Israel
kaymera.com

Kayran (10, 11.1%)
Application Security / Penetration Testing
Nitsanei Oz, Israel
kayran.io

**Numbers in parentheses indicate headcount and % change in 2023.*

Kazuar Advanced Technologies Ltd (37, 0.0%)
Endpoint Security / Dual Use Laptops
Tel Aviv, Israel
kazuar-tech.com

Kela Group (106, 12.8%)
Threat Intelligence / Dark Web
Tel Aviv, Israel
ke-la.com

Kernelios (68, 23.6%)
Training
Rishon LeZion, Israel
kernelios.com

Kodem (38, 81.0%)
Application Security / Runtime Security
Tel Aviv, Israel
kodemsecurity.com

Lasso Security (19, 0.0%)
Data Security
Israel
lasso.security

LayerX (28, 40.0%)
Endpoint Security / Secure Web Browsing
Tel Aviv, Israel
linkedin.com/company/layerx-security/about/www.layerxsecurity.com

Lightspin (41, -29.3%)
Application Security / Software Development Security
Tel Aviv, Israel
lightspin.io

LogDog (8, 0.0%)
Data Security
Tel Aviv, Israel
getlogdog.com

MazeBolt Technologies (35, 2.9%)
Testing / DDoS Defense
Ramat Gan, Israel
mazebolt.com

MediGate (106, -6.2%)
IoT Security / Healthcare
Tel Aviv, Israel
medigate.io

Mend (293, -16.5%)
Application Security / Open Source Security And License Management
Giv'atayim, Israel
whitesourcesoftware.com

Mesh Security (15, 25.0%)
Operations / Posture Management
Tel Aviv, Israel
mesh.security

MindoLife (8, -11.1%)
Network Security / IDS
Haifa, Israel
mindolife.com

Mine (58, 70.6%)
GRC / Compliance Management
Tel Aviv, Israel
saymine.com

Minerva Labs (10, -66.7%)
Endpoint Security / Ransomware Security
Petah Tikva, Israel
minerva-labs.com

Mirato (27, 8.0%)
GRC / Risk Management
Tel Aviv, Israel
mirato.com

Mitiga (84, 1.2%)
MSSP / Incident Management
Tel Aviv, Israel
mitiga.io

Morphisec (126, -17.6%)
Endpoint Security / Obfuscation
Be'er Sheva, Israel
morphisec.com

MyPermissions (6, -14.3%)
Endpoint Security / Data Privacy
Ramat Gan, Israel
mypermissions.com

Myrror Security (17, 30.8%)
Application Security / Code Security
Tel Aviv, Israel
myrror.security

Nanolock (43, 7.5%)
IoT Security / Automotive
Nitsanei Oz, Israel
nanolocksecurity.com

Naval Dome (8, -27.3%)
IoT Security / Security For Ships
Ra'anana, Israel
navaldome.com

Nokod Security (15, 1400.0%)
Application Security / Security For No-code Applications
Tel Aviv, Israel
nokodsecurity.com

nsKnox (46, -4.2%)
Fraud Prevention / Payment Verification
Tel Aviv, Israel
nsknox.net

nSure.ai (49, 13.9%)
Fraud Prevention / Chargeback Prevention
Tel Aviv, Israel
nsureai.com

odix (26, -7.1%)
Data Security / Document Security
Rosh HaAyin, Israel
odi-x.com

Oligo Security (58, 65.7%)
Application Security
Tel Aviv, Israel
oligo.security

Opus Security (31, 24.0%)
Operations / Cloud Security
Tel Aviv, Israel
opus.security

Orca Security (506, 14.7%)
Operations / Vulnerabilities
Tel Aviv, Israel
orca.security

Orchestra Group (45, -16.7%)
IoT Security / Monitoring
Tel Aviv, Israel
orchestragroup.com

OTORIO (94, -2.1%)
IoT Security / OT Security
Tel Aviv, Israel
otorio.com

Ovalsec (10, -9.1%)
Operations / Attack Surface Management
Tel Aviv, Israel
ovalsec.com

OwnID (16, -5.9%)
IAM / Authentication
Tel Aviv, Israel
ownid.com

OX Security (85, 107.3%)
Application Security / Software Development Security
Tel Aviv, Israel
ox.security

oxeye (30, -9.1%)
Application Security / Software Testing For Security
Tel Aviv, Israel
oxeye.io

Paygilant (14, -6.7%)
Fraud Prevention / Transaction Security
Ramat Gan, Israel
paygilant.com

Pentera (was Pcysys) (374, 25.5%)
Operations / Penetration Testing
Petah Tikva, Israel
pcysys.com

Perception Point (126, 1.6%)
Email Security / Defense Against Phishing
Tel Aviv, Israel
perception-point.io

**Numbers in parentheses indicate headcount and % change in 2023.*

Perimeter 81 (206, -14.5%)
Network Security / Gateways
Tel Aviv, Israel
perimeter81.com

PerimeterX (66, -37.1%)
Network Security / Website Security
Tel Aviv, Israel
perimeterx.com

Piiano (27, -6.9%)
GRC / Data Privacy
Tel Aviv, Israel
piiano.com

PlainID (91, -12.5%)
IAM / Authorization
Tel Aviv, Israel
plainid.com

Polar Security (29, -9.4%)
Data Security / Data Management
Tel Aviv, Israel
polar.security

Portnox (66, 0.0%)
Endpoint Security / Device Management
Israel
portnox.com

Portshift (12, 33.3%)
Application Security / Identity-Based Workload Protection
Tel Aviv, Israel
portshift.io

Privya.AI (23, -11.5%)
GRC / Compliance Management
Tel Aviv, Israel
privya.ai

Promisec (31, 0.0%)
Endpoint Security / Endpoint Security Intelligence
Holon, Israel
promisec.com

Protected Media (18, 100.0%)
Network Security / Advertising-related
Petah Tikva, Israel
protected.media

Pynt (17, 13.3%)
API Security / API Testing
Tel Aviv, Israel
pynt.io

QEDit (14, 16.7%)
Data Security / Data Privacy
Tel Aviv, Israel
qed-it.com

QuantLR (10, 25.0%)
Data Security / Quantum
Jerusalem, Israel
quantlr.com

Quttera (5, 0.0%)
Network Security / Website Security
Herzliya Pituach, Israel
quttera.com

RadiFlow (69, 40.8%)
IoT Security / OT Security
Tel Aviv, Israel
radiflow.com

Radware (1472, -1.0%)
Network Security / IPS
Tel Aviv, Israel
radware.com

Raz-Lee Security (22, -8.3%)
Endpoint Security / ISeries
Herzliya, Israel
razlee.com

Reblaze (45, -30.8%)
Application Security / Web App Protection
Tel Aviv, Israel
reblaze.com

Red Access (26, 62.5%)
Network Security / Secure Web Browsing
Tel Aviv, Israel
redaccess.io

Red Button (10, 25.0%)
Network Security / DDoS Defense
Tel Aviv, Israel
red-button.net

Refine Intelligence (20, 0.0%)
Fraud Prevention / Monitoring
Tel Aviv, Israel
refineintelligence.com

Reflectiz (38, 11.8%)
Application Security / Website Security
Ramat Gan, Israel
reflectiz.com

Regulus (15, 25.0%)
IoT Security / Automotive
Haifa, Israel
regulus.com

Reposify (13, -23.5%)
Operations / Asset Management
Bnei Brak, Israel
reposify.com

Rescana (17, 54.5%)
GRC
Tel Aviv, Israel
rescana.com

ReSec Technologies (20, -16.7%)
Data Security / Document Security
Caesarea, Israel
resec.co

RevealSecurity (47, 4.4%)
Application Security / Monitoring
Tel Aviv, Israel
trackerdetect.com

Rezilion (42, -32.3%)
Endpoint Security
Be'er Sheva, Israel
rezilion.co

Riskified (753, -3.2%)
Fraud Prevention / Transaction Security
Tel Aviv, Israel
riskified.com

Safe-T (21, 5.0%)
IAM / Access Security
Herzliya Pituach, Israel
safe-t.com

SafeBreach (134, -20.2%)
Operations / Breach And Attack Simulation
Tel Aviv, Israel
safebreach.com

Safehouse Technologies (66, 10.0%)
Network Security / VPN/Proxy
Tel Aviv, Israel
safehousetech.com

Salvador Technologies (26, 36.8%)
IoT Security
Rehovot, Israel
salvador-tech.com

SAM Seamless Network (74, -7.5%)
Network Security / Gateways
Tel Aviv, Israel
securingsam.com

Sasa Software (32, -5.9%)
Data Security / File Scrubbing
Sasa, Israel
sasa-software.com

Satori Cyber (136, 58.1%)
Data Security / Data Flows
Tel Aviv, Israel
satoricyber.com

Savvy (50, -2.0%)
Operations / SaaS Security
Tel Aviv District, Israel
savvy.security

Sayata Labs (73, 7.3%)
GRC / Risk Management
Tel Aviv, Israel
sayatalabs.com

ScadaFence (56, -15.2%)
IoT Security / OT Security
Tel Aviv, Israel
scadafence.com

**Numbers in parentheses indicate headcount and % change in 2023.*

Scribe Security (33, 37.5%)
Application Security / SBOM
Tel Aviv, Israel
scribesecurity.com

Scytale (54, 25.6%)
GRC / Compliance Management
Tel Aviv, Israel
scytale.ai

Secret Double Octopus (41, -21.1%)
IAM / Authentication
Tel Aviv, Israel
doubleoctopus.com

SecureTeam (11, -8.3%)
Data Security / DRM
Rishon LeZion, Israel
secureteam.net

Securithings (72, 2.9%)
IoT Security / Device Management
Ramat Gan, Israel
securithings.com

SeeMetrics (23, 21.1%)
Operations / Monitoring
Tel Aviv, Tel Aviv, Israel
seemetrics.co

Seemplicity (67, 48.9%)
Operations
Tel Aviv, Israel
seemplicity.io

Sentra (84, 44.8%)
Data Security / Data Discovery
Tel Aviv, Israel
sentra.io

Septier Communication (30, 3.5%)
Network Security / SIGINT Offensive
Petah Tikva, Israel
septier.com

ShieldIOT (17, -15.0%)
IoT Security
Herzliya, Israel
shieldiot.io

Simplex (215, 0.9%)
Fraud Prevention / Transaction Security
Givatayim, Israel
simplex.com

Skyhawk Security (34, 25.9%)
Operations / Breach Detection
Tel Aviv, Israel
skyhawk.security

Slauth.io (4, 0.0%)
GRC / Policy Management
Tel Aviv, Israel
slauth.io

Sling (26, -7.1%)
GRC / Risk Management
Tel Aviv, Israel
slingscore.com

Snowbit (16, 23.1%)
MSSP / MDR
Tel Aviv, Israel
snowbit.io

Solvo (30, 25.0%)
Operations / Configuration Management
Tel Aviv, Israel
solvo.cloud

Source Defense (46, -9.8%)
Network Security / Client-Side Protection Against Third Party Attacks
Be'er Sheva, Israel
sourcedefense.com

Spera Security (34, 0.0%)
IAM / Posture Management
Tel Aviv, Israel
spera.security

Sternum (38, -13.6%)
IoT Security / Healthcare
Tel Aviv, Israel
sternumiot.com

Stream.Security (43, -28.3%)
GRC / Posture Management
Tel Aviv, Israel
stream.security

Surance.io (10, 25.0%)
IoT Security / Home Security
Ramat HaSharon, Israel
surance.io

Suridata (38, 11.8%)
Data Security / SaaS Data Protection
Tel Aviv, Israel
suridata.ai

Sweet Security (20, 0.0%)
Endpoint Security / Workload Protection
Tel Aviv, Israel
sweet.security

Symmetrium (12, 100.0%)
Data Security / Access Security
Tel Aviv, Israel
symmetrium.io

Telemessage (113, 31.4%)
GRC / Secure Communications
Petah Tikva, Israel
telemessage.com

Terafence (15, -11.8%)
IoT Security / Gateways
Haifa, Israel
terafence.com

ThetaRay (160, 26.0%)
Security Analytics
Hod HaSharon, Israel
thetaray.com

TripleCyber (16, 14.3%)
MSSP / SOC
Tel Aviv, Israel
triplecyber.co.il

ULTRA RED (22, 0.0%)
Operations / Breach And Attack Simulation
Tel Aviv, Israel
ultrared.ai

Upstream Security (128, -3.0%)
IoT Security / Automotive
Herzliya, Israel
upstream.auto

Valence Security (49, 36.1%)
API Security
Tel Aviv, Israel
valencesecurity.com

Vdoo (15, -37.5%)
IoT Security / Security For Embedded Systems
Tel Aviv, Israel
vdoo.com

Velotix (39, -4.9%)
Data Security
Tel Aviv, Israel
velotix.ai

Vendict (36, 89.5%)
GRC / Security Questionnaire Automation
Tel Aviv, Israel
vendict.com

Verifyoo (3, 0.0%)
IAM / Authentication
Tel Aviv, Israel
verifyoo.com

Veriti (39, 129.4%)
Operations / Posture Management
Tel Aviv, Israel
veriti.ai

Vicarius (58, 9.4%)
Application Security / Code Security
Jerusalem, Israel
vicarius.io

Vorpal (8, 0.0%)
IoT Security / Drones
Tel Aviv, Israel
vorpal-corp.com

Votiro (57, 23.9%)
Network Security / File Scrubbing
Tel Aviv, Israel
votiro.com

Vulcan Cyber (118, 16.8%)
GRC / Vulnerabilities
Tel Aviv, Israel
vulcan.io

**Numbers in parentheses indicate headcount and % change in 2023.*

Waterfall (124, 25.2%)
IoT Security / Firewalls
Rosh HaAyin, Israel
waterfall-security.com

WIB (70, 25.0%)
API Security
Tel Aviv, Israel
wib.com

Wing Security (44, 2.3%)
Application Security / SaaS Management
Tel Aviv, Israel
wing.security

Wiz (1114, 74.3%)
GRC / Configuration Management
Tel Aviv, Israel
wiz.io

Wizdome (10, -63.0%)
Threat Intelligence / TIP
Tel Aviv, Israel
wizdome.com

XM Cyber (297, 63.2%)
Operations / Breach And Attack Simulation
Herzliya, Israel
xmcyber.com

YazamTech (8, 33.3%)
Data Security
Ra'anana, Israel
yazamtech.com

Yoggie (8, 14.3%)
Network Security / Firewalls
Beth Halevy, Israel
yoggie.com

ZenGo (60, -1.6%)
Data Security / Wallets
Sarona, Israel
zengo.com

Zenity (37, 42.3%)
GRC / No-code/Low-code Security
Tel Aviv, Israel
zenity.io

Zero Networks (54, 35.0%)
Network Security / Segmentation
Tel Aviv, Israel
zeronetworks.com

Italy

Boolebox (13, -18.8%)
Data Security / IRM
Milan, Italy
boolebox.com

Cleafy (54, -6.9%)
Fraud Prevention / Anti-fraud
Milan, Italy
cleafy.com

CY4GATE (132, 5.6%)
Security Analytics / SIEM
Rome, Italy
cy4gate.com

Cyber Guru (80, 33.3%)
GRC / Security Awareness Training
Rome, Italy
cyberguru.it

CyLock (11, 10.0%)
GRC / Penetration Testing
Roma, Italy
cylock.tech/en/home-en

Endian (28, 0.0%)
Network Security / UTM
Bolzano, Italy
endian.com

ERMES Cyber Security (48, 23.1%)
Data Security / DLP
Turin, Italy
ermessecurity.com

Exein (26, 18.2%)
IoT Security
Rome, Italy
exein.io

Libraesva (35, 25.0%)
Email Security
Lecco, Italy
libraesva.com

Minded Security UK Limited (32, 14.3%)
Endpoint Security / Anti-malware
Rome, Italy
mindedsecurity.com

Pikered (6, 0.0%)
Operations / Breach And Attack Simulation
Milan, Italy
pikered.com

Security Mind (4, 0.0%)
GRC / Security Awareness Training
Veneto, Italy
securitymind.cloud

SecurityGen (35, 0.0%)
Network Security / Firewalls
Rome, Italy
secgen.com

Swascan (78, 13.0%)
GRC / Scanning
Cassina de' Pecchi, Italy
swascan.com

TG Soft (10, 0.0%)
Endpoint Security / Anti-virus
Rubano, Italy
tgsoft.it

ToothPic (11, 10.0%)
Operations / Forensics
Turin, Italy
toothpic.eu

Japan

Authlete (29, 38.1%)
IAM / Gateways
Tokyo, Japan
authlete.com

Blue Planet-works (14, -22.2%)
Application Security / Isolation
Tokyo, Japan
blueplanet-works.com

Fujitsu (66402, 15.8%)
MSSP / Managed Security Services
Kawasaki-Shi, Japan
fujitsu.com

Humming Heads (9, 125.0%)
Endpoint Security / Application Whitelisting
Tokyo, Japan
hummingheads.co.jp

Pipeline Security (26, -10.3%)
MSSP
Chuo-ku, Tokyo, Japan
ppln.co

SpiderAF (45, 0.0%)
Fraud Prevention / Advertising-related
Tokyo, Japan
spideraf.com

Vario Secure Networks (12, -14.3%)
MSSP / Managed Security Services
Tokyo, Japan
variosecure.net

Kuwait

Cyberkov (4, 0.0%)
GRC / Risk Management
Kuwait City, Kuwait
cyberkov.com

Latvia

Notakey (3, -25.0%)
IAM / Access Security
Riga, Latvia
notakey.com

Luxembourg

EBRAND (81, 11.0%)
Threat Intelligence / Brand
Leudelange, Luxembourg
ebrand.com

**Numbers in parentheses indicate headcount and % change in 2023.*

Passbolt (28, -15.2%)
IAM / Credential Security
Esch-sur-alzette, Luxembourg
passbolt.com

RCDevs (19, 5.6%)
IAM
Belvaux, Luxembourg
rcdevs.com

Malaysia

Ensign Infosecurity (722, 20.9%)
MSSP / Managed Security Services
Kuala Lumpur, Malaysia
ensigninfosecurity.com

Malta

Acunetix (Invicti) (38, -28.3%)
GRC / Vulnerabilities
Mriehel, Malta
acunetix.com

NoID (12, 33.3%)
Data Security / Secure Communications
St Julians, Malta
noid.ltd

Mexico

Tesseract (5, 25.0%)
Data Security / Encryption
Mexico City, Mexico
tesseract.mx

Tu Identidad (20, 66.7%)
IAM / Authentication
Mexico City, Mexico
tuidentidad.com

Morocco

ADINES MAROC (8, 0.0%)
MSSP / SOC
Casablanca, Casablanca, Morocco
adines.ma

Nepal

Vairav Technology (94, 27.0%)
MSSP / Managed Security Services
Kathmandu, Nepal
vairav.net

Netherlands

3rdRisk (11, 57.1%)
GRC / Risk Management
Amsterdam, Netherlands
3rdrisk.com

AET Europe (58, 18.4%)
IAM / Identity Management
Arnhem, Gelderland, Netherlands
aeteurope.com

Awareways (53, -10.2%)
GRC / Security Awareness Training
Utrecht, Netherlands
awareways.com

Brama Systems (6, 0.0%)
Network Security / Access Security
Utrecht, Netherlands
bramasystems.com

BroadForward (26, 0.0%)
Network Security / Firewalls
Amersfoort, Netherlands
broadforward.com

Codean (7, 0.0%)
Application Security / Code Security
Utrecht, Netherlands
codean.io

Compumatica (19, 0.0%)
Data Security / Secure Remote Access
Uden, Netherlands
compumatica.com

EclecticIQ (82, -35.4%)
Threat Intelligence / Threat Intelligence Platform
Amsterdam, Netherlands
eclecticiq.com

Elastic (3751, 8.4%)
Security Analytics / SIEM
Amsterdam, Netherlands
elastic.co

emproof (13, 18.2%)
IoT Security / Security For Embedded Systems
Eindhoven, Netherlands
emproof.com

Eye Security (99, 32.0%)
MSSP / MDR
Zuid-Holland, Netherlands
eye.security

Fox IT (424, 11.6%)
MSSP / MDR
Delft, Netherlands
fox-it.com

Guardian 360 (13, 30.0%)
GRC / Vulnerabilities
Utrecht, Netherlands
guardian360.nl

Hadrian (79, 31.7%)
Operations / Attack Surface Management
Noord-Holland, Netherlands
hadrian.io

Infosequre (12, 20.0%)
GRC / Security Awareness Training
Hilversum, Netherlands
infosequre.com

Intel 471 (157, 6.1%)
Threat Intelligence / Threat Actor Intelligence
Amsterdam, Netherlands
intel471.com

Irdeto (1094, 5.8%)
IoT Security / Entertainment Systems
Hoofddorp, Netherlands
irdeto.com

iWelcome (10, -23.1%)
IAM / Identity Management
Amersfoort, Netherlands
iwelcome.com

Keytalk - Pki Management Solutions (5, -16.7%)
Data Security / Public Key Infrastructure
Amersfoort, Netherlands
keytalk.com

MMOX (6, 0.0%)
MSSP / SMB Security
The Hague, Netherlands
mmox.co

Networking4All (35, 2.9%)
MSSP / Managed Security Services
de Meern, Utrecht, Netherlands
networking4all.com

ON2IT Cybersecurity (85, 4.9%)
MSSP / Managed Security Services
Zaltbommel, Netherlands
on2it.net

OneLeet (15, 7.1%)
GRC / Penetration Testing
Amsterdam, Netherlands
oneleet.com

OneWelcome (Was Onegini) (4, -50.0%)
IAM / CIAM
Woerden, Netherlands
onegini.com

Profitap (35, 16.7%)
Network Security / Traffic Analysis
Eindhoven, Netherlands
profitap.com

Quiver (3, -40.0%)
Data Security / Secure Data Sharing
Amsterdam, Netherlands
quivercloud.com

ReaQta (14, -48.1%)
Endpoint Security / EDR
Amsterdam, Netherlands
reaqta.com

**Numbers in parentheses indicate headcount and % change in 2023.*

Riscure (173, 1.8%)
Testing / Security For Embedded Systems
Delft, Netherlands
riscure.com

Secureme2 (17, 54.5%)
MSSP / MDR
Rijen, Netherlands
secureme2.eu

Signicat (438, -0.5%)
IAM / Identity Verification
Rotterdam, Netherlands
signicat.nl

Storro (6, 0.0%)
Data Security / Secure Storage
Hengelo, Netherlands
storro.com

Tesorion (122, 2.5%)
MSSP / Managed Security Services
Leusden, Netherlands
tesorion.nl

ThreatFabric (52, 67.7%)
Fraud Prevention / Bot Security
Amsterdam, Netherlands
threatfabric.com

Threatspan (4, -20.0%)
IoT Security / Maritime Security
Rotterdam, Netherlands
threatspan.com

Ubiqu (16, 23.1%)
IAM / Public Key Infrastructure
Delft, Netherlands
ubiqu.com

Zerocopter (45, 2.3%)
Application Security / Hackers For Hire
Amsterdam, Netherlands
zerocopter.com

Zivver (136, -8.7%)
Email Security / Secure Email
Amsterdam, Netherlands
zivver.eu

ZyLAB (61, -18.7%)
GRC / E-discovery
Amsterdam, Netherlands
zylab.com

New Zealand

Authsignal (11, 22.2%)
Fraud Prevention
Auckland, New Zealand
authsignal.com

Blacklock Security (4, -20.0%)
GRC / Penetration Testing
Thorndon, Wellington Region, New Zealand
blacklock.io

Capture The Bug (12, 200.0%)
Application Security / Bugs
Waikato, New Zealand
capturethebug.xyz

DarkScope (8, 300.0%)
Threat Intelligence
Wellington, New Zealand
darkscope.com

Datamasque (15, 36.4%)
Data Security / Data Masking
Auckland, New Zealand
datamasque.com

Endace (89, 7.2%)
Network Security / IDS
Ellerslie, New Zealand
endace.com

Firetrust (3, -57.1%)
Email Security / Anti-spam
Christchurch, New Zealand
firetrust.com

First Watch (18, -5.3%)
IoT Security / OT Security
Hamilton, New Zealand
firstwatchprotect.com

InPhySec (42, -32.3%)
MSSP / Managed Security Services
Wellington, New Zealand
inphysecsecurity.com

Liverton Security (18, 20.0%)
Email Security / Gateways
Wellington, New Zealand
livertonsecurity.com

Mindshift (9, 50.0%)
GRC / Security Awareness Training
New Zealand
mindshift.kiwi

Onwardly (8, 14.3%)
GRC / Policy Management
Aukland, New Zealand
onwardly.io

Quasar Scan (4, 0.0%)
Data Security / Data Discovery
Wellington Region, New Zealand
quasarscan.com

RedShield Security (37, -7.5%)
MSSP / Managed Security Services
Wellington, New Zealand
redshield.co

SafeStack (19, -24.0%)
Training / Software Development Security
Aukland, New Zealand
safestack.io

SAM for Compliance (3, 0.0%)
GRC / Compliance Management
Hastings, New Zealand
samcompliance.co

Sandfly Security (10, 11.1%)
Endpoint Security / EDR
Christchurch, New Zealand
sandflysecurity.com

SMX (26, 44.4%)
Email Security
Auckland, New Zealand
smxemail.com

TamosSoft (4, 0.0%)
Network Security / Monitoring
Christchurch, New Zealand
tamos.com

Theta (282, 10.2%)
Operations / Attack Surface Management
Auckland, New Zealand
theta.co.nz

VTS (36, 227.3%)
IoT Security / IDS
Auckland, New Zealand
vts.energy

Nigera

Dojah (21, 0.0%)
Fraud Prevention / Identity Verification
Lagos, Nigera
dojah.io

Identitypass (20, -16.7%)
IAM / Identity Verification
Lagos, Nigera
myidentitypass.com

Norway

Buypass As (85, 10.4%)
IAM / Public Key Infrastructure
OSLO, Norway
buypass.no

Commfides Norge As (15, -11.8%)
IAM / Public Key Infrastructure
Lysaker, Norway
commfides.com

Mnemonic (383, 17.1%)
MSSP / MDR
Oslo, Norway
mnemonic.no

**Numbers in parentheses indicate headcount and % change in 2023.*

Omny (32, 77.8%)
GRC / Risk Management
Oslo, Norway
omnysecurity.com

Promon (109, 7.9%)
Application Security /
Mobile Device Security
Oslo, Norway
promon.co

River Security (26, 62.5%)
Operations / Attack Surface
Management
Oslo, Norway
riversecurity.eu

Secure-Nok (15, 15.4%)
IoT Security / OT Security
Hamar, Norway
securenok.com

Zwipe (39, -26.4%)
IAM / Authentication
Oslo, Norway
zwipe.com

Panama

NordVPN (75, 29.3%)
Network Security
/ VPN/Proxy
Panama City, Panama
nordvpn.com

Peru

Advanced Systems International (3, -25.0%)
Endpoint Security
Lima, Peru
usb-lock-rp.com

Dreamlab Technologies (142, 21.4%)
Deception / Managed
Security Services
San Isidro, Peru
dreamlab.net

Poland

APT Defend (5, 400.0%)
GRC / Security Awareness Training
Warszawa, Mazowieckie,
Poland
aptdefend.com

Arcabit (3, 0.0%)
Endpoint Security /
Anti-virus
Warsaw, Poland
arcabit.pl

CDeX (27, 0.0%)
Training / Cyber Range
Poznan, Poland
cdex.cloud

Cyberus Labs (7, 0.0%)
IAM / Authentication
Krakow, Poland
cyberuslabs.com

Cypher.Dog (13, -23.5%)
Data Security / Secure
Data Sharing
Wroclaw, Poland
cypher.dog

Digital Core Design (6, 0.0%)
Data Security / Encryption
Bytom, Poland
dcd.pl

ICsec (29, 0.0%)
IoT Security / OT Security
Poznan, Poland
icsec.pl/en/

IDENTT (38, 0.0%)
IAM
Wroclaw, Poland
identt.pl

Inseqr (12, 0.0%)
Network Security
/ VPN/Proxy
Warszawa, Poland
inseqr.pl/en/

Labyrinth (13, 0.0%)
Deception / Decoy Hosts
Zabrze, Poland
labyrinth.tech

Mission: Cybersecurity (7, 0.0%)
Training / Security Awareness Training
Ruda Slaska, Poland
misjacyber.pl/en/

Nethone (106, 2.9%)
Fraud Prevention /
Anti-fraud
Warsaw, Poland
nethone.com

ProDevice (5, 0.0%)
Data Security / Data Erasure
And Destruction
Wieliczka, Poland
pro-device.com/en/pro-device.com/en/

RAWCyber (3, 0.0%)
Endpoint Security / Mobile
Device Security
Warszawa, Poland
rawcyber.pl

Rublon (18, 20.0%)
IAM / Authentication
Zielona Gora, Poland
rublon.com

Secfense (16, 23.1%)
IAM / Access Security
Krakow, Poland
secfense.com

Specfile (4, 0.0%)
Data Security / Encryption
Poznan, Poland
specfile.pl

Portugal

AnubisNetworks (BitSight) (29, 3.6%)
Email Security
Lisbon, Portugal
anubisnetworks.com

ETHIACK (13, 160.0%)
Application Security / Penetration Testing
Coimbra, Portugal
ethiack.com

Immunefi (86, 43.3%)
Application Security / Bugs
Cascais, Portugal
immunefi.com

Multicert (83, 10.7%)
Data Security / Public Key
Infrastructure
Porto Salvo, Portugal
multicert.com

Probely (33, 43.5%)
Application Security
/ Scanning
Lisbon, Portugal
probely.com

Redstout (3, -50.0%)
Network Security / UTM
Lisbon, Portugal
redstout.com

Puerto Rico

GM Sectec (166, 32.8%)
MSSP / Managed
Security Services
San Juan, Puerto Rico
gmsectec.com

Republic of Moldova

Dekart (9, 125.0%)
Data Security / Encryption
Chisinau, Republic
of Moldova
dekart.com

Romania

BitDefender (2110, 4.0%)
Endpoint Security /
Anti-virus
Bucharest, Romania
bitdefender.com

**Numbers in parentheses indicate headcount and % change in 2023.*

CyberGhost (47, -16.1%)
Network Security / VPN/Proxy
Bucharest, Romania
cyberghostvpn.com

east-tec (7, 16.7%)
Data Security / Data Erasure And Destruction
Oradea, Romania
east-tec.com

Softwin SRL (176, -9.7%)
Endpoint Security / Anti-virus
Bucharest, Romania
softwin.com

Russia

Aladdin-RD (43, 4.9%)
IAM / Authentication
Moscow, Russia
aladdin-rd.ru

BI.ZONE (257, 12.7%)
Threat Intelligence / Threat Intel Aggregator
Moscow, Russia
bi.zone

CyberSafe Software (3, 0.0%)
Data Security / Encryption
Krasnodar, Russia
cybersafesoft.com

Ddos-Guard (60, -6.2%)
Network Security / DDoS Defense
Rostov-na-Donu, Russia
ddos-guard.net

Dr. Web (245, -8.9%)
Endpoint Security / Anti-virus
Moscow, Russia
drweb.com

Elcomsoft (15, 0.0%)
Operations / Forensics
Moscow, Russia
elcomsoft.com

Infowatch (193, -3.0%)
GRC / DLP
Moscow, Russia
infowatch.com

Kaspersky (3901, 3.4%)
Endpoint Security / Anti-virus
Moscow, Russia
kaspersky.com

Metascan (6, 0.0%)
GRC / Scanning
Moscow, Russia
metascan.ru

Nano Security (3, -25.0%)
Endpoint Security / Anti-virus
Moscow, Russia
nanoav.pro

R-Vision (114, 2.7%)
Operations / Incident Management
Moscow, Russia
rvision.pro

SearchInform (110, 12.2%)
Operations / Monitoring
Moscow, Russia
searchinform.com

Security Code (123, -3.9%)
Network Security / UTM
Moscow, Russia
securitycode.ru

SolidWall (17, 112.5%)
Application Security / Firewalls
Moscow, Russia
solidwall.io

Xello (7, 75.0%)
Deception
Moscow, Russia
xello.ru

Zecurion (38, 5.6%)
Data Security / Database Security
Moscow, Russia
zecurion.com

Scotland

Ionburst (8, 0.0%)
Data Security
Edinburgh, Scotland
ionburst.io

Lupovis (10, -16.7%)
Deception / Network Decoys
Glasgow, Scotland
lupovis.io

Singapore

AppKnox (73, 19.7%)
Application Security / Mobile Device Security
Singapore, Singapore
appknox.com

Apvera (5, 0.0%)
GRC / Monitoring
Singapore, Singapore
apvera.com

Avnos (3, -50.0%)
Endpoint Security / Application Whitelisting
Singapore, Singapore
avnos.io

Cura Software Solutions (85, 9.0%)
GRC / Risk Management
Singapore, Singapore
curasoftware.com

Dathena Science (6, -40.0%)
Data Security / Data Discovery
Singapore, Singapore
dathena.io

Deep Indentity Pte Ltd. (78, 2.6%)
GRC / Access Security
Singapore, Singapore
deepidentity.com

Digify (45, 21.6%)
Data Security / IRM
Singapore, Singapore
digify.com

Flexible IR (6, 0.0%)
Operations / Incident Management
Singapore, Singapore
flexibleir.com

Ground Labs (44, -6.4%)
GRC / Data Discovery
Singapore, Singapore
groundlabs.com

Group-IB (103, -72.9%)
Threat Intelligence / Dark Web
Central Region, Singapore, Singapore
group-ib.com

Horangi (115, -14.8%)
Network Security / Vulnerabilities
Singapore, Singapore
horangi.com

I-Sprint Innovations (104, -0.9%)
IAM
Singapore, Singapore
i-sprint.com

Invisiron - Cyber Defence Fortified (8, -11.1%)
Network Security / Firewalls
Singapore, Singapore
invisiron.com

MicroSec (35, -16.7%)
IoT Security / OT Security
Central Region, Singapore, Singapore
usec.io

Quantum (11, -47.6%)
MSSP / MDR
Singapore, Singapore
quantum.security

Responsible Cyber (14, -6.7%)
GRC / Risk Management
Central Business District, Singapore
responsible-cyber.com

**Numbers in parentheses indicate headcount and % change in 2023.*

Safeheron (13, 0.0%)
Data Security / Encryption
Singapore City, Singapore
safeheron.com

Scantist (26, -16.1%)
GRC / Vulnerabilities
Singapore, Singapore
scantist.com

Scybers (61, 29.8%)
MSSP / SOC
Singapore
scybers.com

Seconize (17, 6.2%)
GRC / Risk Management
Singapore, Singapore
seconize.co

Silence Laboratories (24, -25.0%)
IAM / Authentication
Central Region, Singapore, Singapore
silencelaboratories.com

SilverLakeMasterSAM (29, -6.5%)
IAM / Access Security
Singapore, Singapore
mastersam.com

SpeQtral (31, 55.0%)
Data Security / Quantum
Singapore, Singapore
speqtral.space

SquareX (15, 1400.0%)
Network Security / Secure Web Browsing
Singapore
sqrx.com

StealthMole (12, 20.0%)
Threat Intelligence / Dark Web
Singapore
stealthmole.com

Sunnic (55, 77.4%)
Data Security / Encryption
Singapore
sunnic-sec.com

Treebox Solutions (17, 21.4%)
Data Security / Secure Communications
Singapore, Singapore
treeboxsolutions.com

Uppsala Security (26, 8.3%)
Data Security / Tracking Of Crypto Currencies
Singapore, Singapore
uppsalasecurity.com

Watchdata (204, 5.2%)
IAM / Public Key Infrastructure
Singapore, Singapore
watchdata.com

watchTowr (21, 5.0%)
Operations / Attack Surface Management
Central Region, Singapore, Singapore
watchtowr.com

Slovakia

Ardaco (25, -16.7%)
Data Security / Secure Communications
Bratislava, Slovakia
ardaco.com

ESET (1719, 5.6%)
Endpoint Security / Anti-virus
Bratislava, Slovakia
eset.com

SaferPass (16, -11.1%)
IAM / Credential Security
Bratislava, Slovakia
saferpass.net

StormWall (26, 8.3%)
Network Security / DDoS Defense
Bratislava, Slovakia
stormwall.network

South Africa

Bowline Security (11, 10.0%)
MSSP / SOC
Durban, KZN, South Africa
bowlinesecurity.co.za

Entersekt (211, 3.4%)
IAM / Authentication
Stellenbosch, South Africa
entersekt.com

Sendmarc (64, 68.4%)
Email Security / Defense Against Phishing
ROSEBANK, Gauteng, South Africa
sendmarc.com

Thinkst Canary (5, 150.0%)
Deception / Target Agents Deployed In Operations
Edinvale, South Africa
canary.tools

ThisIsMe (9, -10.0%)
IAM / Onboarding
Cape Town, South Africa
thisisme.com

VoxCroft (39, -9.3%)
Threat Intelligence / OSINT
Western Cape, South Africa
voxcroft.com

South Korea

Ahnlab (563, 7.8%)
Endpoint Security / Anti-virus
Gyeonggi-do, South Korea
ahnlab.com

Ahope (16, 6.7%)
Application Security / Mobile Device Security
Seoul, South Korea
ahope.net

AI Spera (23, 15.0%)
Threat Intelligence / OSINT
Seoul, South Korea
criminalip.io

AUTOCRYPT (162, 55.8%)
IoT Security / Automotive
Seoul, South Korea
autocrypt.io

CHEQUER (12, -40.0%)
IAM / Access Security
Seoul, South Korea
querypie.com

Cloudbric Corporation (17, -32.0%)
MSSP / Website Security
Seoul, South Korea
cloudbric.com

ESTsoft (314, 3.3%)
Endpoint Security / Anti-virus
Seoul, South Korea
estsoft.ai

Everspin (19, 26.7%)
Endpoint Security / Dynamic Image Replacement
Seoul, South Korea
everspin.global

EYL (4, -81.0%)
Data Security / Quantum
Seoul, South Korea
eylpartners.com

FASOO (105, -3.7%)
GRC / Digital Rights Management
Seoul, South Korea
fasoo.com

Genians (7, 0.0%)
IoT Security / Device Fingerprinting
Anyang-si, South Korea
genians.com

HDN (16, 0.0%)
Network Security / Security Switches
Guro-gu, South Korea
handream.net

Insignary (6, -25.0%)
Application Security / Vulnerabilities
Seoul, South Korea
insignary.com

**Numbers in parentheses indicate headcount and % change in 2023.*

Jiran (44, -2.2%)
GRC / DLP
Daejeon, South Korea
jiran.com

Keypair (10, 42.9%)
IAM / Indentities
Gangnam-gu, South Korea
keypair.co.kr

LABRADOR LABS (16, 14.3%)
Application Security / Code Security
Seoul, South Korea
labradorlabs.ai

Markany (96, 28.0%)
Data Security / DRM
Seoul, South Korea
markany.com

Norma (9, 80.0%)
IoT Security
Seoul, South Korea
norma.co.kr

NPcore (18, 5.9%)
Endpoint Security / EDR
Seoul, South Korea
npcore.com

Octatco (6, 20.0%)
IAM / Authentication
Seongnam, South Korea
octatco.com

Penta Security (81, 0.0%)
Network Security / Firewalls
Seoul, South Korea
pentasecurity.com

Quad Miners (25, 13.6%)
Network Security / Monitoring
Seoul, South Korea
quadminers.com

S2W Inc. (59, -6.3%)
Threat Intelligence / Investigation
Pangyo, South Korea
s2w.inc

SecuLetter (16, 0.0%)
Operations / Malware Analysis
Seongnam-si, South Korea
seculetter.com

Softcamp (29, 3.6%)
Data Security
Eongnam-Si, South Korea
softcamp.co.kr

Somma (8, -27.3%)
Security Analytics / XDR
Seongnam-si, South Korea
somma.kr

Sparrow (19, 26.7%)
Application Security / Code Security
Mapo-gu, South Korea
sparrowfasoo.com

SSenStone (17, 6.2%)
IAM / Authentication
Mapo-Gu, South Korea
ssenstone.com

STEALIEN (37, 8.8%)
Application Security
Seoul, South Korea
stealien.com

Viascope (7, -36.4%)
IAM / Access Security
Seoul, South Korea
viascope.com

Spain

A3Sec Grupo (119, 29.4%)
MSSP
Madrid, Spain
a3sec.com

AIUKEN CYBERSECURITY (85, 14.9%)
MSSP / Managed Security Services
Madrid, Spain
aiuken.com

Alias Robotics (14, 27.3%)
IoT Security / Anti-malware
Vitoria, Basque Country, Spain
aliasrobotics.com

Arexdata (11, 175.0%)
Data Security / Posture Management
Madrid, Spain
arexdata.com

Babel (3080, 19.0%)
MSSP / SOC
Madrid, Spain
babelgroup.com

CounterCraft (48, -21.3%)
Deception
Donostia-San Sebastian, Spain
countercraft.eu

Eneo Tecnologia (9, 50.0%)
Network Security / IPS
Mairena del Aljerafe, Spain
redborder.com

Enigmedia (8, -66.7%)
Data Security / Secure Communications
San Sebastian, Spain
enigmedia.es

Facephi Biometra (261, 17.6%)
IAM / Authentication
Alicante, Spain
facephi.com

Insside Informacion (104, 16.9%)
GRC / GRC Platform
Madrid, Spain
insside.net

IriusRisk (167, 11.3%)
Application Security / Scanning
Cuarte, Spain
iriusrisk.com

Ironchip Telco (29, 20.8%)
IAM / Identity Management
Barakaldo, Spain
ironchip.com

Kymatio (18, -14.3%)
GRC / Security Awareness Training
Madrid, Spain
kymatio.com

Maltiverse (9, 0.0%)
Threat Intelligence / IoC Intelligence
Madrid, Spain
maltiverse.com

Mobbeel (22, 22.2%)
IAM / Authentication
Caceres, Spain
mobbeel.com

OneLayer (30, 0.0%)
Network Security / Cellular Network Security
Galicia, Spain
one-layer.com

Panda Security (402, 0.8%)
Endpoint Security / Anti-virus
Bilbao, Spain
pandasecurity.com

Quside (47, 34.3%)
Data Security / Quantum
Barcelona, Spain
quside.com

Realsec (23, 0.0%)
Data Security / Hardware
Madrid, Spain
realsec.com

Redborder (10, 11.1%)
Network Security / IDS
Sevilla, Spain
redborder.com

S2 Grupo (679, 13.4%)
MSSP / SOC
Valencia, Spain
s2grupo.es

Sealpath (26, 0.0%)
Data Security / IRM
Bilbao, Spain
sealpath.com

Soffid (14, 40.0%)
IAM / Authentication
Palma de Mallorca, Spain
soffid.com

Sofistic (81, -3.6%)
MSSP
Castellon, Spain
sofistic.com

**Numbers in parentheses indicate headcount and % change in 2023.*

SSHTeam (19, 58.3%)
GRC / Penetration Testing
Logroño, La Rioja, Spain
sshteam.com

Veridas (197, 50.4%)
IAM / Authentication
Pamplona, Navarra, Spain
veridas.com

Xygeni (22, 120.0%)
Application Security / SBOM
Madrid, Spain
xygeni.io

Sweden

Advenica (87, 22.5%)
Network Security / Air Gap
Sweden
advenica.com

Allurity (13, 44.4%)
MSSP / SOC
Stockholm, Stockholms Lan, Sweden
allurity.com

Axcrypt (24, 14.3%)
Data Security / Encryption
Stockholm, Sweden
axcrypt.net

Axiomatics (67, 24.1%)
IAM / Access Security
Stockholm, Sweden
axiomatics.com

Baffin Bay Networking (8, -50.0%)
Network Security / Threat Detection
Stockholm, Sweden
baffinbaynetworks.com

Besedo (370, 9.8%)
Fraud Prevention / Scanning
Stockholm, Sweden
besedo.com

Clavister (120, -13.7%)
Network Security / UTM
Ornskoldsvik, Sweden
clavister.com

Covr Security (21, 16.7%)
IAM / Authentication
Sweden
covrsecurity.com

Debricked (29, -23.7%)
Application Security / Vulnerabilities
Sweden
debricked.com

Defentry (17, -15.0%)
Operations / Scanning
Stockholm, Sweden
defentry.com

Detectify (128, -25.6%)
Application Security / Scanning
Stockholm, Sweden
detectify.com

Eyeonid Group Ab (11, 83.3%)
IAM / Theft
Stockholm, Sweden
eyeonid.com

Fingerprint Cards AB (185, -12.3%)
IAM / Authentication
Gothenburg, Sweden
fingerprints.com

Freja eID Group AB (Was Verisec) (45, -13.5%)
IAM / Mobile Identity
Stockholm, Sweden
verisec.com

Halon (32, 23.1%)
Email Security / Anti-spam
Gothenburg, Sweden
halon.io

Holm Security (62, -19.5%)
Network Security / Vulnerabilities
Stockholm, Sweden
holmsecurity.com

InGate (19, 0.0%)
Network Security / Firewalls
Sundbyberg, Sweden
ingate.com

Msab (279, 10.7%)
Endpoint Security / Forensics
Stockholm, Sweden
msab.com

Nexus Group Global (257, 19.0%)
IAM / Identity Management
Stockholm, Sweden
nexusgroup.com

Outpost24 (228, 38.2%)
GRC / Vulnerabilities
Karlskrona, Sweden
outpost24.com

PointSharp AB (58, 13.7%)
Endpoint Security / Mobile Device Security
Stockholm, Sweden
pointsharp.com

PrimeKey Solutions (36, -28.0%)
Data Security / Public Key Infrastructure
Solna, Sweden
primekey.com

Sectra Communications (1363, 21.5%)
Data Security / Secure Communications
Linkoping, Sweden
sectra.com

Securemailbox (3, 0.0%)
Data Security / Secure Communications
Stockholm, Sweden
securemailbox.com

Sentor (78, -6.0%)
MSSP / SIEM
Stockholm, Sweden
sentor.se

Specops Software Inc. (68, -17.1%)
IAM / Credential Security
Stockholm, Sweden
specopssoft.com

Tutus (47, 42.4%)
Data Security / Encryption
Danderyd, Sweden
tutus.se

Veriscan Security (12, 9.1%)
GRC / Security Measurement
Karlstad, Sweden
veriscan.se

Versasec (23, -11.5%)
IAM
Stockholm, Sweden
versasec.com

Yubico (460, 15.3%)
IAM / Authentication
Stockholm, Sweden
yubico.com

Zignsec (26, 4.0%)
IAM / Identity Verification
Solna, Sweden
zignsec.com

Switzerland

AckTao (5, 0.0%)
GRC / Security Awareness Training
Vaud, Switzerland
acktao.com

Acronis (2123, -3.1%)
Data Security / Secure Backup/Recovery
Schaffhausen, Switzerland
acronis.com

AdNovum (638, 7.8%)
IAM / CIAM
Zurich, Switzerland
adnovum.ch

Agora SecureWare (7, 16.7%)
Data Security / Secure Collaboration
Bioggio, Switzerland
agora-secureware.com

Airlock (12, -14.3%)
IAM / Access Security
Zurich, Switzerland
airlock.com

**Numbers in parentheses indicate headcount and % change in 2023.*

AppTec (20, 42.9%)
Endpoint Security / Mobile Device Security
Basel, Switzerland
apptec360.com

ARCANO (4, 0.0%)
Data Security / Secure Data Sharing
Zurich, Switzerland
arcano.app

BinaryEdge (6, 0.0%)
Operations / Scanning
Zurich, Switzerland
binaryedge.io

BioID (14, 7.7%)
IAM / Authentication
Sachseln, Switzerland
bioid.com

Blowfish (18, 260.0%)
Data Security / Wallets
Switzerland
blowfish.xyz

Calvin Risk (17, 13.3%)
Application Security / AI Model Security
Zurich, Switzerland
calvin-risk.com

Compass Security AG (60, -16.7%)
Data Security / Secure Data Sharing
Rapperswil-Jona, Switzerland
compass-security.com

Crypto International AG (43, 43.3%)
Data Security / Hardware
Steinhausen, Switzerland
crypto.ch

CuriX AG (16, 45.5%)
Operations / Monitoring
Baar, Switzerland
curix.ai

CYSEC (50, 13.6%)
Endpoint Security
Lausanne, Vaud, Switzerland
cysec.com

Decentriq (34, -2.9%)
Data Security / Secure Collaboration
Zurich, Switzerland
decentriq.com

DuoKey (7, 0.0%)
Data Security / Encryption
Lausanne, Switzerland
duokey.com

Exeon Analytics (37, 42.3%)
Security Analytics / Monitoring
Zurich, Switzerland
exeon.ch

fidentity (10, 25.0%)
IAM / Identity Verification
Basel, Switzerland
fidentity.ch

Futurae (45, -2.2%)
IAM / Authentication
Zurich, Switzerland
futurae.com

GObugfree AG (20, 0.0%)
Application Security / Hackers For Hire
Zurich, Switzerland
gobugfree.com

Hacking Lab (9, 50.0%)
Training / Cyber Range
Rapperswil-Jona, Switzerland
shop.hacking-lab.com

Id Quantique (110, 5.8%)
Data Security / Quantum
Carouge, Switzerland
idquantique.com

Immuniweb (34, 3.0%)
Application Security / Scanning
Geneva, Switzerland
immuniweb.com

JOESecurity (8, 14.3%)
Operations / Malware Analysis
Reinach, Switzerland
joesecurity.org

Lakera (30, 0.0%)
Data Security / AI Data Security
Zürich, Switzerland
lakera.ai

LUCY Security (20, -25.9%)
GRC / Defense Against Phishing
Zug, Switzerland
lucysecurity.com

MailCleaner (4, 0.0%)
Email Security
Saint-Sulpice, Switzerland
mailcleaner.net

Netsense Gmbh (3, -25.0%)
GRC / Vulnerabilities
Zurich, Switzerland
netsense.ch

OneVisage (7, -12.5%)
IAM / Authentication
Lausanne, Switzerland
onevisage.com

Open Systems (426, -17.6%)
MSSP / Managed Security Services
Zurich, Switzerland
open-systems.com

Privus (7, -22.2%)
Data Security / Secure Communications
Zug, Switzerland
privus.global

Procivis AG (29, 11.5%)
IAM / Credential Security
Zurich, Switzerland
procivis.ch

Prodaft (52, 15.6%)
Threat Intelligence / OSINT
Yverdon-les-Bains, Switzerland
prodaft.com

PXL Vision (34, -2.9%)
IAM / Identity Verification
Zurich, Switzerland
pxl-vision.com

Quantum Integrity (4, -20.0%)
IAM / Identity Verification
Lausanne, Switzerland
q-integrity.com

Quantum Resistant Cryptography (5, 0.0%)
Data Security / Encryption
Lausanne, Switzerland
qrcrypto.ch

Regdata (16, 23.1%)
Data Security / Compliance Management
Geneva, Switzerland
regdata.ch/en/

Saporo (30, 7.1%)
IAM / Identity Management
Lausanne, Vaud, Switzerland
saporo.io

scanmeter (7, 75.0%)
Application Security / Penetration Testing
Zurich, Switzerland
scanmeter.io

Secude (108, -25.0%)
Data Security / SAP
Luzern, Switzerland
secude.com

Securosys (29, 20.8%)
Data Security / Hardware
Zurich, Switzerland
securosys.com

Seppmail (12, 20.0%)
Email Security / Secure Email
Neuenhof, Switzerland
seppmail.com

SHAREKEY (25, -3.9%)
Data Security / Encryption
Zug, Switzerland
sharekey.com

SnowHaze (3, 0.0%)
Endpoint Security / Secure Web Browsing
Zurich, Switzerland
snowhaze.com

Numbers in parentheses indicate headcount and % change in 2023.

Sonar (527, 5.6%)
Application Security /
Code Security
Vernier, Switzerland
sonarsource.com

Strong Network (32, 3.2%)
Application Security / Workspace Security
Lausanne, Switzerland
strong.network

SwissSign Group (90, 12.5%)
Data Security / Public Key Infrastructure
Glattbrugg, Switzerland
swisssign.com

Synergy Quantum (8, 33.3%)
Data Security / Encryption
Geneva, Switzerland
synergyquantum.swiss

TECH5 (61, 29.8%)
IAM / Identity Management
Geneva, Switzerland
tech5.ai

Threatray (12, 20.0%)
Threat Intelligence / IoC Intelligence
Biel/Bienne, Switzerland
threatray.com

Trustless.ai (3, -40.0%)
Endpoint Security /
Secured Devices
Geneva, Switzerland
trustless.ai

Tune Insight (13, 18.2%)
Data Security / Secure Collaboration
Lausanne, Switzerland
tuneinsight.com

United Security Providers (75, -3.9%)
Network Security / Firewalls
Bern, Switzerland
united-security-providers.com

Vereign (17, 13.3%)
IAM
Zug, Switzerland
vereign.com

Wisekey (104, -3.7%)
IoT Security / Hardware
Geneva, Switzerland
wisekey.com

Xorlab (28, 3.7%)
Email Security / Zero Day Defense
Zurich, Switzerland
xorlab.com

ZITADEL (14, -17.6%)
IAM / Identity Management
St. Gallen, Schweiz, Switzerland
zitadel.com

Taiwan

BlockChain Security (20, 66.7%)
Data Security / Blockchain
Taipei, Taipei, Taiwan
chainsecurity.asia

Cellopoint International Corporation (31, -6.1%)
Email Security / Gateways
New Taipei City, Taiwan
cellopoint.com

Cycraft (81, 44.6%)
Operations / Incident Management
Taipei City, Banqiao District, Taiwan
cycraft.com

D-Link Systems (542, 9.1%)
Network Security / UTM
Taipei City, Taiwan
dlink.com

DragonSoft (21, -19.2%)
Application Security
/ Firewalls
New Taipei City, Taiwan
dragonsoft.com.tw

Egis Technology (147, -2.6%)
IAM / Authentication
Taipei, Taiwan
egistec.com

GoTrustID Inc. (16, -15.8%)
IAM / Authentication
Taichung City, Taiwan
gotrustid.com

Nexcom (282, 8.1%)
Network Security
/ Hardware
New Taipei City, Taiwan
nexcom.com

Turkey

BRANDEFENSE (64, 42.2%)
Threat Intelligence /
Managed Security Services
Ankura, Turkey
brandefense.io

CodeThreat (8, 33.3%)
Application Security / SAST
Istanbul, Turkey
codethreat.com

Deepinfo (24, 9.1%)
Operations / Attack Surface Management
Istanbul, Turkey
deepinfo.com

klearis (4, 0.0%)
Data Security / Content Disarm And Reconstruction
Ankara, Turkey
klearis.com

Kondukto (23, 9.5%)
Application Security
Istanbul, Turkey
kondukto.io

Labris Networks (42, 75.0%)
Network Security / UTM
Ankara, Turkey
labrisnetworks.com

Logsign (65, -13.3%)
Security Analytics / SIEM
Istanbul, Turkey
logsign.com

OctoXlabs (10, 66.7%)
GRC / Attack Surface Management
Istanbul, Turkey
octoxlabs.com

Picus Security (234, 8.3%)
Operations / Breach And Attack Simulation
Ankara, Turkey
picussecurity.com

TR7 (25, 38.9%)
Network Security / Firewalls
Ankara, Turkey
tr7.com

Zemana (11, -8.3%)
Endpoint Security / Anti-virus
Ankara, Turkey
zemana.com

Ukraine

RMRF TECH (11, 22.2%)
Deception / Host Environments
Kyiv, Ukraine
rmrf.tech

Romad (21, -12.5%)
Endpoint Security /
Anti-virus
Kiev, Ukraine
romad.io

SOC Prime (99, -10.8%)
Threat Intelligence / Threat Intelligence Platform
Kiev, Ukraine
socprime.com

United Arab Emirates

ANY.RUN (89, 161.8%)
Endpoint Security / Malware Analysis
Dubai, United Arab Emirates
any.run

SpiderSilk (43, 2.4%)
GRC / Attack Surface Management
Dubai, United Arab Emirates
spidersilk.com

**Numbers in parentheses indicate headcount and % change in 2023.*

VirusRescuers (26, -3.7%)
MSSP / MDR
Dubai, United Arab Emirates
virusrescuers.com

United Kingdom

1E (513, 8.2%)
Endpoint Security / Patch Management
London, United Kingdom
1e.com

2T Security (16, 33.3%)
MSSP / Monitoring
Victoria, United Kingdom
2t-security.com

4Secure (17, 41.7%)
Network Security / Firewalls
Northampton, Northamptonshire, United Kingdom
4-secure.com

A&O IT Group (266, 3.5%)
MSSP / MDR
Bracknell, Berkshire, United Kingdom
aoitgroup.com

Acuity Risk Management (16, 14.3%)
GRC / Risk Management
London, United Kingdom
acuityrm.com

Adarma (301, -5.3%)
MSSP / MDR
Edinburgh, United Kingdom
adarma.com

Angoka (34, 21.4%)
IoT Security / Automotive
Belfast, United Kingdom
angoka.io

AppCheck (83, 0.0%)
GRC / Vulnerabilities
Leeds, United Kingdom
appcheck-ng.com

Approov (16, 23.1%)
API Security
Edinburgh, United Kingdom
approov.io

Armadillo Managed Services Limited (55, -6.8%)
MSSP / Managed Security Services
Hayes, United Kingdom
wearearmadillo.com

ArQit (150, -8.5%)
Network Security / Quantum
London, United Kingdom
arqit.io

Assuria (19, 0.0%)
Security Analytics / SIEM
Reading, United Kingdom
assuria.com

AuthLogics (6, -25.0%)
IAM / Authentication
Bracknell, United Kingdom
authlogics.com

Ava Security (81, -24.3%)
Security Analytics / Monitoring
Uxbridge, United Kingdom
avasecurity.com

Aves Netsec (4, -20.0%)
Endpoint Security / Patch Management
London, United Kingdom
avesnetsec.com

B-Secur (76, -2.6%)
IAM / Authentication
Belfast, United Kingdom
b-secur.com

BAE Systems (38342, 6.4%)
MSSP / Managed Security Services
Guildford, United Kingdom
baesystems.com

Becrypt (57, 23.9%)
Data Security / Encryption
London, United Kingdom
becrypt.com

BitNinja (30, -14.3%)
Endpoint Security / Servers
London, United Kingdom
bitninja.io

Blackbelt Smartphone Defence Ltd (33, 57.1%)
Data Security / Data Erasure And Destruction
Kendal, United Kingdom
blackbeltdefence.com

BlackDice Cyber (14, 366.7%)
Network Security / Security For Gateways
Leeds, Horsforth, United Kingdom
blackdice.io

Blacklight by Owlgaze (11, -50.0%)
Operations / Threat Hunting
London, United Kingdom
blacklight.owlgaze.com

Blancco (352, 3.8%)
Data Security / Data Erasure And Destruction
Bishops Stortford, United Kingdom
blancco.com

Blue Team Labs (193, 127.1%)
Training / Cyber Range
London, United Kingdom
blueteamlabs.online

Bluecat Networks (687, 55.1%)
Network Security / DNS Security
Bracknell, United Kingdom
bluecatnetworks.com

Bob's Business (29, 0.0%)
GRC / Security Awareness Training
Barnsley, United Kingdom
bobsbusiness.co.uk

Boldon James (31, -8.8%)
GRC / DLP
Farnborough, United Kingdom
boldonjames.com

Boxphish (25, 19.1%)
GRC / Security Awareness Training
London, United Kingdom
boxphish.com

Bridewell (230, -0.9%)
MSSP / SOC
Reading, United Kingdom
bridewell.com

British Telecom (78799, 7.3%)
MSSP / Managed Security Services
London, United Kingdom
bt.com

BSI Group (8263, 8.3%)
Training / Standards Certification
London, United Kingdom
bsigroup.com

Bulletproof (101, 13.5%)
MSSP / SIEM
Stevenage, United Kingdom
bulletproof.co.uk

BullGuard Ltd. (31, -24.4%)
Endpoint Security / Anti-virus
London, United Kingdom
bullguard.com

C2 Cyber (22, 4.8%)
GRC / Risk Management
London, United Kingdom
c2cyber.com

Cado Security (53, 39.5%)
Operations / Incident Management
London, United Kingdom
cadosecurity.com

Callsign (233, -19.7%)
IAM / Authentication
London, United Kingdom
callsign.com

Cambridge Intelligence (72, -1.4%)
Security Analytics / Data Visualization
Cambridge, United Kingdom
cambridge-intelligence.com

**Numbers in parentheses indicate headcount and % change in 2023.*

Cellcrypt (5, 400.0%)
Data Security / Secure Communications
London, United Kingdom
cellcrypt.com

CensorNet (59, -27.2%)
Network Security / Filtering
Basingstoke, United Kingdom
censornet.com

Cerbos (20, 66.7%)
IAM / Authorization
London, United Kingdom
cerbos.dev

Chorus Intel (38, -13.6%)
Operations / Link Analysis
Woodbridge, United Kingdom
chorusintel.com

Citicus (3, -25.0%)
GRC
London, United Kingdom
citicus.com

Claranet Cyber Security (81, -22.1%)
MSSP
London, United Kingdom
claranetcybersecurity.com

ClearSky Cyber (10, 11.1%)
Threat Intelligence / Threat Analysis
Cambridge, United Kingdom
clearskysec.com

Clearswift (95, -15.9%)
Email Security
Theale, United Kingdom
clearswift.com

Codified Security (4, 33.3%)
Application Security / Code Security
London, United Kingdom
codifiedsecurity.com

Communication Security Group (16, -23.8%)
Data Security / Secure Communications
London, United Kingdom
csghq.com

Contxt (17, 0.0%)
API Security
London, United Kingdom
bycontxt.com

CovertSwarm (32, 88.2%)
Operations / Breach And Attack Simulation
London, United Kingdom
covertswarm.com

Crossword Cybersecurity (71, -12.3%)
GRC / Risk Management
London, United Kingdom
crosswordcybersecurity.com

Crypta Labs (13, -7.1%)
Data Security / Encryption
London, United Kingdom
cryptalabs.com

Crypto Quantique (49, 16.7%)
IoT Security / Security For Embedded Systems
Egham, United Kingdom
cryptoquantique.com

CultureAI (39, 44.4%)
GRC / Security Awareness Training
Manchester, United Kingdom
culture.ai

CyberHive (32, 3.2%)
Network Security / Quantum
Newbury, United Kingdom
cyberhive.com

Cybermaniacs (18, 20.0%)
GRC / Security Awareness Training
London, United Kingdom
thecybermaniacs.com

CyberOwl (51, 18.6%)
GRC / Risk Management
Birmingham, United Kingdom
cyberowl.io

CyberSafe Ltd. (10, 66.7%)
IAM / Access Security
Longford, United Kingdom
cybersafe.com

Cyberseer (10, 11.1%)
MSSP / Threat Intelligence
London, United Kingdom
cyberseer.net

Cybersmart (69, 13.1%)
GRC / Compliance Management
London, United Kingdom
cybersmart.co.uk

CybSafe (105, -5.4%)
GRC / Security Awareness Training
London, United Kingdom
cybsafe.com

Cyjax (33, 6.5%)
Threat Intelligence
London, United Kingdom
cyjax.com

Cynalytica (6, 0.0%)
IoT Security / OT Security
Belfast, United Kingdom
cynalytica.com

CyNation (4, 0.0%)
GRC / Risk Management
London, United Kingdom
cynation.com

Cyphere (3, 50.0%)
MSSP / Vulnerabilities
Greater Manchester, GB, United Kingdom
thecyphere.com

Cyscale (16, -20.0%)
Operations / Posture Management
London, United Kingdom
cyscale.com

Cytix (8, 166.7%)
Operations / Penetration Testing
Manchester, United Kingdom
cytix.io

DarkBeam (7, -22.2%)
Threat Intelligence
London, United Kingdom
darkbeam.com

DarkInvader (9, 80.0%)
Threat Intelligence / Dark Web
Leeds, United Kingdom
darkinvader.io

Data Encryption Systems (5, 25.0%)
Data Security / DRM
Taunton, United Kingdom
des.co.uk

Deep-Secure (23, 15.0%)
Network Security / Air Gap
Malvern, United Kingdom
deep-secure.com

Deepnet Security (24, 84.6%)
IAM / Identity Management
London, United Kingdom
deepnetsecurity.com

DeepView (6, 20.0%)
Data Security / Monitoring
London, United Kingdom
deepview.com

Device Authority (32, -3.0%)
IAM / Authentication
Reading, United Kingdom
deviceauthority.com

DigitalXRAID (52, 13.0%)
MSSP / Monitoring
Doncaster, South Yorkshire, United Kingdom
digitalxraid.com

DynaRisk (19, -13.6%)
GRC / Risk Management
London, United Kingdom
dynarisk.com

Egress (307, 4.1%)
Email Security
London, United Kingdom
egress.com

Elemendar (20, 11.1%)
Threat Intelligence / Threat Intelligence Analysis
Stourbridge, NC, United Kingdom
elemendar.com

**Numbers in parentheses indicate headcount and % change in 2023.*

Elliptic (168, -17.6%)
GRC
London, United Kingdom
elliptic.co

Enclave Networks (9, -10.0%)
Network Security / Zero Trust Networking
London, United Kingdom
enclave.io

Encode (61, -24.7%)
Security Analytics
London, United Kingdom
encodegroup.com

Encore (10, 0.0%)
Operations / Attack Surface Management
Maidenhead, United Kingdom
encore.io

erika (7, 40.0%)
Email Security / Anti-scam
London, United Kingdom
erika.app

ESProfiler (7, 133.3%)
Operations / Security Tool Effectiveness Platform
Manchester, United Kingdom
esprofiler.com

Exacttrak Ltd (8, -11.1%)
Data Security / Managed Devices To Protect Laptop Data
Banbury, United Kingdom
exacttrak.com

eXate (30, -6.2%)
API Security / Monitoring
West End, United Kingdom
exate.com

Exonar (5, -54.5%)
GRC / Data Discovery
Newbury, United Kingdom
exonar.com

EY (345449, -1.6%)
MSSP / Managed Security Services
London, United Kingdom
ey.com

FACT360 (12, 9.1%)
Network Security / Monitoring
Waterlooville, United Kingdom
fact360.co

Falanx Cyber (48, -2.0%)
MSSP / MDR
Reading, Berkshire, United Kingdom
falanxcyber.com

Featurespace (393, -1.3%)
Fraud Prevention
Cambridge, United Kingdom
featurespace.com

forghetti (3, 0.0%)
IAM / Credential Security
Winchester, United Kingdom
forghetti.com

FortKnoxster (4, -33.3%)
Data Security / Encryption
Gibraltar, United Kingdom
fortknoxster.com

Fraud.com (28, 7.7%)
Fraud Prevention / Identity Verification
London, United Kingdom
fraud.com

Galaxkey (33, -5.7%)
Data Security / Secure Data Sharing
London, United Kingdom
galaxkey.com

Garrison (189, 32.2%)
Network Security / Secure Web Browsing
London, United Kingdom
garrison.com

GBMS Tech (16, 0.0%)
Endpoint Security / Monitoring
London, United Kingdom
gbmstech.com

Glasswall Solutions (129, 30.3%)
Operations / Document Security
West End, United Kingdom
glasswallsolutions.com

Goldilock (30, 25.0%)
Network Security / Air Gap
London, United Kingdom
goldilock.com

Hack the Box (1620, 36.4%)
Training / Cyber Range
Kent, United Kingdom
hackthebox.eu

Hicomply (16, -20.0%)
GRC / Compliance Management
Durham, United Kingdom
hicomply.com

HighGround.io (6, 0.0%)
GRC / Compliance Management
Perth, United Kingdom
highground.io

Humio (40, -37.5%)
Security Analytics / Logs
London, United Kingdom
humio.com

idappcom (6, 0.0%)
Network Security / Traffic Analysis
Ludlow, United Kingdom
idappcom.com

Idax Software (5, 25.0%)
IAM
Petersfield, United Kingdom
idaxsoftware.com

IDENprotect (18, 63.6%)
IAM / Authentication
London, United Kingdom
idenprotect.com

Immersive Labs (329, -0.3%)
Training / Cyber Range
Bristol, United Kingdom
immersivelabs.com

incident.io (84, 100.0%)
Operations / Slack Automation
London, United Kingdom
incident.io

Informer (15, -11.8%)
GRC / Attack Surface Management
London, United Kingdom
informer.io

Intruder (70, 59.1%)
GRC / Vulnerabilities
London, United Kingdom
intruder.io

Ioetec (6, 0.0%)
IoT Security / Endpoint Protection
Sheffield, United Kingdom
ioetec.com

iomart (392, 9.5%)
MSSP / Managed Security Services
Glasgow, United Kingdom
iomart.com

IProov (201, 16.2%)
IAM / Authentication
London, United Kingdom
iproov.com

IRM Security (46, -25.8%)
GRC / Risk Management
Cheltenham, United Kingdom
irmsecurity.com

ISARR (8, 60.0%)
GRC / Asset Management
London, United Kingdom
isarr.com

IStorage (27, 0.0%)
Data Security / Hardware
Perivale, United Kingdom
istorage-uk.com

**Numbers in parentheses indicate headcount and % change in 2023.*

ITC Secure Networking (97, -14.9%)
MSSP / Managed Security Services
London, United Kingdom
itcsecure.com

IVPN (8, -20.0%)
Network Security / VPN/Proxy
Gibraltar, United Kingdom
ivpn.net

iZOOlogic (22, 69.2%)
Threat Intelligence
London, United Kingdom
izoologic.com

Jetstack (36, -32.1%)
Operations
United Kingdom
jetstack.io

Keepnet Labs (42, 23.5%)
Email Security
London, United Kingdom
keepnetlabs.com

KETS Quantum Security (29, 20.8%)
Data Security / Secure Communications
Bristol, United Kingdom
kets-quantum.com

Keyless (60, -3.2%)
IAM / Authentication
London, United Kingdom
keyless.io

Kovrr (42, -2.3%)
GRC / Risk Management
London, United Kingdom
kovrr.com

KYND (46, 53.3%)
GRC / Risk Management
London, United Kingdom
kynd.io

Liopa (13, 44.4%)
IAM / Authentication
Belfast, United Kingdom
liopa.ai

Lunio (71, 14.5%)
Fraud Prevention / Advertising-related
Chorley, Lancashire, United Kingdom
ppcprotect.com

Lynx Tech (68, 7.9%)
Fraud Prevention / Monitoring
London, United Kingdom
lynxtech.com

MacKeeper (80, -9.1%)
Endpoint Security / Anti-virus
London, United Kingdom
kromtech.com

Maidsafe (19, 0.0%)
Data Security / Blockchain
Ayr, United Kingdom
maidsafe.net

MetaCompliance (197, 13.9%)
GRC / Compliance Management
London, United Kingdom
metacompliance.com

Meterian (12, 33.3%)
Application Security / Open Source Management
North Kensington, United Kingdom
meterian.io

Metomic (52, 73.3%)
Data Security / Data Discovery
Liverpool, United Kingdom
metomic.io

Micro Focus (5742, -40.3%)
Security Analytics / SIEM
Newbury, United Kingdom
microfocus.com

Mimecast (2355, 7.7%)
Email Security / Microsoft
London, United Kingdom
mimecast.com

MIRACL (20, -13.0%)
IAM / Authentication
London, United Kingdom
miracl.com

My1login (15, 7.1%)
IAM / Identity Management
London, United Kingdom
my1login.com

MyCena (14, 0.0%)
IAM / Credential Security
London, United Kingdom
mycena.co

Mymobilesecurity (4, -20.0%)
Endpoint Security / Mobile Device Security
London, United Kingdom
mymobilesecurity.com

Navaho Technologies (10, 25.0%)
Endpoint Security / Secure Linux
Brockenhurst, United Kingdom
navaho.co.uk

Netacea (72, -28.7%)
Fraud Prevention / Bot Security
Manchester, United Kingdom
netacea.com

Netcraft (167, 29.5%)
GRC / Compliance Management
Bath, United Kingdom
netcraft.com

Nettoken (5, 25.0%)
GRC / Credential Security
London, United Kingdom
nettoken.io

Network Critical (28, 27.3%)
Network Security / IPS
Caversham, United Kingdom
networkcritical.com

Next DLP (86, 4.9%)
GRC / Insider Threats
London, United Kingdom
qush.com

Nexus Industrial Memory (6, 0.0%)
Data Security
West Sussex, United Kingdom
nexusindustrialmemory.com

Nominet (323, 7.7%)
Network Security / Threat Detection
Oxford, United Kingdom
nominet.com

NTT Ltd. (18412, -8.1%)
MSSP / Managed Security Services
London, United Kingdom
hello.global.ntt

Nu Quantum (39, 69.6%)
Data Security / Quantum
London, United Kingdom
nu-quantum.com

Omniquad Ltd. (23, -11.5%)
Endpoint Security / Anti-spyware
London, United Kingdom
omniquad.com

Onfido (588, -17.3%)
Fraud Prevention / Identity Verification
London, United Kingdom
onfido.com

Orpheus Cyber (32, 0.0%)
Threat Intelligence / OSINT
London, United Kingdom
orpheus-cyber.com

Osirium (40, -14.9%)
IAM / Access Security
Theale, United Kingdom
osirium.com

OutThink (43, 34.4%)
GRC / Monitoring
London, United Kingdom
outthink.io

**Numbers in parentheses indicate headcount and % change in 2023.*

Overe.io (4, 0.0%)
Application Security / SaaS Security
London, United Kingdom
overe.io

Oxford Biochronometrics (8, -11.1%)
Fraud Prevention / Click Fraud Prevention
London, United Kingdom
oxford-biochron.com

P3 Audit (5, 0.0%)
GRC / Compliance Management
Covent Garden, United Kingdom
p3audit.com

Palqee (11, -26.7%)
GRC / Compliance Management
London, United Kingdom
palqee.com

Panaseer (135, -2.9%)
Operations / Security Management
London, United Kingdom
panaseer.com

Pervade Software (10, 0.0%)
GRC
Cardiff, United Kingdom
pervade-software.com

Pirean (Echostar) (30, -9.1%)
IAM / Identity Management
London, United Kingdom
pirean.com

PortSwigger (196, 40.0%)
GRC / Vulnerabilities
Knutsford, United Kingdom
portswigger.net

Post-Quantum (9, -25.0%)
IAM / Authentication
London, United Kingdom
post-quantum.com

PQShield Ltd (62, 34.8%)
Data Security / Quantum
Oxford, United Kingdom
pqshield.com

Prevalent AI (136, 6.2%)
GRC / Risk Management
London, United Kingdom
prevalent.ai

Preventon (3, 0.0%)
Endpoint Security / Anti-virus
Mayfair, United Kingdom
preventon.com

Privitar (67, -54.7%)
Data Security / Data Masking
London, United Kingdom
privitar.com

Proteus Cyber (5, 0.0%)
GRC
London, United Kingdom
proteuscyber.com

Pryvate Now (46, 12.2%)
Data Security / Secure Communications
Jersey, United Kingdom
pryvatenow.com

PureID (12, -7.7%)
IAM / Authentication
Heydon, Royston, United Kingdom
pureid.io

Push Security (26, 52.9%)
Operations / Application Security
London, United Kingdom
pushsecurity.com

Qredo (124, -24.9%)
Data Security / Encryption
London, United Kingdom
qredo.com

Quantum Dice (23, 76.9%)
Data Security / Quantum
Oxford, United Kingdom
quantum-dice.com

Quorum Cyber (223, 11.5%)
MSSP / MDR
Edinburgh, United Kingdom
quorumcyber.com

Rawstream (3, 0.0%)
Network Security / DNS Security
London, United Kingdom
rawstream.com

RazorSecure (46, 9.5%)
IoT Security / Automotive
Basingstoke, United Kingdom
razorsecure.com

RealVNC (108, 12.5%)
Network Security / Access Security
Cambridge, United Kingdom
realvnc.com

Red Sift (111, 3.7%)
Endpoint Security / Open Platform
London, United Kingdom
redsift.com

RedScan (87, -23.0%)
MSSP / MDR
London, United Kingdom
redscan.com

Regulativ.ai (7, 16.7%)
GRC / Compliance Management
London, United Kingdom
regulativ.ai

Report-Uri (3, -25.0%)
Network Security / Website Security
Clitheroe, United Kingdom
report-uri.com

Risk Ledger (33, -23.3%)
GRC / Risk Management
London, United Kingdom
riskledger.com

Risk.Ident (74, 5.7%)
Fraud Prevention / Fraud Detection
London, United Kingdom
riskident.com

Rootshell Security (46, 12.2%)
GRC
Basingstoke, Hampshire, United Kingdom
rootshellsecurity.net

Runecast Solutions (68, -8.1%)
Operations / Vulnerabilities
London, United Kingdom
runecast.com

S2T (51, 21.4%)
Threat Intelligence / Dark Web
Slough, United Kingdom
s2t.ai

SaltDNA (16, -20.0%)
Data Security / Secure Communications
Belfast, United Kingdom
saltdna.com

Salviol Global Analytics (22, 15.8%)
Fraud Prevention / Fraud Detection
Reading, United Kingdom
salviol.com

Sealit (11, -15.4%)
Data Security / Secure Communications
London, United Kingdom
sealit.id

Searchlight Cyber (57, 26.7%)
Threat Intelligence / Dark Web
Portsmouth, United Kingdom
slcyber.io

Secon Cyber (211, 74.4%)
MSSP / MDR
Surrey, United Kingdom
seconcyber.com

SecuPi (50, 21.9%)
Application Security / Monitoring
London, United Kingdom
secupi.com

**Numbers in parentheses indicate headcount and % change in 2023.*

SecureEnvoy (3, -25.0%)
GRC / DLP
Cardiff, United Kingdom
geolang.com

SecureFlag (24, 33.3%)
Training
London, United Kingdom
secureflag.com

SecurEnvoy (24, 0.0%)
IAM / Authentication
Basingstoke,
United Kingdom
securenvoy.com

SecurityHQ (383, 26.0%)
MSSP / MDR
London, United Kingdom
securityhq.com

SecurityZONES (5, -28.6%)
Threat Intelligence
/ Spamhaus
London, United Kingdom
securityzones.net

Secuware (9, -25.0%)
Data Security / Database
Security
London, United Kingdom
secuware.com

Seedata (5, -28.6%)
Deception / Leaked Data
London, United Kingdom
seedata.io

Senseon (83, -1.2%)
Security Analytics / Incident
Management
London, United Kingdom
senseon.io

SentryBay (32, -11.1%)
Endpoint Security /
Anti-malware
London, United Kingdom
sentrybay.com

Sharkgate (12, -20.0%)
Network Security / Firewalls
London, United Kingdom
sharkgate.net

Silobreaker (66, -1.5%)
Threat Intelligence / Threat
Intelligence Management
London, United Kingdom
silobreaker.com

SIRP (21, 31.2%)
Operations
London, United Kingdom
sirp.io

Sitehop (13, 85.7%)
Network Security
Sheffield, United Kingdom
sitehop.co.uk

Skurio (33, -13.2%)
Threat Intelligence / Brand
Belfast, United Kingdom
skurio.com

Smoothwall (151, 11.8%)
Network Security / UTM
Leeds, United Kingdom
smoothwall.com

Snyk (1128, -11.5%)
Application Security /
Vulnerabilities
London, United Kingdom
snyk.io

SOCAutomation (6, 50.0%)
Operations / XDR
Witney, United Kingdom
socautomation.com

Socura (22, 15.8%)
MSSP / MDR
London, United Kingdom
socura.co.uk

SolSoft (24, 4.3%)
Operations / Policy
Management
Bristol, United Kingdom
solsoft.co.uk

Sophos (4592, -1.3%)
Endpoint Security /
Anti-virus
Abingdon, United Kingdom
sophos.com

Soveren (28, -12.5%)
API Security / Compliance
Management
London, United Kingdom
soveren.io

Spirent Communications (2053, -1.0%)
Testing / Security
Instrumentation
Crawley, United Kingdom
spirent.com

Strata Security Solutions (7, 16.7%)
GRC / Asset Management
Croydon, United Kingdom
stratasecurity.co.uk

Strike.sh (36, -2.7%)
GRC / Penetration Testing
London, United Kingdom
strike.sh

Surevine (23, -8.0%)
Data Security / Secure
Collaboration
Guildford, United Kingdom
surevine.com

Surf Security (36, 157.1%)
Network Security / Secure
Web Browsing
London, United Kingdom
surf.security/

swIDch (9, -10.0%)
IAM
London, United Kingdom
swidch.com

SwivelSecure (39, -11.4%)
IAM / Authentication
Wetherby, United Kingdom
swivelsecure.com

Sword Active Risk (56, -20.0%)
GRC / Risk Management
Maidenhead,
United Kingdom
sword-activerisk.com

Teskalabs (18, 5.9%)
Network Security / Gateways
London, United Kingdom
teskalabs.com

The Cyberfort Group (107, 15.1%)
MSSP / SOC
Thatcham, United Kingdom
cyberfortgroup.com

Think Cyber Security (14, 55.6%)
GRC / Security Aware-
ness Training
London, United Kingdom
thinkcyber.co.uk

ThreatAware (19, 0.0%)
Operations / Asset
Management
London, United Kingdom
threataware.com

ThreatSpike (20, 17.6%)
MSSP / MDR
London, United Kingdom
threatspike.com

Titania Ltd. (90, 57.9%)
GRC / Configuration
Management
Worcester, United Kingdom
titania.com

Torsion Information Security (12, -25.0%)
Data Security / Monitoring
London, United Kingdom
torsionis.com

Tricerion (4, -20.0%)
IAM / Credential Security
Reading, United Kingdom
tricerion.com

TryHackMe (2118, 45.4%)
Training / Cyber Range
London, United Kingdom
tryhackme.com

Tyk (156, -22.4%)
API Security / Gateways
London, United Kingdom
tyk.io

**Numbers in parentheses indicate headcount and % change in 2023.*

UM-Labs (9, 12.5%)
Endpoint Security / Operating System Security
London, United Kingdom
um-labs.com

usecure (40, 25.0%)
GRC / Security Awareness Training
Manchester, United Kingdom
usecure.io

Vaultmatix (4, 0.0%)
Data Security / Data Rooms
London, United Kingdom
vaultmatix.com

Venari Security (51, -3.8%)
Network Security / Traffic Analysis
London, United Kingdom
venarisecurity.com

Wault (9, 28.6%)
Data Security / Secure Data Sharing
London, United Kingdom
wault.com

Yes Security (9, 800.0%)
Application Security
United Kingdom
yes-security.com

Yoti (390, 5.4%)
Fraud Prevention / Identity Verification
London, United Kingdom
yoti.com

United States of America (See Next Section)

Venezuela

Inteligensa (125, 9.7%)
IAM / Smart Card Solutions
Caracas, Venezuela
inteligensa.com

Vietnam

1LINK (3, -40.0%)
GRC / Vulnerabilities
Ha Noi, Ba Dinh, Vietnam
1link.vn

SecurityBox (4, -33.3%)
Network Security / Gateways
Hanoi, Vietnam
securitybox.vn

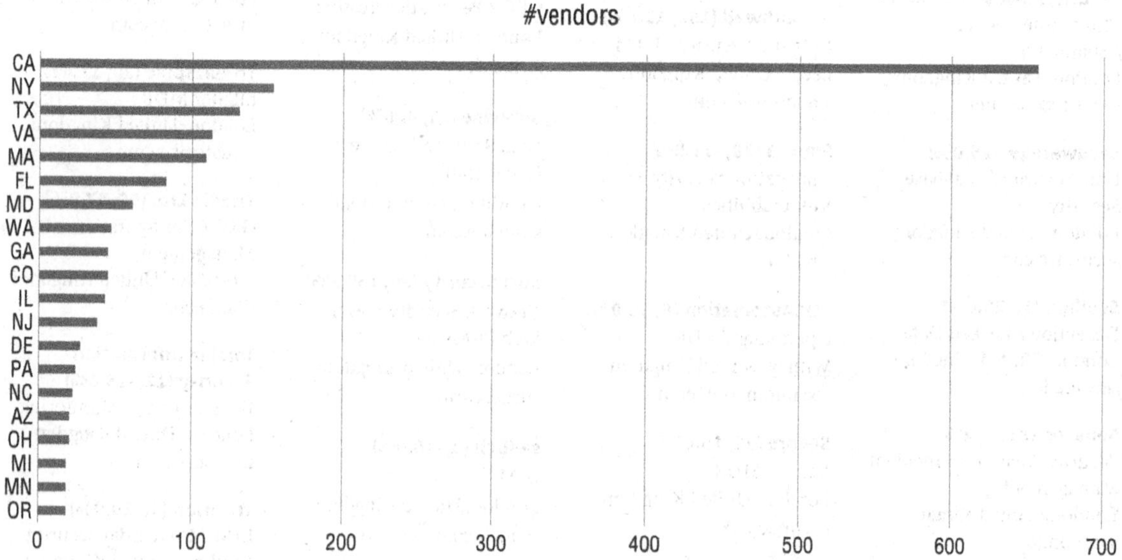

Vendors by US State

State	Number of Vendors
CA	657
NY	154
TX	131
VA	113
MA	109
FL	83
MD	61
WA	47
GA	45
CO	45
IL	43
NJ	38
DE	27
PA	24
NC	22
AZ	20
OH	20
MI	18
MN	18
OR	18
UT	17
DC	17
CT	16
NV	15
WI	9
KS	8
TN	8
MO	7
AL	6
SC	6
NH	5
ID	5
IN	4
IA	3
MT	3
LA	3
SD	3
OK	3
NE	2
ME	2
NM	2
WY	2
WV	1
KY	1
VT	1
AR	1
MS	1

Alabama

Adtran Inc. (2052, 26.0%)
Network Security / Firewalls
Huntsville, AL
adtran.com

Cyber Operations LLC (5, -28.6%)
Operations / Access Security
Pelham, AL
cyberoperations.com

Diamond Fortress Technologies (3, -25.0%)
IAM / Authentication
Birmingham, AL
diamondfortress.com

PhishFirewall (11, -15.4%)
GRC / Security Awareness Training
Huntsville, AL
phishfirewall.com

Sentar (313, 3.3%)
Application Security / Code Security
Huntsville, AL
sentar.com

Arkansas

Bastazo (6, 0.0%)
GRC / Vulnerabilities
Fayetteville, AR
bastazo.com

Arizona

Avertium (209, -10.3%)
MSSP / Managed Security Services
Phoenix, AZ
avertium.com

Axway (1729, -4.9%)
GRC / Secure Data Sharing
Phoenix, AZ
axway.com

Bishop Fox (389, -8.2%)
Operations / Breach And Attack Simulation
Tempe, AZ
bishopfox.com

Celltrust Corporation (20, 11.1%)
Data Security / Secure Communications
Scottsdale, AZ
celltrust.com

Early Warning (1308, 12.5%)
Fraud Prevention / Assurance
Scottsdale, AZ
earlywarning.com

Edgio (1161, -9.3%)
Network Security / DDoS Defense
Scottsdale, AZ
edg.io

Gen Digital (2011, 44.0%)
Endpoint Security / Anti-virus
Tempe, AZ
gendigital.com

Lumifi Cyber (69, 35.3%)
MSSP / MDR
Scottsdale, AZ
lumificyber.com

MegaplanIT (28, -3.5%)
MSSP / Managed Security Services
Scottsdale, AZ
megaplanit.com

Mosaic451 (25, -58.3%)
MSSP / SOC
Phoenix, AZ
mosaic451.com

Privoro (55, 0.0%)
Endpoint Security / Hardened Cases For Mobile Phones
Chandler, AZ
privoro.com

SiteLock (98, -10.1%)
Network Security / Website Security
Scottsdale, AZ
sitelock.com

Stealth Software (5, 25.0%)
Data Security / Encryption
Scottsdale, AZ
stealth-soft.com

Synsaber (8, -27.3%)
IoT Security / Monitoring
Chandler, AZ
synsaber.com

Trusona (37, 0.0%)
IAM / Authentication
Scottsdale, AZ
trusona.com

VIA3 Corperation (4, -66.7%)
Data Security / Secure Communications
Scottsdale, AZ
via3.com

California

0pass (7, 133.3%)
IAM / Authentication
Los Angeles, CA
0pass.com

42Crunch (44, -13.7%)
API Security
Irvine, CA
42crunch.com

4CRisk (29, -6.5%)
GRC / Compliance Management
San Francisco, CA
4crisk.ai

A10 Networks (721, -1.1%)
Network Security / DDoS Defense
San Jose, CA
a10networks.com

Abnormal Security (584, 2.8%)
Email Security / Defense Against Phishing
San Francisco, CA
abnormalsecurity.com

Abusix (35, -5.4%)
Threat Intelligence
San Jose, CA
abusix.com

Acalvio Technologies (75, 2.7%)
Deception
Santa Clara, CA
acalvio.com

Accuknox (146, 49.0%)
Endpoint Security
Cupertino, CA
accuknox.com

Accurics (10, -16.7%)
GRC / Policy Management
Pleasanton, CA
accurics.com

Active Cypher (15, 7.1%)
Network Security / DLP
Newport Beach,, CA
activecypher.com

ActZero (65, -30.1%)
MSSP / MDR
Menlo Park, CA
actzero.ai

Aegify (12, -7.7%)
GRC / Risk Management
San Jose, CA
aegify.com

Afero (47, -2.1%)
IoT Security / Hardware
Los Altos, CA
afero.io

Agari (65, 41.3%)
Email Security
Foster City, CA
agari.com

Aiprise (10, 400.0%)
Fraud Prevention / Identity Verification
Santa Clara, CA
aiprise.com

Airgap Networks (45, 25.0%)
Network Security / Segmentation
Santa Clara, CA
airgap.io

**Numbers in parentheses indicate headcount and % change in 2023.*

AKITRA (42, 50.0%)
GRC / Compliance Management
Sunnyvale, CA
akitra.com

Akto (15, 114.3%)
Application Security / Visibility
Palo Alto, CA
www.akto.io

Alcatraz.ai (97, 14.1%)
IAM / Authentication
Cupertino, CA
alcatraz.ai

AlertEnterprise (268, 20.7%)
IAM / Physical IAM
Fremont, CA
alertenterprise.com

alertsec (6, 20.0%)
GRC / Monitoring
Palo Alto, CA
alertsec.com

Allgress (23, -8.0%)
GRC / Compliance Management
Livermore, CA
allgress.com

Allied Telesis (926, 5.3%)
Network Security / Firewalls
San Jose, CA
alliedtelesis.com

Allthenticate (12, 0.0%)
IAM / Authentication
Goleta, CA
allthenticate.net

AlphaGuardian Networks (5, -16.7%)
IoT Security / OT Security
San Ramon, CA
alphaguardian.net

AlphaSOC (18, 80.0%)
Operations / Security Analytics
San Francisco, CA
alphasoc.com

Altitude Networks (3, -50.0%)
Data Security / Monitoring
San Francisco, CA
altitudenetworks.com

Ananda Networks (4, 0.0%)
Network Security / Segmentation
San Francisco, CA
ananda.net

AnChain.ai (36, -5.3%)
Security Analytics / Forensics
San Jose, CA
anchain.ai

Anchorage (336, -11.3%)
Data Security / Secure Storage
San Francisco, CA
anchorage.com

Anchore (82, 28.1%)
Endpoint Security / Container Security
Montecito, CA
anchore.com

anecdotes (109, 31.3%)
GRC / Compliance Management
Palo Alto, CA
anecdotes.ai

Anetac (16, 0.0%)
Stealth
Los Altos, CA
anetac.com

Anjuna (50, -29.6%)
Data Security / Runtime Security
Palo Alto, CA
anjuna.io

Anomali (286, -1.0%)
Threat Intelligence / Threat Intelligence Platform
Redwood City, CA
anomali.com

Anvilogic (81, 15.7%)
Operations / SOC
Palo Alto, CA
anvilogic.com

APIsec.ai (53, 1.9%)
API Security
San Francisco, CA
apisec.ai

Apollo Information Systems (63, 65.8%)
MSSP / Managed Security Services
Los Gatos, CA
apollo-is.com

Apolloshield (5, 0.0%)
IoT Security / Drones
Palo Alto, CA
apolloshield.com

Apona (12, 50.0%)
Application Security / SAST
Roseville, CA
apona.ai

Apozy (17, -41.4%)
Endpoint Security / Filtering
San Francisco, CA
apozy.com

Appaegis (31, 24.0%)
IAM / Access Security
Palo Alto, CA
appaegis.com

AppOmni (208, 48.6%)
Operations / Configuration Management
San Francisco, CA
appomni.com

AppSealing (8, 33.3%)
Application Security
Los Angeles, CA
appsealing.com

AppVision (5, -16.7%)
Application Security / Code Security
San Francisco, CA
appvision.net

Apricorn (31, 10.7%)
Data Security / Secure Storage
Poway, CA
apricorn.com

Aptible (29, 0.0%)
GRC / Compliance Management
San Francisco, CA
aptible.com

Araali Networks (7, -53.3%)
Application Security / Container Security
Fremont, CA
araalinetworks.com

Arista Networks (4079, 12.5%)
Network Security / NDR
Santa Clara, CA
arista.com

Arkose Labs (214, -11.6%)
Fraud Prevention / Bot Security
San Francisco, CA
arkoselabs.com

Armis (764, 8.2%)
IoT Security / Asset Management
Palo Alto, CA
armis.com

Armorblox (34, -71.4%)
Email Security / Defense Against Phishing
Cupertino, CA
armorblox.com

ArmorCode (125, 71.2%)
Application Security / Posture Management
Palo Alto, CA
armorcode.com

Array Networks (OSS Corp.) (219, 7.3%)
Network Security / VPN/Proxy
Milpitas, CA
arraynetworks.com

Aruba Networks (5710, 3.7%)
Network Security / Monitoring
Santa Clara, CA
arubanetworks.com

**Numbers in parentheses indicate headcount and % change in 2023.*

Aryaka (589, 1.2%)
Network Security / SASE
San Mateo, CA
aryaka.com

Asimily (66, 43.5%)
IoT Security / Healthcare
Sunnyvale, CA
asimily.com

AT&T Cybersecurity (62, -10.1%)
Security Analytics / SIEM
San Mateo, CA
cybersecurity.att.com

At-Bay (325, 12.8%)
GRC / Cyber Insurance
San Francisco, CA
at-bay.com

Atricore (8, 14.3%)
IAM
Sausalito, CA
atricore.com

AttackFlow (3, -25.0%)
Application Security / Code Security
San Francisco, CA
attackflow.com

AttackIQ (151, -1.9%)
Testing / Security Instrumentation
San Diego, CA
attackiq.com

Attivo Networks (91, -32.6%)
Deception
Fremont, CA
attivonetworks.com

AuditBoard (781, 20.3%)
GRC / GRC Platform
Cerritos, CA
auditboard.com

Auth Armor (5, -16.7%)
IAM / Authentication
Los Angeles, CA
autharmor.com

Authentic8 (134, 8.9%)
Network Security / Secure Web Browsing
Redwood City, CA
authentic8.com

Autonomic Software (9, 0.0%)
Endpoint Security / Patch Management
Danville, CA
autonomic-software.com

Avatier (39, 11.4%)
IAM / Identity Management
Pleasanton, CA
avatier.com

Avaya (13587, -2.8%)
Network Security / VPN/Proxy
Santa Clara, CA
avaya.com

Avi Networks (38, -29.6%)
Network Security / Firewalls
Santa Clara, CA
avinetworks.com

Aviatrix (390, -8.9%)
Network Security / Firewalls
Palo Alto, CA
aviatrix.com

Avocado Systems (20, -48.7%)
Application Security / App Hardening
San Jose, CA
avocadosys.com

Awake Security (50, -3.9%)
Network Security / Monitoring
Sunnyvale, CA
awakesecurity.com

Axiad IDS (62, 3.3%)
IAM / Authentication
Santa Clara, CA
axiadids.com

Axiado (62, 19.2%)
Endpoint Security / Hardware
San Jose, CA
axiado.com

Axiom (22, 4.8%)
IAM / Identity Management
San Francisco, CA
axiom.security

Axis Security (268, 103.0%)
IAM / Access Security
San Mateo, CA
axissecurity.com

Azul (416, -22.5%)
Application Security / Runtime Security
Sunnyvale, CA
azul.com

Baffle (54, 14.9%)
Data Security / Database Security
Santa Clara, CA
baffle.io

Balbix (146, 29.2%)
GRC / Asset Management
San Jose, CA
balbix.com

Banyan Cloud (54, 25.6%)
Operations / Posture Management
San Jose, CA
banyancloud.io

Banyan Security (64, -1.5%)
Network Security / Zero Trust Networking
San Francisco, CA
banyansecurity.io

Barracuda Networks (2146, 17.0%)
Network Security / Anti-spam
Campbell, CA
barracuda.com

Beachhead Solutions (14, 0.0%)
Endpoint Security / Device Management
San Jose, CA
beachheadsolutions.com

Bearer (29, 20.8%)
Application Security
San Francisco, CA
bearer.com

Bedrock (21, 40.0%)
Data Security / Posture Management
San Francisco, CA
bedrock.security

Behaviosec (24, -36.8%)
Fraud Prevention / Monitoring
San Francisco, CA
behaviosec.com

Belkasoft (21, -8.7%)
Operations / Forensics
Palo Alto, CA
belkasoft.com

Beyond Security (33, -10.8%)
GRC / Vulnerabilities
San Jose, CA
beyondsecurity.com

BeyondID (191, 0.5%)
MSSP / Managed Security Services
San Francisco, CA
beyondid.com

Binarly (26, 30.0%)
Endpoint Security / Firmware
Pasadena, CA
binarly.io

Bionic (103, -8.8%)
API Security / Posture Management
Palo Alto, CA
bionic.ai

**Numbers in parentheses indicate headcount and % change in 2023.*

Bitdiscovery (3, 0.0%)
GRC / Asset Management
Santa Clara, CA
bitdiscovery.com

BitGlass (36, -36.8%)
Security Analytics / Incident Management
Campbell, CA
bitglass.com

Bitwarden (162, 46.0%)
IAM / Credential Security
Santa Barbara, CA
bitwarden.com

BlastWave (19, 11.8%)
Network Security / Segmentation
Mountain View, CA
blastwaveinc.com

Bloombase (18, -28.0%)
Data Security / Encryption
Redwood City, CA
bloombase.com

BluBracket (6, -60.0%)
Application Security / Software Development Security
Palo Alto, CA
blubracket.com

Blue Lava (12, -76.5%)
GRC / Security Program Management
Menlo Park, CA
blue-lava.net

BlueCedar (44, 41.9%)
Endpoint Security / Mobile Device Security
San Francisco, CA
bluecedar.com

BOLDEND (17, 13.3%)
Stealth
San Diego, CA
boldend.com

Bolster (75, 27.1%)
Email Security / Defense Against Phishing
Los Altos, CA
bolster.ai

Borneo (142, 144.8%)
GRC / Compliance Management
San Francisco, CA
borneo.io

Bornio (12, 0.0%)
Data Security / Data Flows
Menlo Park, CA
bornio.com

BreachRx (17, 21.4%)
GRC / Incident Management
San Francisco, CA
breachrx.com

Bridgecrew (10, -56.5%)
Application Security / Configuration Management
San Francisco, CA
bridgecrew.io

Britive (58, -12.1%)
IAM / Access Security
Glendale, CA
britive.com

Broadcom (24651, 1.8%)
Network Security / Hardware
San Jose, CA
broadcom.com

Btech - IT Security for Credit Unions (9, 0.0%)
MSSP / Managed Security Services
Pasadena, CA
btechonline.com

Bugcrowd (2461, 18.7%)
Operations / Bugs
San Francisco, CA
bugcrowd.com

Buoyant (25, 4.2%)
Network Security / Segmentation
San Francisco, CA
buoyant.io

Bureau (115, 3.6%)
Fraud Prevention / Identity Verification
San Francisco, CA
bureau.id

C1Risk (7, 0.0%)
GRC / Policy Management
San Francisco, CA
c1risk.com

Calypso AI (51, 13.3%)
Data Security / Safe AI/ML Data
San Francisco, CA
calypsoai.com

Caplinked (14, -12.5%)
Data Security / Secure Data Sharing
Manhattan Beach, CA
caplinked.com

Castle (27, 22.7%)
Fraud Prevention / Access Security
San Francisco, CA
castle.io

Cavirin Systems (16, -15.8%)
GRC / Compliance Management
Santa Clara, CA
cavirin.com

Celestix (23, 15.0%)
IAM
Fremont, CA
celestix.com

Cequence Security (167, 4.4%)
API Security
Sunnyvale, CA
cequence.ai

Cerby (93, 55.0%)
IAM / Credential Security
Alameda, CA
cerby.com

Chronicle (part of Google) (45, 80.0%)
Security Analytics / SIEM
Mountain View, CA
chronicle.security

Ciphertex (8, 33.3%)
Data Security / Secure Storage
San Fernando, CA
ciphertex.com

ciphertrace (110, 17.0%)
Fraud Prevention / Anti-money Laudering
Menlo Park, CA
ciphertrace.com

Cisco (99793, 2.6%)
Network Security / Firewalls
San Jose, CA
cisco.com

Civic Technologies (33, -8.3%)
Data Security / Wallets
San Francisco, CA
civic.com

Clare Computing Solutions (51, 6.2%)
MSSP / Managed Security Services
San Ramon, CA
clarecomputer.com

ClearSkye (38, -17.4%)
IAM / Governance
Emeryville, CA
clearskye.com

Cloud Raxak (7, 0.0%)
GRC / Compliance Management
Los Gatos, CA
cloudraxak.com

Clouddefense.ai (36, 28.6%)
Application Security / Code Security
Palo Alto, CA
clouddefense.ai

Cloudera (2987, -9.7%)
Operations / Cloud Security
Palo Alto, CA
cloudera.com

Cloudflare (4009, 18.1%)
Network Security / DDoS Defense
San Francisco, CA
cloudflare.com

**Numbers in parentheses indicate headcount and % change in 2023.*

Cloudmark Inc. (68, 0.0%)
Network Security / DNS Security
San Francisco, CA
cloudmark.com

Cloudmatos (12, -29.4%)
GRC / Compliance Management
Livermore, CA
cloudmatos.com

Coalition (638, 11.0%)
GRC / Cyber Insurance
San Francisco, CA
coalitioninc.com

Cobalt (444, -3.3%)
Application Security / Software Testing For Security
San Francisco, CA
cobalt.io

Cognito (12, 20.0%)
Fraud Prevention / Authentication
Palo Alto, CA
cognitohq.com

Cohesity (2221, -3.1%)
Data Security
San Jose, CA
cohesity.com

ColorTokens (270, -13.5%)
Network Security / Zero Trust Networking
Santa Clara, CA
colortokens.com

Comae Technologies (5, -16.7%)
Endpoint Security / Forensics
San Francisco, CA
comae.com

CommandK.Dev (13, 85.7%)
Data Security / Secrets Management
San Francisco, CA
commandk.dev

ComplianceCow (20, 53.9%)
GRC
Fremont, CA
compliancecow.com

Concentric AI (59, 37.2%)
Data Security / Data Classification
San Jose, CA
concentric.ai

Confidently (28, 211.1%)
GRC / Employee Protection
San Francisco, CA
confidently.com

Confluera (7, -46.1%)
Security Analytics / Incident Management
Palo Alto, CA
confluera.com

Constella Intelligence (143, -16.4%)
Threat Intelligence / Stolen Identities
Los Altos, CA
constellaintelligence.com

Containn (4, 0.0%)
Application Security / Container Security
Bay Area, CA
containn.com

Contrast Security (304, -22.4%)
Application Security / Software Testing For Security
Los Altos, CA
contrastsecurity.com

Conveyor (24, 14.3%)
GRC
San Francisco, CA
conveyor.com

Coralogix (295, 30.5%)
Operations / OP- Configuration Management
San Francisco, CA
coralogix.com

Corelight (273, -1.8%)
Network Security / Traffic Analysis
San Francisco, CA
corelight.com

Corgea (4, 0.0%)
Application Security
San Francisco, CA
corgea.com

cPacket (119, -4.8%)
Network Security / Traffic Analysis
San Jose, CA
cpacket.com

Cribl (671, 37.8%)
Operations / Data Process Flow
San Francisco, CA
cribl.io

CrowdStrike (7569, 11.8%)
Endpoint Security / EDR
Sunnyvale, CA
crowdstrike.com

Crown Sterling (29, 26.1%)
Data Security / Encryption
Newport Beach, CA
crownsterling.io

Crysp (3, 200.0%)
IAM / Authentication
San Francisco, CA
crysp.com

Cujo AI (171, 6.9%)
Network Security / Home Security
El Segundo, CA
getcujo.com

Culinda (26, 13.0%)
IoT Security / Healthcare
Irvine, CA
culinda.io

Cupp Computing (5, 0.0%)
Endpoint Security
Palo Alto, CA
cuppcomputing.com

Curtail (4, -20.0%)
Application Security / Software Development Security
Anaheim, CA
curtail.com

CyberCube (117, 11.4%)
GRC / Risk Management
San Francisco, CA
cybcube.com

CyberForza (10, -16.7%)
Endpoint Security / Endpoint Protection
Santa Clara, CA
cyberforza.com

CyberProof (377, 20.1%)
MSSP / Managed Security Services
Aliso Viejo, CA
cyberproof.com

Cycognito (162, -15.6%)
GRC / Vulnerabilities
Palo Alto, CA
cycognito.com

Cycuity (38, 2.7%)
Endpoint Security
San Diego, CA
cycuity.com

Cyder (6, 50.0%)
Data Security / Data Privacy
San Francisco, CA
getcyder.com

CYGNVS (103, 56.1%)
Operations / Crisis Response Platform
Los Altos, CA
cygnvs.com

Cyral (47, -24.2%)
Data Security / Access Security
Redwood City, CA
cyral.com

Cyrus (28, -45.1%)
Data Security / Personal Cybersecurity
San Francisco, CA
cyrus.app

Cytellix (22, 22.2%)
GRC / MDR
Aliso Viejo, CA
cytellix.com

**Numbers in parentheses indicate headcount and % change in 2023.*

Cyvatar.Ai (26, 13.0%)
MSSP / Full Service
Irvine, CA
cyvatar.ai

Darktrace (2529, 6.4%)
Security Analytics / Incident Management
San Francisco, CA
darktrace.com

Darwinium (30, 76.5%)
Fraud Prevention / Monitoring
San Francisco, CA
darwinium.com

Dasera (46, 21.1%)
Data Security / Monitoring
Mountain View, CA
dasera.com

Data Theorem (91, 167.7%)
Application Security / Mobile Device Security
Palo Alto, CA
datatheorem.com

DataGrail (127, 5.0%)
GRC / Data Privacy
San Francisco, CA
datagrail.io

Datatron (8, -42.9%)
Operations / AI Operations
San Francisco, CA
datatron.com

Datavisor (129, 13.2%)
Fraud Prevention
Mountain View, CA
datavisor.com

Datawiza (9, -10.0%)
IAM / Access Security
Santa Clara, CA
datawiza.com

Datiphy (13, 8.3%)
GRC / Monitoring
San Jose, CA
datiphy.com

Dazz (107, 40.8%)
Operations / Vulnerabilities
Palo Alto, CA
dazz.io

Dedrone (137, 45.7%)
Network Security / Drones
San Francisco, CA
dedrone.com

Deepfactor (40, -2.4%)
Application Security / Runtime Security
San Jose, CA
deepfactor.io

Deepfence (27, -3.6%)
Network Security / IPS
Milpitas, CA
deepfence.io

DeepSource (19, -57.8%)
Application Security / Code Security
San Francisco, CA
deepsource.io

Defined Networking (11, 10.0%)
Network Security / Zero Trust Networking
Santa Monica, CA
defined.net

Delinea (956, 21.5%)
IAM / Access Security
Redwood City, CA
delinea.com

Dellfer (11, -26.7%)
IoT Security / Automotive
Novato, CA
dellfer.com

Delphix (628, 0.2%)
Data Security / Data Management
Redwood City, CA
delphix.com

Denexus (46, 2.2%)
GRC / Risk Management
Sausalito, CA
denexus.io

Descope (43, 34.4%)
IAM / Authentication
Los Altos, CA
descope.com

Digital Shadows (45, -64.6%)
Threat Intelligence / Dark Web
San Francisco, CA
digitalshadows.com

Disconnect (12, -36.8%)
Network Security / VPN/Proxy
San Francisco, CA
disconnect.me

Docker Scout (798, 1.8%)
Application Security / SBOM
San Francisco, CA
docker.com

dope.security (37, 19.4%)
Endpoint Security / Gateways
Mountain View, CA
dope.security

Doppler (34, 0.0%)
Data Security / Secrets Management
San Francisco, CA
doppler.com

Dragonfly Cyber (3, 0.0%)
Data Security
San Diego, CA
dragonflycyber.com

Drata (552, -10.1%)
GRC / Compliance Management
San Diego, CA
drata.com

Druva (1220, -1.3%)
Endpoint Security / Secure Secure Backup/Recovery
Sunnyvale, CA
druva.com

DTEX Systems (118, 32.6%)
GRC / Insider Threats
San Jose, CA
dtexsystems.com

DuploCloud Inc. (72, 84.6%)
Application Security / Configuration Management
San Jose, CA
duplocloud.com

Eclipz (18, -37.9%)
Data Security / IPSec Tools
Los Gatos, CA
eclipz.io

EdgeBit (5, 66.7%)
Application Security / SBOM
San Mateo, CA
edgebit.io

Egnyte (1065, 31.3%)
Data Security / Secure Data Sharing
Mountain View, CA
egnyte.com

Ekran System (27, -6.9%)
GRC / Insider Threats
Newport Beach, CA
ekransystem.com

Elevate Security (42, -14.3%)
GRC / Security Awareness Training
Berkeley, CA
elevatesecurity.com

Elisity (69, 27.8%)
IAM / Access Security
Milpitas, CA
elisity.com

Elysium Analytics (27, 12.5%)
Operations / Security Analytics
Santa Clara, CA
elysiumanalytics.ai

Endor Labs (74, 85.0%)
Application Security / Dependency Management
Palo Alto, CA
endorlabs.com

**Numbers in parentheses indicate headcount and % change in 2023.*

Engage Black (4, -20.0%)
Data Security / Code Security
Aptos, CA
engageblack.com

Ensighten (28, -17.6%)
Fraud Prevention / Bot Security
Menlo Park, CA
ensighten.com

Enso Security (21, -40.0%)
Application Security / Code Security
Mill Valley, CA
enso.security

Entreda (9, -10.0%)
Endpoint Security / Monitoring
Santa Clara, CA
entreda.com

Exabeam (760, 5.0%)
Security Analytics / Monitoring
San Mateo, CA
exabeam.com

Exium (37, 15.6%)
Network Security / SASE
Palo Alto, CA
exium.net

Expanse (33, -8.3%)
GRC / Vulnerabilities
San Francisco, CA
expanse.co

Extreme Networks (3881, 7.8%)
IAM / Access Security
San Jose, CA
extremenetworks.com

Farsight Security (17, -15.0%)
Threat Intelligence / Threat Intelligence From DNS
San Mateo, CA
farsightsecurity.com

Fastly (1279, 12.3%)
Network Security / DDoS Defense
San Francisco, CA
fastly.com

Feedly (56, 0.0%)
Threat Intelligence / Feeds
Redwood City, CA
feedly.com

Feedzai (582, -20.1%)
Fraud Prevention / Anti-fraud
San Mateo, CA
feedzai.com

FileOpen Systems (7, -36.4%)
Data Security / DRM
Santa Cruz, CA
fileopen.com

Filestring (55, 7.8%)
Data Security / IRM
Santa Cruz, CA
filestring.com

Firewalla (18, 12.5%)
Network Security / Firewalls
San Jose, CA
firewalla.com

Firezone (7, 40.0%)
Network Security / VPN/Proxy
Mountain View, CA
firezone.dev

Fleet (55, 37.5%)
Endpoint Security / Asset Management
San Francisco, CA
fleetdm.com

Fletch.AI (69, 187.5%)
Operations / SOC
San Francisco, CA
fletch.ai

Flowmon Networks (65, -5.8%)
Network Security / Monitoring
San Diego, CA
flowmon.com

Fluid Attacks (156, 34.5%)
Application Security / Scanning
San Francisco, CA
fluidattacks.com

Flying Cloud Technology (15, 0.0%)
Data Security / Data Flows
Santa Cruz, CA
flyingcloudtech.com

ForeScout Technologies (1048, 3.2%)
Network Security / Access Security
San Jose, CA
forescout.com

ForgeRock (896, -6.1%)
IAM
San Francisco, CA
forgerock.com

Fortanix (273, 28.8%)
Data Security / Confidential Computing
Mountain View, CA
fortanix.com

Fortify 24x7 (5, -16.7%)
MSSP / Managed Security Services
Los Angeles, CA
fortify24x7.com

Fortinet (13793, 11.5%)
Network Security / UTM
Sunnyvale, CA
fortinet.com

Forward Networks (150, 74.4%)
Network Security / Attack Surface Management
Santa Clara, CA
forwardnetworks.com

Fossa (72, -19.1%)
Application Security / Vulnerabilities
San Francisco, CA
fossa.com

Foxpass (6, -45.5%)
IAM / Authentication
San Francisco, CA
foxpass.com

Fudo Security (56, 12.0%)
IAM / Access Security
Newark, CA
fudosecurity.com

Garner Products (22, -18.5%)
Data Security / Data Erasure And Destruction
Roseville, CA
garnerproducts.com

GeoTrust Inc. (31, -16.2%)
Data Security / Encryption
Mountain View, CA
geotrust.com

GhangorCloud (20, 53.9%)
GRC / DLP
San Jose, CA
ghangorcloud.com

Gigamon (1175, 2.7%)
Network Security / Span Port Mirroring
Santa Clara, CA
gigamon.com

Github (5327, -0.1%)
Application Security / Vulnerabilities
San Francisco, CA
github.com

GitLab (2351, 1.9%)
Application Security / Code Security
San Francisco, CA
about.gitlab.com

Green Hills Software (258, 0.4%)
Endpoint Security / Operating System Security
Santa Barbara, CA
ghs.com

Green Rocket Security Inc. (5, 400.0%)
IAM / Authentication
San Jose, CA
greenrocketsecurity.com

**Numbers in parentheses indicate headcount and % change in 2023.*

Gretel.ai (72, 35.9%)
Data Security /
Data Masking
San Diego, CA
gretel.ai

GTB Technologies (60, -1.6%)
GRC / Leaked Data
Newport Beach, CA
gttb.com

Guardian (10, 100.0%)
Endpoint Security / Firewalls
San Francisco, CA
guardianapp.com

Guidewire (3358, 2.8%)
GRC / Security Ratings
Foster City, CA
guidewire.com

GuruCul (200, 25.0%)
Security Analytics
El Segundo, CA
gurucul.com

HackerOne (4418, 21.4%)
Operations / Research
San Francisco, CA
hackerone.com

HashiCorp (2339, -5.4%)
Data Security / Secrets
Management
San Francisco, CA
hashicorp.com

Hexnode (112, 6.7%)
Endpoint Security / Device
Management
San Francisco, CA
hexnode.com

Hideez (12, 0.0%)
IAM / Hardware
Redwood City, CA
hideez.com

Hillstone Networks (388, 11.2%)
Network Security / Firewalls
Santa Clara, CA
hillstonenet.com

Hive Pro (68, 36.0%)
GRC / Vulnerabilities
Milpitas, CA
hivepro.com

Horizon3.ai (111, 3.7%)
Network Security /
Penetration Testing
San Francisco, CA
horizon3.ai

i2Chain (8, -20.0%)
Data Security
San Francisco, CA
i2chain.com

Iconix (23, 4.5%)
Email Security / Sender
Verification
San Jose, CA
iconix.com

Idemeum (10, 11.1%)
IAM / Access Security
Palo Alto, CA
idemeum.com

Identity Science (8, 60.0%)
Application Security / Software Development Security
Sunnyvale, CA
identityscience.ai

Identiv (277, 9.5%)
IAM / Credential Security
Fremont, CA
identiv.com

IdenTrust (part of HID Global) (66, -1.5%)
Data Security / Public Key
Infrastructure
Fremont, CA
identrust.com

Illumio (591, 2.2%)
Endpoint Security /
Monitoring
Sunnyvale, CA
illumio.com

ImageWare (47, -17.5%)
IAM / Authentication
San Diego, CA
iwsinc.com

Immunant (5, 25.0%)
Application Security /
Code Security
Irvine, CA
immunant.com

Impart Security (16, 128.6%)
API Security
Los Angeles, CA
impart.security

Imperva (1751, 3.1%)
Network Security / Firewalls
Redwood Shores, CA
imperva.com

Incode (340, 17.6%)
IAM / Identity Management
San Francisco, CA
incode.com

Incognia (178, 23.6%)
Fraud Prevention /
Authentication
Palo Alto, CA
incognia.com

Indeni (28, -22.2%)
Operations / Automation
San Francisco, CA
indeni.com

IndyKite (54, -3.6%)
IAM / Identity Management
San Francisco, CA
indykite.com

Infiot (5, -44.4%)
Network Security / Secure
Remote Access
San Jose, CA
infiot.com

Infisical (9, 12.5%)
Data Security / Secrets
Management
San Francisco, CA
infisical.com

Infoblox (2186, 4.7%)
Network Security /
DNS Security
Santa Clara, CA
infoblox.com

InfoExpress Inc. (30, -31.8%)
IAM / Access Security
Santa Clara, CA
infoexpress.com

Informatica (5720, -4.9%)
Data Security /
Data Masking
Redwood City, CA
informatica.com

Inigo (12, 50.0%)
API Security /
GraphQL Security
Palo Alto, CA
inigo.io

Inpixon (128, -39.9%)
Network Security / Rogue
Wifi AP Location
Palo Alto, CA
inpixon.com

Inside-Out Defense (6, 0.0%)
IAM / Access Security
Palo Alto, CA
insideoutdefense.com

Interface Masters Technologies (60, -17.8%)
Network Security / IPS
San Jose, CA
interfacemasters.com

Intertrust Technologies (197, 0.5%)
IoT Security / Public Key
Infrastructure
Sunnyvale, CA
intertrust.com

Intrinsic-ID (45, 2.3%)
IAM / Authentication
Sunnyvale, CA
intrinsic-id.com

Ionu (3, 0.0%)
Data Security / Data
Management
Los Gatos, CA
ionu.com

**Numbers in parentheses indicate headcount and % change in 2023.*

Isovalent (157, 52.4%)
Endpoint Security / Container Security
Mountain View, CA
isovalent.com

JFrog (1567, 15.1%)
Application Security / Software Development Security
Sunnyvale, CA
jfrog.com

Jscrambler (100, 8.7%)
Application Security / Code Security
San Francisco, CA
jscrambler.com

Jumio (714, -22.2%)
Fraud Prevention / Identity Verification
Palo Alto, CA
jumio.com

Juniper Networks (11835, 5.1%)
Network Security / Firewalls
Sunnyvale, CA
juniper.net

K2 Cyber Security (10, 0.0%)
Application Security
San Jose, CA
k2io.com

Kameleon Security (5, 0.0%)
Endpoint Security
Mountain View, CA
kameleonsec.com

Kandji (315, -4.3%)
Endpoint Security / Device Management
San Diego, CA
kandji.io

KeepSafe (22, 10.0%)
Data Security / Encryption
San Francisco, CA
getkeepsafe.com

Kenna Security (rebranded from Risk I/O) (46, -25.8%)
GRC / Feeds
San Francisco, CA
kennasecurity.com

Ketch (93, 20.8%)
GRC / Compliance Management
San Francisco, CA
ketch.com

Keysight (was Ixia) (522, -6.6%)
Network Security / Visibility
Calabasas, CA
keysight.com

Kingston Technology (1496, 11.3%)
Data Security / Secure Storage
Fountain Valley, CA
kingston.com

Kiteworks (239, 6.7%)
Data Security / IRM
Palo Alto, CA
kiteworks.com

Kriptos (50, 16.3%)
Data Security / Data Classification
Sausalito, CA
kriptos.io

KSOC (36, 5.9%)
Endpoint Security / Kubernetes Security
San Francisco, CA
ksoc.com

Lacework (823, -15.8%)
Application Security / Cloud Security
Mountain View, CA
lacework.com

LastLine (VMware) (8, -27.3%)
Threat Intelligence / IoC Intelligence
Redwood City, CA
lastline.com

Lastwall (26, 36.8%)
IAM / Access Security
Mountain View, CA
lastwall.com

LeakSignal (8, 33.3%)
API Security / Leaked Data
Menlo Park, CA
leaksignal.com

LeapFILE (6, 0.0%)
Data Security / Secure Data Sharing
Cupertino, CA
leapfile.com

LeapYear Technologies (5, -86.5%)
Data Security / Analyze Private Information
Berkeley, CA
leapyear.ai

Legit Security (79, 12.9%)
GRC / Risk Management
Palo Alto, CA
legitsecurity.com

Licel (15, 25.0%)
Application Security / Mobile Device Security
Los Angeles, CA
licelus.com

LimaCharlie/Refraction Point (21, 40.0%)
Network Security / SASE
Walnut, CA
limacharlie.io

Live Action (138, -13.8%)
Network Security / NDR
Palo Alto, CA
liveaction.com

LMNTRIX (47, 56.7%)
MSSP / MDR
Orange, CA
lmntrix.com

LogicHub (17, -55.3%)
Operations / Incident Management
Mountain View, CA
logichub.com

LoginID (45, -6.2%)
IAM / Authentication
San Mateo, CA
loginid.io

LoginRadius (154, 12.4%)
IAM / CIAM
San Francisco, CA
loginradius.com

Lookout (830, -9.6%)
Endpoint Security / Mobile Device Security
San Francisco, CA
lookout.com

Lucent Sky (3, 0.0%)
Application Security / Code Security
San Francisco, CA
lucentsky.com

Lucidum (20, 11.1%)
Operations / Asset Management
San Jose, CA
lucidum.io

Lynx Software Technologies (91, 3.4%)
Endpoint Security / Container Security
San Jose, CA
lynx.com

MagicCube (28, -22.2%)
IAM / Transaction Security
Santa Clara, CA
magiccube.co

Mailshell (8, 14.3%)
Email Security / Anti-spam
San Francisco, CA
mailshell.com

Malwarebytes (768, -12.4%)
Endpoint Security / Anti-virus
Santa Clara, CA
malwarebytes.org

Mammoth Cyber (31, 34.8%)
Network Security / Secure Web Browsing
Palo Alto, CA
mammothcyber.com

**Numbers in parentheses indicate headcount and % change in 2023.*

ManageEngine (Zoho Corp.) (300, 55.4%)
GRC / Security Management
Pleasanton, CA
manageengine.com

Mandiant (1394, 4.2%)
Security Analytics / XDR
Milpitas, CA
mandiant.com

MarkMonitor (178, 3.5%)
Threat Intelligence / Brand
San Francisco, CA
markmonitor.com

Marvell (7744, -3.9%)
Data Security / Hardware
Santa Clara, CA
marvell.com

Material Security (107, 87.7%)
Email Security / ATO Prevention
Redwood City, CA
material.security

Mattermost (158, -31.0%)
Operations / Incident Management
Palo Alto, CA
mattermost.com

McAfee (5641, -6.0%)
Endpoint Security / Anti-virus
Santa Clara, CA
mcafee.com

Medcrypt (59, 68.6%)
IoT Security / Healthcare
Encinitas, CA
medcrypt.co

Mender (39, 69.6%)
IoT Security / Linux Devices
Palo Alto, CA
mender.io

Menlo Security (380, -11.8%)
Network Security / Secure Web Browsing
Palo Alto, CA
menlosecurity.com

Merit (258, 69.7%)
IAM
Sunnyvale, CA
merits.com

MessageSolution Inc. (17, -10.5%)
GRC / Email Archiving
Milpitas, CA
messagesolution.com

METABASE Q (94, 27.0%)
GRC / Compliance Management
San Francisco, CA
metabaseq.com

MetricStream (1385, -5.3%)
GRC
Palo Alto, CA
metricstream.com

Mezmo (115, -25.8%)
Security Analytics / Logs
Mountain View, CA
mezmo.com

Microsec.AI (35, -18.6%)
Operations / Posture Management
Santa Clara, CA
microsec.ai

MixMode (81, 47.3%)
Operations / Forensics
San Diego, CA
mixmode.ai

Mobile Helix (3, 0.0%)
Data Security / Encryption
Mountain View, CA
mobilehelix.com

MobileHop (8, 33.3%)
Network Security / VPN/Proxy
Los Angeles, CA
mobilehop.com

Mobolize (13, -13.3%)
Network Security / Mobile Wireless Protection
Santa Monica, CA
mobolize.com

Mocana Corporation (29, 7.4%)
Application Security / Mobile Device Security
Sunnyvale, CA
mocana.com

Monad (36, 50.0%)
GRC / Vulnerabilities
San Francisco, CA
monad.security

Mondoo (40, 25.0%)
GRC / Risk Management
San Francisco, CA
mondoo.io

Msecure Data Labs (13, -7.1%)
Endpoint Security / Anti-virus
Walnut, CA
msecuredatalabs.com

MyWorkDrive (10, 0.0%)
Data Security / Secure Storage
San Francisco, CA
myworkdrive.com

NanoVMs (8, -27.3%)
Endpoint Security / Container Security
San Francisco, CA
nanovms.com

NCP Engineering (18, -5.3%)
Network Security / VPN/Proxy
Mountain View, CA
ncp-e.com

Netenrich (885, 3.1%)
Operations / Logs
San Jose, CA
netenrich.com

NetFlow Logic (5, -16.7%)
Network Security / Traffic Analysis
Atherton, CA
netflowlogic.com

Netography (47, 6.8%)
Network Security / DDoS Defense
San Francisco, CA
netography.com

NetSkope (2439, 13.7%)
Application Security
Santa Clara, CA
netskope.com

NetSTAR (11, 10.0%)
Network Security / Gateways
San Mateo, CA
netstar-inc.com

Netswitch Technology Management (16, 6.7%)
MSSP / MDR
San Francisco, CA
netswitch.net

NetWrix Corporation (751, 18.8%)
GRC / Auditing
Irvine, CA
netwrix.com

NeuShield (10, 42.9%)
Data Security / Ransomware Security
Fremont, CA
neushield.com

NeuVector (17, -5.6%)
Endpoint Security / Container Security
San Jose, CA
neuvector.com

NextLabs (163, 19.0%)
Data Security / IRM
San Mateo, CA
nextlabs.com

NexusFlow AI (6, 50.0%)
Security Analytics / AI Security
Palo Alto, CA
nexusflow.ai

ngrok (84, 0.0%)
IAM / Access Security
San Francisco, CA
ngrok.com

**Numbers in parentheses indicate headcount and % change in 2023.*

Niagra Networks (64, -8.6%)
Network Security / Monitoring
San Jose, CA
niagaranetworks.com

Nightfall AI (114, 11.8%)
Data Security / Data Discovery
San Francisco, CA
nightfall.ai

NightVision (25, 47.1%)
API Security / Vulnerabilities
Los Angeles, CA
nightvision.net

NINJIO (60, -6.2%)
GRC / Security Awareness Training
Westlake Village, CA
ninjio.com

Nira (33, 10.0%)
Data Security
Redwood City, CA
nira.com

Nirmata (73, 4.3%)
GRC / Kubernetes Security
San Jose, CA
nirmata.com

NodeSource (18, 5.9%)
Application Security / Serverless
San Francisco, CA
nodesource.com

Nok Nok Labs (36, -16.3%)
IAM / Authentication
San Jose, CA
noknok.com

noname security (499, 41.4%)
API Security
Palo Alto, CA
nonamesecurity.com

Noq (4, 0.0%)
IAM / Identity As Code
Irvine, CA
noq.dev

Normalyze (66, 112.9%)
Data Security / Data Discovery
Los Altos, CA
normalyze.ai

Notebook Labs (5, 0.0%)
IAM / Identity Management
Stanford, CA
notebooklabs.xyz

Nozomi Networks (268, -30.2%)
IoT Security / OT Security
San Francisco, CA
nozominetworks.com

NSFocus (369, -47.5%)
Network Security / DDoS Defense
Santa Clara, CA
nsfocus.com

NXM Labs (17, 13.3%)
IoT Security / Endpoint Protection
San Francisco, CA
nxmlabs.com

Oasis Labs (32, -25.6%)
Data Security / Governance
San Francisco, CA
oasislabs.com

ObserveID (10, 42.9%)
IAM / Monitoring
Los Angeles, CA
observeid.com

Obsidian Security (144, 22.0%)
Network Security / Cloud Security
Newport Beach, CA
obsidiansecurity.com

Ockam (24, 26.3%)
Data Security / Orchestration
San Francisco, CA
ockam.io

Okera (24, -72.4%)
Data Security / Governance
San Francisco, CA
okera.com

Okta (7108, -12.4%)
IAM
San Francisco, CA
okta.com

Oloid (46, 9.5%)
IAM / Identity Management
Sunnyvale, CA
oloid.ai

One Identity (596, 1.5%)
IAM / Identity Management
Aliso Viejo, CA
oneidentity.com

OneLogin (100, -17.4%)
IAM / Identity Management
San Francisco, CA
onelogin.com

Ontinue (197, 99.0%)
MSSP / MDR
Redwood City, CA
ontinue.com

Opal Dev (50, 51.5%)
IAM / Identity Management
San Francisco, CA
opal.dev

Open Zeppelin (92, 10.8%)
Application Security / Blockchain
San Francisco, CA
openzeppelin.com

OpenVPN (164, 9.3%)
Network Security / VPN/Proxy
Pleasanton, CA
openvpn.net

Operant AI (23, 21.1%)
Application Security / Runtime Security
San Francisco, CA
operant.ai

Opora (14, -54.8%)
Threat Intelligence / Adversary Tracking
San Francisco, CA
opora.io

Opscura (28, 12.0%)
IoT Security
CA
opscura.io

OPSWAT (732, 11.4%)
Endpoint Security / SDKs
San Francisco, CA
opswat.com

Optimeyes (65, 62.5%)
GRC / Risk Management
San Diego, CA
optimeyes.ai

Oracle (201930, -1.7%)
IAM
Redwood Shores, CA
oracle.com

Ordr (121, 21.0%)
IoT Security / Device Management
Santa Clara, CA
ordr.net

Outseer (216, -3.1%)
Fraud Prevention / Authentication
Palo Alto, CA
outseer.com

P0 Security (11, 22.2%)
IAM / Access Security
San Francisco, CA
p0.dev

Paladin Cyber (36, 89.5%)
Email Security / Defense Against Phishing
San Francisco, CA
meetpaladin.com

Palantir Technologies (4031, 0.1%)
Security Analytics / Link Analysis
Palo Alto, CA
palantir.com

Palo Alto Networks (14805, 5.8%)
Network Security / UTM
Santa Clara, CA
paloaltonetworks.com

**Numbers in parentheses indicate headcount and % change in 2023.*

Pangea (56, 80.7%)
Operations / Security APIs
Palo Alto, CA
pangea.cloud

Pango (91, 26.4%)
IAM / VPN/Proxy
Redwood City, CA
pango.co

Panther (245, 17.2%)
Security Analytics / SIEM
San Francisco, CA
runpanther.io

Parablu (44, 29.4%)
Data Security / Secure Backup/Recovery
Santa Clara, CA
parablu.com

Parasoft (271, 0.0%)
Application Security / Software Testing For Security
Monrovia, CA
parasoft.com

Passware (25, 8.7%)
Operations / Red Team Tools
Mountain View, CA
passware.com

Paubox (51, -16.4%)
Email Security / Secure Email
San Francisco, CA
paubox.com

Permiso Security (33, 17.9%)
Operations / Vulnerabilities
Palo Alto, CA
permiso.io

Persona (280, 27.3%)
IAM / Identity Verification
San Francisco, CA
withpersona.com

Phantom (127, 89.5%)
Data Security / Wallets
San Francisco, CA
phantom.app

Phoenix Security (6, 20.0%)
Endpoint Security
Los Altos, CA
r6security.com

Phoenix Technologies (726, 31.8%)
Endpoint Security / Secured Devices
Campbell, CA
phoenix.com

PNF Software (3, 0.0%)
Application Security / Reverse Engineering
Redwood City, CA
pnfsoftware.com

PolySwarm (24, -11.1%)
Endpoint Security / Anti-malware
San Diego, CA
polyswarm.io

Prancer (27, 50.0%)
Operations / Vulnerabilities
San Diego, CA
prancer.io

Prismo Systems (5, -72.2%)
Network Security / Zero Trust Networking
San Francisco, CA
prismosystems.com

Privacera (140, -1.4%)
Data Security / Governance
Fremont, CA
privacera.com

Privado (173, 130.7%)
Application Security / Code Security
San Francisco, CA
privado.ai

Procyon (17, 325.0%)
IAM / Access Security
Santa Clara, CA
procyon.ai

Proficio (242, 22.2%)
MSSP / MDR
Carlsbad, CA
proficio.com

Proofpoint (4508, 4.3%)
Email Security / Defense Against Phishing
Sunnyvale, CA
proofpoint.com

PropelAuth (6, -14.3%)
IAM / Authentication
Redwood City, CA
propelauth.com

Protecto (26, 0.0%)
Data Security / Posture Management
Cupertino, CA
protecto.ai

Proxim (130, -4.4%)
Network Security / Wireless Security
San Jose, CA
proxim.com

Psafe Technology (3, -80.0%)
Endpoint Security / Anti-virus
San Francisco, CA
psafe.com

Pulse Secure (151, -18.4%)
IAM / Authentication
San Jose, CA
pulsesecure.net

qikfox (35, 94.4%)
Fraud Prevention / Secure Web Browsing
San Mateo, CA
qikfox.com

Qualys (2528, 11.6%)
GRC / Vulnerabilities
Foster City, CA
qualys.com

Quantum Knight (10, 400.0%)
Data Security / Quantum
Palo Alto, CA
quantumknight.io

Quest Software (3736, -4.1%)
IAM / Access Security
Aliso Viejo, CA
quest.com

Qusecurity (76, 7.0%)
Data Security
San Mateo, CA
qusecure.com

Qustodio (89, 1.1%)
Endpoint Security / Mobile Parental Controls
Redondo Beach, CA
qustodio.com

Qwiet AI (42, -22.2%)
Application Security / Code Security
Santa Clara, CA
shiftleft.io

Radiant Logic (166, 23.9%)
IAM / Authentication
Novato, CA
radiantlogic.com

Radiant Security (41, 78.3%)
Operations / SOC
San Francisco, CA
radiantsecurity.ai

Rambus (973, -6.8%)
Data Security / Semiconductor Security R&D
Sunnyvale, CA
rambus.com

Raonsecure (78, 36.8%)
IAM / Authentication
Santa Clara, CA
raonsecure.com

RapidFort Inc. (33, 32.0%)
Application Security / Attack Surface Management
Sunnyvale, CA
rapidfort.com

RavenWhite Security (3, 0.0%)
IAM / Cookies
Menlo Park, CA
ravenwhite.com

**Numbers in parentheses indicate headcount and % change in 2023.*

Reach Security (11, 0.0%)
Operations
San Francisco, CA
reach.security

RealDefense (40, 37.9%)
Endpoint Security / Microsoft
Pasadena, CA
realdefen.se

Reciprocity (90, -46.4%)
GRC / Risk Management
San Francisco, CA
reciprocity.com

RedSeal (178, 7.2%)
GRC / Posture Management
San Jose, CA
redseal.net

RedShift Networks (35, -10.3%)
Network Security / VoIP Security
San Ramon, CA
redshiftnetworks.com

Relyance AI (70, 0.0%)
GRC / Compliance Management
Mountain View, CA
relyance.ai

Remediant (9, -66.7%)
IAM / Access Security
San Francisco, CA
remediant.com

remote.it (16, -23.8%)
Network Security / Zero Trust Networking
Palo Alto, CA
remote.it

Remy Security (4, -33.3%)
Operations
San Francisco, CA
remysec.com

Resecurity (85, 57.4%)
Endpoint Security / EDR
Los ANgelas, CA
resecurity.com

Resilient Network Systems (3, 0.0%)
IAM / Access Security
San Francisco, CA
resilient-networks.com

Resolve (127, -19.6%)
Operations / Orchestration
Campbell, CA
resolve.io

Resourcely (28, 12.0%)
Operations / Technology Deployment Management
San Francisco, CA
resourcely.io

Revelstoke (9, -82.7%)
Operations / Orchestration
San Jose, CA
revelstoke.io

revyz (11, 83.3%)
Data Security
Fremont, CA
revyz.io

Ridge Security (33, 50.0%)
GRC / Penetration Testing
Santa Clara, CA
ridgesecurity.ai

Riot (34, 54.5%)
GRC / Security Awareness Training
San Francisco, CA
tryriot.com

Robust Intelligence (72, 4.3%)
GRC / Governance
San Francisco, CA
robustintelligence.com

Rootly (35, -7.9%)
Operations / Incident Management
San Francisco, CA
rootly.com

Rubrik (3540, 14.7%)
Data Security / Data Discovery
Palo Alto, CA
rubrik.com

Saaspass (11, -8.3%)
IAM
San Francisco, CA
saaspass.com

Safe Security (301, -34.6%)
GRC / Risk Management
Palo Alto, CA
safe.security

SafeBase (72, 56.5%)
GRC / Secure Storage
San Francisco, CA
safebase.io

SafeLogic (13, 18.2%)
Data Security / Cryptographic Libraries
Palo Alto, CA
safelogic.com

Salt Security (202, -1.0%)
API Security
Palo Alto, CA
salt.security

Saviynt (845, -5.0%)
IAM / Governance
El Segundo, CA
saviynt.com

Seagate Technology (16127, -2.7%)
Data Security / Encryption
Cupertino, CA
seagate.com

Seclytics (15, 0.0%)
Security Analytics / Threat Intelligence
San Diego, CA
seclytics.com

SECNOLOGY (14, -6.7%)
Security Analytics / Big Data
El Granada, CA
secnology.com

SecuGen (18, -14.3%)
IAM / Authentication
Santa Clara, CA
secugen.com

Secureauth Corporation (175, -8.4%)
IAM / Access Security
Irvine, CA
secureauth.com

Secured Communications (12, -55.6%)
Data Security / Secure Communications
San Francisco, CA
securedcommunications.com

SecureData (57, -26.0%)
Data Security / Secure Storage
Los Angeles, CA
securedata.com

Secureframe (153, 5.5%)
GRC / Compliance Management
San Francisco, CA
secureframe.com

SecureThings (26, 23.8%)
IoT Security / Automotive
Sunnyvale, CA
securethings.ai

Securiti (703, 34.4%)
Data Security / Data Discovery
San Jose, CA
securiti.ai

Security Mentor (5, 25.0%)
GRC / Security Awareness Training
Pacific Grove, CA
securitymentor.com

SecurityTrails (17, -39.3%)
Operations / Asset Inventory
Los Angeles, CA
securitytrails.com

Semgrep (147, 0.0%)
Application Security / Code Security
San Francisco, CA
semgrep.dev

**Numbers in parentheses indicate headcount and % change in 2023.*

Sendio (17, -5.6%)
Email Security / Anti-spam
Newport Beach, CA
sendio.com

Sennovate (73, -16.1%)
MSSP / Managed Security Services
San Ramon, CA
sennovate.com

SentiLink (101, 16.1%)
Fraud Prevention / Anti-fraud
San Francisco, CA
sentilink.com

SentinelOne (2293, 20.7%)
Endpoint Security / Endpoint Protection
Mountain View, CA
sentinelone.com

ServiceNow (24941, 14.4%)
Operations / Orchestration
Santa Clara, CA
servicenow.com

Seworks (28, 133.3%)
Operations / Penetration Testing
San Francisco, CA
se.works

ShareVault (38, 2.7%)
Data Security / Secure Storage
Los Gatos, CA
sharevault.com

Shield (157, 6.8%)
Fraud Prevention / Device Fingerprinting
San Francisco, CA
shield.com

Sierraware (13, -13.3%)
Endpoint Security / Mobile Device Security
Sunnyvale, CA
sierraware.com

Sift (369, 14.9%)
Fraud Prevention / Identity Verification
San Francisco, CA
sift.com

Signal Science (24, 26.3%)
API Security / Bot Security
Culver City, CA
signalsciences.com

Signifyd (555, 2.0%)
Fraud Prevention / E-Commerce Fraud Prevention
San Jose, CA
signifyd.com

Silicon Forensics (11, 22.2%)
Operations / Forensics
Pomona, CA
siliconforensics.com

Silk Security (25, 66.7%)
GRC / Risk Management
Santa Clara, CA
silk.security

Singular Security (8, 14.3%)
GRC
Tustin, CA
singularsecurity.com

SixMap (26, 420.0%)
Operations / Attack Surface Management
San Francisco, CA
sixmap.io

Skiff (30, 30.4%)
Data Security / Secure Communications
San Francisco, CA
skiff.org

Skybox Security (300, -7.4%)
Operations / Security Management
San Jose, CA
skyboxsecurity.com

Skyflow (132, 17.9%)
Data Security / Secure Storage
Palo Alto, CA
skyflow.com

Skyhigh Security (620, -2.4%)
Network Security / Gateways
Santa Clara, CA
skyhighsecurity.com

SlashNext (168, 31.2%)
Email Security / Defense Against Phishing
Pleasanton, CA
slashnext.com

Smallstep (22, -18.5%)
Data Security / Public Key Infrastructure
San Francisco, CA
smallstep.com

Somansa (38, -9.5%)
GRC / DLP
San Jose, CA
somansatech.com

Sonet.io (12, 33.3%)
IAM / Access Security
San Jose, CA
sonet.io

SonicWall (1944, 3.9%)
Network Security / UTM
Milpitas, CA
sonicwall.com

SpecTrust (81, 68.8%)
Fraud Prevention
San Jose, CA
spec-trust.com

Spherical Defence (4, 0.0%)
API Security
San Francisco, CA
sphericaldefence.com

Spin Technology (76, 5.6%)
GRC / Risk Management
Palo Alto, CA
spin.ai

SplashData (10, 0.0%)
IAM / Authentication
Los Gatos, CA
splashdata.com

SplitByte (4, 0.0%)
Data Security / Shards
Los Gatos, CA
splitbyte.com

Splunk (8893, 1.9%)
Security Analytics / SIEM
San Francisco, CA
splunk.com

Spring Labs (68, 28.3%)
Data Security / Data Masking
Marina del Rey, CA
springlabs.com

Sprinto (227, 83.1%)
GRC / Compliance Management
San Francisco, CA
sprinto.com

SS8 (124, 6.9%)
Security Analytics
Milpitas, CA
ss8.com

Stack Identity (33, 57.1%)
Operations / Access Security
Los Gatos, CA
stackidentity.com

Stairwell (65, 6.6%)
Security Analytics / Graph Search
Palo Alto, CA
stairwell.com

Stellar Cyber (120, 29.0%)
Security Analytics / Threat Detection
Santa Clara, CA
stellarcyber.ai

StrikeReady (35, -2.8%)
Operations / SOC
Fremont, CA
strikeready.co

strongDM (108, -26.5%)
IAM / Access Security
Burlingame, CA
strongdm.com

Styra (61, -38.4%)
Endpoint Security / Access Security
Redwood City, CA
styra.com

Stytch (64, -19.0%)
IAM
San Francisco, CA
stytch.com

**Numbers in parentheses indicate headcount and % change in 2023.*

Sucuri (51, 4.1%)
Network Security / Website Security
Menifee, CA
sucuri.net

Sumo Logic (914, -15.2%)
Security Analytics / SIEM
Redwood City, CA
sumologic.com

Sunny Valley Networks (9, -18.2%)
Network Security / Firewalls
Cupertino, CA
sunnyvalley.io

Susteen (36, 12.5%)
Endpoint Security / Forensics
Irvine, CA
susteen.com

Sym (36, 63.6%)
Operations / Workflow Automation
San Francisco, CA
symops.com

Symantec (13600, -3.3%)
Endpoint Security / Anti-virus
San Jose, CA
broadcom.com/products/cybersecurity

Symmetry Systems. (47, -6.0%)
Data Security / Monitoring
San Francisco, CA
symmetry-systems.com

Symphony (769, 8.3%)
Data Security / Secure Collaboration
Palo Alto, CA
symphony.com

Synack (264, -22.8%)
Testing
Redwood City, CA
synack.com

Syncplicity by Axway (36, 56.5%)
Data Security / Secure Storage
Santa Clara, CA
syncplicity.com

Synopsys (18348, 7.5%)
Application Security / Software Testing For Security
Mountain View, CA
synopsys.com

Sysdig (879, 3.8%)
Endpoint Security / Kubernetes Security
Davis, CA
sysdig.com

Syxsense (81, 15.7%)
Operations / Vulnerabilities
Aliso Viejo, CA
syxsense.com

TAC Security (155, 31.4%)
GRC
San Francisco, CA
tacsecurity.com

Tala Secure (6, -14.3%)
GRC / Compliance Management
Mountain View, CA
talasecure.com

Tanium (1952, -4.4%)
Endpoint Security / Visibility
Emeryville, CA
tanium.com

Tascent (8, -61.9%)
IAM / Authentication
Los Gatos, CA
tascent.com

Teleport (153, -27.1%)
IAM / Access Security
Oakland, CA
goteleport.com

TeleSign Corporation (773, 9.7%)
IAM / Identity Verification
Marina del Rey, CA
telesign.com

TerraTrue (38, -22.4%)
GRC / Software Development Security
San Francisco, CA
terratrue.com

Tetrate (126, -2.3%)
Operations / Posture Management
Milpitas, CA
tetrate.io

The DigiTrust Group (19, -5.0%)
MSSP / Firewalls
Los Angeles, CA
digitrustgroup.com

Theom (25, 4.2%)
Data Security / Posture Management
San Francisco, CA
theom.ai

Theon (5, -68.8%)
Data Security / Quantum
Newport Beach, CA
theontechnology.com

Theta Lake (92, -8.0%)
GRC / Compliance Management
Santa Barbara, CA
thetalake.com

Thistle Technologies (6, -40.0%)
IoT Security / Security For Embedded Systems
San Francisco, CA
thistle.tech

ThreatOptix (12, 33.3%)
Operations / XDR
San Francisco, CA
threatoptix.ai

ThreatSTOP (20, 5.3%)
Network Security / Reputation
Carlsbad, CA
threatstop.com

TIBCO Software Inc. (3470, -22.4%)
Data Security / Big Data
Palo Alto, CA
tibco.com

Tigera (124, -9.5%)
Endpoint Security / Kubernetes Security
San Francisco, CA
tigera.io

Titaniam (31, 0.0%)
Data Security / Encryption
San Jose, CA
titaniam.io

Tonic.ai (98, -6.7%)
Data Security / Data Masking
San Francisco, CA
tonic.ai

Traceable (186, 24.0%)
API Security / API Security Cloud
San Francisco, CA
traceable.ai

Trellix (3353, 8.7%)
Security Analytics / XDR
Milpitas, CA
trellix.com

TriagingX (9, -10.0%)
Operations / Sandbox
San Jose, CA
triagingx.com

Tromzo (27, 80.0%)
Application Security / Software Development Security
Mountain View, CA
tromzo.com

TrueVault (16, -5.9%)
Data Security / Secure Storage
San Francisco, CA
truevault.com

Truffle Security (31, 24.0%)
Data Security / Secrets Management
San Francisco, CA
trufflesecurity.com

**Numbers in parentheses indicate headcount and % change in 2023.*

TrustArc (396, -7.9%)
GRC / Privacy Assessments
San Francisco, CA
trustarc.com

Trustero (12, -36.8%)
GRC / Compliance Management
Palo Alto, CA
trustero.com

TrustLayer (45, 0.0%)
GRC / Risk Management
San Francisco, CA
trustlayer.io

Trustle (14, 16.7%)
IAM / Access Security
Walnut Creek, CA
trustle.io

TrustLogix (18, 38.5%)
GRC / Governance
Mountain View, CA
trustlogix.io

Trustlook (9, -25.0%)
Endpoint Security / Malware Analysis
San Jose, CA
trustlook.com

TruU (69, 21.1%)
IAM / Authentication
Palo Alto, CA
truu.ai

Twingate (78, 11.4%)
IAM / Access Security
Redwood City, CA
twingate.com

Ubiq Security (23, -17.9%)
Data Security / Encryption
San Diego, CA
ubiqsecurity.com

UnifyID (5, -28.6%)
IAM / Authentication
Redwood City, CA
unify.id

Unit21 (125, 0.8%)
GRC / Compliance Management
San Francisco, CA
unit21.ai

Uno (14, 16.7%)
Operations / Threat Analysis
Palo Alto, CA
uno.ai

Untangle (18, -18.2%)
Network Security / UTM
San Jose, CA
untangle.com

Upfort (36, 9.1%)
Email Security / SMB Security
San Francisco, CA
upfort.com

UpGuard (195, 48.9%)
GRC / Monitoring
Mountain View, CA
upguard.com

V5 Systems (30, -21.1%)
IoT Security / OT Security
Fremont, CA
v5systems.us

Vade Secure (264, 16.8%)
Email Security / Defense Against Phishing
San Francisco, CA
vadesecure.com

Valimail (109, 6.9%)
Email Security / Defense Against Phishing
San Francisco, CA
valimail.com

Valtix (22, -42.1%)
Network Security / Zero Trust Networking
Santa Clara, CA
valtix.com

Vanta (484, 33.7%)
GRC / Compliance Management
San Francisco, CA
vanta.com

vArmour (91, -34.5%)
Endpoint Security / Servers
Mountain View, CA
varmour.com

Vault Security (3, -66.7%)
IAM / Authentication
CA
linktr.ee/vault_security

Vault12 (14, -6.7%)
Data Security / Wallets
Mountain View, CA
vault12.com

Vaultize (10, -23.1%)
Data Security / IRM
San Francisco, CA
vaultize.com

Vectra AI (624, 0.3%)
Security Analytics / Incident Management
San Jose, CA
vectra.ai

Vehere (155, 14.0%)
Network Security / NDR
San Francisco, CA
vehere.com

Vera (19, -9.5%)
Data Security / IRM
Palo Alto, CA
vera.com

Veracity Industrial Networks (7, 16.7%)
IoT Security / OT Security
Aliso Viejo, CA
veracity.io

Verimatrix (280, -3.1%)
Data Security / DRM
San Diego, CA
verimatrix.com

Versa (662, 4.6%)
Network Security / SDN
San Jose, CA
versa-networks.com

Very Good Security (233, 34.7%)
GRC / Secure Storage
San Francisco, CA
verygoodsecurity.com

Veza Technologies (195, 77.3%)
IAM / Access Security
Palo Alto, CA
veza.com

Viakoo (22, -4.3%)
IoT Security / Vulnerabilities
Mountain View, CA
viakoo.com

Vir2us (6, 0.0%)
Endpoint Security / Virtualization
Petaluma, CA
vir2us.com

Virsec Systems (150, -14.8%)
Application Security / Web App Protection
San Jose, CA
virsec.com

Viso Trust (45, 15.4%)
GRC / Risk Management
San Francisco, CA
visotrust.com

VMWare (30796, -12.7%)
Endpoint Security / EDR
Palo Alto, CA
vmware.com

Wallarm (112, 21.7%)
API Security
San Francisco, CA
wallarm.com

Wazuh (197, 26.3%)
Operations / SOC
San Jose, CA
wazuh.com

White Hawk Software (4, 0.0%)
Application Security / Tamper Proofing
Palo Alto, CA
whitehawksoftware.com

Whiteswan (8, 700.0%)
IAM / Access Security
Belmont, CA
whiteswansecurity.com

**Numbers in parentheses indicate headcount and % change in 2023.*

WhoisXML API (31, 6.9%)
Threat Intelligence / DNS Security
Covina, CA
whoisxmlapi.com

Wickr (22, -29.0%)
Data Security / Secure Communications
San Francisco, CA
wickr.com

WireX Systems (21, 16.7%)
Operations / Forensics
Sunnyvale, CA
wirexsystems.com

WootCloud (3, -40.0%)
Endpoint Security / Endpoint Control
San Jose, CA
wootcloud.com

Workspot (158, -6.0%)
Operations / Secure Remote Access
Campbell, CA
workspot.com

Xage Security (102, 54.5%)
IoT Security / OT Security
Palo Alto, CA
xage.com

Xantrion (84, 5.0%)
MSSP / Managed Security Services
Oakland, CA
xantrion.com

Xaptum (4, -20.0%)
Network Security
Palo Alto, CA
xaptum.com

Xiid (5, 25.0%)
IAM / Identity Management
Cupertino, CA
xiid.com

XQmessage (30, -25.0%)
Data Security / IRM
Oakland, CA
xqmsg.co

YouAttest (20, -9.1%)
GRC / Governance
Newport Beach, CA
youattest.com

ZecOps (16, -30.4%)
Operations / Automated Defense
San Francisco, CA
zecops.com

Zentera Systems (19, -24.0%)
Network Security / Zero Trust Networking
San Jose, CA
zentera.net

ZeroTier (16, 33.3%)
Network Security / Segmentation
Irvine, CA
zerotier.com

Zettaset (16, -5.9%)
Data Security / Encryption
Mountain View, CA
zettaset.com

Zluri (239, 151.6%)
Operations / Asset Management
San Francisco, CA
zluri.com

ZPE Systems (143, 19.2%)
Network Security / Access Security
Fremont, CA
zpesystems.com

Zscaler (7050, 11.3%)
Network Security / Cloud Security
San Jose, CA
zscaler.com

Zumigo (28, 33.3%)
IAM / Identity Verification
San Jose, CA
zumigo.com

Zymbit (12, 71.4%)
IoT Security / Device Security Modules
Santa Barbara, CA
zymbit.com

ZyXEL Communications Corp. (18, 5.9%)
Network Security / Firewalls
Anaheim, CA
zyxel.com

Colorado

Absio (5, 0.0%)
Data Security / Software-Defined Distributed Key Cryptography (SDKC)
Denver, CO
absio.com

AerPass (6, -33.3%)
IAM / Authentication
Boulder, CO
aerpass.com

Alpha Recon (22, 0.0%)
Threat Intelligence / Threat Intelligence Platform
Colorado Springs, CO
alpharecon.com

Anonos (69, 81.6%)
Data Security / Secure Data Sharing
Boulder, CO
anonos.com

Automox (227, -12.0%)
GRC / Patch Management
Boulder, CO
automox.com

Botdoc (13, 8.3%)
Data Security / Secure Data Sharing
Monument, CO
botdoc.io

Casa (68, 6.2%)
Data Security
Denver, CO
keys.casa

Circadence (76, -20.0%)
Training / Cyber Range
Boulder, CO
circadence.com

Cloudrise (56, 3.7%)
MSSP / Security Platform Management
Grand Junction, CO
cloudrise.com

Coalfire (984, -8.2%)
GRC / Vulnerabilities
Westminster, CO
coalfire.com

CyberGRX (107, -44.0%)
GRC / Risk Management
Denver, CO
cybergrx.com

Dapple (3, 0.0%)
IAM / Authentication
Centennial, CO
dapplesecurity.com

DarkOwl (26, -31.6%)
Threat Intelligence / Dark Web
Denver, CO
darkowl.com

deepwatch (395, 7.9%)
MSSP / MDR
Denver, CO
deepwatch.com

DH2i (12, 20.0%)
Network Security / Zero Trust Networking
Fort Collins, CO
dh2i.com

Enzoic (19, 0.0%)
Fraud Prevention / Credential Security
Boulder, CO
enzoic.com

FusionAuth (30, 20.0%)
IAM / CIAM
Broomfield, CO
fusionauth.io

FYEO (10, -56.5%)
Threat Intelligence / Threat Intelligence From DNS
Denver, CO
gofyeo.com

**Numbers in parentheses indicate headcount and % change in 2023.*

Jumpcloud (697, 5.9%)
IAM / Directory Services
Louisville, CO
jumpcloud.com

Keyavi (41, -2.4%)
Data Security / IRM
Denver, CO
keyavi.com

LogRhythm (544, -11.4%)
Security Analytics / Logs
Boulder, CO
logrhythm.com

Managed Methods (37, 23.3%)
GRC / Access Security
Boulder, CO
managedmethods.com

Mantix4 (4, 0.0%)
Security Analytics / Threat Hunting
Englewood, CO
mantix4.com

NeoCertified (8, 0.0%)
Email Security / Secure Email
Centennial, CO
neocertified.com

Optiv (2381, -2.6%)
MSSP / Managed Security Services
Denver, CO
optiv.com

Patch My PC (86, 8.9%)
GRC / Patch Management
Castle Rock, CO
patchmypc.com

Phylum (22, -33.3%)
Application Security / Code Security
Evergreen, CO
phylum.io

Ping Identity Corporation (1387, -0.2%)
IAM
Denver, CO
pingidentity.com

Red Canary (418, -5.6%)
MSSP / MDR
Denver, CO
redcanary.com

Sectrio (39, 34.5%)
IoT Security / Segmentation
CO
sectrio.com

Secure64 (41, 0.0%)
Network Security / DNS Security
Fort Collins, CO
secure64.com

Solutions-II (85, 11.8%)
MSSP / Monitoring
Littleton, CO
solutions-ii.com

StackHawk (56, 3.7%)
Application Security / Vulnerabilities
Denver, CO
stackhawk.com

Strata Identity (70, 6.1%)
IAM / Orchestration
Boulder, CO
strata.io

Swimlane (238, 30.1%)
Operations / Incident Management
Louisville, CO
swimlane.com

ThreatX (63, -4.5%)
API Security / Firewalls
Louisville, CO
threatx.com

TruKno (8, 0.0%)
Threat Intelligence / TIP
Denver, CO
trukno.com

Vault Vision (3, 0.0%)
IAM
Denver, CO
vaultvision.com

VirtualArmour (48, 6.7%)
MSSP / Managed Security Services
Centennial, CO
virtualarmour.com

YeshID (17, 54.5%)
IAM / Identity Management
Denver, CO
yeshid.com

Zvelo (40, -4.8%)
Network Security / URL Categorization
Greenwood VillageCO, CO
zvelo.com

Connecticut

1touch.io (78, 39.3%)
GRC / Data Discovery
Stamford, CT
1touch.io

Aceiss (10, 25.0%)
IAM / Access Security
New Canaan, CT
aceiss.com

Awareness Technologies (36, 5.9%)
Operations / Monitoring
Westport, CT
awarenesstechnologies.com

Datto (1193, -31.8%)
Email Security / Microsoft
Norwalk, CT
datto.com

Interguard (6, 0.0%)
Operations / Monitoring
Westport, CT
interguardsoftware.com

Kyber Security (16, -5.9%)
MSSP / Managed Security Services
Fairfield, CT
kybersecure.com

Netlib (4, 0.0%)
Data Security
Stamford, CT
netlibsecurity.com

Owl Cyber Defense (163, -11.9%)
Network Security / Air Gap
Danbury, CT
owlcyberdefense.com

Polarity (34, -15.0%)
Operations / Onscreen Data Augmentation
Farmington, CT
polarity.io

Protegrity (369, -1.6%)
Application Security
Stamford, CT
protegrity.com

SDG Corporation (577, 10.3%)
GRC
Norwalk, CT
sdgc.com

Truops (19, -5.0%)
GRC / Risk Management
Norwalk, CT
truops.com

Veridify Security (20, 11.1%)
IoT Security / Authentication
Shelton, CT
veridify.com

Zorus (25, -16.7%)
Network Security / VPN/Proxy
Monroe, CT
zorustech.com

California

Upwind (72, 53.2%)
Operations
California
upwind.io

DC

Adlumin (119, 35.2%)
Security Analytics / SIEM
Washington, DC
adlumin.com

**Numbers in parentheses indicate headcount and % change in 2023.*

DNSFilter (161, 30.9%)
Network Security / Filtering
Washington DC, DC
dnsfilter.com

Enveil (67, -10.7%)
Data Security / Encryption
Washington, DC
enveil.com

GreyNoise (62, 5.1%)
Threat Intelligence / Dark Web
Washington, DC
greynoise.io

Ion Channel (4, -69.2%)
Application Security / SBOM
DC
ionchannel.io

KeyCaliber (13, -23.5%)
GRC / Asset Inventory
Washington DC, DC
keycaliber.com

Picnic (38, -17.4%)
Data Security / Employee Protection
Washington, DC
getpicnic.com

Stacklet (25, -34.2%)
GRC / Policy Management
Washington, DC
stacklet.io

Star Lab (42, -2.3%)
Application Security / Research
Washington, DC
starlab.io

Sttarx (4, 33.3%)
Data Security / Encryption
Washington, DC
sttarx.com

Tidal Cyber (25, 25.0%)
Threat Intelligence / OSINT
Washington, DC
tidalcyber.com

ValeVPN (4, 100.0%)
Network Security / VPN/Proxy
Washington, DC
valevpn.com

Virtru (178, -3.3%)
Data Security / Secure Communications
Washington, DC
virtru.com

WWN Software LLC (7, -12.5%)
Data Security / Secure Data Sharing
Washington, DC
wwnsoftware.com

ZERODIUM (5, 400.0%)
Application Security / Bugs
Washington, DC
zerodium.com

Delaware

Anlyz (9, -66.7%)
Operations / SIEM
Lewes, DE
anlyz.co

Apphaz Security Solutions (5, -16.7%)
GRC / Penetration Testing
Bear, DE
apphaz.com

Arcanna AI (24, -4.0%)
Operations / SOC
Dover, DE
arcanna.ai

Aries Security (14, 7.7%)
Training / Cyber Range
Wilmington, DE
ariessecurity.com

EasyDMARC (74, 23.3%)
Email Security / DNS Security
Middletown, DE
easydmarc.com

InCyber (3, 0.0%)
Operations / Monitoring
Cherry Hill Township, DE
incyber1.com

IS3 (opens as Stopzilla) (26, 13.0%)
Endpoint Security / Anti-virus
Dover, DE
stopzilla.com

kloudle (11, -21.4%)
Operations / OP- Configuration Management
Wilmington, DE
kloudle.com

Nelysis (11, 37.5%)
IoT Security / Monitoring
Wilmington, DE
nelysis.com

Phin Security (32, 146.2%)
GRC / Security Awareness Training
Newark, DE
phinsec.io

Resmo (17, 6.2%)
Operations
Wilmington, DE
resmo.com

Right-Hand Security (48, 54.8%)
GRC / Security Awareness Training
Lewes, DE
right-hand.ai

Scalarr (21, -27.6%)
Fraud Prevention / Advertising-related
Wilmington, DE
scalarr.io

Securden (75, 31.6%)
IAM / Access Security
Newark, DE
securden.com

Seraphic Security (29, 31.8%)
Network Security / Secure Web Browsing
Wilmington, DE
seraphicsecurity.com

ShadowDragon (48, 71.4%)
Threat Intelligence / OSINT
Wilmington, DE
shadowdragon.io

Siga OT Solutions (35, 9.4%)
IoT Security / Monitoring
Wilmington, DE
sigasec.com

SOCRadar (166, 19.4%)
Threat Intelligence / TIP
Middletown, DE
socradar.io

STASH Global (4, 0.0%)
Data Security / DRM
Wilmington, DE
stash.global

ThreatMate (8, 700.0%)
Operations
Dover, DE
threatmate.com

Tophat Security (4, 0.0%)
MSSP / SIEM
Wilmington, DE
tophatsecurity.com

Trickest (15, 15.4%)
Operations / Penetration Testing
Dover, DE
trickest.com

vFeed (3, -25.0%)
GRC / Vulnerabilities
Middletow, DE
vfeed.io

Vulners (3, -25.0%)
Threat Intelligence / Vulnerabilities
Wilmington, DE
vulners.com

Florida

3wSecurity (4, -20.0%)
GRC / Penetration Testing
Tampa, FL
3wsecurity.com

**Numbers in parentheses indicate headcount and % change in 2023.*

A-Lign (644, -0.5%)
GRC / Compliance Management
Tampa, FL
a-lign.com

Abacode (70, 18.6%)
MSSP / MDR
Tampa, FL
abacode.com

Adsero Security (3, 0.0%)
MSSP / Managed Security Services
Tampa, FL
adserosecurity.com

Aegis IT Solutions (7, 16.7%)
MSSP / Managed Security Services
Boca Raton, FL
aegisitsolutions.net

Aerobyte (11, 0.0%)
Network Security / Zero Trust Networking
Boca Raton, FL
aerobyte.com

Airiam (62, -17.3%)
MSSP / MDR
Miami Beach, FL
airiam.com

Appgate (372, -11.2%)
IAM / Access Security
Coral Gables, FL
appgate.com

AppRiver (149, -20.7%)
Email Security
Gulf Breeze, FL
appriver.com

ASPG (31, 40.9%)
Data Security / Encryption
Naples, FL
aspg.com

BlackCloak (50, 56.2%)
Threat Intelligence / Protection For Executives And Celebrities
Orlando, FL
blackcloak.io

BlueShift Cybersecurity (12, -7.7%)
MSSP / MDR
Fort Myers, FL
blueshiftcyber.com

Cienaga Systems (5, 25.0%)
Security Analytics / Cyber Threat Management
Lakewood Ranch, FL
cienagasystems.net

Cigent (20, -9.1%)
Network Security / Monitoring
Fort Myers, FL
cigent.com

CIPHER Security (341, 27.7%)
MSSP / Managed Security Services
Miami, FL
cipher.com

Citrix Systems (6105, -27.2%)
Network Security / Access Security
Fort Lauderdale, FL
citrix.com

Cloud24X7 (25, 8.7%)
MSSP / MSSP Enablement
Fort Lauderdale, FL
cloud24x7.us

Code-X (16, -5.9%)
Data Security / Shards
Tampa, FL
teamcode-x.com

ComplyUp (4, 0.0%)
GRC / Compliance Management
Tampa, FL
complyup.com

Compuquip (59, 0.0%)
MSSP / SOC
Miami, FL
compuquip.com

Corellium (53, 23.3%)
Application Security / Virtualization
Boynton Beach, FL
corellium.com

CyberFOX (64, 8.5%)
IAM / Access Security
Tampa, FL
cyberfox.com

Cyborg Security (32, 23.1%)
Threat Intelligence / TIP
Orlando, FL
cyborgsecurity.com

Cybral (24, 33.3%)
Operations / Breach And Attack Simulation
Miami, FL
cybral.com

CybrHawk (11, -8.3%)
Operations / Data Management
Fort Lauderdale, FL
cybrhawk.com

Cygna Labs Corp (80, 56.9%)
GRC / Auditing
Miami Beach, FL
cygnalabs.com

Cyxtera Technologies (622, -9.7%)
Network Security / Zero Trust Networking
Coral Gables, FL
cyxtera.com

Digital Hands (69, 9.5%)
MSSP / Managed Security Services
Tampa, FL
digitalhands.com

ELK Analytics (18, 20.0%)
MSSP / Managed Security Services
Naples, FL
elkanalytics.com

ERMProtect (14, -22.2%)
GRC / Security Awareness Training
Coral Gables, FL
ermprotect.com

Faraday (47, 14.6%)
Operations / Manager Of Managers
Miami, FL
faradaysec.com

Fischer International Identity (69, -6.8%)
IAM
Naples, FL
fischeridentity.com

Fortress Information Security (248, 6.0%)
GRC / Risk Management
Oralndo, FL
fortressinfosec.com

Fraudlogix (17, -5.6%)
Fraud Prevention
Hallandale Beach, FL
fraudlogix.com

Gatefy (6, -14.3%)
Email Security
Miami, FL
gatefy.com

GigaNetworks (13, 8.3%)
MSSP / Managed Security Services
Miami, FL
giganetworks.com

ID Agent (20, 5.3%)
Threat Intelligence / Dark Web
Miami, FL
idagent.com

Identite (43, -21.8%)
IAM / Authentication
Clearwater, FL
identite.us

Immunity (27, -18.2%)
GRC / Vulnerabilities
Miami, FL
immunityinc.com

**Numbers in parentheses indicate headcount and % change in 2023.*

Ironwifi (3, -25.0%)
IAM / Authentication
Orlando, FL
ironwifi.com

KnowBe4 (1856, 4.9%)
GRC / Security Awareness Training
Clearwater, FL
knowbe4.com

Lumu Technologies (121, 12.0%)
Security Analytics / Incident Management
Doral, FL
lumu.io

Moderne (33, 37.5%)
Application Security
Miami, FL
moderne.io

New Net Technologies (28, 21.7%)
Operations / Workflow Automation
Naples, FL
newnettechnologies.com

Nucleon Cyber (6, -33.3%)
Threat Intelligence / Aggregation
Tampa, FL
nucleon.sh

Nucleus Security (73, 1.4%)
GRC / Vulnerabilities
Sarasota, FL
nucleussec.com

Optimal IdM (11, 0.0%)
IAM / Authentication
Lutz, FL
optimalidm.com

Perch (9, -30.8%)
MSSP / SOC
Tampa, FL
perchsecurity.com

ProtectStar (3, 50.0%)
Data Security / Data Erasure And Destruction
Miami, FL
protectstar.com

Q6 Cyber (51, 4.1%)
Threat Intelligence / Dark Web
Miami, FL
q6cyber.com

Quadrant Information Security (41, 17.1%)
MSSP / SIEM
Jacksonville, FL
quadrantsec.com

Quicklaunch (41, 13.9%)
IAM / Identity Management
Miami, FL
quicklaunch.io

Reliaquest (1002, 5.1%)
Operations / Threat Hunting
Tampa, FL
reliaquest.com

RiskWatch International (12, -7.7%)
GRC / Risk Management
Sarasota, FL
riskwatch.com

Secberus (20, -33.3%)
GRC / Compliance Management
Miami, FL
secberus.com

SecLogic (38, 46.1%)
GRC / Posture Management
Jacksonville, FL
seclogic.io

Secnap (18, 12.5%)
MSSP / Managed Security Services
Fort Lauderdale, FL
secnap.com

Sensible Vision (4, -20.0%)
IAM / Authentication
Cape Coral, FL
sensiblevision.com

SPAMfighter (16, -11.1%)
Endpoint Security / Anti-spam
Miami, FL
spamfighter.com

Spirion (was Identity Finder) (81, -17.4%)
GRC / Data Discovery
St. Petersburg, FL
spirion.com

Spur (7, 0.0%)
Fraud Prevention / Reputation
Mount Dora, FL
spur.us

SurePass ID (13, 8.3%)
IAM / Authentication
Winter Garden, FL
surepassid.com

Surety (45, 40.6%)
Data Security
Naples, FL
surety.com

Tauruseer (23, 155.6%)
Operations / Code Security
Jacksonville Beach, FL
tauruseer.com

Team Cymru (128, 1.6%)
Threat Intelligence / IoC Intelligence
Lake Mary, FL
team-cymru.com

Teramind (104, 50.7%)
Operations / Monitoring
Aventura, FL
teramind.co

Thales (666, 12.1%)
Data Security / Authentication
Plantation, FL
thalesesecurity.com

ThreatLocker (314, 34.8%)
Endpoint Security / Application Whitelisting
Maitland, FL
threatlocker.com

Trapezoid (9, -30.8%)
IoT Security / Firmware
Miami, FL
trapezoid.com

VantagePoint (53, 1.9%)
Operations
Wesley Chapel, FL
thevantagepoint.com

Veriato (22, -4.3%)
Operations / Monitoring
Palm Beach Gardens, FL
veriato.com

Vigiles (4, 33.3%)
GRC / Security Awareness Training
Miami, FL
vigiles.cloud

Vijilan Security (52, -3.7%)
MSSP / SIEM
Ft. Lauderdale, FL
vijilan.com

Vipre (182, 15.2%)
Endpoint Security / Anti-virus
Clearwater, FL
vipre.com

Wavecrest Computing (16, 14.3%)
Network Security / Gateways
Melbourne, FL
wavecrest.net

Georgia

AMI (1980, 44.6%)
Endpoint Security / Firmware
Duluth, GA
ami.com

Apptega (54, 1.9%)
GRC / Compliance Management
Atlanta, GA
apptega.com

arnica (25, -26.5%)
Operations / Software Development Security
Alpharetta, GA
arnica.io

Arpeggio Software (3, 0.0%)
Data Security / ISeries
Atlanta, GA
arpeggiosoftware.com

**Numbers in parentheses indicate headcount and % change in 2023.*

Bastille (64, 39.1%)
Network Security / Wireless Security
Atlanta, GA
bastille.net

BeyondTrust (1452, 4.5%)
IAM / Access Security
Johns Creek, GA
beyondtrust.com

C1Secure (19, -20.8%)
GRC / Compliance Management
Atlanta, GA
c1secure.com

Cloudnosys (13, 0.0%)
Operations / Posture Management
Roswell, GA
cloudnosys.com

ControlScan (35, -14.6%)
MSSP / Managed Security Services
Alpharetta, GA
controlscan.com

Core Security (112, 3.7%)
GRC / Vulnerabilities
Roswell, GA
coresecurity.com

CORL Technologies (81, -22.9%)
GRC
Atlanta, GA
corltech.com

Curricula (12, 0.0%)
GRC / Security Awareness Training
Atlanta, GA
curricula.com

Cyble (185, 58.1%)
Threat Intelligence / Dark Web
Alpharetta, GA
cyble.io

Cybraics (11, -50.0%)
Security Analytics
Atlanta, GA
cybraics.com

Cybriant (24, 0.0%)
MSSP / MDR
Alpharetta, GA
cybriant.com

Cynamics (31, 6.9%)
Network Security / Traffic Analysis
Peachtree Corners, GA
cynamics.ai

DefenseStorm (103, 0.0%)
GRC / Compliance Management
Atlanta, GA
defensestorm.com

Digital Envoy (69, 7.8%)
Network Security / Reputation
Peachtree Corners, GA
digitalenvoy.net

Diligent eSecurity International (4, 33.3%)
GRC / Monitoring
Atlanta, GA
desintl.com

Dispersive Networks (14, -30.0%)
Network Security / VPN/Proxy
Alpharetta, GA
dispersive.io

Evident ID (69, -19.8%)
IAM / Identity Verification
Atlanta, GA
evidentid.com

FortifyData (19, -36.7%)
GRC / Risk Management
Kennesaw, GA
fortifydata.com

Fortiphyd Logic (6, 0.0%)
IoT Security / OT Security
Norcross, GA
fortiphyd.com

Fraudmarc (5, 25.0%)
Fraud Prevention / Email Fraud Prevention
Atlanta, GA
fraudmarc.com

IDology (184, 85.9%)
IAM / Authentication
Atlanta, GA
idology.com

IntelliSystems (29, 11.5%)
MSSP / Managed Security Services
Augusta, GA
intellisystems.com

IoT Secure (10, 25.0%)
IoT Security / Asset Management
Duluth, GA
iotsecure.io

Iris Network Systems (19, 11.8%)
Network Security / Traffic Analysis
Alpharetta, GA
irisns.com

M2Sys Technology (86, -8.5%)
IAM / Authentication
Atlanta, GA
m2sys.com

Nevatech (4, -33.3%)
API Security
Atlanta, GA
nevatech.com

OnePath (356, -5.3%)
MSSP / Managed Security Services
Kennesaw, GA
1path.com

OneTrust (2500, -5.2%)
GRC / Risk Management
Atlanta, GA
onetrust.com

Privacy4Cars (32, 33.3%)
Data Security / Automotive
Kennesaw, GA
privacy4cars.com

RealTheory (7, -12.5%)
Endpoint Security / Container Security
Atlanta, GA
realtheory.io

SecurEnds (62, -26.2%)
IAM / Governance
Atlanta, GA
securends.com

SecureWorks (1903, -21.8%)
MSSP / Managed Security Services
Atlanta, GA
secureworks.com

Simeio Solutions (719, 1.8%)
IAM
Atlanta, GA
simeiosolutions.com

Telemate Software (23, 15.0%)
Security Analytics / SIEM
Norcross, GA
telemate.net

Vonahi Security (16, -11.1%)
Operations / Penetration Testing
Atlanta, GA
vonahi.io

WiKID Systems (4, 0.0%)
IAM / Authentication
Atlanta, GA
wikidsystems.com

WitFoo (11, -21.4%)
Operations / Security Operations Platform
Dunwoody, GA
witfoo.com

Iowa

FastPath (109, 13.5%)
GRC / Authorization
Des Moines, IA
gofastpath.com

IdRamp (4, 0.0%)
IAM / Authentication
Indianola, IA
idramp.com

**Numbers in parentheses indicate headcount and % change in 2023.*

PC Matic (63, 8.6%)
Endpoint Security / Application Whitelisting
Sioux City, IA
pcmatic.com

Idaho

AppDetex (218, 7.4%)
Threat Intelligence / Brand
Boise, ID
appdetex.com

Gravwell (16, 14.3%)
Security Analytics / Data Analysis
Coeur dAlene, ID
gravwell.io

Kount (265, 0.4%)
Fraud Prevention / Identity Verification
Boise, ID
kount.com

Plextrac (95, -15.9%)
GRC / Security Report Management Platform
Boise, ID
plextrac.com

ULedger (21, 5.0%)
Data Security / Blockchain
Boise, ID
uledger.co

Illinois

Accertify (330, 9.6%)
Fraud Prevention
Itasca, IL
accertify.com

Armarius Software (8, 0.0%)
Data Security / DLP
Warrenville, IL
armariussoftware.com

Ascend Technologies (246, -5.0%)
MSSP / Managed Security Services
Chicago, IL
teamascend.com

Cohesive Networks (18, 0.0%)
Network Security / Cloud Tunnels Over IPSec
Chicago, IL
cohesive.net

CYFIRMA (98, 27.3%)
Threat Intelligence
Oak Park, IL
cyfirma.com

DealRoom (27, -18.2%)
Data Security / Deal Room
Chicago, IL
dealroom.net

DefendEdge (124, 12.7%)
MSSP / Managed Security Services
Rosemont, IL
defendedge.com

Emsisoft (28, 7.7%)
Endpoint Security / Anti-virus
Chicago, IL
emsisoft.com

EventSentry (4, 0.0%)
Security Analytics / SIEM
Chicago, IL
eventsentry.com

Fingerprint (115, 2.7%)
Fraud Prevention / Device Identification
Chicago, IL
fingerprint.com

FingerprintJS (115, -21.2%)
Fraud Prevention / Device Characteristics
Chicago, IL
fingerprintjs.com

HALOCK Security Labs (33, 10.0%)
Operations / Incident Management
Schaumburg, IL
halock.com

Havoc Shield (13, 18.2%)
GRC / SMB Security
Chicago, IL
havocshield.com

Ilantus (175, -8.4%)
IAM / Identity Management
Schaumburg, IL
ilantus.com

Infinite Convergence Solutions (110, 7.8%)
Data Security / Secure Communications
Arlington Heights, IL
infinite-convergence.com

Information Security Corporation (21, 16.7%)
Data Security / Public Key Infrastructure
Oak Park, IL
infoseccorp.com

Jemurai (8, 0.0%)
Operations / Security Program Dashboard
Chicago, IL
jemurai.com

Keeper Security (347, -7.2%)
IAM / Credential Security
Chicago, IL
keepersecurity.com

LogicGate (271, 3.4%)
GRC
Chicago, IL
logicgate.com

Mako Networks Ltd. (70, 9.4%)
MSSP / Managed Security Services
Elgin, IL
makonetworks.com

Metmox (106, -22.6%)
MSSP / SOC
Schaumburg, IL
metmox.com

Mutare (40, -18.4%)
Data Security / Secure Communications
Rolling Meadows, IL
mutare.com

Network Perception (47, -21.7%)
GRC / Configuration Management
Chicago, IL
network-perception.com

NorthStar.io (16, -5.9%)
GRC / Vulnerabilities
Chicago, IL
northstar.io

NowSecure (137, -16.5%)
Endpoint Security / Mobile Device Security
Chicago, IL
nowsecure.com

Nullafi (15, 0.0%)
Data Security / Secure Storage
Chicago, IL
nullafi.com

Nuts Technologies Inc. (6, 0.0%)
Data Security / Encryption
Chicago Area, IL
nutstechnologies.com

OneSpan (741, -1.5%)
IAM
Chicago, IL
onespan.com

onShore Security (41, -2.4%)
MSSP / Managed Security Services
Chicago, IL
onShore.com

Pinochle.AI (15, -40.0%)
Operations / XDR
Vernon Hills, IL
pinochle.ai

**Numbers in parentheses indicate headcount and % change in 2023.*

RedLegg (58, 18.4%)
MSSP / Managed Security Services
Geneva, IL
redlegg.com

Rippleshot (20, -9.1%)
Fraud Prevention / Fraud Detection
Chicago, IL
rippleshot.com

Runtime Verification (48, 17.1%)
Application Security / Code Security
Urbana, IL
runtimeverification.com

SlashID (14, 0.0%)
IAM / Access Security
Chicago, IL
slashid.dev

ThirdPartyTrust (16, -71.4%)
GRC / Risk Management
Chicago, IL
thirdpartytrust.com

TruGrid (6, -14.3%)
IAM / Access Security
Schaumburg, IL
trugrid.com

TrustWave (a Singtel Company) (1202, -7.4%)
MSSP / Managed Security Services
Chicago, IL
trustwave.com

UncommonX (22, 0.0%)
MSSP / MDR
Chicago, IL
uncommonx.com

Verve (134, 0.8%)
IoT Security / OT Security
Chicago, IL
verveindustrial.com

VikingCloud (574, 9.8%)
MSSP / MDR
Chicago, IL
vikingcloud.com

Indiana

Cimcor (22, 0.0%)
GRC
Merrillville, IN
cimcor.com

IdentityLogix (3, 0.0%)
IAM / Access Security
Crown Point, IN
identitylogix.com

Stamus Networks (24, 20.0%)
Network Security / NDR
Indianapolis, IN
stamus-networks.com

Kansas

Archer (661, 36.3%)
GRC / Risk Management
Overland Park, KS
archerirm.com

DataLocker (55, -3.5%)
Data Security / Secure Storage
Overland Park, KS
datalocker.com

FireMon (235, -8.2%)
Operations / Policy Management
Overland Park, KS
firemon.com

Foresite MSP (63, -14.9%)
MSSP / Managed Security Services
Overland Park, KS
foresite.com

Onspring (85, 6.2%)
GRC / Auditing
Overland Park, KS
onspring.com

SendThisFile (8, 60.0%)
Data Security / Secure Data Sharing
Wichita, KS
sendthisfile.com

SOFTwarfare (31, 63.2%)
Application Security / Integration Security
Prairie Village, KS
softwarfare.com

Spideroak (38, 0.0%)
Data Security
Mission, KS
spideroak.com

Kentucky

Venminder (236, -3.3%)
GRC / Risk Management
Elizabethtown, KY
venminder.com

Louisiana

CenturyLink (25991, -5.1%)
MSSP / Monitoring
Monroe, LA
centurylink.com

CyberReef Solutions (21, -30.0%)
IoT Security / OT Security
Shreveport, LA
cyberreef.com

TraceSecurity (108, 1.9%)
GRC
Baton Rouge, LA
tracesecurity.com

Massachusetts

Accolade Technology (8, 14.3%)
Network Security / Network Appliance Security
Franklin, MA
accoladetechnology.com

Akamai Technologies (9270, 5.7%)
Network Security / DDoS Defense
Cambridge, MA
akamai.com

Allegro Software (6, -25.0%)
IoT Security / Security For Embedded Systems
Boxborough, MA
allegrosoft.com

Aquila Technology (31, 14.8%)
Email Security / Defense Against Phishing
Burlington, MA
aquilatc.com

Aura (733, 13.8%)
Endpoint Security / Data Privacy
Boston, MA
aura.com

Basis Technology (75, -44.4%)
Operations / Forensics
Cambridge, MA
basistech.com

BastionZero (14, -26.3%)
IAM / Gateways
Boston, MA
bastionzero.com

Belarc Inc. (14, -12.5%)
GRC / Asset Management
Maynard, MA
belarc.com

Biscom (202, 9.2%)
Data Security / Secure Data Sharing
Chelmsford, MA
biscom.com

BitSight (805, 0.6%)
GRC / Security Ratings
Boston, MA
bitsight.com

Blind Hash (3, 0.0%)
IAM / Credential Security
Boston, MA
blindhash.com

BlueRisc (10, -16.7%)
Application Security / Code Security
Amherst, MA
bluerisc.com

**Numbers in parentheses indicate headcount and % change in 2023.*

Censinet (39, 34.5%)
GRC
Boston, MA
censinet.com

Ceritas (8, 0.0%)
IoT Security / Vulnerabilities
Cambridge, MA
ceritas.ai

Cloaked (50, 16.3%)
Data Security
Lowell, MA
cloaked.app

CloudTruth (15, 25.0%)
Application Security / Configuration Management
Boston, MA
cloudtruth.com

CODA Intelligence (11, 22.2%)
GRC / Vulnerabilities
Boston, MA
codaintelligence.com

Corero Network Security (117, 13.6%)
Network Security / DDoS Defense
Marlborough, MA
corero.com

Covered Security (3, -25.0%)
GRC / Security Awareness Training
Boston, MA
coveredsecurity.com

CSPi (125, 10.6%)
Network Security / Traffic Analysis
Lowell, MA
cspi.com

Cybereason (814, -17.4%)
Security Analytics / Incident Management
Boston, MA
cybereason.com

Cyberhaven (116, 22.1%)
Network Security / Monitoring
Boston, MA
cyberhaven.io

CyberSaint (43, -20.4%)
GRC / Risk Management
Boston, MA
cybersaint.io

CyGlass (12, -47.8%)
Security Analytics
Littleton, MA
cyglass.com

CYTRIO (17, -15.0%)
GRC / Rights Management
Boston, MA
cytrio.com

DeleteMe (110, 74.6%)
Data Security / Data Removal
Somerville, MA
joindeleteme.com

Devo (675, 4.7%)
Security Analytics / SIEM
Cambridge, MA
devo.com

Digital Guardian (204, -10.5%)
GRC / DLP
Waltham, MA
digitalguardian.com

Digital Immunity (3, 0.0%)
Endpoint Security / System Hardening
Burlington, MA
digitalimmunity.com

Dover Microsystems (10, 11.1%)
IoT Security / Firmware
Waltham, MA
dovermicrosystems.com

DTonomy (8, 100.0%)
Security Analytics / AI Applied To Alerts
Cambridge, MA
dtonomy.com

Dynatrace (4639, 8.9%)
Application Security / Vulnerabilities
Waltham, MA
dynatrace.com

FireCompass (81, 8.0%)
Operations / Attack Surface Management
Boston, MA
firecompass.com

Fiverity (21, 10.5%)
Fraud Prevention / Fraud Detection
Boston, MA
fiverity.com

Foregenix (91, 1.1%)
GRC / Vulnerabilities
Boston, MA
foregenix.com

ForumSystems (35, 12.9%)
Network Security / Firewalls
Needham, MA
forumsys.com

FullArmor (24, 0.0%)
Network Security / Policy Management
Boston, MA
fullarmor.com

Getvisibility (51, 34.2%)
Data Security / Data Discovery
Cambridge, MA
getvisibility.com

GreatHorn (23, -41.0%)
Email Security / Defense Against Phishing
Waltham, MA
greathorn.com

HAProxy Technologies (100, 5.3%)
Network Security / Firewalls
Waltham, MA
haproxy.com

iboss (307, 1.3%)
Network Security / Gateways
Boston, MA
iboss.com

Imprivata (1058, 36.2%)
IAM
Lexington, MA
imprivata.com

Industrial Defender (43, -2.3%)
IoT Security
Foxborough, MA
industrialdefender.com

JetPatch (14, -17.6%)
Operations / Patch Management
Boston, MA
jetpatch.com

KabaCorp (5, 400.0%)
Endpoint Security / Secure Web Browsing
Boston, MA
kabacorp.com

Keytos Security (7, 16.7%)
IAM / Authentication
Boston, MA
keytos.io

Kintent (70, -6.7%)
GRC / Compliance Management
Boston, MA
kintent.com

Kolide (35, 25.0%)
Endpoint Security / Slack Community For Security Updates
Somerville, MA
kolide.com

LogMeIn (1337, -19.8%)
IAM / Credential Security
Boston, MA
logmein.com

Logz.io (184, -17.1%)
Security Analytics / Logs
Boston, MA
logz.io

Lux Scientiae (43, 0.0%)
Data Security / Secure Communications
Medfield, MA
luxsci.com

Maxmind (80, 27.0%)
Fraud Prevention / Geolocation
Waltham, MA
maxmind.com

**Numbers in parentheses indicate headcount and % change in 2023.*

Mobb (25, 38.9%)
Application Security / Vulnerabilities
Acton, MA
mobb.ai

NetScout (2816, 1.9%)
Network Security / Incident Management
Westford, MA
netscout.com

NetWitness (196, 56.8%)
Operations / XDR
Bedford, MA
netwitness.com

Nimbusddos (4, 0.0%)
Testing / DDoS Defense
Newton, MA
nimbusddos.com

Noetic (52, 4.0%)
GRC / Asset Management
Waltham, MA
noeticcyber.com

Onapsis Inc. (345, -5.0%)
Data Security / SAP
Boston, MA
onapsis.com

Onpage (31, 0.0%)
Operations / Security Alerts
Waltham, MA
OnPage.com

Oort (29, -37.0%)
IAM / Incident Management
Boston, MA
www.oort.io

Perygee (9, 28.6%)
IoT Security / OT Security
Boston, MA
perygee.com

PiiqMedia (5, -16.7%)
GRC / Security Awareness Training
Cambridge, MA
piiqmedia.com

PortSys (6, -25.0%)
IAM / Access Security
Marlborough, MA
portsys.com

PreVeil (61, 17.3%)
Data Security / Encryption
Boston, MA
preveil.com

Privafy (83, -3.5%)
IAM / Access Security
Burlington, MA
privafy.com

Process Software (15, 7.1%)
Email Security
Framingham, MA
process.com

ProcessUnity (174, 28.9%)
GRC / Risk Management
Concord, MA
processunity.com

Progress (3516, 6.3%)
Network Security / Secure Data Sharing
Bedford, MA
progress.com

Proof Authentication (12, 50.0%)
IAM / Application Authenticity
Boston, MA
proofauthentication.com

Quantum Xchange (17, 13.3%)
Data Security / Quantum
Newton, MA
quantumxc.com

Randori (90, -6.2%)
GRC / Attack Surface Management
Waltham, MA
randori.com

Rapid7 (2825, -0.2%)
GRC / Vulnerabilities
Boston, MA
rapid7.com

RealCISO (6, -25.0%)
GRC
Boston, MA
realciso.io

Recorded Future (1104, 9.5%)
Threat Intelligence
Somerville, MA
recordedfuture.com

Reversing Labs (298, 13.3%)
Operations / Malware Analysis
Cambridge, MA
reversinglabs.com

Rezonate (27, 50.0%)
IAM / Identity Management
Boston, MA
rezonate.io

RSA Security (Symphony Technology Group) (2826, 0.3%)
IAM / Authentication
Bedford, MA
rsa.com

Seceon (121, 9.0%)
Security Analytics / SIEM
Westford, MA
seceon.com

Security Innovation (225, 22.3%)
Training / Cyber Range
Wilmington, MA
securityinnovation.com

SecZetta (17, -56.4%)
IAM
Fall River, MA
seczetta.com

SideChannel (34, 3.0%)
Network Security / Segmentation
Worcester, MA
sidechannel.com

SimSpace (173, -13.9%)
Training / Cyber Range
Boston, MA
simspace.com

Slim.AI (38, -9.5%)
Application Security / Container Security
Acton, MA
slim.ai

solo.io (229, 2.7%)
Network Security / Segmentation
Cambridge, MA
solo.io

Sotero (19, -36.7%)
Data Security / Encryption
Burlington, MA
soterosoft.com

Tausight (29, 31.8%)
GRC / Healthcare
Boston, MA
tausight.com

Technical Communications Corporation (15, -28.6%)
Data Security / Secure Communications
Concord, MA
tccsecure.com

Threat Stack (8, -68.0%)
Network Security / Monitoring
Boston, MA
threatstack.com

ThreatNG (11, 120.0%)
Threat Intelligence / Dark Web
Shrewsbury, MA
threatngsecurity.com

Tidelift (66, -17.5%)
Application Security / SBOM
Boston, MA
tidelift.com

Timus Networks (66, 106.2%)
Network Security
Boston, MA
timusnetworks.com

**Numbers in parentheses indicate headcount and % change in 2023.*

Transmit Security (324, -11.7%)
Fraud Prevention / Anti-fraud
Boston, MA
transmitsecurity.com

Tufin (462, -12.3%)
Operations / Policy Management
Boston, MA
tufin.com

Unitrends (156, -6.6%)
Data Security / Encryption
Burlington, MA
unitrends.com

Uptycs (344, 18.6%)
Security Analytics / OSQuery
Waltham, MA
uptycs.com

Veracode (692, -13.6%)
Application Security / Code Security
Burlington, MA
veracode.com

Veridium (42, -2.3%)
IAM / Authentication
Boston, MA
veridiumid.com

VMRay (118, 11.3%)
Security Analytics / Threat Analysis
Boston, MA
vmray.com

VulnCheck (13, 116.7%)
Threat Intelligence / Vulnerabilities
Lexington, MA
vulncheck.com

Wabbi (16, -5.9%)
Application Security / Software Development Security
Boston, MA
wabbisoft.com

XTN Cognitive Security (25, 0.0%)
IAM / Identity Verification
Boston, MA
xtn-lab.com

Yottaa (103, -18.2%)
Network Security / DDoS Defense
Waltham, MA
yottaa.com

Zeronorth (5, -28.6%)
GRC / Vulnerabilities
Boston, MA
zeronorth.io

Zilla Security (41, 28.1%)
GRC / Compliance Management
Boston, MA
zillasecurity.com

Maryland

ADF Solutions (25, 19.1%)
GRC / Forensics
Bethesda, MD
adfsolutions.com

Aembit (21, 162.5%)
IAM / Identity Management
Silver Spring, MD
aembit.io

Amtel (78, 6.8%)
Endpoint Security / Mobile Device Security
Rockville, MD
amtelnet.com

Anchor Technologies (16, -11.1%)
GRC / Risk Management
Columbia, MD
anchortechnologies.com

Archon (Was Attila Security) (17, 13.3%)
IoT Security / Firewalls
Fulton, MD
attilasec.com

arctonyx (7, 0.0%)
Operations / Attack Surface Management
Baltimore, MD
arctonyx.com

Ardent Privacy (15, 25.0%)
GRC / Data Privacy
Catonsville, MD
ardentprivacy.ai

AuthMind (31, 55.0%)
GRC / Risk Management
Bethesda, MD
authmind.com

Balance Theory (16, 45.5%)
Operations / Secure Collaboration
Columbia, MD
balancetheory.io

Bandura Cyber (30, 0.0%)
Network Security / Firewalls
Columbia, MD
bandurasystems.com

Blackpoint (169, 83.7%)
MSSP / MDR
Ellicott City, MD
blackpointcyber.com

Bricata (10, -23.1%)
Network Security / IPS
Columbia, MD
bricata.com

Brivo (405, 38.7%)
IAM / Identity Management
Bethesda, MD
brivo.com

Carson & Saint (Was Saint Corporation) (25, 8.7%)
GRC / Vulnerabilities
Bethesda, MD
carson-saint.com

Corsica Technologies (138, 9.5%)
MSSP / Managed Security Services
Centreville, MD
corsicatech.com

Cyber Crucible (12, -20.0%)
Security Analytics / Incident Management
Severna Park, MD
cybercrucible.com

Cyber Reliant (6, 0.0%)
Data Security / Encryption
Annapolis, MD
cyberreliant.com

Cyber Skyline (16, 77.8%)
Training / Continuous Training
College Park, MD
cyberskyline.com

CyberPoint International (3, 0.0%)
Endpoint Security / File Artifact Detection (mostly PS)
Baltimore, MD
cyberpointllc.com

CyberSecure IPS (10, 25.0%)
Network Security / IPS
Upper Marlboro, MD
cybersecureips.com

Cybrary (213, -13.1%)
GRC / Training
College Park, MD
cybrary.it

Dragos (553, -4.3%)
IoT Security / OT Security
Hanover, MD
dragos.com

Envieta (18, -5.3%)
Data Security / Hardware
Columbia, MD
envieta.com

Fidelis Cybersecurity (Skyview) (150, -23.9%)
Security Analytics
Bethesda, MD
fidelissecurity.com

Fluency Security (7, 0.0%)
Security Analytics / SIEM
College Park, MD
fluencysecurity.com

Fornetix (49, 8.9%)
Data Security / Key Management
Frederick, MD
fornetix.com

GateKeeper Access (19, 5.6%)
IAM / Authentication
College Park, MD
gkaccess.com

**Numbers in parentheses indicate headcount and % change in 2023.*

Hopr (8, 0.0%)
Operations / Key Rotation
Columbia, MD
hopr.co

Huntress Labs (335, 19.6%)
Operations / Anti-malware
Baltimore, MD
huntresslabs.com

Immuta (265, -8.6%)
Data Security / Access Security
College Park, MD
immuta.com

Inky (48, -11.1%)
Email Security / Defense Against Phishing
Rockville, MD
inky.com

Interpres Security (26, 136.4%)
Operations / Attack Surface Management
Bethesda, MD
interpressecurity.com

IronNet Cybersecurity (84, -55.8%)
Network Security / Traffic Analysis
Fulton, MD
ironnet.com

Kion (80, 33.3%)
GRC / Compliance Management
Fulton, MD
kion.io

KoolSpan (33, 10.0%)
Data Security / Secure Communications
Bethesda, MD
koolspan.com

OnSystem Logic (6, 0.0%)
Endpoint Security / Application Hardening
Catonsville, MD
onsystemlogic.com/

Protenus (101, -11.4%)
GRC / Healthcare
Baltimore, MD
protenus.com

Racktop Systems (59, 1.7%)
Data Security / Secure Storage
Fulton, MD
racktopsystems.com

Rampart Communications (55, 66.7%)
Network Security / Wireless Security
Hanover, MD
rampartcommunications.com

RedJack (36, 33.3%)
Network Security / Monitoring
Silver Spring, MD
redjack.com

Ridgeback Network Defense (9, -18.2%)
Deception
Baltimore, MD
ridgebacknet.com

RioRey (16, 0.0%)
Network Security / DDoS Defense
Bethesda, MD
riorey.com

Room 40 Labs (27, 145.4%)
Operations
Bethesda, MD
room40labs.com

Saf.ai (6, 0.0%)
Data Security / IRM
Bethesda, MD
saf.ai

Sepio Systems (69, -15.8%)
IoT Security / Asset Management
Gaithersburg, MD
sepiocyber.com

Sicura (26, 8.3%)
GRC / Compliance Management
Baltimore, MD
sicura.us

SnapAttack (26, 0.0%)
Operations / Threat Hunting
Columbia, MD
snapattack.com

SOCSoter (21, 16.7%)
MSSP / Managed Security Services
Hagerstown, MD
socsoter.com

Sonatype (573, -10.5%)
Application Security / Code Security
Fulton, MD
sonatype.com

South River Technologies (17, -10.5%)
Data Security / Secure Data Sharing
Annapolis, MD
southrivertech.com

Telesoft Technologies (109, 34.6%)
Network Security / Monitoring
Annapolis Junction, MD
telesoft-technologies.com

Tenable (2219, 7.9%)
GRC / Vulnerabilities
Columbia, MD
tenable.com

Tresys (28, -3.5%)
Data Security / Data Erasure And Destruction
Columbia, MD
tresys.com

ZeroFOX (823, 30.0%)
Threat Intelligence / Monitoring
Baltimore, MD
zerofox.com

Zuul (11, 0.0%)
IoT Security / OT Security
Columbia, MD
zuuliot.com

Maine

Defendify (26, -3.7%)
GRC
Portland, ME
defendify.io

Plixer (96, -6.8%)
Network Security / Traffic Analysis
Kennebunk, ME
plixer.com

Michigan

AaDya Security (31, 6.9%)
MSSP / SMB Security
Plymouth, MI
aadyasecurity.com

BitLyft (20, 17.6%)
MSSP / SIEM
Lansing, MI
bitlyft.com

Blacksands (8, -11.1%)
Network Security / Software Defined Perimeter
Ann Arbor, MI
blacksandsinc.com

Blumira (63, 21.1%)
Security Analytics / SIEM
Ann Arbor, MI
blumira.com

Censys (129, 14.2%)
GRC / Asset Management
Ann Arbor, MI
censys.io

Cybernet (32, -8.6%)
GRC / Security Manager
Ann Arbor, MI
cybernet.com

DryvIQ (44, -18.5%)
GRC / Risk Management
Ann Arbor, MI
dryviq.com

**Numbers in parentheses indicate headcount and % change in 2023.*

DuoSecurity (now part of Cisco) (641, -11.0%)
IAM / Authentication
Ann Arbor, MI
duo.com

Ensure Technologies (21, 0.0%)
IAM
Ypsilanti, MI
ensuretech.com

Greenview Data (7, 0.0%)
MSSP / Managed Security Services
Ann Arbor, MI
greenviewdata.com

Interlink Networks (5, 0.0%)
IAM
Ann Arbor, MI
interlinknetworks.com

Nemassis (Was MicroWorld) (13, 116.7%)
GRC / Vulnerabilities
Novi, MI
nemasisva.com

Nuspire (183, -9.0%)
MSSP / Managed Security Services
Commerce, MI
nuspire.com

SensCy (17, 6.2%)
GRC / Healthcare
Ann Arbor, MI
senscy.com

Tenacity (7, -46.1%)
Operations / Posture Management
Ann Arbor, MI
tenacitycloud.com

ToucanX (3, -25.0%)
Endpoint Security / Sandbox
Southfield, MI
toucanx.com

Trustpage (3, -81.2%)
Data Security / Secure Storage
Detroit, MI
trustpage.com

Minnesota

Akana By Perforce (51, -1.9%)
API Security / API Management
Minneapolis, MN
akana.com

Arctic Wolf Networks (2251, 8.9%)
MSSP / MDR
Eden Prarie, MN
arcticwolf.com

CloudCover (19, 26.7%)
GRC / Compliance Management
Saint Paul, MN
cloudcover.net

Code 42 Software (294, -32.4%)
Operations / Secure Backup/Recovery
Minneapolis, MN
code42.com

Datakey (ATEK Access Technologies LLC) (11, 22.2%)
IAM / Authentication
Eden Prairie, MN
datakey.com

Fortra (313, -26.7%)
Endpoint Security / ISeries
Eden Prairie, MN
fortra.com

Great Bay Software (3, 0.0%)
IAM / Access Security
Bloomington, MN
greatbaysoftware.com

Id Insight (19, 26.7%)
Fraud Prevention / Identity Verification
Minneapolis, MN
idinsight.com

Jamf (2746, 3.6%)
Endpoint Security / Device Management
Minneapolis, MN
jamf.com

KinectIQ (14, 27.3%)
IAM / Encryption
Woodbury, MN
knectiq.com

NetSPI (537, 33.2%)
GRC / Vulnerabilities
Minneapolis, MN
netspi.com

Onda (39, 457.1%)
GRC / Risk Management
Minneapolis, MN
onda.ai

Secured2 (5, -16.7%)
Data Security / Secure Storage
Minneapolis, MN
secured2.com

SecurityStudio (13, -35.0%)
GRC / Risk Management
Minnetonka, MN
securitystudio.com

Senserva (7, 16.7%)
GRC / Posture Management
St Paul, MN
senserva.com

Software Diversified Services (20, 17.6%)
Endpoint Security / Z/OS Security
Minneapolis, MN
sdsusa.com

TrustMAPP (14, -6.7%)
GRC / Monitoring
Minneapolis, MN
trustmapp.com

Missouri

Cyderes (715, -1.8%)
MSSP / Managed Security Services
Kansas City, MO
cyderes.com

DisruptOps (6, -25.0%)
Operations / Cloud Security
Kansas City, MO
disruptops.com

Goldkey (19, -52.5%)
Data Security / Secure Storage
Kansas City, MO
goldkey.com

Pareto Cyber (12, -20.0%)
GRC / Risk Management
St. Louis, MO
paretosecurity.com

Q-Net Security (16, 0.0%)
Network Security / Segmentation
St. Louis, MO
qnetsecurity.com

TripleBlind (53, -15.9%)
Data Security / Secure Data Sharing
Kansas City, MO
tripleblind.ai

Mississippi

Applied Technology Group (6, 0.0%)
MSSP / Managed Security Services
Brandon, MS
atgconsults.com

Montana

Hoplite Industries (15, 7.1%)
Operations / Security Alerts
Bozeman, MT
hopliteindustries.com

Neuro-ID (74, -11.9%)
Fraud Prevention / Monitoring
Whitefish, MT
neuro-id.com

TeraDact (9, 12.5%)
Data Security / Secure Data Sharing
Missoula, MT
teradact.com

**Numbers in parentheses indicate headcount and % change in 2023.*

North Carolina

aPersona (3, -25.0%)
IAM / Authentication
Raleigh, NC
apersona.com

appNovi (8, 60.0%)
Application Security
Durham, NC
appnovi.com

Bayshore Networks (14, 0.0%)
IoT Security / OT Security
Durham, NC
bayshorenetworks.com

Calyptix Security Corporation (11, 10.0%)
Network Security / UTM
Charlotte, NC
calyptix.com

Corvid Cyberdefense (24, 20.0%)
MSSP / MDR
Mooresville, NC
corvidcyberdefense.com

CoSoSys (156, 0.0%)
Network Security / DLP
Raleigh, NC
endpointprotector.com

Cymatic (5, -37.5%)
Security Analytics / Monitoring
Raleigh, NC
cymatic.io

Data443 Risk Mitigation (23, 43.8%)
Data Security / Data Management
Morrisville, NC
data443.com

Dmarcian (33, 0.0%)
Email Security / Technology Deployment Management
Brevard, NC
dmarcian.com

JupiterOne (141, -25.8%)
Operations / Posture Management
Morrisville, NC
jupiterone.com

N-Able (1644, 23.6%)
Endpoint Security
Morrisville, NC
n-able.com

Netfoundry (78, 8.3%)
Network Security / Zero Trust Networking
Charlotte, NC
NetFoundry.io

Profian (9, -40.0%)
Data Security / Hardware
Raleigh, NC
profian.com

Quantinuum (397, 13.4%)
Data Security / Quantum
Charlotte, NC
quantinuum.com

SaaS Alerts (35, 20.7%)
Operations / Monitoring
Wilmington, NC
saasalerts.com

Salem Security (8, 0.0%)
Operations
Winston-Salem, NC
salemcyber.com

SAS Institute (16426, 2.9%)
Fraud Prevention / Anti-fraud
Cary, NC
sas.com

Security Journey (60, -3.2%)
Training / Software Development Security
Raleigh, NC
securityjourney.com

SilverSky (417, 27.5%)
MSSP / Managed Security Services
Durham, NC
silversky.com

SolonTek (4, -55.6%)
GRC / Configuration Management
Raleigh, NC
solontek.net

StrongKey (12, 20.0%)
Data Security / Key Management
Durham, NC
strongkey.com

Tavve Software (21, 40.0%)
Network Security / Packet Routing
Morrisville, NC
tavve.com

Nebraska

OpsCompass (24, 14.3%)
Operations / Posture Management
Omaha, NE
opscompass.com

SecureSky (19, 18.8%)
MSSP / MDR
Omaha, NE
securesky.com

New Hampshire

Bottomline (2461, 6.0%)
Data Security
Portsmouth, NH
bottomline.com

ComplianceRisk (5, 0.0%)
GRC
Dover, NH
compliancerisk.io

CyberHoot (5, 0.0%)
GRC / Security Awareness Training
Hampton, NH
cyberhoot.com

GlobalSign (475, 3.5%)
IAM / Authentication
Portsmouth, NH
globalsign.com

WWPass (19, 26.7%)
IAM / Authentication
Nashua, NH
wwpass.com

New Jersey

11:11 Systems (794, 40.5%)
MSSP / MDR
Fairfield, NJ
1111systems.com

1Kosmos (92, 15.0%)
IAM / Authentication
Somerset, NJ
1kosmos.com

Acreto Cloud (20, 25.0%)
IoT Security / Segmentation
Jersey City, NJ
acreto.io

Aspire Technology Partners (150, 5.6%)
MSSP / Managed Security Services
Eatontown, NJ
aspiretransforms.com

Aujas (897, 9.0%)
IAM / Identity Management
Jersey City, NJ
aujas.com

Authomate (4, 0.0%)
IAM / Authentication
Morganville, NJ
authomate.com

Avepoint (1466, 9.7%)
Data Security / Secure Backup/Recovery
Jersey City, NJ
avepoint.com

BIO-key (72, -13.2%)
IAM / Authentication
Wall, NJ
bio-key.com

Calamu (27, -12.9%)
Data Security / Shards
Clinton, NJ
calamu.com

**Numbers in parentheses indicate headcount and % change in 2023.*

Clearnetwork (10, 11.1%)
MSSP / SOC
Hazlet, NJ
clearnetwork.com

Communication Devices Inc (10, 25.0%)
Operations / Remote Devices
Boonton, NJ
commdevices.com

CommVault (3022, 3.9%)
Operations / Secure Backup/Recovery
Tinton Falls, NJ
commvault.com

Comodo (663, -2.8%)
Data Security / Public Key Infrastructure
Clifton, NJ
comodo.com

Cranium (32, 166.7%)
GRC / AI Discovery
Short Hills, NJ
cranium.ai

CyberShark (Was Black Stratus) (26, -7.1%)
MSSP / SOC
Piscataway, NJ
cybersharkinc.com

DataMotion (41, -10.9%)
Email Security
Florham Park, NJ
datamotion.com

FCI Cyber (128, -22.4%)
MSSP / Device Management
Bloomfield, NJ
fcicyber.com

Guardian Digital Inc. (5, -28.6%)
Endpoint Security / Secure Linux
Midland Park, NJ
guardiandigital.com

NICE Actimize (1357, 6.8%)
Fraud Prevention / Fraud Detection
Hoboken, NJ
niceactimize.com

NIKSUN (334, 30.5%)
Network Security / NBAD
Princeton, NJ
niksun.com

OwnData (1264, -10.8%)
Data Security
Englewood Cliffs, NJ
owndata.com

Paperclip (26, -3.7%)
Data Security / Document Security
Hackensack, NJ
paperclip.com

PivotPoint Security (31, -20.5%)
GRC / Risk Management
Hamilton, NJ
pivotpointsecurity.com

Prevalent Networks (152, 23.6%)
GRC / Risk Management
Warren, NJ
prevalent.net

SafeLiShare (13, 160.0%)
Data Security
Morristown, NJ
safelishare.com

Sectigo (410, 25.0%)
Data Security / Public Key Infrastructure
Roseland, NJ
sectigo.com

SPHERE Technology Solutions (109, 34.6%)
IAM / Access Security
Hoboken, NJ
sphereco.com

Stealthbits (61, -25.6%)
Security Analytics / Threat Prevention
Hawthorne, NJ
stealthbits.com

StrikeForce Technologies (25, 13.6%)
IAM / Authentication
Edison, NJ
strikeforcetech.com

SysCloud (138, -9.2%)
Data Security / Secure Backup/Recovery
Red Bank, NJ
syscloud.com

TELEGRID Technologies (5, -44.4%)
Data Security / Monitoring
Florham Park, NJ
telegrid.com

ThreatModeler Software (53, 8.2%)
Application Security / Vulnerabilities
Jersey City, NJ
threatmodeler.com

TrueFort (89, 6.0%)
Application Security / Monitoring
Weehawken, NJ
truefort.com

Uniken (163, 14.0%)
IAM / Authentication
Chatham Twp., NJ
uniken.com

Verizon Business Security Solutions (17038, -14.2%)
MSSP / Managed Security Services
Basking Ridge, NJ
verizon.com

Xcitium (139, 6.9%)
Endpoint Security
Bloomfield, NJ
xcitium.com

New Mexico

RiskSense (27, -12.9%)
GRC / Vulnerabilities
Albuquerque, NM
risksense.com

Vandyke Software (18, -5.3%)
Data Security / Secure Data Sharing
Albuquerque, NM
vandyke.com

Nevada

Anomalix (6, 0.0%)
IAM / Identity Analysis
Las Vegas, NV
anomalix.com

Axiom Cyber Solutions (3, -25.0%)
GRC / Vulnerabilities
Las Vegas, NV
axiomcyber.com

Cryptyk (10, -9.1%)
Data Security / Secure Storage
Las Vegas, NV
cryptyk.io

Crytica Security (29, 3.6%)
Endpoint Security / Anti-malware
Reno, NV
cryticasecurity.com

Equiinet (11, 10.0%)
Network Security / UTM
Las Vegas, NV
equiinet.com

IPQualityScore (33, 200.0%)
Fraud Prevention / IP Intelligence
Las Vegas, NV
ipqualityscore.com

SecSign (4, 0.0%)
IAM / Authentication
Henderson, NV
secsign.com

SecureMac (6, 0.0%)
Endpoint Security / Anti-malware
Las Vegas, NV
securemac.com

Sharktech (21, 40.0%)
Network Security / DDoS Defense
Las Vegas, NV
sharktech.net

**Numbers in parentheses indicate headcount and % change in 2023.*

Squadra Technologies (27, 3.9%)
GRC / DLP
Las Vegas, NV
squadratechnologies.com

Tego Cyber (17, 70.0%)
Threat Intelligence / TIP
Las Vegas, NV
tegocyber.com

Traitware (18, 5.9%)
IAM / Credential Security
Reno, NV
traitware.com

Trustifi (27, 0.0%)
Email Security / Encryption
Las Vegas, NV
trustifi.com

Vanguard Integrity Professionals (91, 8.3%)
GRC / Monitoring
Las Vegas, NV
go2vanguard.com

VirnetX (24, 4.3%)
Network Security / Zero Trust Networking
Zephyr Cove, NV
virnetx.com

New York

1Fort (7, 0.0%)
GRC / Cyber Insurance
New York City, NY
1fort.com

Agency (11, 37.5%)
MSSP
New York, NY
getagency.com

Allure Security (36, -12.2%)
Deception / Document Security
New York, NY
alluresecurity.com

Anonybit (22, 15.8%)
IAM / Shards
New York, NY
anonybit.io

AppMobi (14, 0.0%)
Endpoint Security / Mobile Device Security
Poughkeepsie, NY
appmobi.com

Assured Information Security (186, 3.9%)
Network Security / Dual Domain Control
Rome, NY
ainfosec.com

Atakama (43, -4.4%)
Data Security / Encryption
New York, NY
atakama.com

AuthID (32, 0.0%)
IAM / Authentication
Long Beach, NY
authid.ai

Avalon Cyber (425, 3.7%)
MSSP / Managed Security Services
Buffalo, NY
avaloncybersecurity.com

Avanan (93, 8.1%)
Email Security / Technology Deployment Management
New York, NY
avanan.com

Axio (91, 26.4%)
GRC / Risk Management
New York, NY
axio.com

Axonius (600, -6.2%)
GRC / Asset Management
New York, NY
axonius.com

Barricade IT Security (3, 200.0%)
MSSP / Managed Security Services
Islip, NY
barricadeitsecurity.com

Bettercloud (267, -22.8%)
Network Security / Monitoring
New York, NY
bettercloud.com

Beyond Identity (146, -18.0%)
IAM / Authentication
New York, NY
beyondidentity.com

Bindle Systems (17, -19.1%)
IAM / Identity Management
Ardsley, NY
bindlesystems.com

BlueVoyant (604, 2.5%)
MSSP / MDR
New York, NY
bluevoyant.com

Breachlock (90, 1.1%)
GRC / Penetration Testing
New York, NY
breachlock.com

Capsule8 (4, -55.6%)
Endpoint Security / Linux Security
New York, NY
capsule8.com

Carve Systems (16, -30.4%)
GRC / Risk Management
New York, NY
carvesystems.com

Centraleyes (20, -13.0%)
GRC / Risk Management
New York, NY
centraleyes.com

CertiK (206, -14.9%)
Data Security / Blockchain
New York, NY
certik.com

Chainalysis (842, -7.3%)
Fraud Prevention / Crypto Investigations
New York, NY
chainalysis.com

Cinder (27, 107.7%)
GRC / Insider Abuse Management
New York, NY
cinder.co

CipherTechs (58, -33.3%)
MSSP / Managed Security Services
New York, NY
ciphertechs.com

Claroty (484, 16.6%)
IoT Security / OT Security
New York, NY
claroty.com

Cloud Storage Security (17, 70.0%)
Operations / Anti-virus
Rochester, NY
cloudstoragesec.com

Cloudcheckr (61, -51.2%)
GRC / Configuration Management
Rochester, NY
cloudcheckr.com

Cobwebs (164, 16.3%)
Threat Intelligence / All Source
New York, NY
cobwebs.com

Confiant Inc (46, -11.5%)
Endpoint Security / Advertising-related
New York, NY
confiant.com

Continuity (63, 0.0%)
Data Security / Hygiene For Storage
New York, NY
continuitysoftware.com

Coro (330, 24.5%)
MSSP / SMB Security
New York, NY
coro.net

**Numbers in parentheses indicate headcount and % change in 2023.*

Criptext (8, 0.0%)
Email Security / Secure Email
New York, NY
criptext.com

Crosswire (15, -16.7%)
IAM / Access Security
New York, NY
crosswire.io

Cybera (20, -25.9%)
Fraud Prevention / Financial Crime
New York, NY
cybera.io

CyberConvoy (18, 0.0%)
MSSP / MDR
New York, NY
cyberconvoy.com

Cyberlitica (8, -33.3%)
Threat Intelligence / Dark Web
New York, NY
cyberlitica.com

CyberMDX (18, -64.7%)
IoT Security / Healthcare
New York, NY
cybermdx.com

Cybersafe Solutions (56, 1.8%)
MSSP / MDR
Jericho, NY
cybersafesolutions.com

Cyberwrite (14, 0.0%)
GRC / Risk Management
Manhattan, NY
cyberwrite.com

CyFlare (42, 61.5%)
MSSP / Managed Security Services
Victor, NY
cyflare.com

Cylera (44, 22.2%)
IoT Security / Healthcare
New York, NY
cylera.com

Cyviation (18, 0.0%)
IoT Security / Trains, Planes, And Tanks
New York, NY
cyviation.aero

Cyware (248, -6.1%)
Threat Intelligence / TIP
New York, NY
cyware.com

Dashlane (353, -13.9%)
IAM / Credential Security
New York, NY
dashlane.com

DataDog (5821, 14.1%)
Application Security / Logs
New York, NY
datadoghq.com

DataDome (179, 21.8%)
Fraud Prevention / Bot Security
New York, NY
datadome.co

Deep Instinct (271, 0.0%)
Endpoint Security / Endpoint Machine Learning
New York, NY
deepinstinct.com

DefensX (21, 16.7%)
Endpoint Security
NY
defensx.com

Diligent Corporation (2240, -0.3%)
GRC / GRC Platform
New York, NY
diligent.com

DoControl (71, -5.3%)
Data Security / Access Security
New York, NY
docontrol.io

Drawbridge (98, 27.3%)
GRC / GRC Platform
New York, NY
drawbridgeco.com

DuskRise (47, -33.8%)
Network Security / Segmentation
New York, NY
duskrise.com

Entitle (34, 9.7%)
IAM
NY
entitle.io

Ethyca (29, -14.7%)
GRC / Privacy Tools
New York, NY
ethyca.com

Findings (34, 9.7%)
GRC / Risk Management
New York, NY
findings.co

Fireblocks (649, 25.5%)
Data Security / Blockchain
New York, NY
fireblocks.com

Flashpoint (398, 0.0%)
Threat Intelligence / Dark Web
New York, NY
flashpoint-intel.com

FortMesa (10, 42.9%)
GRC / Risk Management
Austerlitz, NY
fortmesa.com

Fraud.net (45, 12.5%)
Fraud Prevention / Fraud Management
New York, NY
fraud.net

Garland Technology (49, 16.7%)
IoT Security / Network Taps
Buffalo, NY
garlandtechnology.com

Gem (65, 225.0%)
Operations / Incident Management
NY
gem.security

GeoEdge (69, -2.8%)
Application Security / Advertising-related
New York, NY
geoedge.com

Gomboc (12, 50.0%)
Operations / Configuration Management
New York, NY
gomboc.ai

GrammaTech (65, -52.2%)
Application Security / Code Security
Ithaca, NY
grammatech.com

HacWare (8, -27.3%)
GRC / Security Awareness Training
Brooklyn, NY
hacware.com

Human (481, 17.3%)
Fraud Prevention / Bot Security
New York, NY
humansecurity.com

HYPR (132, -7.7%)
IAM / Authentication
New York, NY
hypr.com

IBM (307605, 1.0%)
MSSP / Managed Security Services
Armonk, NY
ibm.com

ID R&D Inc. (56, 30.2%)
IAM / Authentication
New York, NY
idrnd.net

ideaBOX (4, 0.0%)
MSSP
New Rochelle, NY
ideabox.com

illusive Networks (58, -55.4%)
Deception
New York, NY
illusivenetworks.com

**Numbers in parentheses indicate headcount and % change in 2023.*

Infor (20055, 3.7%)
GRC / Monitoring
New York, NY
infor.com

Inpher (33, 13.8%)
Data Security / Data Privacy
New York, NY
inpher.io

Intezer (42, -6.7%)
Operations / Run-time Security
New York, NY
intezer.com

Intsights (45, -43.0%)
Threat Intelligence / Dark Web
New York, NY
intsights.com

IronVest (25, 0.0%)
IAM / Authentication
New York, NY
ironvest.com

Kaseya (4862, 95.1%)
IAM / Authentication
New York, NY
kaseya.com

KPMG (230145, -0.4%)
MSSP / Managed Security Services
New York, NY
kpmg.com

Kroll (5960, 9.9%)
MSSP / Risk Management
New York, NY
kroll.com

Laika (185, -7.5%)
GRC / Compliance Management
NY
heylaika.com

Laminar (74, -12.9%)
Data Security / Data Discovery
New York, NY
lmnr.io

Mage (Was Mentis) (91, 12.3%)
Data Security / Data Masking
New York, NY
magedata.ai

Netspark Ltd (77, 28.3%)
Network Security / Filtering
New York, NY
netspark.com

Nopsec (53, 12.8%)
GRC / Vulnerabilities
Brooklyn, NY
nopsec.com

NS1 (126, -25.9%)
Network Security / DNS Security
New York, NY
ns1.com

Nubo Software (8, 0.0%)
Endpoint Security / Virtualization
New York, NY
nubosoftware.com

Occamsec (37, -2.6%)
GRC / Penetration Testing
New York, NY
occamsec.com

Offensive Security (964, 11.1%)
Training / Cyber Range
New York, NY
offensive-security.com

Onyxia Cyber (21, 40.0%)
Operations
NY
onyxia.io

OpenIAM (11, 37.5%)
IAM / Identity Management
Cortlandt Manor, NY
openiam.com

Panorays (147, -2.0%)
GRC / Vulnerabilities
New York, NY
panorays.com

PIXM (11, -8.3%)
Email Security / Defense Against Phishing
Brooklyn, NY
pixm.net

Polymer (24, 9.1%)
GRC / DLP
New York, NY
polymerhq.io

Prelude (31, 3.3%)
Testing / Breach And Attack Simulation
New York, NY
prelude.org

Presidio (3799, 3.8%)
MSSP / Managed Security Services
New York, NY
presidio.com

Prove (414, 35.3%)
Fraud Prevention / Anti-fraud
New York, NY
payfone.com

Qrypt (52, 6.1%)
Data Security / Quantum
New York, NY
qrypt.com

RangeForce (80, -8.1%)
Training / Cyber Range
White Plains, NY
rangeforce.com

Reco Labs (62, 29.2%)
Data Security / Secure Collaboration
NY
recolabs.ai

Red Balloon Security (25, 0.0%)
Endpoint Security / Security For Embedded Systems
New York, NY
redballoonsecurity.com

RevBits (13, 0.0%)
Endpoint Security
Mineola, NY
revbits.com

Safeguard Privacy (27, 42.1%)
GRC / Compliance Management
New York, NY
safeguardprivacy.com

SaferVPN (3, 0.0%)
Network Security / VPN/Proxy
New York, NY
safervpn.com

SandboxAQ (219, 71.1%)
Data Security / Quantum
New York, NY
sandboxaq.com

Securco (24, 33.3%)
Data Security / Secure Communications
New York, NY
secureco.com

Secure Decisions (4, 0.0%)
Security Analytics / Visualization
Northport, NY
securedecisions.com

SecurityScorecard (544, -0.2%)
GRC / Risk Management
New York, NY
securityscorecard.com

Semperis (396, 14.4%)
IAM / Active Directory
New York, NY
semperis.com

SendSafely (34, 9.7%)
Data Security / Secure Data Sharing
New York, NY
sendsafely.com

SessionGuardian (14, 27.3%)
IAM / Identity Verification
New York, NY
sessionguardian.com

ShardSecure (35, 29.6%)
Data Security / Shards
New York, NY
go.shardsecure.com

**Numbers in parentheses indicate headcount and % change in 2023.*

SIEMonster (14, 75.0%)
Security Analytics
New York, NY
siemonster.com

Skopenow (45, -6.2%)
Threat Intelligence / OSINT
New York, NY
skopenow.com

Skout Cybersecurity (20, -20.0%)
Security Analytics / Data Analysis
New York, NY
getskout.com

Smarttech247 (190, 38.7%)
MSSP / MDR
New York, NY
smarttech247.com

Social Links (96, 100.0%)
Operations / OSINT
New York, NY
sociallinks.io

Socure (440, -8.0%)
IAM / Identity Verification
New York, NY
socure.com

Software Engineering of America (85, -5.6%)
Endpoint Security / ISeries
Garden City, NY
seasoft.com

Sonrai Security (90, -21.1%)
IAM / Data Security
New York, NY
sonraisecurity.com

SpeechPro (25, -26.5%)
IAM / Authentication
New York, NY
speechpro-usa.com

SpruceID (25, 4.2%)
IAM / Credential Security
New York, NY
spruceid.com

Supplywisdon (115, -5.7%)
GRC
New York, NY
supplywisdom.com

Talon Cyber Security (147, 54.7%)
Network Security / Secure Web Browsing
New York, NY
talon-sec.com

Tessian (212, -17.8%)
Email Security / Defense Against Phishing
New York, NY
tessian.com

Thoropass (185, 0.5%)
GRC / Compliance Management
New York, NY
thoropass.com

ThreatKey (12, 20.0%)
GRC / Configuration Management
New York, NY
threatkey.com

Todyl (67, 67.5%)
Network Security / Access Security
New York, NY
todyl.com

Token (40, 11.1%)
IAM / Authentication
Rochester, NY
tokenring.com

Total Defense (27, -3.6%)
Endpoint Security / PC, Mobile & Internet Security
Hauppauge, NY
totaldefense.com

Trail of Bits (105, 4.0%)
Data Security / Vulnerabilities
New York, NY
trailofbits.com

Turbot (46, 2.2%)
IAM / Encryption
New York, NY
turbot.com

TwoSense (13, -13.3%)
IAM / Authentication
New York, NY
twosense.ai

Typing DNA (144, -11.7%)
IAM / Authentication
New York, NY
typingdna.com

UnderDefense (104, 31.6%)
MSSP / MDR
New York, NY
underdefense.com

Valid Networks (8, -38.5%)
Application Security / Blockchain
New York, NY
valid.network

Varonis (2207, 5.2%)
Data Security / Secure Collaboration
New York, NY
varonis.com

Verificient Technologies (215, -11.9%)
IAM / Identity Verification
New York, NY
verificient.com

VisibleRisk (5, -70.6%)
GRC / Risk Management
New York, NY
visiblerisk.com

WetStone Technologies (14, 40.0%)
Data Security / Forensics
Cortland, NY
wetstonetech.com

Xeol (3, 0.0%)
API Security
New York, NY
xeol.io

Ohio

AgileBlue (36, 2.9%)
MSSP / Managed Security Services
Cleveland, OH
agileblue.com

AwareHQ (159, -5.9%)
Network Security / Monitoring
Columbus, OH
awarehq.com

Axuall (92, 95.7%)
IAM / Identity Verification
Cleveland, OH
axuall.com

Binary Defense (178, 26.2%)
MSSP / SOC
Stow, OH
binarydefense.com

Buckler (8, 0.0%)
GRC / Compliance Management
Columbus, OH
buckler.app

Cerdant (26, -25.7%)
MSSP / Managed Security Services
Dublin, OH
cerdant.com

Cyberstanc (9, -35.7%)
Operations
Delaware, OH
cyberstanc.com

Datanchor (32, 18.5%)
Data Security / Document Security
Columbus, OH
anchormydata.com

Everykey (19, 11.8%)
IAM / Authentication
Cleveland, OH
everykey.com

**Numbers in parentheses indicate headcount and % change in 2023.*

Finite State (58, -10.8%)
IoT Security / Firmware
Columbus, OH
finitestate.io

Fortress SRM (53, 1.9%)
MSSP / Managed Security Services
Cleveland, OH
fortresssrm.com

Heureka Software (5, -37.5%)
GRC / Data Discovery
Cleveland, OH
heurekasoftware.com

Keyfactor (416, 12.4%)
Data Security / Public Key Infrastructure
Independence, OH
keyfactor.com

OpenVRM (6, 0.0%)
GRC / Risk Management
Columbus, OH
openvrm.com

PreEmptive Solutions (44, 76.0%)
Application Security / App Hardening
Mayfield Village, OH
preemptive.com

Redwall Technologies (5, 0.0%)
Endpoint Security / Mobile Device Security
Beavercreek, OH
redwall.us

TechR2 (36, 12.5%)
Data Security / Data Erasure And Destruction
Reynoldsburg, OH
techr2.com

Oklahoma

Secpod (112, 21.7%)
Endpoint Security / Endpoint Management
Tulsa, OK
secpod.com

TokenEx (90, 11.1%)
Data Security / Tokenization
Edmond, OK
tokenex.com

True Digital Security (10, -41.2%)
MSSP / SIEM
Tulsa, OK
truedigitalsecurity.com

Oregon

Acceptto (9, -43.8%)
Fraud Prevention / Identity Verification
Portland, OR
acceptto.com

Anitian (66, -17.5%)
GRC / Compliance Management
Portland, OR
anitian.com

Apcon (231, 5.0%)
Network Security / Traffic Analysis
Wilsonville, OR
apcon.com

Biomio (4, -20.0%)
IAM / Authentication
Portland, OR
biom.io

ConductorOne (57, 72.7%)
GRC
Portland, OR
conductorone.com

Cryptium (3, 50.0%)
IAM / Authentication
Portland, OR
cryptium.com

CTCI (4, 0.0%)
Threat Intelligence / OSINT
Beaverton, OR
ctci.ai

DeepSurface (19, -13.6%)
GRC / Vulnerabilities
Portland, OR
deepsurface.com

Eclypsium (100, 6.4%)
Endpoint Security / Firmware
Beaverton, OR
eclypsium.com

IDX (71, -27.6%)
GRC / Data Privacy
Portland, OR
idx.us

Manifest (13, 44.4%)
Application Security / SBOM
Remote, OR
manifestcyber.com

NAVEX (1340, 2.6%)
GRC / GRC Platform
Lake Oswego, OR
navex.com

Radarfirst (63, -14.9%)
Operations / Incident Management
Portland, OR
radarfirst.com

Stratus Digital Systems (3, 0.0%)
Endpoint Security / Servers
Eugene, OR
stratusdigitalsystems.com

thatDot (17, 21.4%)
Fraud Prevention / Fraud Analytics
Portland, OR
thatdot.com

Torq (126, 0.8%)
Operations / Automation
Portland, OR
torq.io

Tozny (19, 18.8%)
IAM / Secure Identity
Portland, OR
tozny.com

TripWire (Fortra) (202, -20.8%)
GRC / Monitoring
Portland, OR
tripwire.com

Pennsylvania

Appalachia Technologies (49, 0.0%)
MSSP / Managed Security Services
Mechanicsburg, PA
appalachiatech.com

Certes Networks (46, 4.5%)
Network Security / VPN/Proxy
Pittsburgh, PA
certesnetworks.com

Clone Systems (16, -11.1%)
MSSP / Monitoring
Philadelphia, PA
clone-systems.com

Core Business Solutions (66, 0.0%)
GRC / CMCC Tools
Lewisburg, PA
thecoresolution.com

CyberconIQ (31, 63.2%)
GRC / Security Awareness Training
York, PA
cyberconiq.com

Deduce (26, -25.7%)
Fraud Prevention / ATO Defense
Philadelphia, PA
deduce.com

EfficientIP (231, -10.5%)
Network Security / DNS Security
West Chester, PA
efficientip.com

ForAllSecure (42, -22.2%)
Application Security / Software Testing For Security
Pittsburgh, PA
forallsecure.com

Mira Security (19, -5.0%)
Network Security / Traffic Analysis
Cranberry Township, PA
mirasecurity.com

**Numbers in parentheses indicate headcount and % change in 2023.*

Myota (19, 58.3%)
Data Security / IRM
Blue Bell, PA
myota.io

Omega Systems (173, 0.0%)
MSSP / SIEM
Reading, PA
omegasystemscorp.com

PacketViper (16, 0.0%)
Deception
Pittsburgh, PA
packetviper.com

Privakey (7, 75.0%)
Fraud Prevention / Transaction Security
Philadelphia, PA
privakey.com

Ricoh USA (18703, -1.1%)
IAM / Authentication
Exton, PA
ricoh-usa.com

SecureAge Technology (37, -9.8%)
Data Security / Encryption
West Chester, PA
secureage.com

Unisys Stealth (24225, 4.5%)
Network Security / Cloaking
Blue Bell, PA
unisys.com

Verif-y (29, 7.4%)
IAM / Identity Verification
Philadelphia, PA
verif-y.com

VigilantOps (3, 0.0%)
GRC / Healthcare
Pittsburgh, PA
vigilant-ops.com

South Carolina

Akku (19, 1800.0%)
IAM / Identity Platform
Rock Hill, SC
akku.work

Convergent Information Security Solutions (7, 16.7%)
MSSP / Managed Security Services
Columbia, SC
convergesecurity.com

Hook Security (26, 52.9%)
GRC / Security Awareness Training
Greenville, SC
hooksecurity.co

Human Presence (8, -33.3%)
Network Security / Bot Security
Greenville, SC
humanpresence.io

PhishLabs (109, -18.7%)
GRC / Defense Against Phishing
Charleston, SC
phishlabs.com

South Dakota

Active Countermeasures (10, 25.0%)
Security Analytics / Threat Hunting
Spearfish, SD
activecountermeasures.com

Mailprotector (42, 5.0%)
Email Security / Managed Security Services
Greenville, SD
mailprotector.com

Query.Ai (42, 2.4%)
Operations / Search
Brookings, SD
query.ai

Tennessee

ARMS Cyber (4, 0.0%)
Endpoint Security
Nashville, TN
armscyber.com

Clearwater (250, 110.1%)
GRC / Compliance Management
Nashville, TN
clearwatercompliance.com

Cloud Range (22, 0.0%)
Training / Cyber Range
Nashville, TN
cloudrangecyber.com

CyberMaxx (117, 244.1%)
MSSP / Managed Security Services
Nashville, TN
cybermaxx.com

Msignia (14, 7.7%)
Data Security / Public Key Infrastructure
Franklin, TN
mSIGNIA.com

Phosphorus (62, 10.7%)
IoT Security / Patch Management
Nashville, TN
phosphorus.io

PolicyCo (8, -46.7%)
GRC / Policy Management
Nashville, TN
policyco.io

Sertinty (20, 0.0%)
Data Security / IRM
Nashville, TN
sertainty.com

Texas

443ID (22, -8.3%)
IAM / Identity Verification
Austin, TX
443id.com

9Star (31, 40.9%)
IAM / Managed Security Services
Austin, TX
9starinc.com

Accountable (6, -25.0%)
GRC / Compliance Management
Fort Worth, TX
accountablehq.com

Accudata Systems (98, -14.0%)
Operations / Security Management
Houston, TX
accudatasystems.com

Acumera (201, 21.1%)
MSSP / Firewalls
Austin, TX
acumera.net

Adaptus (11, 37.5%)
Operations
Austin, TX
adaptus.com

Alert Logic (319, -30.4%)
Security Analytics / Logs
Houston, TX
alertlogic.com

AllClear ID (55, 1.9%)
Fraud Prevention / Identity Protection Service
Austin, TX
allclearid.com

Altr (72, 18.0%)
Data Security / Data Discovery
Austin, TX
altr.com

Armor (151, 16.1%)
MSSP / Cloud Security
Richardson, TX
armor.com

Backbox (63, 16.7%)
Operations / Orchestration
Dallas, TX
backbox.com

BalkanID (27, 35.0%)
IAM / Auditing
Austin, TX
balkan.id

**Numbers in parentheses indicate headcount and % change in 2023.*

Biometric Signature-Id (15, 7.1%)
IAM / Authentication
Lewisville, TX
biosig-id.com

Bizzy Labs (8, -11.1%)
IoT Security / Vulnerabilities
Irving, TX
bizzylabs.tech

Blocmount (3, 50.0%)
IoT Security / OT Security
San Antonio, TX
blocmount.com

Blue Lance Inc. (11, -21.4%)
GRC / Asset Management
Houston, TX
bluelance.com

BMC Software (9786, 1.8%)
Security Analytics / SIEM
Houston, TX
bmc.com

BreachQuest (9, -35.7%)
Security Analytics / Incident Management
Dallas, TX
breachquest.com

Brinqa (98, -10.1%)
GRC / Risk Management
Austin, TX
brinqa.com

CheckRed (48, 60.0%)
Operations / Posture Management
Frisco, TX
checkred.com

ClearDATA (186, -3.1%)
MSSP / HIPAA Cloud Hosting
Austin, TX
cleardata.com

Codenotary (17, -26.1%)
Application Security / SBOM
Bellaire, TX
codenotary.com

Command Zero (28, 27.3%)
Stealth
Austin, TX
cmdzero.io

ContraForce (21, 0.0%)
Security Analytics / XDR
Dallas, TX
contraforce.com

Critical Start (281, 2.9%)
MSSP / MDR
Plano, TX
criticalstart.com

Cyber adAPT (23, 0.0%)
Security Analytics / Monitoring
Dallas, TX
cyberadapt.com

Cyber Defense Labs (36, -40.0%)
MSSP / Managed Security Services
Dallas, TX
cyberdefenselabs.com

Cybernance (4, 0.0%)
GRC / Risk Management
Austin, TX
cybernance.com

Cysiv (27, -63.5%)
MSSP / SOC
Irving, TX
cysiv.com

Cyturus Technologies (12, 20.0%)
GRC / Risk Management
Addison, TX
cyturus.com

Delta Risk (22360, 2.0%)
MSSP / MDR
San Antonio, TX
deltarisk.com

DeUmbra (4, 0.0%)
Security Analytics / Visualization
Austin, TX
deumbra.com

Digital Defense (44, -24.1%)
GRC / Vulnerabilities
San Antonio, TX
digitaldefense.com

Digital.ai (923, 13.4%)
Endpoint Security / Mobile Device Security
Plano, TX
digital.ai

Dispel (37, 5.7%)
IoT Security / Remote Devices
Austin, TX
dispel.io

DryRun Security (6, 500.0%)
Application Security / Software Development Security
Austin, TX
dryrun.security

Edgile (214, -2.7%)
MSSP / Managed Security Services
Austin, TX
edgile.com

Elemental Cyber Security (5, 0.0%)
GRC / Vulnerabilities
Dallas, TX
elementalsecurity.com

Evo Security (28, 27.3%)
IAM / Identity Management
Austin, TX
evosecurity.com

Exodus Intelligence (45, 36.4%)
Application Security / Research
Austin, TX
exodusintel.com

FaceFirst (65, 109.7%)
Fraud Prevention / Non-authentication Biometrics
Austin, TX
FaceFirst.com

FileCloud (117, 7.3%)
Data Security / IRM
Austin, TX
filecloud.com

ForcePoint (2199, -0.1%)
GRC / DLP
Austin, TX
forcepoint.com

FutureX (134, 36.7%)
Data Security / Hardware
Bulverde, TX
futurex.com

GFI Software (220, -0.9%)
Email Security / Anti-spam
Austin, TX
gfi.com

Ghost Security (28, 27.3%)
Application Security / Asset Management
TX
ghost.security

GlassWire (3, -40.0%)
Endpoint Security / Firewalls
Austin, TX
glasswire.com

Globalscape (59, -6.3%)
Network Security / Secure Data Sharing
San Antonio, TX
globalscape.com

Gluu (22, -18.5%)
IAM / Access Security
Austin, TX
gluu.org

Gradiant Cyber (46, 15.0%)
GRC / Risk Management
Dallas, TX
gradientcyber.com

Graylog (108, -4.4%)
Operations / Logs
Houston, TX
graylog.org

**Numbers in parentheses indicate headcount and % change in 2023.*

HackNotice (26, -40.9%)
GRC / Security Awareness Training
Austin, TX
hacknotice.com

Halcyon (105, 72.1%)
Endpoint Security / Ransomware Security
Austin, TX
halcyon.ai

Hawk Network Defense (3, -25.0%)
Security Analytics
Dallas, TX
hawkdefense.com

HID Global (3416, 9.6%)
IAM / Authentication
Austin, TX
hidglobal.com

HiddenLayer (78, 271.4%)
Application Security / ML Security
Austin, TX
hiddenlayer.com

Hopzero (9, 0.0%)
Network Security / Hop Minimization
Austin, TX
hopzero.com

Hypori (114, 2.7%)
Endpoint Security / Device Management
Austin, TX
hypori.com

Identity Automation (83, -17.0%)
IAM / Identity Management
Houston, TX
identityautomation.com

Idera (270, 1.5%)
GRC / Compliance Management
Houston, TX
idera.com

Intrusion Inc. (55, -19.1%)
Network Security / IDS
Richardson, TX
intrusion.com

Invicti Security (318, -17.0%)
Application Security / Scanning
Austin, TX
invicti.com

IPVanish (7, -12.5%)
Network Security / VPN/Proxy
Dallas, TX
ipvanish.com

Ironwood Cyber (19, -13.6%)
MSSP / Scanning
Fort Worth, TX
ironwoodcyber.com

Island (413, 163.1%)
Network Security / Secure Web Browsing
Dallas, TX
island.io

Keep Aware (12, 200.0%)
Endpoint Security
Austin, TX
keepaware.co

Kiuwan (29, 0.0%)
Application Security / Code Security
Houston, TX
kiuwan.com

Lavabit (132, -1.5%)
Email Security / Secure Email
Dallas, TX
lavabit.com

Lepide (157, -4.8%)
GRC / Data Discovery
Austin, TX
lepide.com

Living Security (68, -16.1%)
GRC / Security Awareness Training
Austin, TX
livingsecurity.com

Longbow Security (31, 0.0%)
GRC / Vulnerabilities
Austin, TX
longbow.security

Masergy (684, 3.5%)
MSSP / Managed Security Services
Plano, TX
masergy.com

Maxxsure (32, 6.7%)
GRC / Risk Management
Richardson, TX
maxxsure.com

MDaemon Technologies (34, -2.9%)
Network Security / Gateways
Grapevine, TX
altn.com

Merlincryption (5, 0.0%)
Data Security / Encryption
Austin, TX
MerlinCryption.com

Mi-Token (63, 0.0%)
IAM / Authentication
Austin, TX
mi-token.com

Netgate (126, 37.0%)
Network Security
Austin, TX
netgate.com

NetRise (36, 33.3%)
Application Security / Firmware
Austin, TX
netrise.io

Netsurion (263, -9.3%)
MSSP / Managed Security Services
Houston, TX
netsurion.com

Network Box USA (9, -10.0%)
MSSP / Managed Security Services
Houston, TX
networkboxusa.com

NinjaOne (908, 47.2%)
Endpoint Security / Endpoint Management
Austin, TX
ninjaone.com

Nudge Security (19, 26.7%)
GRC
Austin, TX
nudgesecurity.com

Ontic (188, 12.6%)
Threat Intelligence / Personal Protection Platform
Austin, TX
ontic.co

Osano (107, 78.3%)
Data Security / Compliance Management
Austin, TX
osano.com

Passage (4, -66.7%)
IAM / Authentication
Austin, TX
passage.id

Praetorian (141, 6.0%)
Operations / Secure Remote Access
Austin, TX
praetorian.com

Riscosity (26, 52.9%)
GRC
Austin, TX
riscosity.com

Rocketcyber (22, 4.8%)
Operations / SOC
Dallas, TX
rocketcyber.com

runZero (57, -29.6%)
Network Security / Asset Management
Austin, TX
runzero.com

SailPoint (2464, 9.2%)
IAM / Governance
Austin, TX
sailpoint.com

**Numbers in parentheses indicate headcount and % change in 2023.*

SaltyCloud (10, -9.1%)
Operations / Workflow Automation
Austin, TX
saltycloud.com

SCIS Security (62, -1.6%)
MSSP / MDR
Houston, TX
scissecurity.com

ScoutDNS (3, 0.0%)
Network Security / DNS Security
Grand Prairie, TX
scoutdns.com

SecureLink (132, -21.0%)
IAM / Access Security
Austin, TX
securelink.com

SecureLogix Corporation (77, 0.0%)
Network Security / VoIP Security
San Antonio, TX
securelogix.com

Securonix (750, -20.6%)
Security Analytics / Monitoring
Addison, TX
securonix.com

Sentinel IPS (9, 0.0%)
MSSP / Firewalls
Dallas, TX
sentinelips.com

Sevco Security (63, 21.1%)
GRC / Asset Management
Austin, TX
sevco.io

Shodan (12, 50.0%)
IoT Security / Attack Surface Management
Austin, TX
beta.shodan.io

SignaCert (6, 0.0%)
Endpoint Security / Whitelisting OEM
Austin, TX
signacert.com

Softex (22, 266.7%)
IAM / Authentication
Austin, TX
softexinc.com

Solarwinds (2540, 0.2%)
Security Analytics / SIEM
Austin, TX
solarwinds.com

SolCyber (34, 0.0%)
MSSP / Managed Security Services
Dallas, TX
solcyber.com

SparkCognition (309, -17.8%)
Endpoint Security / Anti-virus
Austin, TX
sparkcognition.com

Specialized Security Services Inc. (66, -20.5%)
MSSP / Managed Security Services
Plano, TX
s3security.com

SpyCloud (213, 27.5%)
Threat Intelligence / Dark Web
Austin, TX
spycloud.com

Spyderbat (26, 8.3%)
Operations / Runtime Security
Austin, TX
spyderbat.com

SSL.com (43, 26.5%)
Data Security / Public Key Infrastructure
Houston, TX
ssl.com

StackPath (249, -18.4%)
Network Security / DDoS Defense
Dallas, TX
stackpath.com

StratoKey (4, 0.0%)
Data Security / Encryption
Austin, TX
stratokey.com

Strobes (53, 15.2%)
GRC / Vulnerabilities
Frisco, TX
strobes.co

SureCloud (99, -18.2%)
GRC / Cloud Security
Plano, TX
surecloud.com

The Whisper Company (3, 0.0%)
IAM / Authentication
Austin, TX
thewhispercompany.com

Threatrix (14, -12.5%)
GRC / Supply Chain Security
Dallas, TX
threatrix.io

ThreatWarrior (13, -23.5%)
Network Security / Monitoring
Austin, TX
threatwarrior.com

Trend Micro (7735, 1.8%)
Endpoint Security / Anti-virus
Irving, TX
trendmicro.com

Trustonic (109, 14.7%)
Endpoint Security / Mobile Device Security
Austin, TX
trustonic.com

Visual Click Software (12, 0.0%)
GRC / Auditing
Austin, TX
visualclick.com

White Cloud Security (15, 0.0%)
Endpoint Security / Application Whitelisting
Austin, TX
whitecloudsecurity.com

Zartech (41, 20.6%)
GRC / GRC Platform
Dallas, TX
zartech.net/grc

Zero Day Initiative (Trend Micro) (13, 30.0%)
Application Security / Bugs
Austin, TX
zerodayinitiative.com

Zimperium (228, -4.2%)
Endpoint Security / Mobile Device Security
Dallas, TX
zimperium.com

Ziperase (5, 0.0%)
Data Security / Data Erasure And Destruction
Austin, TX
ziperase.com

Zix Corp. (275, -13.2%)
Data Security / Secure Communications
Dallas, TX
zixcorp.com

Zyston (66, 20.0%)
MSSP / Managed Security Services
Dallas, TX
zyston.com

Utah

alphaMountain.ai (9, 28.6%)
Threat Intelligence / DNS Security
Salt Lake City, UT
alphamountain.ai

Anonyome Labs (128, 18.5%)
Data Security / Secure Communications
Salt Lake City, UT
anonyome.com

DATASHIELD (24, -17.2%)
MSSP / Managed Security Services
Salt Lake City, UT
datashieldprotect.com

**Numbers in parentheses indicate headcount and % change in 2023.*

DigiCert (1368, 7.3%)
Data Security / Public Key Infrastructure
Lehi, UT
digicert.com

Evernym (6, -40.0%)
IAM / Identity Attestation
Herriman, UT
evernym.com

HEROIC Cybersecurity (25, 19.1%)
Threat Intelligence / Monitoring
Provo, UT
heroic.com

Ivanti (3050, -1.3%)
Endpoint Security / Endpoint Management
South Jordan, UT
ivanti.com

Monarx (18, 5.9%)
Network Security / Webshell Detection And Blocking
Cottonwood Heights, UT
monarx.com

Ostrich (21, 61.5%)
GRC / Risk Management
Cottonwood Heights, UT
ostrichcyber-risk.com

RiskRecon (118, 0.8%)
GRC / Risk Management
Salt Lake City, UT
riskrecon.com

Security Weaver (59, -21.3%)
Data Security / IRM
Lehi, UT
securityweaver.com

SecurityMetrics (260, 0.8%)
GRC / Vulnerabilities
Orem, UT
securitymetrics.com

TrustBrands (61, -1.6%)
GRC / Scanning
Ogden, UT
trustbrands.com

Venafi (430, -10.0%)
Data Security / Key Management
Salt Lake City, UT
venafi.com

Whistic (84, -34.9%)
Operations / Vendor Management
Pleasant Grove, UT
whistic.com

WipeDrive (Was White Canyon Inc.) (10, -16.7%)
Data Security / Data Erasure And Destruction
American Fork, UT
whitecanyon.com

Virginia

418 Intelligence (11, 37.5%)
Threat Intelligence / Threat Intelligence Gamification
Reston, VA
418intelligence.com

Advanced Network Systems (22, -38.9%)
MSSP / MDR
Charlottesville, VA
getadvanced.net

Airside (17, -39.3%)
IAM / Mobile Identity
Herndon, VA
airsidemobile.com

Analyst1 (35, 59.1%)
Threat Intelligence / Threat Intelligence Platform
Reston, VA
analyst1.com

AppGuard (22, -15.4%)
Endpoint Security / Application Containment
Chantilly, VA
appguard.us

Armortext (12, 0.0%)
Data Security / Secure Collaboration
McLean, VA
armortext.com

Assura (46, 12.2%)
MSSP / Managed Security Services
Richmond, VA
assurainc.com

Assured Enterprises Inc (10, 0.0%)
GRC / Vulnerabilities
Vienna, VA
assured.enterprises

Atomicorp (11, -8.3%)
Endpoint Security / IPS
Chantilly, VA
atomicorp.com

Black Kite (115, -2.5%)
GRC / Security Scores
Vienna, VA
normshield.com

Blue Ridge Networks (36, 2.9%)
Network Security / Segmentation
Chantilly, VA
blueridgenetworks.com

BluVector (13, 0.0%)
Network Security / IDS
Arlington, VA
bluvector.io

CACI International Inc. (19442, 7.4%)
MSSP / Managed Security Services
Arlington, VA
caci.com

Caveonix (33, 43.5%)
GRC / Risk Management
Falls Church, VA
caveonix.com

Centripetal (91, 30.0%)
Network Security / Firewalls
Herndon, VA
centripetalnetworks.com

CertiPath (43, 10.3%)
Data Security / Public Key Infrastructure
Reston, VA
certipath.com

Cocoon Data (23, -17.9%)
Data Security / Secure Data Sharing
Arlington, VA
cocoondata.com

Cofense (was Phishme) (312, -26.4%)
GRC / Defense Against Phishing
Leesburg, VA
cofense.com

Comtech (94, 32.4%)
GRC / Credential Security
Reston, VA
comtechllc.com

Corsha (34, 54.5%)
API Security
Vienna, VA
corsha.com

CYBER RANGES (54, 35.0%)
Training / Cyber Range
Stafford, VA
cyberranges.com

Cyph (3, 0.0%)
Data Security / Secure Collaboration
McLean, VA
cyph.com

Cyren (67, -69.0%)
Threat Intelligence / Reputation
McLean, VA
cyren.com

Daon (271, 1.1%)
IAM / Assurance
Reston, VA
daon.com

Dark Cubed (10, -58.3%)
Security Analytics / Monitoring
Charlottesville, VA
darkcubed.com

DXC Technology (91269, 5.9%)
MSSP / Managed Security Services
Tysons, VA
dxc.technology

**Numbers in parentheses indicate headcount and % change in 2023.*

Expel (516, 1.0%)
MSSP / SOC
Herndon, VA
expel.io

Fend Incorporated (9, -10.0%)
IoT Security / Firewalls
Arlington, VA
fend.tech

FireTail (20, 100.0%)
API Security / Authentication
McLean, VA
firetail.io

General Dynamics Information Technology (24128, 6.3%)
MSSP / Managed Security Services
Drive Falls Church, VA
gdit.com

Gold Comet (7, 75.0%)
Email Security / Secure Email
Alexandria, VA
goldcomet.com

Greymatter (37, -26.0%)
API Security
Arlington, VA
greymatter.io

GroupSense (38, -11.6%)
Threat Intelligence / Dark Web
Arlington, VA
groupsense.io

Guidepoint Security (869, 25.4%)
MSSP / Managed Security Services
Herndon, VA
guidepointsecurity.com

Haystax (42, 27.3%)
Security Analytics / Threat Analysis
McLean, VA
haystax.com

Hubble Technology (19, 5.6%)
Operations / Asset Management
Reston, VA
hubble.net

Hushmesh (9, 50.0%)
Data Security / Key Management
Falls Church, VA
hushmesh.com

ID.me (875, -2.7%)
IAM / Credential Security
McLean, VA
id.me

IDEMIA (12850, 10.6%)
IAM / Identity Augmentation
Reston, VA
idemia.com

InQuest (30, 15.4%)
Data Security / DLP
Arlington, VA
inquest.net

Intelligent Waves (206, 21.2%)
Network Security / Secure Web Browsing
Reston, VA
intelligentwaves.com

IntelliGRC (18, 38.5%)
GRC / GRC Platform
Fairfax, VA
intelligrc.com

Intensity Analytics (9, -10.0%)
IAM / Monitoring
Warrenton, VA
intensityanalytics.com

Internet 2.0 (14, -17.6%)
Network Security / UTM
Alexandria, VA
internet2-0.com

Interos (229, -16.7%)
GRC / Risk Management
Arlington, VA
interos.ai

LastPass (704, 16.0%)
IAM / Credential Security
Fairfax, VA
lastpass.com

LetsDefend (52, 40.5%)
Training / Cyber Range
Sterling, VA
letsdefend.io

Logmeonce (8, -20.0%)
IAM / Identity Management
McLean, VA
LogmeOnce.com

Lookingglass Cyber Solutions (102, -37.0%)
Threat Intelligence
Reston, VA
lookingglasscyber.com

Mantis Networks (6, 0.0%)
Network Security / Visibility
Reston, VA
mantisnet.com

MeasuredRisk (21, -8.7%)
GRC / Risk Management
Arlington, VA
measuredrisk.com

MicroStrategy (3405, -2.0%)
IAM / Mobile Identity
Tysons Corner, VA
microstrategy.com

Mission Secure (30, -23.1%)
IoT Security / OT Security
Charlottesville, VA
missionsecure.com

Neustar (1449, -29.2%)
Network Security / DDoS Defense
Sterling, VA
home.neustar

Nisos (115, 18.6%)
Threat Intelligence / Managed Security Services
Alexandria, VA
nisos.com

Novetta (411, -23.0%)
Network Security / Monitoring
McLean, VA
novetta.com

NTrepid (179, -6.3%)
Operations / Forensics
Herndon, VA
ntrepidcorp.com

Onclave Networks (19, -32.1%)
IoT Security / OT Security
North Mclean, VA
onclave.net

Ostendio (37, -21.3%)
GRC / Compliance Management
Arlington, VA
ostendio.com

Paraben Corporation (17, -10.5%)
GRC / Forensics
Aldie, VA
paraben.com

Personam (3, 200.0%)
Network Security / Insider Threats
McLean, VA
PersonamInc.com

PFP Cybersecurity (25, -3.9%)
Endpoint Security / Endpoint Protection
Vienna, VA
pfpcyber.com

Privo (39, 8.3%)
GRC / Data Privacy
Dumfries, VA
privo.com

Privva (8, -20.0%)
GRC / Risk Management
Arlington, VA
privva.com

PwC (277228, 6.5%)
MSSP / Managed Security Services
Mclean, VA
pwc.com

**Numbers in parentheses indicate headcount and % change in 2023.*

Qmulos (87, 11.5%)
GRC
Arlington, VA
qmulos.com

Qomplx (92, 31.4%)
Security Analytics / Incident Management
Reston, VA
qomplx.com

R&K Cyber Solutions (6, 0.0%)
MSSP / Managed Security Services
Manassas, VA
rkcybersolutions.com

RegScale (55, 96.4%)
GRC / Compliance Management
Tysons, VA
regscale.com

Risk Based Security (4, -20.0%)
GRC / Vulnerabilities
Richmond, VA
riskbasedsecurity.com

RunSafe Security (18, 5.9%)
Application Security / Application Hardening
McLean, VA
runsafesecurity.com

SafeDNS (21, 31.2%)
Network Security / DNS Security
Alexandria, VA
safedns.com

SafeGuard Cyber (62, -13.9%)
GRC / Employee Social Media Management
Charlottesville, VA
safeguardcyber.com

SCIT Labs (8, -11.1%)
Endpoint Security / Servers
Clifton, VA
scitlabs.com

SCYTHE (32, -33.3%)
Testing / Breach And Attack Simulation
Arlington, VA
scythe.io

Sera-Brynn (13, 44.4%)
GRC / Risk Management
Suffolk, VA
sera-brynn.com

Shift5 (114, 28.1%)
IoT Security / Trains, Planes, And Tanks
Arlington, VA
shift5.io

Silent Circle (23, 0.0%)
Data Security / Secure Communications
Fairfax, VA
silentcircle.com

Silent Push (28, 55.6%)
Threat Intelligence / OSINT
Reston, VA
silentpush.com

Spanalytics (11, -8.3%)
IoT Security / Wireless Security
Glen Allen, VA
spanalytics.com

SpecterOps (115, 51.3%)
IAM
Alexandria, VA
specterops.io

stackArmor (49, 11.4%)
GRC / Monitoring
Tysons, VA
stackarmor.com

SteelCloud (66, 3.1%)
GRC / Configuration Management
Ashburn, VA
steelcloud.com

Strivacity (50, 31.6%)
IAM / Customer Registration
Herndon, VA
strivacity.com

Syncdog (12, -36.8%)
Endpoint Security / Mobile Device Security
Reston, VA
syncdog.com

TecSec (45, 80.0%)
Data Security / Key Management
McLean, VA
tecsec.com

Telos (736, -4.5%)
GRC / Compliance Management
Ashburn, VA
telos.com

The Media Trust (69, -4.2%)
Fraud Prevention / Advertising-related
McLean, VA
themediatrust.com

ThreatConnect (168, 5.0%)
Threat Intelligence
Arlington, VA
threatconnect.com

ThreatQuotient (106, -9.4%)
Threat Intelligence / Threat Intelligence Platform
Reston, VA
threatquotient.com

Tychon (49, 36.1%)
GRC / Risk Management
Fredericksburg, VA
tychon.io

UltraViolet Cyber (205, 15.8%)
MSSP / MDR
McLean, VA
uvcyber.com

Vali Cyber (32, 23.1%)
Endpoint Security / Linux Security
Charlottesville, VA
valicyber.com

VectorZero (22, 83.3%)
Data Security / Secure Storage
Reston, VA
vectorzero.ai

Virgil Security (15, -6.2%)
Data Security / Encryption
Manassas, VA
virgilsecurity.com

Volexity (41, 13.9%)
Data Security / Forensics
Reston, VA
volexity.com

Wirewheel (20, -57.5%)
Data Security / Customer Data Security
Arlington, VA
wirewheel.io

WiTopia (9, 12.5%)
Network Security / VPN/Proxy
Reston, VA
witopia.com

Zeva (25, -7.4%)
Data Security / Encryption
Fairfax, VA
zevainc.com

Vermont

Soos (15, -6.2%)
Application Security / SBOM
Winooski, VT
soos.io

Washington

Adaptiva (90, -10.9%)
Endpoint Security / Configuration Management
Kirkland, WA
adaptiva.com

AppViewX (575, 10.8%)
Data Security / Encryption
Seattle, WA
appviewx.com

Aserto (17, 0.0%)
IAM / Access Security
Redmond, WA
aserto.com

Atonomi (10, 25.0%)
IoT Security / Blockchain
Seattle, WA
atonomi.io

**Numbers in parentheses indicate headcount and % change in 2023.*

Auth0 (448, -17.2%)
IAM / Authentication
Bellevue, WA
auth0.com

Authenticid (96, -20.7%)
Fraud Prevention / Identity Verification
Kirkland, WA
authenticid.co

C2SEC (6, 0.0%)
GRC / Risk Management
Redmond, WA
c2sec.com

Chainguard (97, 67.2%)
Application Security / Code Security
Kirkland, WA
chainguard.dev

CI Security (90, 8.4%)
MSSP / MDR
Seattle, WA
ci.security

Cloudentity (45, -35.7%)
IAM / Identity Management
Seattle, WA
cloudentity.com

CodeProof (18, 20.0%)
Application Security / Mobile Device Security
Bellevue, WA
codeproof.com

ControlMap (10, -33.3%)
GRC / Compliance Management
Bellevue, WA
controlmap.io

Cyemptive Technologies Inc. (83, 36.1%)
MSSP / Managed Security Services
Snohomish, WA
cyemptive.com

DarkLight.ai (19, -20.8%)
Security Analytics
Bellevue, WA
darklight.ai

DataSunrise (117, 10.4%)
Data Security / Database Security
Mercer Island, WA
datasunrise.com

DigitSec (9, 12.5%)
Application Security / Scanning
Seattle, WA
digitsec.com

DomainTools (123, 5.1%)
Threat Intelligence / Threat Intelligence From DNS
Seattle, WA
domaintools.com

ExtraHop Networks (671, 0.6%)
Security Analytics / Incident Management
Seattle, WA
extrahop.com

F5 Networks (6174, -3.0%)
Network Security / Firewalls
Seattle, WA
f5.com

Hyperproof (150, 48.5%)
GRC / Compliance Management
Bellevue, WA
hyperproof.io

Intego Inc. (56, 16.7%)
Network Security / Firewalls
Seattle, WA
intego.com

IONIX (83, 38.3%)
GRC / Attack Surface Management
Kirkland, WA
cyberpion.com

Microsoft (224857, -1.4%)
IAM
Redmond, WA
microsoft.com

Nametag (19, 11.8%)
IAM / Authentication
Seattle, WA
getnametag.com

NetMotion (134, 4.7%)
Network Security / SASE
Seattle, WA
netmotionwireless.com

Open Raven (38, -19.1%)
Data Security / Data Discovery
Olympia, WA
openraven.com

OpsHelm (12, 50.0%)
Operations / Configuration Management
Seattle, WA
opshelm.com

PhishCloud (9, 12.5%)
Email Security / Defense Against Phishing
Renton, WA
phishcloud.com

Polyverse (6, 0.0%)
Endpoint Security / Operating System Security
Bellevue, WA
polyverse.io

Protect AI (38, 153.3%)
Data Security
Seattle, WA
protectai.com

RiskLens (14, -79.4%)
GRC / Risk Management
Spokane, WA
risklens.com

Rthreat (23, -14.8%)
Operations / Breach And Attack Simulation
Bellingham, WA
rthreat.net

SecureW2 (73, 0.0%)
IAM / Authentication
Seattle, WA
securew2.com

Strac (6, 20.0%)
Data Security / DLP
Bellevue, WA
strac.io

Strike Graph (44, -15.4%)
GRC / Compliance Management
Seattle, WA
strikegraph.com

Tamnoon (19, 137.5%)
MSSP / Managed Security Services
Remote, WA
tamnoon.io

Topia Technology (23, 9.5%)
Data Security / Encryption
Tacoma, WA
topiatechnology.com

Townsend Security (13, 0.0%)
Data Security / Encryption
Olympia, WA
townsendsecurity.com

Trovares (11, 57.1%)
Security Analytics / Graph Analytics
Seattle, WA
trovares.com

VeriClouds (9, -10.0%)
Fraud Prevention / Credential Security
Seattle, WA
vericlouds.com

Virta Laboratories (4, 0.0%)
IoT Security / Healthcare
Seattle, WA
virtalabs.com

WatchGuard (1023, 9.1%)
Network Security / UTM
Seattle, WA
watchguard.com

Widevine Technologies (6, -14.3%)
Data Security / DRM
Kirkland, WA
widevine.com

wolfSSL (41, 5.1%)
Network Security / Open Source Internet Security
Edmonds, WA
wolfssl.com

**Numbers in parentheses indicate headcount and % change in 2023.*

Wisconsin

Cereus (4, 33.3%)
GRC / Compliance Management
Eau Claire, WI
cereus.io

Locknet Managed IT (53, 8.2%)
MSSP / Managed Security Services
Onalaska, WI
locknetmanagedit.com

PKWARE (149, 4.2%)
Data Security / Data Privacy
Milwaukee, WI
pkware.com

Sergeant Laboratories (15, 0.0%)
GRC / Risk Management
Onalaska, WI
sgtlabs.com

Sprocket Security (18, 80.0%)
GRC / Penetration Testing
Madison, WI
sprocketsecurity.com

SynerComm (50, 6.4%)
Network Security / Network & Security Infrastructure
Brookdfield, WI
synercomm.com

Tascet (7, 0.0%)
GRC / Risk Management
Madison, WI
tascet.com

Tetra Defense (46, -57.4%)
MSSP / MDR
Madison, WI
tetradefense.com

West Virginia

SecurLinx (9, -10.0%)
IAM / Authentication
Morgantown, WV
securlinx.com

Wyoming

BlackFog (21, 23.5%)
Endpoint Security / EDR
Cheyenne, WY
blackfog.com

**Numbers in parentheses indicate headcount and % change in 2023.*

CHAPTER 21

Directory by Category

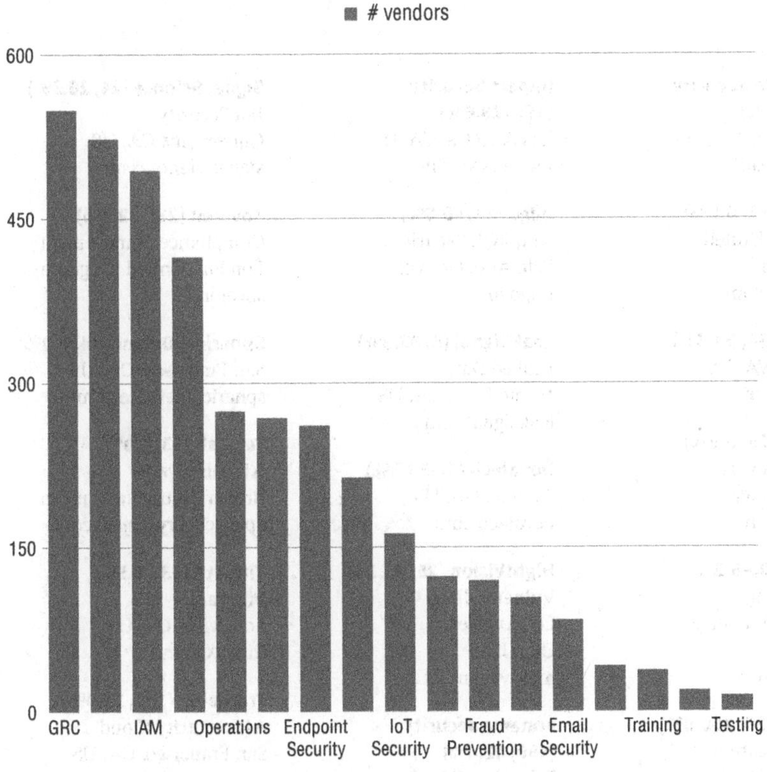

Vendors by Category

Category	Number of Vendors
GRC	549
Data Security	523
IAM	494
Network Security	415
Operations	274

(continued)

Vendors by Category (continued)

Category	Number of Vendors
MSSP	268
Endpoint Security	261
Application Security	213
IoT Security	162
Threat Intelligence	123
Fraud Prevention	119
Security Analytics	103
Email Security	83
API Security	41
Training	37
Deception	19
Testing	14

API Security

42Crunch (44, -13.7%)
Irvine, CA, US
42crunch.com

Aiculus (8, 14.3%)
Melbourne, Australia
aiculus.co

Akana By Perforce (51, -1.9%)
API Management
Minneapolis, MN, US
akana.com

Apiiro (126, 22.3%)
Software Development Security
Tel Aviv, Israel
apiiro.com

APIsec.ai (53, 1.9%)
San Francisco, CA, US
apisec.ai

Approov (16, 23.1%)
Edinburgh, United Kingdom
approov.io

Balasys (39, -27.8%)
Budapest, Hungary
balasys.hu

Bionic (103, -8.8%)
Posture Management
Palo Alto, CA, US
bionic.ai

Cequence Security (167, 4.4%)
Sunnyvale, CA, US
cequence.ai

Contxt (17, 0.0%)
London, United Kingdom
bycontxt.com

Corsha (34, 54.5%)
Vienna, VA, US
corsha.com

Escape (18, 5.9%)
API Discovery
Paris, France
escape.tech

eXate (30, -6.2%)
Monitoring
West End, United Kingdom
exate.com

FireTail (20, 100.0%)
Authentication
McLean, VA, US
firetail.io

Gravitee.io (110, 1.9%)
Access Security
France
gravitee.io

Greymatter (37, -26.0%)
Arlington, VA, US
greymatter.io

Impart Security (16, 128.6%)
Los Angeles, CA, US
impart.security

Inigo (12, 50.0%)
GraphQL Security
Palo Alto, CA, US
inigo.io

LeakSignal (8, 33.3%)
Leaked Data
Menlo Park, CA, US
leaksignal.com

Nevatech (4, -33.3%)
Atlanta, GA, US
nevatech.com

NightVision (25, 47.1%)
Vulnerabilities
Los Angeles, CA, US
nightvision.net

noname security (499, 41.4%)
Palo Alto, CA, US
nonamesecurity.com

Pynt (17, 13.3%)
API Testing
Tel Aviv, Israel
pynt.io

Salt Security (202, -1.0%)
Palo Alto, CA, US
salt.security

Signal Science (24, 26.3%)
Bot Security
Culver City, CA, US
signalsciences.com

Soveren (28, -12.5%)
Compliance Management
London, United Kingdom
soveren.io

Spherical Defence (4, 0.0%)
San Francisco, CA, US
sphericaldefence.com

TeejLab (13, 0.0%)
API Discovery
British Columbia, Canada
apidiscovery.teejlab.com

ThreatX (63, -4.5%)
Firewalls
Louisville, CO, US
threatx.com

Traceable (186, 24.0%)
API Security Cloud
San Francisco, CA, US
traceable.ai

Tyk (156, -22.4%)
Gateways
London, United Kingdom
tyk.io

UBIKA (74, 32.1%)
Firewalls
Meudon, France
ubikasec.com

**Numbers in parentheses indicate headcount and % change in 2023.*

Valence Security (49, 36.1%)
Tel Aviv, Israel
valencesecurity.com

Wallarm (112, 21.7%)
San Francisco, CA, US
wallarm.com

WIB (70, 25.0%)
Tel Aviv, Israel
wib.com

Xeol (3, 0.0%)
New York, NY, US
xeol.io

Application Security

Adversa (3, -25.0%)
Tel Aviv, Israel
adversa.ai

Ahope (16, 6.7%)
Mobile Device Security
Seoul, South Korea
ahope.net

Aikido (20, 11.1%)
Vulnerabilities
Ghent, Belgium
aikido.dev

Akeero (5, -44.4%)
Software Development Security
County Cork, Ireland
akeero.com

Akto (15, 114.3%)
Visibility
Palo Alto, CA, US
www.akto.io

Anxinsec (34, 100.0%)
Runtime Security
Beijing, China
anxinsec.com

Apona (12, 50.0%)
SAST
Roseville, CA, US
apona.ai

AppDome (154, 28.3%)
Tel Aviv, Israel
appdome.com

AppKnox (73, 19.7%)
Mobile Device Security
Singapore
appknox.com

appNovi (8, 60.0%)
Durham, NC, US
appnovi.com

AppSealing (8, 33.3%)
Los Angeles, CA, US
appsealing.com

AppSec Labs (15, 0.0%)
Mobile Device Security
Kfar Saba, Israel
appsec-labs.com

AppSecure Security (14, 27.3%)
Software Testing For Security
Bangalore, Karnataka, India
appsecure.security

AppVision (5, -16.7%)
Code Security
San Francisco, CA, US
appvision.net

Araali Networks (7, -53.3%)
Container Security
Fremont, CA, US
araalinetworks.com

ArmorCode (125, 71.2%)
Posture Management
Palo Alto, CA, US
armorcode.com

Astra (54, 63.6%)
Web App Protection
New Delhi, India
getastra.com

AttackFlow (3, -25.0%)
Code Security
San Francisco, CA, US
attackflow.com

Attify (5, 0.0%)
Mobile Device Security
Bangalore, India
attify.com

Avocado Systems (20, -48.7%)
App Hardening
San Jose, CA, US
avocadosys.com

Azul (416, -22.5%)
Runtime Security
Sunnyvale, CA, US
azul.com

Beagle Security (35, 16.7%)
Penetration Testing
Thiruvananthapuram, Kerala, India
beaglesecurity.com

Bearer (29, 20.8%)
San Francisco, CA, US
bearer.com

BluBracket (6, -60.0%)
Software Development Security
Palo Alto, CA, US
blubracket.com

Blue Planet-works (14, -22.2%)
Isolation
Tokyo, Japan
blueplanet-works.com

BlueRisc (10, -16.7%)
Code Security
Amherst, MA, US
bluerisc.com

Boost Security (27, 28.6%)
Software Development Security
Montreal, QU, Canada
boostsecurity.io

Bosch AIShield (13, 30.0%)
Koramangala, Bengaluru, India
boschaishield.com

Bridgecrew (10, -56.5%)
Configuration Management
San Francisco, CA, US
bridgecrew.io

Bright Security (162, 65.3%)
Code Security
Tel Aviv, Israel
brightsec.com

Build38 (67, 52.3%)
Mobile Device Security
Munich, Germany
build38.com

Calvin Risk (17, 13.3%)
AI Model Security
Zurich, Switzerland
calvin-risk.com

Canonic (14, -50.0%)
Tel Aviv, Israel
canonic.security

Capture The Bug (12, 200.0%)
Bugs
Waikato, New Zealand
capturethebug.xyz

Capzul (3, 0.0%)
Toronto, ON, Canada
capzul.net

Chainguard (97, 67.2%)
Code Security
Kirkland, WA, US
chainguard.dev

Checkmarx (919, -1.8%)
Software Development Security
Ramat Gan, Israel
checkmarx.com

Cider Security (30, -64.3%)
Software Development Security
Tel Aviv, Israel
cidersecurity.io

Clouddefense.ai (36, 28.6%)
Code Security
Palo Alto, CA, US
clouddefense.ai

**Numbers in parentheses indicate headcount and % change in 2023.*

CloudTruth (15, 25.0%)
Configuration Management
Boston, MA, US
cloudtruth.com

Cobalt (444, -3.3%)
Software Testing For Security
San Francisco, CA, US
cobalt.io

Code Intelligence (62, -3.1%)
Bonn, Germany
code-intelligence.com

Codean (7, 0.0%)
Code Security
Utrecht, Netherlands
codean.io

Codenotary (17, -26.1%)
SBOM
Bellaire, TX, US
codenotary.com

CodeProof (18, 20.0%)
Mobile Device Security
Bellevue, WA, US
codeproof.com

CodeThreat (8, 33.3%)
SAST
Istanbul, Turkey
codethreat.com

Codified Security (4, 33.3%)
Code Security
London, United Kingdom
codifiedsecurity.com

Containn (4, 0.0%)
Container Security
Bay Area, CA, US
containn.com

Contrast Security (304, -22.4%)
Software Testing For Security
Los Altos, CA, US
contrastsecurity.com

Corellium (53, 23.3%)
Virtualization
Boynton Beach, FL, US
corellium.com

Corgea (4, 0.0%)
San Francisco, CA, US
corgea.com

Curtail (4, -20.0%)
Software Development Security
Anaheim, CA, US
curtail.com

Cybeats (41, 28.1%)
SBOM
Aurora, Canada
cybeats.com

Cycode (122, 15.1%)
Code Security
Tel Aviv, Israel
cycode.com

Data Theorem (91, 167.7%)
Mobile Device Security
Palo Alto, CA, US
datatheorem.com

DataDog (5821, 14.1%)
Logs
New York, NY, US
datadoghq.com

Debricked (29, -23.7%)
Vulnerabilities
Sweden
debricked.com

Deepfactor (40, -2.4%)
Runtime Security
San Jose, CA, US
deepfactor.io

DeepSource (19, -57.8%)
Code Security
San Francisco, CA, US
deepsource.io

Detectify (128, -25.6%)
Scanning
Stockholm, Sweden
detectify.com

DigitSec (9, 12.5%)
Scanning
Seattle, WA, US
digitsec.com

Docker Scout (798, 1.8%)
SBOM
San Francisco, CA, US
docker.com

DragonSoft (21, -19.2%)
Firewalls
New Taipei City, Taiwan
dragonsoft.com.tw

DryRun Security (6, 500.0%)
Software Development Security
Austin, TX, US
dryrun.security

DuploCloud Inc. (72, 84.6%)
Configuration Management
San Jose, CA, US
duplocloud.com

Dynatrace (4639, 8.9%)
Vulnerabilities
Waltham, MA, US
dynatrace.com

eCyLabs (8, 60.0%)
Software Testing For Security
Coimbatore, India
ecylabs.com

EdgeBit (5, 66.7%)
SBOM
San Mateo, CA, US
edgebit.io

edgescan (90, 11.1%)
Vulnerabilities
Dublin, Ireland
edgescan.com

Endor Labs (74, 85.0%)
Dependency Management
Palo Alto, CA, US
endorlabs.com

Enso Security (21, -40.0%)
Code Security
Mill Valley, CA, US
enso.security

ETHIACK (13, 160.0%)
Penetration Testing
Coimbra, Portugal
ethiack.com

Exodus Intelligence (45, 36.4%)
Research
Austin, TX, US
exodusintel.com

Feroot Security (22, 0.0%)
Scanning
Toronto, Canada
feroot.com

Fluid Attacks (156, 34.5%)
Scanning
San Francisco, CA, US
fluidattacks.com

ForAllSecure (42, -22.2%)
Software Testing For Security
Pittsburgh, PA, US
forallsecure.com

Fossa (72, -19.1%)
Vulnerabilities
San Francisco, CA, US
fossa.com

GeoEdge (69, -2.8%)
Advertising-related
New York, NY, US
geoedge.com

Ghost Security (28, 27.3%)
Asset Management
TX, US
ghost.security

Github (5327, -0.1%)
Vulnerabilities
San Francisco, CA, US
github.com

GitLab (2351, 1.9%)
Code Security
San Francisco, CA, US
about.gitlab.com

GObugfree AG (20, 0.0%)
Hackers For Hire
Zurich, Switzerland
gobugfree.com

GrammaTech (65, -52.2%)
Code Security
Ithaca, NY, US
grammatech.com

**Numbers in parentheses indicate headcount and % change in 2023.*

Guardio (85, 21.4%)
Scanning
Tel Aviv, Israel
guard.io

Guardsquare (149, 16.4%)
Mobile Device Security
Leuven, Belgium
guardsquare.com

HiddenLayer (78, 271.4%)
ML Security
Austin, TX, US
hiddenlayer.com

Identity Science (8, 60.0%)
Software Development Security
Sunnyvale, CA, US
identityscience.ai

illustria.io (14, 27.3%)
Code Security
Tel Aviv, Israel
illustria.io

Immunant (5, 25.0%)
Code Security
Irvine, CA, US
immunant.com

Immunefi (86, 43.3%)
Bugs
Cascais, Portugal
immunefi.com

Immuniweb (34, 3.0%)
Scanning
Geneva, Switzerland
immuniweb.com

Insignary (6, -25.0%)
Vulnerabilities
Seoul, South Korea
insignary.com

Invicti Security (318, -17.0%)
Scanning
Austin, TX, US
invicti.com

Ion Channel (4, -69.2%)
SBOM
Washington, DC, US
ionchannel.io

IriusRisk (167, 11.3%)
Scanning
Cuarte, Spain
iriusrisk.com

JFrog (1567, 15.1%)
Software Development Security
Sunnyvale, CA, US
jfrog.com

Jit.io (64, 42.2%)
Open Source Tools
Tel Aviv, Israel
jit.io

Jscrambler (100, 8.7%)
Code Security
San Francisco, CA, US
jscrambler.com

K2 Cyber Security (10, 0.0%)
San Jose, CA, US
k2io.com

Kayran (10, 11.1%)
Penetration Testing
Nitsanei Oz, Israel
kayran.io

Kiuwan (29, 0.0%)
Code Security
Houston, TX, US
kiuwan.com

Kodem (38, 81.0%)
Runtime Security
Tel Aviv, Israel
kodemsecurity.com

Kondukto (23, 9.5%)
Istanbul, Turkey
kondukto.io

LABRADOR LABS (16, 14.3%)
Code Security
Seoul, South Korea
labradorlabs.ai

Lacework (823, -15.8%)
Cloud Security
Mountain View, CA, US
lacework.com

Licel (15, 25.0%)
Mobile Device Security
Los Angeles, CA, US
licelus.com

Lightspin (41, -29.3%)
Software Development Security
Tel Aviv, Israel
lightspin.io

Lucent Sky (3, 0.0%)
Code Security
San Francisco, CA, US
lucentsky.com

Manifest (13, 44.4%)
SBOM
Remote, OR, US
manifestcyber.com

Mend (293, -16.5%)
Open Source Security And License Management
Giv'atayim, Israel
whitesourcesoftware.com

Meterian (12, 33.3%)
Open Source Management
North Kensington, United Kingdom
meterian.io

Mobb (25, 38.9%)
Vulnerabilities
Acton, MA, US
mobb.ai

Mocana Corporation (29, 7.4%)
Mobile Device Security
Sunnyvale, CA, US
mocana.com

Moderne (33, 37.5%)
Miami, FL, US
moderne.io

Moresec (49, 0.0%)
Scanning
Hangzhou, China
moresec.cn

Myrror Security (17, 30.8%)
Code Security
Tel Aviv, Israel
myrror.security

NetRise (36, 33.3%)
Firmware
Austin, TX, US
netrise.io

NetSkope (2439, 13.7%)
Santa Clara, CA, US
netskope.com

NodeSource (18, 5.9%)
Serverless
San Francisco, CA, US
nodesource.com

Nokod Security (15, 1400.0%)
Security For No-code Applications
Tel Aviv, Israel
nokodsecurity.com

Oligo Security (58, 65.7%)
Tel Aviv, Israel
oligo.security

Open Zeppelin (92, 10.8%)
Blockchain
San Francisco, CA, US
openzeppelin.com

Operant AI (23, 21.1%)
Runtime Security
San Francisco, CA, US
operant.ai

Overe.io (4, 0.0%)
SaaS Security
London, United Kingdom
overe.io

OX Security (85, 107.3%)
Software Development Security
Tel Aviv, Israel
ox.security

oxeye (30, -9.1%)
Software Testing For Security
Tel Aviv, Israel
oxeye.io

Parasoft (271, 0.0%)
Software Testing For Security
Monrovia, CA, US
parasoft.com

**Numbers in parentheses indicate headcount and % change in 2023.*

Patronus.io (3, 0.0%)
Scanning
Berlin, Germany
patronus.io

Phylum (22, -33.3%)
Code Security
Evergreen, CO, US
phylum.io

PNF Software (3, 0.0%)
Reverse Engineering
Redwood City, CA, US
pnfsoftware.com

Portshift (12, 33.3%)
Identity-Based Workload Protection
Tel Aviv, Israel
portshift.io

PreEmptive Solutions (44, 76.0%)
App Hardening
Mayfield Village, OH, US
preemptive.com

Privado (173, 130.7%)
Code Security
San Francisco, CA, US
privado.ai

Probely (33, 43.5%)
Scanning
Lisbon, Portugal
probely.com

Promon (109, 7.9%)
Mobile Device Security
Oslo, Norway
promon.co

Protegrity (369, -1.6%)
Stamford, CT, US
protegrity.com

Purplemet (4, 0.0%)
Scanning
Paris, France
purplemet.com

Quarkslab (93, 0.0%)
Code Security
Paris, France
quarkslab.com

Qwiet AI (42, -22.2%)
Code Security
Santa Clara, CA, US
shiftleft.io

RapidFort Inc. (33, 32.0%)
Attack Surface Management
Sunnyvale, CA, US
rapidfort.com

Reblaze (45, -30.8%)
Web App Protection
Tel Aviv, Israel
reblaze.com

Reflectiz (38, 11.8%)
Website Security
Ramat Gan, Israel
reflectiz.com

RevealSecurity (47, 4.4%)
Monitoring
Tel Aviv, Israel
trackerdetect.com

RunSafe Security (18, 5.9%)
Application Hardening
McLean, VA, US
runsafesecurity.com

Runtime Verification (48, 17.1%)
Code Security
Urbana, IL, US
runtimeverification.com

SafeHats (7, 16.7%)
Bugs
Bangalore, India
safehats.com

scanmeter (7, 75.0%)
Penetration Testing
Zurich, Switzerland
scanmeter.io

Scribe Security (33, 37.5%)
SBOM
Tel Aviv, Israel
scribesecurity.com

SEC Consult (137, 0.0%)
Code Security
Vienna, Austria
sec-consult.com

SecuPi (50, 21.9%)
Monitoring
London, United Kingdom
secupi.com

SecurityBridge (43, 65.4%)
SAP
Ingolstadt, Germany
securitybridge.com

Semgrep (147, 0.0%)
Code Security
San Francisco, CA, US
semgrep.dev

Sentar (313, 3.3%)
Code Security
Huntsville, AL, US
sentar.com

Slim.AI (38, -9.5%)
Container Security
Acton, MA, US
slim.ai

Snyk (1128, -11.5%)
Vulnerabilities
London, United Kingdom
snyk.io

SoBug (3, 0.0%)
Bugs
Shenzhen, China
sobug.com

SOFTwarfare (31, 63.2%)
Integration Security
Prairie Village, KS, US
softwarfare.com

SolidWall (17, 112.5%)
Firewalls
Moscow, Russia
solidwall.io

Sonar (527, 5.6%)
Code Security
Vernier, Switzerland
sonarsource.com

Sonatype (573, -10.5%)
Code Security
Fulton, MD, US
sonatype.com

Soos (15, -6.2%)
SBOM
Winooski, VT, US
soos.io

Sparrow (19, 26.7%)
Code Security
Mapo-gu, South Korea
sparrowfasoo.com

Sqreen (4, -42.9%)
Monitoring
Saint-Cloud, France
sqreen.com

StackHawk (56, 3.7%)
Vulnerabilities
Denver, CO, US
stackhawk.com

Star Lab (42, -2.3%)
Research
Washington, DC, US
starlab.io

STEALIEN (37, 8.8%)
Seoul, South Korea
stealien.com

Strong Network (32, 3.2%)
Workspace Security
Lausanne, Switzerland
strong.network

Sudoviz (8, 100.0%)
US
sudoviz.com

Syhunt (7, 40.0%)
Code Security
Rio de Janeiro, Brazil
syhunt.com

Synopsys (18348, 7.5%)
Software Testing For Security
Mountain View, CA, US
synopsys.com

ThreatModeler Software (53, 8.2%)
Vulnerabilities
Jersey City, NJ, US
threatmodeler.com

**Numbers in parentheses indicate headcount and % change in 2023.*

Tidelift (66, -17.5%)
SBOM
Boston, MA, US
tidelift.com

Tromzo (27, 80.0%)
Software Development Security
Mountain View, CA, US
tromzo.com

TrueFort (89, 6.0%)
Monitoring
Weehawken, NJ, US
truefort.com

Valid Networks (8, -38.5%)
Blockchain
New York, NY, US
valid.network

Veracode (692, -13.6%)
Code Security
Burlington, MA, US
veracode.com

Vicarius (58, 9.4%)
Code Security
Jerusalem, Israel
vicarius.io

Virsec Systems (150, -14.8%)
Web App Protection
San Jose, CA, US
virsec.com

Wabbi (16, -5.9%)
Software Development Security
Boston, MA, US
wabbisoft.com

Waratek (31, -20.5%)
Dublin, Ireland
waratek.com

White Hawk Software (4, 0.0%)
Tamper Proofing
Palo Alto, CA, US
whitehawksoftware.com

Wing Security (44, 2.3%)
SaaS Management
Tel Aviv, Israel
wing.security

Xygeni (22, 120.0%)
SBOM
Madrid, Spain
xygeni.io

Yes Security (9, 800.0%)
South Yorkshire, United Kingdom
yes-security.com

Zero Day Initiative (Trend Micro) (13, 30.0%)
Bugs
Austin, TX, US
zerodayinitiative.com

Zerocopter (45, 2.3%)
Hackers For Hire
Amsterdam, Netherlands
zerocopter.com

ZERODIUM (5, 400.0%)
Bugs
Washington, DC, US
zerodium.com

Data Security

Absio (5, 0.0%)
Software-Defined Distributed Key Cryptography (SDKC)
Denver, CO, US
absio.com

Acronis (2123, -3.1%)
Secure Backup/Recovery
Schaffhausen, Switzerland
acronis.com

Agora SecureWare (7, 16.7%)
Secure Collaboration
Bioggio, Switzerland
agora-secureware.com

Aircloak (5, -28.6%)
Data Masking
Berlin, Germany
aircloak.com

Akeyless (95, 11.8%)
Key Management
Tel Aviv, Israel
akeyless.io

Altitude Networks (3, -50.0%)
Monitoring
San Francisco, CA, US
altitudenetworks.com

Altr (72, 18.0%)
Data Discovery
Austin, TX, US
altr.com

Anchorage (336, -11.3%)
Secure Storage
San Francisco, CA, US
anchorage.com

Anjuna (50, -29.6%)
Runtime Security
Palo Alto, CA, US
anjuna.io

Anonos (69, 81.6%)
Secure Data Sharing
Boulder, CO, US
anonos.com

Anonyome Labs (128, 18.5%)
Secure Communications
Salt Lake City, UT, US
anonyome.com

AppViewX (575, 10.8%)
Encryption
Seattle, WA, US
appviewx.com

Apricorn (31, 10.7%)
Secure Storage
Poway, CA, US
apricorn.com

ARCANO (4, 0.0%)
Secure Data Sharing
Zurich, Switzerland
arcano.app

Ardaco (25, -16.7%)
Secure Communications
Bratislava, Slovakia
ardaco.com

Arexdata (11, 175.0%)
Posture Management
Madrid, Spain
arexdata.com

Armarius Software (8, 0.0%)
DLP
Warrenville, IL, US
armariussoftware.com

Armortext (12, 0.0%)
Secure Collaboration
McLean, VA, US
armortext.com

Arpeggio Software (3, 0.0%)
ISeries
Atlanta, GA, US
arpeggiosoftware.com

Asigra (85, 13.3%)
Secure Backup/Recovery
Toronto, Canada
asigra.com

Asparna Ltd. (5, 0.0%)
Encrypted File Sync And Social Conversations
Afula, Israel
asparna.com

ASPG (31, 40.9%)
Encryption
Naples, FL, US
aspg.com

Astran (26, 8.3%)
Secure Storage
Paris, France
astran.io

Atakama (43, -4.4%)
Encryption
New York, NY, US
atakama.com

Avepoint (1466, 9.7%)
Secure Backup/Recovery
Jersey City, NJ, US
avepoint.com

Axcrypt (24, 14.3%)
Encryption
Stockholm, Sweden
axcrypt.net

Baffle (54, 14.9%)
Database Security
Santa Clara, CA, US
baffle.io

**Numbers in parentheses indicate headcount and % change in 2023.*

Becrypt (57, 23.9%)
Encryption
London, United Kingdom
becrypt.com

Bedrock (21, 40.0%)
Posture Management
San Francisco, CA, US
bedrock.security

BicDroid (7, 0.0%)
Encryption
Waterloo, Canada
bicdroid.com

Biscom (202, 9.2%)
Secure Data Sharing
Chelmsford, MA, US
biscom.com

Bittium (1526, -4.4%)
Secure Communications
Oulu, Finland
bittium.com

Blackbelt Smartphone Defence Ltd (33, 57.1%)
Data Erasure And Destruction
Kendal, United Kingdom
blackbeltdefence.com

Blancco (352, 3.8%)
Data Erasure And Destruction
Bishops Stortford, United Kingdom
blancco.com

BlockChain Security (20, 66.7%)
Blockchain
Taipei, Taiwan
chainsecurity.asia

Bloombase (18, -28.0%)
Encryption
Redwood City, CA, US
bloombase.com

Blowfish (18, 260.0%)
Wallets
Switzerland
blowfish.xyz

Boolebox (13, -18.8%)
IRM
Milan, Italy
boolebox.com

Bornio (12, 0.0%)
Data Flows
Menlo Park, CA, US
bornio.com

Botdoc (13, 8.3%)
Secure Data Sharing
Monument, CO, US
botdoc.io

Bottomline (2461, 6.0%)
Portsmouth, NH, US
bottomline.com

Boxcryptor (10, -44.4%)
Encryption
Augsburg, Germany
boxcryptor.com

Brainloop (67, 3.1%)
Secure Collaboration
Munich, Germany
brainloop.com

brighter AI (44, -4.3%)
Video/Image Anonymization
Berlin, Germany
brighter.ai

BYSTAMP (19, 0.0%)
Paris, France
bystamp.com

Calamu (27, -12.9%)
Shards
Clinton, NJ, US
calamu.com

Calypso AI (51, 13.3%)
Safe AI/ML Data
San Francisco, CA, US
calypsoai.com

Caplinked (14, -12.5%)
Secure Data Sharing
Manhattan Beach, CA, US
caplinked.com

Casa (68, 6.2%)
Denver, CO, US
keys.casa

CBL Data Recovery Technologies Inc. (39, 11.4%)
Data Recovery
Markham, Canada
cbldata.com

Cellcrypt (5, 400.0%)
Secure Communications
London, United Kingdom
cellcrypt.com

Celltrust Corporation (20, 11.1%)
Secure Communications
Scottsdale, AZ, US
celltrust.com

Certicom (123, -2.4%)
Encryption
Mississauga, Canada
certicom.com

CertiK (206, -14.9%)
Blockchain
New York, NY, US
certik.com

CertiPath (43, 10.3%)
Public Key Infrastructure
Reston, VA, US
certipath.com

Certora (74, 8.8%)
Blockchain
Tel Aviv, Israel
certora.com

CipherStash (19, 18.8%)
Encryption
Sydney, Australia
cipherstash.com

Ciphertex (8, 33.3%)
Secure Storage
San Fernando, CA, US
ciphertex.com

Civic Technologies (33, -8.3%)
Wallets
San Francisco, CA, US
civic.com

Cloaked (50, 16.3%)
Lowell, MA, US
cloaked.app

Cocoon Data (23, -17.9%)
Secure Data Sharing
Arlington, VA, US
cocoondata.com

Code-X (16, -5.9%)
Shards
Tampa, FL, US
teamcode-x.com

Cognni (28, 0.0%)
Data Discovery
Tel Aviv, Israel
cognni.ai

Cohesity (2221, -3.1%)
San Jose, CA, US
cohesity.com

CommandK.Dev (13, 85.7%)
Secrets Management
San Francisco, CA, US
commandk.dev

Communication Security Group (16, -23.8%)
Secure Communications
London, United Kingdom
csghq.com

Comodo (663, -2.8%)
Public Key Infrastructure
Clifton, NJ, US
comodo.com

Compass Security AG (60, -16.7%)
Secure Data Sharing
Rapperswil-Jona, Switzerland
compass-security.com

Compumatica (19, 0.0%)
Secure Remote Access
Uden, Netherlands
compumatica.com

Concentric AI (59, 37.2%)
Data Classification
San Jose, CA, US
concentric.ai

Continuity (63, 0.0%)
Hygiene For Storage
New York, NY, US
continuitysoftware.com

**Numbers in parentheses indicate headcount and % change in 2023.*

Cord3 Innovation Inc. (9, 0.0%)
Encryption
Ottawa, Canada
cord3inc.com

Cosmian (20, 25.0%)
Paris, France
cosmian.com

Crown Sterling (29, 26.1%)
Encryption
Newport Beach, CA, US
crownsterling.io

Crypta Labs (13, -7.1%)
Encryption
London, United Kingdom
cryptalabs.com

Crypto International AG (43, 43.3%)
Hardware
Steinhausen, Switzerland
crypto.ch

Crypto4A Inc. (25, 8.7%)
Entropy As A Service
Ottawa, Canada
crypto4a.com

Cryptomathic (102, -1.9%)
Key Management
Aarhus, Denmark
cryptomathic.com

Cryptomill Cybersecurity Solutions (21, -22.2%)
Toronto, Canada
cryptomill.com

cryptovision (59, 40.5%)
Public Key Infrastructure
Gelsenkirchen, Germany
cryptovision.com

Cryptshare (57, -1.7%)
Secure Data
Freiburg, Germany
cryptshare.com

Cryptsoft Pty Ltd. (15, 0.0%)
Public Key Infrastructure
Greenslopes, Australia
cryptsoft.com

Cryptyk (10, -9.1%)
Secure Storage
Las Vegas, NV, US
cryptyk.io

Cyber Reliant (6, 0.0%)
Encryption
Annapolis, MD, US
cyberreliant.com

CyberSafe Software (3, 0.0%)
Encryption
Krasnodar, Russia
cybersafesoft.com

Cybersense (10, 25.0%)
Deception
North Rhine-Westphalia, Germany
cybersense.ai

Cyder (6, 50.0%)
Data Privacy
San Francisco, CA, US
getcyder.com

Cyera (180, 164.7%)
Data Management
Tel Aviv, Israel
cyera.io

Cyph (3, 0.0%)
Secure Collaboration
McLean, VA, US
cyph.com

Cypher.Dog (13, -23.5%)
Secure Data Sharing
Wroclaw, Poland
cypher.dog

Cyral (47, -24.2%)
Access Security
Redwood City, CA, US
cyral.com

Cyrus (28, -45.1%)
Personal Cybersecurity
San Francisco, CA, US
cyrus.app

Dasera (46, 21.1%)
Monitoring
Mountain View, CA, US
dasera.com

Data Encryption Systems (5, 25.0%)
DRM
Taunton, United Kingdom
des.co.uk

Data443 Risk Mitigation (23, 43.8%)
Data Management
Morrisville, NC, US
data443.com

DataLocker (55, -3.5%)
Secure Storage
Overland Park, KS, US
datalocker.com

Datamasque (15, 36.4%)
Data Masking
Auckland, New Zealand
datamasque.com

Datanchor (32, 18.5%)
Document Security
Columbus, OH, US
anchormydata.com

DataPassports (9, -52.6%)
IRM
Toronto, Canada
datapassports.com

DataSunrise (117, 10.4%)
Database Security
Mercer Island, WA, US
datasunrise.com

Datex Inc. (52, 20.9%)
DLP
Mississauga, Canada
datex.ca

Dathena Science (6, -40.0%)
Data Discovery
Singapore, Singapore
dathena.io

Dawizz (9, 0.0%)
Data Discovery
Vannes, France
dawizz.fr

DealRoom (27, -18.2%)
Deal Room
Chicago, IL, US
dealroom.net

Decentriq (34, -2.9%)
Secure Collaboration
Zurich, Switzerland
decentriq.com

Deepkeep (20, 66.7%)
Safe AI/ML Data
Tel Aviv, Israel
deepkeep.ai

DeepView (6, 20.0%)
Monitoring
London, United Kingdom
deepview.com

Dekart (9, 125.0%)
Encryption
Chisinau, Republic of Moldova
dekart.com

Dekko Secure (10, 25.0%)
Encryption
Sydney, Australia
dekkosecure.com

DeleteMe (110, 74.6%)
Data Removal
Somerville, MA, US
joindeleteme.com

Delphix (628, 0.2%)
Data Management
Redwood City, CA, US
delphix.com

Dig Security (80, 48.1%)
Data Discovery
Tel Aviv, Israel
dig.security

DigiCert (1368, 7.3%)
Public Key Infrastructure
Lehi, UT, US
digicert.com

Digify (45, 21.6%)
IRM
Singapore, Singapore
digify.com

Digital Core Design (6, 0.0%)
Encryption
Bytom, Poland
dcd.pl

**Numbers in parentheses indicate headcount and % change in 2023.*

Digitronic (11, 22.2%)
Encryption
Chemnitz, Sachsen, Germany
digitronic.net

DigitTrade (6, -14.3%)
Teutschenthal, Germany
digittrade.de

DoControl (71, -5.3%)
Access Security
New York, NY, US
docontrol.io

Doppler (34, 0.0%)
Secrets Management
San Francisco, CA, US
doppler.com

DRACOON (97, 19.8%)
Secure Data Sharing
Regensburg, Germany
dracoon.com

Dragonfly Cyber (3, 0.0%)
San Diego, CA, US
dragonflycyber.com

Drooms (174, 1.2%)
Data Rooms
Frankfurt, Germany
drooms.com

DuoKey (7, 0.0%)
Encryption
Lausanne, Switzerland
duokey.com

east-tec (7, 16.7%)
Data Erasure And Destruction
Oradea, Romania
east-tec.com

Eclipz (18, -37.9%)
IPSec Tools
Los Gatos, CA, US
eclipz.io

Egnyte (1065, 31.3%)
Secure Data Sharing
Mountain View, CA, US
egnyte.com

enclaive (9, 50.0%)
Confidential Computing
Berlin, Germany
enclaive.io

Engage Black (4, -20.0%)
Code Security
Aptos, CA, US
engageblack.com

Enigmedia (8, -66.7%)
Secure Communications
San Sebastian, Spain
enigmedia.es

Enov8 (29, 7.4%)
Data Masking
New South Wales, Australia
enov8.com

Entro Security (24, 71.4%)
Secrets Management
Tel Aviv, Israel
entro.security

Enveil (67, -10.7%)
Encryption
Washington, DC, US
enveil.com

Envieta (18, -5.3%)
Hardware
Columbia, MD, US
envieta.com

eperi (26, 8.3%)
Encryption
Pfungstadt, Germany
eperi.de

ERMES Cyber Security (48, 23.1%)
DLP
Turin, Italy
ermessecurity.com

eureka (38, 11.8%)
Data Discovery
Tel Aviv, Israel
eureka.security

Exacttrak Ltd (8, -11.1%)
Managed Devices To Protect Laptop Data
Banbury, United Kingdom
exacttrak.com

ExcelSecu (51, -17.7%)
Public Key Infrastructure
Shenzhen, China
excelsecu.com

EYL (4, -81.0%)
Quantum
Seoul, South Korea
eylpartners.com

FileCloud (117, 7.3%)
IRM
Austin, TX, US
filecloud.com

FileOpen Systems (7, -36.4%)
DRM
Santa Cruz, CA, US
fileopen.com

Filestring (55, 7.8%)
IRM
Santa Cruz, CA, US
filestring.com

Fireblocks (649, 25.5%)
Blockchain
New York, NY, US
fireblocks.com

Flow Security (33, 32.0%)
Data Flows
Tel Aviv, Israel
flowsecurity.com

Flying Cloud Technology (15, 0.0%)
Data Flows
Santa Cruz, CA, US
flyingcloudtech.com

Fornetix (49, 8.9%)
Key Management
Frederick, MD, US
fornetix.com

Fortanix (273, 28.8%)
Confidential Computing
Mountain View, CA, US
fortanix.com

FortKnoxster (4, -33.3%)
Encryption
Gibraltar, United Kingdom
fortknoxster.com

FutureX (134, 36.7%)
Hardware
Bulverde, TX, US
futurex.com

Galaxkey (33, -5.7%)
Secure Data Sharing
London, United Kingdom
galaxkey.com

Garner Products (22, -18.5%)
Data Erasure And Destruction
Roseville, CA, US
garnerproducts.com

GBS (37, -15.9%)
Karlsruhe, Germany
gbs.com

GeoTrust Inc. (31, -16.2%)
Encryption
Mountain View, CA, US
geotrust.com

Getvisibility (51, 34.2%)
Data Discovery
Cambridge, MA, US
getvisibility.com

GK8 (48, 23.1%)
Wallets
Tel Aviv, Israel
gk8.io

Gold Lock (6, 0.0%)
Mobile Device Security
Ramat Gan, Israel
goldlock.com.br

Goldkey (19, -52.5%)
Secure Storage
Kansas City, MO, US
goldkey.com

Gretel.ai (72, 35.9%)
Data Masking
San Diego, CA, US
gretel.ai

Gsmk Cryptophone (12, -14.3%)
Secure Communications
Berlin, Germany
cryptophone.de

**Numbers in parentheses indicate headcount and % change in 2023.*

HashiCorp (2339, -5.4%)
Secrets Management
San Francisco, CA, US
hashicorp.com

HUB Security (141, -11.3%)
Encryption
Tel Aviv, Israel
hubsecurity.com

Hushmail (256, 0.4%)
Secure Communications
Vancouver, Canada
hushmail.com

Hushmesh (9, 50.0%)
Key Management
Falls Church, VA, US
hushmesh.com

i2Chain (8, -20.0%)
San Francisco, CA, US
i2chain.com

Id Quantique (110, 5.8%)
Quantum
Carouge, Switzerland
idquantique.com

IdenTrust (part of HID Global) (66, -1.5%)
Public Key Infrastructure
Fremont, CA, US
identrust.com

Immuta (265, -8.6%)
Access Security
College Park, MD, US
immuta.com

Infinite Convergence Solutions (110, 7.8%)
Secure Communications
Arlington Heights, IL, US
infinite-convergence.com

Infisical (9, 12.5%)
Secrets Management
San Francisco, CA, US
infisical.com

Infobay (10, 0.0%)
Secure Data Sharing
Petah Tikva, Israel
infobaysec.com

Informatica (5720, -4.9%)
Data Masking
Redwood City, CA, US
informatica.com

Information Security Corporation (21, 16.7%)
Public Key Infrastructure
Oak Park, IL, US
infoseccorp.com

Infosec Global (35, 2.9%)
Public Key Infrastructure
North York, Canada
infosecglobal.com

Inpher (33, 13.8%)
Data Privacy
New York, NY, US
inpher.io

InQuest (30, 15.4%)
DLP
Arlington, VA, US
inquest.net

Inspeere (8, 100.0%)
Secure Backup/Recovery
Poitiers, France
inspeere.com

Ionburst (8, 0.0%)
Edinburgh, Scotland
ionburst.io

Ionu (3, 0.0%)
Data Management
Los Gatos, CA, US
ionu.com

Ironblocks (14, 40.0%)
Blockchain
Tel Aviv, Israel
ironblocks.com

ISARA (18, -47.1%)
Encryption
Waterloo, Canada
isara.com

IStorage (27, 0.0%)
Hardware
Perivale,
United Kingdom
istorage-uk.com

ITsMine (24, -4.0%)
Secure Storage
Rishon Lezion, Israel
itsmine.io

IXDen (12, -7.7%)
Tel Aviv, Israel
ixden.com

Janusnet (9, 12.5%)
Data Classification
Milsons Point, Australia
janusnet.com

Jetico Inc. Oy (14, -6.7%)
Encryption
Espoo, Finland
jetico.com

KeeeX (9, 12.5%)
Document Security
Marseille, France
keeex.me

KeepSafe (22, 10.0%)
Encryption
San Francisco, CA, US
getkeepsafe.com

KEEQuant (16, 45.5%)
Quantum
Fürth, Germany
keequant.com

KETS Quantum Security (29, 20.8%)
Secure Communications
Bristol, United Kingdom
kets-quantum.com

Keyavi (41, -2.4%)
IRM
Denver, CO, US
keyavi.com

Keyfactor (416, 12.4%)
Public Key Infrastructure
Independence, OH, US
keyfactor.com

Keytalk - Pki Management Solutions (5, -16.7%)
Public Key Infrastructure
Amersfoort, Netherlands
keytalk.com

Kingston Technology (1496, 11.3%)
Secure Storage
Fountain Valley, CA, US
kingston.com

Kiteworks (239, 6.7%)
IRM
Palo Alto, CA, US
kiteworks.com

klearis (4, 0.0%)
Content Disarm And Reconstruction
Ankara, Turkey
klearis.com

KoolSpan (33, 10.0%)
Secure Communications
Bethesda, MD, US
koolspan.com

Kriptos (50, 16.3%)
Data Classification
Sausalito, CA, US
kriptos.io

Kryptus (130, 8.3%)
Hardware
Campinas Sao Paulo, Brazil
kryptus.com

Lakera (30, 0.0%)
AI Data Security
Zürich, Switzerland
lakera.ai

Laminar (74, -12.9%)
Data Discovery
New York, NY, US
lmnr.io

Lasso Security (19, 0.0%)
Israel
lasso.security

Leanear (8, 0.0%)
Cloud Security
Paris, France
leanear.io

LeapFILE (6, 0.0%)
Secure Data Sharing
Cupertino, CA, US
leapfile.com

**Numbers in parentheses indicate headcount and % change in 2023.*

LeapYear Technologies (5, -86.5%)
Analyze Private Information
Berkeley, CA, US
leapyear.ai

Ledger (732, 0.1%)
Wallets
Paris, France
ledger.com

LogDog (8, 0.0%)
Tel Aviv, Israel
getlogdog.com

LSoft Technologies (7, 0.0%)
Data Erasure And Destruction
Mississauga, Canada
lsoft.net

Lux Scientiae (43, 0.0%)
Secure Communications
Medfield, MA, US
luxsci.com

Mage (Was Mentis) (91, 12.3%)
Data Masking
New York, NY, US
magedata.ai

Maidsafe (19, 0.0%)
Blockchain
Ayr, United Kingdom
maidsafe.net

Markany (96, 28.0%)
DRM
Seoul, South Korea
markany.com

Marvell (7744, -3.9%)
Hardware
Santa Clara, CA, US
marvell.com

Materna Virtual Solution (102, 21.4%)
Secure Communications
Munich, Germany
virtual-solution.com

Merlincryption (5, 0.0%)
Encryption
Austin, TX, US
MerlinCryption.com

Metomic (52, 73.3%)
Data Discovery
Liverpool, United Kingdom
metomic.io

Mithril Security (17, -15.0%)
AI Training Security
Paris, France
mithrilsecurity.io

Mobile Helix (3, 0.0%)
Encryption
Mountain View, CA, US
mobilehelix.com

Mode (21, 250.0%)
Quantum
Calgary, Canada
mode.io

Mostly.AI (61, 3.4%)
Data Masking
Vienna, Wien, Austria
mostly.ai

Msignia (14, 7.7%)
Public Key Infrastructure
Franklin, TN, US
mSIGNIA.com

Multicert (83, 10.7%)
Public Key Infrastructure
Porto Salvo, Portugal
multicert.com

Mutare (40, -18.4%)
Secure Communications
Rolling Meadows, IL, US
mutare.com

Myntex (9, 0.0%)
Secure Communications
Calgary, Canada
myntex.com

Myota (19, 58.3%)
IRM
Blue Bell, PA, US
myota.io

MyWorkDrive (10, 0.0%)
Secure Storage
San Francisco, CA, US
myworkdrive.com

Netlib (4, 0.0%)
Stamford, CT, US
netlibsecurity.com

Neurocat (36, 2.9%)
Safe AI/ML Data
Berlin, Germany
neurocat.ai

NeuShield (10, 42.9%)
Ransomware Security
Fremont, CA, US
neushield.com

NextLabs (163, 19.0%)
IRM
San Mateo, CA, US
nextlabs.com

Nexus Industrial Memory (6, 0.0%)
West Sussex, United Kingdom
nexusindustrialmemory.com

Nightfall AI (114, 11.8%)
Data Discovery
San Francisco, CA, US
nightfall.ai

Nira (33, 10.0%)
Redwood City, CA, US
nira.com

NitroKey (6, 50.0%)
Encryption
Berlin, Germany
nitrokey.com

NoID (12, 33.3%)
Secure Communications
St Julians, Malta
noid.ltd

Normalyze (66, 112.9%)
Data Discovery
Los Altos, CA, US
normalyze.ai

Nu Quantum (39, 69.6%)
Quantum
London, United Kingdom
nu-quantum.com

Nullafi (15, 0.0%)
Secure Storage
Chicago, IL, US
nullafi.com

Nuts Technologies Inc. (6, 0.0%)
Encryption
Chicago Area, IL, US
nutstechnologies.com

Nym (55, 22.2%)
Encryption
Neuchatel, China
nymtech.net

Oasis Labs (32, -25.6%)
Governance
San Francisco, CA, US
oasislabs.com

Oblivious (32, 88.2%)
Secure Data Sharing
Dublin, Ireland
oblivious.ai

Ockam (24, 26.3%)
Orchestration
San Francisco, CA, US
ockam.io

odix (26, -7.1%)
Document Security
Rosh HaAyin, Israel
odi-x.com

Okera (24, -72.4%)
Governance
San Francisco, CA, US
okera.com

Onapsis Inc. (345, -5.0%)
SAP
Boston, MA, US
onapsis.com

OneKey (12, 500.0%)
Wallets
Hong Kong Island, Hong Kong
onekey.so

Oodrive (415, -1.9%)
Secure Backup/Recovery
Paris, France
oodrive.com

**Numbers in parentheses indicate headcount and % change in 2023.*

Open Raven (38, -19.1%)
Data Discovery
Olympia, WA, US
openraven.com

Osano (107, 78.3%)
Compliance
Management
Austin, TX, US
osano.com

OwnData (1264, -10.8%)
Englewood Cliffs,
NJ, US
owndata.com

Paperclip (26, -3.7%)
Document Security
Hackensack, NJ, US
paperclip.com

Parablu (44, 29.4%)
Secure Backup/Recovery
Santa Clara, CA, US
parablu.com

Penten (110, 5.8%)
Encryption
Braddon, Australia
penten.com

Phantom (127, 89.5%)
Wallets
San Francisco, CA, US
phantom.app

Picnic (38, -17.4%)
Employee Protection
Washington, DC, US
getpicnic.com

PKWARE (149, 4.2%)
Data Privacy
Milwaukee, WI, US
pkware.com

Polar Security (29, -9.4%)
Data Management
Tel Aviv, Israel
polar.security

PQShield Ltd (62, 34.8%)
Quantum
Oxford, United Kingdom
pqshield.com

PreVeil (61, 17.3%)
Encryption
Boston, MA, US
preveil.com

PrimeKey Solutions (36, -28.0%)
Public Key Infrastructure
Solna, Sweden
primekey.com

Primx (48, -2.0%)
Encryption
Lyon, France
primx.eu/en

Privacera (140, -1.4%)
Governance
Fremont, CA, US
privacera.com

Privacy Analytics (98, -4.8%)
Healthcare
Ottawa, Canada
privacy-analytics.com

Privacy4Cars (32, 33.3%)
Automotive
Kennesaw, GA, US
privacy4cars.com

Privitar (67, -54.7%)
Data Masking
London, United Kingdom
privitar.com

Privus (7, -22.2%)
Secure Communications
Zug, Switzerland
privus.global

Privy (721, 8.6%)
Jakarta Selatan, DKI Jakarta,
Indonesia
privy.id

ProDevice (5, 0.0%)
Data Erasure And Destruction
Wieliczka, Poland
pro-device.com/en/pro-device.com/en/

Profian (9, -40.0%)
Hardware
Raleigh, NC, US
profian.com

Protect AI (38, 153.3%)
Seattle, WA, US
protectai.com

Protecto (26, 0.0%)
Posture Management
Cupertino, CA, US
protecto.ai

ProtectStar (3, 50.0%)
Data Erasure And Destruction
Miami, FL, US
protectstar.com

Pryvate Now (46, 12.2%)
Secure Communications
Jersey, United Kingdom
pryvatenow.com

QEDit (14, 16.7%)
Data Privacy
Tel Aviv, Israel
qed-it.com

QEYnet (11, 22.2%)
Vaughan, Canada
qeynet.com

Qredo (124, -24.9%)
Encryption
London, United Kingdom
qredo.com

Qrypt (52, 6.1%)
Quantum
New York, NY, US
qrypt.com

Quantinuum (397, 13.4%)
Quantum
Charlotte, NC, US
quantinuum.com

QuantLR (10, 25.0%)
Quantum
Jerusalem, Israel
quantlr.com

Quantropi (31, 0.0%)
Quantum
Ontario, Canada
quantropi.com

Quantum Dice (23, 76.9%)
Quantum
Oxford, United Kingdom
quantum-dice.com

Quantum Knight (10, 400.0%)
Quantum
Palo Alto, CA, US
quantumknight.io

Quantum Resistant Cryptography (5, 0.0%)
Encryption
Lausanne, Switzerland
qrcrypto.ch

Quantum Xchange (17, 13.3%)
Quantum
Newton, MA, US
quantumxc.com

Quasar Scan (4, 0.0%)
Data Discovery
Wellington Region,
New Zealand
quasarscan.com

QuintessenceLabs (48, -7.7%)
Quantum
Deakin, Australia
quintessencelabs.com

Quiver (3, -40.0%)
Secure Data Sharing
Amsterdam,
Netherlands
quivercloud.com

Qusecurity (76, 7.0%)
San Mateo, CA, US
qusecure.com

Quside (47, 34.3%)
Quantum
Barcelona, Spain
quside.com

Racktop Systems (59, 1.7%)
Secure Storage
Fulton, MD, US
racktopsystems.com

Raito (15, -6.2%)
Access Security
Brussels, Belgium
raito.io

**Numbers in parentheses indicate headcount and % change in 2023.*

Rambus (973, -6.8%)
Semiconductor
Security R&D
Sunnyvale, CA, US
rambus.com

Ravel Technologies (10, -16.7%)
Encryption
Paris, France
raveltech.io

Realsec (23, 0.0%)
Hardware
Madrid, Spain
realsec.com

Reco Labs (62, 29.2%)
Secure Collaboration
New York, NY, US
recolabs.ai

Regdata (16, 23.1%)
Compliance Management
Geneva, Switzerland
regdata.ch/en/

ReSec Technologies (20, -16.7%)
Document Security
Caesarea, Israel
resec.co

revyz (11, 83.3%)
Fremont, CA, US
revyz.io

Rubrik (3540, 14.7%)
Data Discovery
Palo Alto, CA, US
rubrik.com

Saf.ai (6, 0.0%)
IRM
Bethesda, MD, US
saf.ai

Safeheron (13, 0.0%)
Encryption
Singapore City, Singapore
safeheron.com

SafeLiShare (13, 160.0%)
Morristown, NJ, US
safelishare.com

SafeLogic (13, 18.2%)
Cryptographic Libraries
Palo Alto, CA, US
safelogic.com

Safetica (94, -8.7%)
DLP
Brno, Czechia
safetica.com

SafeUM (3, 50.0%)
Secure Communications
Iceland
safeum.com

SaltDNA (16, -20.0%)
Secure Communications
Belfast, United Kingdom
saltdna.com

SandboxAQ (219, 71.1%)
Quantum
New York, NY, US
sandboxaq.com

Sasa Software (32, -5.9%)
File Scrubbing
Sasa, Israel
sasa-software.com

Satori Cyber (136, 58.1%)
Data Flows
Tel Aviv, Israel
satoricyber.com

Scram Software (3, -25.0%)
Encryption
Melbourne, Australia
scramsoft.com

Seagate Technology (16127, -2.7%)
Encryption
Cupertino, CA, US
seagate.com

Seald (10, 25.0%)
Paris, France
seald.io

Sealit (11, -15.4%)
Secure Communications
London, United Kingdom
sealit.id

Sealpath (26, 0.0%)
IRM
Bilbao, Spain
sealpath.com

Searchguard (6, 50.0%)
Security For Elasticsearch
Berlin, Germany
search-guard.com

Seclab (20, -13.0%)
Secure Data Sharing
Montpellier, France
seclab-security.com

Seclore (325, 15.7%)
IRM
Mumbai, India
seclore.com

Sectigo (410, 25.0%)
Public Key Infrastructure
Roseland, NJ, US
sectigo.com

Sectra Communications (1363, 21.5%)
Secure Communications
Linkoping, Sweden
sectra.com

Secude (108, -25.0%)
SAP
Luzern, Switzerland
secude.com

secunet (762, 47.4%)
Germany
secunet.com

Securco (24, 33.3%)
Secure Communications
New York, NY, US
secureco.com

Secure Exchanges (10, 42.9%)
Document Security
Canada
secure-exchanges.com

SecureAge Technology (37, -9.8%)
Encryption
West Chester, PA, US
secureage.com

Secured Communications (12, -55.6%)
Secure Communications
San Francisco, CA, US
securedcommunications.com

Secured2 (5, -16.7%)
Secure Storage
Minneapolis, MN, US
secured2.com

SecureData (57, -26.0%)
Secure Storage
Los Angeles, CA, US
securedata.com

SecurelyShare (24, -22.6%)
Secure Storage
Indira Nagar, India
securelyshare.com

Securemailbox (3, 0.0%)
Secure Communications
Stockholm, Sweden
securemailbox.com

SecureTeam (11, -8.3%)
DRM
Rishon LeZion, Israel
secureteam.net

Securiti (703, 34.4%)
Data Discovery
San Jose, CA, US
securiti.ai

Security Weaver (59, -21.3%)
IRM
Lehi, UT, US
securityweaver.com

Securosys (29, 20.8%)
Hardware
Zurich, Switzerland
securosys.com

Secutech Solutions (8, -20.0%)
USB Token Security
North Ryde, Australia
esecutech.com

Secuware (9, -25.0%)
Database Security
London, United Kingdom
secuware.com

**Numbers in parentheses indicate headcount and % change in 2023.*

SendSafely (34, 9.7%)
Secure Data Sharing
New York, NY, US
sendsafely.com

SendThisFile (8, 60.0%)
Secure Data Sharing
Wichita, KS, US
sendthisfile.com

Senetas Corporation Limited (41, -8.9%)
Encryption
South Melbourne, Australia
senetas.com

Sentra (84, 44.8%)
Data Discovery
Tel Aviv, Israel
sentra.io

Sepior (8, 33.3%)
Encryption
Aarhus, Denmark
sepior.com

Sertinty (20, 0.0%)
IRM
Nashville, TN, US
sertainty.com

Set In Stone (3, 0.0%)
IRM
Paris, France
setinstone.io

ShardSecure (35, 29.6%)
Shards
New York, NY, US
go.shardsecure.com

SHAREKEY (25, -3.9%)
Encryption
Zug, Switzerland
sharekey.com

ShareVault (38, 2.7%)
Secure Storage
Los Gatos, CA, US
sharevault.com

SideDrawer (27, 22.7%)
Secure Data Sharing
Toronto, Canada
sidedrawer.com

SigmaRed (16, 60.0%)
AI Debiasing
Toronto, ON, Canada
sigmared.ai

Silent Circle (23, 0.0%)
Secure Communications
Fairfax, VA, US
silentcircle.com

SISA (638, -12.7%)
Data Discovery
Bengaluru, India
sisainfosec.com

Skiff (30, 30.4%)
Secure Communications
San Francisco, CA, US
skiff.org

Skyflow (132, 17.9%)
Secure Storage
Palo Alto, CA, US
skyflow.com

Skymatic (5, 25.0%)
Sankt Augustin, Germany
skymatic.de

Smallstep (22, -18.5%)
Public Key Infrastructure
San Francisco, CA, US
smallstep.com

Softcamp (29, 3.6%)
Eongnam-Si, South Korea
softcamp.co.kr

Sotero (19, -36.7%)
Encryption
Burlington, MA, US
soterosoft.com

South River Technologies (17, -10.5%)
Secure Data Sharing
Annapolis, MD, US
southrivertech.com

Specfile (4, 0.0%)
Encryption
Poznan, Poland
specfile.pl

SpeQtral (31, 55.0%)
Quantum
Singapore, Singapore
speqtral.space

Spideroak (38, 0.0%)
Mission, KS, US
spideroak.com

SplitByte (4, 0.0%)
Shards
Los Gatos, CA, US
splitbyte.com

Spring Labs (68, 28.3%)
Data Masking
Marina del Rey, CA, US
springlabs.com

SSH Communications Security (516, -4.3%)
Secure Data Sharing
Helsinki, Finland
ssh.com

SSL.com (43, 26.5%)
Public Key Infrastructure
Houston, TX, US
ssl.com

STASH Global (4, 0.0%)
DRM
Wilmington, DE, US
stash.global

Stealth Software (5, 25.0%)
Encryption
Scottsdale, AZ, US
stealth-soft.com

Steganos (11, -8.3%)
Encryption
Munich, Germany
steganos.com

Storro (6, 0.0%)
Secure Storage
Hengelo, Netherlands
storro.com

Strac (6, 20.0%)
DLP
Bellevue, WA, US
strac.io

StratoKey (4, 0.0%)
Encryption
Austin, TX, US
stratokey.com

StrongKey (12, 20.0%)
Key Management
Durham, NC, US
strongkey.com

Sttarx (4, 33.3%)
Encryption
Washington, DC, US
sttarx.com

Sunnic (55, 77.4%)
Encryption
Singapore
sunnic-sec.com

Surety (45, 40.6%)
Naples, FL, US
surety.com

Surevine (23, -8.0%)
Secure Collaboration
Guildford, United Kingdom
surevine.com

Suridata (38, 11.8%)
SaaS Data Protection
Tel Aviv, Israel
suridata.ai

SwissSign Group (90, 12.5%)
Public Key Infrastructure
Glattbrugg, Switzerland
swisssign.com

Symmetrium (12, 100.0%)
Access Security
Tel Aviv, Israel
symmetrium.io

Symmetry Systems. (47, -6.0%)
Monitoring
San Francisco, CA, US
symmetry-systems.com

Symphony (769, 8.3%)
Secure Collaboration
Palo Alto, CA, US
symphony.com

**Numbers in parentheses indicate headcount and % change in 2023.*

Syncplicity by Axway (36, 56.5%)
Secure Storage
Santa Clara, CA, US
syncplicity.com

Synergy Quantum (8, 33.3%)
Encryption
Geneva, Switzerland
synergyquantum.swiss

SysCloud (138, -9.2%)
Secure Backup/Recovery
Red Bank, NJ, US
syscloud.com

Technical Communications Corporation (15, -28.6%)
Secure Communications
Concord, MA, US
tccsecure.com

TechR2 (36, 12.5%)
Data Erasure And Destruction
Reynoldsburg, OH, US
techr2.com

TecSec (45, 80.0%)
Key Management
McLean, VA, US
tecsec.com

TELEGRID Technologies (5, -44.4%)
Monitoring
Florham Park, NJ, US
telegrid.com

TeraDact (9, 12.5%)
Secure Data Sharing
Missoula, MT, US
teradact.com

Tesseract (5, 25.0%)
Encryption
Mexico City, Mexico
tesseract.mx

Thales (666, 12.1%)
Authentication
Plantation, FL, US
thalesesecurity.com

Theom (25, 4.2%)
Posture Management
San Francisco, CA, US
theom.ai

Theon (5, -68.8%)
Quantum
Newport Beach, CA, US
theontechnology.com

TIBCO Software Inc. (3470, -22.4%)
Big Data
Palo Alto, CA, US
tibco.com

Titaniam (31, 0.0%)
Encryption
San Jose, CA, US
titaniam.io

TokenEx (90, 11.1%)
Tokenization
Edmond, OK, US
tokenex.com

Tonic.ai (98, -6.7%)
Data Masking
San Francisco, CA, US
tonic.ai

Topia Technology (23, 9.5%)
Encryption
Tacoma, WA, US
topiatechnology.com

Torsion Information Security (12, -25.0%)
Monitoring
London, United Kingdom
torsionis.com

Townsend Security (13, 0.0%)
Encryption
Olympia, WA, US
townsendsecurity.com

Trail of Bits (105, 4.0%)
Vulnerabilities
New York, NY, US
trailofbits.com

Treebox Solutions (17, 21.4%)
Secure Communications
Singapore, Singapore
treeboxsolutions.com

Tresorit (130, -1.5%)
Secure Data Sharing
Budapest, Hungary
tresorit.com

Tresys (28, -3.5%)
Data Erasure And Destruction
Columbia, MD, US
tresys.com

TripleBlind (53, -15.9%)
Secure Data Sharing
Kansas City, MO, US
tripleblind.ai

TrueVault (16, -5.9%)
Secure Storage
San Francisco, CA, US
truevault.com

Truffle Security (31, 24.0%)
Secrets Management
San Francisco, CA, US
trufflesecurity.com

Trustpage (3, -81.2%)
Secure Storage
Detroit, MI, US
trustpage.com

Tune Insight (13, 18.2%)
Secure Collaboration
Lausanne, Switzerland
tuneinsight.com

Tutus (47, 42.4%)
Encryption
Danderyd, Sweden
tutus.se

Ubiq Security (23, -17.9%)
Encryption
San Diego, CA, US
ubiqsecurity.com

ULedger (21, 5.0%)
Blockchain
Boise, ID, US
uledger.co

Unitrends (156, -6.6%)
Encryption
Burlington, MA, US
unitrends.com

Uppsala Security (26, 8.3%)
Tracking Of Crypto Currencies
Singapore, Singapore
uppsalasecurity.com

Utimaco (510, 14.6%)
Hardware
Aachen, Germany
utimaco.com

Vandyke Software (18, -5.3%)
Secure Data Sharing
Albuquerque, NM, US
vandyke.com

Varonis (2207, 5.2%)
Secure Collaboration
New York, NY, US
varonis.com

Vault12 (14, -6.7%)
Wallets
Mountain View, CA, US
vault12.com

Vaultize (10, -23.1%)
IRM
San Francisco, CA, US
vaultize.com

Vaultmatix (4, 0.0%)
Data Rooms
London, United Kingdom
vaultmatix.com

Vaultree (64, 3.2%)
Encryption
Cork, Ireland
vaultree.com

VectorZero (22, 83.3%)
Secure Storage
Reston, VA, US
vectorzero.ai

Velotix (39, -4.9%)
Tel Aviv, Israel
velotix.ai

**Numbers in parentheses indicate headcount and % change in 2023.*

Venafi (430, -10.0%)
Key Management
Salt Lake City, UT, US
venafi.com

Vera (19, -9.5%)
IRM
Palo Alto, CA, US
vera.com

Verimatrix (280, -3.1%)
DRM
San Diego, CA, US
verimatrix.com

VIA3 Corperation (4, -66.7%)
Secure Communications
Scottsdale, AZ, US
via3.com

Virgil Security (15, -6.2%)
Encryption
Manassas, VA, US
virgilsecurity.com

Virtru (178, -3.3%)
Secure Communications
Washington, DC, US
virtru.com

Vitrium (28, 27.3%)
DRM
Vancouver, Canada
vitrium.com

Volexity (41, 13.9%)
Forensics
Reston, VA, US
volexity.com

Wault (9, 28.6%)
Secure Data Sharing
London, United Kingdom
wault.com

WetStone Technologies (14, 40.0%)
Forensics
Cortland, NY, US
wetstonetech.com

Wickr (22, -29.0%)
Secure Communications
San Francisco, CA, US
wickr.com

Widevine Technologies (6, -14.3%)
DRM
Kirkland, WA, US
widevine.com

WinMagic Inc. (89, 2.3%)
Encryption
Mississauga, Canada
winmagic.com

WipeDrive (Was White Canyon Inc.) (10, -16.7%)
Data Erasure And Destruction
American Fork, UT, US
whitecanyon.com

Wirewheel (20, -57.5%)
Customer Data Security
Arlington, VA, US
wirewheel.io

Woleet (3, -62.5%)
Blockchain
Rennes, France
woleet.io

WoSign (5, -44.4%)
Public Key Infrastructure
Shenzhen, China
wosign.com

WWN Software LLC (7, -12.5%)
Secure Data Sharing
Washington, DC, US
wwnsoftware.com

X-Ways Software (5, 66.7%)
Forensics
Germany
x-ways.net

Xahive (12, 20.0%)
Secure Communications
Ottawa, Canada
xahive.com

Xiphera (16, 14.3%)
Encryption
Espoo, Finland
xiphera.com

XQmessage (30, -25.0%)
IRM
Oakland, CA, US
xqmsg.co

YazamTech (8, 33.3%)
Ra'anana, Israel
yazamtech.com

Zama (92, 37.3%)
Encryption
Paris, France
zama.ai

Zecurion (38, 5.6%)
Database Security
Moscow, Russia
zecurion.com

ZenGo (60, -1.6%)
Wallets
Sarona, Israel
zengo.com

Zettaset (16, -5.9%)
Encryption
Mountain View, CA, US
zettaset.com

Zeva (25, -7.4%)
Encryption
Fairfax, VA, US
zevainc.com

Ziperase (5, 0.0%)
Data Erasure And Destruction
Austin, TX, US
ziperase.com

Ziroh Labs (74, -6.3%)
Data Discovery
Bangalore, India
ziroh.com

Zix Corp. (275, -13.2%)
Secure Communications
Dallas, TX, US
zixcorp.com

Deception

Acalvio Technologies (75, 2.7%)
Santa Clara, CA, US
acalvio.com

Allure Security (36, -12.2%)
Document Security
New York, NY, US
alluresecurity.com

Attivo Networks (91, -32.6%)
Fremont, CA, US
attivonetworks.com

CounterCraft (48, -21.3%)
Donostia-San Sebastian, Spain
countercraft.eu

CYBERTRAP (14, -6.7%)
Wiener Neustadt, Austria
cybertrap.com

Deceptive Bytes (6, 20.0%)
Holon, Israel
deceptivebytes.com

Dreamlab Technologies (142, 21.4%)
Managed Security Services
San Isidro, Peru
dreamlab.net

Illuria Security (5, -16.7%)
Yerevan, Armenia
illuriasecurity.com

illusive Networks (58, -55.4%)
New York, NY, US
illusivenetworks.com

Labyrinth (13, 0.0%)
Decoy Hosts
Zabrze, Poland
labyrinth.tech

Lupovis (10, -16.7%)
Network Decoys
Glasgow, Scotland
lupovis.io

PacketViper (16, 0.0%)
Pittsburgh, PA, US
packetviper.com

Ridgeback Network Defense (9, -18.2%)
Baltimore, MD, US
ridgebacknet.com

**Numbers in parentheses indicate headcount and % change in 2023.*

RMRF TECH (11, 22.2%)
Host Environments
Kyiv, Ukraine
rmrf.tech

Seedata (5, -28.6%)
Leaked Data
London, United Kingdom
seedata.io

Thinkst Canary (5, 150.0%)
Target Agents Deployed In Operations
Edinvale, South Africa
canary.tools

Xello (7, 75.0%)
Moscow, Russia
xello.ru

Email Security

Abnormal Security (584, 2.8%)
Defense Against Phishing
San Francisco, CA, US
abnormalsecurity.com

Agari (65, 41.3%)
Foster City, CA, US
agari.com

AnubisNetworks (BitSight) (29, 3.6%)
Lisbon, Portugal
anubisnetworks.com

AppRiver (149, -20.7%)
Gulf Breeze, FL, US
appriver.com

Aquila Technology (31, 14.8%)
Defense Against Phishing
Burlington, MA, US
aquilatc.com

Armorblox (34, -71.4%)
Defense Against Phishing
Cupertino, CA, US
armorblox.com

Avanan (93, 8.1%)
Technology Deployment Management
New York, NY, US
avanan.com

Bolster (75, 27.1%)
Defense Against Phishing
Los Altos, CA, US
bolster.ai

Cellopoint International Corporation (31, -6.1%)
Gateways
New Taipei City, Taiwan
cellopoint.com

Clearswift (95, -15.9%)
Theale, United Kingdom
clearswift.com

Cloudmask (4, 0.0%)
Ottawa, Canada
cloudmask.com

comcrypto (13, 8.3%)
Secure Email
Chemnitz, Sachsen, Germany
comcrypto.de

Criptext (8, 0.0%)
Secure Email
New York, NY, US
criptext.com

Cybernite (10, -28.6%)
Defense Against Phishing
Tel Aviv, Israel
cybernite.com

Cybonet (27, -12.9%)
Sandbox
Matam, Israel
cybonet.com

DataMotion (41, -10.9%)
Florham Park, NJ, US
datamotion.com

Datto (1193, -31.8%)
Microsoft
Norwalk, CT, US
datto.com

Dmarcian (33, 0.0%)
Technology Deployment Management
Brevard, NC, US
dmarcian.com

EasyDMARC (74, 23.3%)
DNS Security
Middletown, DE, US
easydmarc.com

Echoworx (89, 4.7%)
Secure Email
Toronto, Canada
echoworx.com

Egress (307, 4.1%)
London, United Kingdom
egress.com

erika (7, 40.0%)
Anti-scam
London, United Kingdom
erika.app

Firetrust (3, -57.1%)
Anti-spam
Christchurch, New Zealand
firetrust.com

Gatefy (6, -14.3%)
Miami, FL, US
gatefy.com

GFI Software (220, -0.9%)
Anti-spam
Austin, TX, US
gfi.com

Gold Comet (7, 75.0%)
Secure Email
Alexandria, VA, US
goldcomet.com

GreatHorn (23, -41.0%)
Defense Against Phishing
Waltham, MA, US
greathorn.com

Halon (32, 23.1%)
Anti-spam
Gothenburg, Sweden
halon.io

Hornetsecurity (346, 11.6%)
Managed Security Services
Hannover, Germany
hornetsecurity.com

Iconix (23, 4.5%)
Sender Verification
San Jose, CA, US
iconix.com

IDECSI (31, 14.8%)
Auditing
Paris, France
idecsi.com

Inky (48, -11.1%)
Defense Against Phishing
Rockville, MD, US
inky.com

Keepnet Labs (42, 23.5%)
London, United Kingdom
keepnetlabs.com

Lavabit (132, -1.5%)
Secure Email
Dallas, TX, US
lavabit.com

Libraesva (35, 25.0%)
Lecco, Italy
libraesva.com

Liverton Security (18, 20.0%)
Gateways
Wellington, New Zealand
livertonsecurity.com

Mailchannels (17, 6.2%)
SMTP Relay
Vancouver, Canada
mailchannels.com

MailCleaner (4, 0.0%)
Saint-Sulpice, Switzerland
mailcleaner.net

Mailfence (6, 0.0%)
Secure Email
Brussels, Belgium
mailfence.com

MailInBlack (106, 20.4%)
Anti-spam
Marseille, France
mailinblack.com

Mailprotector (42, 5.0%)
Managed Security Services
Greenville, SD, US
mailprotector.com

Mailshell (8, 14.3%)
Anti-spam
San Francisco, CA, US
mailshell.com

Material Security (107, 87.7%)
ATO Prevention
Redwood City, CA, US
material.security

**Numbers in parentheses indicate headcount and % change in 2023.*

Mesh (16, 128.6%)
Sandyford, Dublin, Ireland
meshsecurity.io

Messageware (11, 0.0%)
OWA Security
Mississauga, Canada
messageware.com

Mimecast (2355, 7.7%)
Microsoft
London, United Kingdom
mimecast.com

NeoCertified (8, 0.0%)
Secure Email
Centennial, CO, US
neocertified.com

Paladin Cyber (36, 89.5%)
Defense Against Phishing
San Francisco, CA, US
meetpaladin.com

Paubox (51, -16.4%)
Secure Email
San Francisco, CA, US
paubox.com

Perception Point (126, 1.6%)
Defense Against Phishing
Tel Aviv, Israel
perception-point.io

Perseus. (41, -21.1%)
Defense Against Phishing
Berlin, Germany
perseus.de

PhishCloud (9, 12.5%)
Defense Against Phishing
Renton, WA, US
phishcloud.com

PIXM (11, -8.3%)
Defense Against Phishing
Brooklyn, NY, US
pixm.net

Process Software (15, 7.1%)
Framingham, MA, US
process.com

Proofpoint (4508, 4.3%)
Defense Against Phishing
Sunnyvale, CA, US
proofpoint.com

Sendio (17, -5.6%)
Anti-spam
Newport Beach, CA, US
sendio.com

Sendmarc (64, 68.4%)
Defense Against Phishing
ROSEBANK, Gauteng,
South Africa
sendmarc.com

Seppmail (12, 20.0%)
Secure Email
Neuenhof,
Switzerland
seppmail.com

SlashNext (168, 31.2%)
Defense Against Phishing
Pleasanton, CA, US
slashnext.com

SMX (26, 44.4%)
Auckland, New Zealand
smxemail.com

Tessian (212, -17.8%)
Defense Against Phishing
New York, NY, US
tessian.com

Trustifi (27, 0.0%)
Encryption
Las Vegas, NV, US
trustifi.com

Upfort (36, 9.1%)
SMB Security
San Francisco, CA, US
upfort.com

Vade Secure (264, 16.8%)
Defense Against Phishing
San Francisco,
CA, US
vadesecure.com

Valimail (109, 6.9%)
Defense Against Phishing
San Francisco,
CA, US
valimail.com

Vircom (31, 0.0%)
Threat Prevention
Montreal, Canada
vircom.com

Xorlab (28, 3.7%)
Zero Day Defense
Zurich, Switzerland
xorlab.com

ZeroSpam (4, -42.9%)
Anti-spam
Montreal, Canada
zerospam.ca

Zertificon Solutions (62, -15.1%)
Secure Email
Berlin, Germany
zertificon.com

Zivver (136, -8.7%)
Secure Email
Amsterdam, Netherlands
zivver.eu

Endpoint Security

1E (513, 8.2%)
Patch Management
London, United Kingdom
1e.com

3Frames Software labs (50, 19.1%)
Mobile Device Security
Bangalore, India
3frameslab.com

42Gears (437, 12.1%)
Mobile Device Security
Bangalore, India
42gears.com

Absolute Software (981, 14.6%)
Mobile Device Security
Vancouver, Canada
absolute.com

Accuknox (146, 49.0%)
Cupertino, CA, US
accuknox.com

Adaptiva (90, -10.9%)
Configuration Management
Kirkland, WA, US
adaptiva.com

Adaptive Mobile (91, -33.1%)
Mobile Device Security
Dublin, Ireland
adaptivemobile.com

Adaware (13, 0.0%)
Anti-virus
Montreal, Canada
adaware.com

Advanced Systems International (3, -25.0%)
Lima, Peru
usb-lock-rp.com

Ahnlab (563, 7.8%)
Anti-virus
Gyeonggi-do, South Korea
ahnlab.com

Airlock Digital (37, 42.3%)
Application Whitelisting
Unley, Australia
airlockdigital.com

AMI (1980, 44.6%)
Firmware
Duluth, GA, US
ami.com

Amtel (78, 6.8%)
Mobile Device Security
Rockville, MD, US
amtelnet.com

Anchore (82, 28.1%)
Container Security
Montecito, CA, US
anchore.com

ANY.RUN (89, 161.8%)
Malware Analysis
Dubai, United
Arab Emirates
any.run

Apozy (17, -41.4%)
Filtering
San Francisco, CA, US
apozy.com

AppGuard (22, -15.4%)
Application Containment
Chantilly, VA, US
appguard.us

AppMobi (14, 0.0%)
Mobile Device Security
Poughkeepsie, NY, US
appmobi.com

**Numbers in parentheses indicate headcount and % change in 2023.*

AppTec (20, 42.9%)
Mobile Device Security
Basel, Switzerland
apptec360.com

Aqua Security (605, -4.4%)
Container Security
Ramat Gan, Israel
aquasec.com

Arcabit (3, 0.0%)
Anti-virus
Warsaw, Poland
arcabit.pl

Armo Security (59, 25.5%)
Container Security
Tel Aviv, Israel
armosec.io

ARMS Cyber (4, 0.0%)
Nashville, TN, US
armscyber.com

Assac Networks (15, 25.0%)
Mobile Device Security
Ramat HaSharon, Israel
assacnetworks.com

Atomicorp (11, -8.3%)
IPS
Chantilly, VA, US
atomicorp.com

Aura (733, 13.8%)
Data Privacy
Boston, MA, US
aura.com

Autonomic Software (9, 0.0%)
Patch Management
Danville, CA, US
autonomic-software.com

Avast Software (1057, -29.4%)
Anti-virus
Prague, Czech Republic
avast.com

Aves Netsec (4, -20.0%)
Patch Management
London, United Kingdom
avesnetsec.com

Avira (202, -0.5%)
Anti-virus
Tettnang, Germany
avira.com

Avnos (3, -50.0%)
Application Whitelisting
Singapore, Singapore
avnos.io

Axiado (62, 19.2%)
Hardware
San Jose, CA, US
axiado.com

Beachhead Solutions (14, 0.0%)
Device Management
San Jose, CA, US
beachheadsolutions.com

Binarly (26, 30.0%)
Firmware
Pasadena, CA, US
binarly.io

BitDefender (2110, 4.0%)
Anti-virus
Bucharest, Romania
bitdefender.com

BitNinja (30, -14.3%)
Servers
London, United Kingdom
bitninja.io

Blackberry (3314, -7.4%)
Mobile Device Security
Waterloo, Canada
BlackBerry.com

BlackFog (21, 23.5%)
EDR
Cheyenne, WY, US
blackfog.com

BlueCedar (44, 41.9%)
Mobile Device Security
San Francisco, CA, US
bluecedar.com

Bufferzone (19, 11.8%)
Sandbox
Giv'atayim, Israel
bufferzonesecurity.com

BullGuard Ltd. (31, -24.4%)
Anti-virus
London, United Kingdom
bullguard.com

CalCom (52, 20.9%)
Servers
Lod, Israel
calcomsoftware.com

Capsule8 (4, -55.6%)
Linux Security
New York, NY, US
capsule8.com

Ceedo (34, -2.9%)
Secured Devices
Herzliya, Israel
ceedo.com

Cellebrite (1081, 5.5%)
Forensics
Petah Tikva, Israel
cellebrite.com

Cellrox (14, -30.0%)
Virtualization
Tel Aviv, Israel
cellrox.com

certgate (11, -8.3%)
Mobile Device Security
Germany
airid.com

Chili Security (32, 0.0%)
Anti-virus
Odense, Denmark
chilisecurity.dk

Comae Technologies (5, -16.7%)
Forensics
San Francisco, CA, US
comae.com

CommuniTake Technologies (17, -10.5%)
Mobile Device Security
Yokneam, Israel
communitake.com

Confiant Inc (46, -11.5%)
Advertising-related
New York, NY, US
confiant.com

Corrata (8, -20.0%)
Mobile Device Security
Blackrock, Ireland
corrata.com

CrowdStrike (7569, 11.8%)
EDR
Sunnyvale, CA, US
crowdstrike.com

Crytica Security (29, 3.6%)
Anti-malware
Reno, NV, US
cryticasecurity.com

Cubed Mobile (5, -16.7%)
Mobile Device Security
Kibbutz Einat, Drom HaSharon Regional Council, Israel
cubedmobile.com

Cupp Computing (5, 0.0%)
Palo Alto, CA, US
cuppcomputing.com

Currentware Inc. (24, 4.3%)
Monitoring
Toronto, Canada
currentware.com

Cybellum (95, 33.8%)
In-Memory Prevention
Tel Aviv, Israel
cybellum.com

CyberForza (10, -16.7%)
Endpoint Protection
Santa Clara, CA, US
cyberforza.com

CyberPoint International (3, 0.0%)
File Artifact Detection (mostly PS)
Baltimore, MD, US
cyberpointllc.com

Cycuity (38, 2.7%)
San Diego, CA, US
cycuity.com

CYSEC (50, 13.6%)
Lausanne, Vaud, Switzerland
cysec.com

**Numbers in parentheses indicate headcount and % change in 2023.*

Deep Instinct (271, 0.0%)
Endpoint Machine Learning
New York, NY, US
deepinstinct.com

DefensX (21, 16.7%)
New York, NY, US
defensx.com

Digital Immunity (3, 0.0%)
System Hardening
Burlington, MA, US
digitalimmunity.com

Digital.ai (923, 13.4%)
Mobile Device Security
Plano, TX, US
digital.ai

Domdog (5, 150.0%)
Secure Web Browsing
Chennai, India
domdog.io

dope.security (37, 19.4%)
Gateways
Mountain View, CA, US
dope.security

Dr. Web (245, -8.9%)
Anti-virus
Moscow, Russia
drweb.com

DriveLock (58, 18.4%)
DLP
Munich, Germany
drivelock.com

Druva (1220, -1.3%)
Secure Secure Backup / Recovery
Sunnyvale, CA, US
druva.com

Eclypsium (100, 6.4%)
Firmware
Beaverton, OR, US
eclypsium.com

Emsisoft (28, 7.7%)
Anti-virus
Chicago, IL, US
emsisoft.com

Entreda (9, -10.0%)
Monitoring
Santa Clara, CA, US
entreda.com

EScan (204, 33.3%)
Anti-virus
Mumbai, India
escanav.com

ESET (1719, 5.6%)
Anti-virus
Bratislava, Slovakia
eset.com

ESTsoft (314, 3.3%)
Anti-virus
Seoul, South Korea
estsoft.ai

Everspin (19, 26.7%)
Dynamic Image Replacement
Seoul, South Korea
everspin.global

Faronics Technologies Inc. (116, 2.6%)
Vancouver, Canada
faronics.com

FirstPoint Mobile Guard (17, -34.6%)
Mobile Device Security
Netanya, Israel
firstpoint-mg.com

FixMeStick (12, -7.7%)
Anti-virus
Montreal, Canada
fixmestick.com

Fleet (55, 37.5%)
Asset Management
San Francisco, CA, US
fleetdm.com

Fortra (313, -26.7%)
ISeries
Eden Prairie, MN, US
fortra.com

G Data Software (116, -10.8%)
Anti-virus
Bochum, Germany
gdata.de

GBMS Tech (16, 0.0%)
Monitoring
London, United Kingdom
gbmstech.com

Gen Digital (2011, 44.0%)
Anti-virus
Tempe, AZ, US
gendigital.com

GlassWire (3, -40.0%)
Firewalls
Austin, TX, US
glasswire.com

Graphite Software (3, 0.0%)
Container Security
Ottawa, Canada
graphitesoftware.com

Green Hills Software (258, 0.4%)
Operating System Security
Santa Barbara, CA, US
ghs.com

Guardian (10, 100.0%)
Firewalls
San Francisco, CA, US
guardianapp.com

Guardian Digital Inc. (5, -28.6%)
Secure Linux
Midland Park, NJ, US
guardiandigital.com

Halcyon (105, 72.1%)
Ransomware Security
Austin, TX, US
halcyon.ai

HarfangLab (85, 49.1%)
EDR
Paris, France
harfanglab.io

Hexnode (112, 6.7%)
Device Management
San Francisco, CA, US
hexnode.com

Humming Heads (9, 125.0%)
Application Whitelisting
Tokyo, Japan
hummingheads.co.jp

Hypori (114, 2.7%)
Device Management
Austin, TX, US
hypori.com

Hysolate (7, -22.2%)
Secure Workspace
Tel Aviv, Israel
hysolate.com

Ikarus Security Software GmbH (45, 21.6%)
Anti-virus
Vienna, Austria
ikarussecurity.com

Illumio (591, 2.2%)
Monitoring
Sunnyvale, CA, US
illumio.com

Infinipoint (21, -25.0%)
Device Identity
Tel Aviv, Israel
infinipoint.io

IS3 (opens as Stopzilla) (26, 13.0%)
Anti-virus
Dover, DE, US
stopzilla.com

Isovalent (157, 52.4%)
Container Security
Mountain View, CA, US
isovalent.com

itWatch (17, -5.6%)
DLP
Munich, Germany
itwatch.info

Ivanti (3050, -1.3%)
Endpoint Management
South Jordan, UT, US
ivanti.com

Jamf (2746, 3.6%)
Device Management
Minneapolis, MN, US
jamf.com

Jio Security (60073, -2.8%)
Anti-virus
Navi Mumbai, India
jio.com

**Numbers in parentheses indicate headcount and % change in 2023.*

K7Computing (416, 5.6%)
Anti-virus
Sholinganallur, India
k7computing.com

KabaCorp (5, 400.0%)
Secure Web Browsing
Boston, MA, US
kabacorp.com

Kameleon Security (5, 0.0%)
Mountain View, CA, US
kameleonsec.com

Kandji (315, -4.3%)
Device Management
San Diego, CA, US
kandji.io

Kaspersky (3901, 3.4%)
Anti-virus
Moscow, Russia
kaspersky.com

Kaymera (33, -17.5%)
Mobile Device Security
Herzliya, Israel
kaymera.com

Kazuar Advanced Technologies Ltd (37, 0.0%)
Dual Use Laptops
Tel Aviv, Israel
kazuar-tech.com

Keep Aware (12, 200.0%)
Austin, TX, US
keepaware.co

Kolide (35, 25.0%)
Slack Community For Security Updates
Somerville, MA, US
kolide.com

KSOC (36, 5.9%)
Kubernetes Security
San Francisco, CA, US
ksoc.com

LayerX (28, 40.0%)
Secure Web Browsing
Tel Aviv, Israel
linkedin.com/company/layerx-security/about/www.layerxsecurity.com

Lookout (830, -9.6%)
Mobile Device Security
San Francisco, CA, US
lookout.com

Lynx Software Technologies (91, 3.4%)
Container Security
San Jose, CA, US
lynx.com

MacKeeper (80, -9.1%)
Anti-virus
London, United Kingdom
kromtech.com

Malwarebytes (768, -12.4%)
Anti-virus
Santa Clara, CA, US
malwarebytes.org

Matrix42 (384, 9.4%)
EDR
Paris, France
matrix42.com

Max Secure Software (75, 2.7%)
Endpoint Protection
Pune, India
maxpcsecure.com

McAfee (5641, -6.0%)
Anti-virus
Santa Clara, CA, US
mcafee.com

Minded Security UK Limited (32, 14.3%)
Anti-malware
Rome, Italy
mindedsecurity.com

Minerva Labs (10, -66.7%)
Ransomware Security
Petah Tikva, Israel
minerva-labs.com

Miradore (60, -18.9%)
Device Management
Vantaa, Finland
miradore.com

Morphisec (126, -17.6%)
Obfuscation
Be'er Sheva, Israel
morphisec.com

Msab (279, 10.7%)
Forensics
Stockholm, Sweden
msab.com

Msecure Data Labs (13, -7.1%)
Anti-virus
Walnut, CA, US
msecuredatalabs.com

Mymobilesecurity (4, -20.0%)
Mobile Device Security
London, United Kingdom
mymobilesecurity.com

MyPermissions (6, -14.3%)
Data Privacy
Ramat Gan, Israel
mypermissions.com

N-Able (1644, 23.6%)
Morrisville, NC, US
n-able.com

Nano Security (3, -25.0%)
Anti-virus
Moscow, Russia
nanoav.pro

NanoVMs (8, -27.3%)
Container Security
San Francisco, CA, US
nanovms.com

Navaho Technologies (10, 25.0%)
Secure Linux
Brockenhurst, United Kingdom
navaho.co.uk

Net Protector Antivirus (121, 18.6%)
Anti-virus
Karvenagar, India
npav.net

NeuVector (17, -5.6%)
Container Security
San Jose, CA, US
neuvector.com

NinjaOne (908, 47.2%)
Endpoint Management
Austin, TX, US
ninjaone.com

Nokia (82184, 4.5%)
Mobile Device Security
Espoo, Finland
networks.nokia.com

NowSecure (137, -16.5%)
Mobile Device Security
Chicago, IL, US
nowsecure.com

NPcore (18, 5.9%)
EDR
Seoul, South Korea
npcore.com

Nubo Software (8, 0.0%)
Virtualization
New York, NY, US
nubosoftware.com

Omniquad Ltd. (23, -11.5%)
Anti-spyware
London, United Kingdom
omniquad.com

OnSystem Logic (6, 0.0%)
Application Hardening
Catonsville, MD, US
onsystemlogic.com/

OPSWAT (732, 11.4%)
SDKs
San Francisco, CA, US
opswat.com

Panda Security (402, 0.8%)
Anti-virus
Bilbao, Spain
pandasecurity.com

PC Matic (63, 8.6%)
Application Whitelisting
Sioux City, IA, US
pcmatic.com

PFP Cybersecurity (25, -3.9%)
Endpoint Protection
Vienna, VA, US
pfpcyber.com

Phoenix Security (6, 20.0%)
Los Altos, CA, US
r6security.com

**Numbers in parentheses indicate headcount and % change in 2023.*

Phoenix Technologies (726, 31.8%)
Secured Devices
Campbell, CA, US
phoenix.com

PointSharp AB (58, 13.7%)
Mobile Device Security
Stockholm, Sweden
pointsharp.com

PolySwarm (24, -11.1%)
Anti-malware
San Diego, CA, US
polyswarm.io

Polyverse (6, 0.0%)
Operating System Security
Bellevue, WA, US
polyverse.io

Portnox (66, 0.0%)
Device Management
Israel
portnox.com

Preventon (3, 0.0%)
Anti-virus
Mayfair, United Kingdom
preventon.com

Privoro (55, 0.0%)
Hardened Cases For Mobile Phones
Chandler, AZ, US
privoro.com

Promisec (31, 0.0%)
Endpoint Security Intelligence
Holon, Israel
promisec.com

Protectt.ai (54, 35.0%)
Mobile Device Security
Gurgaon, Haryana, India
protectt.ai

Psafe Technology (3, -80.0%)
Anti-virus
San Francisco, CA, US
psafe.com

QI-ANXIN (87, 13.0%)
Anti-virus
Beijing, China
qianxin.com

Qihoo 360 Total Security (3044, 18.7%)
Anti-virus
Beijing, China
360.cn

Quick Heal (1513, 5.1%)
UTM
Pune, India
quickheal.com

Qustodio (89, 1.1%)
Mobile Parental Controls
Redondo Beach, CA, US
qustodio.com

RAWCyber (3, 0.0%)
Mobile Device Security
Warszawa, Poland
rawcyber.pl

Raz-Lee Security (22, -8.3%)
ISeries
Herzliya, Israel
razlee.com

RealDefense (40, 37.9%)
Microsoft
Pasadena, CA, US
realdefen.se

RealTheory (7, -12.5%)
Container Security
Atlanta, GA, US
realtheory.io

ReaQta (14, -48.1%)
EDR
Amsterdam, Netherlands
reaqta.com

Red Balloon Security (25, 0.0%)
Security For Embedded Systems
New York, NY, US
redballoonsecurity.com

Red Sift (111, 3.7%)
Open Platform
London, United Kingdom
redsift.com

Redwall Technologies (5, 0.0%)
Mobile Device Security
Beavercreek, OH, US
redwall.us

Resecurity (85, 57.4%)
EDR
Los ANgelas, CA, US
resecurity.com

RevBits (13, 0.0%)
Mineola, NY, US
revbits.com

Rezilion (42, -32.3%)
Be'er Sheva, Israel
rezilion.co

Romad (21, -12.5%)
Anti-virus
Kiev, Ukraine
romad.io

Sandfly Security (10, 11.1%)
EDR
Christchurch, New Zealand
sandflysecurity.com

SCIT Labs (8, -11.1%)
Servers
Clifton, VA, US
scitlabs.com

Secpod (112, 21.7%)
Endpoint Management
Tulsa, OK, US
secpod.com

SecureMac (6, 0.0%)
Anti-malware
Las Vegas, NV, US
securemac.com

SentinelOne (2293, 20.7%)
Endpoint Protection
Mountain View, CA, US
sentinelone.com

SentryBay (32, -11.1%)
Anti-malware
London, United Kingdom
sentrybay.com

Seqrite (171, 185.0%)
Encryption
Pune, India
seqrite.com

Sequretek (353, 4.8%)
Anti-virus
Mumbai, India
sequretek.com

Sierraware (13, -13.3%)
Mobile Device Security
Sunnyvale, CA, US
sierraware.com

SignaCert (6, 0.0%)
Whitelisting OEM
Austin, TX, US
signacert.com

SnowHaze (3, 0.0%)
Secure Web Browsing
Zurich, Switzerland
snowhaze.com

Software Diversified Services (20, 17.6%)
Z/OS Security
Minneapolis, MN, US
sdsusa.com

Software Engineering of America (85, -5.6%)
ISeries
Garden City, NY, US
seasoft.com

Softwin SRL (176, -9.7%)
Anti-virus
Bucharest, Romania
softwin.com

Sophos (4592, -1.3%)
Anti-virus
Abingdon, United Kingdom
sophos.com

SPAMfighter (16, -11.1%)
Anti-spam
Miami, FL, US
spamfighter.com

SparkCognition (309, -17.8%)
Anti-virus
Austin, TX, US
sparkcognition.com

**Numbers in parentheses indicate headcount and % change in 2023.*

Stratus Digital Systems (3, 0.0%)
Servers
Eugene, OR, US
stratusdigitalsystems.com

Styra (61, -38.4%)
Access Security
Redwood City, CA, US
styra.com

Subgraph (5, 25.0%)
Operating System Security
Montreal, Canada
subgraph.com

Susteen (36, 12.5%)
Forensics
Irvine, CA, US
susteen.com

Sweet Security (20, 0.0%)
Workload Protection
Tel Aviv, Israel
sweet.security

Symantec (13600, -3.3%)
Anti-virus
San Jose, CA, US
broadcom.com/products/cybersecurity

Syncdog (12, -36.8%)
Mobile Device Security
Reston, VA, US
syncdog.com

Sysdig (879, 3.8%)
Kubernetes Security
Davis, CA, US
sysdig.com

Tanium (1952, -4.4%)
Visibility
Emeryville, CA, US
tanium.com

Tencent (108056, -0.3%)
Anti-virus
Shenzhen, China
tencent.com

TG Soft (10, 0.0%)
Anti-virus
Rubano, Italy
tgsoft.it

ThinScale (57, -28.8%)
Remote Desktop Agent
Dublin, Ireland
thinscale.com

ThreatLocker (314, 34.8%)
Application Whitelisting
Maitland, FL, US
threatlocker.com

Tiempo (31, 34.8%)
Hardware
Montbonnot-Saint-Martin, France
tiempo-secure.com

Tigera (124, -9.5%)
Kubernetes Security
San Francisco, CA, US
tigera.io

Total Defense (27, -3.6%)
PC, Mobile & Internet Security
Hauppauge, NY, US
totaldefense.com

ToucanX (3, -25.0%)
Sandbox
Southfield, MI, US
toucanx.com

Trapmine (4, -77.8%)
Tallinn, Estonia
trapmine.com

Trend Micro (7735, 1.8%)
Anti-virus
Irving, TX, US
trendmicro.com

Trustless.ai (3, -40.0%)
Secured Devices
Geneva, Switzerland
trustless.ai

Trustlook (9, -25.0%)
Malware Analysis
San Jose, CA, US
trustlook.com

Trustonic (109, 14.7%)
Mobile Device Security
Austin, TX, US
trustonic.com

UM-Labs (9, 12.5%)
Operating System Security
London, United Kingdom
um-labs.com

Unistal Systems (231, 2.2%)
Anti-virus
Mumbai, India
unistal.in

V-Key (122, 16.2%)
Sandbox
Ottawa, Canada
v-key.com

Vali Cyber (32, 23.1%)
Linux Security
Charlottesville, VA, US
valicyber.com

vArmour (91, -34.5%)
Servers
Mountain View, CA, US
varmour.com

Vipre (182, 15.2%)
Anti-virus
Clearwater, FL, US
vipre.com

Vir2us (6, 0.0%)
Virtualization
Petaluma, CA, US
vir2us.com

VirusBlokAda (15, 25.0%)
Anti-virus
Minsk, Belarus
anti-virus.by

VMWare (30796, -12.7%)
EDR
Palo Alto, CA, US
vmware.com

White Cloud Security (15, 0.0%)
Application Whitelisting
Austin, TX, US
whitecloudsecurity.com

WithSecure (1671, 63.3%)
Anti-virus
Helsinki, Finland
withsecure.com

WootCloud (3, -40.0%)
Endpoint Control
San Jose, CA, US
wootcloud.com

Xcitium (139, 6.9%)
Bloomfield, NJ, US
xcitium.com

Zemana (11, -8.3%)
Anti-virus
Ankara, Turkey
zemana.com

Zimperium (228, -4.2%)
Mobile Device Security
Dallas, TX, US
zimperium.com

Fraud Prevention

Acceptto (9, -43.8%)
Identity Verification
Portland, OR, US
acceptto.com

Accertify (330, 9.6%)
Itasca, IL, US
accertify.com

Actus Mobile Solutions (4, -20.0%)
Bray, Ireland
actusmobile.com

Adjust (646, -5.0%)
Bot Security
Berlin, Germany
adjust.com

Aiprise (10, 400.0%)
Identity Verification
Santa Clara, CA, US
aiprise.com

AllClear ID (55, 1.9%)
Identity Protection Service
Austin, TX, US
allclearid.com

Arkose Labs (214, -11.6%)
Bot Security
San Francisco, CA, US
arkoselabs.com

**Numbers in parentheses indicate headcount and % change in 2023.*

AUTHADA (22, -12.0%)
Authentication
Darmstadt, Germany
authada.de

Authenteq (5, -58.3%)
Identity Verification
Reykjavik, Iceland
authenteq.com

Authenticid (96, -20.7%)
Identity Verification
Kirkland, WA, US
authenticid.co

Authsignal (11, 22.2%)
Auckland, New Zealand
authsignal.com

Behaviosec (24, -36.8%)
Monitoring
San Francisco,
CA, US
behaviosec.com

Besedo (370, 9.8%)
Scanning
Stockholm, Sweden
besedo.com

BioCatch (297, 20.7%)
Authentication
Tel Aviv, Israel
biocatch.com

BotGuard (31, 0.0%)
Bot Security
Tallinn, Estonia
botguard.net/en/home

BrandShield (82, 9.3%)
Brand
Ramat HaSharon, Israel
brandshield.com

Bureau (115, 3.6%)
Identity Verification
San Francisco, CA, US
bureau.id

Castle (27, 22.7%)
Access Security
San Francisco,
CA, US
castle.io

Chainalysis (842, -7.3%)
Crypto Investigations
New York, NY, US
chainalysis.com

Cheq (263, 2.7%)
Advertising-related
Tel Aviv, Israel
cheq.ai

ciphertrace (110, 17.0%)
Anti-money Laudering
Menlo Park, CA, US
ciphertrace.com

Cleafy (54, -6.9%)
Anti-fraud
Milan, Italy
cleafy.com

Cognito (12, 20.0%)
Authentication
Palo Alto, CA, US
cognitohq.com

Consistec (31, 14.8%)
Saarland, Germany
consistec.de

Customerxps (236, 5.8%)
Bangalore, India
clari5.com

Cybera (20, -25.9%)
Financial Crime
New York, NY, US
cybera.io

Darwinium (30, 76.5%)
Monitoring
San Francisco, CA, US
darwinium.com

DataDome (179, 21.8%)
Bot Security
New York, NY, US
datadome.co

Datavisor (129, 13.2%)
Mountain View, CA, US
datavisor.com

Deduce (26, -25.7%)
ATO Defense
Philadelphia, PA, US
deduce.com

Dojah (21, 0.0%)
Identity Verification
Lagos, Nigera
dojah.io

Early Warning (1308, 12.5%)
Assurance
Scottsdale, AZ, US
earlywarning.com

EFTsure (145, 39.4%)
EFT Protection
North Sydney, Australia
home.eftsure.com.au

Ensighten (28, -17.6%)
Bot Security
Menlo Park, CA, US
ensighten.com

Enzoic (19, 0.0%)
Credential Security
Boulder, CO, US
enzoic.com

Ethoca (171, 4.3%)
Transaction Security
Toronto, Canada
ethoca.com

EverCompliant (153, -13.6%)
Banking Security
Tel Aviv, Israel
everc.com

FaceFirst (65, 109.7%)
Non-authentication
Biometrics
Austin, TX, US
FaceFirst.com

Featurespace (393, -1.3%)
Cambridge, United Kingdom
featurespace.com

Feedzai (582, -20.1%)
Anti-fraud
San Mateo, CA, US
feedzai.com

Fingerprint (115, 2.7%)
Device Identification
Chicago, IL, US
fingerprint.com

FingerprintJS (115, -21.2%)
Device Characteristics
Chicago, IL, US
fingerprintjs.com

FinLock Technologies (3, -62.5%)
Personal Protection
South Delhi, New Delhi,
India
finlock.in

Fiverity (21, 10.5%)
Fraud Detection
Boston, MA, US
fiverity.com

Forter (611, -1.3%)
Tel Aviv, Israel
forter.com

Fraud.com (28, 7.7%)
Identity Verification
London, United Kingdom
fraud.com

Fraud.net (45, 12.5%)
Fraud Management
New York, NY, US
fraud.net

Fraudlogix (17, -5.6%)
Hallandale Beach, FL, US
fraudlogix.com

Fraudmarc (5, 25.0%)
Email Fraud Prevention
Atlanta, GA, US
fraudmarc.com

Fraugster (9, -87.5%)
Transaction Security
Berlin, Germany
fraugster.com

Friendly Captcha (15, 150.0%)
Bot Security
Munich, Germany
friendlycaptcha.com

FRS Labs (23, 9.5%)
Fraud Detection
Bangalore, India
frslabs.com

**Numbers in parentheses indicate headcount and % change in 2023.*

Human (481, 17.3%)
Bot Security
New York, NY, US
humansecurity.com

Id Insight (19, 26.7%)
Identity Verification
Minneapolis, MN, US
idinsight.com

IDnow (321, 6.6%)
Identity Verification
Munich, Bayern, Germany
idnow.io

idwall (361, -10.2%)
Fraud Detection
Sao Paulo, Brazil
idwall.co

Incognia (178, 23.6%)
Authentication
Palo Alto, CA, US
incognia.com

IPQualityScore (33, 200.0%)
IP Intelligence
Las Vegas, NV, US
ipqualityscore.com

Iris Analytics Gmbh (47, 34.3%)
Urbar, Germany
iris.de

Jumio (714, -22.2%)
Identity Verification
Palo Alto,
CA, US
jumio.com

Kasada (113, 15.3%)
Bot Security
Sydney, Australia
kasada.io

Konduto (73, -17.1%)
Fraud Detection
Sao Paulo, Brazil
konduto.com

Kount (265, 0.4%)
Identity Verification
Boise, ID, US
kount.com

Lunio (71, 14.5%)
Advertising-related
Chorley, United Kingdom
ppcprotect.com

Lynx Tech (68, 7.9%)
Monitoring
London, United Kingdom
lynxtech.com

Maxmind (80, 27.0%)
Geolocation
Waltham,
MA, US
maxmind.com

Netacea (72, -28.7%)
Bot Security
Manchester, United Kingdom
netacea.com

Nethone (106, 2.9%)
Anti-fraud
Warsaw, Poland
nethone.com

Neuro-ID (74, -11.9%)
Monitoring
Whitefish, MT, US
neuro-id.com

NICE Actimize (1357, 6.8%)
Fraud Detection
Hoboken, NJ, US
niceactimize.com

nsKnox (46, -4.2%)
Payment Verification
Tel Aviv, Israel
nsknox.net

nSure.ai (49, 13.9%)
Chargeback Prevention
Tel Aviv, Israel
nsureai.com

NuData Security (52, -42.9%)
Fraud Detection
Vancouver, Canada
nudatasecurity.com

Onfido (588, -17.3%)
Identity Verification
London, United Kingdom
onfido.com

Outseer (216, -3.1%)
Authentication
Palo Alto, CA, US
outseer.com

Oxford Biochronometrics (8, -11.1%)
Click Fraud Prevention
London, United Kingdom
oxford-biochron.com

Paygilant (14, -6.7%)
Transaction Security
Ramat Gan, Israel
paygilant.com

Privakey (7, 75.0%)
Transaction Security
Philadelphia, PA, US
privakey.com

Prove (414, 35.3%)
Anti-fraud
New York, NY, US
payfone.com

qikfox (35, 94.4%)
Secure Web Browsing
San Mateo, CA, US
qikfox.com

Refine Intelligence (20, 0.0%)
Monitoring
Tel Aviv, Israel
refineintelligence.com

Rippleshot (20, -9.1%)
Fraud Detection
Chicago, IL, US
rippleshot.com

Risk.Ident (74, 5.7%)
Fraud Detection
London, United Kingdom
riskident.com

Riskified (753, -3.2%)
Transaction Security
Tel Aviv, Israel
riskified.com

Salviol Global Analytics (22, 15.8%)
Fraud Detection
Reading, United Kingdom
salviol.com

SAS Institute (16426, 2.9%)
Anti-fraud
Cary, NC, US
sas.com

Scalarr (21, -27.6%)
Advertising-related
Wilmington, DE, US
scalarr.io

SentiLink (101, 16.1%)
Anti-fraud
San Francisco, CA, US
sentilink.com

Seon (254, -13.9%)
Fraud Detection
Budapest, Hungary
seon.io

Shield (157, 6.8%)
Device Fingerprinting
San Francisco, CA, US
shield.com

Sift (369, 14.9%)
Identity Verification
San Francisco,
CA, US
sift.com

Signifyd (555, 2.0%)
E-Commerce Fraud Prevention
San Jose, CA, US
signifyd.com

Simplex (215, 0.9%)
Transaction Security
Givatayim, Israel
simplex.com

SpecTrust (81, 68.8%)
San Jose, CA, US
spec-trust.com

SpiderAF (45, 0.0%)
Advertising-related
Tokyo, Japan
spideraf.com

Spur (7, 0.0%)
Reputation
Mount Dora, FL, US
spur.us

**Numbers in parentheses indicate headcount and % change in 2023.*

thatDot (17, 21.4%)
Fraud Analytics
Portland, OR, US
thatdot.com

The Media Trust (69, -4.2%)
Advertising-related
McLean, VA, US
themediatrust.com

Threat Mark (82, -19.6%)
Identity Verification
Brno, Czechia
threatmark.com

ThreatFabric (52, 67.7%)
Bot Security
Amsterdam, Netherlands
threatfabric.com

Transmit Security (324, -11.7%)
Anti-fraud
Boston, MA, US
transmitsecurity.com

Ubble.ai (70, -26.3%)
Identity Verification
Paris, France
ubble.ai

Verafin (802, -2.8%)
Fraud Management
St. John's, Canada
verafin.com

VeriClouds (9, -10.0%)
Credential Security
Seattle, WA, US
vericlouds.com

Veriff (380, -24.8%)
Identity Verification
Tallinn, Estonia
veriff.com

Wontok (24, 4.3%)
Anti-fraud
Pyrmont, Australia
wontok.com

Yoti (390, 5.4%)
Identity Verification
London, United Kingdom
yoti.com

GRC

1Fort (7, 0.0%)
Cyber Insurance
New York, NY, US
1fort.com

1LINK (3, -40.0%)
Vulnerabilities
Ha Noi, Ba Dinh, Vietnam
1link.vn

1touch.io (78, 39.3%)
Data Discovery
Stamford, CT, US
1touch.io

3rdRisk (11, 57.1%)
Risk Management
Amsterdam, Netherlands
3rdrisk.com

3wSecurity (4, -20.0%)
Penetration Testing
Tampa, FL, US
3wsecurity.com

4CRisk (29, -6.5%)
Compliance Management
San Francisco, CA, US
4crisk.ai

6clicks (61, 24.5%)
Compliance Management
Melbourne, Australia
6clicks.io

A-Lign (644, -0.5%)
Compliance Management
Tampa, FL, US
a-lign.com

Accountable (6, -25.0%)
Compliance Management
Fort Worth, TX, US
accountablehq.com

Accurics (10, -16.7%)
Policy Management
Pleasanton, CA, US
accurics.com

AckTao (5, 0.0%)
Security Awareness Training
Vaud, Switzerland
acktao.com

Actifile (22, 4.8%)
DLP
Herzliya, Israel
actifile.com

ActiveFence (293, -6.1%)
Monitoring
Tel Aviv, Israel
activefence.com

Acuity Risk Management (16, 14.3%)
Risk Management
London, United Kingdom
acuityrm.com

Acunetix (Invicti) (38, -28.3%)
Vulnerabilities
Mriehel, Malta
acunetix.com

ADF Solutions (25, 19.1%)
Forensics
Bethesda, MD, US
adfsolutions.com

Aegify (12, -7.7%)
Risk Management
San Jose, CA, US
aegify.com

Akarion (15, 7.1%)
Compliance Management
Munich, Germany
akarion.com

AKITRA (42, 50.0%)
Compliance Management
Sunnyvale, CA, US
akitra.com

alertsec (6, 20.0%)
Monitoring
Palo Alto, CA, US
alertsec.com

Alfahive (30, -16.7%)
Posture Management
Mississauga, Canada
alfahive.com

ALL4TEC (26, -3.7%)
Risk Management
Massy, France
all4tec.com

Allgress (23, -8.0%)
Compliance Management
Livermore, CA, US
allgress.com

Alyne (22, -24.1%)
Risk Management
Munich, Germany
alyne.com

Amplify Intelligence (3, 0.0%)
Vulnerabilities
Melbourne, Victoria, Australia
amplifyintelligence.com

Anchor Technologies (16, -11.1%)
Risk Management
Columbia, MD, US
anchortechnologies.com

anecdotes (109, 31.3%)
Compliance Management
Palo Alto, CA, US
anecdotes.ai

Anitian (66, -17.5%)
Compliance Management
Portland, OR, US
anitian.com

AppCheck (83, 0.0%)
Vulnerabilities
Leeds, United Kingdom
appcheck-ng.com

Apphaz Security Solutions (5, -16.7%)
Penetration Testing
Bear, DE, US
apphaz.com

Apptega (54, 1.9%)
Compliance Management
Atlanta, GA, US
apptega.com

APT Defend (5, 400.0%)
Security Awareness Training
Warszawa, Mazowieckie, Poland
aptdefend.com

**Numbers in parentheses indicate headcount and % change in 2023.*

Aptible (29, 0.0%)
Compliance Management
San Francisco, CA, US
aptible.com

Apvera (5, 0.0%)
Monitoring
Singapore, Singapore
apvera.com

Arama Tech (6, -14.3%)
Compliance Management
Glostrop, Denmark
aramatech.com

Archer (661, 36.3%)
Risk Management
Overland Park, KS, US
archerirm.com

Arcon (551, 53.9%)
Rights Management
Mumbai, India
arconnet.com

Ardent Privacy (15, 25.0%)
Data Privacy
Catonsville, MD, US
ardentprivacy.ai

Assured Enterprises Inc (10, 0.0%)
Vulnerabilities
Vienna, VA, US
assured.enterprises

Astrix Security (63, 90.9%)
Risk Management
Tel Aviv, Israel
astrix.security

At-Bay (325, 12.8%)
Cyber Insurance
San Francisco, CA, US
at-bay.com

AuditBoard (781, 20.3%)
GRC Platform
Cerritos, CA, US
auditboard.com

AuthMind (31, 55.0%)
Risk Management
Bethesda, MD, US
authmind.com

Automox (227, -12.0%)
Patch Management
Boulder, CO, US
automox.com

Avertro (22, 57.1%)
Risk Management
Sydney, NSW, Australia
avertro.com

Aware7 (34, 183.3%)
Security Awareness Training
Gelsenkirchen, Germany
aware7.com

Awareways (53, -10.2%)
Security Awareness Training
Utrecht, Netherlands
awareways.com

Axio (91, 26.4%)
Risk Management
New York, NY, US
axio.com

Axiom Cyber Solutions (3, -25.0%)
Vulnerabilities
Las Vegas, NV, US
axiomcyber.com

Axonius (600, -6.2%)
Asset Management
New York, NY, US
axonius.com

Axway (1729, -4.9%)
Secure Data Sharing
Phoenix, AZ, US
axway.com

Balbix (146, 29.2%)
Asset Management
San Jose, CA, US
balbix.com

Baramundi Software (209, 14.8%)
Endpoint Management
Augsburg, Germany
baramundi.com

Bastazo (6, 0.0%)
Vulnerabilities
Fayetteville, AR, US
bastazo.com

Beauceron (44, -22.8%)
Defense Against Phishing
Fredericton, Canada
beauceronsecurity.com

Belarc Inc. (14, -12.5%)
Asset Management
Maynard, MA, US
belarc.com

Beyond Security (33, -10.8%)
Vulnerabilities
San Jose, CA, US
beyondsecurity.com

BigID (543, 0.2%)
Data Discovery
Tel Aviv, Israel
bigid.com

Bitdiscovery (3, 0.0%)
Asset Management
Santa Clara, CA, US
bitdiscovery.com

BitSight (805, 0.6%)
Security Ratings
Boston, MA, US
bitsight.com

Black Kite (115, -2.5%)
Security Scores
Vienna, VA, US
normshield.com

Blacklock Security (4, -20.0%)
Penetration Testing
Thorndon, Wellington Region, New Zealand
blacklock.io

Blue Lance Inc. (11, -21.4%)
Asset Management
Houston, TX, US
bluelance.com

Blue Lava (12, -76.5%)
Security Program Management
Menlo Park, CA, US
blue-lava.net

Bob's Business (29, 0.0%)
Security Awareness Training
Barnsley, United Kingdom
bobsbusiness.co.uk

Boldon James (31, -8.8%)
DLP
Farnborough, United Kingdom
boldonjames.com

Borneo (142, 144.8%)
Compliance Management
San Francisco, CA, US
borneo.io

Boxphish (25, 19.1%)
Security Awareness Training
London, United Kingdom
boxphish.com

Brainwave Grc (32, -37.2%)
Identity Analytics
Asnieres-sur-Seine, France
brainwaveGRC.com

Breachlock (90, 1.1%)
Penetration Testing
New York, NY, US
breachlock.com

BreachRx (17, 21.4%)
Incident Management
San Francisco, CA, US
breachrx.com

Brinqa (98, -10.1%)
Risk Management
Austin, TX, US
brinqa.com

Buckler (8, 0.0%)
Compliance Management
Columbus, OH, US
buckler.app

C1Risk (7, 0.0%)
Policy Management
San Francisco, CA, US
c1risk.com

C1Secure (19, -20.8%)
Compliance Management
Atlanta, GA, US
c1secure.com

C2 Cyber (22, 4.8%)
Risk Management
London, United Kingdom
c2cyber.com

**Numbers in parentheses indicate headcount and % change in 2023.*

C2SEC (6, 0.0%)
Risk Management
Redmond, WA, US
c2sec.com

Camel Secure (8, -27.3%)
Santiago, Chile
camelsecure.com

Carson & Saint (Was Saint Corporation) (25, 8.7%)
Vulnerabilities
Bethesda, MD, US
carson-saint.com

Carve Systems (16, -30.4%)
Risk Management
New York, NY, US
carvesystems.com

Cavelo Inc (20, 25.0%)
Data Discovery
Kitchener, Canada
cavelo.com

Caveonix (33, 43.5%)
Risk Management
Falls Church, VA, US
caveonix.com

Cavirin Systems (16, -15.8%)
Compliance Management
Santa Clara, CA, US
cavirin.com

Censinet (39, 34.5%)
Boston, MA, US
censinet.com

Censys (129, 14.2%)
Asset Management
Ann Arbor, MI, US
censys.io

Centraleyes (20, -13.0%)
Risk Management
New York, NY, US
centraleyes.com

Cereus (4, 33.3%)
Compliance Management
Eau Claire, WI, US
cereus.io

Cimcor (22, 0.0%)
Merrillville, IN, US
cimcor.com

Cinder (27, 107.7%)
Insider Abuse Management
New York, NY, US
cinder.co

CISOteria (7, 0.0%)
Risk Management
Ra'ananna, Israel
cisoteria.com

Citalid (43, 87.0%)
Versailles, France
citalid.com

Citicus (3, -25.0%)
London, United Kingdom
citicus.com

Clearwater (250, 110.1%)
Compliance Management
Nashville, TN, US
clearwatercompliance.com

Cloud Raxak (7, 0.0%)
Compliance Management
Los Gatos, CA, US
cloudraxak.com

Cloudcheckr (61, -51.2%)
Configuration Management
Rochester, NY, US
cloudcheckr.com

CloudCover (19, 26.7%)
Compliance Management
Saint Paul, MN, US
cloudcover.net

Cloudmatos (12, -29.4%)
Compliance Management
Livermore, CA, US
cloudmatos.com

Coalfire (984, -8.2%)
Vulnerabilities
Westminster, CO, US
coalfire.com

Coalition (638, 11.0%)
Cyber Insurance
San Francisco, CA, US
coalitioninc.com

CODA Intelligence (11, 22.2%)
Vulnerabilities
Boston, MA, US
codaintelligence.com

Cofense (was Phishme) (312, -26.4%)
Defense Against Phishing
Leesburg, VA, US
cofense.com

CoGuard (5, 25.0%)
Configuration Management
Waterloo, Canada
coguard.io

Commugen (25, 8.7%)
Risk Management
Tel Aviv, Israel
commugen.com

ComplianceCow (20, 53.9%)
Fremont, CA, US
compliancecow.com

ComplianceRisk (5, 0.0%)
Dover, NH, US
compliancerisk.io

ComplyCloud (91, 7.1%)
GDPR
Copenhagen, Denmark
complycloud.com

ComplyUp (4, 0.0%)
Compliance Management
Tampa, FL, US
complyup.com

Comtech (94, 32.4%)
Credential Security
Reston, VA, US
comtechllc.com

ConductorOne (57, 72.7%)
Portland, OR, US
conductorone.com

Confidently (28, 211.1%)
Employee Protection
San Francisco, CA, US
confidently.com

ControlMap (10, -33.3%)
Compliance Management
Bellevue, WA, US
controlmap.io

Conveyor (24, 14.3%)
San Francisco, CA, US
conveyor.com

Core Business Solutions (66, 0.0%)
CMCC Tools
Lewisburg, PA, US
thecoresolution.com

Core Security (112, 3.7%)
Vulnerabilities
Roswell, GA, US
coresecurity.com

CORL Technologies (81, -22.9%)
Atlanta, GA, US
corltech.com

Covered Security (3, -25.0%)
Security Awareness Training
Boston, MA, US
coveredsecurity.com

Cranium (32, 166.7%)
AI Discovery
Short Hills, NJ, US
cranium.ai

Crossword Cybersecurity (71, -12.3%)
Risk Management
London, United Kingdom
crosswordcybersecurity.com

CultureAI (39, 44.4%)
Security Awareness Training
Manchester, United Kingdom
culture.ai

Cura Software Solutions (85, 9.0%)
Risk Management
Singapore, Singapore
curasoftware.com

Curricula (12, 0.0%)
Security Awareness Training
Atlanta, GA, US
curricula.com

**Numbers in parentheses indicate headcount and % change in 2023.*

Cyber Guru (80, 33.3%)
Security Awareness Training
Rome, Italy
cyberguru.it

Cyber Observer Ltd. (6, -60.0%)
Security Management
Caesarea, Israel
cyber-observer.com

Cyber Risk Aware (6, -14.3%)
Security Awareness Training
Dublin, Ireland
cyberriskaware.com

Cyber Risk International (3, -40.0%)
Risk Management
Kinsealy, Ireland
cyberriskinternational.com

Cyberaware (3, -25.0%)
Security Awareness Training
Melbourne, Australia
cyberaware.com

CyberCNS (7, -22.2%)
Vulnerabilities
Surrey, BC, Canada
cybercns.com

CyberconIQ (31, 63.2%)
Security Awareness Training
York, PA, US
cyberconiq.com

CyberCube (117, 11.4%)
Risk Management
San Francisco, CA, US
cybcube.com

Cybeready (36, 5.9%)
Defense Against Phishing
Tel Aviv, Israel
cybeready.com

CyberEye Research Labs & Security Solutions (15, 0.0%)
Security Awareness Training
Hyderabad, India
cybereye.io

CyberGRX (107, -44.0%)
Risk Management
Denver, CO, US
cybergrx.com

CyberHoot (5, 0.0%)
Security Awareness Training
Hampton, NH, US
cyberhoot.com

Cyberkov (4, 0.0%)
Risk Management
Kuwait City, Kuwait
cyberkov.com

Cybermaniacs (18, 20.0%)
Security Awareness Training
London, United Kingdom
thecybermaniacs.com

Cybernance (4, 0.0%)
Risk Management
Austin, TX, US
cybernance.com

Cybernet (32, -8.6%)
Security Manager
Ann Arbor, MI, US
cybernet.com

CyberOwl (51, 18.6%)
Risk Management
Birmingham, United Kingdom
cyberowl.io

CyberSaint (43, -20.4%)
Risk Management
Boston, MA, US
cybersaint.io

Cybersmart (69, 13.1%)
Compliance Management
London, United Kingdom
cybersmart.co.uk

CyberVadis (89, 7.2%)
Risk Management
Paris, France
cybervadis.com

Cyberwatch (27, -3.6%)
Paris, France
cyberwatch.fr

Cyberwrite (14, 0.0%)
Risk Management
Manhattan, NY, US
cyberwrite.com

Cybrary (213, -13.1%)
Training
College Park, MD, US
cybrary.it

CybSafe (105, -5.4%)
Security Awareness Training
London, United Kingdom
cybsafe.com

Cycognito (162, -15.6%)
Vulnerabilities
Palo Alto, CA, US
cycognito.com

Cygna Labs Corp (80, 56.9%)
Auditing
Miami Beach, FL, US
cygnalabs.com

CyLock (11, 10.0%)
Penetration Testing
Roma, Italy
cylock.tech/en/home-en

CyNation (4, 0.0%)
Risk Management
London, United Kingdom
cynation.com

Cypago (35, 34.6%)
Compliance Management
Tel Aviv, Israel
cypago.com

Cysmo (3, 50.0%)
Risk Management
Hambueg, Germany
cysmo.de

Cytellix (22, 22.2%)
MDR
Aliso Viejo, CA, US
cytellix.com

CYTRIO (17, -15.0%)
Rights Management
Boston, MA, US
cytrio.com

Cyturus Technologies (12, 20.0%)
Risk Management
Addison, TX, US
cyturus.com

Data Sentinel (31, -11.4%)
Risk Management
Concord, Canada
data-sentinel.com

DataGrail (127, 5.0%)
Data Privacy
San Francisco, CA, US
datagrail.io

Dataships (18, -10.0%)
Compliance Management
Dublin, Ireland
dataships.io

Datiphy (13, 8.3%)
Monitoring
San Jose, CA, US
datiphy.com

Dcoya (23, 64.3%)
Defense Against Phishing
Tel Aviv, Israel
dcoya.com

Decision Focus (54, 46.0%)
Compliance Management
Birkerod, Denmark
decisionfocus.com

Deep Indentity Pte Ltd. (78, 2.6%)
Access Security
Singapore, Singapore
deepidentity.com

DeepSurface (19, -13.6%)
Vulnerabilities
Portland, OR, US
deepsurface.com

Defendify (26, -3.7%)
Portland, ME, US
defendify.io

DefenseStorm (103, 0.0%)
Compliance Management
Atlanta, GA, US
defensestorm.com

Denexus (46, 2.2%)
Risk Management
Sausalito, CA, US
denexus.io

**Numbers in parentheses indicate headcount and % change in 2023.*

DGC (9, -25.0%)
Vulnerabilities
Flensburg, Germany
dgc.org

Digital Confidence Ltd. (4, 0.0%)
DLP
Tel Aviv, Israel
digitalconfidence.com

Digital Defense (44, -24.1%)
Vulnerabilities
San Antonio, TX, US
digitaldefense.com

Digital Guardian (204, -10.5%)
DLP
Waltham, MA, US
digitalguardian.com

Diligent (104, -30.7%)
Risk Management
Vancouver, Canada
wegalvanize.com

Diligent Corporation (2240, -0.3%)
GRC Platform
New York, NY, US
diligent.com

Diligent eSecurity International (4, 33.3%)
Monitoring
Atlanta, GA, US
desintl.com

DocAuthority (7, 0.0%)
DLP
Ra'anana, Israel
docauthority.com

Drata (552, -10.1%)
Compliance Management
San Diego, CA, US
drata.com

Drawbridge (98, 27.3%)
GRC Platform
New York, NY, US
drawbridgeco.com

DryvIQ (44, -18.5%)
Risk Management
Ann Arbor, MI, US
dryviq.com

DTEX Systems (118, 32.6%)
Insider Threats
San Jose, CA, US
dtexsystems.com

DynaRisk (19, -13.6%)
Risk Management
London, United Kingdom
dynarisk.com

EGERIE (144, 63.6%)
Risk Management
Toulon, France
egerie.eu

Ekran System (27, -6.9%)
Insider Threats
Newport Beach, CA, US
ekransystem.com

Elba (32, 113.3%)
Security Awareness Training
Paris, France
elba.security

Elemental Cyber Security (5, 0.0%)
Vulnerabilities
Dallas, TX, US
elementalsecurity.com

Elevate Security (42, -14.3%)
Security Awareness Training
Berkeley, CA, US
elevatesecurity.com

Elliptic (168, -17.6%)
London, United Kingdom
elliptic.co

Enginsight (28, 3.7%)
Vulnerabilities
Jena, Germany
enginsight.com

ERMProtect (14, -22.2%)
Security Awareness Training
Coral Gables, FL, US
ermprotect.com

ESNC (4, 0.0%)
SAP
Berlin, Germany
esnc.de

Ethyca (29, -14.7%)
Privacy Tools
New York, NY, US
ethyca.com

Exonar (5, -54.5%)
Data Discovery
Newbury, United Kingdom
exonar.com

Expanse (33, -8.3%)
Vulnerabilities
San Francisco, CA, US
expanse.co

FASOO (105, -3.7%)
Digital Rights Management
Seoul, South Korea
fasoo.com

FastPath (109, 13.5%)
Authorization
Des Moines, IA, US
gofastpath.com

Findings (34, 9.7%)
Risk Management
New York, NY, US
findings.co

Fixnix (39, -9.3%)
SMB Security
Ashok Nagar, India
fixnix.co

ForcePoint (2199, -0.1%)
DLP
Austin, TX, US
forcepoint.com

Foregenix (91, 1.1%)
Vulnerabilities
Boston, MA, US
foregenix.com

FortifyData (19, -36.7%)
Risk Management
Kennesaw, GA, US
fortifydata.com

FortMesa (10, 42.9%)
Risk Management
Austerlitz, NY, US
fortmesa.com

Fortress Information Security (248, 6.0%)
Risk Management
Oralndo, FL, US
fortressinfosec.com

Gat Labs (17, 0.0%)
Monitoring
Dublin, Ireland
gatlabs.com

GetData Forensics (12, 0.0%)
Forensics
Kogarah, Australia
forensicexplorer.com

GhangorCloud (20, 53.9%)
DLP
San Jose, CA, US
ghangorcloud.com

GORISCON (5, 25.0%)
Compliance Management
Rosenheim, Bayern, Germany
goriscon.de

Gradiant Cyber (46, 15.0%)
Risk Management
Dallas, TX, US
gradientcyber.com

Granite (26, 8.3%)
Risk Management
Tampere, Finland
granitegrc.com

Ground Labs (44, -6.4%)
Data Discovery
Singapore, Singapore
groundlabs.com

GTB Technologies (60, -1.6%)
Leaked Data
Newport Beach, CA, US
gttb.com

Guardian 360 (13, 30.0%)
Vulnerabilities
Utrecht, Netherlands
guardian360.nl

Guardtime (106, 3.9%)
Assurance
Tallinn, Estonia
guardtime.com

**Numbers in parentheses indicate headcount and % change in 2023.*

GuardYoo (6, 0.0%)
Compromise Assessment
Cork, Ireland
guardyoo.com

Guidewire (3358, 2.8%)
Security Ratings
Foster City, CA, US
guidewire.com

Gytpol (33, 57.1%)
Configuration Management
Tel Aviv, Israel
gytpol.com

Hackmetrix (58, 11.5%)
Compliance Management
Santiago, Chile
hackmetrix.com

HackNotice (26, -40.9%)
Security Awareness Training
Austin, TX, US
hacknotice.com

Hackuity (51, 24.4%)
Vulnerabilities
Lyon, France
hackuity.io

HacWare (8, -27.3%)
Security Awareness Training
Brooklyn, NY, US
hacware.com

Havoc Shield (13, 18.2%)
SMB Security
Chicago, IL, US
havocshield.com

Heureka Software (5, -37.5%)
Data Discovery
Cleveland, OH, US
heurekasoftware.com

Hicomply (16, -20.0%)
Compliance Management
Durham, United Kingdom
hicomply.com

HighGround.io (6, 0.0%)
Compliance Management
Perth, United Kingdom
highground.io

Hive Pro (68, 36.0%)
Vulnerabilities
Milpitas, CA, US
hivepro.com

Hook Security (26, 52.9%)
Security Awareness Training
Greenville, SC, US
hooksecurity.co

Hoxhunt (142, -7.8%)
Security Awareness Training
Helsinki, Finland
hoxhunt.com

Hyperproof (150, 48.5%)
Compliance Management
Bellevue, WA, US
hyperproof.io

Idera (270, 1.5%)
Compliance Management
Houston, TX, US
idera.com

IDX (71, -27.6%)
Data Privacy
Portland, OR, US
idx.us

IGLOO Software (125, -9.4%)
Security Management
Kitchener, Canada
igloosoftware.com

Immunity (27, -18.2%)
Vulnerabilities
Miami, FL, US
immunityinc.com

Infor (20055, 3.7%)
Monitoring
New York, NY, US
infor.com

Informer (15, -11.8%)
Attack Surface Management
London, United Kingdom
informer.io

Infosequre (12, 20.0%)
Security Awareness Training
Hilversum, Netherlands
infosequre.com

Infowatch (193, -3.0%)
DLP
Moscow, Russia
infowatch.com

Innosec (16, 33.3%)
DLP
Hod HaSharon, Israel
innosec.com

Insside Informacion (104, 16.9%)
GRC Platform
Madrid, Spain
insside.net

IntelliGRC (18, 38.5%)
GRC Platform
Fairfax, VA, US
intelligrc.com

Interos (229, -16.7%)
Risk Management
Arlington, VA, US
interos.ai

Intruder (70, 59.1%)
Vulnerabilities
London, United Kingdom
intruder.io

IONIX (83, 38.3%)
Attack Surface Management
Kirkland, WA, US
cyberpion.com

IRM Security (46, -25.8%)
Risk Management
Cheltenham, United Kingdom
irmsecurity.com

IronScales (138, -13.8%)
Defense Against Phishing
Tel Aviv, Israel
ironscales.com

ISARR (8, 60.0%)
Asset Management
London, United Kingdom
isarr.com

iTrust (83, 36.1%)
Vulnerabilities
Labege, France
itrust.fr

Jiran (44, -2.2%)
DLP
Daejeon, South Korea
jiran.com

Kenna Security (rebranded from Risk I/O) (46, -25.8%)
Feeds
San Francisco, CA, US
kennasecurity.com

Ketch (93, 20.8%)
Compliance Management
San Francisco, CA, US
ketch.com

KeyCaliber (13, -23.5%)
Asset Inventory
Washington, DC, US
keycaliber.com

Kintent (70, -6.7%)
Compliance Management
Boston, MA, US
kintent.com

Kion (80, 33.3%)
Compliance Management
Fulton, MD, US
kion.io

KnowBe4 (1856, 4.9%)
Security Awareness Training
Clearwater, FL, US
knowbe4.com

Kovrr (42, -2.3%)
Risk Management
London, United Kingdom
kovrr.com

Kratikal Tech (138, 7.8%)
Risk Management
Noida, India
kratikal.com

Kriptone (4, 300.0%)
Monitoring
Navsari, India
kriptone.com

Kymatio (18, -14.3%)
Security Awareness Training
Madrid, Spain
kymatio.com

**Numbers in parentheses indicate headcount and % change in 2023.*

KYND (46, 53.3%)
Risk Management
London, United Kingdom
kynd.io

Laika (185, -7.5%)
Compliance Management
New York, NY, US
heylaika.com

Legit Security (79, 12.9%)
Risk Management
Palo Alto, CA, US
legitsecurity.com

Lepide (157, -4.8%)
Data Discovery
Austin, TX, US
lepide.com

Living Security (68, -16.1%)
Security Awareness Training
Austin, TX, US
livingsecurity.com

LocateRisk (18, 28.6%)
Risk Management
Darmstadt, Germany
locaterisk.com

LogicGate (271, 3.4%)
Chicago, IL, US
logicgate.com

Longbow Security (31, 0.0%)
Vulnerabilities
Austin, TX, US
longbow.security

LUCY Security (20, -25.9%)
Defense Against Phishing
Zug, Switzerland
lucysecurity.com

Make IT Safe (15, -25.0%)
Auditing
Rezé, France
makeitsafe.fr

Managed Methods (37, 23.3%)
Access Security
Boulder, CO, US
managedmethods.com

ManageEngine (Zoho Corp.) (300, 55.4%)
Security Management
Pleasanton, CA, US
manageengine.com

Maxxsure (32, 6.7%)
Risk Management
Richardson, TX, US
maxxsure.com

MeasuredRisk (21, -8.7%)
Risk Management
Arlington, VA, US
measuredrisk.com

MessageSolution Inc. (17, -10.5%)
Email Archiving
Milpitas, CA, US
messagesolution.com

METABASE Q (94, 27.0%)
Compliance Management
San Francisco, CA, US
metabaseq.com

MetaCompliance (197, 13.9%)
Compliance Management
London, United Kingdom
metacompliance.com

Metascan (6, 0.0%)
Scanning
Moscow, Russia
metascan.ru

MetricStream (1385, -5.3%)
Palo Alto, CA, US
metricstream.com

Mindshift (9, 50.0%)
Security Awareness Training
Aotearoa, New Zealand
mindshift.kiwi

Mine (58, 70.6%)
Compliance Management
Tel Aviv, Israel
saymine.com

Mirato (27, 8.0%)
Risk Management
Tel Aviv, Israel
mirato.com

Mobiledit (Was Compelson Labs) (24, 33.3%)
Forensics
Prague, Czech Republic
mobiledit.com

Modulo (182, 9.0%)
Rio de Janeiro, Brazil
modulo.com

Monad (36, 50.0%)
Vulnerabilities
San Francisco, CA, US
monad.security

Mondoo (40, 25.0%)
Risk Management
San Francisco, CA, US
mondoo.io

Nanitor (20, 17.6%)
Iceland
nanitor.com

NAVEX (1340, 2.6%)
GRC Platform
Lake Oswego, OR, US
navex.com

Nemassis (Was MicroWorld) (13, 116.7%)
Vulnerabilities
Novi, MI, US
nemasisva.com

Netcraft (167, 29.5%)
Compliance Management
Bath, United Kingdom
netcraft.com

Netsense Gmbh (3, -25.0%)
Vulnerabilities
Zurich, Switzerland
netsense.ch

NetSPI (537, 33.2%)
Vulnerabilities
Minneapolis, MN, US
netspi.com

Nettoken (5, 25.0%)
Credential Security
London, United Kingdom
nettoken.io

Network Perception (47, -21.7%)
Configuration Management
Chicago, IL, US
network-perception.com

NetWrix Corporation (751, 18.8%)
Auditing
Irvine, CA, US
netwrix.com

Neupart (21, 50.0%)
Secure ISMS
Soborg, Denmark
neupart.com

Next DLP (86, 4.9%)
Insider Threats
London, United Kingdom
qush.com

Nimbusec (14, 16.7%)
Scanning
Linz, Austria
nimbusec.com

NINJIO (60, -6.2%)
Security Awareness Training
Westlake Village, CA, US
ninjio.com

Nirmata (73, 4.3%)
Kubernetes Security
San Jose, CA, US
nirmata.com

Noetic (52, 4.0%)
Asset Management
Waltham, MA, US
noeticcyber.com

Nopsec (53, 12.8%)
Vulnerabilities
Brooklyn, NY, US
nopsec.com

NorthStar.io (16, -5.9%)
Vulnerabilities
Chicago, IL, US
northstar.io

Nucleus Security (73, 1.4%)
Vulnerabilities
Sarasota, FL, US
nucleussec.com

**Numbers in parentheses indicate headcount and % change in 2023.*

Nudge Security (19, 26.7%)
Austin, TX, US
nudgesecurity.com

Occamsec (37, -2.6%)
Penetration Testing
New York, NY, US
occamsec.com

OctoXlabs (10, 66.7%)
Attack Surface Management
Istanbul, Turkey
octoxlabs.com

Omny (32, 77.8%)
Risk Management
Oslo, Norway
omnysecurity.com

Onda (39, 457.1%)
Risk Management
Minneapolis, MN, US
onda.ai

OneLeet (15, 7.1%)
Penetration Testing
Amsterdam, Netherlands
oneleet.com

OneTrust (2500, -5.2%)
Risk Management
Atlanta, GA, US
onetrust.com

Onspring (85, 6.2%)
Auditing
Overland Park, KS, US
onspring.com

Onwardly (8, 14.3%)
Policy Management
Aukland, New Zealand
onwardly.io

OpenVRM (6, 0.0%)
Risk Management
Columbus, OH, US
openvrm.com

Optimeyes (65, 62.5%)
Risk Management
San Diego, CA, US
optimeyes.ai

Ostendio (37, -21.3%)
Compliance Management
Arlington, VA, US
ostendio.com

Ostrich (21, 61.5%)
Risk Management
Cottonwood Heights, UT, US
ostrichcyber-risk.com

Outpost24 (228, 38.2%)
Vulnerabilities
Karlskrona, Sweden
outpost24.com

OutThink (43, 34.4%)
Monitoring
London, United Kingdom
outthink.io

P3 Audit (5, 0.0%)
Compliance Management
Covent Garden, United Kingdom
p3audit.com

Palqee (11, -26.7%)
Compliance Management
London, United Kingdom
palqee.com

Panorays (147, -2.0%)
Vulnerabilities
New York, NY, US
panorays.com

Paraben Corporation (17, -10.5%)
Forensics
Aldie, VA, US
paraben.com

Pareto Cyber (12, -20.0%)
Risk Management
St. Louis, MO, US
paretosecurity.com

Patch My PC (86, 8.9%)
Patch Management
Castle Rock, CO, US
patchmypc.com

Pervade Software (10, 0.0%)
Cardiff, United Kingdom
pervade-software.com

Phin Security (32, 146.2%)
Security Awareness Training
Newark, DE, US
phinsec.io

PhishFirewall (11, -15.4%)
Security Awareness Training
Huntsville, AL, US
phishfirewall.com

PhishLabs (109, -18.7%)
Defense Against Phishing
Charleston, SC, US
phishlabs.com

PhishX (20, 5.3%)
Security Awareness Training
Cotia, Brazil
phishx.io

Piiano (27, -6.9%)
Data Privacy
Tel Aviv, Israel
piiano.com

PiiqMedia (5, -16.7%)
Security Awareness Training
Cambridge, MA, US
piiqmedia.com

PivotPoint Security (31, -20.5%)
Risk Management
Hamilton, NJ, US
pivotpointsecurity.com

PixAlert (10, 0.0%)
Data Discovery
Dublin, Ireland
pixalert.com

Plextrac (95, -15.9%)
Security Report Management Platform
Boise, ID, US
plextrac.com

PolicyCo (8, -46.7%)
Policy Management
Nashville, TN, US
policyco.io

Polymer (24, 9.1%)
DLP
New York, NY, US
polymerhq.io

PortSwigger (196, 40.0%)
Vulnerabilities
Knutsford, United Kingdom
portswigger.net

Prevalent AI (136, 6.2%)
Risk Management
London, United Kingdom
prevalent.ai

Prevalent Networks (152, 23.6%)
Risk Management
Warren, NJ, US
prevalent.net

Privacy Engine (34, 6.2%)
Data Privacy
Blackrock, Ireland
privacyengine.io

Private AI (81, 113.2%)
Data Discovery
Toronto, Canada
private-ai.com

Privo (39, 8.3%)
Data Privacy
Dumfries, VA, US
privo.com

Privva (8, -20.0%)
Risk Management
Arlington, VA, US
privva.com

Privya.AI (23, -11.5%)
Compliance Management
Tel Aviv, Israel
privya.ai

ProcessUnity (174, 28.9%)
Risk Management
Concord, MA, US
processunity.com

**Numbers in parentheses indicate headcount and % change in 2023.*

Prohacktive.Io (9, -30.8%)
Vulnerabilities
Gap, France
prohacktive.io

Protenus (101, -11.4%)
Healthcare
Baltimore, MD, US
protenus.com

Proteus Cyber (5, 0.0%)
London, United Kingdom
proteuscyber.com

Protexxa (70, 2233.3%)
Security Awareness Training
Toronto, ON, Canada
protexxa.com

Qmulos (87, 11.5%)
Arlington, VA, US
qmulos.com

Qohash (43, -21.8%)
Data Discovery
Quebec, Canada
qohash.com

Qontrol (12, 71.4%)
Compliance Management
Paris, France
qontrol.io

Qualys (2528, 11.6%)
Vulnerabilities
Foster City, CA, US
qualys.com

Quotium (12, -20.0%)
Monitoring
Paris, France
quotium.com

Randori (90, -6.2%)
Attack Surface Management
Waltham, MA, US
randori.com

Rapid7 (2825, -0.2%)
Vulnerabilities
Boston, MA, US
rapid7.com

RealCISO (6, -25.0%)
Boston, MA, US
realciso.io

Reciprocity (90, -46.4%)
Risk Management
San Francisco, CA, US
reciprocity.com

RedSeal (178, 7.2%)
Posture Management
San Jose, CA, US
redseal.net

RegScale (55, 96.4%)
Compliance Management
Tysons, VA, US
regscale.com

Regulativ.ai (7, 16.7%)
Compliance Management
London, United Kingdom
regulativ.ai

Relyance AI (70, 0.0%)
Compliance Management
Mountain View, CA, US
relyance.ai

Rescana (17, 54.5%)
Tel Aviv, Israel
rescana.com

Resolver (363, 13.4%)
Risk Management
Toronto, Canada
resolver.com

Responsible Cyber (14, -6.7%)
Risk Management
Central Business District, Singapore
responsible-cyber.com

Ridge Security (33, 50.0%)
Penetration Testing
Santa Clara, CA, US
ridgesecurity.ai

Right-Hand Security (48, 54.8%)
Security Awareness Training
Lewes, DE, US
right-hand.ai

Riot (34, 54.5%)
Security Awareness Training
San Francisco, CA, US
tryriot.com

Riscosity (26, 52.9%)
Austin, TX, US
riscosity.com

Risk Based Security (4, -20.0%)
Vulnerabilities
Richmond, VA, US
riskbasedsecurity.com

Risk Ledger (33, -23.3%)
Risk Management
London, United Kingdom
riskledger.com

RiskLens (14, -79.4%)
Risk Management
Spokane, WA, US
risklens.com

RiskRecon (118, 0.8%)
Risk Management
Salt Lake City, UT, US
riskrecon.com

RiskSense (27, -12.9%)
Vulnerabilities
Albuquerque, NM, US
risksense.com

RiskWatch International (12, -7.7%)
Risk Management
Sarasota, FL, US
riskwatch.com

Robust Intelligence (72, 4.3%)
Governance
San Francisco, CA, US
robustintelligence.com

Rootshell Security (46, 12.2%)
Basingstoke, Hampshire, United Kingdom
rootshellsecurity.net

Safe Security (301, -34.6%)
Risk Management
Palo Alto, CA, US
safe.security

SafeBase (72, 56.5%)
Secure Storage
San Francisco, CA, US
safebase.io

SafeGuard Cyber (62, -13.9%)
Employee Social Media Management
Charlottesville, VA, US
safeguardcyber.com

Safeguard Privacy (27, 42.1%)
Compliance Management
New York, NY, US
safeguardprivacy.com

SAM for Compliance (3, 0.0%)
Compliance Management
Hastings, New Zealand
samcompliance.co

Sayata Labs (73, 7.3%)
Risk Management
Tel Aviv, Israel
sayatalabs.com

Scantist (26, -16.1%)
Vulnerabilities
Singapore, Singapore
scantist.com

Scrut Automation (145, 119.7%)
Compliance Management
Bangalore, Karnataka, India
scrut.io

Scytale (54, 25.6%)
Compliance Management
Tel Aviv, Israel
scytale.ai

SDG Corporation (577, 10.3%)
Norwalk, CT, US
sdgc.com

Secberus (20, -33.3%)
Compliance Management
Miami, FL, US
secberus.com

Secfix (21, 50.0%)
Compliance Management
Berlin, Germany
secfix.com

**Numbers in parentheses indicate headcount and % change in 2023.*

SecLogic (38, 46.1%)
Posture Management
Jacksonville, FL, US
seclogic.io

Seconize (17, 6.2%)
Risk Management
Singapore, Singapore
seconize.co

SecOps Solution (10, -9.1%)
Vulnerabilities
Bengaluru, India
secopsolution.com

SecPoint (15, -11.8%)
Vulnerabilities
Copenhagen, Denmark
secpoint.com

SecureEnvoy (3, -25.0%)
DLP
Cardiff, United Kingdom
geolang.com

Secureframe (153, 5.5%)
Compliance Management
San Francisco, CA, US
secureframe.com

SecureStack (8, 33.3%)
Configuration Management
Docklands, Australia
securestack.com

Securicy (Now Carbide) (34, -27.7%)
Policy Management
Sydney, Canada
securicy.com

Security Compass (259, 13.1%)
Compliance Management
Toronto, Canada
securitycompass.com

Security Mentor (5, 25.0%)
Security Awareness Training
Pacific Grove, CA, US
securitymentor.com

Security Mind (4, 0.0%)
Security Awareness Training
Veneto, Italy
securitymind.cloud

SecurityMetrics (260, 0.8%)
Vulnerabilities
Orem, UT, US
securitymetrics.com

SecurityScorecard (544, -0.2%)
Risk Management
New York, NY, US
securityscorecard.com

SecurityStudio (13, -35.0%)
Risk Management
Minnetonka, MN, US
securitystudio.com

SensCy (17, 6.2%)
Healthcare
Ann Arbor, MI, US
senscy.com

Senserva (7, 16.7%)
Posture Management
St Paul, MN, US
senserva.com

Sera-Brynn (13, 44.4%)
Risk Management
Suffolk, VA, US
sera-brynn.com

Sergeant Laboratories 15, 0.0%)
Risk Management
Onalaska, WI, US
sgtlabs.com

Sevco Security (63, 21.1%)
Asset Management
Austin, TX, US
sevco.io

Sicura (26, 8.3%)
Compliance Management
Baltimore, MD, US
sicura.us

Silk Security (25, 66.7%)
Risk Management
Santa Clara, CA, US
silk.security

Silverskin Information Security (20, -9.1%)
Compliance Management
Helsinki, Finland
silverskin.com

Singular Security (8, 14.3%)
Tustin, CA, US
singularsecurity.com

Slauth.io (4, 0.0%)
Policy Management
Tel Aviv, Israel
slauth.io

Sling (26, -7.1%)
Risk Management
Tel Aviv, Israel
slingscore.com

Smartfense (32, -8.6%)
Security Awareness Training
Cordoba, Argentina
smartfense.com

SolonTek (4, -55.6%)
Configuration Management
Raleigh, NC, US
solontek.net

Somansa (38, -9.5%)
DLP
San Jose, CA, US
somansatech.com

SoSafe (403, 12.6%)
Security Awareness Training
Cologne, North Rhine-Westphalia, Germany
sosafe-awareness.com

SpiderSilk (43, 2.4%)
Attack Surface Management
Dubai, United Arab Emirates
spidersilk.com

Spin Technology (76, 5.6%)
Risk Management
Palo Alto, CA, US
spin.ai

Spirion (was Identity Finder) (81, -17.4%)
Data Discovery
St. Petersburg, FL, US
spirion.com

Sprinto (227, 83.1%)
Compliance Management
San Francisco, CA, US
sprinto.com

Sprocket Security (18, 80.0%)
Penetration Testing
Madison, WI, US
sprocketsecurity.com

Squadra Technologies (27, 3.9%)
DLP
Las Vegas, NV, US
squadratechnologies.com

SSHTeam (19, 58.3%)
Penetration Testing
LogroÃƒÆ'Ã‚Â±o, La Rioja, Spain
sshteam.com

stackArmor (49, 11.4%)
Monitoring
Tysons, VA, US
stackarmor.com

StackGuardian (21, 75.0%)
Compliance Management
Munich, Germany
beta.stackguardian.io

Stacklet (25, -34.2%)
Policy Management
Washington, DC, US
stacklet.io

SteelCloud (66, 3.1%)
Configuration Management
Ashburn, VA, US
steelcloud.com

Strata Security Solutions (7, 16.7%)
Asset Management
Croydon, United Kingdom
stratasecurity.co.uk

Stream.Security (43, -28.3%)
Posture Management
Tel Aviv, Israel
stream.security

Strike Graph (44, -15.4%)
Compliance Management
Seattle, WA, US
strikegraph.com

**Numbers in parentheses indicate headcount and % change in 2023.*

Strike.sh (36, -2.7%)
Penetration Testing
London, United Kingdom
strike.sh

Strobes (53, 15.2%)
Vulnerabilities
Frisco, TX, US
strobes.co

Supplywisdon (115, -5.7%)
New York, NY, US
supplywisdom.com

SureCloud (99, -18.2%)
Cloud Security
Plano, TX, US
surecloud.com

Swascan (78, 13.0%)
Scanning
Cassina de' Pecchi, Italy
swascan.com

Sword Active Risk (56, -20.0%)
Risk Management
Maidenhead, United Kingdom
sword-activerisk.com

TAC Security (155, 31.4%)
San Francisco, CA, US
tacsecurity.com

Tala Secure (6, -14.3%)
Compliance Management
Mountain View, CA, US
talasecure.com

Tascet (7, 0.0%)
Risk Management
Madison, WI, US
tascet.com

Tausight (29, 31.8%)
Healthcare
Boston, MA, US
tausight.com

Telemessage (113, 31.4%)
Secure Communications
Petah Tikva, Israel
telemessage.com

Telos (736, -4.5%)
Compliance Management
Ashburn, VA, US
telos.com

Tempest Security Intelligence (425, -7.0%)
Data Discovery
Recife, Brazil
tempest.com.br

Tenable (2219, 7.9%)
Vulnerabilities
Columbia, MD, US
tenable.com

Tenchi Security (45, 60.7%)
Risk Management
Sao Paulo, Brazil
tenchisecurity.com

TerraTrue (38, -22.4%)
Software Development Security
San Francisco, CA, US
terratrue.com

Theta Lake (92, -8.0%)
Compliance Management
Santa Barbara, CA, US
thetalake.com

Think Cyber Security (14, 55.6%)
Security Awareness Training
London, United Kingdom
thinkcyber.co.uk

ThirdPartyTrust (16, -71.4%)
Risk Management
Chicago, IL, US
thirdpartytrust.com

Thoropass (185, 0.5%)
Compliance Management
New York, NY, US
thoropass.com

ThreatKey (12, 20.0%)
Configuration Management
New York, NY, US
threatkey.com

Threatrix (14, -12.5%)
Supply Chain Security
Dallas, TX, US
threatrix.io

Titania Ltd. (90, 57.9%)
Configuration Management
Worcester, United Kingdom
titania.com

TITUS (73, -4.0%)
DLP
Ottawa, Canada
titus.com

TraceSecurity (108, 1.9%)
Baton Rouge, LA, US
tracesecurity.com

trackd (9, 80.0%)
Vulnerabilities
US
trackd.com

TripWire (Fortra) (202, -20.8%)
Monitoring
Portland, OR, US
tripwire.com

TrojAI (19, 5.6%)
Governance
New Brunswick, Canada
troj.ai

Truops (19, -5.0%)
Risk Management
Norwalk, CT, US
truops.com

TrustArc (396, -7.9%)
Privacy Assessments
San Francisco, CA, US
trustarc.com

TrustBrands (61, -1.6%)
Scanning
Ogden, UT, US
trustbrands.com

Trustero (12, -36.8%)
Compliance Management
Palo Alto, CA, US
trustero.com

TrustLayer (45, 0.0%)
Risk Management
San Francisco, CA, US
trustlayer.io

TrustLogix (18, 38.5%)
Governance
Mountain View, CA, US
trustlogix.io

TrustMAPP (14, -6.7%)
Monitoring
Minneapolis, MN, US
trustmapp.com

TrustSpace (6, -33.3%)
Compliance Management
Berlin, Germany
trustspace.io

Tychon (49, 36.1%)
Risk Management
Fredericksburg, VA, US
tychon.io

Unit21 (125, 0.8%)
Compliance Management
San Francisco, CA, US
unit21.ai

UpGuard (195, 48.9%)
Monitoring
Mountain View, CA, US
upguard.com

usecure (40, 25.0%)
Security Awareness Training
Manchester, United Kingdom
usecure.io

Vanguard Integrity Professionals (91, 8.3%)
Monitoring
Las Vegas, NV, US
go2vanguard.com

Vanta (484, 33.7%)
Compliance Management
San Francisco, CA, US
vanta.com

Velona Systems (5, 0.0%)
Scanning
Cork, Ireland
velonasystems.com

**Numbers in parentheses indicate headcount and % change in 2023.*

Vendict (36, 89.5%)
Security Questionnaire Automation
Tel Aviv, Israel
vendict.com

Venminder (236, -3.3%)
Risk Management
Elizabethtown, KY, US
venminder.com

Veriscan Security (12, 9.1%)
Security Measurement
Karlstad, Sweden
veriscan.se

Very Good Security (233, 34.7%)
Secure Storage
San Francisco, CA, US
verygoodsecurity.com

vFeed (3, -25.0%)
Vulnerabilities
Middletown, DE, US
vfeed.io

VigilantOps (3, 0.0%)
Healthcare
Pittsburgh, PA, US
vigilant-ops.com

Vigiles (4, 33.3%)
Security Awareness Training
Miami, FL, US
vigiles.cloud

VigiTrust (129, 16.2%)
Risk Management
Dublin, Ireland
vigitrust.com

VisibleRisk (5, -70.6%)
Risk Management
New York, NY, US
visiblerisk.com

Viso Trust (45, 15.4%)
Risk Management
San Francisco, CA, US
visotrust.com

Visual Click Software (12, 0.0%)
Auditing
Austin, TX, US
visualclick.com

Vulcan Cyber (118, 16.8%)
Vulnerabilities
Tel Aviv, Israel
vulcan.io

WaryMe (16, 6.7%)
Cesson-Sevigne, France
waryme.com

Wiz (1114, 74.3%)
Configuration Management
Tel Aviv, Israel
wiz.io

YouAttest (20, -9.1%)
Governance
Newport Beach, CA, US
youattest.com

Zartech (41, 20.6%)
GRC Platform
Dallas, TX, US
zartech.net/grc

Zenity (37, 42.3%)
No-code/Low-code Security
Tel Aviv, Israel
zenity.io

Zeronorth (5, -28.6%)
Vulnerabilities
Boston, MA, US
zeronorth.io

Zilla Security (41, 28.1%)
Compliance Management
Boston, MA, US
zillasecurity.com

ZyLAB (61, -18.7%)
E-discovery
Amsterdam, Netherlands
zylab.com

IAM

0pass (7, 133.3%)
Authentication
Los Angeles, CA, US
0pass.com

1Kosmos (92, 15.0%)
Authentication
Somerset, NJ, US
1kosmos.com

1Password (1707, 89.0%)
Credential Security
Toronto, Canada
1password.com

443ID (22, -8.3%)
Identity Verification
Austin, TX, US
443id.com

9Star (31, 40.9%)
Managed Security Services
Austin, TX, US
9starinc.com

A3BC (11, -35.3%)
Authentication
Rennes, France
a3bc.io

Accops Systems (243, 25.9%)
Access Security
Pune, Maharastra, India
accops.com

accSenSe (18, 0.0%)
Secure Backup/Recovery
Ra'anana, Israel
accsense.io

Aceiss (10, 25.0%)
Access Security
New Canaan, CT, US
aceiss.com

Acsense (19, 0.0%)
Tel Aviv, Israel
acsense.com

AdNovum (638, 7.8%)
CIAM
Zurich, Switzerland
adnovum.ch

Aembit (21, 162.5%)
Identity Management
Silver Spring, MD, US
aembit.io

AerPass (6, -33.3%)
Authentication
Boulder, CO, US
aerpass.com

AET Europe (58, 18.4%)
Identity Management
Arnhem, Gelderland, Netherlands
aeteurope.com

Airlock (12, -14.3%)
Access Security
Zurich, Switzerland
airlock.com

Airside (17, -39.3%)
Mobile Identity
Herndon, VA, US
airsidemobile.com

Akku (19, 1800.0%)
Identity Platform
Rock Hill, SC, US
akku.work

Aladdin-RD (43, 4.9%)
Authentication
Moscow, Russia
aladdin-rd.ru

Alcatraz.ai (97, 14.1%)
Authentication
Cupertino, CA, US
alcatraz.ai

AlertEnterprise (268, 20.7%)
Physical IAM
Fremont, CA, US
alertenterprise.com

AllowMe (65, 22.6%)
Identity Management
Sao Paulo, Brazil
allowme.cloud

Allthenticate (12, 0.0%)
Authentication
Goleta, CA, US
allthenticate.net

Anomalix (6, 0.0%)
Identity Analysis
Las Vegas, NV, US
anomalix.com

Anonybit (22, 15.8%)
Shards
New York, NY, US
anonybit.io

**Numbers in parentheses indicate headcount and % change in 2023.*

aPersona (3, -25.0%)
Authentication
Raleigh, NC, US
apersona.com

Apono (28, 27.3%)
Rights Management
Tel Aviv, Israel
apono.io

Appaegis (31, 24.0%)
Access Security
Palo Alto, CA, US
appaegis.com

Appgate (372, -11.2%)
Access Security
Coral Gables, FL, US
appgate.com

Apporetum (4, 0.0%)
Canberra, Australia
apporetum.com.au

Aserto (17, 0.0%)
Access Security
Redmond, WA, US
aserto.com

Atos Group (81052, -12.7%)
Bezons, France
atos.net

Atricore (8, 14.3%)
Sausalito, CA, US
atricore.com

Au10Tix (199, 1.0%)
Identity Management
Hod HaSharon, Israel
au10tix.com

Auconet (9, -25.0%)
Access Security
Berlin, Germany
auconet.com

Aujas (897, 9.0%)
Identity Management
Jersey City, NJ, US
aujas.com

Auth Armor (5, -16.7%)
Authentication
Los Angeles, CA, US
autharmor.com

Auth0 (448, -17.2%)
Authentication
Bellevue, WA, US
auth0.com

AuthID (32, 0.0%)
Authentication
Long Beach, NY, US
authid.ai

Authlete (29, 38.1%)
Gateways
Tokyo, Japan
authlete.com

AuthLogics (6, -25.0%)
Authentication
Bracknell, United Kingdom
authlogics.com

Authomate (4, 0.0%)
Authentication
Morganville, NJ, US
authomate.com

Authomize (47, 0.0%)
Monitoring
Tel Aviv, Israel
authomize.com

Avatier (39, 11.4%)
Identity Management
Pleasanton, CA, US
avatier.com

Axiad IDS (62, 3.3%)
Authentication
Santa Clara, CA, US
axiadids.com

Axiom (22, 4.8%)
Identity Management
San Francisco,
CA, US
axiom.security

Axiomatics (67, 24.1%)
Access Security
Stockholm, Sweden
axiomatics.com

**Axis Security
(268, 103.0%)**
Access Security
San Mateo, CA, US
axissecurity.com

Axuall (92, 95.7%)
Identity Verification
Cleveland, OH, US
axuall.com

B-Secur (76, -2.6%)
Authentication
Belfast, United Kingdom
b-secur.com

BAAR (57, 23.9%)
Identity Management
Mississauga, Canada
baar.ai

BalkanID (27, 35.0%)
Auditing
Austin, TX, US
balkan.id

**BankVault Cybersecurity
(14, 75.0%)**
Authentication
West Perth, Australia
bankvault.com

BastionZero (14, -26.3%)
Gateways
Boston, MA, US
bastionzero.com

BAYOOSOFT (22, 29.4%)
Darmstadt, Germany
bayoosoft.com

**Beta Systems Software AG
(327, 14.3%)**
Berlin, Germany
betasystems.com

**Beyond Identity
(146, -18.0%)**
Authentication
New York, NY, US
beyondidentity.com

**BeyondTrust
(1452, 4.5%)**
Access Security
Johns Creek, GA, US
beyondtrust.com

**Bindle Systems
(17, -19.1%)**
Identity Management
Ardsley, NY, US
bindlesystems.com

BIO-key (72, -13.2%)
Authentication
Wall, NJ, US
bio-key.com

BioConnect (50, 21.9%)
Authentication
Toronto, Canada
bioconnect.com

BioEnable (76, 0.0%)
Access Security
Pune, India
bioenabletech.com

BioID (14, 7.7%)
Authentication
Sachseln, Switzerland
bioid.com

**Biometric Signature-Id
(15, 7.1%)**
Authentication
Lewisville, TX, US
biosig-id.com

Biomio (4, -20.0%)
Authentication
Portland, OR, US
biom.io

Bitwarden (162, 46.0%)
Credential Security
Santa Barbara,
CA, US
bitwarden.com

Blind Hash (3, 0.0%)
Credential Security
Boston, MA, US
blindhash.com

Bluink (24, 9.1%)
Authentication
Ottawa, Canada
bluink.ca

Britive (58, -12.1%)
Access Security
Glendale, CA, US
britive.com

Brivo (405, 38.7%)
Identity Management
Bethesda, MD, US
brivo.com

**Numbers in parentheses indicate headcount and % change in 2023.*

Bundesdruckerei (1373, 30.0%)
Public Key Infrastructure
Berlin, Germany
bundesdruckerei.de

Buypass As (85, 10.4%)
Public Key Infrastructure
OSLO, Norway
buypass.no

Callsign (233, -19.7%)
Authentication
London, United Kingdom
callsign.com

Celestix (23, 15.0%)
Fremont, CA, US
celestix.com

Cerbos (20, 66.7%)
Authorization
London, United Kingdom
cerbos.dev

Cerby (93, 55.0%)
Credential Security
Alameda, CA, US
cerby.com

CHEQUER (12, -40.0%)
Access Security
Seoul, South Korea
querypie.com

ClearSkye (38, -17.4%)
Governance
Emeryville, CA, US
clearskye.com

Cloudcodes Software (21, -12.5%)
Pune, India
cloudcodes.com

Cloudentity (45, -35.7%)
Identity Management
Seattle, WA, US
cloudentity.com

Cognitum-Software (11, 0.0%)
Lower Saxony, Germany
cognitum-software.com

Commfides Norge As (15, -11.8%)
Public Key Infrastructure
Lysaker, Norway
commfides.com

Covr Security (21, 16.7%)
Authentication
Sweden
covrsecurity.com

Crosswire (15, -16.7%)
Access Security
New York, NY, US
crosswire.io

Cryptium (3, 50.0%)
Authentication
Portland, OR, US
cryptium.com

CryptoPhoto (4, 0.0%)
Authentication
Australia
cryptophoto.com

Cryptr (9, -10.0%)
Authentication
Lille, France
cryptr.co

Crysp (3, 200.0%)
Authentication
San Francisco, CA, US
crysp.com

Csi Tools (7, -36.4%)
SAP
Herent, Belgium
csi-tools.com

CSIT Finland Oy (13, 85.7%)
Helsinki, Finland
csit.fi

CyberArk Software (3188, 15.2%)
Access Security
Petah Tikva, Israel
cyberark.com

CyberFOX (64, 8.5%)
Access Security
Tampa, FL, US
cyberfox.com

CyberQP (68, 54.5%)
Access Security
North Vancouver, Canada
cyberqp.com

CyberSafe Ltd. (10, 66.7%)
Access Security
Longford, United Kingdom
cybersafe.com

Cyberus Labs (7, 0.0%)
Authentication
Krakow, Poland
cyberuslabs.com

Cyolo (93, 0.0%)
Access Security
Tel Aviv, Israel
cyolo.io

D-ID (123, 95.2%)
Non-authentication Biometrics
Tel Aviv, Israel
deidentification.co

Daon (271, 1.1%)
Assurance
Reston, VA, US
daon.com

Dapple (3, 0.0%)
Authentication
Centennial, CO, US
dapplesecurity.com

Dashlane (353, -13.9%)
Credential Security
New York, NY, US
dashlane.com

Datakey (ATEK Access Technologies LLC) (11, 22.2%)
Authentication
Eden Prairie, MN, US
datakey.com

Datawiza (9, -10.0%)
Access Security
Santa Clara, CA, US
datawiza.com

Deepnet Security (24, 84.6%)
Identity Management
London, United Kingdom
deepnetsecurity.com

Delinea (956, 21.5%)
Access Security
Redwood City, CA, US
delinea.com

Descope (43, 34.4%)
Authentication
Los Altos, CA, US
descope.com

Detack (13, 0.0%)
Credential Security
Ludwigsburg, Germany
detack.de

Device Authority (32, -3.0%)
Authentication
Reading, United Kingdom
deviceauthority.com

Devolutions (175, 34.6%)
Quebec, Canada
devolutions.net

Diamond Fortress Technologies (3, -25.0%)
Authentication
Birmingham, AL, US
diamondfortress.com

DuoSecurity (now part of Cisco) (641, -11.0%)
Authentication
Ann Arbor, MI, US
duo.com

Egis Technology (147, -2.6%)
Authentication
Taipei, Taiwan
egistec.com

Elimity (6, 50.0%)
CIAM
Mechelen, Antwerpen, Belgium
elimity.com

Elisity (69, 27.8%)
Access Security
Milpitas, CA, US
elisity.com

**Numbers in parentheses indicate headcount and % change in 2023.*

Ensure Technologies (21, 0.0%)
Ypsilanti, MI, US
ensuretech.com

Ensurity (28, -6.7%)
Authentication
Hyderabad, India
ensurity.com

Entersekt (211, 3.4%)
Authentication
Stellenbosch, South Africa
entersekt.com

Entitle (34, 9.7%)
New York, NY, US
entitle.io

Ermetic (106, -45.1%)
Access Security
Tel Aviv, Israel
ermetic.com

esatus (40, 8.1%)
Langen, Hessen, Germany
esatus.com

essentry (16, 77.8%)
Eschborn, Hessen, Germany
essentry.com

Evernym (6, -40.0%)
Identity Attestation
Herriman, UT, US
evernym.com

Everykey (19, 11.8%)
Authentication
Cleveland, OH, US
everykey.com

Evident ID (69, -19.8%)
Identity Verification
Atlanta, GA, US
evidentid.com

Evo Security (28, 27.3%)
Identity Management
Austin, TX, US
evosecurity.com

Extreme Networks (3881, 7.8%)
Access Security
San Jose, CA, US
extremenetworks.com

Eyeonid Group Ab (11, 83.3%)
Theft
Stockholm, Sweden
eyeonid.com

FACEKI (15, 0.0%)
Manama, Al Manamah, Bahrain
faceki.com

Facephi Biometra (261, 17.6%)
Authentication
Alicante, Spain
facephi.com

FastpassCorp (69, -2.8%)
Credential Security
Kongens Lyngby, Denmark
fastpasscorp.com

Feitian Technologies (101, 6.3%)
Beijing, China
ftsafe.com

fidentity (10, 25.0%)
Identity Verification
Basel, Switzerland
fidentity.ch

Fileflex (19, -17.4%)
Access Security
Toronto, ON, Canada
fileflex.com

Fingerprint Cards AB (185, -12.3%)
Authentication
Gothenburg, Sweden
fingerprints.com

Fischer International Identity (69, -6.8%)
Naples, FL, US
fischeridentity.com

ForgeRock (896, -6.1%)
San Francisco, CA, US
forgerock.com

forghetti (3, 0.0%)
Credential Security
Winchester, United Kingdom
forghetti.com

Fortifyedge (5, -16.7%)
Tasmania, Australia
fortifyedge.com

Foxpass (6, -45.5%)
Authentication
San Francisco, CA, US
foxpass.com

Freja eID Group AB (Was Verisec) (45, -13.5%)
Mobile Identity
Stockholm, Sweden
verisec.com

Fudo Security (56, 12.0%)
Access Security
Newark, CA, US
fudosecurity.com

FusionAuth (30, 20.0%)
CIAM
Broomfield, CO, US
fusionauth.io

Futurae (45, -2.2%)
Authentication
Zurich, Switzerland
futurae.com

GateKeeper Access (19, 5.6%)
Authentication
College Park, MD, US
gkaccess.com

Geetest (64, -8.6%)
Captchas
Wuhan, China
geetest.com

getidee (17, 0.0%)
Authentication
München, Germany
getidee.com

GitGuardian (162, 50.0%)
Monitoring
Paris, France
gitguardian.com

GlobalSign (475, 3.5%)
Authentication
Portsmouth, NH, US
globalsign.com

Gluu (22, -18.5%)
Access Security
Austin, TX, US
gluu.org

GoTrustID Inc. (16, -15.8%)
Authentication
Taichung City, Taiwan
gotrustid.com

Great Bay Software (3, 0.0%)
Access Security
Bloomington, MN, US
greatbaysoftware.com

Green Rocket Security Inc. (5, 400.0%)
Authentication
San Jose, CA, US
greenrocketsecurity.com

Grip Security (100, 37.0%)
Access Security
Tel Aviv, Israel
grip.security

Hexagate (12, 500.0%)
Access Security
Israel
hexagate.com

heylogin (12, 20.0%)
Braunschweig, Germany
heylogin.com

HIAsecure (5, 0.0%)
Authentication
Courbevoie, France
hiasecure.com

HID Global (3416, 9.6%)
Authentication
Austin, TX, US
hidglobal.com

Hideez (12, 0.0%)
Hardware
Redwood City, CA, US
hideez.com

Hitachi ID Systems (80, -18.4%)
Calgary, Canada
hitachi-id.com

**Numbers in parentheses indicate headcount and % change in 2023.*

Hypersecu Information Systems (7, 0.0%)
OTP
Canada
hypersecu.com

HYPR (132, -7.7%)
Authentication
New York, NY, US
hypr.com

I Am I (4, 33.3%)
Authentication
Markham, Canada
useiami.com

I-Sprint Innovations (104, -0.9%)
Singapore, Singapore
i-sprint.com

ID R&D Inc. (56, 30.2%)
Authentication
New York, NY, US
idrnd.net

ID.me (875, -2.7%)
Credential Security
McLean, VA, US
id.me

Idax Software (5, 25.0%)
Petersfield, United Kingdom
idaxsoftware.com

IDEE (17, 0.0%)
Identity Platform
Munich, Germany
getidee.com

Idemeum (10, 11.1%)
Access Security
Palo Alto, CA, US
idemeum.com

IDEMIA (12850, 10.6%)
Identity Augmentation
Reston, VA, US
idemia.com

IDENprotect (18, 63.6%)
Authentication
London, United Kingdom
idenprotect.com

Identiq (59, -7.8%)
Identity Validation
Tel Aviv, Israel
identiq.com

Identite (43, -21.8%)
Authentication
Clearwater, FL, US
identite.us

Identity Automation (83, -17.0%)
Identity Management
Houston, TX, US
identityautomation.com

IdentityLogix (3, 0.0%)
Access Security
Crown Point, IN, US
identitylogix.com

Identitypass (20, -16.7%)
Identity Verification
Lagos, Nigera
myidentitypass.com

Identiv (277, 9.5%)
Credential Security
Fremont, CA, US
identiv.com

Identos Inc. (60, 9.1%)
Mobile Identity
Toronto, Canada
identos.com

IDENTT (38, 0.0%)
Wroclaw, Poland
identt.pl

IDmelon Technologies Inc. (12, 71.4%)
Vancouver, Canada
idmelon.com

IDology (184, 85.9%)
Authentication
Atlanta, GA, US
idology.com

IdRamp (4, 0.0%)
Authentication
Indianola, IA, US
idramp.com

Ilantus (175, -8.4%)
Identity Management
Schaumburg, IL, US
ilantus.com

ImageWare (47, -17.5%)
Authentication
San Diego, CA, US
iwsinc.com

Imprivata (1058, 36.2%)
Lexington, MA, US
imprivata.com

InBay Technologies (8, -33.3%)
Authentication
Kanata, Canada
inbaytech.com

Incode (340, 17.6%)
Identity Management
San Francisco, CA, US
incode.com

IndyKite (54, -3.6%)
Identity Management
San Francisco, CA, US
indykite.com

Infineon (37071, 17.6%)
Smart Card Solutions
Neubiberg, Germany
infineon.com

InfoExpress Inc. (30, -31.8%)
Access Security
Santa Clara, CA, US
infoexpress.com

Inside-Out Defense (6, 0.0%)
Access Security
Palo Alto, CA, US
insideoutdefense.com

Integrated Corporation (19, 171.4%)
Sheungwan, Hong Kong
integrated.com

Inteligensa (125, 9.7%)
Smart Card Solutions
Caracas, Venezuela
inteligensa.com

Intensity Analytics (9, -10.0%)
Monitoring
Warrenton, VA, US
intensityanalytics.com

Interlink Networks (5, 0.0%)
Ann Arbor, MI, US
interlinknetworks.com

Intrinsic-ID (45, 2.3%)
Authentication
Sunnyvale, CA, US
intrinsic-id.com

inWebo (5, -91.4%)
Authentication
Paris, France
inwebo.com

IPification (26, -13.3%)
Hong Kong
ipification.com

IProov (201, 16.2%)
Authentication
London, United Kingdom
iproov.com

Iraje (61, 17.3%)
Access Security
Mumbai, India
iraje.com

Ironchip Telco (29, 20.8%)
Identity Management
Barakaldo, Spain
ironchip.com

IronVest (25, 0.0%)
Authentication
New York, NY, US
ironvest.com

Ironwifi (3, -25.0%)
Authentication
Orlando, FL, US
ironwifi.com

IS Decisions (43, 4.9%)
Access Security
Bidart, France
isdecisions.com

**Numbers in parentheses indicate headcount and % change in 2023.*

ITConcepts (36, 0.0%)
Bonn, Germany
itconcepts.net

iWelcome (10, -23.1%)
Identity Management
Amersfoort, Netherlands
iwelcome.com

Jumpcloud (697, 5.9%)
Directory Services
Louisville, CO, US
jumpcloud.com

Kaseya (4862, 95.1%)
Authentication
New York, NY, US
kaseya.com

Keeper Security (347, -7.2%)
Credential Security
Chicago, IL, US
keepersecurity.com

Keyless (60, -3.2%)
Authentication
London, United Kingdom
keyless.io

Keypair (10, 42.9%)
Indentities
Gangnam-gu, South Korea
keypair.co.kr

Keytos Security (7, 16.7%)
Authentication
Boston, MA, US
keytos.io

KinectIQ (14, 27.3%)
Encryption
Woodbury, MN, US
knectiq.com

KOBIL Systems (179, 20.1%)
Authentication
Worms, Germany
kobil.com

LastPass (704, 16.0%)
Credential Security
Fairfax, VA, US
lastpass.com

Lastwall (26, 36.8%)
Access Security
Mountain View, CA, US
lastwall.com

Liopa (13, 44.4%)
Authentication
Belfast, United Kingdom
liopa.ai

LoginID (45, -6.2%)
Authentication
San Mateo, CA, US
loginid.io

LoginRadius (154, 12.4%)
CIAM
San Francisco, CA, US
loginradius.com

LoginTC (8, -11.1%)
Authentication
Kanata, Canada
logintc.com

LogMeIn (1337, -19.8%)
Credential Security
Boston, MA, US
logmein.com

Logmeonce (8, -20.0%)
Identity Management
McLean, VA, US
LogmeOnce.com

M2Sys Technology (86, -8.5%)
Authentication
Atlanta, GA, US
m2sys.com

MagicCube (28, -22.2%)
Transaction Security
Santa Clara, CA, US
magiccube.co

Mantra (621, 15.9%)
Authentication
Ahmedabad, India
mantratec.com

MATESO (11, -63.3%)
Credential Security
Neusäß, Germany
passwordsafe.com

Merit (258, 69.7%)
Sunnyvale, CA, US
merits.com

Mi-Token (63, 0.0%)
Authentication
Austin, TX, US
mi-token.com

Microsoft (224857, -1.4%)
Redmond, WA, US
microsoft.com

MicroStrategy (3405, -2.0%)
Mobile Identity
Tysons Corner, VA, US
microstrategy.com

Mideye (6, 200.0%)
Authentication
Espoo, Finland
mideye.com

miniOrange (293, 148.3%)
Authentication
Pune, India
miniorange.com

MIRACL (20, -13.0%)
Authentication
London, United Kingdom
miracl.com

Mobbeel (22, 22.2%)
Authentication
Caceres, Spain
mobbeel.com

My1login (15, 7.1%)
Identity Management
London, United Kingdom
my1login.com

MyCena (14, 0.0%)
Credential Security
London, United Kingdom
mycena.co

Nametag (19, 11.8%)
Authentication
Seattle, WA, US
getnametag.com

neoEYED (3, -57.1%)
Authentication
Bangalore, India
neoeyed.com

NewBanking (17, 6.2%)
Copenhagen, Denmark
newbanking.com

Nexus Group Global (257, 19.0%)
Identity Management
Stockholm, Sweden
nexusgroup.com

ngrok (84, 0.0%)
Access Security
San Francisco, CA, US
ngrok.com

Nok Nok Labs (36, -16.3%)
Authentication
San Jose, CA, US
noknok.com

Noq (4, 0.0%)
Identity As Code
Irvine, CA, US
noq.dev

Notakey (3, -25.0%)
Access Security
Riga, Latvia
notakey.com

Notebook Labs (5, 0.0%)
Identity Management
Stanford, CA, US
notebooklabs.xyz

ObserveID (10, 42.9%)
Monitoring
Los Angeles, CA, US
observeid.com

Octatco (6, 20.0%)
Authentication
Seongnam, South Korea
octatco.com

Odyssey Technologies (155, 14.8%)
Public Key Infrastructure
Chennai, India
odysseytec.com

**Numbers in parentheses indicate headcount and % change in 2023.*

Okta (7108, -12.4%)
San Francisco,
CA, US
okta.com

Oloid (46, 9.5%)
Identity Management
Sunnyvale, CA, US
oloid.ai

Omada (322, 20.1%)
Copenhagen, Denmark
omada.net

One Identity (596, 1.5%)
Identity Management
Aliso Viejo, CA, US
oneidentity.com

OneLogin (100, -17.4%)
Identity Management
San Francisco, CA, US
onelogin.com

OneSpan (741, -1.5%)
Chicago, IL, US
onespan.com

OneVisage (7, -12.5%)
Authentication
Lausanne, Switzerland
onevisage.com

OneWave (29, -9.4%)
Authentication
Rennes, France
onewave.io

OneWelcome (Was Onegini) (4, -50.0%)
CIAM
Woerden, Netherlands
onegini.com

Oort (29, -37.0%)
Incident Management
Boston, MA, US
www.oort.io

Opal Dev (50, 51.5%)
Identity Management
San Francisco, CA, US
opal.dev

OpenIAM (11, 37.5%)
Identity Management
Cortlandt Manor,
NY, US
openiam.com

OpenText (21752, 45.1%)
Federated Identity
Waterloo, Canada
opentext.com

Optimal IdM (11, 0.0%)
Authentication
Lutz, FL, US
optimalidm.com

Oracle (201930, -1.7%)
Redwood Shores,
CA, US
oracle.com

Ory (25, -34.2%)
Munich, Germany
ory.sh

Osirium (40, -14.9%)
Access Security
Theale, United Kingdom
osirium.com

OwnID (16, -5.9%)
Authentication
Tel Aviv, Israel
ownid.com

P0 Security (11, 22.2%)
Access Security
San Francisco, CA, US
p0.dev

P3KI (6, -25.0%)
Access Security
Berlin, Germany
p3ki.com

Pango (91, 26.4%)
VPN/Proxy
Redwood City, CA, US
pango.co

Passage (4, -66.7%)
Authentication
Austin, TX, US
passage.id

Passbase (5, -83.9%)
User Verification
Berlin, Germany
passbase.com

Passbolt (28, -15.2%)
Credential Security
Esch-sur-alzette,
Luxembourg
passbolt.com

PassMark Software Pvt Ltd. (8, 0.0%)
Surry Hills, Australia
passmark.com

Password Depot (13, 8.3%)
Credential Security
Darmstadt, Germany
password-depot.de

Persona (280, 27.3%)
Identity Verification
San Francisco, CA, US
withpersona.com

Ping Identity Corporation (1387, -0.2%)
Denver, CO, US
pingidentity.com

Pirean (Echostar) (30, -9.1%)
Identity Management
London, United Kingdom
pirean.com

PlainID (91, -12.5%)
Authorization
Tel Aviv, Israel
plainid.com

Plurilock (45, -8.2%)
Authentication
Victoria, Canada
plurilock.com

PortSys (6, -25.0%)
Access Security
Marlborough, MA, US
portsys.com

Post-Quantum (9, -25.0%)
Authentication
London, United
Kingdom
post-quantum.com

Privafy (83, -3.5%)
Access Security
Burlington, MA, US
privafy.com

Procivis AG (29, 11.5%)
Credential Security
Zurich, Switzerland
procivis.ch

Procyon (17, 325.0%)
Access Security
Santa Clara, CA, US
procyon.ai

Proof Authentication (12, 50.0%)
Application Authenticity
Boston, MA, US
proofauthentication.com

PropelAuth (6, -14.3%)
Authentication
Redwood City, CA, US
propelauth.com

Protectimus Ltd (49, 13.9%)
Authentication
Dublin, Ireland
protectimus.com

Pulse Secure (151, -18.4%)
Authentication
San Jose, CA, US
pulsesecure.net

PureID (12, -7.7%)
Authentication
Heydon, Royston, United
Kingdom
pureid.io

PXL Vision (34, -2.9%)
Identity Verification
Zurich, Switzerland
pxl-vision.com

**Numbers in parentheses indicate headcount and % change in 2023.*

Quantum Integrity (4, -20.0%)
Identity Verification
Lausanne, Switzerland
q-integrity.com

Quest Software (3736, -4.1%)
Access Security
Aliso Viejo, CA, US
quest.com

Quicklaunch (41, 13.9%)
Identity Management
Miami, FL, US
quicklaunch.io

Quickpass (67, 67.5%)
Access Security
North Vancouver, Canada
getquickpass.com

Radiant Logic (166, 23.9%)
Authentication
Novato, CA, US
radiantlogic.com

Raonsecure (78, 36.8%)
Authentication
Santa Clara, CA, US
raonsecure.com

RavenWhite Security (3, 0.0%)
Cookies
Menlo Park, CA, US
ravenwhite.com

RCDevs (19, 5.6%)
Belvaux, Luxembourg
rcdevs.com

Remediant (9, -66.7%)
Access Security
San Francisco, CA, US
remediant.com

Resilient Network Systems (3, 0.0%)
Access Security
San Francisco, CA, US
resilient-networks.com

Rezonate (27, 50.0%)
Identity Management
Boston, MA, US
rezonate.io

Ricoh USA (18703, -1.1%)
Authentication
Exton, PA, US
ricoh-usa.com

Route 1 (43, -12.2%)
Toronto, Canada
route1.com

RSA Security (Symphony Technology Group) (2826, 0.3%)
Authentication
Bedford, MA, US
rsa.com

Rublon (18, 20.0%)
Authentication
Zielona Gora, Poland
rublon.com

Saaspass (11, -8.3%)
San Francisco, CA, US
saaspass.com

Safe-T (21, 5.0%)
Access Security
Herzliya Pituach, Israel
safe-t.com

SaferPass (16, -11.1%)
Credential Security
Bratislava, Slovakia
saferpass.net

SailPoint (2464, 9.2%)
Governance
Austin, TX, US
sailpoint.com

Saporo (30, 7.1%)
Identity Management
Lausanne, Vaud, Switzerland
saporo.io

Saviynt (845, -5.0%)
Governance
El Segundo, CA, US
saviynt.com

Secfense (16, 23.1%)
Access Security
Krakow, Poland
secfense.com

Secret Double Octopus (41, -21.1%)
Authentication
Tel Aviv, Israel
doubleoctopus.com

SecSign (4, 0.0%)
Authentication
Henderson, NV, US
secsign.com

Sectona (56, 21.7%)
Access Security
Mumbai, Maharashtra, India
sectona.com

SecuGen (18, -14.3%)
Authentication
Santa Clara, CA, US
secugen.com

Securden (75, 31.6%)
Access Security
Newark, DE, US
securden.com

Secureauth Corporation (175, -8.4%)
Access Security
Irvine, CA, US
secureauth.com

SecureLink (132, -21.0%)
Access Security
Austin, TX, US
securelink.com

SecurEnds (62, -26.2%)
Governance
Atlanta, GA, US
securends.com

SecurEnvoy (24, 0.0%)
Authentication
Basingstoke, United Kingdom
securenvoy.com

SecureW2 (73, 0.0%)
Authentication
Seattle, WA, US
securew2.com

SecurLinx (9, -10.0%)
Authentication
Morgantown, WV, US
securlinx.com

SecZetta (17, -56.4%)
Fall River, MA, US
seczetta.com

Sedicii (12, -33.3%)
Authentication
Carriganore, Ireland
sedicii.com

Semperis (396, 14.4%)
Active Directory
New York, NY, US
semperis.com

Sensible Vision (4, -20.0%)
Authentication
Cape Coral, FL, US
sensiblevision.com

SensiPass (7, 0.0%)
Authentication
Dublin, Ireland
sensipass.com

SessionGuardian (14, 27.3%)
Identity Verification
New York, NY, US
sessionguardian.com

SharePass (5, 66.7%)
CIAM
Melbourne, Victoria, Australia
sharepass.com

Signicat (438, -0.5%)
Identity Verification
Rotterdam, Netherlands
signicat.nl

Silence Laboratories (24, -25.0%)
Authentication
Central Region, Singapore, Singapore
silencelaboratories.com

**Numbers in parentheses indicate headcount and % change in 2023.*

SilverLakeMasterSAM (29, -6.5%)
Access Security
Singapore, Singapore
mastersam.com

Simeio Solutions (719, 1.8%)
Atlanta, GA, US
simeiosolutions.com

SlashID (14, 0.0%)
Access Security
Chicago, IL, US
slashid.dev

Socure (440, -8.0%)
Identity Verification
New York, NY, US
socure.com

Soffid (14, 40.0%)
Authentication
Palma de Mallorca, Spain
soffid.com

Softex (22, 266.7%)
Authentication
Austin, TX, US
softexinc.com

Sonet.io (12, 33.3%)
Access Security
San Jose, CA, US
sonet.io

Sonrai Security (90, -21.1%)
Data Security
New York, NY, US
sonraisecurity.com

Specops Software Inc. (68, -17.1%)
Credential Security
Stockholm, Sweden
specopssoft.com

SpecterOps (115, 51.3%)
Alexandria, VA, US
specterops.io

SpeechPro (25, -26.5%)
Authentication
New York, NY, US
speechpro-usa.com

Spera Security (34, 0.0%)
Posture Management
Tel Aviv, Israel
spera.security

SPHERE Technology Solutions (109, 34.6%)
Access Security
Hoboken, NJ, US
sphereco.com

SplashData (10, 0.0%)
Authentication
Los Gatos, CA, US
splashdata.com

SpruceID (25, 4.2%)
Credential Security
New York, NY, US
spruceid.com

SSenStone (17, 6.2%)
Authentication
Mapo-Gu, South Korea
ssenstone.com

StickyPassword (7, 0.0%)
Brno, Czech Republic
stickypassword.com

Strata Identity (70, 6.1%)
Orchestration
Boulder, CO, US
strata.io

StrikeForce Technologies (25, 13.6%)
Authentication
Edison, NJ, US
strikeforcetech.com

Strivacity (50, 31.6%)
Customer Registration
Herndon, VA, US
strivacity.com

strongDM (108, -26.5%)
Access Security
Burlingame, CA, US
strongdm.com

Stytch (64, -19.0%)
San Francisco, CA, US
stytch.com

SurePass ID (13, 8.3%)
Authentication
Winter Garden, FL, US
surepassid.com

swIDch (9, -10.0%)
London, United Kingdom
swidch.com

SwivelSecure (39, -11.4%)
Authentication
Wetherby, United Kingdom
swivelsecure.com

Systancia (115, -3.4%)
Sausheim, France
systancia.com

Tascent (8, -61.9%)
Authentication
Los Gatos, CA, US
tascent.com

TECH5 (61, 29.8%)
Identity Management
Geneva, Switzerland
tech5.ai

Teleport (153, -27.1%)
Access Security
Oakland, CA, US
goteleport.com

TeleSign Corporation (773, 9.7%)
Identity Verification
Marina del Rey, CA, US
telesign.com

The Whisper Company (3, 0.0%)
Authentication
Austin, TX, US
thewhispercompany.com

ThisIsMe (9, -10.0%)
Onboarding
Cape Town, South Africa
thisisme.com

Token (40, 11.1%)
Authentication
Rochester, NY, US
tokenring.com

TokenOne (3, 0.0%)
Sydney, Australia
tokenone.com

Tozny (19, 18.8%)
Secure Identity
Portland, OR, US
tozny.com

Traitware (18, 5.9%)
Credential Security
Reno, NV, US
traitware.com

Tricerion (4, -20.0%)
Credential Security
Reading, United Kingdom
tricerion.com

TruGrid (6, -14.3%)
Access Security
Schaumburg, IL, US
trugrid.com

Trulioo (398, 3.1%)
Identity Verification
Vancouver, Canada
trulioo.com

Trusona (37, 0.0%)
Authentication
Scottsdale, AZ, US
trusona.com

TrustBuilder (62, 82.3%)
CIAM
Ghent, Flemish Region, Belgium
trustbuilder.com

Trustle (14, 16.7%)
Access Security
Walnut Creek, CA, US
trustle.io

TruU (69, 21.1%)
Authentication
Palo Alto, CA, US
truu.ai

Tu Identidad (20, 66.7%)
Authentication
Mexico City, Mexico
tuidentidad.com

**Numbers in parentheses indicate headcount and % change in 2023.*

Turbot (46, 2.2%)
Encryption
New York, NY, US
turbot.com

Twingate (78, 11.4%)
Access Security
Redwood City, CA, US
twingate.com

TwinSoft (33, 10.0%)
Authentication
Darmstadt, Hessen, Germany
twinsoft-biometrics.de

TwoSense (13, -13.3%)
Authentication
New York, NY, US
twosense.ai

Typing DNA (144, -11.7%)
Authentication
New York, NY, US
typingdna.com

Ubiqu (16, 23.1%)
Public Key Infrastructure
Delft, Netherlands
ubiqu.com

Ubisecure (66, 15.8%)
Espoo, Finland
ubisecure.com

unico (1031, -3.6%)
Authentication
Sao Paulo, Brazil
unico.io

UnifyID (5, -28.6%)
Authentication
Redwood City,
CA, US
unify.id

Uniken (163, 14.0%)
Authentication
Chatham Twp., NJ, US
uniken.com

Uniqkey (56, 5.7%)
Credential Security
Herlev, Hovedstaden,
Denmark
uniqkey.eu

Universign (85, -8.6%)
Authentication
Paris, France
universign.com

Usercube (17, -37.0%)
Marseille, France
usercube.com

Vault Security (3, -66.7%)
Authentication
CA, US
linktr.ee/vault_security

Vault Vision (3, 0.0%)
Denver, CO, US
vaultvision.com

Vereign (17, 13.3%)
Zug, Switzerland
vereign.com

Veridas (197, 50.4%)
Authentication
Pamplona, Navarra, Spain
veridas.com

Veridium (42, -2.3%)
Authentication
Boston, MA, US
veridiumid.com

Verif-y (29, 7.4%)
Identity Verification
Philadelphia, PA, US
verif-y.com

Verificient Technologies (215, -11.9%)
Identity Verification
New York, NY, US
verificient.com

Verifyoo (3, 0.0%)
Authentication
Tel Aviv, Israel
verifyoo.com

Verimi (107, 0.9%)
Identity Management
Berlin, Germany
verimi.de

Versasec (23, -11.5%)
Stockholm, Sweden
versasec.com

Veza Technologies (195, 77.3%)
Access Security
Palo Alto, CA, US
veza.com

Viascope (7, -36.4%)
Access Security
Seoul, South Korea
viascope.com

Vkansee (5, 0.0%)
Authentication
Beijing, China
vkansee.com

VU Security (180, -28.0%)
VPN/Proxy
Buenos Aires, Argentina
vusecurity.com

Wallix (261, 11.1%)
Access Security
Paris, France
wallix.com

Watchdata (204, 5.2%)
Public Key Infrastructure
Singapore, Singapore
watchdata.com

Whiteswan (8, 700.0%)
Access Security
Belmont, CA, US
whiteswansecurity.com

WiKID Systems (4, 0.0%)
Authentication
Atlanta, GA, US
wikidsystems.com

WWPass (19, 26.7%)
Authentication
Nashua, NH, US
wwpass.com

XignSys (18, 0.0%)
Authentication
Gelsenkirchen,
NRW, Germany
xignsys.com

Xiid (5, 25.0%)
Identity Management
Cupertino, CA, US
xiid.com

XTN Cognitive Security (25, 0.0%)
Identity Verification
Boston, MA, US
xtn-lab.com

YeshID (17, 54.5%)
Identity Management
Denver, CO, US
yeshid.com

Yubico (460, 15.3%)
Authentication
Stockholm, Sweden
yubico.com

Zafehouze (5, 150.0%)
Roskilde, Denmark
zafehouze.com

Zertid (24, 71.4%)
Melbourne, Australia
zertid.com

Zighra (11, 10.0%)
Authentication
Ottawa, Canada
zighra.com

Zignsec (26, 4.0%)
Identity Verification
Solna, Sweden
zignsec.com

ZITADEL (14, -17.6%)
Identity Management
St. Gallen, Schweiz,
Switzerland
zitadel.com

Zoloz (4, -55.6%)
Authentication
Haidian District, China
zoloz.com

Zumigo (28, 33.3%)
Identity Verification
San Jose, CA, US
zumigo.com

Zwipe (39, -26.4%)
Authentication
Oslo, Norway
zwipe.com

**Numbers in parentheses indicate headcount and % change in 2023.*

IoT Security

Acreto Cloud (20, 25.0%)
Segmentation
Jersey City, NJ, US
acreto.io

aDolas (30, 15.4%)
Assurance
Victoria, Canada
adolus.com

Afero (47, -2.1%)
Hardware
Los Altos, CA, US
afero.io

Agilicus (13, -13.3%)
Access Security
Kitchener, Canada
agilicus.com

Alias Robotics (14, 27.3%)
Anti-malware
Vitoria, Basque Country, Spain
aliasrobotics.com

Allegro Software (6, -25.0%)
Security For Embedded Systems
Boxborough, MA, US
allegrosoft.com

AlphaGuardian Networks (5, -16.7%)
OT Security
San Ramon, CA, US
alphaguardian.net

AmynaSec Labs (12, -7.7%)
Vulnerabilities
Pune, Maharashtra, India
amynasec.io

Angoka (34, 21.4%)
Automotive
Belfast, United Kingdom
angoka.io

APERIO Systems (35, 25.0%)
OT Security
Haifa, Israel
aperio-systems.com

Apolloshield (5, 0.0%)
Drones
Palo Alto, CA, US
apolloshield.com

Archon (Was Attila Security) (17, 13.3%)
Firewalls
Fulton, MD, US
attilasec.com

Argus Cyber Security (210, 11.1%)
Automotive
Tel Aviv, Israel
argus-sec.com

Armis (764, 8.2%)
Asset Management
Palo Alto, CA, US
armis.com

Asimily (66, 43.5%)
Healthcare
Sunnyvale, CA, US
asimily.com

asvin (23, 15.0%)
Device Management
Stuttgart, Germany
asvin.io

Atonomi (10, 25.0%)
Blockchain
Seattle, WA, US
atonomi.io

AUTOCRYPT (162, 55.8%)
Automotive
Seoul, South Korea
autocrypt.io

Ayyeka (34, -5.6%)
Remote Devices
Jerusalem, Israel
ayyeka.com

Bayshore Networks (14, 0.0%)
OT Security
Durham, NC, US
bayshorenetworks.com

Binare.io (8, 14.3%)
Firmware
Finland
binare.io

Bizzy Labs (8, -11.1%)
Vulnerabilities
Irving, TX, US
bizzylabs.tech

Blocmount (3, 50.0%)
OT Security
San Antonio, TX, US
blocmount.com

BugProve (12, 9.1%)
Vulnerabilities
Budapest, Hungary
bugprove.com

C2A Security (39, 18.2%)
Automotive
Jerusalem, Israel
c2a-sec.com

Ceritas (8, 0.0%)
Vulnerabilities
Cambridge, MA, US
ceritas.ai

Cervello (36, 28.6%)
Railway
Tel Aviv, Israel
cervellosec.com

Claroty (484, 16.6%)
OT Security
New York, NY, US
claroty.com

Cog (19, 5.6%)
Virtualization
Sydney, Australia
cog.systems

Critifence (4, 100.0%)
OT Security
Herzliya, Israel
critifence.com

Crypto Quantique (49, 16.7%)
Security For Embedded Systems
Egham, United Kingdom
cryptoquantique.com

Culinda (26, 13.0%)
Healthcare
Irvine, CA, US
culinda.io

CyberMDX (18, -64.7%)
Healthcare
New York, NY, US
cybermdx.com

CyberReef Solutions (21, -30.0%)
OT Security
Shreveport, LA, US
cyberreef.com

Cydome (25, 66.7%)
Maritime Security
Tel Aviv, Israel
cydome.io

Cylera (44, 22.2%)
Healthcare
New York, NY, US
cylera.com

Cylus (67, -11.8%)
Railway
Tel Aviv, Israel
cylus.com

Cymotive (197, 0.0%)
Automotive
Tel Aviv, Israel
cymotive.com

Cynalytica (6, 0.0%)
OT Security
Belfast, United Kingdom
cynalytica.com

Cynerio (66, 1.5%)
Healthcare
Ramat Gan, Israel
cynerio.co

Cyviation (18, 0.0%)
Trains, Planes, And Tanks
New York, NY, US
cyviation.aero

D-Fend Solutions (145, 2.1%)
Drones
Ra'anana, Israel
d-fendsolutions.com

Dellfer (11, -26.7%)
Automotive
Novato, CA, US
dellfer.com

**Numbers in parentheses indicate headcount and % change in 2023.*

DeviceTotal (12, -14.3%)
Vulnerabilities
Tel Aviv, Israel
devicetotal.com

Dispel (37, 5.7%)
Remote Devices
Austin, TX, US
dispel.io

Dover Microsystems (10, 11.1%)
Firmware
Waltham, MA, US
dovermicrosystems.com

Dragos (553, -4.3%)
OT Security
Hanover, MD, US
dragos.com

DroneSec (11, -8.3%)
Drones
Melbourne, Victoria, Australia
dronesec.com

Dull (11, 22.2%)
Secure Remote Access
Melbourne, Australia
dull.net

emproof (13, 18.2%)
Security For Embedded Systems
Eindhoven, Netherlands
emproof.com

Enigmatos (11, -8.3%)
Automotive
Yavne, Israel
enigmatos.com

Exein (26, 18.2%)
Rome, Italy
exein.io

Fend Incorporated (9, -10.0%)
Firewalls
Arlington, VA, US
fend.tech

Fijowave (8, -11.1%)
Remote Devices
Dublin, Ireland
fijowave.com

Finite State (58, -10.8%)
Firmware
Columbus, OH, US
finitestate.io

FireDome (27, -47.1%)
IoT Security For Device Manufacturers
Tel Aviv, Israel
firedome.io

First Watch (18, -5.3%)
OT Security
Hamilton, New Zealand
firstwatchprotect.com

Fortiphyd Logic (6, 0.0%)
OT Security
Norcross, GA, US
fortiphyd.com

Garland Technology (49, 16.7%)
Network Taps
Buffalo, NY, US
garlandtechnology.com

Genians (7, 0.0%)
Device Fingerprinting
Anyang-si, South Korea
genians.com

GuardKnox (74, -1.3%)
Automotive
Tel Aviv, Israel
guardknox.com

HENSOLDT Cyber (15, -40.0%)
Taufkirchen, Germany
hensoldt-cyber.com

ICsec (29, 0.0%)
OT Security
Poznan, Poland
icsec.pl/en/

Industrial Defender (43, -2.3%)
Foxborough, MA, US
industrialdefender.com

InfiniDome (27, 8.0%)
Automotive
Caesarea, Israel
infinidome.com

Intertrust Technologies (197, 0.5%)
Public Key Infrastructure
Sunnyvale, CA, US
intertrust.com

Ioetec (6, 0.0%)
Endpoint Protection
Sheffield, United Kingdom
ioetec.com

IoT Secure (10, 25.0%)
Asset Management
Duluth, GA, US
iotsecure.io

Irdeto (1094, 5.8%)
Entertainment Systems
Hoofddorp, Netherlands
irdeto.com

Karamba Security (44, 10.0%)
Automotive
Hod HaSharon, Israel
karambasecurity.com

MB Connect Line (20, -20.0%)
Firewalls
Germany
mbconnectline.com

Medcrypt (59, 68.6%)
Healthcare
Encinitas, CA, US
medcrypt.co

MediGate (106, -6.2%)
Healthcare
Tel Aviv, Israel
medigate.io

Mender (39, 69.6%)
Linux Devices
Palo Alto, CA, US
mender.io

MicroSec (35, -16.7%)
OT Security
Central Region, Singapore, Singapore
usec.io

Mission Secure (30, -23.1%)
OT Security
Charlottesville, VA, US
missionsecure.com

MTG AG (28, 27.3%)
OT Security
Darmstadt, Germany
mtg.de

Nanolock (43, 7.5%)
Automotive
Nitsanei Oz, Israel
nanolocksecurity.com

Naval Dome (8, -27.3%)
Security For Ships
Ra'anana, Israel
navaldome.com

Nelysis (11, 37.5%)
Monitoring
Wilmington, DE, US
nelysis.com

Norma (9, 80.0%)
Seoul, South Korea
norma.co.kr

Nova Leah (21, 0.0%)
Healthcare
Dundalk, Ireland
novaleah.com

Nozomi Networks (268, -30.2%)
OT Security
San Francisco, CA, US
nozominetworks.com

NXM Labs (17, 13.3%)
Endpoint Protection
San Francisco, CA, US
nxmlabs.com

Onclave Networks (19, -32.1%)
OT Security
North Mclean, VA, US
onclave.net

Ondeso - Industrial It Made In Germany (22, -15.4%)
OT Security
Regensburg, Germany
ondeso.com

**Numbers in parentheses indicate headcount and % change in 2023.*

Opscura (28, 12.0%)
CA, US
opscura.io

Orchestra Group (45, -16.7%)
Monitoring
Tel Aviv, Israel
orchestragroup.com

Ordr (121, 21.0%)
Device Management
Santa Clara, CA, US
ordr.net

OTORIO (94, -2.1%)
OT Security
Tel Aviv, Israel
otorio.com

Perygee (9, 28.6%)
OT Security
Boston, MA, US
perygee.com

Phosphorus (62, 10.7%)
Patch Management
Nashville, TN, US
phosphorus.io

PHYSEC (40, -13.0%)
OT Security
Bochum, Nordrhein-Westfalen, Germany
physec.de

RadiFlow (69, 40.8%)
OT Security
Tel Aviv, Israel
radiflow.com

RazorSecure (46, 9.5%)
Automotive
Basingstoke, United Kingdom
razorsecure.com

Regulus (15, 25.0%)
Automotive
Haifa, Israel
regulus.com

Rhebo (36, 0.0%)
OT Security
Leipzig, Germany
rhebo.com

Salvador Technologies (26, 36.8%)
Rehovot, Israel
salvador-tech.com

ScadaFence (56, -15.2%)
OT Security
Tel Aviv, Israel
scadafence.com

Seckiot (34, 6.2%)
Paris, France
seckiot.fr

Secomea A/S (101, 5.2%)
Remote Devices
Herlev, Denmark
secomea.com

Sectrio (39, 34.5%)
Segmentation
CO, US
sectrio.com

Secure-Nok (15, 15.4%)
OT Security
Hamar, Norway
securenok.com

SecureIC (112, 2.8%)
Hardware
France
secure-ic.com

SecureThings (26, 23.8%)
Automotive
Sunnyvale, CA, US
securethings.ai

Securithings (72, 2.9%)
Device Management
Ramat Gan, Israel
securithings.com

Sepio Systems (69, -15.8%)
Asset Management
Gaithersburg, MD, US
sepiocyber.com

ShieldIOT (17, -15.0%)
Herzliya, Israel
shieldiot.io

Shift5 (114, 28.1%)
Trains, Planes, And Tanks
Arlington, VA, US
shift5.io

Shodan (12, 50.0%)
Attack Surface Management
Austin, TX, US
beta.shodan.io

Siga OT Solutions (35, 9.4%)
Monitoring
Wilmington, DE, US
sigasec.com

Spanalytics (11, -8.3%)
Wireless Security
Glen Allen, VA, US
spanalytics.com

Sternum (38, -13.6%)
Healthcare
Tel Aviv, Israel
sternumiot.com

Surance.io (10, 25.0%)
Home Security
Ramat HaSharon, Israel
surance.io

Synsaber (8, -27.3%)
Monitoring
Chandler, AZ, US
synsaber.com

Terafence (15, -11.8%)
Gateways
Haifa, Israel
terafence.com

Thistle Technologies (6, -40.0%)
Security For Embedded Systems
San Francisco, CA, US
thistle.tech

Threatspan (4, -20.0%)
Maritime Security
Rotterdam, Netherlands
threatspan.com

Tosibox (77, 28.3%)
Remote Devices
Oulu, Finland
tosibox.com

Trapezoid (9, -30.8%)
Firmware
Miami, FL, US
trapezoid.com

Trusted Objects (13, 8.3%)
Aix-en-Provence, France
trusted-objects.com

Ubirch (28, -34.9%)
OT Security
Berlin, Germany
ubirch.de

Upstream Security (128, -3.0%)
Automotive
Herzliya, Israel
upstream.auto

V5 Systems (30, -21.1%)
OT Security
Fremont, CA, US
v5systems.us

Vdoo (15, -37.5%)
Security For Embedded Systems
Tel Aviv, Israel
vdoo.com

Veracity Industrial Networks (7, 16.7%)
OT Security
Aliso Viejo, CA, US
veracity.io

Veridify Security (20, 11.1%)
Authentication
Shelton, CT, US
veridify.com

Verve (134, 0.8%)
OT Security
Chicago, IL, US
verveindustrial.com

Viakoo (22, -4.3%)
Vulnerabilities
Mountain View, CA, US
viakoo.com

Virta Laboratories (4, 0.0%)
Healthcare
Seattle, WA, US
virtalabs.com

**Numbers in parentheses indicate headcount and % change in 2023.*

Vorpal (8, 0.0%)
Drones
Tel Aviv, Israel
vorpal-corp.com

VTS (36, 227.3%)
IDS
Auckland, New Zealand
vts.energy

Waterfall (124, 25.2%)
Firewalls
Rosh HaAyin, Israel
waterfall-security.com

Wisekey (104, -3.7%)
Hardware
Geneva, Switzerland
wisekey.com

Xage Security (102, 54.5%)
OT Security
Palo Alto, CA, US
xage.com

Zuul (11, 0.0%)
OT Security
Columbia, MD, US
zuuliot.com

Zymbit (12, 71.4%)
Device Security Modules
Santa Barbara, CA, US
zymbit.com

MSSP

11:11 Systems (794, 40.5%)
MDR
Fairfield, NJ, US
1111systems.com

2T Security (16, 33.3%)
Monitoring
Victoria, United Kingdom
2t-security.com

360 Security (23, 35.3%)
Managed Security Services
Bogota, Colombia
360sec.com

A&O IT Group (266, 3.5%)
MDR
Bracknell, Berkshire, United Kingdom
aoitgroup.com

A3Sec Grupo (119, 29.4%)
Madrid, Spain
a3sec.com

AaDya Security (31, 6.9%)
SMB Security
Plymouth, MI, US
aadyasecurity.com

Abacode (70, 18.6%)
MDR
Tampa, FL, US
abacode.com

Accenture (548423, 1.2%)
MDR
Dublin, Ireland
accenture.com

Achilleas (13, 333.3%)
MDR
Brazil
achilleas.com.br

ActZero (65, -30.1%)
MDR
Menlo Park, CA, US
actzero.ai

Acumera (201, 21.1%)
Firewalls
Austin, TX, US
acumera.net

Adarma (301, -5.3%)
MDR
Edinburgh, United Kingdom
adarma.com

Adcy.io (5, -16.7%)
Managed Security Services
Trivandrum, Kerala, India
adcy.io

ADINES MAROC (8, 0.0%)
SOC
Casablanca, Morocco
adines.ma

Adsero Security (3, 0.0%)
Managed Security Services
Tampa, FL, US
adserosecurity.com

Advanced Network Systems (22, -38.9%)
MDR
Charlottesville, VA, US
getadvanced.net

Advens (477, 32.5%)
SOC
Paris, France
advens.fr

Aegis IT Solutions (7, 16.7%)
Managed Security Services
Boca Raton, FL, US
aegisitsolutions.net

Agency (11, 37.5%)
New York, NY, US
getagency.com

AgileBlue (36, 2.9%)
Managed Security Services
Cleveland, OH, US
agileblue.com

Airiam (62, -17.3%)
MDR
Miami Beach, FL, US
airiam.com

AIUKEN CYBERSECURITY (85, 14.9%)
Managed Security Services
Madrid, Spain
aiuken.com

Allgeier IT (82, -6.8%)
Managed Security Services
Bremen, Germany
allgeier-it.de

Allurity (13, 44.4%)
SOC
Stockholm, Stockholms Lan, Sweden
allurity.com

Apollo Information Systems (63, 65.8%)
Managed Security Services
Los Gatos, CA, US
apollo-is.com

Appalachia Technologies (49, 0.0%)
Managed Security Services
Mechanicsburg, PA, US
appalachiatech.com

Applied Technology Group (6, 0.0%)
Managed Security Services
Brandon, MS, US
atgconsults.com

Arctic Wolf Networks (2251, 8.9%)
MDR
Eden Prarie, MN, US
arcticwolf.com

Armadillo Managed Services Limited (55, -6.8%)
Managed Security Services
Hayes, United Kingdom
wearearmadillo.com

Armor (151, 16.1%)
Cloud Security
Richardson, TX, US
armor.com

Ascend Technologies (246, -5.0%)
Managed Security Services
Chicago, IL, US
teamascend.com

Aspire Technology Partners (150, 5.6%)
Managed Security Services
Eatontown, NJ, US
aspiretransforms.com

Assura (46, 12.2%)
Managed Security Services
Richmond, VA, US
assurainc.com

Avalon Cyber (425, 3.7%)
Managed Security Services
Buffalo, NY, US
avaloncybersecurity.com

**Numbers in parentheses indicate headcount and % change in 2023.*

Avertium (209, -10.3%)
Managed Security Services
Phoenix, AZ, US
avertium.com

Babel (3080, 19.0%)
SOC
Madrid, Spain
babelgroup.com

BAE Systems (38342, 6.4%)
Managed Security Services
Guildford, United Kingdom
baesystems.com

Barricade IT Security (3, 200.0%)
Managed Security Services
Islip, NY, US
barricadeitsecurity.com

BDO Cyber Security (46, 27.8%)
SIEM
Hamburg, Germany
bdosecurity.de

BeyondID (191, 0.5%)
Managed Security Services
San Francisco, CA, US
beyondid.com

Binary Defense (178, 26.2%)
SOC
Stow, OH, US
binarydefense.com

BitLyft (20, 17.6%)
SIEM
Lansing, MI, US
bitlyft.com

Blackpoint (169, 83.7%)
MDR
Ellicott City, MD, US
blackpointcyber.com

Blu Sapphire (85, 97.7%)
Threat Hunting
Madhapur, India
blusapphire.com

BlueShift Cybersecurity (12, -7.7%)
MDR
Fort Myers, FL, US
blueshiftcyber.com

BlueVoyant (604, 2.5%)
MDR
New York, NY, US
bluevoyant.com

Bowline Security (11, 10.0%)
SOC
Durban, KZN, South Africa
bowlinesecurity.co.za

Bridewell (230, -0.9%)
SOC
Reading, United Kingdom
bridewell.com

British Telecom (78799, 7.3%)
Managed Security Services
London, United Kingdom
bt.com

Btech - IT Security for Credit Unions (9, 0.0%)
Managed Security Services
Pasadena, CA, US
btechonline.com

Bugsec Group (77, -6.1%)
Managed Security Services
Rishon LeZion, Israel
bugsec.com

Bulletproof (101, 13.5%)
SIEM
Stevenage, United Kingdom
bulletproof.co.uk

CACI International Inc. (19442, 7.4%)
Managed Security Services
Arlington, VA, US
caci.com

Capgemini (290105, 2.4%)
Managed Security Services
Paris, France
capgemini.com

CenturyLink (25991, -5.1%)
Monitoring
Monroe, LA, US
centurylink.com

Cerdant (26, -25.7%)
Managed Security Services
Dublin, OH, US
cerdant.com

CI Security (90, 8.4%)
MDR
Seattle, WA, US
ci.security

CIPHER Security (341, 27.7%)
Managed Security Services
Miami, FL, US
cipher.com

CipherTechs (58, -33.3%)
Managed Security Services
New York, NY, US
ciphertechs.com

Claranet Cyber Security (81, -22.1%)
London, United Kingdom
claranetcybersecurity.com

Clare Computing Solutions (51, 6.2%)
Managed Security Services
San Ramon, CA, US
clarecomputer.com

ClearDATA (186, -3.1%)
HIPAA Cloud Hosting
Austin, TX, US
cleardata.com

Clearnetwork (10, 11.1%)
SOC
Hazlet, NJ, US
clearnetwork.com

Clone Systems (16, -11.1%)
Monitoring
Philadelphia, PA, US
clone-systems.com

Cloud24X7 (25, 8.7%)
MSSP Enablement
Fort Lauderdale, FL, US
cloud24x7.us

Cloudbric Corporation (17, -32.0%)
Website Security
Seoul, South Korea
cloudbric.com

Cloudrise (56, 3.7%)
Security Platform Management
Grand Junction, CO, US
cloudrise.com

Commsec (22, -4.3%)
Managed Security Services
Dublin, Ireland
commsec.ie

Compuquip (59, 0.0%)
SOC
Miami, FL, US
compuquip.com

ControlScan (35, -14.6%)
Managed Security Services
Alpharetta, GA, US
controlscan.com

Convergent Information Security Solutions (7, 16.7%)
Managed Security Services
Columbia, SC, US
convergesecurity.com

Coro (330, 24.5%)
SMB Security
New York, NY, US
coro.net

Corsica Technologies (138, 9.5%)
Managed Security Services
Centreville, MD, US
corsicatech.com

**Numbers in parentheses indicate headcount and % change in 2023.*

Corvid Cyberdefense (24, 20.0%)
MDR
Mooresville, NC, US
corvidcyberdefense.com

Critical Start (281, 2.9%)
MDR
Plano, TX, US
criticalstart.com

CSIS Security Group (117, 11.4%)
MDR
Denmark
csisgroup.com

Cyber Defense Labs (36, -40.0%)
Managed Security Services
Dallas, TX, US
cyberdefenselabs.com

CyberConvoy (18, 0.0%)
MDR
New York, NY, US
cyberconvoy.com

CyberCX (1263, 14.4%)
Managed Security Services
Melbourne, Australia
cybercx.com.au

CyberMaxx (117, 244.1%)
Managed Security Services
Nashville, TN, US
cybermaxx.com

Cyberpoint (64, 60.0%)
SOC
Baku, Azerbaijan
cyberpoint.az

CyberProof (377, 20.1%)
Managed Security Services
Aliso Viejo, CA, US
cyberproof.com

Cybersafe Solutions (56, 1.8%)
MDR
Jericho, NY, US
cybersafesolutions.com

Cyberseer (10, 11.1%)
Threat Intelligence
London, United Kingdom
cyberseer.net

CyberShark (Was Black Stratus) (26, -7.1%)
SOC
Piscataway, NJ, US
cybersharkinc.com

Cybriant (24, 0.0%)
MDR
Alpharetta, GA, US
cybriant.com

Cyderes (715, -1.8%)
Managed Security Services
Kansas City, MO, US
cyderes.com

Cyemptive Technologies Inc. (83, 36.1%)
Managed Security Services
Snohomish, WA, US
cyemptive.com

CyFlare (42, 61.5%)
Managed Security Services
Victor, NY, US
cyflare.com

Cyphere (3, 50.0%)
Vulnerabilities
Greater Manchester, GB, United Kingdom
thecyphere.com

Cyrebro (150, -5.1%)
SOC
Tel Aviv, Israel
cyberhat.com

Cysiv (27, -63.5%)
SOC
Irving, TX, US
cysiv.com

Cyvatar.Ai (26, 13.0%)
Full Service
Irvine, CA, US
cyvatar.ai

Dacoso (139, 10.3%)
SOC
Langen, Germany
dacoso.com

DATAKOM (16, -23.8%)
Managed Security Services
Ismaning, Bayern, Germany
datakom.de

DATASHIELD (24, -17.2%)
Managed Security Services
Salt Lake City, UT, US
datashieldprotect.com

Davinsi Labs (68, 21.4%)
MDR
Antwerp, Belgium
davinsi.com

deepwatch (395, 7.9%)
MDR
Denver, CO, US
deepwatch.com

DefendEdge (124, 12.7%)
Managed Security Services
Rosemont, IL, US
defendedge.com

Delta Risk (22360, 2.0%)
MDR
San Antonio, TX, US
deltarisk.com

Difenda (77, 2.7%)
MDR
Oakville, Canada
difenda.com

Digital Hands (69, 9.5%)
Managed Security Services
Tampa, FL, US
digitalhands.com

DigitalXRAID (52, 13.0%)
Monitoring
Doncaster, South Yorkshire, United Kingdom
digitalxraid.com

DXC Technology (91269, 5.9%)
Managed Security Services
Tysons, VA, US
dxc.technology

Edgile (214, -2.7%)
Managed Security Services
Austin, TX, US
edgile.com

Ekco (311, 9.1%)
MDR
Dublin, Ireland
ek.co

ELK Analytics (18, 20.0%)
Managed Security Services
Naples, FL, US
elkanalytics.com

Ensign Infosecurity (722, 20.9%)
Managed Security Services
Kuala Lumpur, Malaysia
ensigninfosecurity.com

eSentire (577, -5.1%)
MDR
Cambridge, Canada
esentire.com

Expel (516, 1.0%)
SOC
Herndon, VA, US
expel.io

EY (345449, -1.6%)
Managed Security Services
London, United Kingdom
ey.com

Eye Security (99, 32.0%)
MDR
Zuid-Holland, Netherlands
eye.security

Falanx Cyber (48, -2.0%)
MDR
Reading, Berkshire, United Kingdom
falanxcyber.com

FCI Cyber (128, -22.4%)
Device Management
Bloomfield, NJ, US
fcicyber.com

Field Effect Software (161, 9.5%)
MDR
Ottawa, Canada
fieldeffect.com

Foresite MSP (63, -14.9%)
Managed Security Services
Overland Park, KS, US
foresite.com

Fortify 24x7 (5, -16.7%)
Managed Security Services
Los Angeles, CA, US
fortify24x7.com

**Numbers in parentheses indicate headcount and % change in 2023.*

Fortress SRM (53, 1.9%)
Managed Security Services
Cleveland, OH, US
fortresssrm.com

Fox IT (424, 11.6%)
MDR
Delft, Netherlands
fox-it.com

Fujitsu (66402, 15.8%)
Managed Security Services
Kawasaki-Shi, Japan
fujitsu.com

General Dynamics Information Technology (24128, 6.3%)
Managed Security Services
Drive Falls Church, VA, US
gdit.com

GigaNetworks (13, 8.3%)
Managed Security Services
Miami, FL, US
giganetworks.com

GM Sectec (166, 32.8%)
Managed Security Services
San Juan, Puerto Rico
gmsectec.com

GoSecure (177, -6.3%)
Managed Security Services
Montreal, Canada
gosecure.net

Greenview Data (7, 0.0%)
Managed Security Services
Ann Arbor, MI, US
greenviewdata.com

Guidepoint Security (869, 25.4%)
Managed Security Services
Herndon, VA, US
guidepointsecurity.com

HCL Technologies (254393, 15.3%)
Managed Security Services
Noida, India
hcltech.com

I-Tracing (443, 51.2%)
Managed Security Services
Puteaux, France
i-tracing.com

IBM (307605, 1.0%)
Managed Security Services
Armonk, NY, US
ibm.com

Iceberg Cyber (5, 25.0%)
Personal Protection
Toronto, ON, Canada
icebergcyber.com

ideaBOX (4, 0.0%)
New Rochelle, NY, US
ideabox.com

Infopercept (136, 46.2%)
MDR
Ahmedabad, Gujarat, India
infopercept.com

Infosys (324937, 7.1%)
Managed Security Services
Bangalore, India
infosys.com

InPhySec (42, -32.3%)
Managed Security Services
Wellington, New Zealand
inphysecsecurity.com

Inspira Enterprise (1557, 8.9%)
MDR
Mumbai, India
inspiraenterprise.com

Integrity360 (357, 89.9%)
MDR
Dublin, Ireland
integrity360.com

IntelliSystems (29, 11.5%)
Managed Security Services
Augusta, GA, US
intellisystems.com

iomart (392, 9.5%)
Managed Security Services
Glasgow, United Kingdom
iomart.com

IPV Security (19, -13.6%)
Monitoring
Ra'anana, Israel
ipvsecurity.com

Ironwood Cyber (19, -13.6%)
Scanning
Fort Worth, TX, US
ironwoodcyber.com

ITC Secure Networking (97, -14.9%)
Managed Security Services
London, United Kingdom
itcsecure.com

ITUS Security Technologies (4, 0.0%)
Managed Security Services
Letterkenny, Ireland
itus-tech.com

Kobalt (24, 60.0%)
Managed Security Services
Vancouver, Canada
kobalt.io

Konika Minolta (519, 7.2%)
Managed Security Services
Mississauga, Canada
konicaminolta.ca

KPMG (230145, -0.4%)
Managed Security Services
New York, NY, US
kpmg.com

Kroll (5960, 9.9%)
Risk Management
New York, NY, US
kroll.com

Kyber Security (16, -5.9%)
Managed Security Services
Fairfield, CT, US
kybersecure.com

LMNTRIX (47, 56.7%)
MDR
Orange, CA, US
lmntrix.com

Locknet Managed IT (53, 8.2%)
Managed Security Services
Onalaska, WI, US
locknetmanagedit.com

Loop Secure (27, -41.3%)
Managed Security Services
Melbourne, Australia
loopsec.com.au

Lumifi Cyber (69, 35.3%)
MDR
Scottsdale, AZ, US
lumificyber.com

Mako Networks Ltd. (70, 9.4%)
Managed Security Services
Elgin, IL, US
makonetworks.com

Masergy (684, 3.5%)
Managed Security Services
Plano, TX, US
masergy.com

MegaplanIT (28, -3.5%)
Managed Security Services
Scottsdale, AZ, US
megaplanit.com

Metmox (106, -22.6%)
SOC
Schaumburg, IL, US
metmox.com

Mitiga (84, 1.2%)
Incident Management
Tel Aviv, Israel
mitiga.io

MMOX (6, 0.0%)
SMB Security
The Hague, Netherlands
mmox.co

Mnemonic (383, 17.1%)
MDR
Oslo, Norway
mnemonic.no

**Numbers in parentheses indicate headcount and % change in 2023.*

Mosaic451 (25, -58.3%)
SOC
Phoenix, AZ, US
mosaic451.com

NetSecurity (82, 12.3%)
Managed Security Services
Sao Paulo, Brazil
netsecurity.com.br

Netsurion (263, -9.3%)
Managed Security Services
Houston, TX, US
netsurion.com

Netswitch Technology Management (16, 6.7%)
MDR
San Francisco, CA, US
netswitch.net

Network Box USA (9, -10.0%)
Managed Security Services
Houston, TX, US
networkboxusa.com

Networking4All (35, 2.9%)
Managed Security Services
de Meern, Utrecht, Netherlands
networking4all.com

Nixu Corporation (414, 5.3%)
Managed Security Services
Espoo, Finland
nixu.com

nostra (229, 36.3%)
Managed Security Services
Dublin, Ireland
nostra.ie

NTT Ltd. (18412, -8.1%)
Managed Security Services
London, United Kingdom
hello.global.ntt

Nuspire (183, -9.0%)
Managed Security Services
Commerce, MI, US
nuspire.com

Octiga (5, 0.0%)
Managed Security Services
Galway, Ireland
octiga.io

Omega Systems (173, 0.0%)
SIEM
Reading, PA, US
omegasystemscorp.com

On Security (3, 50.0%)
SOC
Sao Paulo, Brazil
on-security.com

ON2IT Cybersecurity (85, 4.9%)
Managed Security Services
Zaltbommel, Netherlands
on2it.net

OnePath (356, -5.3%)
Managed Security Services
Kennesaw, GA, US
1path.com

onShore Security (41, -2.4%)
Managed Security Services
Chicago, IL, US
onShore.com

Ontinue (197, 99.0%)
MDR
Redwood City, CA, US
ontinue.com

Open Systems (426, -17.6%)
Managed Security Services
Zurich, Switzerland
open-systems.com

Optiv (2381, -2.6%)
Managed Security Services
Denver, CO, US
optiv.com

Orange Cyberdefense (3449, 14.4%)
Managed Security Services
Nanterre, France
orangecyberdefense.com

Peloton Cyber Security (16, -20.0%)
SOC
Brunswick, Australia
pelotoncyber.com.au

Perch (9, -30.8%)
SOC
Tampa, FL, US
perchsecurity.com

Pipeline Security (26, -10.3%)
Chuo-ku, Tokyo, Japan
ppln.co

Presidio (3799, 3.8%)
Managed Security Services
New York, NY, US
presidio.com

Proficio (242, 22.2%)
MDR
Carlsbad, CA, US
proficio.com

PwC (277228, 6.5%)
Managed Security Services
Mclean, VA, US
pwc.com

Quadrant Information Security (41, 17.1%)
SIEM
Jacksonville, FL, US
quadrantsec.com

Quantum (11, -47.6%)
MDR
Singapore, Singapore
quantum.security

Quorum Cyber (223, 11.5%)
MDR
Edinburgh, United Kingdom
quorumcyber.com

R&K Cyber Solutions (6, 0.0%)
Managed Security Services
Manassas, VA, US
rkcybersolutions.com

Red Canary (418, -5.6%)
MDR
Denver, CO, US
redcanary.com

RedLegg (58, 18.4%)
Managed Security Services
Geneva, IL, US
redlegg.com

RedScan (87, -23.0%)
MDR
London, United Kingdom
redscan.com

RedShield Security (37, -7.5%)
Managed Security Services
Wellington, New Zealand
redshield.co

S2 Grupo (679, 13.4%)
SOC
Valencia, Spain
s2grupo.es

SCIS Security (62, -1.6%)
MDR
Houston, TX, US
scissecurity.com

Scybers (61, 29.8%)
SOC
Singapore
scybers.com

Seccom Global (46, -4.2%)
Managed Security Services
Sydney, Australia
seccomglobal.com

Secnap (18, 12.5%)
Managed Security Services
Fort Lauderdale, FL, US
secnap.com

Secon Cyber (211, 74.4%)
MDR
Surrey, United Kingdom
seconcyber.com

**Numbers in parentheses indicate headcount and % change in 2023.*

Secureme2 (17, 54.5%)
MDR
Rijen, Netherlands
secureme2.eu

SecureSky (19, 18.8%)
MDR
Omaha, NE, US
securesky.com

SecureWorks (1903, -21.8%)
Managed Security Services
Atlanta, GA, US
secureworks.com

SecurityHQ (383, 26.0%)
MDR
London, United Kingdom
securityhq.com

Sennovate (73, -16.1%)
Managed Security Services
San Ramon, CA, US
sennovate.com

Sentinel IPS (9, 0.0%)
Firewalls
Dallas, TX, US
sentinelips.com

Sentor (78, -6.0%)
SIEM
Stockholm, Sweden
sentor.se

SilverSky (417, 27.5%)
Managed Security Services
Durham, NC, US
silversky.com

Smarttech247 (190, 38.7%)
MDR
New York, NY, US
smarttech247.com

Snowbit (16, 23.1%)
MDR
Tel Aviv, Israel
snowbit.io

SOCSoter (21, 16.7%)
Managed Security Services
Hagerstown, MD, US
socsoter.com

Socura (22, 15.8%)
MDR
London, United Kingdom
socura.co.uk

Sofistic (81, -3.6%)
Castellon, Spain
sofistic.com

SolCyber (34, 0.0%)
Managed Security Services
Dallas, TX, US
solcyber.com

Solutions-II (85, 11.8%)
Monitoring
Littleton, CO, US
solutions-ii.com

Specialized Security Services Inc. (66, -20.5%)
Managed Security Services
Plano, TX, US
s3security.com

Stratejm (69, 21.1%)
SOC
Ontario, Canada
stratejm.com

suresecure (79, 16.2%)
SOC
Nordrhein-Westfalen, Germany
suresecure.de

Tamnoon (19, 137.5%)
Managed Security Services
Remote, WA, US
tamnoon.io

Tata Communications (15430, 9.9%)
Managed Security Services
Mumbai, India
tatacommunications.com

Tata Consultancy Services (583267, -8.1%)
Managed Security Services
Nariman Point, India
on.tcs.com

Telstra (35161, 5.5%)
Managed Security Services
Melbourne, Australia
telstra.com

Tesorion (122, 2.5%)
Managed Security Services
Leusden, Netherlands
tesorion.nl

Tetra Defense (46, -57.4%)
MDR
Madison, WI, US
tetradefense.com

The Cyberfort Group (107, 15.1%)
SOC
Thatcham, United Kingdom
cyberfortgroup.com

The DigiTrust Group (19, -5.0%)
Firewalls
Los Angeles, CA, US
digitrustgroup.com

Thinking Objects (59, 7.3%)
SOC
Stuttgart, Germany
to.com

Threatscape (36, 28.6%)
MDR
Dublin, Ireland
threatscape.com

ThreatSpike (20, 17.6%)
MDR
London, United Kingdom
threatspike.com

Tophat Security (4, 0.0%)
SIEM
Wilmington, DE, US
tophatsecurity.com

TripleCyber (16, 14.3%)
SOC
Tel Aviv, Israel
triplecyber.co.il

True Digital Security (10, -41.2%)
SIEM
Tulsa, OK, US
truedigitalsecurity.com

TrustWave (a Singtel Company) (1202, -7.4%)
Managed Security Services
Chicago, IL, US
trustwave.com

UltraViolet Cyber (205, 15.8%)
MDR
McLean, VA, US
uvcyber.com

UncommonX (22, 0.0%)
MDR
Chicago, IL, US
uncommonx.com

UnderDefense (104, 31.6%)
MDR
New York, NY, US
underdefense.com

Vairav Technology (94, 27.0%)
Managed Security Services
Kathmandu, Nepal
vairav.net

Vario Secure Networks (12, -14.3%)
Managed Security Services
Tokyo, Japan
variosecure.net

Verizon Business Security Solutions (17038, -14.2%)
Managed Security Services
Basking Ridge, NJ, US
verizon.com

Vijilan Security (52, -3.7%)
SIEM
Ft. Lauderdale, FL, US
vijilan.com

**Numbers in parentheses indicate headcount and % change in 2023.*

VikingCloud (574, 9.8%)
MDR
Chicago, IL, US
vikingcloud.com

Vinca Cyber (128, 10.3%)
Bangalore, India
vincacyber.com

VirtualArmour (48, 6.7%)
Managed Security Services
Centennial, CO, US
virtualarmour.com

VirusRescuers (26, -3.7%)
MDR
Dubai, United Arab Emirates
virusrescuers.com

Wipro Limited (237905, -18.9%)
Managed Security Services
Bangalore, India
wipro.com

Xantrion (84, 5.0%)
Managed Security Services
Oakland, CA, US
xantrion.com

Zyston (66, 20.0%)
Managed Security Services
Dallas, TX, US
zyston.com

Network Security

4Secure (17, 41.7%)
Firewalls
Northampton, Northamptonshire, United Kingdom
4-secure.com

6cure (16, 23.1%)
DDoS Defense
Herouville-Saint-Clair, France
6cure.com

6WIND (112, 17.9%)
VPN/Proxy
Montigny-le-Bretonneux, France
6wind.com

A10 Networks (721, -1.1%)
DDoS Defense
San Jose, CA, US
a10networks.com

Accedian (336, -11.3%)
Monitoring
Montreal, QU, Canada
accedian.com

Accolade Technology (8, 14.3%)
Network Appliance Security
Franklin, MA, US
accoladetechnology.com

Active Cypher (15, 7.1%)
DLP
Newport Beach, CA, US
activecypher.com

ADAMnetworks (5, 25.0%)
Access Security
London, Canada
adamnet.works

Adtran Inc. (2052, 26.0%)
Firewalls
Huntsville, AL, US
adtran.com

ADVA Optical Networking (2011, -10.7%)
Secure Switching
Munich, Germany
advaoptical.com

Advenica (87, 22.5%)
Air Gap
Sweden
advenica.com

Aerobyte (11, 0.0%)
Zero Trust Networking
Boca Raton, FL, US
aerobyte.com

Agat Software (32, 14.3%)
Security For Unified Comms
Jerusalem, Israel
agatsoftware.com

Aireye (27, -27.0%)
Wireless Security
Tel Aviv, Israel
AirEye.tech

Airgap Networks (45, 25.0%)
Segmentation
Santa Clara, CA, US
airgap.io

Akamai Technologies (9270, 5.7%)
DDoS Defense
Cambridge, MA, US
akamai.com

Allied Telesis (926, 5.3%)
Firewalls
San Jose, CA, US
alliedtelesis.com

Allot (955, -4.3%)
Filtering
Hod HaSharon, Israel
allot.com

Alsid (14, -30.0%)
Active Directory
Paris, France
alsid.com

Ananda Networks (4, 0.0%)
Segmentation
San Francisco, CA, US
ananda.net

AnexGATE (25, 25.0%)
UTM
Bangalore, India
anexgate.com/

Apcon (231, 5.0%)
Traffic Analysis
Wilsonville, OR, US
apcon.com

Arbit Security (12, 20.0%)
Data Diode
Hvidovre, Denmark
arbitcds.com

Arista Networks (4079, 12.5%)
NDR
Santa Clara, CA, US
arista.com

ArQit (150, -8.5%)
Quantum
London, United Kingdom
arqit.io

Array Networks (OSS Corp.) (219, 7.3%)
VPN/Proxy
Milpitas, CA, US
arraynetworks.com

Aruba Networks (5710, 3.7%)
Monitoring
Santa Clara, CA, US
arubanetworks.com

Aryaka (589, 1.2%)
SASE
San Mateo, CA, US
aryaka.com

Assured Information Security (186, 3.9%)
Dual Domain Control
Rome, NY, US
ainfosec.com

Authentic8 (134, 8.9%)
Secure Web Browsing
Redwood City, CA, US
authentic8.com

Avaya (13587, -2.8%)
VPN/Proxy
Santa Clara, CA, US
avaya.com

Avi Networks (38, -29.6%)
Firewalls
Santa Clara, CA, US
avinetworks.com

Aviatrix (390, -8.9%)
Firewalls
Palo Alto, CA, US
aviatrix.com

**Numbers in parentheses indicate headcount and % change in 2023.*

Awake Security (50, -3.9%)
Monitoring
Sunnyvale, CA, US
awakesecurity.com

AwareHQ (159, -5.9%)
Monitoring
Columbus, OH, US
awarehq.com

Baffin Bay Networking (8, -50.0%)
Threat Detection
Stockholm, Sweden
baffinbaynetworks.com

Bandura Cyber (30, 0.0%)
Firewalls
Columbia, MD, US
bandurasystems.com

Banyan Security (64, -1.5%)
Zero Trust Networking
San Francisco, CA, US
banyansecurity.io

Barracuda Networks (2146, 17.0%)
Anti-spam
Campbell, CA, US
barracuda.com

Bastille (64, 39.1%)
Wireless Security
Atlanta, GA, US
bastille.net

Bettercloud (267, -22.8%)
Monitoring
New York, NY, US
bettercloud.com

BlackDice Cyber (14, 366.7%)
Security For Gateways
Leeds, Horsforth, United Kingdom
blackdice.io

Blacksands (8, -11.1%)
Software Defined Perimeter
Ann Arbor, MI, US
blacksandsinc.com

BlastWave (19, 11.8%)
Segmentation
Mountain View, CA, US
blastwaveinc.com

Block Armour (36, 24.1%)
Zero Trust Networking
Mumbai, India
blockarmour.com

Blockdos (4, 0.0%)
DDoS Defense
Mississauga, Canada
blockdos.net

Blue Ridge Networks (36, 2.9%)
Segmentation
Chantilly, VA, US
blueridgenetworks.com

Bluecat Networks (687, 55.1%)
DNS Security
Bracknell, United Kingdom
bluecatnetworks.com

BluVector (13, 0.0%)
IDS
Arlington, VA, US
bluvector.io

Brama Systems (6, 0.0%)
Access Security
Utrecht, Netherlands
bramasystems.com

Bricata (10, -23.1%)
IPS
Columbia, MD, US
bricata.com

Broadcom (24651, 1.8%)
Hardware
San Jose, CA, US
broadcom.com

BroadForward (26, 0.0%)
Firewalls
Amersfoort, Netherlands
broadforward.com

Buoyant (25, 4.2%)
Segmentation
San Francisco, CA, US
buoyant.io

Byos (29, -6.5%)
Segmentation
Halifax, Canada
byos.io

Calyptix Security Corporation (11, 10.0%)
UTM
Charlotte, NC, US
calyptix.com

Cato Networks (813, 22.4%)
Cloud Security
Tel Aviv, Israel
catonetworks.com

CensorNet (59, -27.2%)
Filtering
Basingstoke, United Kingdom
censornet.com

Centripetal (91, 30.0%)
Firewalls
Herndon, VA, US
centripetalnetworks.com

Certes Networks (46, 4.5%)
VPN/Proxy
Pittsburgh, PA, US
certesnetworks.com

CGS Tower Networks (15, 7.1%)
Network Taps
Rosh HaAyin, Israel
cgstowernetworks.com

Check Point Software (7468, 9.2%)
UTM
Tel Aviv, Israel
checkpoint.com

Cigent (20, -9.1%)
Monitoring
Fort Myers, FL, US
cigent.com

Cisco (99793, 2.6%)
Firewalls
San Jose, CA, US
cisco.com

Citrix Systems (6105, -27.2%)
Access Security
Fort Lauderdale, FL, US
citrix.com

Clavister (120, -13.7%)
UTM
Ornskoldsvik, Sweden
clavister.com

Cloudcoffer (4, -20.0%)
UTM
Taipei, China
cloudcoffer.com

Cloudflare (4009, 18.1%)
DDoS Defense
San Francisco, CA, US
cloudflare.com

Cloudmark Inc. (68, 0.0%)
DNS Security
San Francisco, CA, US
cloudmark.com

Cohesive Networks (18, 0.0%)
Cloud Tunnels Over IPSec
Chicago, IL, US
cohesive.net

Collax Inc. (6, 20.0%)
UTM
Ismaning, Germany
collax.com

ColorTokens (270, -13.5%)
Zero Trust Networking
Santa Clara, CA, US
colortokens.com

ContentKeeper (34, -20.9%)
Filtering
Braddon, Australia
contentkeeper.com

Corelight (273, -1.8%)
Traffic Analysis
San Francisco, CA, US
corelight.com

Corero Network Security (117, 13.6%)
DDoS Defense
Marlborough, MA, US
corero.com

**Numbers in parentheses indicate headcount and % change in 2023.*

Corsa (27, 8.0%)
Zero Trust Networking
Ottawa, Canada
corsa.com

CoSoSys (156, 0.0%)
DLP
Raleigh, NC, US
endpointprotector.com

cPacket (119, -4.8%)
Traffic Analysis
San Jose, CA, US
cpacket.com

CrowdSec (40, 42.9%)
IPS
Paris, France
crowdsec.net

CSPi (125, 10.6%)
Traffic Analysis
Lowell, MA, US
cspi.com

Cubro (32, -3.0%)
Traffic Analysis
Vienna, Austria
cubro.com

Cujo AI (171, 6.9%)
Home Security
El Segundo, CA, US
getcujo.com

CYAN Network Security (4, 33.3%)
Gateways
Vienna, Austria
cyannetworks.com

CyberGhost (47, -16.1%)
VPN/Proxy
Bucharest, Romania
cyberghostvpn.com

Cyberhaven (116, 22.1%)
Monitoring
Boston, MA, US
cyberhaven.io

CyberHive (32, 3.2%)
Quantum
Newbury, United Kingdom
cyberhive.com

CyberSecure IPS (10, 25.0%)
IPS
Upper Marlboro, MD, US
cybersecureips.com

Cynamics (31, 6.9%)
Traffic Analysis
Peachtree Corners, GA, US
cynamics.ai

CySight (5, 25.0%)
Monitoring
Sydney, Australia
netflowauditor.com

Cyxtera Technologies (622, -9.7%)
Zero Trust Networking
Coral Gables, FL, US
cyxtera.com

D-Link Systems (542, 9.1%)
UTM
Taipei City, Taiwan
dlink.com

Data Resolve Technologies (80, -2.4%)
Monitoring
Noida, India
dataresolve.com

Ddos-Guard (60, -6.2%)
DDoS Defense
Rostov-na-Donu, Russia
ddos-guard.net

Dedrone (137, 45.7%)
Drones
San Francisco, CA, US
dedrone.com

Deep-Secure (23, 15.0%)
Air Gap
Malvern, United Kingdom
deep-secure.com

Deepfence (27, -3.6%)
IPS
Milpitas, CA, US
deepfence.io

Defined Networking (11, 10.0%)
Zero Trust Networking
Santa Monica, CA, US
defined.net

DH2i (12, 20.0%)
Zero Trust Networking
Fort Collins, CO, US
dh2i.com

Digital Envoy (69, 7.8%)
Reputation
Peachtree Corners, GA, US
digitalenvoy.net

Disconnect (12, -36.8%)
VPN/Proxy
San Francisco, CA, US
disconnect.me

Dispersive Networks (14, -30.0%)
VPN/Proxy
Alpharetta, GA, US
dispersive.io

Ditno (9, -25.0%)
Firewalls
Sydney, Australia
ditno.com

DNSFilter (161, 30.9%)
Filtering
Washington, DC, US
dnsfilter.com

DOSarrest (12, -7.7%)
DDoS Defense
Canada
dosarrest.com

Dream Security (67, 570.0%)
Tel Aviv, Israel
dream-security.com

DuskRise (47, -33.8%)
Segmentation
New York, NY, US
duskrise.com

Edgio (1161, -9.3%)
DDoS Defense
Scottsdale, AZ, US
edg.io

EfficientIP (231, -10.5%)
DNS Security
West Chester, PA, US
efficientip.com

Enclave Networks (9, -10.0%)
Zero Trust Networking
London, United Kingdom
enclave.io

Endace (89, 7.2%)
IDS
Ellerslie, New Zealand
endace.com

Endian (28, 0.0%)
UTM
Bolzano, Italy
endian.com

Eneo Tecnologia (9, 50.0%)
IPS
Mairena del Aljerafe, Spain
redborder.com

Equiinet (11, 10.0%)
UTM
Las Vegas, NV, US
equiinet.com

evolutionQ (32, 45.5%)
Quantum
Ontario, Canada
evolutionq.com

Exium (37, 15.6%)
SASE
Palo Alto, CA, US
exium.net

ExpressVPN (266, -7.3%)
VPN/Proxy
Tortola, British Virgin Islands
expressvpn.com

F5 Networks (6174, -3.0%)
Firewalls
Seattle, WA, US
f5.com

FACT360 (12, 9.1%)
Monitoring
Waterlooville, United Kingdom
fact360.co

**Numbers in parentheses indicate headcount and % change in 2023.*

Fastly (1279, 12.3%)
DDoS Defense
San Francisco, CA, US
fastly.com

Firewalla (18, 12.5%)
Firewalls
San Jose, CA, US
firewalla.com

Firezone (7, 40.0%)
VPN/Proxy
Mountain View, CA, US
firezone.dev

Flowmon Networks (65, -5.8%)
Monitoring
San Diego, CA, US
flowmon.com

ForeScout Technologies (1048, 3.2%)
Access Security
San Jose, CA, US
forescout.com

Fortinet (13793, 11.5%)
UTM
Sunnyvale, CA, US
fortinet.com

ForumSystems (35, 12.9%)
Firewalls
Needham, MA, US
forumsys.com

Forward Networks (150, 74.4%)
Attack Surface Management
Santa Clara, CA, US
forwardnetworks.com

FullArmor (24, 0.0%)
Policy Management
Boston, MA, US
fullarmor.com

GajShield (72, -4.0%)
Firewalls
Mumbai, India
gajshield.com

Garrison (189, 32.2%)
Secure Web Browsing
London, United Kingdom
garrison.com

GateWatcher (118, 34.1%)
Threat Detection
Paris, France
gatewatcher.com

genua (226, 14.7%)
IoT Security
Kirchheim, Germany
genua.de

Gigamon (1175, 2.7%)
Span Port Mirroring
Santa Clara, CA, US
gigamon.com

Gita Technologies (41, 5.1%)
SIGINT Offensive
Tel Aviv, Israel
gitatechnologies.com

Globalscape (59, -6.3%)
Secure Data Sharing
San Antonio, TX, US
globalscape.com

Goldilock (30, 25.0%)
Air Gap
London, United Kingdom
goldilock.com

GreyCortex (33, 22.2%)
Traffic Analysis
Brno, Czech Republic
greycortex.com

H3C (4064, -0.9%)
Gateways
Beijing, China
h3c.com

Haltdos (26, 8.3%)
DDoS Defense
Noida, India
haltdos.com

HAProxy Technologies (100, 5.3%)
Firewalls
Waltham, MA, US
haproxy.com

HDN (16, 0.0%)
Security Switches
Guro-gu, South Korea
handream.net

Heimdal Security (281, 48.7%)
IPS
Copenhagen, Denmark
heimdalsecurity.com

Hillstone Networks (388, 11.2%)
Firewalls
Santa Clara, CA, US
hillstonenet.com

HOB Networking (40, 17.6%)
VPN/Proxy
Cadolzburg, Germany
hob.de

Holm Security (62, -19.5%)
Vulnerabilities
Stockholm, Sweden
holmsecurity.com

Hopzero (9, 0.0%)
Hop Minimization
Austin, TX, US
hopzero.com

Horangi (115, -14.8%)
Vulnerabilities
Singapore, Singapore
horangi.com

Horizon3.ai (111, 3.7%)
Penetration Testing
San Francisco, CA, US
horizon3.ai

Huawei (174232, 0.5%)
Firewalls
Shenzhen, China
huawei.com

Human Presence (8, -33.3%)
Bot Security
Greenville, SC, US
humanpresence.io

iboss (307, 1.3%)
Gateways
Boston, MA, US
iboss.com

idappcom (6, 0.0%)
Traffic Analysis
Ludlow, United Kingdom
idappcom.com

Imperva (1751, 3.1%)
Firewalls
Redwood Shores, CA, US
imperva.com

Indusface (155, 0.7%)
Firewalls
Vodadora, India
indusface.com

Infiot (5, -44.4%)
Secure Remote Access
San Jose, CA, US
infiot.com

Infoblox (2186, 4.7%)
DNS Security
Santa Clara, CA, US
infoblox.com

Infodas (157, 11.3%)
Air Gap
Cologne, Germany
infodas.com

InGate (19, 0.0%)
Firewalls
Sundbyberg, Sweden
ingate.com

Inpixon (128, -39.9%)
Rogue Wifi AP Location
Palo Alto, CA, US
inpixon.com

Inseqr (12, 0.0%)
VPN/Proxy
Warszawa, Poland
inseqr.pl/en/

Insta DefSec Oy (643, -13.0%)
VPN/Proxy
Tampere, Finland
insta.fi

Instasafe (81, 11.0%)
Gateways
Bangalore, India
instasafe.com

Intego Inc. (56, 16.7%)
Firewalls
Seattle, WA, US
intego.com

**Numbers in parentheses indicate headcount and % change in 2023.*

Intelligent Waves (206, 21.2%)
Secure Web Browsing
Reston, VA, US
intelligentwaves.com

Interface Masters Technologies (60, -17.8%)
IPS
San Jose, CA, US
interfacemasters.com

Internet 2.0 (14, -17.6%)
UTM
Alexandria, VA, US
internet2-0.com

Intrusion Inc. (55, -19.1%)
IDS
Richardson, TX, US
intrusion.com

Invisiron - Cyber Defence Fortified (8, -11.1%)
Firewalls
Singapore, Singapore
invisiron.com

InvizBox (4, -33.3%)
VPN/Proxy
Dublin, Ireland
invizbox.com

IPVanish (7, -12.5%)
VPN/Proxy
Dallas, TX, US
ipvanish.com

Iris Network Systems (19, 11.8%)
Traffic Analysis
Alpharetta, GA, US
irisns.com

IronNet Cybersecurity (84, -55.8%)
Traffic Analysis
Fulton, MD, US
ironnet.com

Island (413, 163.1%)
Secure Web Browsing
Dallas, TX, US
island.io

IVPN (8, -20.0%)
VPN/Proxy
Gibraltar, United Kingdom
ivpn.net

Jimber (20, -16.7%)
Secure Web Browsing
Oostkamp, Belgium
jimber.io

Juniper Networks (11835, 5.1%)
Firewalls
Sunnyvale, CA, US
juniper.net

Keysight (was Ixia) (522, -6.6%)
Visibility
Calabasas, CA, US
keysight.com

Labris Networks (42, 75.0%)
UTM
Ankara, Turkey
labrisnetworks.com

LimaCharlie/Refraction Point (21, 40.0%)
SASE
Walnut, CA, US
limacharlie.io

Link11 (59, 31.1%)
DDoS Defense
Frankfurt, Germany
link11.de

Live Action (138, -13.8%)
NDR
Palo Alto, CA, US
liveaction.com

Macmon (53, 8.2%)
Access Security
Berlin, Germany
macmon.eu

Mammoth Cyber (31, 34.8%)
Secure Web Browsing
Palo Alto, CA, US
mammothcyber.com

Mantis Networks (6, 0.0%)
Visibility
Reston, VA, US
mantisnet.com

MDaemon Technologies (34, -2.9%)
Gateways
Grapevine, TX, US
altn.com

Menlo Security (380, -11.8%)
Secure Web Browsing
Palo Alto, CA, US
menlosecurity.com

Merox (7, -12.5%)
DNS Security
Montpellier, France
merox.io

MindoLife (8, -11.1%)
IDS
Haifa, Israel
mindolife.com

Mira Security (19, -5.0%)
Traffic Analysis
Cranberry Township, PA, US
mirasecurity.com

MobileHop (8, 33.3%)
VPN/Proxy
Los Angeles, CA, US
mobilehop.com

Mobolize (13, -13.3%)
Mobile Wireless Protection
Santa Monica, CA, US
mobolize.com

Monarx (18, 5.9%)
Webshell Detection And Blocking
Cottonwood Heights, UT, US
monarx.com

Myra Security (60, 5.3%)
Web Security
Munich, Germany
myracloud.com

Nano Corp. (20, 5.3%)
Traffic Analysis
Paris, France
nanocorp.fr

NCP Engineering (18, -5.3%)
VPN/Proxy
Mountain View, CA, US
ncp-e.com

Netdeep (6, 20.0%)
Firewalls
Brazil
netdeep.com.br

NetFlow Logic (5, -16.7%)
Traffic Analysis
Atherton, CA, US
netflowlogic.com

Netfoundry (78, 8.3%)
Zero Trust Networking
Charlotte, NC, US
NetFoundry.io

Netgate (126, 37.0%)
Austin, TX, US
netgate.com

NetLinkz (24, 100.0%)
Zero Trust Networking
Sydney, Australia
netlinkz.com

NetMotion (134, 4.7%)
SASE
Seattle, WA, US
netmotionwireless.com

Netography (47, 6.8%)
DDoS Defense
San Francisco, CA, US
netography.com

NetScout (2816, 1.9%)
Incident Management
Westford, MA, US
netscout.com

Netspark Ltd (77, 28.3%)
Filtering
New York, NY, US
netspark.com

NetSTAR (11, 10.0%)
Gateways
San Mateo, CA, US
netstar-inc.com

Netsweeper (70, 0.0%)
Filtering
Waterloo, Canada
netsweeper.com

**Numbers in parentheses indicate headcount and % change in 2023.*

Network Box Deutschland (13, 8.3%)
UTM
Nordrhein-Westfalen, Germany
network-box.eu

Network Critical (28, 27.3%)
IPS
Caversham, United Kingdom
networkcritical.com

Neustar (1449, -29.2%)
DDoS Defense
Sterling, VA, US
home.neustar

Nexcom (282, 8.1%)
Hardware
New Taipei City, Taiwan
nexcom.com

Nexusguard (136, -2.9%)
DDoS Defense
Tsuen Wan, Hong Kong
nexusguard.com

Niagra Networks (64, -8.6%)
Monitoring
San Jose, CA, US
niagaranetworks.com

NIKSUN (334, 30.5%)
NBAD
Princeton, NJ, US
niksun.com

Nominet (323, 7.7%)
Threat Detection
Oxford, United Kingdom
nominet.com

NordVPN (75, 29.3%)
VPN/Proxy
Panama City, Panama
nordvpn.com

Novetta (411, -23.0%)
Monitoring
McLean, VA, US
novetta.com

NoviFlow (50, -3.9%)
SDN
Montreal, Canada
noviflow.com

NS1 (126, -25.9%)
DNS Security
New York, NY, US
ns1.com

NSFocus (369, -47.5%)
DDoS Defense
Santa Clara, CA, US
nsfocus.com

Obsidian Security (144, 22.0%)
Cloud Security
Newport Beach, CA, US
obsidiansecurity.com

Olfeo (55, 12.2%)
Gateways
Paris, France
olfeo.com

OneLayer (30, 0.0%)
Cellular Network Security
Galicia, Spain
one-layer.com

OpenVPN (164, 9.3%)
VPN/Proxy
Pleasanton, CA, US
openvpn.net

Owl Cyber Defense (163, -11.9%)
Air Gap
Danbury, CT, US
owlcyberdefense.com

Palitronica (16, -11.1%)
IDS
Ontario, Canada
palitronica.com

Palo Alto Networks (14805, 5.8%)
UTM
Santa Clara, CA, US
paloaltonetworks.com

Penta Security (81, 0.0%)
Firewalls
Seoul, South Korea
pentasecurity.com

Perimeter 81 (206, -14.5%)
Gateways
Tel Aviv, Israel
perimeter81.com

PerimeterX (66, -37.1%)
Website Security
Tel Aviv, Israel
perimeterx.com

Personam (3, 200.0%)
Insider Threats
McLean, VA, US
PersonamInc.com

Pingsafe (69, 109.1%)
Posture Management
Bengaluru, India
pingsafe.com

Plixer (96, -6.8%)
Traffic Analysis
Kennebunk, ME, US
plixer.com

Prismo Systems (5, -72.2%)
Zero Trust Networking
San Francisco, CA, US
prismosystems.com

Profitap (35, 16.7%)
Traffic Analysis
Eindhoven, Netherlands
profitap.com

Progress (3516, 6.3%)
Secure Data Sharing
Bedford, MA, US
progress.com

Protected Media (18, 100.0%)
Advertising-related
Petah Tikva, Israel
protected.media

Proxim (130, -4.4%)
Wireless Security
San Jose, CA, US
proxim.com

Purevpn (205, 75.2%)
VPN/Proxy
Hong Kong, Hong Kong
purevpn.com

Pyramid Computer GmbH (72, 2.9%)
Firewalls
Freiburg, Germany
pyramid-computer.com

Q-Net Security (16, 0.0%)
Segmentation
St. Louis, MO, US
qnetsecurity.com

Qgroup (21, 10.5%)
Firewalls
Frankfurt am Main, Germany
qgroup.de

Qrator Labs (34, 0.0%)
DDoS Defense
Prague, Czech Republic
qrator.net

Quad Miners (25, 13.6%)
Monitoring
Seoul, South Korea
quadminers.com

Quttera (5, 0.0%)
Website Security
Herzliya Pituach, Israel
quttera.com

Radware (1472, -1.0%)
IPS
Tel Aviv, Israel
radware.com

Rampart Communications (55, 66.7%)
Wireless Security
Hanover, MD, US
rampartcommunications.com

Rawstream (3, 0.0%)
DNS Security
London, United Kingdom
rawstream.com

**Numbers in parentheses indicate headcount and % change in 2023.*

RealVNC (108, 12.5%)
Access Security
Cambridge, United Kingdom
realvnc.com

Red Access (26, 62.5%)
Secure Web Browsing
Tel Aviv, Israel
redaccess.io

Red Button (10, 25.0%)
DDoS Defense
Tel Aviv, Israel
red-button.net

Red Piranha (59, 3.5%)
UTM
Melbourne, Australia
redpiranha.net

Redborder (10, 11.1%)
IDS
Sevilla, Spain
redborder.com

RedJack (36, 33.3%)
Monitoring
Silver Spring, MD, US
redjack.com

RedShift Networks (35, -10.3%)
VoIP Security
San Ramon, CA, US
redshiftnetworks.com

Redstout (3, -50.0%)
UTM
Lisbon, Portugal
redstout.com

remote.it (16, -23.8%)
Zero Trust Networking
Palo Alto, CA, US
remote.it

Report-Uri (3, -25.0%)
Website Security
Clitheroe, United Kingdom
report-uri.com

RioRey (16, 0.0%)
DDoS Defense
Bethesda, MD, US
riorey.com

Rugged Tooling (8, 0.0%)
Monitoring
Oulu, Finland
ruggedtooling.com

runZero (57, -29.6%)
Asset Management
Austin, TX, US
runzero.com

SafeDNS (21, 31.2%)
DNS Security
Alexandria, VA, US
safedns.com

Safehouse Technologies (66, 10.0%)
VPN/Proxy
Tel Aviv, Israel
safehousetech.com

SaferVPN (3, 0.0%)
VPN/Proxy
New York, NY, US
safervpn.com

SAM Seamless Network (74, -7.5%)
Gateways
Tel Aviv, Israel
securingsam.com

Sangfor (2101, -0.5%)
UTM
Shenzhen, China
sangfor.com

ScoutDNS (3, 0.0%)
DNS Security
Grand Prairie, TX, US
scoutdns.com

Secure64 (41, 0.0%)
DNS Security
Fort Collins, CO, US
secure64.com

SecureLogix Corporation (77, 0.0%)
VoIP Security
San Antonio, TX, US
securelogix.com

Security Code (123, -3.9%)
UTM
Moscow, Russia
securitycode.ru

SecurityBox (4, -33.3%)
Gateways
Hanoi, Vietnam
securitybox.vn

SecurityGen (35, 0.0%)
Firewalls
Rome, Italy
secgen.com

Sensor Fleet (9, -10.0%)
Monitoring
Oulu, Finland
sensorfleet.com

Septier Communication (30, 3.5%)
SIGINT Offensive
Petah Tikva, Israel
septier.com

Seraphic Security (29, 31.8%)
Secure Web Browsing
Wilmington, DE, US
seraphicsecurity.com

Sharkgate (12, -20.0%)
Firewalls
London, United Kingdom
sharkgate.net

Sharktech (21, 40.0%)
DDoS Defense
Las Vegas, NV, US
sharktech.net

SideChannel (34, 3.0%)
Segmentation
Worcester, MA, US
sidechannel.com

Sitehop (13, 85.7%)
Sheffield, United Kingdom
sitehop.co.uk

SiteLock (98, -10.1%)
Website Security
Scottsdale, AZ, US
sitelock.com

Skyhigh Security (620, -2.4%)
Gateways
Santa Clara, CA, US
skyhighsecurity.com

Smoothwall (151, 11.8%)
UTM
Leeds, United Kingdom
smoothwall.com

Snowpack (16, 45.5%)
VPN/Proxy
Orsay, France
snowpack.eu

solo.io (229, 2.7%)
Segmentation
Cambridge, MA, US
solo.io

SonicWall (1944, 3.9%)
UTM
Milpitas, CA, US
sonicwall.com

Source Defense (46, -9.8%)
Client-Side Protection Against Third Party Attacks
Be'er Sheva, Israel
sourcedefense.com

SquareX (15, 1400.0%)
Secure Web Browsing
Singapore
sqrx.com

StackPath (249, -18.4%)
DDoS Defense
Dallas, TX, US
stackpath.com

Stamus Networks (24, 20.0%)
NDR
Indianapolis, IN, US
stamus-networks.com

StormShield (was NetASQ/Arcoon) (384, 4.9%)
UTM
Issy-les-Moulineaux, France
stormshield.com

**Numbers in parentheses indicate headcount and % change in 2023.*

StormWall (26, 8.3%)
DDoS Defense
Bratislava,
Slovakia
stormwall.network

SubpicoCat (5, 0.0%)
IPS
Sydney, Australia
subpicocat.com

Sucuri (51, 4.1%)
Website Security
Menifee, CA, US
sucuri.net

Sunny Valley Networks (9, -18.2%)
Firewalls
Cupertino, CA, US
sunnyvalley.io

Surf Security (36, 157.1%)
Secure Web Browsing
London, United Kingdom
surf.security/

SYlink (24, 4.3%)
UTM
Clermont-Ferrand,
France
sylink.fr

SynerComm (50, 6.4%)
Network & Security
Infrastructure
Brookdfield, WI, US
synercomm.com

Tailscale (122, 87.7%)
Zero Trust Networking
Toronto, Canada
tailscale.com

Talon Cyber Security (147, 54.7%)
Secure Web Browsing
New York, NY, US
talon-sec.com

TamosSoft (4, 0.0%)
Monitoring
Christchurch,
New Zealand
tamos.com

Tavve Software (21, 40.0%)
Packet Routing
Morrisville, NC, US
tavve.com

Tehama (29, -47.3%)
Virtualization
Ottawa, Canada
tehama.io

Telesoft Technologies (109, 34.6%)
Monitoring
Annapolis Junction, MD, US
telesoft-technologies.com

Teskalabs (18, 5.9%)
Gateways
London, United Kingdom
teskalabs.com

TheGreenBow (32, 10.3%)
VPN/Proxy
Paris, France
thegreenbow.com

Threat Stack (8, -68.0%)
Monitoring
Boston, MA, US
threatstack.com

ThreatSTOP (20, 5.3%)
Reputation
Carlsbad, CA, US
threatstop.com

ThreatWarrior (13, -23.5%)
Monitoring
Austin, TX, US
threatwarrior.com

Timus Networks (66, 106.2%)
Boston, MA, US
timusnetworks.com

TitanHQ (158, 9.0%)
DNS Security
Galway, Ireland
titanhq.com

Todyl (67, 67.5%)
Access Security
New York, NY, US
todyl.com

Topsec Network Security (152, -0.7%)
Firewalls
Haidian District,
China
topsec.com.cn

TR7 (25, 38.9%)
Firewalls
Ankara, Turkey
tr7.com

TunnelBear (14, 7.7%)
VPN/Proxy
Toronto, Canada
tunnelbear.com

Unisys Stealth (24225, 4.5%)
Cloaking
Blue Bell,
PA, US
unisys.com

United Security Providers (75, -3.9%)
Firewalls
Bern, Switzerland
united-security-providers.com

Unmukti (8, -33.3%)
Firewalls
New Delhi, India
unmukti.in

Untangle (18, -18.2%)
UTM
San Jose, CA, US
untangle.com

ValeVPN (4, 100.0%)
VPN/Proxy
Washington, DC, US
valevpn.com

Valtix (22, -42.1%)
Zero Trust Networking
Santa Clara,
CA, US
valtix.com

Vehere (155, 14.0%)
NDR
San Francisco,
CA, US
vehere.com

Venari Security (51, -3.8%)
Traffic Analysis
London, United Kingdom
venarisecurity.com

Venustech (368, -18.0%)
UTM
China
venustech.com.cn

Versa (662, 4.6%)
SDN
San Jose, CA, US
versa-networks.com

VirnetX (24, 4.3%)
Zero Trust Networking
Zephyr Cove, NV, US
virnetx.com

Votiro (57, 23.9%)
File Scrubbing
Tel Aviv, Israel
votiro.com

WatchGuard (1023, 9.1%)
UTM
Seattle, WA, US
watchguard.com

Wavecrest Computing (16, 14.3%)
Gateways
Melbourne, FL, US
wavecrest.net

WebTitan (TitanHQ) (5, -16.7%)
Filtering
Salthill, Ireland
webtitan.com

Wedge Networks (34, -5.6%)
Calgary, Canada
wedgenetworks.com

WiJungle (53, 76.7%)
UTM
Gurugram, Haryana, India
wijungle.com

WiTopia (9, 12.5%)
VPN/Proxy
Reston, VA, US
witopia.com

**Numbers in parentheses indicate headcount and % change in 2023.*

wolfSSL (41, 5.1%)
Open Source Internet Security
Edmonds, WA, US
wolfssl.com

Xaptum (4, -20.0%)
Palo Alto, CA, US
xaptum.com

XplicitTrust (6, 0.0%)
Karlsruhe, Germany
xplicittrust.com

Yoggie (8, 14.3%)
Firewalls
Beth Halevy, Israel
yoggie.com

Yottaa (103, -18.2%)
DDoS Defense
Waltham, MA, US
yottaa.com

Zentera Systems (19, -24.0%)
Zero Trust Networking
San Jose, CA, US
zentera.net

Zero Networks (54, 35.0%)
Segmentation
Tel Aviv, Israel
zeronetworks.com

ZeroTier (16, 33.3%)
Segmentation
Irvine, CA, US
zerotier.com

Zorus (25, -16.7%)
VPN/Proxy
Monroe, CT, US
zorustech.com

ZPE Systems (143, 19.2%)
Access Security
Fremont, CA, US
zpesystems.com

Zscaler (7050, 11.3%)
Cloud Security
San Jose, CA, US
zscaler.com

Zvelo (40, -4.8%)
URL Categorization
Greenwood Village, CO, US
zvelo.com

ZyXEL Communications Corp. (18, 5.9%)
Firewalls
Anaheim, CA, US
zyxel.com

Operations

Accudata Systems (98, -14.0%)
Security Management
Houston, TX, US
accudatasystems.com

Adaptive Shield (79, 19.7%)
Posture Management
Tel Aviv, Israel
adaptive-shield.com

Adaptus (11, 37.5%)
Austin, TX, US
adaptus.com

AIS (16, 33.3%)
Attack Surface Management
Saarland, Germany
ais-security.de

Algosec (504, 4.6%)
Policy Management
Petah Tikva, Israel
algosec.com

AlphaSOC (18, 80.0%)
Security Analytics
San Francisco, CA, US
alphasoc.com

AMOSSYS (66, 8.2%)
Breach And Attack Simulation
Rennes, Bretagne, France
amossys.fr

Anlyz (9, -66.7%)
SIEM
Lewes, DE, US
anlyz.co

Anvilogic (81, 15.7%)
SOC
Palo Alto, CA, US
anvilogic.com

AppOmni (208, 48.6%)
Configuration Management
San Francisco, CA, US
appomni.com

Arcanna AI (24, -4.0%)
SOC
Dover, DE, US
arcanna.ai

arctonyx (7, 0.0%)
Attack Surface Management
Baltimore, MD, US
arctonyx.com

arnica (25, -26.5%)
Software Development Security
Alpharetta, GA, US
arnica.io

AssetNote (11, 22.2%)
Monitoring
Brisbane, Queensland, Australia
assetnote.io

Atmosec (17, -32.0%)
Application Security
Tel Aviv, Israel
atmosec.com

Attack Forge (7, 0.0%)
Penetration Testing
Melbourne, Australia
attackforge.com

Avalor (74, 39.6%)
Data Management
Tel Aviv, Israel
avalor.io

Awareness Technologies (36, 5.9%)
Monitoring
Westport, CT, US
awarenesstechnologies.com

Backbox (63, 16.7%)
Orchestration
Dallas, TX, US
backbox.com

Badrap Oy (4, -33.3%)
Security Playbooks
Oulu, Finland
badrap.io

Balance Theory (16, 45.5%)
Secure Collaboration
Columbia, MD, US
balancetheory.io

Banyan Cloud (54, 25.6%)
Posture Management
San Jose, CA, US
banyancloud.io

Basis Technology (75, -44.4%)
Forensics
Cambridge, MA, US
basistech.com

Belkasoft (21, -8.7%)
Forensics
Palo Alto, CA, US
belkasoft.com

Binalyze (83, -4.6%)
Forensics
Tallinn, Harjumaa, Estonia
binalyze.com

BinaryEdge (6, 0.0%)
Scanning
Zurich, Switzerland
binaryedge.io

Bishop Fox (389, -8.2%)
Breach And Attack Simulation
Tempe, AZ, US
bishopfox.com

Bitahoy (5, -37.5%)
Saarland, Germany
bitahoy.com

**Numbers in parentheses indicate headcount and % change in 2023.*

Blacklight by Owlgaze (11, -50.0%)
Threat Hunting
London, United Kingdom
blacklight.owlgaze.com

Blink Ops (55, 17.0%)
Automation
Tel Aviv, Israel
blinkops.com

Bugcrowd (2461, 18.7%)
Bugs
San Francisco, CA, US
bugcrowd.com

Cado Security (53, 39.5%)
Incident Management
London, United Kingdom
cadosecurity.com

CardinalOps (50, 0.0%)
Automated Control Checks
Tel Aviv, Israel
cardinalops.com

Ceeyu (10, -16.7%)
Attack Surface Management
Belgium
ceeyu.io

Cenobe (12, 0.0%)
Penetration Testing
Athens, Greece
cenobe.com

CheckRed (48, 60.0%)
Posture Management
Frisco, TX, US
checkred.com

Chorus Intel (38, -13.6%)
Link Analysis
Woodbridge, United Kingdom
chorusintel.com

Cloud Storage Security (17, 70.0%)
Anti-virus
Rochester, NY, US
cloudstoragesec.com

Cloudanix (10, 0.0%)
Posture Management
Pune, India
cloudanix.com

Cloudera (2987, -9.7%)
Cloud Security
Palo Alto, CA, US
cloudera.com

Cloudnosys (13, 0.0%)
Posture Management
Roswell, GA, US
cloudnosys.com

CloudWize (9, 28.6%)
Cloud Security
Netanya, Israel
cloudwize.io

Code 42 Software (294, -32.4%)
Secure Backup/Recovery
Minneapolis, MN, US
code42.com

Communication Devices Inc (10, 25.0%)
Remote Devices
Boonton, NJ, US
commdevices.com

CommVault (3022, 3.9%)
Secure Backup/Recovery
Tinton Falls, NJ, US
commvault.com

Coralogix (295, 30.5%)
OP - Configuration Management
San Francisco, CA, US
coralogix.com

CovertSwarm (32, 88.2%)
Breach And Attack Simulation
London, United Kingdom
covertswarm.com

Cribl (671, 37.8%)
Data Process Flow
San Francisco, CA, US
cribl.io

CuriX AG (16, 45.5%)
Monitoring
Baar, Switzerland
curix.ai

CybelAngel (156, -17.9%)
Attack Surface Management
Paris, France
cybelangel.com

Cyber Operations LLC (5, -28.6%)
Access Security
Pelham, AL, US
cyberoperations.com

Cyberstanc (9, -35.7%)
Delaware, OH, US
cyberstanc.com

Cybral (24, 33.3%)
Breach And Attack Simulation
Miami, FL, US
cybral.com

CybrHawk (11, -8.3%)
Data Management
Fort Lauderdale, FL, US
cybrhawk.com

Cyclops (25, 38.9%)
Data Management
Tel Aviv, Israel
cyclops.security

Cycraft (81, 44.6%)
Incident Management
Taipei City, Banqiao District, Taiwan
cycraft.com

Cydarm (18, -21.7%)
Incident Management
Docklands, Australia
cydarm.com

CYE (185, 2.2%)
Breach And Attack Simulation
Herzliya, Israel
cyesec.com

CYGNVS (103, 56.1%)
Crisis Response Platform
Los Altos, CA, US
cygnvs.com

Cymulate (237, 2.2%)
Breach And Attack Simulation
Holon, Israel
cymulate.com

CYNC (14, 0.0%)
Vulnerabilities
Tel Aviv, Israel
cyncsecure.com

Cynergy (11, 10.0%)
Monitoring
Tel Aviv, Israel
cynergy.app

Cynet (257, -8.2%)
APT Discovery
Rishon LeZion, Israel
cynet.com

Cyscale (16, -20.0%)
Posture Management
London, United Kingdom
cyscale.com

Cytix (8, 166.7%)
Penetration Testing
Manchester, United Kingdom
cytix.io

CyTwist (19, 35.7%)
Threat Hunting
Ramat Gan, Israel
cytwist.com

D3 Security (171, 17.9%)
Incident Management
Vancouver, Canada
d3security.com

Datatron (8, -42.9%)
AI Operations
San Francisco, CA, US
datatron.com

**Numbers in parentheses indicate headcount and % change in 2023.*

Dazz (107, 40.8%)
Vulnerabilities
Palo Alto, CA, US
dazz.io

Deepinfo (24, 9.1%)
Attack Surface Management
Istanbul, Turkey
deepinfo.com

Defence Intelligence (20, -48.7%)
Anti-malware
Kanata, Canada
defintel.com

Defentry (17, -15.0%)
Scanning
Stockholm, Sweden
defentry.com

Detexian (11, 10.0%)
Monitoring
Docklands, Australia
detexian.com

Devicie (22, 46.7%)
Sydney, Australia
devicie.com

DevOcean Security (22, 15.8%)
Tel Aviv, Israel
devocean.security

DisruptOps (6, -25.0%)
Cloud Security
Kansas City, MO, US
disruptops.com

DNIF (65, -1.5%)
SIEM
Mumbai, India
dnif.it

Elcomsoft (15, 0.0%)
Forensics
Moscow, Russia
elcomsoft.com

Elysium Analytics (27, 12.5%)
Security Analytics
Santa Clara, CA, US
elysiumanalytics.ai

Encore (10, 0.0%)
Attack Surface Management
Maidenhead, United Kingdom
encore.io

ESProfiler (7, 133.3%)
Security Tool Effectiveness Platform
Manchester, United Kingdom
esprofiler.com

Faddom (37, -22.9%)
Segmentation
Ramat Gan, Israel
faddom.com

Faraday (47, 14.6%)
Manager Of Managers
Miami, FL, US
faradaysec.com

FireCompass (81, 8.0%)
Attack Surface Management
Boston, MA, US
firecompass.com

Firefly (46, 43.8%)
Asset Management
Tel Aviv, Israel
gofirefly.io

FireMon (235, -8.2%)
Policy Management
Overland Park, KS, US
firemon.com

FirstWave (55, 5.8%)
SOC
North Sydney, New South Wales, Australia
firstwave.com

Flare (59, 3.5%)
Attack Surface Management
Montreal, QU, Canada
flare.systems

Fletch.AI (69, 187.5%)
SOC
San Francisco, CA, US
fletch.ai

Flexible IR (6, 0.0%)
Incident Management
Singapore, Singapore
flexibleir.com

FourCore (9, 28.6%)
Breach And Attack Simulation
New Delhi, Delhi, India
fourcore.io

Gem (65, 225.0%)
Incident Management
New York, NY, US
gem.security

Glasswall Solutions (129, 30.3%)
Document Security
West End, United Kingdom
glasswallsolutions.com

GLIMPSE (50, 47.1%)
Malware Analysis
Cesson-Sevigne, France
glimps.fr

Gomboc (12, 50.0%)
Configuration Management
New York, NY, US
gomboc.ai

Graylog (108, -4.4%)
Logs
Houston, TX, US
graylog.org

Gutsy (35, 29.6%)
Tel Aviv, Israel
gutsy.com

HackerOne (4418, 21.4%)
Research
San Francisco, CA, US
hackerone.com

Hadrian (79, 31.7%)
Attack Surface Management
Noord-Holland, Netherlands
hadrian.io

HALOCK Security Labs (33, 10.0%)
Incident Management
Schaumburg, IL, US
halock.com

Hoplite Industries (15, 7.1%)
Security Alerts
Bozeman, MT, US
hopliteindustries.com

Hopr (8, 0.0%)
Key Rotation
Columbia, MD, US
hopr.co

Hubble Technology (19, 5.6%)
Asset Management
Reston, VA, US
hubble.net

Huntress Labs (335, 19.6%)
Anti-malware
Baltimore, MD, US
huntresslabs.com

incident.io (84, 100.0%)
Slack Automation
London, United Kingdom
incident.io

InCyber (3, 0.0%)
Monitoring
Cherry Hill Township, DE, US
incyber1.com

Indeni (28, -22.2%)
Automation
San Francisco, CA, US
indeni.com

Innefu Labs Pvt Ltd. (190, 31.9%)
Security Analytics
New Delhi, India
innefu.com

**Numbers in parentheses indicate headcount and % change in 2023.*

Interguard (6, 0.0%)
Monitoring
Westport, CT, US
interguardsoftware.com

Interpres Security (26, 136.4%)
Attack Surface Management
Bethesda, MD, US
interpressecurity.com

Intezer (42, -6.7%)
Runtime Security
New York, NY, US
intezer.com

Jemurai (8, 0.0%)
Security Program Dashboard
Chicago, IL, US
jemurai.com

JetPatch (14, -17.6%)
Patch Management
Boston, MA, US
jetpatch.com

Jetstack (36, -32.1%)
United Kingdom
jetstack.io

JOESecurity (8, 14.3%)
Malware Analysis
Reinach, Switzerland
joesecurity.org

JupiterOne (141, -25.8%)
Posture Management
Morrisville, NC, US
jupiterone.com

kloudle (11, -21.4%)
OP - Configuration Management
Wilmington, DE, US
kloudle.com

Lansweeper (323, 19.6%)
Asset Management
Dendermonde, Belgium
lansweeper.com

LogicHub (17, -55.3%)
Incident Management
Mountain View, CA, US
logichub.com

Lucidum (20, 11.1%)
Asset Management
San Jose, CA, US
lucidum.io

Magnet Forensics (566, 23.6%)
Forensics
Waterloo, Canada
magnetforensics.com

Maltego Technologies (130, 32.6%)
Maltego Enhancement
Munich, Germany
maltego.com

Mattermost (158, -31.0%)
Incident Management
Palo Alto, CA, US
mattermost.com

Mesh Security (15, 25.0%)
Posture Management
Tel Aviv, Israel
mesh.security

Microsec.AI (35, -18.6%)
Posture Management
Santa Clara, CA, US
microsec.ai

Mindflow (33, 83.3%)
SOAR
Paris, France
mindflow.io

Mitigant (14, 55.6%)
Posture Management
Potsdam, Germany
mitigant.io

MixMode (81, 47.3%)
Forensics
San Diego, CA, US
mixmode.ai

Muninn (39, 56.0%)
Monitoring
Kongens Lyngby, Denmark
muninn.ai

Napatech (94, -3.1%)
Network Acceleration Cards
Soeborg, Denmark
napatech.com

Netenrich (885, 3.1%)
Logs
San Jose, CA, US
netenrich.com

NetWitness (196, 56.8%)
XDR
Bedford, MA, US
netwitness.com

Network Intelligence (668, 12.3%)
Policy Management
Mumbai, India
niiconsulting.com

New Net Technologies (28, 21.7%)
Workflow Automation
Naples, FL, US
newnettechnologies.com

NTrepid (179, -6.3%)
Forensics
Herndon, VA, US
ntrepidcorp.com

Onpage (31, 0.0%)
Security Alerts
Waltham, MA, US
OnPage.com

Onyxia Cyber (21, 40.0%)
New York, NY, US
onyxia.io

OpsCompass (24, 14.3%)
Posture Management
Omaha, NE, US
opscompass.com

OpsHelm (12, 50.0%)
Configuration Management
Seattle, WA, US
opshelm.com

Opus Security (31, 24.0%)
Cloud Security
Tel Aviv, Israel
opus.security

Orca Security (506, 14.7%)
Vulnerabilities
Tel Aviv, Israel
orca.security

Ovalsec (10, -9.1%)
Attack Surface Management
Tel Aviv, Israel
ovalsec.com

OverSOC (26, 44.4%)
Attack Surface Management
Lille, France
oversoc.com

Panaseer (135, -2.9%)
Security Management
London, United Kingdom
panaseer.com

Pangea (56, 80.7%)
Security APIs
Palo Alto, CA, US
pangea.cloud

Passware (25, 8.7%)
Red Team Tools
Mountain View, CA, US
passware.com

Patrowl (20, 11.1%)
Attack Surface Management
Paris, France
patrowl.io

Pentera (was Pcysys) (374, 25.5%)
Penetration Testing
Petah Tikva, Israel
pcysys.com

Permiso Security (33, 17.9%)
Vulnerabilities
Palo Alto, CA, US
permiso.io

Picus Security (234, 8.3%)
Breach And Attack Simulation
Ankara, Turkey
picussecurity.com

**Numbers in parentheses indicate headcount and % change in 2023.*

Pikered (6, 0.0%)
Breach And Attack Simulation
Milan, Italy
pikered.com

Pinochle.AI (15, -40.0%)
XDR
Vernon Hills, IL, US
pinochle.ai

Polarity (34, -15.0%)
Onscreen Data Augmentation
Farmington, CT, US
polarity.io

Praetorian (141, 6.0%)
Secure Remote Access
Austin, TX, US
praetorian.com

Prancer (27, 50.0%)
Vulnerabilities
San Diego, CA, US
prancer.io

Prevasio (5, 0.0%)
Container Security
Sydney, Australia
prevasio.com

Prophecy International (78, 14.7%)
Logs
Adelaide, Australia
prophecyinternational.com

Push Security (26, 52.9%)
Application Security
London, United Kingdom
pushsecurity.com

Qingteng (101, -1.9%)
Asset Management
Beijing, China
qingteng.cn

Query.Ai (42, 2.4%)
Search
Brookings, SD, US
query.ai

R-Vision (114, 2.7%)
Incident Management
Moscow, Russia
rvision.pro

Radarfirst (63, -14.9%)
Incident Management
Portland, OR, US
radarfirst.com

Radiant Security (41, 78.3%)
SOC
San Francisco, CA, US
radiantsecurity.ai

Reach Security (11, 0.0%)
San Francisco, CA, US
reach.security

Reliaquest (1002, 5.1%)
Threat Hunting
Tampa, FL, US
reliaquest.com

Remy Security (4, -33.3%)
San Francisco, CA, US
remysec.com

Reposify (13, -23.5%)
Asset Management
Bnei Brak, Israel
reposify.com

Resmo (17, 6.2%)
Wilmington, DE, US
resmo.com

Resolve (127, -19.6%)
Orchestration
Campbell, CA, US
resolve.io

Resourcely (28, 12.0%)
Technology Deployment Management
San Francisco, CA, US
resourcely.io

Revelstoke (9, -82.7%)
Orchestration
San Jose, CA, US
revelstoke.io

Reversing Labs (298, 13.3%)
Malware Analysis
Cambridge, MA, US
reversinglabs.com

River Security (26, 62.5%)
Attack Surface Management
Oslo, Norway
riversecurity.eu

Rocketcyber (22, 4.8%)
SOC
Dallas, TX, US
rocketcyber.com

Room 40 Labs (27, 145.4%)
Bethesda, MD, US
room40labs.com

Rootly (35, -7.9%)
Incident Management
San Francisco, CA, US
rootly.com

Rthreat (23, -14.8%)
Breach And Attack Simulation
Bellingham, WA, US
rthreat.net

Rudder (46, 228.6%)
Configuration Management
Paris, France
rudder.io

Runecast Solutions (68, -8.1%)
Vulnerabilities
London, United Kingdom
runecast.com

SaaS Alerts (35, 20.7%)
Monitoring
Wilmington, NC, US
saasalerts.com

SafeBreach (134, -20.2%)
Breach And Attack Simulation
Tel Aviv, Israel
safebreach.com

Salem Security (8, 0.0%)
Winston-Salem, NC, US
salemcyber.com

SaltyCloud (10, -9.1%)
Workflow Automation
Austin, TX, US
saltycloud.com

Savvy (50, -2.0%)
SaaS Security
Tel Aviv District, Israel
savvy.security

SearchInform (110, 12.2%)
Monitoring
Moscow, Russia
searchinform.com

SecuLetter (16, 0.0%)
Malware Analysis
Seongnam-si, South Korea
seculetter.com

SecurityTrails (17, -39.3%)
Asset Inventory
Los Angeles, CA, US
securitytrails.com

SeeMetrics (23, 21.1%)
Monitoring
Tel Aviv, Israel
seemetrics.co

Seemplicity (67, 48.9%)
Tel Aviv, Israel
seemplicity.io

Senser (16, -5.9%)
Workload Security
Ramat Gan, India
senser.tech

ServiceNow (24941, 14.4%)
Orchestration
Santa Clara, CA, US
servicenow.com

Seworks (28, 133.3%)
Penetration Testing
San Francisco, CA, US
se.works

Silicon Forensics (11, 22.2%)
Forensics
Pomona, CA, US
siliconforensics.com

**Numbers in parentheses indicate headcount and % change in 2023.*

SIRP (21, 31.2%)
London, United Kingdom
sirp.io

SixMap (26, 420.0%)
Attack Surface Management
San Francisco, CA, US
sixmap.io

Skybox Security (300, -7.4%)
Security Management
San Jose, CA, US
skyboxsecurity.com

Skyhawk Security (34, 25.9%)
Breach Detection
Tel Aviv, Israel
skyhawk.security

SnapAttack (26, 0.0%)
Threat Hunting
Columbia, MD, US
snapattack.com

SOCAutomation (6, 50.0%)
XDR
Witney, United Kingdom
socautomation.com

Social Links (96, 100.0%)
OSINT
New York, NY, US
sociallinks.io

SolSoft (24, 4.3%)
Policy Management
Bristol, United Kingdom
solsoft.co.uk

Solvo (30, 25.0%)
Configuration Management
Tel Aviv, Israel
solvo.cloud

Spyderbat (26, 8.3%)
Runtime Security
Austin, TX, US
spyderbat.com

Stack Identity (33, 57.1%)
Access Security
Los Gatos, CA, US
stackidentity.com

StrikeReady (35, -2.8%)
SOC
Fremont, CA, US
strikeready.co

Swimlane (238, 30.1%)
Incident Management
Louisville, CO, US
swimlane.com

Sym (36, 63.6%)
Workflow Automation
San Francisco, CA, US
symops.com

Syxsense (81, 15.7%)
Vulnerabilities
Aliso Viejo, CA, US
syxsense.com

Tauruseer (23, 155.6%)
Code Security
Jacksonville Beach, FL, US
tauruseer.com

Tenacity (7, -46.1%)
Posture Management
Ann Arbor, MI, US
tenacitycloud.com

Tenzir (16, 23.1%)
Data Management
Hamburg, Germany
tenzir.com

Teramind (104, 50.7%)
Monitoring
Aventura, FL, US
teramind.co

Tetrate (126, -2.3%)
Posture Management
Milpitas, CA, US
tetrate.io

Theta (282, 10.2%)
Attack Surface Management
Auckland, New Zealand
theta.co.nz

ThreatAware (19, 0.0%)
Asset Management
London, United Kingdom
threataware.com

ThreatMate (8, 700.0%)
Dover, DE, US
threatmate.com

ThreatOptix (12, 33.3%)
XDR
San Francisco, CA, US
threatoptix.ai

Tines (249, 40.7%)
Orchestration
Dublin, Ireland
tines.com

ToothPic (11, 10.0%)
Forensics
Turin, Italy
toothpic.eu

Torq (126, 0.8%)
Automation
Portland, OR, US
torq.io

TriagingX (9, -10.0%)
Sandbox
San Jose, CA, US
triagingx.com

Trickest (15, 15.4%)
Penetration Testing
Dover, DE, US
trickest.com

Tufin (462, -12.3%)
Policy Management
Boston, MA, US
tufin.com

ULTRA RED (22, 0.0%)
Breach And Attack Simulation
Tel Aviv, Israel
ultrared.ai

Uno (14, 16.7%)
Threat Analysis
Palo Alto, CA, US
uno.ai

Unxpose (8, -20.0%)
Attack Surface Management
Sao Paulo, Brazil
unxpose.com

Upwind (72, 53.2%)
CA, US
upwind.io

VantagePoint (53, 1.9%)
Wesley Chapel, FL, US
thevantagepoint.com

Veriato (22, -4.3%)
Monitoring
Palm Beach Gardens, FL, US
veriato.com

Veriti (39, 129.4%)
Posture Management
Tel Aviv, Israel
veriti.ai

Vonahi Security (16, -11.1%)
Penetration Testing
Atlanta, GA, US
vonahi.io

watchTowr (21, 5.0%)
Attack Surface Management
Central Region, Singapore, Singapore
watchtowr.com

Wazuh (197, 26.3%)
SOC
San Jose, CA, US
wazuh.com

Whistic (84, -34.9%)
Vendor Management
Pleasant Grove, UT, US
whistic.com

WireX Systems (21, 16.7%)
Forensics
Sunnyvale, CA, US
wirexsystems.com

WitFoo (11, -21.4%)
Security Operations Platform
Dunwoody, GA, US
witfoo.com

Workspot (158, -6.0%)
Secure Remote Access
Campbell, CA, US
workspot.com

**Numbers in parentheses indicate headcount and % change in 2023.*

XM Cyber (297, 63.2%)
Breach And Attack Simulation
Herzliya, Israel
xmcyber.com

YesWeHack (237, 37.8%)
Bugs
Paris, France
yeswehack.com

Yogosha (189, 41.0%)
Bugs
Paris, France
yogosha.com

ZecOps (16, -30.4%)
Automated Defense
San Francisco, CA, US
zecops.com

Zluri (239, 151.6%)
Asset Management
San Francisco, CA, US
zluri.com

Security Analytics

Active Countermeasures (10, 25.0%)
Threat Hunting
Spearfish, SD, US
activecountermeasures.com

Adlumin (119, 35.2%)
SIEM
Washington, DC, US
adlumin.com

Airtrack (3, -72.7%)
Configuration Management
Melbourne, Victoria, Australia
airtrack.io

Alert Logic (319, -30.4%)
Logs
Houston, TX, US
alertlogic.com

AnChain.ai (36, -5.3%)
Forensics
San Jose, CA, US
anchain.ai

Arc4dia (3, -25.0%)
Incident Management
Montreal, Canada
arc4dia.com

Assuria (19, 0.0%)
SIEM
Reading, United Kingdom
assuria.com

AT&T Cybersecurity (62, -10.1%)
SIEM
San Mateo, CA, US
cybersecurity.att.com

Ava Security (81, -24.3%)
Monitoring
Uxbridge, United Kingdom
avasecurity.com

BitGlass (36, -36.8%)
Incident Management
Campbell, CA, US
bitglass.com

Blumira (63, 21.1%)
SIEM
Ann Arbor, MI, US
blumira.com

BMC Software (9786, 1.8%)
SIEM
Houston, TX, US
bmc.com

BreachQuest (9, -35.7%)
Incident Management
Dallas, TX, US
breachquest.com

Cambridge Intelligence (72, -1.4%)
Data Visualization
Cambridge, United Kingdom
cambridge-intelligence.com

Chronicle (part of Google) (45, 80.0%)
SIEM
Mountain View, CA, US
chronicle.security

Cienaga Systems (5, 25.0%)
Cyber Threat Management
Lakewood Ranch, FL, US
cienagasystems.net

Confluera (7, -46.1%)
Incident Management
Palo Alto, CA, US
confluera.com

ContraForce (21, 0.0%)
XDR
Dallas, TX, US
contraforce.com

CY4GATE (132, 5.6%)
SIEM
Rome, Italy
cy4gate.com

Cyber adAPT (23, 0.0%)
Monitoring
Dallas, TX, US
cyberadapt.com

Cyber Crucible (12, -20.0%)
Incident Management
Severna Park, MD, US
cybercrucible.com

Cybereason (814, -17.4%)
Incident Management
Boston, MA, US
cybereason.com

Cybraics (11, -50.0%)
Atlanta, GA, US
cybraics.com

Cycurity (8, -33.3%)
Tel Aviv, Israel
cycurity.com

CYFOX (31, 0.0%)
XDR
Tel Aviv, Israel
cyfox.com

CyGlass (12, -47.8%)
Littleton, MA, US
cyglass.com

Cymatic (5, -37.5%)
Monitoring
Raleigh, NC, US
cymatic.io

Dark Cubed (10, -58.3%)
Monitoring
Charlottesville, VA, US
darkcubed.com

DarkLight.ai (19, -20.8%)
Bellevue, WA, US
darklight.ai

Darktrace (2529, 6.4%)
Incident Management
San Francisco, CA, US
darktrace.com

DeUmbra (4, 0.0%)
Visualization
Austin, TX, US
deumbra.com

Devo (675, 4.7%)
SIEM
Cambridge, MA, US
devo.com

DTonomy (8, 100.0%)
AI Applied To Alerts
Cambridge, MA, US
dtonomy.com

Elastic (3751, 8.4%)
SIEM
Amsterdam, Netherlands
elastic.co

Elephantastic (6, 200.0%)
Link Analysis
Paris, France
elephantastic.io

Encode (61, -24.7%)
London, United Kingdom
encodegroup.com

EventSentry (4, 0.0%)
SIEM
Chicago, IL, US
eventsentry.com

Exabeam (760, 5.0%)
Monitoring
San Mateo, CA, US
exabeam.com

**Numbers in parentheses indicate headcount and % change in 2023.*

Exeon Analytics (37, 42.3%)
Monitoring
Zurich, Switzerland
exeon.ch

ExtraHop Networks (671, 0.6%)
Incident Management
Seattle, WA, US
extrahop.com

Fidelis Cybersecurity (Skyview) (150, -23.9%)
Bethesda, MD, US
fidelissecurity.com

Fluency Security (7, 0.0%)
SIEM
College Park, MD, US
fluencysecurity.com

Gravwell (16, 14.3%)
Data Analysis
Coeur dAlene, ID, US
gravwell.io

GuruCul (200, 25.0%)
El Segundo, CA, US
gurucul.com

Hawk Network Defense (3, -25.0%)
Dallas, TX, US
hawkdefense.com

Haystax (42, 27.3%)
Threat Analysis
McLean, VA, US
haystax.com

Humio (40, -37.5%)
Logs
London, United Kingdom
humio.com

Hunters (216, 42.1%)
Incident Management
Tel Aviv, Israel
hunters.ai

Huntsman (22, 10.0%)
SIEM
Chatswood, Australia
huntsmansecurity.com

LogPoint (290, -6.2%)
SIEM
Copenhagen, Denmark
logpoint.com

LogRhythm (544, -11.4%)
Logs
Boulder, CO, US
logrhythm.com

Logsign (65, -13.3%)
SIEM
Istanbul, Turkey
logsign.com

Logstail (3, 0.0%)
Logs
Athens, Greece
logstail.com

Logz.io (184, -17.1%)
Logs
Boston, MA, US
logz.io

Lumu Technologies (121, 12.0%)
Incident Management
Doral, FL, US
lumu.io

Mandiant (1394, 4.2%)
XDR
Milpitas, CA, US
mandiant.com

Mantix4 (4, 0.0%)
Threat Hunting
Englewood, CO, US
mantix4.com

Mezmo (115, -25.8%)
Logs
Mountain View, CA, US
mezmo.com

Micro Focus (5742, -40.3%)
SIEM
Newbury, United Kingdom
microfocus.com

NexusFlow AI (6, 50.0%)
AI Security
Palo Alto, CA, US
nexusflow.ai

Nuix (436, 1.4%)
Investigation
Sydney, Australia
nuix.com

Palantir Technologies (4031, 0.1%)
Link Analysis
Palo Alto, CA, US
palantir.com

Panther (245, 17.2%)
SIEM
San Francisco, CA, US
runpanther.io

Penfield.ai (7, -22.2%)
Threat Analysis
Toronto, Canada
penfield.ai

Qomplx (92, 31.4%)
Incident Management
Reston, VA, US
qomplx.com

Sapien Cyber (10, -56.5%)
Incident Management
Joondalup, Australia
sapiencyber.com.au

Seceon (121, 9.0%)
SIEM
Westford, MA, US
seceon.com

Seclytics (15, 0.0%)
Threat Intelligence
San Diego, CA, US
seclytics.com

SECNOLOGY (14, -6.7%)
Big Data
El Granada, CA, US
secnology.com

Secure Decisions (4, 0.0%)
Visualization
Northport, NY, US
securedecisions.com

Securonix (750, -20.6%)
Monitoring
Addison, TX, US
securonix.com

SEKOIA.IO (115, 30.7%)
SIEM
Paris, France
sekoia.io

Senseon (83, -1.2%)
Incident Management
London, United Kingdom
senseon.io

SIEMonster (14, 75.0%)
New York, NY, US
siemonster.com

Siren (84, 29.2%)
Data Analysis
Galway, Ireland
siren.io

Skout Cybersecurity (20, -20.0%)
Data Analysis
New York, NY, US
getskout.com

Solarwinds (2540, 0.2%)
SIEM
Austin, TX, US
solarwinds.com

Somma (8, -27.3%)
XDR
Seongnam-si, South Korea
somma.kr

Splunk (8893, 1.9%)
SIEM
San Francisco, CA, US
splunk.com

SS8 (124, 6.9%)
Milpitas, CA, US
ss8.com

Stairwell (65, 6.6%)
Graph Search
Palo Alto, CA, US
stairwell.com

Stealthbits (61, -25.6%)
Threat Prevention
Hawthorne, NJ, US
stealthbits.com

**Numbers in parentheses indicate headcount and % change in 2023.*

Stellar Cyber (120, 29.0%)
Threat Detection
Santa Clara, CA, US
stellarcyber.ai

Sumo Logic (914, -15.2%)
SIEM
Redwood City, CA, US
sumologic.com

TEHTRIS (271, 21.0%)
XDR
Paris, France
tehtris.com

Telemate Software (23, 15.0%)
SIEM
Norcross, GA, US
telemate.net

ThetaRay (160, 26.0%)
Hod HaSharon, Israel
thetaray.com

Trellix (3353, 8.7%)
XDR
Milpitas, CA, US
trellix.com

Trovares (11, 57.1%)
Graph Analytics
Seattle, WA, US
trovares.com

Uptycs (344, 18.6%)
OSQuery
Waltham, MA, US
uptycs.com

Vectra AI (624, 0.3%)
Incident Management
San Jose, CA, US
vectra.ai

VMRay (118, 11.3%)
Threat Analysis
Boston, MA, US
vmray.com

VuNet Systems (195, 33.6%)
Logs
Bangalore, India
vunetsystems.com

Stealth

Anetac (16, 0.0%)
Los Altos, CA, US
anetac.com

BOLDEND (17, 13.3%)
San Diego, CA, US
boldend.com

Command Zero (28, 27.3%)
Austin, TX, US
cmdzero.io

Testing

achelos GmbH (57, 21.3%)
TLS Testing
Paderborn, Germany
achelos.de

AttackIQ (151, -1.9%)
Security Instrumentation
San Diego, CA, US
attackiq.com

eShard (38, -11.6%)
Aquitaine, France
eshard.com

Intigriti (422, 11.9%)
Penetration Testing
Antwerp, Belgium
intigriti.com

MazeBolt Technologies (35, 2.9%)
DDoS Defense
Ramat Gan, Israel
mazebolt.com

Nimbusddos (4, 0.0%)
DDoS Defense
Newton, MA, US
nimbusddos.com

Prelude (31, 3.3%)
Breach And Attack Simulation
New York, NY, US
prelude.org

Riscure (173, 1.8%)
Security For Embedded Systems
Delft, Netherlands
riscure.com

SCYTHE (32, -33.3%)
Breach And Attack Simulation
Arlington, VA, US
scythe.io

Spirent Communications (2053, -1.0%)
Security Instrumentation
Crawley, United Kingdom
spirent.com

Synack (264, -22.8%)
Redwood City, CA, US
synack.com

Threat Intelligence

418 Intelligence (11, 37.5%)
Threat Intelligence Gamification
Reston, VA, US
418intelligence.com

Abusix (35, -5.4%)
San Jose, CA, US
abusix.com

AI Spera (23, 15.0%)
OSINT
Seoul, South Korea
criminalip.io

Alpha Recon (22, 0.0%)
Threat Intelligence Platform
Colorado Springs, CO, US
alpharecon.com

alphaMountain.ai (9, 28.6%)
DNS Security
Salt Lake City, UT, US
alphamountain.ai

Altrnativ (19, 11.8%)
Consumer CTI
Nice, France
altrnativ.com

Analyst1 (35, 59.1%)
Threat Intelligence Platform
Reston, VA, US
analyst1.com

Anomali (286, -1.0%)
Threat Intelligence Platform
Redwood City, CA, US
anomali.com

AppDetex (218, 7.4%)
Brand
Boise, ID, US
appdetex.com

Apura (71, 29.1%)
OSINT
Sao Paulo, Brazil
apura.com.br

Arctic Security (24, -4.0%)
Oulu, Finland
arcticsecurity.com

Axur (213, 10.9%)
Brand
Porto Alegre, Brazil
axur.com

Bfore.ai (40, 29.0%)
Domain Prediction
Montpellier, France
bfore.ai

BI.ZONE (257, 12.7%)
Threat Intel Aggregator
Moscow, Russia
bi.zone

BlackCloak (50, 56.2%)
Protection For Executives And Celebrities
Orlando, FL, US
blackcloak.io

BRANDEFENSE (64, 42.2%)
Managed Security Services
Ankura, Turkey
brandefense.io

ClearSky Cyber (10, 11.1%)
Threat Analysis
Cambridge, United Kingdom
clearskysec.com

CloudSEK (166, 4.4%)
Risk Management
Bangalore, India
cloudsek.com

**Numbers in parentheses indicate headcount and % change in 2023.*

Cobwebs (164, 16.3%)
All Source
New York, NY, US
cobwebs.com

Constella Intelligence (143, -16.4%)
Stolen Identities
Los Altos, CA, US
constellaintelligence.com

CTCI (4, 0.0%)
OSINT
Beaverton, OR, US
ctci.ai

CTM360 (92, 55.9%)
Dark Web
Seef, Bahrain
ctm360.com

Cyabra (53, 6.0%)
Fake News Defense
Tel Aviv, Israel
cyabra.com

Cyberint (144, 10.8%)
Petah Tikva, Israel
cyberint.com

Cyberlitica (8, -33.3%)
Dark Web
New York, NY, US
cyberlitica.com

CyberSixgill (112, -16.4%)
Dark Web
Netanya, Israel
cybersixgill.com

Cyble (185, 58.1%)
Dark Web
Alpharetta, GA, US
cyble.io

Cyborg Security (32, 23.1%)
TIP
Orlando, FL, US
cyborgsecurity.com

CYFIRMA (98, 27.3%)
Oak Park, IL, US
cyfirma.com

Cyjax (33, 6.5%)
London, United Kingdom
cyjax.com

Cyren (67, -69.0%)
Reputation
McLean, VA, US
cyren.com

Cyware (248, -6.1%)
TIP
New York, NY, US
cyware.com

DarkBeam (7, -22.2%)
London, United Kingdom
darkbeam.com

DarkInvader (9, 80.0%)
Dark Web
Leeds, United Kingdom
darkinvader.io

DarkOwl (26, -31.6%)
Dark Web
Denver, CO, US
darkowl.com

DarkScope (8, 300.0%)
Wellington, New Zealand
darkscope.com

Digital Shadows (45, -64.6%)
Dark Web
San Francisco, CA, US
digitalshadows.com

DomainTools (123, 5.1%)
Threat Intelligence From DNS
Seattle, WA, US
domaintools.com

EBRAND (81, 11.0%)
Brand
Leudelange, Luxembourg
ebrand.com

Echosec (6, -79.3%)
Intel Gathering Tool
Victoria, Canada
echosec.net

EclecticIQ (82, -35.4%)
Threat Intelligence Platform
Amsterdam, Netherlands
eclecticiq.com

Elemendar (20, 11.1%)
Threat Intelligence Analysis
Stourbridge, United Kingdom
elemendar.com

Farsight Security (17, -15.0%)
Threat Intelligence From DNS
San Mateo, CA, US
farsightsecurity.com

Feedly (56, 0.0%)
Feeds
Redwood City, CA, US
feedly.com

Filigran (35, 250.0%)
Paris, France
filigran.io

FIRCY (3, 0.0%)
Cloud Security
Adelaide, Australia
fircy.co

Flashpoint (398, 0.0%)
Dark Web
New York, NY, US
flashpoint-intel.com

Foresiet (10, 25.0%)
OSINT
Bangalore, India
foresiet.com

FYEO (10, -56.5%)
Threat Intelligence From DNS
Denver, CO, US
gofyeo.com

GreyNoise (62, 5.1%)
Dark Web
Washington, DC, US
greynoise.io

Group-IB (103, -72.9%)
Dark Web
Central Region, Singapore, Singapore
group-ib.com

GroupSense (38, -11.6%)
Dark Web
Arlington, VA, US
groupsense.io

HEROIC Cybersecurity (25, 19.1%)
Monitoring
Provo, UT, US
heroic.com

Hudson Rock (5, 0.0%)
Leaked Data
Tel Aviv, Israel
hudsonrock.com/

Hyas (43, -23.2%)
Attribution Intelligence
Victoria, Canada
hyas.com

ID Agent (20, 5.3%)
Dark Web
Miami, FL, US
idagent.com

Intel 471 (157, 6.1%)
Threat Actor Intelligence
Amsterdam, Netherlands
intel471.com

Intsights (45, -43.0%)
Dark Web
New York, NY, US
intsights.com

iZOOlogic (22, 69.2%)
London, United Kingdom
izoologic.com

Kela Group (106, 12.8%)
Dark Web
Tel Aviv, Israel
ke-la.com

**Numbers in parentheses indicate headcount and % change in 2023.*

LastLine (VMware) (8, -27.3%)
IoC Intelligence
Redwood City, CA, US
lastline.com

LifeRaft (85, 3.7%)
Monitoring
Halifax, Canada
liferaftinc.com

Lookingglass Cyber Solutions (102, -37.0%)
Reston, VA, US
lookingglasscyber.com

Maltiverse (9, 0.0%)
IoC Intelligence
Madrid, Spain
maltiverse.com

Malware Patrol (8, 14.3%)
Feeds
Sao Paulo, Brazil
malwarepatrol.net

MarkMonitor (178, 3.5%)
Brand
San Francisco, CA, US
markmonitor.com

Media Sonar (15, -11.8%)
TIP
London, Canada
mediasonar.com

Nisos (115, 18.6%)
Managed Security Services
Alexandria, VA, US
nisos.com

Nucleon Cyber (6, -33.3%)
Aggregation
Tampa, FL, US
nucleon.sh

Ontic (188, 12.6%)
Personal Protection Platform
Austin, TX, US
ontic.co

Opora (14, -54.8%)
Adversary Tracking
San Francisco, CA, US
opora.io

Orpheus Cyber (32, 0.0%)
OSINT
London, United Kingdom
orpheus-cyber.com

Prodaft (52, 15.6%)
OSINT
Yverdon-les-Bains, Switzerland
prodaft.com

Q6 Cyber (51, 4.1%)
Dark Web
Miami, FL, US
q6cyber.com

QuoIntelligence (45, 15.4%)
Managed Security Services
Frankfurt am Main, Hesse, Germany
quointelligence.eu

Recorded Future (1104, 9.5%)
Somerville, MA, US
recordedfuture.com

S2T (51, 21.4%)
Dark Web
Slough, United Kingdom
s2t.ai

S2W Inc. (59, -6.3%)
Investigation
Pangyo, South Korea
s2w.inc

Searchlight Cyber (57, 26.7%)
Dark Web
Portsmouth, United Kingdom
slcyber.io

SecurityZONES (5, -28.6%)
Spamhaus
London, United Kingdom
securityzones.net

ShadowDragon (48, 71.4%)
OSINT
Wilmington, DE, US
shadowdragon.io

Silent Push (28, 55.6%)
OSINT
Reston, VA, US
silentpush.com

Silobreaker (66, -1.5%)
Threat Intelligence Management
London, United Kingdom
silobreaker.com

Skopenow (45, -6.2%)
OSINT
New York, NY, US
skopenow.com

Skurio (33, -13.2%)
Brand
Belfast, United Kingdom
skurio.com

SOC Prime (99, -10.8%)
Threat Intelligence Platform
Kiev, Ukraine
socprime.com

SOCRadar (166, 19.4%)
TIP
Middletown, DE, US
socradar.io

SpyCloud (213, 27.5%)
Dark Web
Austin, TX, US
spycloud.com

StealthMole (12, 20.0%)
Dark Web
Singapore
stealthmole.com

Sweepatic (16, -15.8%)
Brand
Leuven, Belgium
sweepatic.com

Team Cymru (128, 1.6%)
IoC Intelligence
Lake Mary, FL, US
team-cymru.com

Tego Cyber (17, 70.0%)
TIP
Las Vegas, NV, US
tegocyber.com

Tesseract Intelligence (9, -30.8%)
Dark Web
Sofia, Bulgaria
tesseractintelligence.com

Threat Intelligence (21, 0.0%)
Leaked Data
Sydney Nsw, Australia
threatintelligence.com

ThreatBook (88, 57.1%)
TIP
Haidian District, China
threatbook.cn

ThreatConnect (168, 5.0%)
Arlington, VA, US
threatconnect.com

ThreatNG (11, 120.0%)
Dark Web
Shrewsbury, MA, US
threatngsecurity.com

ThreatQuotient (106, -9.4%)
Threat Intelligence Platform
Reston, VA, US
threatquotient.com

Threatray (12, 20.0%)
IoC Intelligence
Biel/Bienne, Switzerland
threatray.com

Tidal Cyber (25, 25.0%)
OSINT
Washington, DC, US
tidalcyber.com

TruKno (8, 0.0%)
TIP
Denver, CO, US
trukno.com

VoxCroft (39, -9.3%)
OSINT
Western Cape, South Africa
voxcroft.com

**Numbers in parentheses indicate headcount and % change in 2023.*

Vulidity (5, 0.0%)
OSINT
Burghausen, Bayern, Germany
vulidity.de

VulnCheck (13, 116.7%)
Vulnerabilities
Lexington, MA, US
vulncheck.com

Vulners (3, -25.0%)
Vulnerabilities
Wilmington, DE, US
vulners.com

WhoisXML API (31, 6.9%)
DNS Security
Covina, CA, US
whoisxmlapi.com

Wizdome (10, -63.0%)
TIP
Tel Aviv, Israel
wizdome.com

ZeroFOX (823, 30.0%)
Monitoring
Baltimore, MD, US
zerofox.com

Training

Airbus Cybersecurity (293, 1.4%)
Cyber Range
Alancourt, France
airbus-cyber-security.com

Aries Security (14, 7.7%)
Cyber Range
Wilmington, DE, US
ariessecurity.com

Blue Team Labs (193, 127.1%)
Cyber Range
London, United Kingdom
blueteamlabs.online

BSI Group (8263, 8.3%)
Standards Certification
London, United Kingdom
bsigroup.com

CDeX (27, 0.0%)
Cyber Range
Poznan, Poland
cdex.cloud

Circadence (76, -20.0%)
Cyber Range
Boulder, CO, US
circadence.com

Cloud Range (22, 0.0%)
Cyber Range
Nashville, TN, US
cloudrangecyber.com

CYBER RANGES (54, 35.0%)
Cyber Range
Stafford, VA, US
cyberranges.com

Cyber Skyline (16, 77.8%)
Continuous Training
College Park, MD, US
cyberskyline.com

Cyberbit (202, -1.5%)
Cyber Range
Ra'anana, Israel
cyberbit.com

Cybergym (55, 0.0%)
Cyber Range
Hadera, Israel
cybergym.com

Cybexer (40, -14.9%)
Cyber Range
Tallinn, Estonia
cybexer.com

Cympire (17, -5.6%)
Cyber Range
Tel Aviv, Israel
cympire.com

FifthDomain (16, -30.4%)
Cyber Range
Canberra, Australia
fifthdomain.com.au

Hack the Box (1620, 36.4%)
Cyber Range
Kent, United Kingdom
hackthebox.eu

HackersEye (7, 40.0%)
Cyber Range
Ramat Gan, Israel
hackerseye.net

Hacking Lab (9, 50.0%)
Cyber Range
Rapperswil-Jona, Switzerland
shop.hacking-lab.com

Immersive Labs (329, -0.3%)
Cyber Range
Bristol, United Kingdom
immersivelabs.com

Kernelios (68, 23.6%)
Rishon LeZion, Israel
kernelios.com

LetsDefend (52, 40.5%)
Cyber Range
Sterling, VA, US
letsdefend.io

Mission: Cybersecurity (7, 0.0%)
Security Awareness Training
Ruda Slaska, Poland
misjacyber.pl/en/

Offensive Security (964, 11.1%)
Cyber Range
New York, NY, US
offensive-security.com

RangeForce (80, -8.1%)
Cyber Range
White Plains, NY, US
rangeforce.com

Rhea Group (675, 13.4%)
Cyber Range
Wavre, Belgium
rheagroup.com

SafeStack (19, -24.0%)
Software Development Security
Aukland, New Zealand
safestack.io

SecureCode Warrior (259, 2.0%)
Software Development Security
Sydney, Australia
securecodewarrior.com

SecureFlag (24, 33.3%)
London, United Kingdom
secureflag.com

Security Innovation (225, 22.3%)
Cyber Range
Wilmington, MA, US
securityinnovation.com

Security Journey (60, -3.2%)
Software Development Security
Raleigh, NC, US
securityjourney.com

Seela (24, -22.6%)
Interactive Courses
Boulogne Billancourt, France
seela.io

SimSpace (173, -13.9%)
Cyber Range
Boston, MA, US
simspace.com

Terranova Security (107, 4.9%)
Laval, Canada
terranovasecurity.com

TryHackMe (2118, 45.4%)
Cyber Range
London, United Kingdom
tryhackme.com

**Numbers in parentheses indicate headcount and % change in 2023.*